Computer Systems

COMPUTER SYSTEMS
Concepts and Design

GLENN A. GIBSON
Electrical Engineering Department
The University of Texas at El Paso

PRENTICE HALL, Englewood Cliffs, New Jersey 07632

Library of Congress Cataloging-in-Publication Data

Gibson, Glenn A.
  Computer systems : concepts and design / Glenn A. Gibson.
    p.   cm.
  Includes bibliographical references.
  ISBN 0-13-172958-6
  1. System design. 2. Computers—Design and construction.
3. Computer software—Development. I. Title.
QA76.9.S88G43 1991
004.2′1—dc20   89-77266
                                                          CIP

Editorial/production supervision: *bookworks*
Cover design: *Bruce Kenselaar*
Manufacturing buyer: *Lori Bulwin*

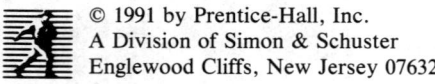

© 1991 by Prentice-Hall, Inc.
A Division of Simon & Schuster
Englewood Cliffs, New Jersey 07632

All rights reserved. No part of this book may be
reproduced, in any form or by any means,
without permission in writing from the publisher.

Printed in the United States of America
10 9 8 7 6 5 4 3 2

ISBN   0-13-172958-6

Prentice-Hall International (UK) Limited, *London*
Prentice-Hall of Australia Pty. Limited, *Sydney*
Prentice-Hall Canada Inc., *Toronto*
Prentice-Hall Hispanoamericana, S.A., *Mexico*
Prentice-Hall of India Private Limited, *New Delhi*
Prentice-Hall of Japan, Inc., *Tokyo*
Simon & Schuster Asia Pte. Ltd., *Singapore*
Editora Prentice-Hall do Brasil, Ltda., *Rio de Janeiro*

To my granddaughter,
Ashley Elizabeth

Contents

Preface xiii

Acknowledgments xvii

1 Introduction 1
    1-1   Computers and Their Applications 2
          1-1-1   Hardware 5
          1-1-2   Software 10
    1-2   About This Book 12

2 Data Representations 16
    2-1   Text Data Types 18
    2-2   Numeric Data Types 20
          2-2-1   Non-negative Integers 21
          2-2-2   Signed Integers 24
          2-2-3   Range and Scaling 34
          2-2-4   Real Numbers 36
          2-2-5   Expression Evaluation 43
    2-3   Design Remarks 47
          References 47
          Exercises 48

3 Computer Circuits 51
    3-1   Electrical Properties 52
          3-1-1   Circuit Effects on Timing 52
          3-1-2   Power Considerations 54

3-2 Combinational Logic Implementations 57
3-3 Important Combinational Circuits 64
    3-3-1 Multiplexers and Demultiplexers 64
    3-3-2 Comparators 66
    3-3-3 Adders and Subtractors 69
    3-3-4 Multipliers 74
    3-3-5 Parity Generation and Detection 75
3-4 Important Sequential Circuits 77
    3-4-1 Counters and Frequency Dividers 77
    3-4-2 Registers 80
    3-4-3 Serial Adders and Subtracters 82
    3-4-4 Multipliers and Dividers 85
3-5 Link Connections 87
3-6 Integrated Circuits and Technologies 91
3-7 Design Remarks 92
References 94
Exercises 95

4 Fundamental Computer Operations 98
4-1 Machine Language Instructions 102
    4-1-1 Instruction Types and Formats 103
    4-1-2 Operation Codes 105
    4-1-3 Operand Fields and Addressing Modes 107
    4-1-4 Instruction and Instruction Set Design 112
    4-1-5 Condition Flags and the PSW 117
4-2 Assembler Language Instructions 119
    4-2-1 Transfer Instructions 122
    4-2-2 Arithmetic Instructions 124
    4-2-3 Branch Instructions 129
    4-2-4 Looping 132
    4-2-5 Logical Instructions 136
    4-2-6 Shift and Rotate Instructions 138
    4-2-7 PSW Instructions 141
4-3 Stacks 142
4-4 Procedures 145
    4-4-1 Calls and Returns 146
    4-4-2 Parameter Passing and Side Effects 149
4-5 Macros 157
4-6 Instruction Execution Time 159
4-7 Design Remarks 161
References 162
Exercises 163

5 Program Creation 169
5-1 Assemblers 170

       5-1-1   Data-related Directives   171
       5-1-2   The Assembly Process   177
- 5-2 **Compilers**   184
- 5-3 **Linking and Address Adjustment**   191
- 5-4 **Loading and Address Adjustment**   195
- 5-5 **Design Remarks**   196
- **References**   197
- **Exercises**   198

6 Input/Output Programming   200

- 6-1 **Programmed I/O**   202
- 6-2 **Interrupt I/O**   207
  - 6-2-1 The Interrupt Process   208
  - 6-2-2 Interrupt Masking   210
  - 6-2-3 Interrupt Example   211
  - 6-2-4 Interrupt Management   214
- 6-3 **Direct Memory Access**   220
  - 6-3-1 Programming Block Transfers   221
  - 6-3-2 Double and Triple Buffering   224
  - 6-3-3 Multichannel Controllers   224
- 6-4 **I/O Elements**   227
  - 6-4-1 Keyboards and Monitors   227
  - 6-4-2 Printers and Plotters   231
  - 6-4-3 Timer/Event Counters   232
  - 6-4-4 A/D and D/A Converters   234
- 6-5 **Design Remarks**   236
- **References**   239
- **Exercises**   239

7 Processing Elements   243

- 7-1 **Macroinstruction Execution**   246
- 7-2 **Internal Bus Transfers**   249
- 7-3 **Detailed Internal Architecture Example**   252
  - 7-3-1 Macroinstruction Execution   253
  - 7-3-2 ALU and PSW Design   257
  - 7-3-3 BCL Logic   261
  - 7-3-4 Control Bus   261
- 7-4 **Microcontrol**   265
  - 7-4-1 Hardwired Control   265
  - 7-4-2 Microprogrammed Control   271
- 7-5 **Reduced Instruction Set Computers**   283
- 7-6 **Packaging**   285
- 7-7 **Other Design Remarks**   288
- **References**   291
- **Exercises**   291

8 Links and Interfaces 294
- 8-1 **System Buses** 296
- 8-2 **Interfaces** 300
  - 8-2-1 Bus Control Logic 301
  - 8-2-2 Link to Link Interfaces 310
- 8-3 **Data Links** 320
  - 8-3-1 Signal Formats 322
  - 8-3-2 Local Data Links 326
  - 8-3-3 Data Link Standards 327
  - 8-3-4 Packets 330
- 8-4 **Summary** 332
- References 333
- Exercises 334

9 Memory Hierarchy 337
- 9-1 **Mass Storage** 339
  - 9-1-1 Magnetic Tape Units 340
  - 9-1-2 Movable Head Disk and Diskette Units 345
  - 9-1-3 Fixed Head Disks and Drums 350
  - 9-1-4 Magnetic Bubble Memory 351
- 9-2 **Main Memory** 352
  - 9-2-1 Static RAM 358
  - 9-2-2 Dynamic RAM 359
  - 9-2-3 Read Only Memory 361
  - 9-2-4 Memory IC Timing 363
  - 9-2-5 Memory Module Interfacing 366
- 9-3 **Multiple-port Memory** 369
- 9-4 **Cache Memory** 371
- 9-5 **Hierarchy Design** 380
- References 383
- Exercises 384

10 Memory Management 388
- 10-1 **Mass Storage Management** 389
- 10-2 **Main Memory Management** 399
- 10-3 **Memory Management Hardware and Virtual Memory** 405
  - 10-3-1 Paging 407
  - 10-3-2 Segmentation 413
  - 10-3-3 Paging Versus Segmentation 416
  - 10-3-4 Memory Management Remarks 417
- References 419
- Exercises 419

11 Operating Systems 422
- 11-1 **Uniprogramming Systems** 423
  - 11-1-1 Memory and File Management 426

    11-1-2 Input/Output 427
    11-1-3 Operating System Services 429
    11-1-4 Systems Programs 429
    11-1-5 Overlapping I/O and Processing 430
  11-2 Multiprogramming Systems 431
  11-3 Organization of a Multiprogramming System 435
    11-3-1 Process Scheduling 435
    11-3-2 Memory Management and Process Loading 438
    11-3-3 I/O Handling 440
  11-4 Sharing Resources 443
  11-5 Areas for Further Study 447
    References 449
    Exercises 450

12 Parallel Processing 452
  12-1 Multiprocessing 454
    12-1-1 Bus Topologies 456
    12-1-2 Non-bus Topologies 461
    12-1-3 Synchronization and Resource Sharing 464
  12-2 Pipelining 469
    12-2-1 Pipeline Performance 472
    12-2-2 Pipeline Design 476
  12-3 Vector and Matrix Processing 482
    12-3-1 Vector Addition 482
    12-3-2 Summing Elements of a Vector 483
    12-3-3 Inner Products 484
    12-3-4 Matrix Operations 486
  12-4 High Performance Computing Summary 487
    References 489
    Exercises 490

Appendix A Number Systems and Conversions 494
    Exercises 498

Appendix B Logic Level Design 499
  B-1 Elementary Logic Gates 500
  B-2 Combinational Logic Design 508
  B-3 Elementary Sequential Circuits 522
    B-3-1 Clocks 524
    B-3-2 Monostable Multivibrators 524
    B-3-3 Flip-flops 526
    References 532
    Exercises 532

Appendix C X16 Summary 537

Index 549

Preface

Over the past forty-five years enormous progress has been made in the design and construction of computers. During that time many avenues have been tried and retried as the economics of building and putting together the various components of computers has changed drastically. Although hardware has undergone the most noticeable changes as we have passed from vacuum tubes to the high density integrated circuits of today, software has also gone through significant improvements.

As important as the hardware and software improvements is the knowledge gained during these forty-five years. Rather than dwelling on specific examples of computers that have been built, it is the intent of this book to draw from this pool of knowledge those facts and ideas that currently seem most pertinent to the design of computer systems. These facts and ideas will be discussed in an implementation independent way with little reference to existing systems. However, much of the middle portion of the book is concerned with the design of an example processing element. This design provides a vehicle for introducing several important points. Basically, the presentation proceeds by introducing a central idea or set of facts and then discussing the related tradeoffs. In many instances there is no speculation as to which choice is "best," because what is best using today's technology may not be best using tomorrow's technology.

The decision to avoid references to existing computers was made after careful consideration. It is the author's belief that computers have evolved to the point where enough fundamentals can fill an introductory text without frequently examining computers that are currently in use. In fact, it is felt that discussions of existing computers would detract from the points being made and, perhaps, make the reader feel that a point is applicable only to a particular computer, even though it may be generally applicable. If a concept is central to computer design, then arguments can be made and tradeoffs presented without the distractions caused by referring to specific computers.

Both hardware and software concepts are considered, and attention is given to the interdependencies between them. Such interdependencies are very important to the design of compilers, multiprogramming systems, and multiprocessing systems and must be considered to make faster, more efficient, and more reliable systems.

This book is designed as an introductory computer systems text for a one-semester course in Electrical Engineering or Computer Science. It could, however, be useful to anyone who wants to learn the fundamentals of computer systems. It is assumed that the reader has a good knowledge of at least one high-level language and some knowledge of how computers are organized (e.g., the reader has taken a course in FORTRAN, C, or Pascal and has used a personal computer). Familiarity with Boolean algebra and the elementary logic gates and flip-flops will be assumed in the body of the text, but for those who lack a background in these areas, a lengthy appendix on this material has been included. There is also a short appendix on number systems.

After the overall concepts and terminology related to computers are introduced in Chapter 1, the second chapter describes the basic data types used by computers and the representations of their elements. The third chapter introduces several of the basic logic circuits needed in constructing a computer. Chapter 4 examines the kinds of operations a computer must perform by presenting short machine and assembler language program segments, and Chapter 5 extends this discussion to the construction of complete programs. In the fourth and fifth chapters the emphasis focuses on the tasks that computers must perform and the instruction combinations needed to do them, with little attention being given to how the instructions and data are physically moved around within the computer or are input to or output from the computer.

Chapter 6 discusses the instructions and techniques computers use to communicate with the external world and introduces a few of the more important input and output hardware elements. Chapters 7 through 9 study the hardware elements for processing, transferring, and storing information. All of these chapters assume a single bus, single processor architecture, such as the architecture found in personal computers. Although the construction of computers and the physical processes that occur during a computer's operation are only minimally considered in Chapters 4 and 5, such topics dominate the discussions in Chapters 6 through 9.

Chapters 10 and 11 are the chapters most concerned with software issues. Chapter 10 introduces the hardware implementation of memory management, whose purpose is to provide better control of the memory hierarchy, and Chapter 11 examines operating systems. It is in the discussion of operating systems that the interdependencies between hardware and software become most apparent.

The final chapter introduces more advanced design topics. In particular, it examines the problems related to parallel processing, which allows a computer to increase the amount of work it can accomplish in a given time. Parallel processing involves either overlapping the stages needed to carry out a computer's operations (pipelining) or concurrently executing operations (multiprocessing).

The amount of material presented in this book that can be covered in a one-semester course depends on the background of the students. If the students have only the minimum background previously indicated, then a typical course would consist of Appendices A and B (which are self-contained and have their own exercises) and Chapters 1 through 9. If the students have already been exposed to data representations and elementary logic, then the appendices would be used for reference purposes only and Chapters 2 and 3 could be scanned or omitted entirely. This scenario would allow the material through Chapter 11 to be covered. Students who also have had some exposure to assembler language programming could scan Chapters 4 and 5 and complete the entire book.

The author would like to thank The University of Auckland in New Zealand, which permitted him to teach computer architecture courses during the early preparation of this book; The University of Texas at El Paso; Dr. Vijay Singh for helping with the material on technologies; Dr. Dan Cooke and the many anonymous reviewers; and Mary Lou Gibson for typing and correcting the manuscript as it was taking shape. He would also like to thank Yu-cheng Liu for giving permission to extract several figures from the book *Microcomputer Systems: The 8086/8088 Family*, which was coauthored by the present author and Dr. Liu.

Glenn A. Gibson

X16 Software to accompany *Computer Systems: Concepts and Design*
by Glenn A. Gibson (ISBN 0-13-172958-6)

The *X16 Assembler, Linker, and Simulator* (for IBM® PCs and compatibles) is provided *free* and site-licensed in conjunction with *Computer Systems: Concepts and Design.*

The Assembler

- can handle macros and includes columns for indicating errors, relocatable addresses, external references, named constants, and macro expansions.
- produces a listing that includes both internal and external symbol tables (similar to listings output by other well-written assemblers).

The Linker

- links several object units produced by the assembler.
- in addition to the load unit, it generates a map that indicates the relative locations of the object units linked and any errors that occurred during linking.

The Simulator

- is the first simulator **designed specifically for instruction and homework assignments.**
- can be used with an overhead projector for classroom demonstrations.
- allows the user to display the activity in various parts of a computer **as the program executes.**
- switches between computer parts with a single keystroke.
- provides **eight variable execution speeds** to step through a program at the instruction level or the individual transfer level.
- allows **start-stop keystroke operation** at the end of each instruction or at the end of each instruction fetch and operand transfer.
- **the primary screen** displays the programming model of the processor, a terminal interface, the portions of the code and data memories being referenced, the system bus, and the instruction being executed, its predecessor and its successor.
- **additional screens** display the activity inside the processor, on the system bus, inside the interface, inside the bus control logic, and DMA transfers.
- all screens use a consistent format and permit the same variable execution speeds.

The *X16 Software* is available in the Instructor's Manual accompanying *Computer Systems: Concepts and Design* or, contact your Prentice Hall Representative for additional information.

Acknowledgments

The following figures are being reproduced with the permission of Prentice-Hall, Inc. (Figure numbers refer to *Computer Systems: Concepts and Design*.)

GIBSON/GIBSON, *Understanding and Selecting Small Business Computers*, © 1986.
   Figures 6-21, 6-22, 9-7(b).
GIBSON/LIU, *Microcomputers for Engineers and Scientists*, 2nd ed., © 1987.
   Figures 2-1, 2-2, 3-23 through 3-28, 3-30, 3-38, 9-12, A-1, A-2, B-4, B-10 through B-21, B-23 through B-27, B-29, Appendix C, and Exercises B-11, B-14, B-17, and B-18.
GIBSON/YOUNG, *Introduction to Programming Using FORTRAN 77*, © 1982.
   Figures 5-11, 9-4, 9-7(a), 9-8.
LIU/GIBSON, *Microcomputer Systems: The 8086/8088 Family, Architecture, Programming, and Design*, 2nd ed., © 1986.
   Figures 4-3, 4-9, 5-6, 8-24 through 8-26, 9-10.

Computer Systems

1

Introduction

The advancement of the human race from its primitive existence in which people had little control over their destinies to its present state has been closely paralleled by its ability to work and communicate with numbers. Indeed, much of our progress has been made possible by our ability to continually refine our quantitative analysis of the world around us. It was the initial realization of numbers that allowed us to progress from the day to day existence of primitive man to a society that could engage in trade. This progression meant that it was no longer necessary for individuals or small groups to provide themselves with everything they needed. Instead, people could specialize in the production of certain items and then barter their goods for the other things they required.

As society became more sophisticated so did its tools—rafts became boats and boats became ships powered by the winds. To assist this advancement, man needed an expanding system of numbers and an improved ability to work with them. As we became civilized we became interested in our surroundings, not just to survive but to satisfy our curiosity and understand our place in the universe. In particular, great strides were made during the 17th, 18th, and 19th centuries when some of our greatest mathematicians and scientists were able to abstract mathematical concepts far beyond our ability to use these concepts in a practical way. Although formulae were hypothesized and tentatively verified by relatively simple experiments, they could not be used fully in a practical sense because of the amount of computation that would be required to produce results from them. For example, Maxwell's equations provided an elegant view of electricity and magnetism, but could be solved for only a very limited number of situations for which analytical solutions existed.

By the 20th century there was considerable pressure to increase our ability to make computations. This pressure was magnified by World War II, whose outcome largely depended on the technical advances of the combatants. During World War II it was fully recognized that further advancement in our use of scientific knowledge would depend on our ability to make computations. In short, we had reached the limits of the human capacity to make calculations, and automatic machinery was needed to assist these calculations. Thus was born the age of electronic computers, an age made possible by the coming together of our accumulated knowledge of mathematics, science, and technology.

Since World War II the progress made in building computers has been astonishing and there is no end in sight. Today a person of modest means can buy more automated computing power than existed in the entire world in the early 1950s. Much of this advancement has been due to improved technology that has taken us from vacuum tubes, to transistors, and finally to integrated circuits of ever-increasing densities. Major obstacles have been overcome in the areas of processing speed, storage capacity, communications, and software development. As each obstacle is struck down, a whole new field of possibilities and applications is opened for exploration.

Although recent progress has caused a departure from the relatively simple views of computers held by the first computer designers, many of the fundamental design concepts are still valid. Because this text is introductory, the emphasis in this book is on the fundamental concepts, but reference will be made to recent developments whenever appropriate. Computers have many faces and the intent here is to provide a basis upon which the reader can expand his or her knowledge in many different directions.

1-1 COMPUTERS AND THEIR APPLICATIONS

The original purpose of computers was to perform calculations rapidly but, because human intervention would inject a relatively slow component into the process, automation was needed to achieve the desired levels of computational speed. Hence, computers are sometimes generically referred to as automatic computing machinery. To eliminate human intervention it is necessary for a computer to be able to store a significant number of instructions and amount of data. Unlike a calculator that requires instructions and data to be fed into it in a step-by-step manner, a computer must be capable of accepting instructions and data in advance and then quickly accessing this information as the need arises. Therefore, in this book, a **computer** is defined to be a machine that is capable of automatically receiving and storing instructions and data, using its instructions to rapidly make its computations, and outputting its results.

Our definition of a computer is quite broad and encompasses **special purpose computers**, which are designed to satisfy a single, narrowly-defined application, and **general purpose computers**, which may be used to solve a wide variety of computational problems. An example of a very limited special purpose computer is shown in Fig. 1-1. It is used as a simple traffic light controller that contains a fixed set of instructions that permit it to input signals from sensors embedded in the road and output signals to relays that control the traffic lights.

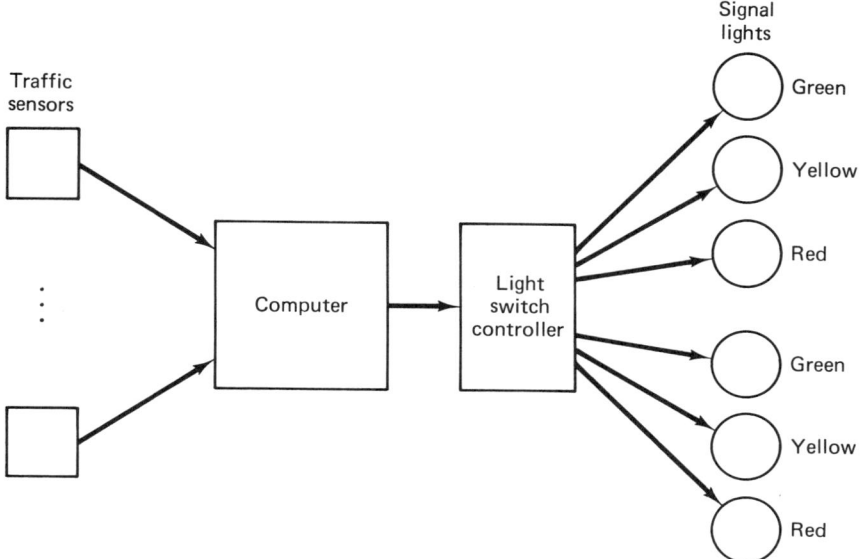

Figure 1-1 Special purpose computer for controlling a set of traffic lights.

At the other extreme is the general purpose computer shown in Fig. 1-2. It is intended to be used as the central computing facility for a university and includes a storage facility capable of storing large quantities of instructions and data. To satisfy the diverse needs of the university it may be called upon to perform a large variety of tasks. It could be used to teach students to program, solve research problems, or provide administrative services for the registrar and business offices. Because of this computer's diverse usage, it would require several different types of equipment for communicating with the world external to it. Much of this communication would be through terminals used by students, faculty, and staff, but printers and plotters would also be needed to provide printed records, and special equipment may be required as well to input experimental data or display results.

It is the broad spectrum of applications that presents computer designers with so many challenges and causes computers to be viewed so differently by different people. The primary physical characteristics of a computer are its speed, storage capacity, and means of communicating with the external world. Which of these characteristics are important depends on the application. For the traffic controller example, very little storage is needed, the input and output of data are minimal, and speed is not critical because traffic movement is slow as compared to the electronic speed of even the slowest computers. On the other hand, for the university computer example, storage must be large to hold all of the university's student and financial records, the amount and variety of input and output equipment must be considerable to accommodate the large number and variety of users, and the computational speed must be high to handle the needs of scientific and technological research.

It is a computer designer's responsibility to identify those characteristics

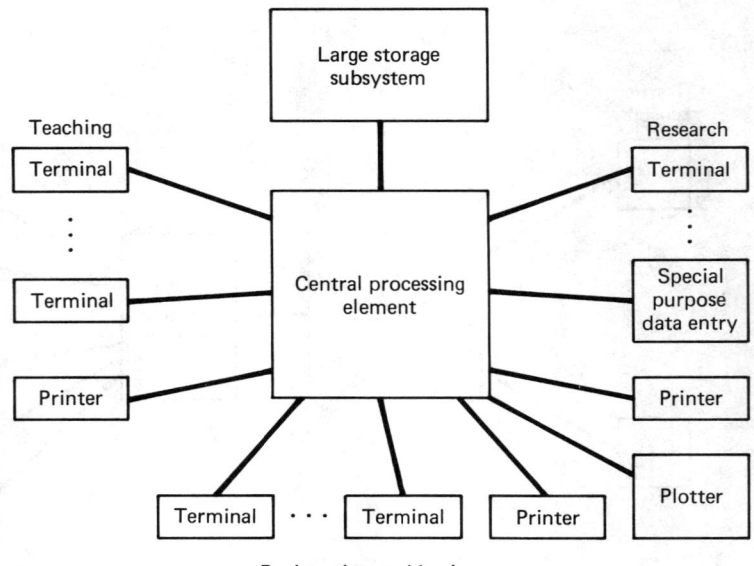

Figure 1-2 General purpose computer.

that are most important to an application or set of applications. The designer must match the applications to the computer in such a way that the overall cost is minimized. Because many applications are ill-defined or not known in advance, one of the major problems a designer must face is establishing requirements from rather nebulous application descriptions. Quite often the best description is to simply state the computer's users or setting. For example, specifications might state that the computer is to be used for scientific work, which tends to imply high computational speed, or, it is to be used in a business setting, which tends to imply large amounts of input, output, and storage. To be competitive, computer manufacturers must normally depend on volume and cannot afford to customize each design. Therefore, they tend to produce general purpose computers with optional components that allow specific computer systems to be shaded toward the requirements of specific applications. For this reason, and because it would be impractical to explore the multitude of individual applications, this book is primarily concerned with general purpose computer design and only occasionally refers to special situations.

It is important to realize that a **computer system** consists of both **hardware**, which is the electronic circuits and mechanical parts that physically make up the computer, and **software**, which is the set of all the instruction combinations used to control the computer. The software consists of a collection of programs, each of which is a set of instruction combinations designed to perform a specific task. Although the physical limitations of the electronic circuits and mechanical devices place an upper bound on the speed of a computer, the software plays an equal role in determining the computer's actual performance. There are many different ways of putting instructions together to perform a given task. Some ways use fewer instructions and are more efficient than others. Sometimes a slight change in the ordering of instructions or the inclusion of hardware that aids the execution of certain instructions will make a computer system enormously more efficient or better suited to a particular application. The overall design of a computer system is multifaceted and the optimal design should take into account not only the hardware and software, but also the interplay between the hardware and software.

1-1-1 Hardware

At the abstract level, computers are constructed from the following fundamental components and the means for connecting these components together:

> **Source,** or **input, devices** that create or input information and then transfer the information to the other components of the computer. The origin of the information is not important; the information may be generated by the device or input from the external world.
> **Sink,** or **output, devices** that receive information from the computer and then output it to the external world.
> **Storage devices** that receive information and then, at a later time (when they are given the proper control signals), provide the same information to other devices in the computer.
> **Conversion devices** that receive information, convert it, and then provide the converted information to other devices in the computer.

The information flowing among these fundamental components may be either instructions or data. In addition to information signals, control signals are communicated among the components and at least some of the conversion devices convert instructions into control signals.

The above devices can be constructed and then connected together in an infinite number of ways. It is the job of the hardware designer to decipher the description of what the computer is to do and then design the individual components and put them into a suitable configuration.

The procedure for designing any complex system, computer or otherwise, begins with a definition of its major components and a description of how these components are to be connected. Then the major components are broken down by defining their principal subcomponents, which are in turn divided into subcomponents. The subdivision process continues until the structure of the system has been completely delineated. This design approach is referred to as **top-down design** and is necessary because of the limited amount of information that the human mind can grasp at one time. It provides an orderly means of arriving at a solution to a complex problem.

Figure 1-3 shows the hierarchy associated with the hardware design of a computer system. Note that the first task is to decide on the major subsystems that are needed and how they should be connected. An example of a subsystem is a set of disk drives and its associated control circuitry. Next, the electronic

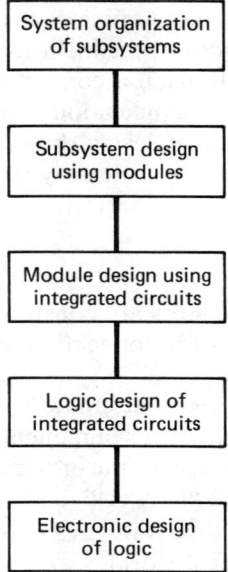

Figure 1-3 Hardware design hierarchy.

portion of each subsystem could be divided into modules. Typically, a module is the electronics on a single printed circuit (PC) board and this level of design includes determining the modules that are required and how they should be connected together. Designing a PC board is a matter of selecting the integrated circuits (ICs) and individual electronic components (transistors, resistors, capacitors, etc.) and laying out the board's conducting surfaces. Each IC is made up of logic elements and, at the lowest design level, each of these elements are constructed from elementary electronic components. The lowest design level would also be concerned with selecting the technology for fabricating the electronics.

Although this book discusses the design considerations of the system and subsystem levels, its emphasis is on the module and logic levels. Except for pertinent references that are useful to the logic level discussions, this book does not consider the electronic level, but leaves this area to books on electronics. However, some attention is paid to the restrictions imposed on a computer system by the physical properties of the electronics.

Module level design can be done by putting together the fundamental devices defined at the beginning of this section, to form the practical components of the computer. From a functional standpoint these components can be divided into the following categories:

Processing element—any hardware element that is primarily used for processing data (i.e., accepting data, performing some operation on the data, and returning results).

Memory element—any element whose primary purpose is to store information (data or instructions). A memory element can accept information, hold it until it is requested, and then output it.

Input/Output (I/O) element—any piece of hardware whose primary purpose is to accept information from or send information to the outside world. By the outside world we mean a person or machine that is distinct from the computer (e.g., a machine tool or another computer).

Link or bus—any connection through which one part of the computer conveys information to or accepts information from another part of the computer.

Interface—any piece of hardware whose primary purpose is to connect together any of the above four types of elements in such a way that the signal levels and timing requirements of the elements are matched by the interface.

In a strict sense, it is difficult to classify a major component as one of the above; therefore, the qualifying word "primary" has been included in these definitions. For example, an element could contain fundamental devices for both processing and storing information as well as internal links over which these devices could communicate, but as a whole, it would be considered a processing element because processing is its primary function. Major components consisting of several subcomponents are classified according to their predominant usage.

Because processing is the primary purpose of a computer, a computer is sometimes considered to be a collection of processing elements with the remainder of the system being viewed simply as support to these elements. The remainder of the system would be charged with communicating with the external world, storing the information needed by the processing elements as well as the results produced by the processing elements, and supplying both data and instructions to the processing elements in a timely fashion. It is the processing elements that contain the conversion devices for converting the instructions into control signals that determine the computer's actions.

Although memory elements have been relegated to a supporting role, they account for much of a computer's hardware. They may be responsible for permanently storing some information and temporarily storing other information. They *must* store the instructions, the data to be operated on, and the results. There are many types of memory elements, and each type serves a specific purpose. It is generally true that, for a given cost, the larger the capacity of a memory element, the more time it takes to access the element (i.e., put information into or take information from the element). As a result, most computers include levels of memory elements. The higher speed elements are the ones most frequently accessed by the processing elements and those that permanently store large quantities of information are slower and more remote from the processing elements. The memory elements that comprise these levels constitute what is known as the computer's **memory hierarchy**. The design of the memory hierarchy is determined by the requirements for supplying instructions and data to the processing elements.

The physical arrangement of the parts of a computer system or subsystem is called its **architecture**. The architecture of a computer can be considered as a whole or by the architecture of one of its major components. Figure 1-4 gives two typical computer architectures. In Fig. 1-4(a), all the elements are connected to a single link, called the **system bus**, and the computer is said to have a **single bus architecture**. This configuration also contains only one processing element and is, therefore, also referred to as a **single processor architecture**. Having a single bus and single processing element considerably simplifies a design and makes it much easier to discuss the basic concepts of computers. It is this type of architecture that is assumed in most of this book.

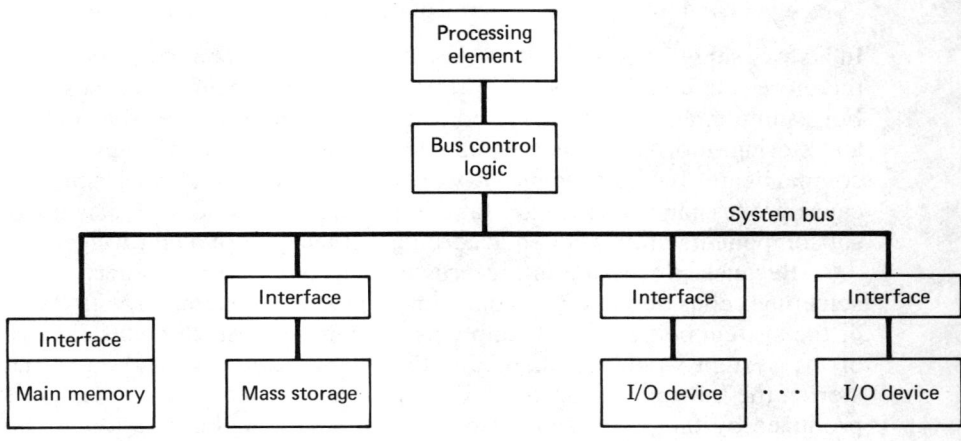

(a) Single bus, single processor system

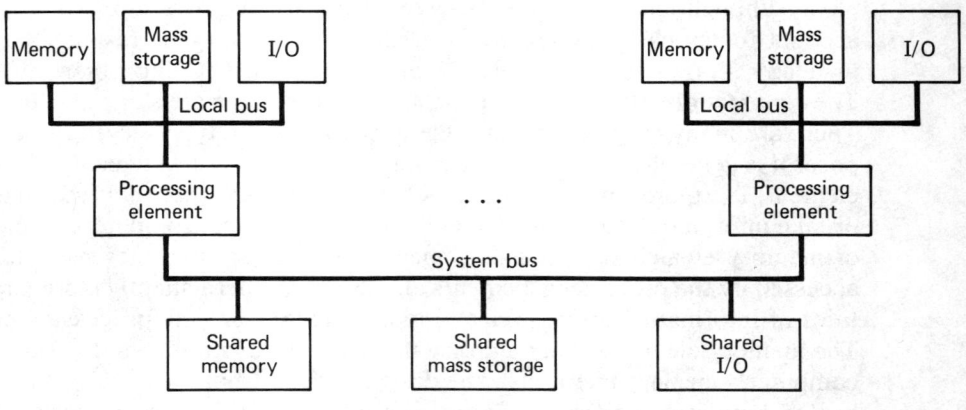

(b) Multiprocessing system

Figure 1-4 Typical computer architectures.

The block in Fig. 1-4(a) that is labeled **mass storage** represents a form of memory that, as the name implies, has a large storage capacity. Typical mass storage elements are diskette, disk, and magnetic tape units. Assuming that the processing element contains a small amount of memory, known as its **register set**, the memory hierarchy for the system in Fig. 1-4(a) consists of its mass storage (which is relatively slow and inexpensive), its memory (which is faster and more expensive), and the processing element's register set (which is very fast and immediately accessible to the processing element's circuitry, but has very limited capacity and is expensive). In order to distinguish the intermediate from other forms of memory, it is sometimes called the **main memory**. A primary concern is to provide a good flow of data and instructions from the mass storage, where they are permanently stored, through the main memory to the processing element, where the data are operated on and the instructions are executed.

Each element attached to the system bus must have an interface to match its electrical characteristics to those of the bus. The interface for the processing element has been given the special name **bus control logic**. Bus control logic is normally charged with regulating bus activity and therefore, is more complex than other interfaces. The memory interface tends to be incorporated into the memory's control circuitry, and this incorporation is illustrated by showing the memory and its interface in a single block.

In contrast, the second configuration shown in Fig. 1-4 includes several processing elements and is a typical example of a **multiprocessing system**. It consists of a subsystem surrounding each processing element and a central link that connects these subsystems together. In a multiprocessing system, the **system bus** is the central link and the links in the subsystems are called **local buses**.

Connected to the system bus of the multiprocessing system are memory and I/O elements accessible to all subsystems. All components of a computer system, both hardware and software and even sets of data, are referred to as **resources**. The elements connected to the system bus and the system bus itself are examples of **shared resources**. The advantage of a multiprocessor architecture is that each subsystem can operate as an independent computer, yet can take advantage of the shared resources. The shared main memory could be used for passing information between subsystems and the shared mass storage could be used to store programs and large quantities of data that are needed by more than one subsystem. These programs and sets of data would also be shared resources. The shared I/O elements tend to be expensive components, such as high-speed printers or large plotters, that are needed by each subsystem but are such that duplication would be an unnecessary expense. The subsystems do not compete with each other when they are accessing information or performing I/O within themselves, but do compete when they are using the shared resources. Competition for shared resources is referred to as **contention**. Although multiprocessing allows the subsystems to act independently while providing an integrated means of communication between several processing elements, the increased level of contention in a multiprocessing system may considerably increase the complexity of its hardware and software.

1-1-2 Software

The basic software unit is the **instruction**. An instruction is a packet of information that is converted into control signals by a processing element's hardware and causes the computer to perform some basic unit of work. The control signals produced by an instruction may be confined to the processing element or transmitted out of the processing element to other parts of the computer. When an instruction is converted into control signals it is said to be **executed**. Prior to being executed, an instruction is moved around and stored within the computer in the same way as data. A computer can perform complex tasks by executing instructions sequentially (i.e., one after the other). The fundamental types of instructions are those that

- Move information around within the computer.
- Perform arithmetic and logical operations.
- Allow the computer to make decisions.
- Allow sequences of instructions to be repeated (i.e., to form loops).
- Permit programs to be subdivided into groups of instructions that perform distinct tasks (i.e., subprograms or procedures).

The latter three instruction types are implemented by **branch instructions** that allow instructions to be executed out of sequence.

Instructions comprise larger units referred to as **programs** that perform complete tasks, and programs comprise the computer's software. There is a wide variation in the amount and types of software needed by a system. A simple traffic light controller, such as the one shown in Fig. 1-1, would require only a small program for accepting inputs from the sensors and outputting to the switch controller. On the other hand, a general purpose computer system would require a program, called its **operating system**, for regulating its overall activity, several system programs that would enable it to create and execute applications programs, and a number of applications programs for performing specific tasks for the users.

An operating system includes a command interpreter for communicating with its users and a variety of subprograms for initializing the system when it is turned on, managing the usage of memory and mass storage, inputting programs to main memory and initiating their execution, controlling the order in which programs are executed, and performing I/O. Operating systems can be classified as single-user or multiprogramming systems. A **single-user system** requires that all user commands and messages be done through a single I/O device, normally a terminal, and can execute only one program at a time. A **multiprogramming system** supports a hardware configuration that may include several terminals, one for each user currently working with the computer. Such a system is designed to have several programs in progress simultaneously. Only one program can use a processing element at a time, but the programs currently in memory can take turns utilizing the processing element. A computer that has more than one processing element and an operating system that allows more than one program to be in progress on each processing element is both a multiprocessing and multiprogramming system.

Figure 1-5 gives a design hierarchy for software that is similar to the one for hardware shown in Fig. 1-3. The highest design level consists of breaking the program down into subprograms and determining the information that must be passed between them and to and from the world outside the computer. The next level is concerned with deciding on the algorithms to be used by the subprograms and the structures of the subprograms.

The actual coding of a program could involve all of the three lower levels, but most programmers rarely become involved with the lower two levels. What we have referred to as instructions are, more specifically, called **machine language instructions** because they are in a form that can be directly decoded by a processing element's logic. However, few people other than hardware designers program at this level. Almost all programming is done using an assembler or high-level language that allows a programmer to use character strings to represent quantities and operations [e.g., the Pascal statement $X := Y + SIN(2*W)$]. This makes the programming much easier but, because the hardware cannot decipher the character strings, translating programs known as assemblers, interpreters, and compilers are needed to covert the character strings into machine language instructions. The difference between an assembler language and a high-level language is that there is, more or less, a one-to-one correspondence between assembler statements and machine language instructions, whereas a high-level language statement may have more in common with verbal language than the machine code

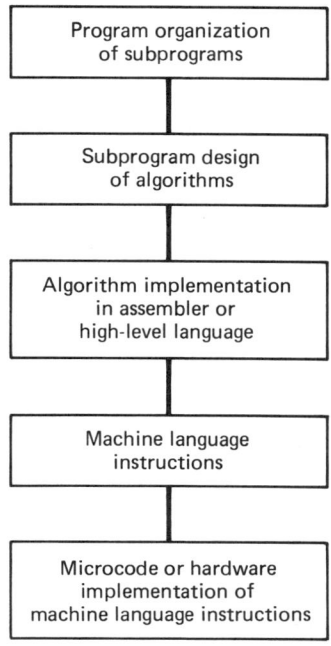

Figure 1-5 Software design hierarchy.

it generates. A single high-level language statement may translate into several machine language instructions.

The lowest level of coding is an integral part of the hardware and is called **microcoding**. Microcode is composed of **microinstructions** that perform very elementary operations. For example, adding two numbers may require only one machine language instruction but several microinstructions. Typically, it would take one microinstruction to transfer the first operand to the arithmetic element, a second to transfer the second operand to the arithmetic element, a third to instruct the arithmetic element to perform the addition, and a fourth to deliver the sum to its destination. Some computers are designed so that their circuitry decodes machine language instructions and directly carries out their operations without resorting to microcode. Even if a computer is designed to use microinstructions, these instructions are a permanent or semipermanent part of the hardware and only the designer of the microcoded element is concerned with them.

Because this book assumes that its readers already know how to program in at least one high-level language, it primarily dwells on the assembler language programming level and the lower two levels shown in Fig. 1-5. However, there are appropriate discussions relating high-level languages and the upper levels shown in Fig. 1-5 to the lower levels and computer hardware. Note that in proceeding from the lower levels to the upper levels, a greater level of abstraction is approached relative to hardware. This higher level permits the person who is implementing an application to work with concepts and not get involved with the details of the hardware. It is left to the system software to convert the abstract form of an application into the form used by the processing element.

1-2 ABOUT THIS BOOK

The purpose of this book is to provide the introductory concepts of computer systems and discuss how these concepts are related to the design of such systems. As with the design of any system, the problem is to determine the basic tradeoffs, make the necessary decisions related to these tradeoffs, and then proceed according to these decisions. Because this book considers so many facets of computers, most of the discussions assume a general purpose setting. Designing a special purpose computer is essentially a matter of restricting a general purpose design to include only those components that are needed and then refining the design to satisfy the specific requirements regarding speed, capacity, cost, and so on.

Any presentation in a learning situation must lay a foundation, then build upon that foundation, and conclude with relatively advanced material and food for future thought. With this in mind, Chaps. 2 through 4 provide background material, Chaps. 5 through 11 discuss the major computer components outlined in Sec. 1-1, and Chap. 12 considers the design approaches to more complex computer systems. Essentially all of the discussion prior to Chap. 10 assumes a single bus, single processor system such as the one shown in Fig. 1-4(a). This simple configuration allows us to focus on the major components one by one. A synopsis of each of the chapters is given below.

Chapter 2

Before presenting a detailed discussion of the internal workings of a computer it is first necessary to examine the types of data a computer operates on, how the data are represented inside the computer, and what operations must be performed on the data. This chapter concentrates on the basic types of data processed by computers and the elementary operations performed on these data. Knowledge of the binary number system is assumed, but Appendix A is provided for those who need a review.

Chapter 3

Although the emphasis in this book is not at the logical design level, some material is needed at this level to provide an appreciation of the physical limitations of electronic circuitry. This is done by showing how the components most basic to all computers are constructed from elementary logic gates and flip-flops. This chapter assumes the reader is already familiar with elementary logic gates and flip-flops, but it is supported by Appendix B, which gives an introduction to combinational and sequential logic design.

Chapter 4

The study of computers as data processors is begun at this point by discussing the types of operations computers must perform and the formats of the instructions needed to carry out these operations. Also, assembler language programming is introduced. The introduction of both machine language instructions and assembler language programming is supported by the development of a hypothetical computer, the X16, which is also used to present examples in subsequent chapters. The details of the X16 are summarized in Appendix C.

Chapter 5

Although Chap. 4 uses the X16 example to provide short segments of code to do simple tasks, no attempt is made to formulate complete programs. Chapter 5 is a continuation of Chap. 4, but considers the development of complete programs. The latter portion of this chapter examines how the major parts of a program are pieced together and then loaded for execution. This material is preparation for the Chap. 11 discussion of operating systems and how they manage programs.

Chapter 6

This chapter describes how a computer communicates with its mass storage and I/O elements. It introduces the instructions and special hardware needed to efficiently transfer information into and out of mass storage or the computer as a whole. The latter part of this chapter begins the examination of the principal components of a computer (i.e., the processing elements, memory elements, I/O elements, links, interfaces, and operating system) by describing the I/O elements that are most often included in a computer system.

Chapter 7

Processing elements do the computing by converting instructions into control signals that direct the computer's activity. Chapter 7 describes how simple processing elements are constructed and the two principal ways of decoding instructions into control signals. Some attention is given to the packaging of processing elements because such packaging can have considerable bearing on speed and cost.

Chapter 8

This chapter discusses the links and interfaces needed to tie the components of a computer together. It begins by describing how transfers are made over the links and by defining the various link classifications. The material on interfaces begins by considering the interfaces between the processing elements and the links to other elements of the computer. This chapter also describes how the control signals generated by the instructions are propagated out of the processing elements to control the system as a whole.

Chapter 9

It is here that the various types of memory elements are examined and the memory hierarchy as a whole is considered. The construction of both main memory and mass storage elements are described and details pertaining to their access times, storage capacity, and cost are given. There is a discussion of the information flow from the outer, slower levels of the hierarchy to and from the inner levels that are close to the processing elements.

Chapter 10

This chapter bridges the gap between the discussion of the memory hierarchy in Chap. 9 and the discussion of operating systems in Chap. 11. A computer's performance and the effectiveness with which it can be programmed is particularly affected by the way its memory elements are managed. Chapter 10 is primarily concerned with the hardware aspects of memory management and leaves the software aspects to the discussion of operating systems.

Chapter 11

Chapter 11 looks at only the most prominent features of an operating system. Much of Chap. 11 concentrates on single-user systems, but an introduction to multiprogramming systems is also included. An operating system is responsible for moving entire blocks of information around within the computer system as it prepares and then executes the various programs. The principal parts of an operating system are those that communicate with the user(s), schedule the execution of the users' programs, and manage the accessing and storing of information in the memory hierarchy.

Chapter 12

The final chapter goes beyond the straightforward design of the single processor, single bus computer and discusses parallel processing, which implies the simultaneous execution of processing operations by more than one set of circuitry. Parallel processing can be achieved either by overlapping the small steps involved in an operation, so that more than one operation can be in the process of being executed at a time, or by simultaneously executing different operations by separate processing elements. The purpose of parallel processing is to increase the overall speed of the computer by more efficiently using each set of circuitry or by using multiple sets of processing circuitry.

2
Data Representations

The purpose of a computer is to process data and, in fact, modern computers are sometimes referred to as **electronic data processors**. It is, therefore, essential that we include a preliminary discussion of data before beginning our examination of computers. In particular, it is important to consider the types of data computers work with, the operations that must be performed on these types of data, and how data are represented inside the computer. In this discussion, keep in mind that, not only must the data be processed by the computer, but they must also be stored within the computer, transmitted between the computer's components, and input from and output to the external world.

A **data type** is defined by its:

- Set of values or elements.
- Set of operations on its elements.

A data type made up of the most fundamental elements is called a **basic** or **atomic data type** and other, more complex data types may be constructed from these basic data types. There are three categories of basic data types of interest in this book—text, numeric, and instruction data types. This chapter is concerned with text and numeric data types. The elements of a computer system's basic instruction data type include the system's machine language instructions, which are discussed in Chap. 4.

The elements of a basic text data type are called **characters**. Characters may be letters, digits, punctuation marks, other printed symbols, and nonprinting characters. Other text data types may be defined by concatenating characters (i.e., placing one character after the other). These concatenations are called **character strings**, or simply **strings**. The principal operations performed on text are comparison, which is used for searching and ordering; concatenation, which is simply a matter of appending one string to another; and extraction and other manipulations that involve substrings. All data that are input from or output to a terminal or printer are in the form of text data types.

The elements of a basic numeric data type are, of course, numbers. More general numeric data types can be defined by groups of numbers such as vectors and matrices. Algebraic operations performed on numbers include the four elementary binary operations—addition, subtraction, multiplication, and division—plus the unary operation negation. Although the decimal digits in text data types represent numbers, they are not treated as numbers and are not usually operated on arithmetically.

There are three ways of viewing data types. A data type may be viewed as a collection of:

- Abstract entities and associated operations that may have no relation to a computer, in which case it is referred to as an **abstract data type**.
- Entities that are defined and operated on by a particular computer language, such as FORTRAN, C, or Pascal, in which case it is referred to as a **virtual data type**.
- Entities that are physically stored in and operated on by a computer's hardware. Such a data type is called a **physical data type**.

The elements and operations of an abstract data type make up the mathematical system that is ideally what should be used to attack a problem and are defined without concern for the computer upon which they will be used. This consideration allows a problem to be initially formulated without taking into account the constraints of a computer or computer language.

If a computer and computer language are to be employed, a programmer must select virtual data types that can be constructed from the language to implement the abstract data types. For example, the basic virtual data types for Pascal are the character, integer, and real data types. The more general Pascal virtual data types can be formed by defining arrays and records. A Pascal programmer need only be concerned with these data types and how they can be used to implement the abstract data types for the problem at hand. Only when a program is translated into its machine language code and executed are the actual representations (i.e., the elements of the physical data types) and operations performed by the computer's hardware of interest. At this level one must be aware of the constraints imposed by both language and hardware.

Because most of this book is concerned with the physical design of computers, it is physical data types that will receive essentially all of the attention. The term "data type" will normally imply from this point forward, that the physical data type is to be assumed. (For a more complete discussion of data types see Stubbs and Webre [1].)

The overriding consideration in representing data elements inside a computer is the binary nature of modern computers. All of the elementary electronic circuits that do the processing and all of the computer's storage cells can take on only one of two states, which are represented by 0 and 1. The underlying reason for this simple representation is reliability. It is much easier to distinguish between one of two voltages, currents, or magnetic fields than one of several because saturation conditions can be used. Also, tolerances can be larger, thus minimizing errors due to aging of the electronic components. If 0 and 5 volts are associated with 0 and 1, respectively, then any voltage less than 1 volt could be treated as a 0, any voltage greater than 3 volts could be taken to be a 1, and there would still be a minimum separation of 2 volts between the 0s and 1s.

A single 0 or 1 is called a **bit** and all data and instructions must be represented by groups of bits. The correspondence between a set of 0-1 combinations and the elements in a basic data type is known as a **code**. The code being used indicates the physical representations of the elements of the data type and a complete set of such coded representations constitutes the set of elements of a physical data type. Except for machine language instructions, the codes for most basic data types are such that all of the elements in the data type are represented by the same number of bits. Such codes are called **fixed length codes**.

Because a single bit can take on only one of two values, groups of bits must be used to represent the elements of practical data types. If the length of a code is n, then the data type can include at most 2^n elements. The most common bit grouping is the **byte**, which contains eight bits and can be used to represent $2^8 = 256$ different entities. The lengths of most codes (at least those that are of interest to us) are an integral number of bytes and, if a data type has more than 256 elements, the length of the code must be two or more bytes.

2-1 TEXT DATA TYPES

The 0-1 representations of a text data type are referred to as an **alphanumeric code**. The most common alphanumeric code is the American Standard Code for Information Interchange (ASCII), which is a fixed length code (7 bits per character) that has become an international standard. It is summarized in Fig. 2-1 and it is the code assumed throughout this book. Figure 2-1 is organized into three groups of three columns each. The first column in each group gives the symbols representing the printing characters or the abbreviations of the nonprinting characters. The second column gives the codes in hexadecimal, and the third gives the names of nonprinting characters. The printing characters include upper-case letters, lower-case letters, the digits 0 through 9, and several punctuation marks and algebraic symbols. The first 33 characters and the last character are nonprinting and include several control characters used for special purposes and for providing spacing. The characters used for spacing are:

BS—for backspacing.
HT—for tabbing horizontally.
LF—for advancing one line.

ASCII Char.	Hex. Code	Control Character	ASCII Char.	Hex. Code	Control Character	ASCII Char.	Hex. Code	Control Character
NUL	00	Null	+	2B		V	56	
SOH	01	Start heading	,	2C		W	57	
STX	02	Start text	-	2D		X	58	
ETX	03	End text	.	2E		Y	59	
EOT	04	End transmission	/	2F		Z	5A	
ENQ	05	Inquiry	0	30		[	5B	
ACK	06	Acknowledgment	1	31		\	5C	
BEL	07	Bell	2	32		]	5D	
BS	08	Backspace	3	33		^	5E	
HT	09	Horizontal tab	4	34		_	5F	
LF	0A	Line feed	5	35		`	60	
VT	0B	Vertical tab	6	36		a	61	
FF	0C	Form feed	7	37		b	62	
CR	0D	Carriage return	8	38		c	63	
SO	0E	Shift out	9	39		d	64	
SI	0F	Shift in	:	3A		e	65	
DLE	10	Data link escape	;	3B		f	66	
DC1	11	Device control 1	<	3C		g	67	
DC2	12	Device control 2	=	3D		h	68	
DC3	13	Device control 3	>	3E		i	69	
DC4	14	Device control 4	?	3F		j	6A	
NAK	15	Neg. acknowledge	@	40		k	6B	
SYN	16	Synchronous/Idle	A	41		l	6C	
ETB	17	End trans. block	B	42		m	6D	
CAN	18	Cancel data	C	43		n	6E	
EM	19	End of medium	D	44		o	6F	
SUB	1A	Start special seq.	E	45		p	70	
ESC	1B	Escape	F	46		q	71	
FS	1C	File separator	G	47		r	72	
GS	1D	Group separator	H	48		s	73	
RS	1E	Record separator	I	49		t	74	
US	1F	Unit separator	J	4A		u	75	
SP	20	Space	K	4B		v	76	
!	21		L	4C		w	77	
"	22		M	4D		x	78	
#	23		N	4E		y	79	
$	24		O	4F		z	7A	
%	25		P	50		{	7B	
&	26		Q	51		|	7C	
'	27		R	52		}	7D	
(	28		S	53		~	7E	
)	29		T	54		DEL	7F	Delete-rubout
*	2A		U	55				

Figure 2-1 ASCII code.

VT—for tabbing vertically.
FF—for advancing to the top of the next page.
CR—for returning to the first column.
SP—for inserting a single space.

Control characters will be discussed as the need arises.

Sec. 2-1   Text Data Types

Because the basic grouping of data in most computers is bytes, ASCII characters are normally extended to eight bits by adding a 0 to the left side. When this addition is made, only 128 of the possible 256 bit combinations are used by the ASCII code and the remainder, those starting with a 1, can be assigned to other characters. They could be used for a different alphabet, such as the Greek alphabet, or a variety of other purposes. Quite often they are used for outputting special graphic characters that provide a means of printing pictures or graphs.

The ASCII code (as well as most other alphanumeric codes) is such that the alphabetic ordering of strings of letters corresponds to the numeric ordering of the coded numeric values of the strings, thereby allowing arithmetic to perform alphabetic ordering. The comparisons needed to search and order character strings are most often done by treating the 0-1 combinations that represent the strings as nonnegative integers, subtracting the two strings, and observing the result to see if it is greater than, less than, or equal to 0.

2-2 NUMERIC DATA TYPES

Ideally, a computer would need to operate on only one set of numbers, the set of real numbers. Real numbers could make up the basic numeric data type and complex numbers, vectors, and so on could form the more general data types. However, the set of real numbers, and even the set of integers, is infinite and each number would require an infinite number of bits to represent it. But computers can work with and store only a finite number of bits. For this reason, computers are sometimes referred to as finite state machines. This finiteness is an underlying problem of all computers and means that they cannot work with the complete set of real numbers, or even the complete set of integers. Therefore, we must be content to work with subsets of real numbers and integers even though this limits the accuracy and magnitudes of the operands and results.

All computers have hardware that can operate directly on numbers in a data type whose basic elements are a subset of the integer number system. Some can even deal directly with a subset of real numbers. Those that do not have the hardware for working with real numbers must somehow accomplish the hardware operations using integer operations. In either case, a computer is normally viewed as being able to utilize two kinds of numeric data types, **integer data types** and **real**, or **floating point, data types**. The exact set of numbers included in these data types depends on the representations of the integers or real numbers.

Codes for numeric data types are almost always of fixed length. However, a computer's hardware or a computer language may include more than one integer or real data type and the different data types may have different lengths. The most obvious example of this representational difference is the inclusion of both single-precision and double-precision real numbers in most high-level languages. Some languages also include both short and long integer data types. As we will see later, the availability of more than one integer or real data type allows the user to select the range and accuracy of the numbers to be used in solving a problem.

2-2-1 Nonnegative Integers

We will first concentrate on the set of nonnegative integers and then generalize the discussion to include negative integers. There are three commonly used ways of representing nonnegative integers in terms of 0-1 combinations. They are the binary, packed binary coded decimal (BCD), and unpacked BCD representations.

Binary representations are constructed using the binary numbering system. The details of the binary numbering system are assumed to be known to the reader, but Appendix A includes a review. This system is the most natural way of representing numbers as 0-1 combinations because numbers in their binary forms can be stored and operated on using the same algorithms as those used when the numbers are in their decimal equivalents. The number "21" in its binary form is

$$1 \times 2^4 + 0 \times 2^3 + 1 \times 2^2 + 0 \times 2 + 1$$

which is written more succinctly as 10101. For addition and subtraction, carries and borrows are handled in the same manner as when working with decimal numbers; multiplication can be performed using alternating shifts and additions; and division can be done using alternating shifts and subtractions. Representative binary computations are given in Fig. 2-2. Particularly note the similarities between binary multiplication and division and the same operations in decimal arithmetic. The usual algorithms for performing arithmetic do not depend on the base, and for multiplication and division the shifting is really multiplying or dividing by the base. Most computer hardware for performing arithmetic assumes that numbers are in their binary form, because this assumption simplifies the hardware design.

Putting a number into its **packed BCD** form is a matter of converting each decimal digit to its 4-bit binary equivalent and placing the 4-bit groupings side by side. For example, the decimal number "8259" would be converted as follows:

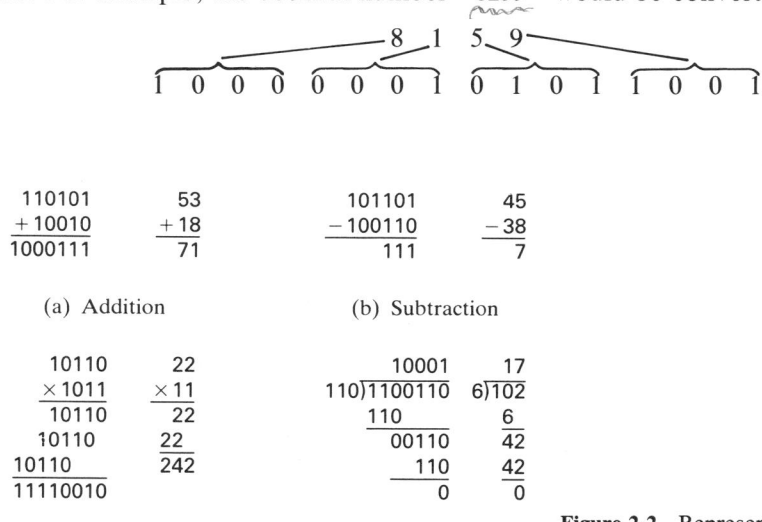

Figure 2-2 Representative binary arithmetic computations.

Hardware that can perform arithmetic on packed BCD numbers is more complex than hardware designed to operate on numbers in binary format. Also, note that it took 16 bits to write the number "8159" in packed BCD, but the same number in binary is 1111111011111, which requires only 13 bits. The main advantage of packed BCD is that it is closer to the alphanumeric codes used for I/O. It is seen from Fig. 2-1 that the ASCII codes for the decimal digits 0 through 9 are 0110000 through 0111001, respectively. The packed BCD representation of a number can be obtained by eliminating the 011 prefix from each character and packing the remaining 4-bit groups two to a byte. For example, the ASCII code to packed BCD conversion for the string "86" (assuming a 0 has been attached to each character to fill out the byte) is

$$00111\underline{1000} \quad 00110\underline{0110}$$
$$\overline{10000110}$$

Chapter 3 will show that it is not difficult to build a packed BCD adder/subtracter, but such a device is more complicated and slower than a binary adder/subtracter. BCD addition can be done by successively adding the binary representations of the digits and adjusting the results. The adjustment rule is:

If the sum of two digits is greater than 9, add 6 to the sum.

Adding 6 causes the unused combinations 1010 through 1111 to be skipped. For example,

```
                    1    0   1
   1748         0001 0111 0100 1000
 + 2925       + 0010 1001 0010 0101
   4673            0000      1101
                    110       110
                0100 0110 0111 0011
```

The problems associated with packed BCD multiplication and division are even more serious than those associated with addition and subtraction. These problems mean that applications that require a lot of I/O and only additions and subtractions, such as point of sales stations, could be based on computers that do only packed BCD addition and subtraction. However, general purpose computers should operate on numbers in their binary forms and have hardware for performing all four arithmetic operations.

The problem with using binary representations for doing calculations is that numbers in a text data form, which include all numbers involved in I/O with terminals and printers, must be converted from the text form to the binary form or vice versa. As shown in Fig. 2-3, this translation is usually done by converting the text input data to BCD, converting the BCD to binary, carrying out the calculations, converting the results to BCD, and then converting the BCD to text output. The algorithm for producing the binary equivalent of a BCD number $d_n \ldots d_0$ is

$$(\ldots((d_n 1010 + d_{n-1})1010 + d_{n-2})\ldots)1010 + d_0$$

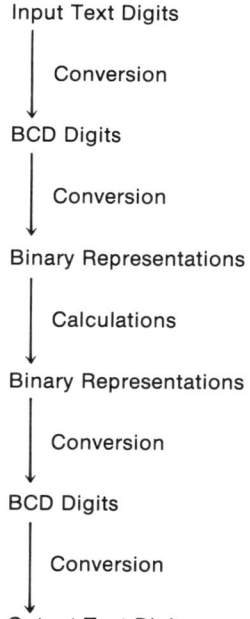

Figure 2-3 Process of getting input text digits into binary form to make calculations and then getting the results into output text form.

where $d_0, \ldots, d_n$ are the BCD digits and 1010 is the binary equivalent of ten. For example, the conversion of "825" to binary would be accomplished as follows:

$$\begin{array}{r} 1000 \\ \times\,1010 \\ \hline 1010000 \\ +\,0010 \\ \hline 1010010 \\ \times\,1010 \\ \hline 1100110100 \\ +\,0101 \\ \hline 1100111001 \end{array}$$

The reverse conversion is done by successive divisions by ten and then using the 4-bit remainders as the BCD digits.

BCD digits that are stored in bytes with the upper four bits set to 0 are called **unpacked BCD digits**. The packing and unpacking of the BCD digits shown in Fig. 2-3 may not be necessary. Without packing, ASCII coded digits can be transformed into BCD digits by simply zeroing the upper 4 bits. For the reverse operation, converting the remainders to ASCII digits is a matter of adding 00110000. As with packed BCD, designing hardware to add and subtract unpacked BCD representations is not difficult, but it is more complex than binary add/subtract hardware. Storing unpacked BCD representations is very inefficient. Again considering the above example, it would require 32 bits to store the number "8159" using unpacked BCD digits.

2-2-2 Signed Integers

Expanding our discussion to include negative integers is not as obvious as one might think. It is possible to include negative integers by using a **sign-magnitude format**, i.e., by denoting the magnitude in the manner described above and attaching a sign designation. When this method is used, normally a 0 in the most significant (leftmost) bit position indicates a nonnegative number and a 1 in this position indicates a negative number. However, there are two other formats that are commonly used because they make hardware design easier, the 2's complement and 1's complement formats. The 2's complement format is more popular. Performing arithmetic operations on sign-magnitude numbers is done by carrying out the operation on the magnitudes using the usual arithmetic algorithms and then assigning the sign of the result according to the rule of signs of algebra. It is the circuitry needed to determine the signs and whether addition or subtraction is needed that make sign-magnitude hardware more complicated.

When considering nonnegative integers or sign-magnitude representations of all integers, length is not important. But when defining the 2's complement or 1's complement, the number of bits is part of the definition. The **n-bit 2's complement** of an integer x is

$$2^n - x$$

and the **n-bit 1's complement** of x is

$$2^n - 1 - x$$

Note that in either case the complement is unique and the complement of the complement returns the original value x, i.e.,

$$2^n - (2^n - x) = x$$

and

$$2^n - 1 - (2^n - 1 - x) = x$$

These properties make it possible to define the negative of an integer to be its complement. Note that, if n is sufficiently large, then all three formats are such that a nonnegative number has a 0 as its most significant bit and a negative number has a 1 in this bit position.

If the 2's complement is used to designate negative integers, the range of x is $-2^{n-1} \leq x < 2^{n-1}$. For the 1's complement, the range is $-2^{n-1} < x < 2^{n-1}$ and there are two representations of 0, one in which all of the bits are 0 and the other in which all of the bits are 1. The binary 4-bit 2's complement and 1's complement representations are listed in Fig. 2-4. Although the fact that the 2's complement format is unbalanced (i.e., the range includes one more negative integer than positive integer), the two 1's complement representations of 0 are even more of a nuisance.

Integer	2's Complement Representation	1's Complement Representation
−8	1000	----
−7	1001	1000
−6	1010	1001
−5	1011	1010
−4	1100	1011
−3	1101	1100
−2	1110	1101
−1	1111	1110
−0	----	1111
0	0000	0000
1	0001	0001
2	0010	0010
3	0011	0011
4	0100	0100
5	0101	0101
6	0110	0110
7	0111	0111

Figure 2-4 Binary 4-bit complement representations.

When using the binary numbering system, $2^n - 1$ is a sequence of n 1s and subtraction from $2^n - 1$ does not require any borrows. In subtracting x, if a bit in x is 0 then the corresponding bit in the difference is 1 and vice versa. In other words, the 1's complement of x is found by complementing the individual bits in x, e.g., if $x = 00101110$, the 8-bit 1's complement of x is

$$
\begin{array}{rl}
11111111 =& 2^8 - 1 \\
- \ 00101110 =& x \\
\hline
11010001 =& \text{1's complement of } x
\end{array}
$$

The 2's complement of x is most easily obtained by adding 1 to the 1's complement of x. Again, if $x = 00101110$ then

$$11010001 + 1 = 11010010 = \text{2's complement of } x$$

Although it is possible to represent negative integers by using complements, for the complement formats to be useful we must be able to perform arithmetic operations on integers expressed in these formats. Also, we must consider finiteness. An **overflow** occurs when the result of an arithmetic operation lies outside the range of the format being used. For an n-bit 2's complement format, because -2^{n-1} has no negative it is possible even for the unary operation negation to produce an overflow.

If no overflow occurs, the addition of 2's complement integers can be done by adding the integers as binary numbers and ignoring the carry from the high order bit, e.g.,

$$\begin{array}{r} 00010110 = 22 \\ \underline{11101100} = -20 \\ 1\ 00000010 = \overline{2} \end{array}$$

↑
Lost ⏎

To prove that this procedure always gives the correct result, we assume x and y are nonnegative and consider the four possible cases:

Case 1:

$$x + y$$

Assuming no overflow, this case is the addition of two binary numbers and there is nothing to prove.

Case 2:

$$x + (-y)$$

If $x \geq y$, then $x + 2^n - y \geq 2^n$ and there is a carry that is lost. Losing the carry is the same as subtracting 2^n. Therefore, the result is

$$x + (2^n - y) - 2^n = x - y$$

which is a positive integer whose magnitude is $x - y$. If $x < y$, there is no carry and the result is

$$x + 2^n - y = 2^n - (y - x)$$

which is a negative integer whose magnitude is $y - x$.

Case 3:

$$(-x) + y$$

Same as Case 2 because addition is commutative.

Case 4:

$$(-x) + (-y)$$

Because $2^n - x + 2^n - y$ is always greater than 2^n, it always produces a carry that is lost. Therefore, the result is

$$(2^n - x) + (2^n - y) - 2^n = 2^n - (x + y)$$

An overflow occurs only if the operands are of the same sign and the sum has the opposite sign. The proof of this statement is left to the reader (see Exercise 14).

Subtraction is accomplished by negating the subtrahend and then adding. An overflow occurs only if the operands have different signs and the difference has the same sign as the subtrahend (see Exercise 15). Sample 4-bit additions and subtractions are given in Fig. 2-5.

Provided no overflow occurs, multiplication of 2's complement operands can also be accomplished by employing the usual algorithm that involves shifting

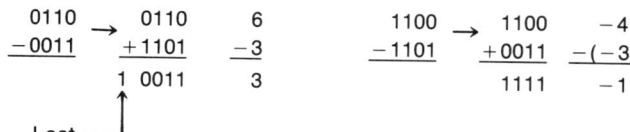

```
1011    −5          1100    −4
+0100   +4         +1110   +(−2)
 1111   −1        1 1010    −6
                   ↑
                   Lost
```

(a) Additions

```
 0110  →  0110    6        1100  →  1100    −4
−0011    +1101   −3       −1101    +0011   −(−3)
        1 0011    3                 1111    −1
        ↑
Lost
```

(b) Subtractions

Figure 2-5 Example 4-bit 2's complement additions and subtractions.

and adding. Once again, assume x and y to be nonnegative and consider the four possible cases:

Case 1:
$$xy$$

This case is just the multiplication of two nonnegative integers and there is nothing to prove.

Case 2:
$$x(-y)$$

If $x \leq 1$ the result is clearly correct. If $x > 1$ then
$$(2^n - y)x = 2^n - xy + 2^n(x - 1)$$

But $2^n(x - 1) \geq 2^n$, and because only the lower n bits are retained this term is lost and the final result is
$$2^n - xy$$

Case 3:
$$(-x)y$$

This case is true by Case 2 and the commutativity of multiplication.

Case 4:
$$(-x)(-y)$$
$$(2^n - x)(2^n - y) = 2^n(2^n - x - y) + xy$$

Because we are assuming an overflow has not occurred, n is large enough that $2^n - x - y > 0$ and the first term consists of bits that are not retained. Thus, the final result is xy.

An overflow occurs if and only if an addition in the shifting and adding process results in an overflow.

With addition and subtraction, an overflow can only be into the next higher bit position, but with multiplication the product can contain twice as many bits as either factor. Therefore, to avoid an overflow, the number of bits reserved for the product should be twice the number needed to express the factors. If the factors are n bits in length, then the result should be $2n$ bits long. Thus, the adder used in the multiplication process must be able to add $2n$ bits. A typical multiplication of two 4-bit 2's complement integers is:

$$
\begin{array}{r}
11111011 = -5 \\
\times 11111010 = \times -6 \\
\hline
00000000 \\
1111011 \\
000000 \\
11011 \\
1011 \\
011 \\
11 \\
1 \\
\hline
\text{Lost} \leftarrow 00011110 = 30
\end{array}
$$

Note that in this example it was necessary to extend the signs of the factors across all eight bits and that seven additions (five not involving zero operands) were required. If the multiplier were nonnegative, it would need to be only four bits in length and the multiplication could be performed as follows:

$$
\begin{array}{r}
11111011 \quad -5 \\
\times 0110 \quad \times 6 \\
\hline
00000000 \\
1111011 \\
111011 \\
00000 \\
\hline
\text{Lost} \leftarrow 11100010 = -30
\end{array}
$$

In this example, only one addition involving a nonzero number is required, although it would still need to be an 8-bit addition. Therefore, on the average more than half of the additions could be saved by applying the rule:

Multiply directly if the multiplier is nonnegative, but negate both factors if the multiplier is negative.

Because additions and negations take up most of the time needed to perform a multiplication, saving these operations considerably reduces multiplication time.

The multiplication algorithm assumed above involved only adding and shifting. If the bit positions are indexed with 0, 1, 2, . . . beginning with the bit that is furthest to the right (the least significant bit), then this algorithm is equivalent

to
$$xy = \sum_{i \in S} 2^i x$$

where S is the set of indices for the bit positions in y that contain 1, e.g.,

$$-5 \times 6 = 2^2(-5) + 2^1(-5) = 11101100 + 11110110$$
$$= 11100010 = -30$$

The restriction of using addition only (and not subtraction) is not necessary. A well-known multiplication algorithm, called **Booth's algorithm**, is derived from the above summation of $2^i x$ terms using the fact that

$$2^i = 2 \times 2^i - 2^i = 2^{i+1} - 2^i$$

to obtain an expression of the form

$$xy = \sum_{i \in S} (2^{i+1} - 2^i)x$$

Replacing a single term with two terms may seem inefficient, but in sequences with runs of adjacent 1s, all but two of the terms in each run cancel. For example,

$$6 \times 7 = (2^3 - 2^2)6 + (2^2 - 2^1)6 + (2^1 - 2^0)6$$
$$= (2^3 - 2^2 + 2^2 - 2^1 + 2^1 - 2^0)6$$
$$= (2^3 - 2^0)6$$
$$= 48 - 6$$
$$= 00110000 + 11111010$$
$$= 00101010$$
$$= 42$$

If there are no adjacent 1s, then Booth's algorithm is less efficient than using shifting and adding, and if the average length of runs is two, the efficiency is equal. But, for a random selection of 0s and 1s the average length of a run is greater than two and thus, using Booth's algorithm is superior. Although Booth's algorithm may require more additions and subtractions than straightforward adding and shifting, other similar algorithms can be derived that overcome this weakness (see Hamacher [2]).

An additional benefit of Booth's algorithm is that separate cases are not required for nonnegative and negative multipliers. An example for which the multiplier is negative is:

$$(-5)(-6) = 2^8(-5) - 2^3(-5) + 2^2(-5) - 2(-5)$$
$$= 00101000 + 11101100 + 00001010$$
$$= 00011110$$
$$= 30$$

An important special case that frequently arises is multiplication by a positive power of 2. It is apparent that if the multiplier is 2^m ($m < n$) then, regardless of the sign of the multiplicand, multiplication is equivalent to shifting the multiplicand left by m bits, e.g.,

$$1110110 = -10$$
$$10110000 = (-10) \times 8 = -80$$

In terms of Booth's algorithm, if the multiplier is 2^m, the set of indices S contains only m.

The best known procedure for dividing one n-bit nonnegative integer into another is called the **restoring division algorithm**. This algorithm assumes the divisor is D and there is a $2n + 1$-bit quantity RQ that is made up of an n-bit quantity Q appended to the right side of an $n + 1$-bit quantity R. Initially, R is filled with 0s and Q is filled with the dividend. The procedure consists of repeating the following steps n times:

1. Shift RQ left one bit.
2. Subtract D from R and put the difference into R.
3. If $R - D < 0$, then the right-most bit in Q is set to 0 and D is added back into R; otherwise the right-most bit in Q is set to 1.

This process leaves the quotient in Q and the remainder in R. The restoring-division algorithm is illustrated in Fig. 2-6.

The adding back operation is really not necessary. To demonstrate, reconsider what happens during an iteration beginning with Step 3. If the difference is nonnegative, 1 is inserted in Q and steps 1 and 2 shift RQ left and subtract D (i.e., $2[(RQ) + 1] - 2^n D$ is computed). If the difference is negative, D is added to R and steps 1 and 2 shift RQ left and subtract D (i.e., $2[(RQ) + 2^n D] - 2^n D = 2(RQ) + 2^n D$ is computed). This procedure suggests repeating the following steps 1 and 2 n times and then performing step 3:

1. If $R \geq 0$, shift RQ left one bit and subtract D from R; otherwise, shift RQ left one bit and add D to R.
2. If $R < 0$, set the right-most bit of Q to 0; otherwise set it to 1.
3. Add D to R if the last iteration leaves $R < 0$.

As before, after the procedure is completed, the quotient is in Q and the remainder is in R. This technique is called the **nonrestoring division algorithm** and is demonstrated in Fig. 2-7.

Unfortunately, no known method exists for simply dividing integer representations that may be either negative or nonnegative. Therefore, the operands are first made to be nonnegative and the signs of the quotient and remainder are determined by the law of signs of algebra. The sign given the remainder is normally that of the dividend so that the dividend is always equal to the divisor times the

	R	Q
Initial RQ	00000	1110
Shift RQ	00001	110
Subtract D	101	
	11100	
Add D	101	
Insert 0	00001	1100
Shift RQ	00011	100
Subtract D	101	
	11110	
Add D	101	
Insert 0	00011	1000
Shift RQ	00111	000
Subtract D	101	
Insert 1	00010	0001
Shift RQ	00100	001
Subtract D	101	
	11111	
Add D	101	
Insert 0	00100	0010

$$\begin{array}{r} Q = 10 \\ D = 101 \overline{)\,1110} \\ \underline{101} \\ 100 \\ \underline{000} \\ R = 100 \end{array}$$

Figure 2-6 Division of 14 by 5 using the restoring-division algorithm.

	R	Q
Initial RQ	00000	1110
Shift RQ	00001	110
Subtract D	101	
Insert 0	11100	1100
Shift RQ	11001	100
Add D	101	
Insert 0	11110	1000
Shift RQ	11101	000
Add D	101	
Insert 1	00010	0001
Shift RQ	00100	001
Subtract D	101	
Insert 0	11111	0010
Add D	101	
	00100	0010

Figure 2-7 Division of 14 by 5 using the nonrestoring-division algorithm.

Sec. 2-2   Numeric Data Types

quotient plus the remainder [e.g., -14 divided by 5 produces a quotient of -2 and a remainder of -4 and $(-2)5 + (-4) = -14$].

Because division by zero is undefined, it must be avoided. Most computers are made to detect a zero divisor in advance of the computation and, if there is an operating system, it will print out a warning message and the division will not be performed. If the hardware cannot automatically detect a zero divisor, the program should check the divisor before performing the division.

Except for division by zero, an n-bit by n-bit division cannot produce an overflow if n bits have been reserved for both the quotient and remainder. This case applies if either of the above algorithms is followed, but often the final places for storing the quotient and remainder may be only as long as the dividend. Thus, either the quotient or remainder could produce an overflow.

Just as multiplication by a positive power of 2 can be done by shifting left, division of a nonnegative integer by a positive power of 2 can be done by shifting right. When dividing by 2^m, the shift is m bits to the right and the m bits shifted out constitute the remainder. For example,

$$01101011/1000 = 00001101 \text{ with remainder} = 11$$

$$(\text{i.e., } 107/8 = 13 \text{ with remainder} = 3).$$

If the dividend is negative, special cases (which will not be considered here) must be taken into account.

Let us now consider the addition and subtraction of numbers in their 1's complement format. Unlike 2's complement addition, which throws away carries from the high order bit position, 1's complement addition must take the carry into account by adding it to the result and the carry is called an **end around carry**. To show that end around carries produce correct results, assume x and y are nonnegative and no overflows occur, and consider the following four cases:

Case 1:
$$x + y$$

This case is just binary addition and there is nothing to prove.

Case 2:
$$x + (-y)$$

If $x > y$ then

$$x + 2^n - 1 - y = 2^n - 1 + (x - y) \geq 2^n$$

and an end around carry is produced. Therefore, the final result is

$$2^n - 1 + (x - y) - 2^n + 1 = x - y$$

Otherwise, there is no end around carry and the result is

$$2^n - 1 - (y - x)$$

Case 3:
$$(-x) + y$$

Same as Case 2.

Case 4:
$$(-x) + (-y)$$
$$2^n - 1 - x + 2^n - 1 - y \geq 2^n$$

and an end around carry is always produced. Therefore, the final result is

$$2^n - 1 - x + 2^n - 1 - y - 2^n + 1 = 2^n - 1 - (x + y)$$

The use of end around carries is easy to understand and even easy to implement, but it slightly complicates the circuitry and requires more time for the extra addition. The principal advantage of the 1's complement format is that negation is easier and does not produce an overflow. This advantage simplifies subtraction, which is addition of the negated subtrahend. However, it is not sufficient to offset the addition of the end around carry and the annoyance of either putting up with or eliminating the negative 0 representation. For this reason, the 1's complement format is not used as often as the 2's complement format for representing negative integers. It will not be considered further in this book but was briefly included for completeness.

Sometimes it is not necessary to include negative integers in the data type. If all of the integers in a set are nonnegative, the set is said to be **unsigned**; otherwise, it is **signed**. Also, the operations on these sets are said to be **unsigned** or **signed** accordingly. When performing an operation on an n-bit unsigned integer, all of the bits are, of course, treated as part of the magnitude. If Booth's algorithm is used for multiplication, the same hardware can both perform unsigned and 2's complement signed additions, subtractions, and multiplications. Only with division would the hardware need to know if the operands are unsigned or signed. This advantage is why the 2's complement format is often used over other formats.

Negative packed BCD integers can be expressed in a sign-magnitude format by assigning two of the six unused 4-bit combinations to represent plus and minus. Typically, 1100 represents plus and 1101 represents minus. The 4-bit sign may be appended to either the left or right of the concatenation of digits.

Negative packed BCD integers may also be represented by the 10's complement of their magnitudes. The **n-digit 10's complement** of x is

$$10^n - x$$

Most of the previous discussion concerning 2's complements also applies to 10's complements. In particular, arithmetic algorithms are the same except that the 4-bit representations of the digits replace the individual bits in the 2's complement representations, e.g.,

```
      0000 1001 0010 0101              0925 =      925
      1001 0010 0000 1000             +9208 = +(-792)
      1001 1011 0010 1101        1    0133 =      133
            110      110  Lost ⏌
      1010 0001 0011 0011
       110
    1 0000 0001 0011 0011
Lost ⏌
```

The range of integers that can be expressed using the *n*-digit 10's complement format is $-5 \times 10^{n-1}$ to $5 \times 10^{n-1} - 1$.

2-2-3 Range and Scaling

A fixed length code restricts the number of elements in a data type to 2^n, where n is the length in bits. The undesirable side effect of having a fixed length is that overflows can occur during arithmetic operations. Overflows are particularly troublesome when multiplying because the product may require twice as many bits as factors; or, when dividing because either the quotient or remainder could cause an overflow.

In Sec. 2-2-2 it was tacitly assumed that the 2^n possible elements would be consecutive integers, either from 0 to $2^n - 1$ or approximately from -2^{n-1} to 2^{n-1}. If the set of integers is consecutive, the only way to reduce the probability of an overflow is to increase the range by increasing the length *n*. However, if it is not required that the integers be consecutive, the range could be made larger without increasing n. For example, if a set includes only even, nonnegative integers, then a length of *n* bits would provide a range of 0 to $2^{n+1} - 2$. The obvious disadvantage is that odd integers would not be represented. This omission is not as bad as it may seem. In fact, when working with large numbers, we frequently do not include some of the low order digits in our calculations.

Although the integers retained would not have to be evenly spaced, it would be difficult to work with them if they were unevenly spaced. Hence, even spacing will be assumed here. The quantity

$$\frac{\text{Distance between consecutive numbers}}{\text{Maximum} - \text{minimum}}$$

is defined as the **resolution** and the **maximum error** is half the distance between consecutive numbers. While not representing all of the integers has, for a given length, reduced the probability of overflows, it has introduced the problem of resolution and error. This has created a three-way tradeoff among length, range, and resolution. For the example above in which odd integers are omitted, the resolution would be approximately 2^{-n} and the maximum error is 1. If $n = 16$, the resolution would be 2^{-16} or one part in 64K.

If groups of *n* bits each are used to store numbers from a set that is evenly spaced by an amount s and contains the number 0, then the stored numbers are 1/*s* times the actual numbers. Multiplying all of the numbers in a set by 1/*s* before storing or operating on them is called **scaling** and 1/*s* is called the **scale factor**. When scaling, all numbers would be scaled before they are used in computations and the results would be rescaled to their true values by multiplying them by *s*. Usually the scaling would be done as the numbers are input and the results would be returned to unscaled values just before they are output.

The arithmetic hardware would operate on the numbers as if they were not scaled. This is not a problem for addition or subtraction because

$$\frac{x}{s} \pm \frac{y}{s} = \frac{x \pm y}{s}$$

but for multiplication

$$\frac{x}{s} \cdot \frac{y}{s} = \frac{xy}{s}\left(\frac{1}{s}\right)$$

and all products must be rescaled by multiplying them by s. Also, because

$$\frac{x}{s} \bigg/ \frac{y}{s} = \frac{x}{y}$$

all quotients must be rescaled by dividing them by s.

Remainders present another problem. If $s > 1$, any division by s is likely to produce a nonzero remainder. **Chopping**, which is ignoring the remainder, is not a good solution because it biases the results and increases the average error. **Rounding**, which is replacing the quotient q with the scaled number closest to

$$q + \frac{\text{remainder}}{s}$$

is much better, but does not resolve the case

$$\text{Remainder} = \frac{s}{2}$$

which has two scaled numbers that are equally close to the actual result. One solution is to leave q alone when the remainder is $s/2$. However, after numerous computations a significant error could build up and, in the extreme, when $s = 2$, this rule would be the same as chopping. A better solution would be to alternate between leaving q alone and adding 1 to its magnitude.

In the above discussion, scaling was used to increase the range and $s > 1$ was assumed. But s could be chosen to be the reciprocal of an integer greater than 1. Although this choice would reduce the range associated with a fixed length code, it would allow integer arithmetic to be used on fractions. For example, an accounting program may input and output numbers as dollars, but by letting the scale factor be 100 all internal operations would be performed on cents.

Scaling is equivalent to changing the units of the physical quantities being operated on. In the above example, the units were changed from dollars to cents. The scale factor or its reciprocal could be any positive integer greater than 1 and may be chosen to make sense physically (e.g., dollars to cents or meters to kilometers); however, a scale factor is more often chosen for computational convenience. It is usually a power of 2 because, when using binary representations, multiplication and division are reduced to shifting. Multiplication by 2^m is a matter of shifting left by m bits and division by 2^m is a right shift by m bits. Keep in mind that not only are scale factor adjustments required on the original data and the final results, but they must also be made after each multiplication and division.

If a scale factor is a positive power of 2, the scaled numbers are referred to as **fixed point numbers** because the representations can be visualized as having a binary point (i.e., the binary equivalent of a decimal point) at some fixed position within the representations. The representations are all of the form

$$a_n \cdots a_0 . a_{-1} \cdots a_{-m}$$

where *m* is the same for all representations. For example, if the scale factor is 8, then m = 3 and 01101011 is

$$01101.011 = 13.375$$

2-2-4 Real Numbers

By using a fixed point format, numbers other than integers may be accommodated. The restriction that m be a constant is, for some applications, too severe. Many scientific applications require that both very large and very small numbers be included in a calculation or a related set of calculations and this requirement could be met with a fixed point representation only if its length were very large. Because greater length increases the amount of storage needed for each number, the computation time, and/or amount of circuitry for performing the arithmetic, the length should be kept as small as possible for a given application. When a fixed point format is used, large integral numbers may include several trailing 0s (e.g., 3,433,000) and small fractions may include several leading 0s (e.g., 0.0000575). For most applications involving real numbers, the emphasis is not on representing the numbers precisely, but on representing them to some specified number of significant figures.

Avoiding leading and trailing 0s and retaining a specified number of significant figures is normally accomplished by using some form of scientific notation. For decimal numbers, scientific notation uses multiplication by powers of 10 to avoid leading and trailing 0s. For example,

$$3,433,000 = 3.433 \times 10^6 \quad \text{and} \quad 0.0000575 = 5.75 \times 10^{-5}$$

Because of their binary nature, computers replace *base 10* with a power of 2. Typically, a base of 2, 8, or 16 is used. Regardless of which base is used, the outcome is equivalent to varying the scale factor. The numbers represented in this manner are called **floating point numbers** and a particular pattern for representing floating point numbers is called a **floating point format**.

A floating point format must include two signed numbers, the exponent of the base, called the **exponent** (or **characteristic**), and the multiplier, called the **significand**. The base does not need to be part of the format because it is always the same. To design a floating point format, one must first decide upon the:

- Base.
- Resolution needed to provide the desired accuracy.
- Range of numbers to be represented.

The resolution and range are determined by the number of bits reserved for the significand and exponent, respectively.

Except for those formats used in large IBM computers, the best known are the Institute for Electrical and Electronics Engineer's (IEEE's) standard **single precision** and **double precision formats** shown in Fig. 2-8. Both assume that the numbers being represented are in the form

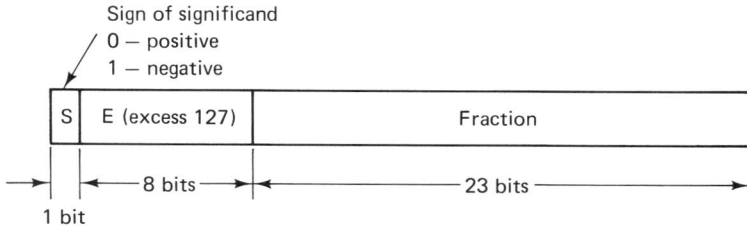

(a) Single precision

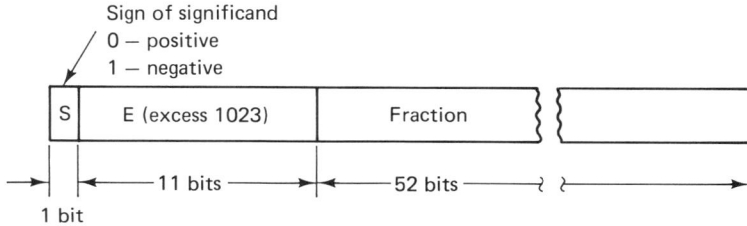

(b) Double precision

*Number E = 0 is reserved for 0 and E = 255 (or 2047) for numbers that are outside of the range.

Figure 2-8 IEEE standard floating point formats.

$$(-1)^S \times 1.\text{fraction} \times 2^{E-N}$$

where S is the value of the sign bit, E is the exponent biased by N, and $N = 127$ for single precision and 1023 for double precision. For example, for the number

$$-5.375 = -101.011 = -1.01011 \times 2^2$$

the

Sign bit = 1

$E = 2 + 127 = 129 = 10000001$

Significand = 1.01011

Fraction = 01011

Sec. 2-2   Numeric Data Types   37

and the complete representation is

$$\underbrace{1}_{\text{Sign}}\ \underbrace{10000001}_{E}\ \underbrace{01011000000000000000000}_{\text{Fraction}}$$

which in hexadecimal is C0AC0000. Conversely,

$$3E600000 = 00111110011000000000000000000000$$

is the number whose

        Sign is positive

        Exponent = $124 - 127 = -3$

        Fraction = .11

        Significand = 1.11

The number is

$$1.11 \times 2^{-3} = 0.00111 = 0.21875$$

For single precision, the 23-bit fraction divides the interval [1,2) into 2^{23} equal subintervals. Therefore, the largest error in the fraction is

$$2^{-23}/2 = 2^{-24} = \frac{1}{16}(2^{10})^{-2} \approx \frac{1}{16} \times 10^{-6} \approx 10^{-7}$$

This statement indicates that the accuracy is better than seven significant figures. The range is approximately from

$$-2 \times 2^{254-127} = -2^{128} \approx -10^{38} \text{ to } 10^{38}$$

If the magnitude of an arithmetic result is outside the range, an **exponent overflow** is said to occur.

Also of interest is the smallest positive number that can be represented. For the single precision format it is $2^{-126} \approx 10^{-38}$. If an arithmetic result has a smaller nonzero magnitude, an **exponent underflow** is said to occur. The actions taken when an exponent overflow or underflow occurs is part of a system's design. Usually, in a computer with an operating system, an exponent underflow will cause the result to be set to 0 and a message to be sent to the user. An overflow will normally cause a message to be sent and may cause a special bit pattern, referred to as **infinity**, to be substituted for the result.

For double precision, the 52-bit fraction guarantees that an error in the fraction cannot exceed

$$2^{-53} = \frac{1}{8}(2^{10})^{-5} \approx \frac{1}{8} 10^{-15} \approx 10^{-16}$$

and the accuracy is approximately 16 significant figures. The range is approximately $\pm 10^{307}$ and the smallest positive number is approximately 10^{-307}.

Note that instead of using a sign-magnitude or complement format to represent an exponent, exponents are biased by the constant 127 (or 1023). For the single precision IEEE format, positive exponents correspond to numbers greater than 127, a zero exponent to 127, and negative exponents to numbers less than 127.

A format that biases by an amount n is called an **excess n format**. Although other formats have been used to represent exponents, excess formats predominate today. It will be seen in a later discussion that the operations performed on exponents are comparison, subtraction, and addition, and when an excess format is used, these operations are unsigned.

The IEEE standard formats use sign-magnitude representations for the significands. This is normal for significands. In the IEEE standard, the fraction is always appended to a 1 that is not stored, thus making a complement format more difficult to implement. Many of the incentives for using 2's complements are not valid when working with exponents and significands. They no longer apply because of the rigid relationship between the exponent and significand, particularly the fact that the exponent must be adjusted so that the binary point is in a specific position.

For the IEEE standard format, the exponent is such that there is exactly one 1 and no 0s to the left of the binary point. If a result does not conform to this format, then the exponent is changed so that the binary point will move to its correct position. For example, the sum resulting from the addition

$$\begin{aligned} 3.75 &= 1.111 \times 2^1 \\ +(-3.375) &= -1.1011 \times 2^1 \\ \hline .375 &= 0.0011 \times 2^1 \end{aligned}$$

is not in the proper form and must be changed to 1.1×2^{-2}. The process of adjusting the exponent to get the binary point in the correct position is called **normalization**. Some computers allow numbers to sometimes be stored in an unnormalized form. Unnormalized numbers must be **prenormalized** before they are operated on. A result may be **postnormalized**.

A flowchart showing the steps required to add or subtract two floating point numbers is given in Fig. 2-9. Before the addition or subtraction can be done, one of the operands may need to be shifted until the exponents are equal. This shifting is called **alignment**. The following addition demonstrates these steps:

3FA00000 = 1.25	Operands
BF400000 = − .75	
01111111 − 01111110 = 1	Subtract exponents
1.10 → 0.11	Align by shifting significand of the second operand by 1
1.01 + (−0.11) = 0.1	Add significands
01111111 − 1 = 01111110	Normalize by subtracting 1 from the exponent and shifting significand by 1
0.1 → 1.0	
3F000000 = 0.5	Result

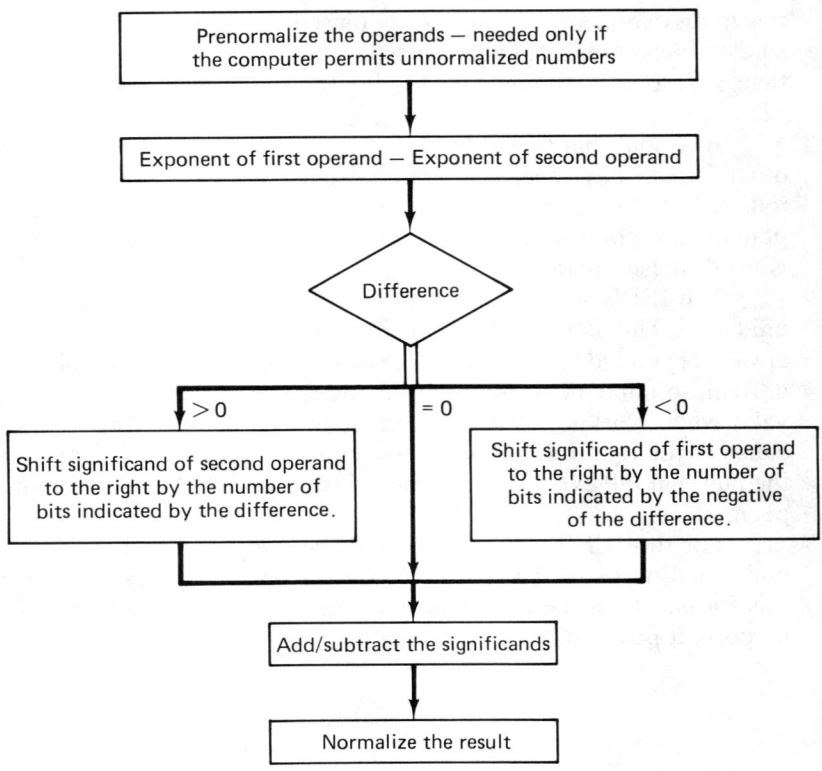

Figure 2-9 Flowchart of floating point addition/subtraction.

Multiplication is flowcharted in Fig. 2-10(a) and division in Fig. 2-10(b). Alignment is not needed in multiplication or division. The exponent of the unnormalized result is determined from the operand exponents by the laws of exponents (i.e., the operand exponents are added for multiplication and subtracted for division). However, if an excess format is used, adding the exponents produces an excess amount that must be subtracted. Subtracting the exponents cancels the excesses and the excess must be added back into the difference. For example, consider the following multiplication:

41380000 = 11.5	Operands
3F400000 = 0.75	
10000010 + 01111110 = 100000000	Add exponent fields
100000000 − 01111111 = 10000001	Subtract excess
1.0111 × 1.1 = 10.00101	Multiply significands
10000001 + 1 = 10000010	Normalize
10.00101 → 1.000101	
410A0000 = 8.625	Result

40   Data Representations   Chap. 2

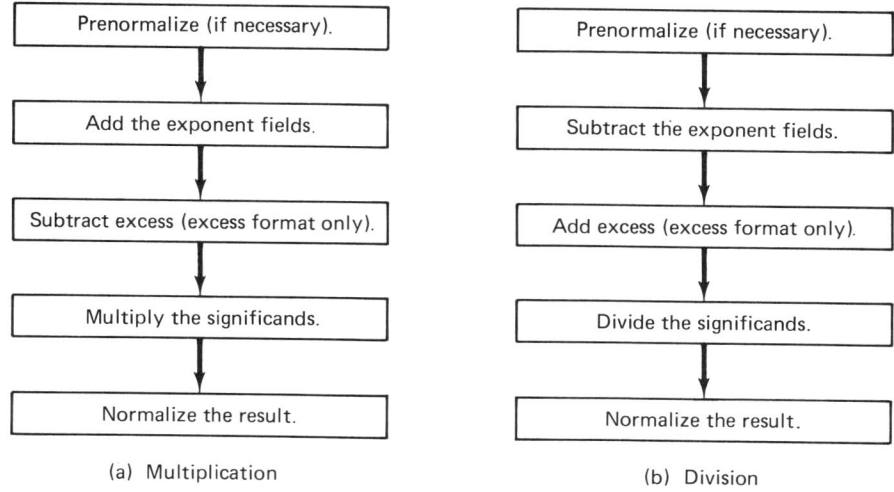

Figure 2-10 Steps needed to perform floating point multiplication and division.

An example of division is:

C0A80000 = −5.25	Operands
40E00000 = 7.0	
10000001 − 10000001 = 0	Subtract exponent fields
0 + 01111111 = 01111111	Add excess
1.0101/1.11 = 0.11	Divide significands
01111111 − 1 = 01111110	Normalize
0.11 → 1.1	
BF400000 = 0.75	Result

Figures 2-9 and 2-10 and the above examples show that integer operations and shifting are used to compute the significand and exponent of the result. Floating point operations, in general, are computed using binary arithmetic and shifting. Some computers have floating point hardware that automatically performs the steps indicated in Figs. 2-9 and 2-10, but others do not and floating point operations must be executed using the machine language instructions that perform shifts and integer operations (see Chap. 4).

Zero divisors are handled in the same way as when dividing integers. Most computers automatically detect a zero divisor in advance of a computation and leave it to the operating system to take the appropriate action.

Although the numbers in the above examples could be expressed exactly, this is certainly not always true. The division of one by ten produces the number

$$0.1_{10} = 0.0001100110011\ldots$$

which in the IEEE standard format is 3DCCCCCC.... Because only a finite

Sec. 2-2 Numeric Data Types

number of bits stores the fraction, only an approximation of the number one tenth can be stored. This problem is not unique to division. Because normalization may require a shift to the right, any of the four binary arithmetic operations may result in bits being lost. The problem we are faced with here is the same as the one introduced by scaling. As with scaling, either chopping or rounding could be used, but, because accuracy is so important when working with floating point numbers, chopping is not considered a viable solution.

Most floating point hardware is constructed so that during a computation, extra bits, called **guard bits**, are retained. Guard bits are additional bits attached to the right side of a fraction and provide a temporary means of increasing the resolution (e.g., if a fraction normally contains 23 bits and the hardware produces 4 guard bits, the fractional part of a result temporarily consists of 27 bits). Guard bits can be used either for

- Rounding or
- Retaining accuracy in the event that normalization requires a left shift.

Just how guard bits are used for rounding depends on the computer. A typical rule that avoids biasing is:

> If the guard bits are all 0, do not change the retained bits, but, if any of the guard bits are 1, set the least significant retained bit to 1.

This rule is known as **Von Neumann rounding**. If the guard bits are all 0, the retained bits are exactly correct and are left alone. Now assume that the least significant retained bit b is purely random (like flipping a coin) and that the 0-1 combinations for the guard bits occur with equal frequency. If the guard bits are viewed as a fraction f (e.g., 0101 = 5/16), then half of the time $b = 1$ and f will be lost and half of the time $b = 0$ and $1 - f$ will be gained. Because the average of f is the same as the average of $1 - f$, the average error is 0. The largest possible error is the amount represented by the least significant retained bit.

For the IEEE standard, the rule for rounding is:

> If the guard bits are not 10 . . . 0, leave the retained bits alone if the most significant guard bit is 0 and add 1 to the retained bits if the most significant guard bit is 1. When the guard bits are 10 . . . 0, set the retained bits to the nearest even number.

This algorithm is also unbiased, but is more difficult to implement. The largest error, however, is half the amount of the least significant retained bit.

The floating point formats used on the IBM 360/370 model computers are given in Fig. 2-11. The most notable differences between these formats and those of the IEEE standard are:

- The base is 16.
- The exponent for both single and double precision is represented by seven bits.

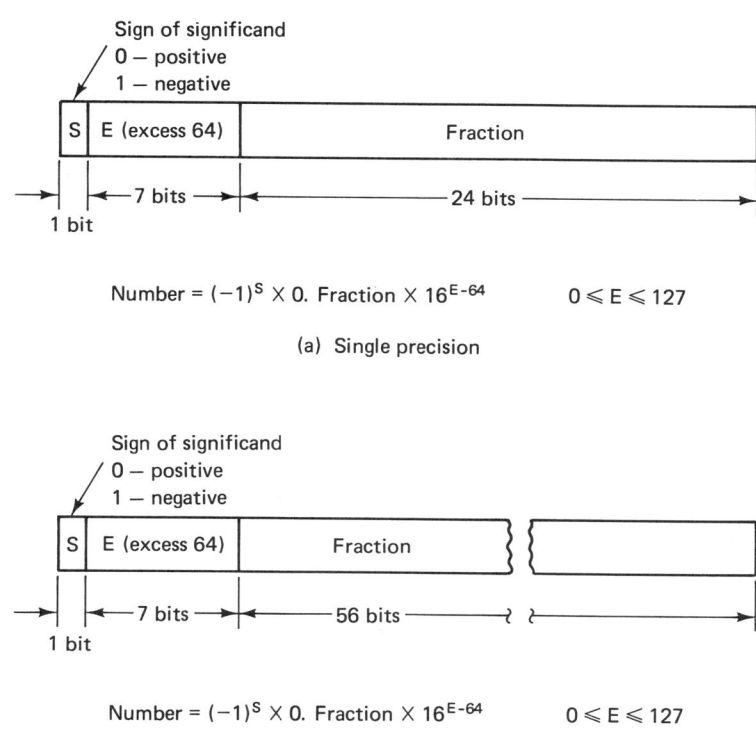

Figure 2-11 IBM 360/370 floating point formats.

- Numbers are normalized so that their fractions are greater than or equal to one sixteenth and less than one.

The range of normalized numbers is from -16^{63} to 16^{63} (approximately $\pm 10^{76}$), even though only seven bits are reserved for the exponent. Although a base of 16 yields a greater range than a base of 2, it introduces the problem of leading 0s in the fraction. In the worst case, there are only 21 significant bits in a normalized fraction. The IBM 360/370 models do permit unnormalized fractions and prenormalization may be necessary.

2-2-5 Expression Evaluation

The previous discussions have concentrated on the binary operations addition, subtraction, multiplication, and division, plus the unary operation negation. With rare exceptions, these are the only operations that can be done by a computer's arithmetic hardware. However, there are frequently other mathematical operations, such as taking the sine of an angle or evaluating an exponential, that must be performed and many computations, particularly scientific computations, require a combination of several operations. Clearly, if a computer can perform only simple arithmetic, then all operations and combinations of operations must be approximated using elementary arithmetic. It is known that:

Any expression that includes only addition, subtraction, multiplication, division, and negation can be reduced to a multivariable rational function, e.g., an expression of the form

$$\frac{a + b*c(d + e)}{f*(g + h)}$$

Any analytic function can be approximated as closely as desired by a multivariable rational function with the accuracy of the approximation being related to the complexity of the rational function (i.e., the number of operations included in the rational function).

Because of these facts, our discussions in this section are concerned only with the evaluation of rational functions.

When writing an algebraic expression, it is normal to use parentheses to indicate the order in which the elementary operations are to be carried out. By convention, it is possible to omit some of the parentheses [e.g., $a + bc$ means $a + (bc)$], but the requirement for ordering the computations is always present, be it explicit or implicit. If the ordering is specified by using parentheses, then the expression is said to use **infix notation** because the binary operators are placed between their operands. An alternative is to use **postfix**, or **reverse Polish**, **notation**, where the operators are placed after their operands. For example, if an expression is written

$$[a + b*c(d + e)]/[f*(g - h)]$$

using infix notation, then it is written

$$abc*de + *+ fgh - */$$

using postfix notation. An expression in postfix notation requires no parentheses, but is evaluated according to the rule

Scan the expression from left to right. Each time a binary operator (i.e., $+$, $-$, $*$, or $/$) is encountered, perform the operation on the two operands that appear just prior to the operator and then replace these operands and the operator with the result. For negation, only the last operand and the negative operator are replaced by the result.

For the above expression, if $s = bc$, $t = d + e$, $u = st$, $v = a + u$, $w = g - h$, $x = fw$, and $y = v/x$, then the computation would proceed as follows:

$$abc*de + *+ fgh - */ = asde + *+ fgh - */$$

$$= ast* + fgh - */$$

$$= au + fgh - */$$
$$= vfgh - */$$
$$= vfw*/$$
$$= vx/$$
$$= y$$

The evaluation of postfix expressions is aided by the use of a temporary storage facility known as a **last-in/first-out (LIFO) stack**. A LIFO stack stores its items (e.g., operands) in such a way that the last item stored is always the first item retrieved. A LIFO stack is analogous to a stack of dishes on which each new dish is placed on the stack of previous dishes and from which dishes are removed by always taking the dish from the top of the stack. Putting an item onto a LIFO stack is called a **push** and retrieving an item is called a **pop**. If a LIFO stack is used, the above rule for evaluating a postfix expression becomes

> Scan the expression from left to right. Each time an operand is encountered, push it onto the stack, and each time a binary operator is encountered, pop the top two operands from the stack, perform the operation, and push the result back onto the stack. For negation, pop the operand from the top of the stack, negate it, and push the result.

Figure 2-12 shows the contents of the stack during the various stages of the evaluation of the expression in the above example.

All of the commonly used high-level languages use infix notation to specify algebraic expressions because it is the notation used by mathematicians, scientists, and engineers. But some computers are constructed with hardware that facilitates the use of stacks (see Chap. 4) and are naturally suited to the postfix procedure for evaluating expressions. When the high-level language being used employs the infix notation, and machine language programs use the postfix pro-

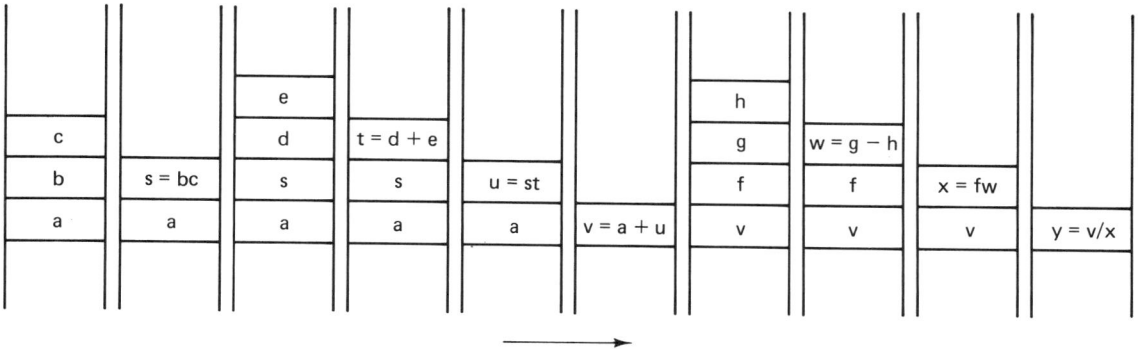

Figure 2-12 Stack contents as the postfix expression $abc*de++*fgh-*/$ is evaluated.

Sec. 2-2 Numeric Data Types

Text Data Types:
  Basic
    Alphanumeric codes - characters
      Fixed length - ASCII (7-bit)
      Variable length
  General - character strings

Numeric Data Types:
  Basic
    Integers
      Representation
        Binary
          Sign-magnitude
          2's complement
          1's complement
        Packed BCD
          Sign-magnitude
          10's complement
        Unpacked BCD
      Types of arithmetic operations
        Unsigned
        Signed
      Length in bits
      Range
        Unscaled
        Scaled - resolution
          Scale factor less than 1
          Scale factor greater than 1 (fixed point format)
    Real numbers
      Representation
        IEEE standard formats
        IBM formats
      Format properties
        Sign of fraction (normally a sign-magnitude format)
        Resolution of fraction
        Base
        Normalization method
        Exponent representation (normally an excess is used)
        Exponent range
        Precision (length of fraction)
          Single
          Double
      Procedures for performing arithmetic operations
      Rounding method (use of guard bits)
        Von Neumann
        IEEE standard
  General - vectors, matrices, and so on

Instruction Data Types (see Chap. 4).

Figure 2-13 Summary of the data type topics discussed in this chapter.

cedure, an infix-to-postfix conversion must be performed by a translating program (see Stallings [6]). However, such conversions would be employed only if the computer includes hardware stack facilities.

As a set of conceptual rules, a stack is an abstract data type that consists of a collection of objects that must be accessed according to certain rules. A hardware stack facility provides the means for working with a stack as a physical data type.

2-3 DESIGN REMARKS

Because the purpose of a computer is to process data, the decisions as to how the data are to be represented and operated on are the first decisions that must be resolved when designing a computer. At the beginning of the design process, one must determine the codes for the basic data types, particularly their lengths because it is the length that determines the size of the set to be represented. For numeric data types, the length also has a direct bearing on the range and resolution. However, as length increases, so does the amount of circuitry needed to store and operate on the data and the time required to make calculations.

Of equal importance is the determination of the operations to be performed and the algorithms for carrying out those operations. Although selection of the 0-1 representations of the basic data types is indicated as being of premier importance, it may be affected by the operations needed and the algorithms used. A general purpose computer would require all of the arithmetic operations—negation, addition, subtraction, multiplication, and division—and may need to perform these operations on packed BCD or floating point numbers as well as integers represented using a binary format. It may be possible to execute floating point operations using integer arithmetic, or, the speed of floating point hardware may be needed.

The important data types and related topics discussed in this chapter are outlined in Fig. 2-13. The items in the outline indicate choices that must be made while designing the circuits that must work with and store the elements of the data types. These choices determine the extent of the text data types and the accuracies and ranges of the numeric data types, which, in turn, dictate the amount of storage and processing circuitry needed.

REFERENCES

1. Stubbs, Daniel F., and Neil W. Webre, *Data Structures with Abstract Data Types and Pascal* (Monterey, California: Brooks/Cole Publishing Company, 1984).
2. Hamacher, V. Carl, Zvonko G. Vranesic, and Safwat G. Zaky, *Computer Organization*, 2nd ed. (New York: McGraw-Hill Book Company, 1984).
3. Struble, George, *Assembler Language Programming: The IBM System/360 and 370*, 2nd ed., (Reading, Massachusetts: Addison Wesley Publishing Company, 1975).

4. Gibson, Glenn A., and Yu-cheng Liu, *Microcomputers for Engineers and Scientists*, 2nd ed. (Englewood Cliffs, New Jersey: Prentice Hall, Inc., 1987).
5. Hwang, Kai, and Faye A. Briggs, *Computer Architecture and Parallel Processing* (New York: McGraw-Hill Book Company, 1984).
6. Stallings, William, *Computer Organization and Architecture* (New York: Macmillan Publishing Company, 1987).

EXERCISES

1. If the length of a code is 12, how many elements are in the basic data type? If 48 bits are used to represent consecutive nonnegative integers beginning with 0, what is the value of the largest integer?
2. Use hexadecimal to give the ASCII equivalents of the following strings:
    (a) JOE   (b) LIU, CHI-NAM   (c) 91 Elm St.   (d) P.O. Box 5 Wink, TX
3. For each of the following ways of specifying real numbers using decimal digits, determine the range and accuracy of the representations and discuss the space needed to write the numbers and the time needed to make calculations using the numbers:
    (a) Four digits and a sign, but no decimal point.
    (b) Eight digits, but no sign or decimal point.
    (c) Eight digits, a sign, and a decimal point that is always three digits from the right.
4. What are the binary and decimal equivalents of the following hexadecimal numbers:
    (a) 62B4   (b) C8015   (c) 10052A2F
5. How many bits would it take to represent the decimal number 72560:
    (a) In binary?   (b) In packed BCD?   (c) In unpacked BCD?
6. Determine the 0-1 combination that represents the decimal number 1052 in
    (a) Binary format   (b) Packed BCD format   (c) ASCII format
7. Determine the packed BCD and ASCII (decimal digit) string representations of the binary number 0110100111010011.
8. Assume the following binary numbers:

    $$A = 1101 \quad B = 1001 \quad C = 1101001$$

    Using the same algorithms as used in decimal arithmetic, compute
    (a) $A + B$ (b) $A - B$ (c) AB (d) C/B (e) AC
9. Use binary arithmetic and adjustment to add the packed BCD numbers 3586 and 5195.
10. Convert the following ASCII coded number to packed BCD and then convert the result to binary:

    $$1862 = 00110001\ 00111000\ 00110110\ 00110010$$

11. Convert the following binary number to packed BCD and then convert it to an ASCII coded string:

    $$0100110111001000$$

12. Find the negative of 01001101 assuming the:
    (a) 8-bit 2's complement format
    (b) 8-bit 1's complement format

13. Assume that in the 8-bit 2's complement format

$$A = 00011011 \quad B = 00101010 \quad C = 11100011$$

Compute the following by adding the negative to perform subtraction:
(a) $A + B$ (b) $A + C$ (c) $A - B$ (d) $A - C$ (e) $C - C$ (f) $B - A$ (g) $B - C$
(h) $C - A$ (i) $C - B$

Check your answers by carrying out the operations using signed decimal numbers.

14. Prove that, when adding numbers in their 2's complement format, an overflow has occurred if and only if the operands have the same sign and the sum has the opposite sign.

15. Prove that, when subtracting numbers in their 2's complement format, an overflow occurs if and only if the operands have opposite signs and the difference has the same sign as the subtrahend.

16. Prove that if a multiplier can be expressed using the $n/2$-bit 2's complement format (n even) while its multiplicand and product use n bits, an $n/2$- by n-bit multiplication could be done by shifting and adding provided that, if the multiplier is negative, $2^{n/2}$ times the multiplicand is subtracted from the result. (Hint: Break the proof into cases.)

17. Assume that

$$A = 0100 \quad B = 0111 \quad C = 1011$$

are 4-bit 2's complement integers and compute
(a) AB using simple shifting and adding.
(b) BC using simple shifting and adding.
(c) $(-A)C$ using simple shifting and adding.
(d) BC using the algorithm proved in Exercise 16.
(e) $(-A)C$ using the algorithm proved in Exercise 16.
(f) AB using Booth's algorithm.
(g) BC using Booth's algorithm.
(h) $(-B)C$ using Booth's algorithm.
(i) CB using Booth's algorithm.

18. Assume that

$$A = 1101 \quad B = 0111 \quad C = 0011$$

are unsigned integers and compute
(a) A/B using restoring division.
(b) A/C using restoring division.
(c) A/B using nonrestoring division.
(d) A/C using nonrestoring division.
(e) B/A using nonrestoring division.

19. Assume the 8-bit 1's complement format and repeat Exercise 13.

20. Suppose that 20 bits are used to represent every tenth integer beginning with 0. What is the range, resolution, and maximum error of the set being represented?

21. Suppose that it is necessary to represent every eighth integer from -100000_{10} through 100000_{10}. How many bits are required?

22. If a scale factor of $1/s$ is used, list every operation, including the scale factor adjustments, needed to complete the computation:

$$U/V + W(X + Y)$$

23. Given that the numbers in the following expression are scaled by a scale factor of 10, what are the scaled and unscaled results?

$$4(8 - 6)/2 + 7$$

In carrying out the computation, show the individual scale factor adjustments.

24. Assume the single precision IEEE standard format and find the decimal equivalents of:
    (a) 40A00000   (b) C1280000   (c) BE700000

25. Given the numbers
    (a) -12.5 (b) 112.6875   (c) 1.1
    find their representations in the IEEE standard single precision format.

26. Assume the IEEE standard double precision format and rework Exercise 25.

27. For each of the following, use Von Neumann rounding and determine the retained bits:

	Other bits	Guard bits
(a)	1101	0000
(b)	1010	0001
(c)	1001	1111
(d)	1110	1000
(e)	1111	1000

28. Repeat Exercise 27 using IEEE standard rounding. Note that for Part (e), normalization after rounding is necessary.

29. Assume the IBM single-precision floating point format and find the decimal equivalents of:
    (a) C0600000   (b) 42900000   (c) 3F180000

30. Repeat Exercise 25, but find the IBM single precision representations.

31. For the worst case, how many significant figures (in decimal) are kept when using the IBM single precision format?

32. Give the postfix expressions corresponding to the following infix expressions:
    (a) $(a + b*c)/(d*e - f*g)$
    (b) $a + b(c*d/(e + f*g))$

33. If a stack is used to evaluate the postfix expression

$$ab + cd +/efg + * -$$

show the stack activity as the computation is being performed (see Fig. 2-12).

3

Computer Circuits

As discussed in Chap. 2, all processing and data storage is accomplished using binary representations and all of a computer's circuits are of a binary, or two-state, nature. Binary circuits have two notable characteristics:

- Their useful states are extreme, or saturation, states which are relatively insensitive to input changes, such as no current or nearly the maximum current that the circuit can handle.
- Changes between these states cannot occur instantaneously.

The first characteristic is what makes binary circuits so reliable and the second is one of the two main factors preventing the construction of an infinitely fast computer. The time it takes an elementary binary circuit to change from one of its states to the other is called its **switching time**. The other factor that restricts the speed of a computer is the times, called **propagation delays**, that it takes for electromagnetic signals to travel through the computer's circuits and links. The switching times and propagation delays of a computer's circuits and links are the ultimate limits of the computer's speed.

This chapter concentrates on fundamental computer circuits and the problems and restrictions, such as switching times, propagation delays, and power consumption, that affect their design. It assumes a basic knowledge of digital logic. For those who are not familiar with (or need to review) Boolean algebra, logic gates, Karnaugh maps, and flip-flops, Appendix B contains a review of this material. It examines very elementary circuits. The computer circuits considered here are those such as decoders, comparators, and adders that are constructed from these elementary circuits.

3-1 ELECTRICAL PROPERTIES

The three passive parameters in any electrical circuit are resistance, capacitance, and inductance. The active device in computer circuitry is the transistor. The purpose of this section is not to analyze computer circuits in detail, but to relate these passive parameters and the characteristics of transistors to the fundamental electrical limitations of computer design.

3-1-1 Circuit Effects on Timing

We begin with the simplified model of a transistor and its associated voltage source and load shown in Fig. 3-1. In this model, R_i (which may be infinite for some technologies) and C represent the internal resistance and capacitance of the transistor, R_s is the equivalent resistance of the voltage source applied to the input, g_m is the gain of the transistor (i.e., the amount by which the transistor's input is magnified), and R_L is the resistance of the load connected to the output. Because our interest lies with the binary properties of the transistor, let us assume the input is an abrupt change between the two voltage levels 0 and V_s as shown in Fig. 3-2(a). (For convenience, one of the levels is taken to be 0. However, the analysis is the same regardless of the two levels.) From network theory (see Nilsson [6]) it can be shown that

$$v_0(t) = V_0(1 - e^{-t/RC})$$

where V_0 is a constant that depends on V_s, the passive parameters, and the gain g_m, and R is an equivalent resistance that depends on R_i and R_s. A graph of $v_0(t)$ is given in Fig. 3-2(b). A measure of how quickly the output reacts to the change at the input is the length of time it takes for the output to attain $1 - 1/e \approx 0.63$ of its final value. This time is $\tau = RC$ and is called the circuit's **time constant**. The switching time of the transistor is approximately two time constants. The switching time is proportional to the internal capacitance of the transistor and demonstrates the importance of this capacitance.

A gate may be made up of several transistors and a model of a gate may include numerous resistances and capacitances. However the output voltage tends

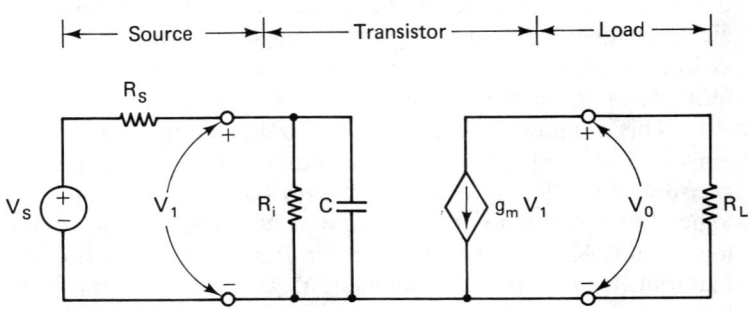

Figure 3-1 Simplified transistor model.

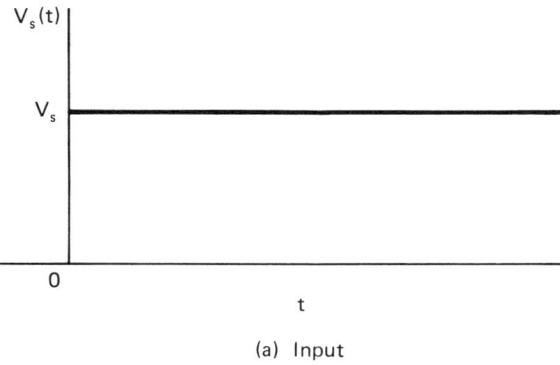

(a) Input

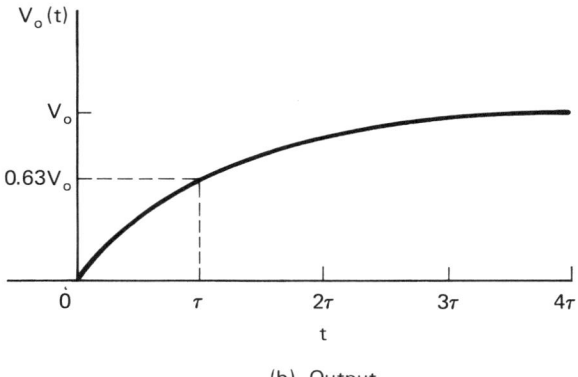

(b) Output

Figure 3-2 Transistor output response to a step change.

to have the same form as that shown in Fig. 3-2(b) and the reaction time is proportional to a dominant time constant that depends on the resistances and capacitances in the gate. Capacitances and the resistances through which the capacitances must be charged significantly contribute to the time constants and hence, the switching times. Typical gate switching times are from 0.1 to 50 nS.

Now consider the model of a conductor connected to a voltage source, such as a gate, shown in Fig. 3-3. The resistance R is the combined resistances of the voltage source driving the conductor and of the conductor itself, and C represents the combined capacitance of the conductor, the source's output, the load's input, and the connections to the conductor. This model is rather crude, but is reasonably accurate for frequencies whose wavelengths are long compared to the length of the conductor. (The wavelength of a one gigahertz signal is approximately 30 cm; therefore, except for very high speed computers, the model would be suitable for conductors on a single PC board and would be good enough for all conductors internal to an IC.) Because this model is also a resistance/capacitance circuit, the response at the end of the conductor to a step change at the input would have the same exponential shape as in Fig. 3-2(b). Therefore, the propagation delay would be proportional to the time constant RC, once again demonstrating that

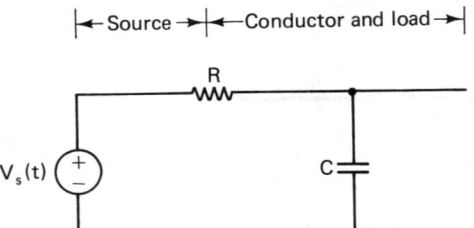

Figure 3-3 Source-driven conductor model.

keeping the capacitance small increases the speed with which the final state is reached.

Because pulses are often applied to link conductors, Fig. 3-4 is included to illustrate the pulse shapes at the output as the width of the source pulse becomes shorter. Because the shape of the response to a step change at the input is always the same, the decline of the output has the same exponential shape as the rise, except that it is inverted. Note that as long as the width is several times the time constant, the output is almost a square pulse except that the edges are not entirely sharp. As the input pulse becomes shorter the output deteriorates until it is no longer a recognizable pulse.

The second major effect on timing is due to the finite speed of electromagnetic propagation, which is not only theoretically bounded by the speed of light, but is also limited by the presence of inductance and capacitance. In a lossless conductor the speed of propagation is $1/\sqrt{LC}$ m/S, where L and C are the per meter distributed inductance and capacitance along the conductor. For the conductors within an IC, both L and C are small and the distances are short so that propagation delays along the conductors are small compared to the gate switching times. But, as conductors are extended between ICs, PC boards, or subsystems, the problem of propagation delays becomes increasingly serious, particularly if the longer lengths are coupled with an increase in L and/or C. For distances over a few meters the designer must contend with both propagation delays and deterioration of the signal (i.e., rounding of the edges) due to the resistance/capacitance effects.

In addition to the loss of time associated with propagation delays, the delays in the conductors in a bus may not be the same. The phenomenon of two or more signals traveling between a source and a destination or one signal traveling to different destinations having different delays is called **skew**. It may be because of the different lengths, different parametric values, or the inclusion of additional circuitry in some of the conductor links; but, whatever the cause, skew forces a design to account for the worst case delay.

3-1-2 Power Considerations

Much of the power consumed by an IC is due to the currents needed to charge the capacitances inherent to the circuit. These currents must flow through resistances and this, of course, generates heat. Consider the simple RC series circuit

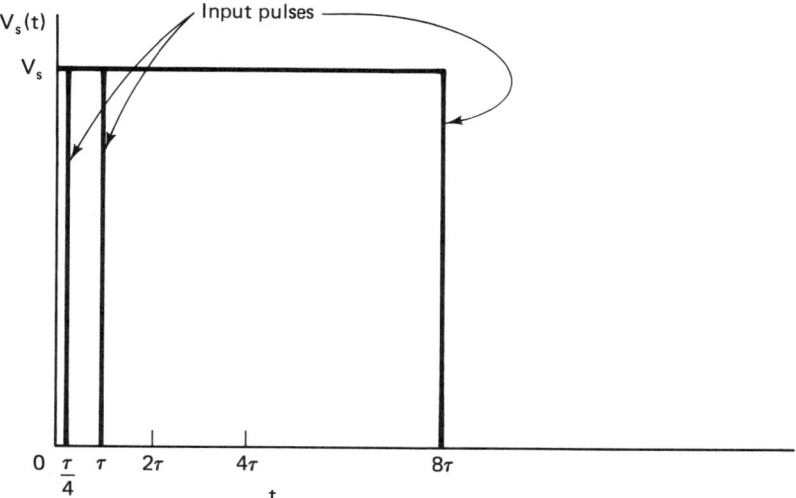

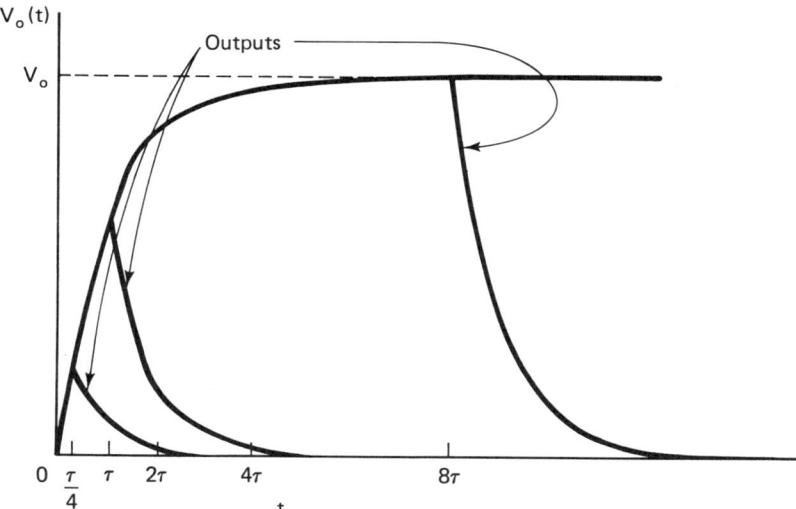

Figure 3-4 Output responses to input pulses applied to a conductor.

shown in Fig. 3-5. If the capacitor initially contains no charge and the input voltage is raised from 0 to V, then, using network theory (see Nilsson [6]), it can be shown that the energy dissipated by the resistor is

$$\frac{1}{2} CV^2$$

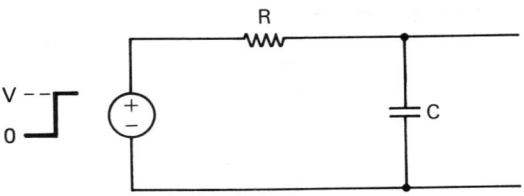

Figure 3-5 Heat dissipation of an RC circuit.

If an input pulse is of sufficient width to charge the capacitor until the voltage across it is essentially V, then the total energy expended in charging and discharging the capacitor is CV^2. When a train of pulses is applied with frequency f, then the power consumed is

$$P = fCV^2$$

As in our discussion of time constants, a circuit consisting of one or more gates may include numerous resistance/capacitance combinations, but the overall effect is the same as that of a simple RC circuit. The power consumed is

$$P = f\sum_i C_i V_i^2$$

where the C_is are the individual capacitances and the V_is are the maximum voltages across them. Because this power is proportional to frequency and must be dissipated as heat, the speed of an IC could be restricted by the power dissipation requirements and not the switching times of the transistors. Within the limits of a given technology, speed can be increased arbitrarily by increasing power, but the more power being consumed by each transistor, the fewer the number of transistors the IC can contain. This is the classical speed versus power tradeoff.

The above power equation also applies to the model of a voltage driven conductor that may include source, line, and load capacitances. In this case, there is only one voltage and one capacitance to be concerned with, and only the total effective capacitance and average frequency of changes needs to be estimated. The voltage would normally be known. For a typical conductor between two ICs, $V = 5$ V and the total $C = 100$ pF; thus the power needed to drive the conductor at 8 MHz is

$$P = 8 \times 10^6 \times 100 \times 10^{-12} \times 5^2 = 20 \text{ mW}$$

To drive 32 such conductors would require 0.64 W, most of which would appear as heat to be radiated from the IC. This heat is not an insignificant amount to dissipate from a single IC. A rule of thumb is:

An IC that consumes more than 2 W may need special means for dissipating its heat.

Other problems related to power consumption are those of fan-in and fan-out. Physical considerations relating to power consumption and voltage differences place a maximum on the number of inputs to a gate. This maximum is referred to as the gate's **fan-in capacity**. Similarly, there is a maximum number of gates or other electronic devices that can be connected to a gate's output, and this maximum is the gate's **fan-out capacity**. The fan-in and/or fan-out capability of a gate depends on its construction and can be quite restrictive. The effects of limited fan-in and fan-out will become evident as we proceed.

3-2 COMBINATIONAL LOGIC IMPLEMENTATIONS

As shown in Fig. 3-6, any combinational logic circuit is a device that physically maps 0-1 input combinations into 0-1 output combinations. It is well known (see Appendix B) that any combinational logic circuit can be described as a sum of products, where each product is a minterm, or as a product of sums, where each sum is a maxterm. For example, the output X defined by the Karnaugh map in Fig. 3-7(a) can be written

$$X = \overline{A}B\overline{C} + ABC + AB\overline{C} + A\overline{B}C$$

or

$$X = (A + B + C)(A + B + \overline{C})(A + \overline{B} + \overline{C})(\overline{A} + B + \overline{C})$$

The corresponding logic diagrams are shown in Figs. 3-7(b) and 3-7(c). It is apparent from this example that a sum of products implementation can always be obtained from the variables and their complements by including an AND gate for each minterm and then ORing the minterms. Similarly, a product of a sums circuit can be obtained from the variables and their complements by including an OR gate for each maxterm and ANDing the maxterms.

One criterion for minimizing a logic circuit is to ignore inversions and minimize the number of other gate inputs. (The reasoning behind this criterion is that generally, each input requires at least one transistor.) It is seen from Fig. 3-7 that, with no reduction, both the sum of products and product of sums require 16 AND and OR gate inputs. From the Karnaugh map, it is clear that X could be expressed

$$X = AB + A\overline{C} + B\overline{C}$$

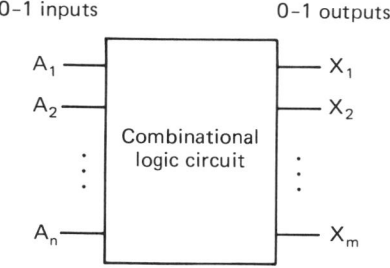

Figure 3-6 General combinational logic circuit.

Sec. 3-2   Computational Logic Implementations   57

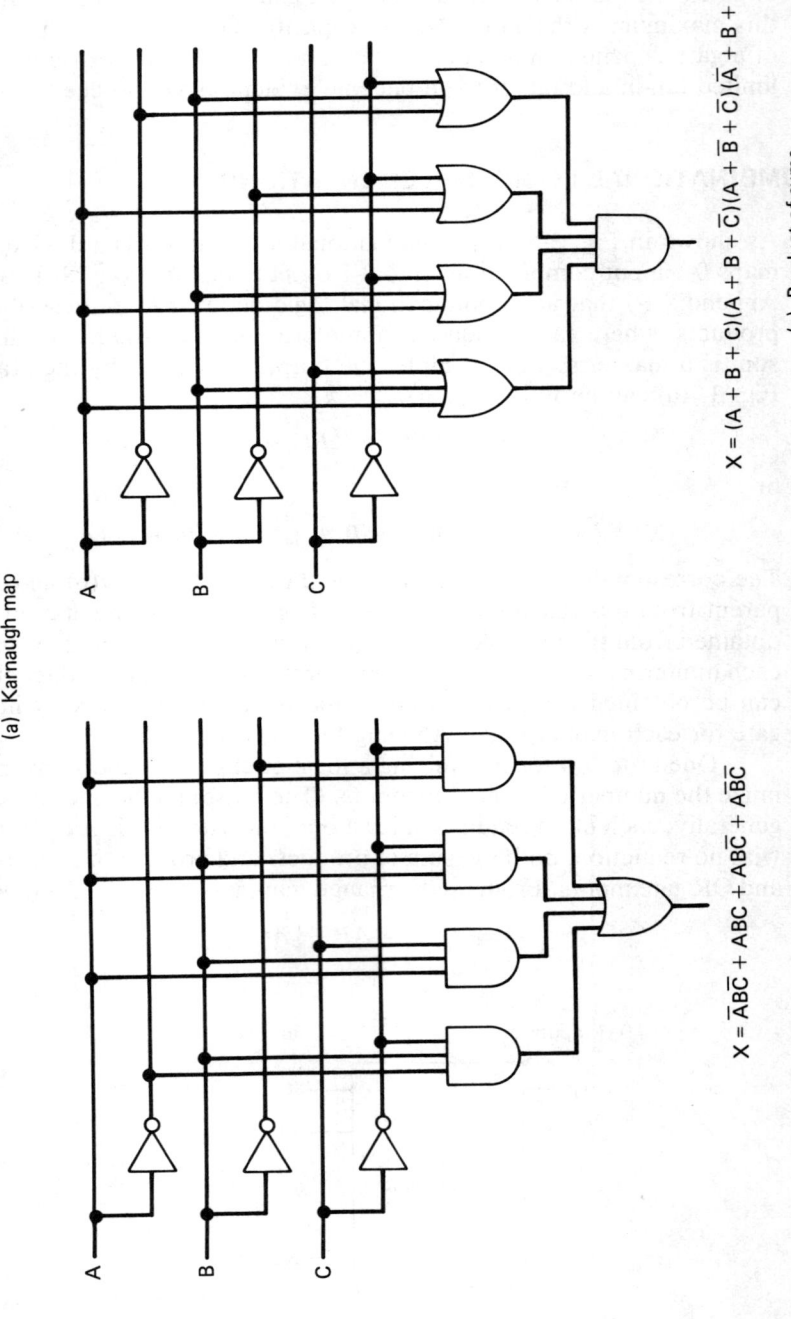

Figure 3-7 Example combinational logic implementations.

or
$$X = (A + B)(A + \overline{C})(B + \overline{C})$$
which, in both cases, would reduce the number of inputs to 9. The logic diagram for the reduced sum of products is shown in Fig. 3-8(a). By factoring A from the

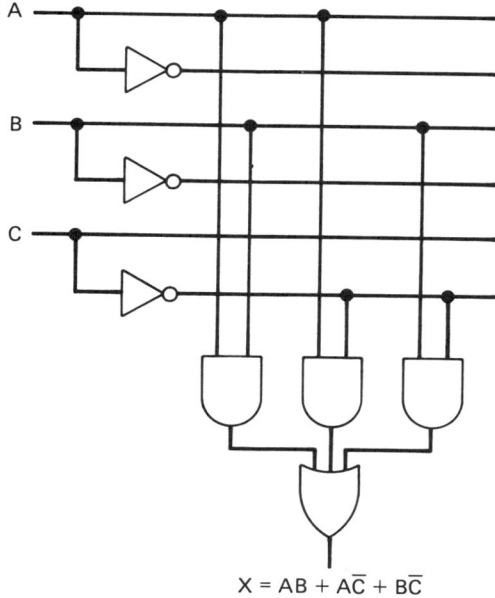

(a) Reduced sum of products

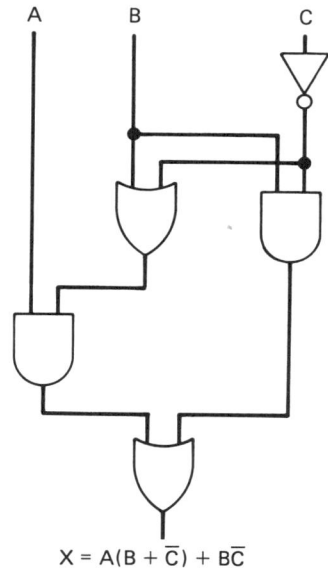

$X = A(B + \overline{C}) + B\overline{C}$

(b) Additional reduction by factoring

Figure 3-8 Minimizing the number of gate inputs.

Sec. 3-2   Computational Logic Implementations

first two terms of the sum of products to get

$$X = A(B + \overline{C}) + B\overline{C}$$

the logic diagram can be reduced to the one shown in Fig. 3-8(b), which includes only eight gate inputs.

It appears that the logic diagram in Fig. 3-8(b) is optimal, but there is a second criterion for optimizing a circuit—to minimize the total amount of delay due to switching times between the time the inputs are applied and the time the output has stabilized to its final state. For cascaded gates, the total delay is the maximum, taken over all possible paths, of the sum of the delays in each path. If each gate in Fig. 3-8 has a delay of 10 nS, the total delay for the circuit in Fig. 3-8(b) (ignoring inversions) is 30 nS, which is a 50% increase over the 20 nS delay for the circuit in Fig. 3-8(a).

Figure 3-9 gives a second example for which the reduction in inputs is from

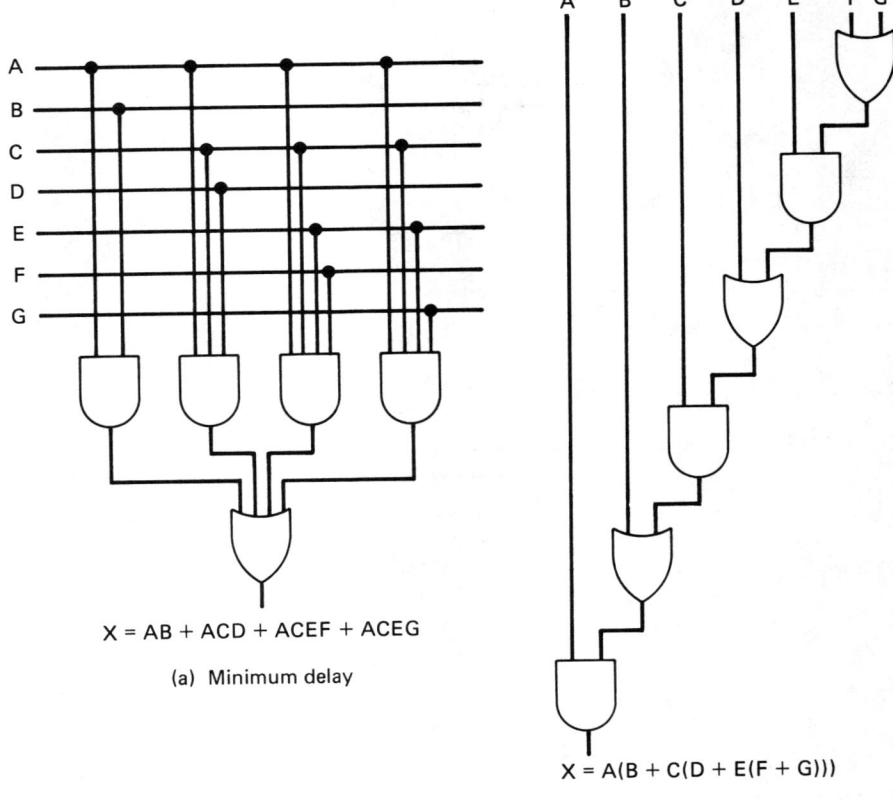

Figure 3-9 Example of the minimum number of inputs versus minimum delay tradeoff.

17 to 12 and the increase in delay time is from 20 to 60 nS (again assuming a 10 nS delay per gate). This is an even more pronounced example of the minimum number of inputs versus minimum delay tradeoff. One should realize, however, that the minimum delay alternative can be affected by fan-in. For example, in Fig. 3-9, if the fan-in were 3, some factoring would be necessary. By factoring out A, the fan-in problem could be resolved and the number of inputs could be reduced by 3, but the delay would be increased by 10 nS.

Using the number of inputs to judge the complexity of a circuit is a rather crude gauge because there are so many ways to construct a logic circuit electronically. The accuracy of this gauge depends on whether the application warrants a customized design or off-the-shelf discrete logic packages are to be used. Minimizing the number of inputs is more applicable to the latter case because each input requires not only a transistor but a solder connection.

Another reason for using the straightforward constructions shown in Fig. 3-7, is the regularity of their patterns. When manufacturing an IC, the electronics can be simplified and packed much more densely if they are patterned instead of being irregular as in Fig. 3-8(b). This simplification is especially useful for circuits that include thousands of gates.

When building complex logic circuits there is considerable incentive for electronically designing the circuit as a whole, as opposed to first designing the logic gates and then putting them together. Designing the circuit as a whole allows optimization of the amount of electronic circuitry and/or the delay time. On the other hand, the more complicated a circuit, the more limited its application. This problem does not apply to customized circuits, but for general manufacture one would like the application to be as broad as possible. What is needed is a logic product that either can be easily built to a user's specifications or is manufactured in a set pattern that can be easily modified by the user. There are two such products available; the read only memory and programmable logic array.

Before defining read only memories and programmable logic arrays let us introduce the two circuits on which they depend. A **decoder** is a logic circuit whose outputs are minterms of the inputs and therefore, exactly one output is 1 at any given time. If n is the number of inputs and m the number of outputs then $2^n \geq m$. A 3-input decoder design is illustrated in Fig. 3-10(a). The truth table for this decoder is

A_1	A_2	A_3	X_1	X_2	X_3	X_4	X_5	X_6	X_7	X_8
0	0	0	1	0	0	0	0	0	0	0
0	0	1	0	1	0	0	0	0	0	0
0	1	0	0	0	1	0	0	0	0	0
0	1	1	0	0	0	1	0	0	0	0
1	0	0	0	0	0	0	1	0	0	0
1	0	1	0	0	0	0	0	1	0	0
1	1	0	0	0	0	0	0	0	1	0
1	1	1	0	0	0	0	0	0	0	1

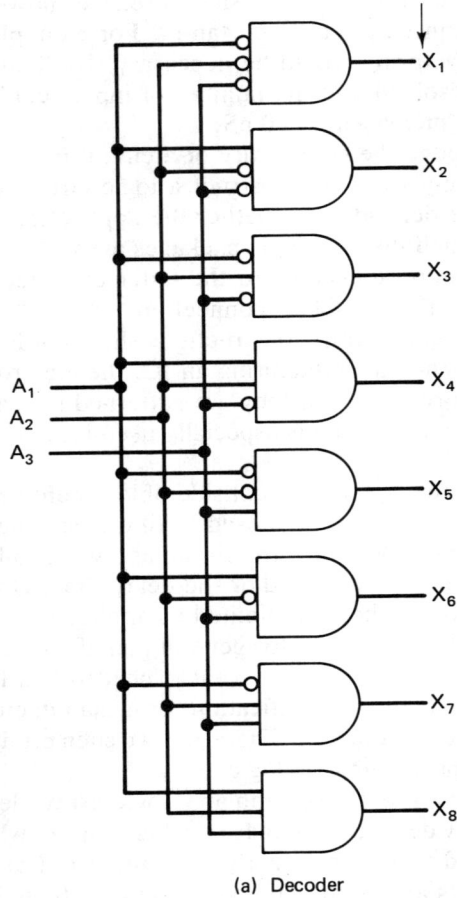

(a) Decoder

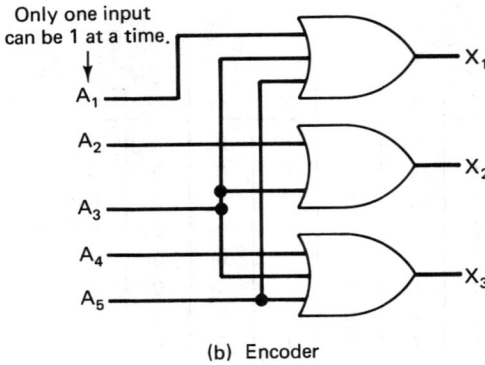

(b) Encoder

Figure 3-10 Decoder and encoder implementations.

An **encoder** is the opposite of a decoder in that only one input can be 1 at a time. A 3-output encoder design is illustrated in Fig. 3-10(b). The corresponding truth table is

A_1	A_2	A_3	A_4	A_5	X_1	X_2	X_3
1	0	0	0	0	1	0	0
0	1	0	0	0	0	1	0
0	0	1	0	0	1	1	1
0	0	0	1	0	0	0	1
0	0	0	0	1	1	0	1

(The input combinations not included are invalid.)

A **read only memory (ROM)** is depicted in Fig. 3-11(a) and is a circuit that is equivalent to a decoder that outputs all possible minterms followed by an encoder. For a ROM, the output combinations are permanently embedded in its circuitry and the inputs serve to select one of these combinations. A **programmable logic array (PLA)** is similar, except that, as seen from Fig. 3-11(b), the decoder does not necessarily produce all of the minterms. Although the theoretical dif-

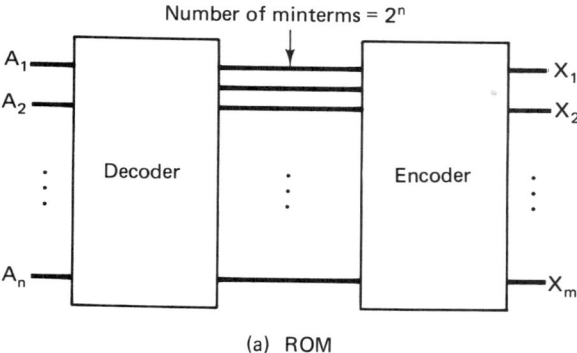

(a) ROM

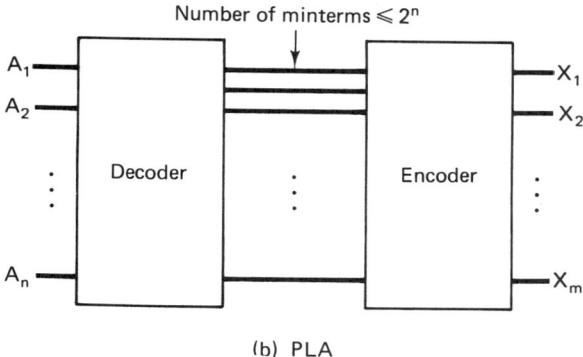

(b) PLA

Figure 3-11 Definitions of ROMs and PLAs.

Sec. 3-2 Computational Logic Implementations

ference between a ROM and PLA is minor, their constructions may differ considerably. Because a ROM must produce *all* minterms, its decoder portion is fixed by n. Its encoder portion however, depends on both m and the way in which the outputs of the decoder are used to generate the final ROM outputs. On the other hand, the designer of a PLA is free to specify the construction of both the decoder and encoder.

For example, suppose that the decoder and encoder of a PLA are constructed from AND and OR gates as indicated in Fig. 3-10. If it has p AND gates, by properly connecting the PLA inputs to the AND gate inputs, up to p specified minterms could be produced. If it has m OR gates, by properly connecting the AND gate outputs to the OR gate inputs, up to m specified sums of minterms could be the outputs of the PLA. It is possible to order custom PLAs from an IC manufacturer by designating the minterms and outputs, but a number of manufacturers produce standard PLA circuits that can be programmed by the buyer. Standard PLAs are manufactured with all possible AND and OR gate connections made and, by using special programming equipment, the buyer can delete unwanted connections. Thereby, the buyer can customize the standard PLA to match his or her specific requirements.

ROMs can also be custom ordered or be such that they can be programmed (customized) by their buyers. However, ROMs are not normally constructed of AND and OR gates as shown in Fig. 3-10, but are made from arrays of diodes. ROMs are discussed further in Chap. 9.

For both ROMs and PLAs the circuitry follows a regular pattern and can be packed very densely within an IC. However, these devices are intended to implement complex logic and, if only a few gates are required, then much of the circuitry of a ROM or PLA would not be used. In such cases, it may be better to use individual logic gates to customize the design. As with all logic, ROMs and PLAs have delays associated with them. Just how extensive these delays are depends on the construction method used and the complexity of the ROM or PLA.

3-3 IMPORTANT COMBINATIONAL CIRCUITS

There are a number of combinational circuits that are fundamental to the construction of any computer. This section examines some of them, including those used for performing the operations of selection, comparison, addition, subtraction, multiplication, and error detection. Although it is possible to implement division with a combinational circuit, such circuits include so many gates that usually, sequential circuits are used to provide division.

3-3-1 Multiplexers and Demultiplexers

A **multiplexer**, or **data selector**, selects one of several sets of inputs and passes the selected inputs to the outputs. A symbol representing a general multiplexer is shown in Fig. 3-12(a). (For the notation being used in this book see Fig. B-38

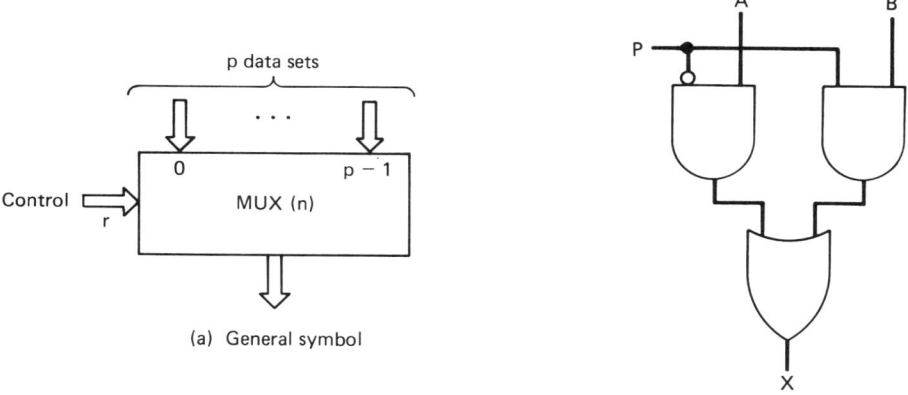

(a) General symbol

(b) Simple 2-to-1 multiplexer

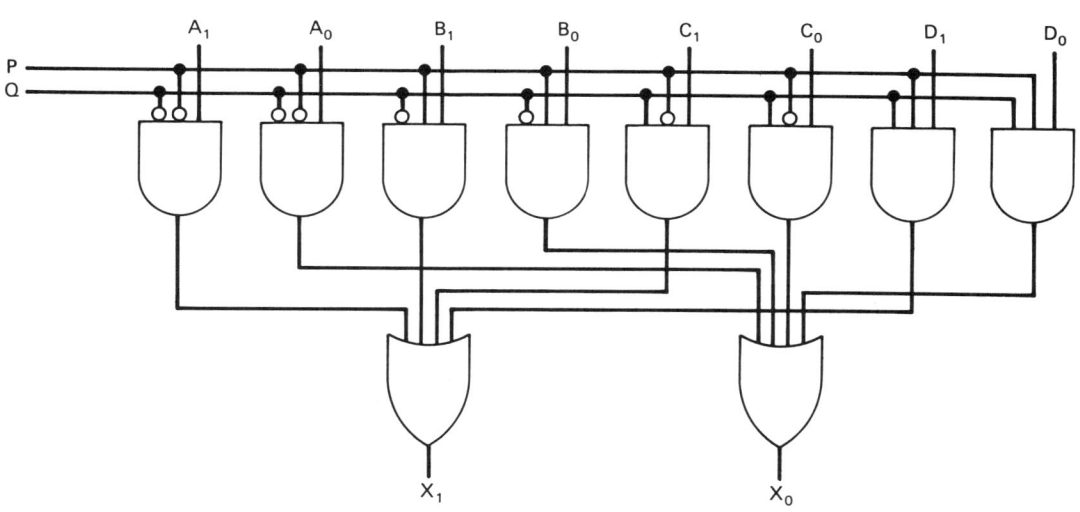

(c) Dual 4-to-1 multiplexer

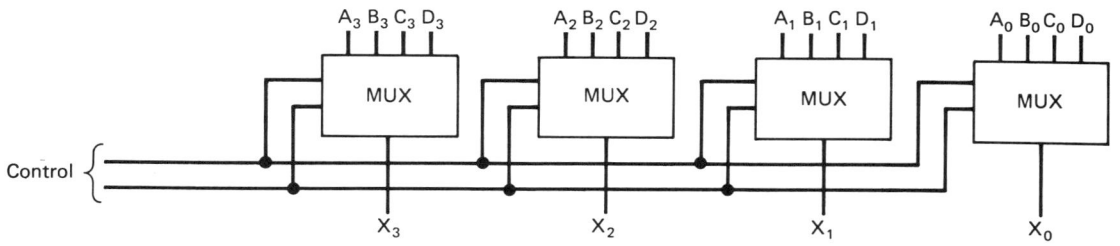

(d) Quad 4-to-1 multiplexer

Figure 3-12 Multiplexer designs.

in Appendix B.) A multiplexer has two types of inputs—control inputs and data inputs. There may be several sets of data inputs, and exactly one set is designated by the control inputs to become the set of outputs.

A logic diagram of the simplest multiplexer is shown in Fig. 3-12(b). It has only two data inputs, one control input, and one output, and is referred to as a 2 to 1 multiplexer. When the control signal P is 0, the output X is equal to A and, when $P = 1$, $X = B$. Figure 3-12(c) is a logic diagram of a dual 4 to 1 multiplexer, which has four sets of two inputs each, two control inputs, and a set of two outputs. Note that, in general, if there are p sets of data inputs, the number of control inputs r must be such that

$$2^r \geq p$$

Both of the logic designs in Figs. 3-12(b) and 3-12(c) use AND gates to perform their selecting and both are such that the controls are input to each AND gate. The AND gate inputs may be direct or inverted and there are at most 2^r input combinations. Figure 3-12(d) shows how a quad 4 to 1 multiplexer, which has four sets of inputs and four outputs, could be made from four simple 4 to 1 multiplexers.

The function of a demultiplexer is opposite that of a multiplexer. A demultiplexer has one set of data inputs, two or more sets of outputs, and a set of control inputs whose purpose is to select the set of outputs to transmit the inputs. The other outputs are 0. A general demultiplexer symbol is shown in Fig. 3-13(a) and a simple 1 to 2 demultiplexer logic diagram is given in Fig. 3-13(b). Other demultiplexer designs are left to the exercises (see Exercises 7 and 8).

3-3-2 Comparators

A comparator is a circuit that compares two sets of inputs and outputs a 1 if the comparison is satisfied. A symbol for a comparator is shown in Fig. 3-14(a). The possible comparisons are those using the relations $=$, $\neq$, $>$, $\leq$, $<$, and $\geq$. For relations other than $=$ and $\neq$, the two sets of inputs are considered to represent

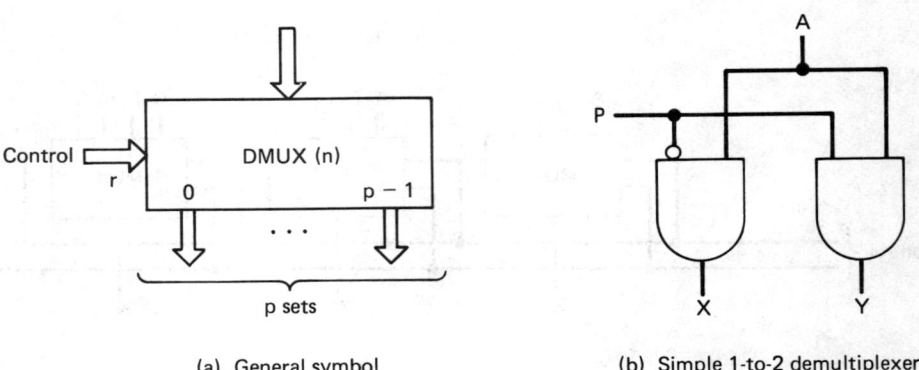

(a) General symbol (b) Simple 1-to-2 demultiplexer

Figure 3-13 Demultiplexers.

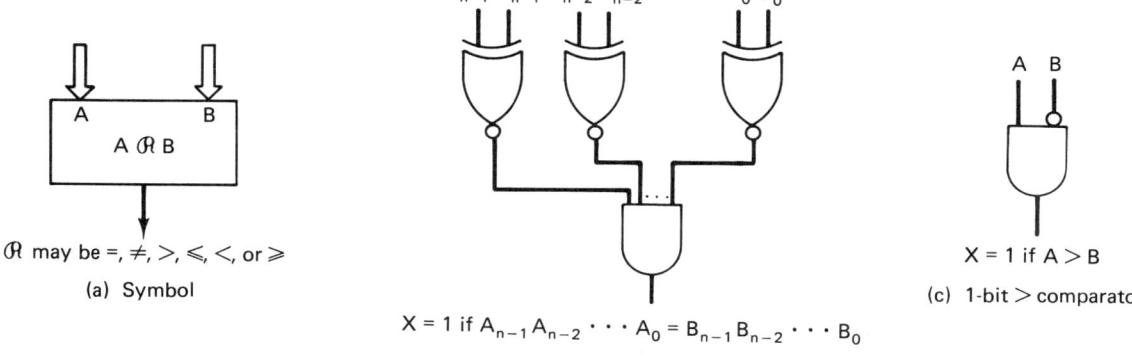

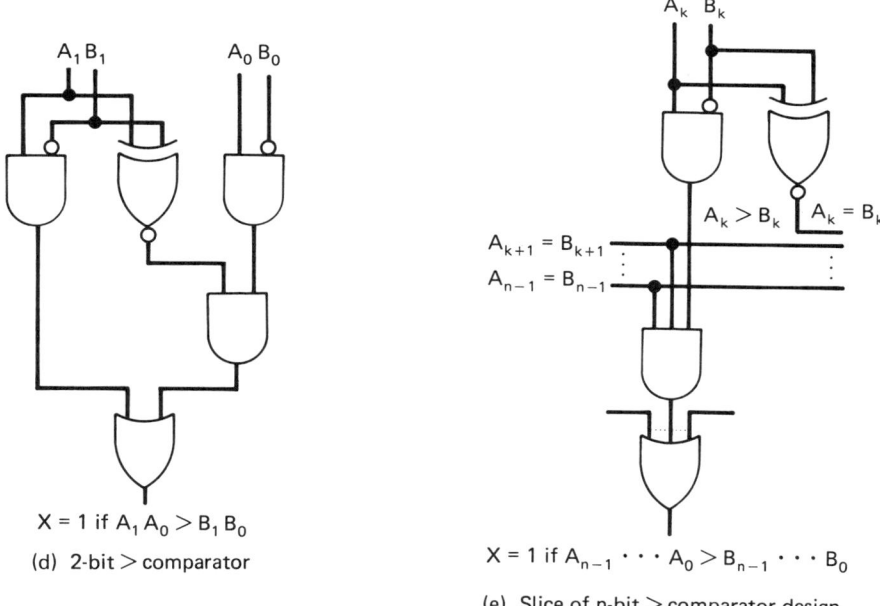

Figure 3-14 Comparator design.

binary integers. The comparator designs developed here (as well as most available comparators) assume the inputs are unsigned, but the modifications needed for comparing 2's complement signed integers are minor (see Exercise 9).

Figure 3-14(b) is the logic diagram of an n-bit equality comparator. This design consists of an XNOR gate for each corresponding pair of input bits and an AND gate that ANDs the XNOR outputs. It can be easily extended to cover any number of bits and, regardless of the number of bits, the delay is the sum of only two gate delays. Fan-in may force the use of more than one AND gate, which would increase the number of gate delays. Figures 3-14(c) and 3-14(d) show 1- and 2-bit > comparators. As the 2-bit > design is developed, the following rule for an n-bit > design begins to emerge:

$A_{n-1} \cdots A_0 > B_{n-1} \cdots B_0$ if and only if there is a

$k = 0, \ldots, n - 1$, for which $A_k > B_k$ and $A_i = B_i$ for all $i > k$.

The logic needed to implement one bit of an n-bit > comparator using this rule is shown in Fig. 3-14(e).

Figure 3-15 is a logic diagram of a 4-bit comparator with both = and > outputs. It includes a carry input that permits it to be chained to other comparators as shown in Fig. 3-16. Figure 3-15 shows that when using the above design rule, the total delay is only three gate delays regardless of the number of bits. We know that theoretically a sum of products involving only two gate delays is always possible, but this approach can, and in the design of a > comparator does, require

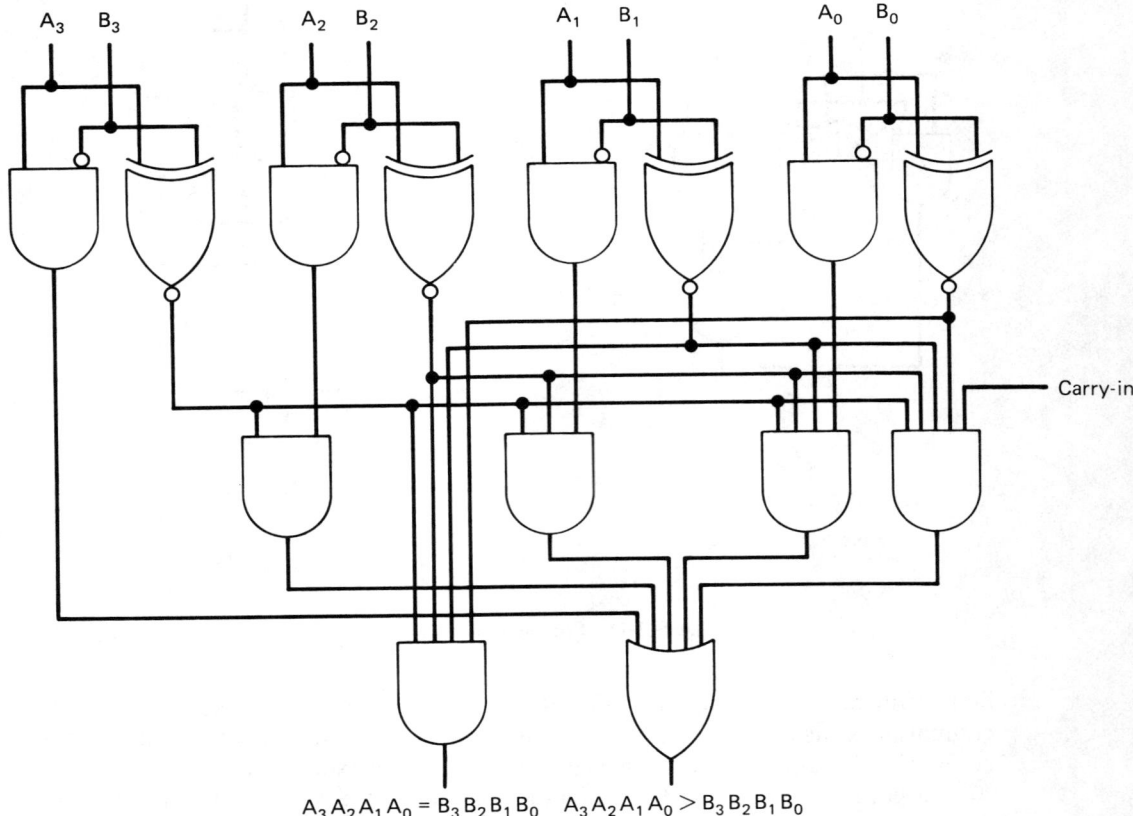

Figure 3-15 4-bit comparator with carry input and = and > outputs.

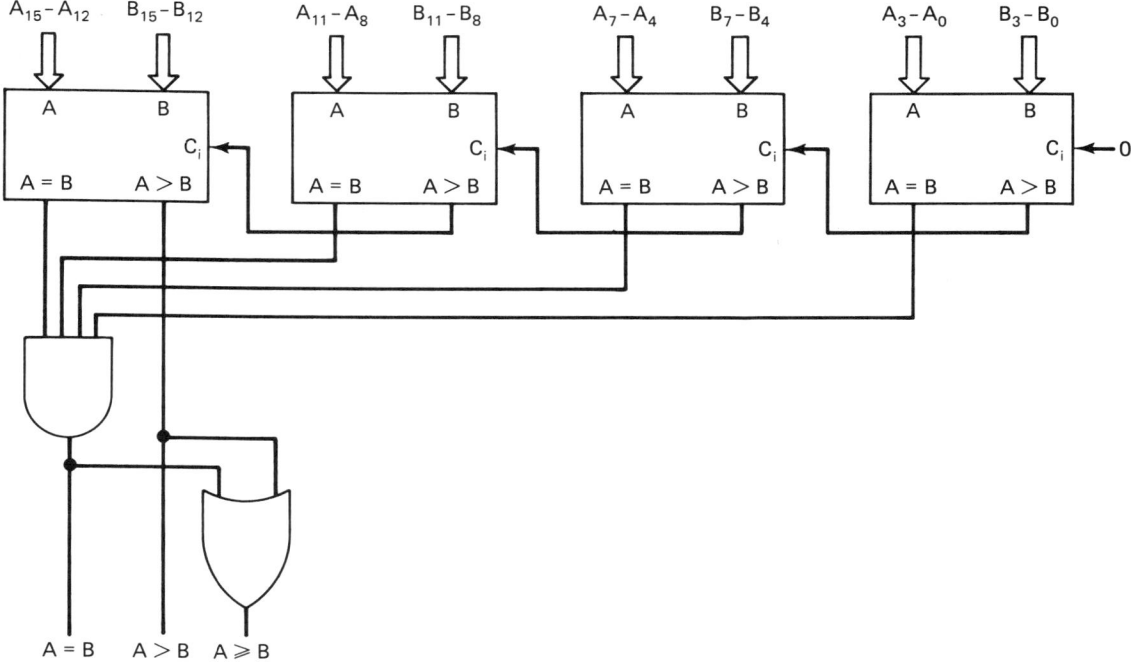

Figure 3-16 16-bit comparator with $=$, $>$, and $\geq$ outputs constructed from 4-bit comparators.

a much larger number of gate inputs (see Fig. B-21 in Appendix B). Therefore, the design in Fig. 3-15 is a good compromise. It does, however, have a serious drawback. Note that, even without the carry input, the rightmost AND gate in the second row of gates and the OR gates have four inputs. In general, for an n-bit comparator, this AND gate and the OR gates would have n inputs. This means that n cannot exceed the fan-in capability of the electronic gate design. If the fan-in is five, then a 4-bit comparator could accommodate a carry input that would allow the chaining shown in Fig. 3-16. (Exercise 10 asks the reader to show that chaining produces the correct result.) The problem introduced by chaining is that it increases the total delay, which is proportional to the number of comparators in the chain.

Also included in the design in Fig. 3-16 is a $\geq$ output that is obtained by ORing the $>$ and $=$ outputs. A $\leq$ or $<$ comparison could be accomplished by either reversing the inputs or complementing the $>$ or $\geq$ output.

3-3-3 Adders and Subtracters

A circuit for adding two 1-bit quantities, called a **half adder**, is illustrated in Fig. 3-17(a). For two multibit quantities, only the lowest order bits can be added using a half adder; the other bits must be added while accounting for a carry bit.

A circuit that does this is called a **full adder**. A typical full adder design is shown in Fig. 3-17(b). An n-bit adder that is obtained by chaining together n − 1 full adders and a half adder is shown in Fig. 3-18(a). In this design, the half adder could be replaced with a full adder whose carry-in input is held at 0. This is significant because, as shown in Fig. 3-18(b), large adders are sometimes made up of identical small adders by chaining the high order carry-out output of each small adder into the carry-in of the succeeding small adder in the chain.

The primary drawback of the designs in Fig. 3-18, which are referred to as **ripple adders**, is the propagation of the carry from the addition of the low order bits up through the higher order bits. Even if a sum of products design is used, a full adder would require two gate delays to produce the carry. Therefore, an n-

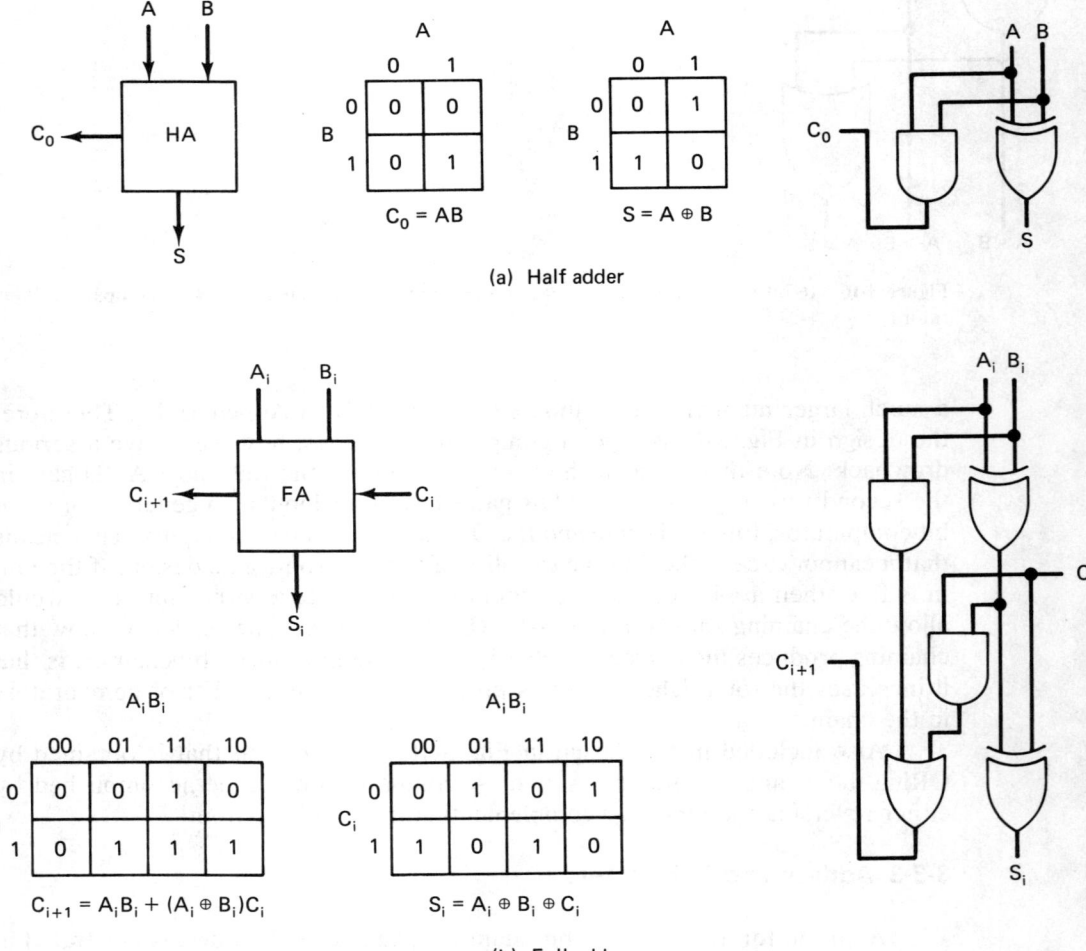

(a) Half adder

(b) Full adder

Figure 3-17 Elementary adder designs.

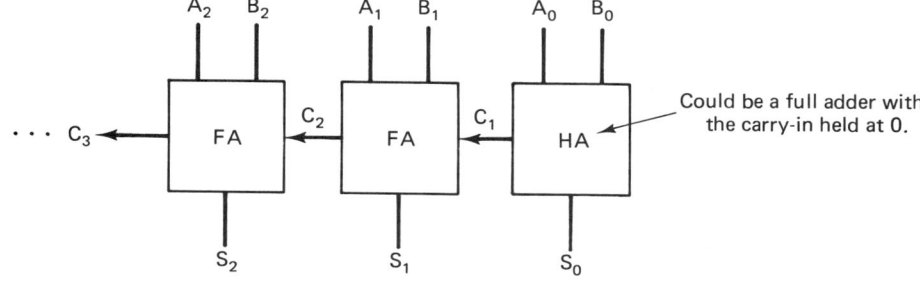

(a) Basic ripple carry adder

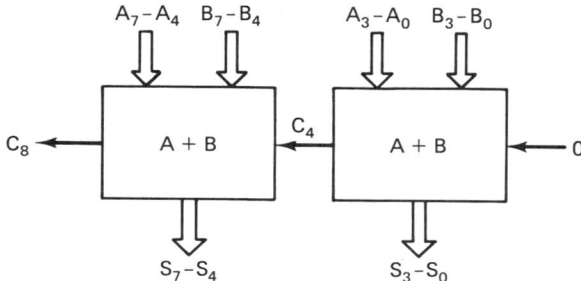

(b) 8-bit ripple carry adder designed from 4-bit adders

Figure 3-18 Ripple carry adders.

bit adder with a carry input would take at least 2n gate delays before the carry from the high order bit becomes stable.

To alleviate this problem, let us re-examine the Karnaugh map for the carry given in Fig. 3-17(b). An alternate means of getting the carry is

$$C_{i+1} = G_i + P_iC_i$$

where $G_i = A_iB_i$ and $P_i = A_i + B_i$. A full adder based on this expression is shown in Fig. 3-19(a). Although this design requires one more gate than the one in Fig. 3-17(b), it, along with the recursive nature of the above expression, introduces a solution to the ripple effect of the carry. By replacing the AND gate in the dashed box with a **look ahead carry circuit**, whose inputs are the lowest order input carry C_0 and the G_j and P_j signals generated by the lower order adders as shown in Fig. 3-19(b), it is possible to eliminate the ripple effect. To illustrate this point, note that

$$C_1 = G_0 + P_0C_0$$
$$C_2 = G_1 + P_1G_0 + P_1P_0C_0$$
$$C_3 = G_2 + P_2G_1 + P_2P_1G_0 + P_2P_1P_0C_0$$
$$\vdots$$

The look ahead carry circuit for $i = 2$ is shown in Fig. 3-19(c).

Sec. 3-3   Important Combinational Circuits

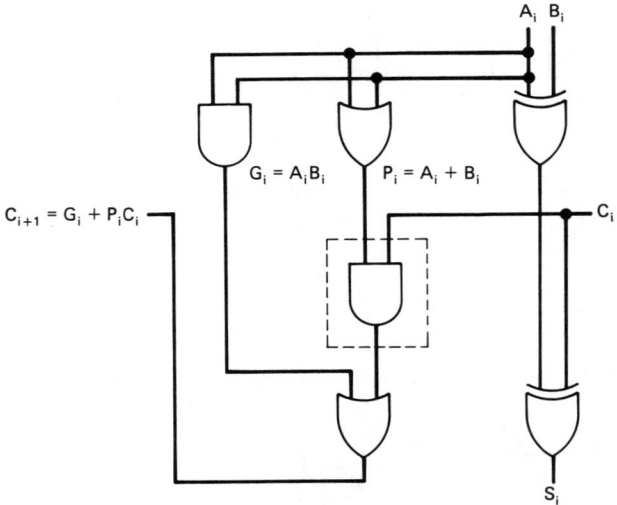

(a) Alternate full adder design

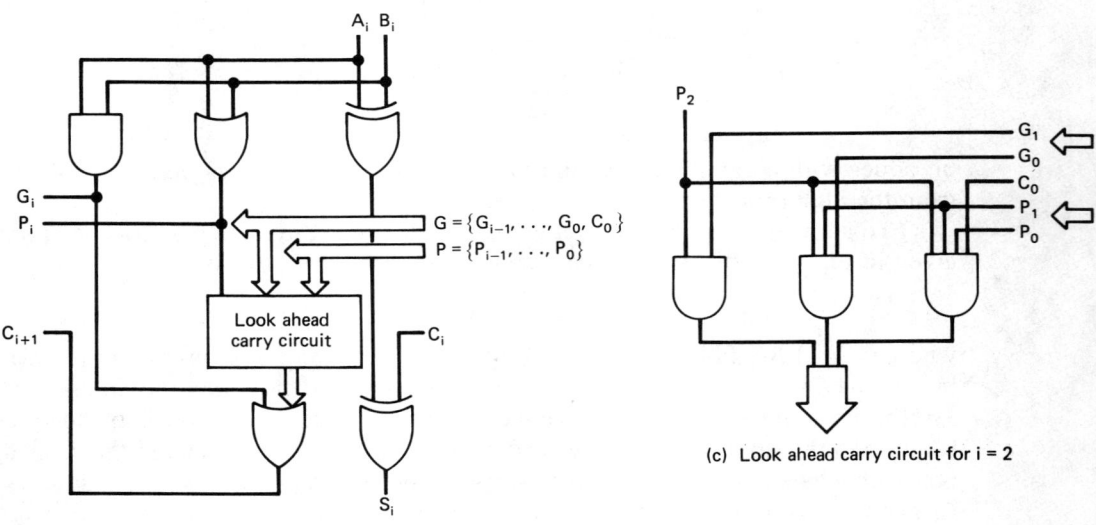

(b) Look ahead carry insertion

(c) Look ahead carry circuit for i = 2

Figure 3-19 Look ahead carry adder.

Although this approach guarantees that the maximum number of gate delays over all carries is three, its problem is obvious. As i increases, the number of gate inputs for the ith adder rapidly becomes impractical. A good compromise is to build 4-bit look ahead carry adders and chain them as shown in Fig. 3-18(b). If this is done, the number of gate delays before C_8 of an 8-bit adder is stable is

6, while for a purely ripple carry design it is at least 16. It is also possible to use the look ahead carry idea to connect the 4-bit adders and thereby, further reduce delay time (see Hamacher, Vranesic, and Zaky [1]).

Addition of packed BCD integers is not nearly as important as addition of binary numbers, but is sometimes done. A 1-digit packed BCD adder that is made from two binary 4-bit adders and a comparator is shown in Fig. 3-20. This design is based on the rule discussed in Sec. 2-2-1 (i.e., add 6 if the result is greater than 9). The total delay time is the sum of the delay of these three circuits. The delay time could be reduced by customizing the design instead of relying on binary adders, but the resulting circuit would be more complex and require more gate inputs.

From Chap. 2, we know that if the 2's complement is used to represent negative numbers, then no changes to the addition/subtraction hardware are required. The correct sum or difference can always be obtained simply by ignoring the carry out of the high order bit. We also know that subtraction can be done by inverting the bits in the subtrahend and adding 1 and the minuend to the result. A circuit that can both add and subtract 2's complement integers is given in Fig. 3-21. It consists of an adder with an $\overline{\text{Add}}$/subtract input and a bank of XOR gates

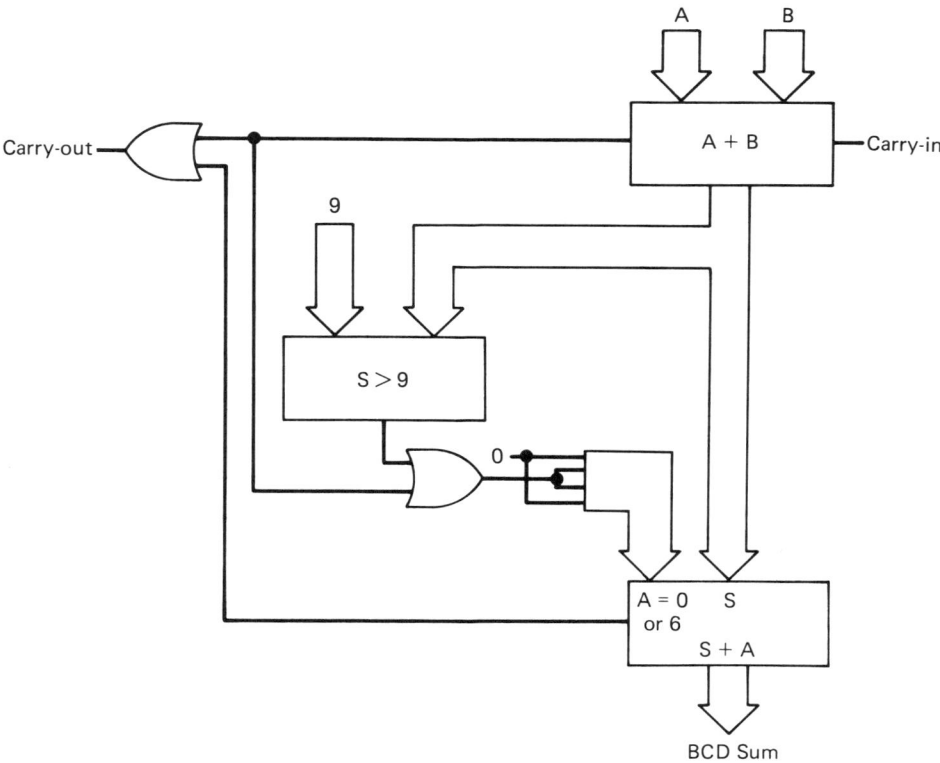

Figure 3-20 Circuit for adding BCD digits.

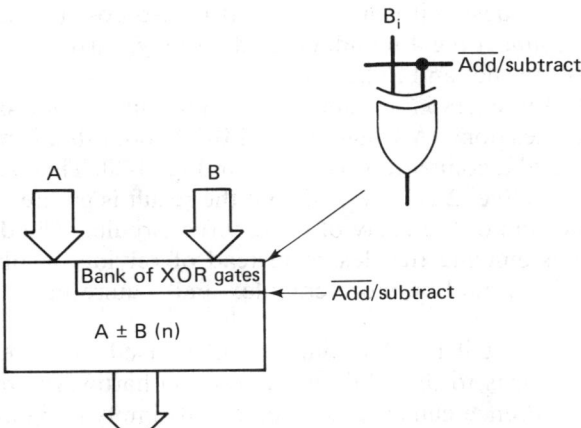

Figure 3-21 2's complement adder/subtracter.

at the addend/subtrahend input. The $\overline{\text{Add}}$/subtract input, which is 0 for addition and 1 for subtraction, is connected to the lower order carry-in and one side of each XOR. When subtraction is being performed it causes the subtrahend bits to be inverted and a 1 to be added through the carry-in. It would be easy to design a separate subtracter but, if both addition and subtraction are needed, the combined adder/subtracter would require less total logic and be almost as fast (see Exercise 15).

3-3-4 Multipliers

Figure 3-22 shows a design of a 4-bit by 4-bit unsigned multiplier that contains only combinational logic. The circuit consists of several rows and columns of identical circuits, called **cells**, consisting of an AND gate and a full adder. Each row is controlled by a bit from the multiplier and performs an addition of either zero or the multiplicand, depending on whether the multiplier bit is 0 or 1, to the row above it. The shifting of the multiply algorithm is attained by offsetting the rows.

The multiplier in Fig. 3-22 is a simple example of a **systolic array**, which is defined as an array of identical cells that are capable of performing some elementary operation and are interconnected so that each cell, except for those on the boundary of the array, can communicate only with its neighbors (Hwang and Briggs [2]). In some systolic arrays the cell operation is very simple, such as the one considered here, while in others, cell operation is complex and may be a complete arithmetic operation or combination of arithmetic operations. Systolic arrays have found important applications in the design of very fast computers. Their advantage is that the results are generated by a steady flow of information through the circuits. More is said about the importance of having steady and continual information flows in Chap. 12. The major disadvantage in a systolic array is the extraordinary amount of logic that may be required. It is apparent

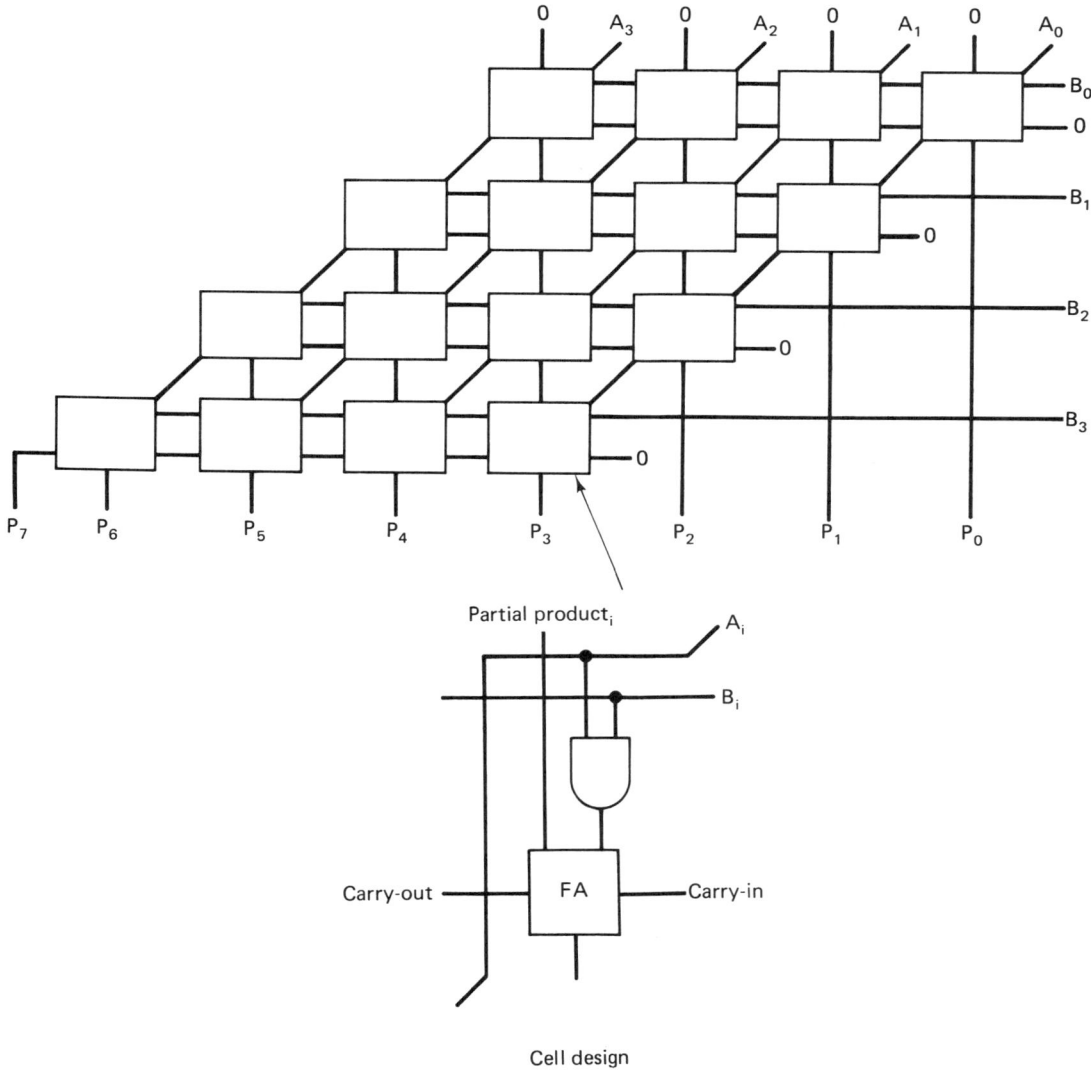

Figure 3-22 Combinational multiplier design.

from Fig. 3-22 that a 32-bit by 32-bit multiplier would require 1024 cells, each containing six gates [see Fig. 3-17(b)].

3-3-5 Parity Generation and Detection

When transmitting or storing data, there is always a chance that an error will occur due to electromagnetic noise or physical damage to the storage medium. If an error should occur, it is highly desirable that it be detected or possibly even corrected. Therefore, if data are to be transmitted more than a very short distance or are to be stored, they should include some type of error-protection scheme. The only way of providing data with error protection is to build in some form of redundancy.

By far the most common type of error protection is single-bit detection. This protection can be attained by adding only one bit to the data. This bit is called the **parity bit** and it is set according to one of the following two rules:

Even Parity—The parity bit is set if an odd number of 1s occurs in the data bits; otherwise, it is cleared. Therefore, the total number of 1s is even.

Odd Parity—The parity bit is set if an even number of 1s in the data occurs; otherwise, it is cleared. Therefore, the total number of 1s is odd.

As an example, suppose that even parity is to be used. Before proceeding with the design, consider the situation depicted in Fig. 3-23. If, as illustrated in this figure, two networks having the property

The output is 1 if and only if there is an odd number of input 1s.

are connected to the inputs of an exclusive OR gate, it can be shown simply by considering the four possible cases that the resulting overall network will also have this property. Because an exclusive OR gate has this property, an even parity bit for 4-bit data can be generated by the logic shown in Fig. 3-24(a). The corresponding 5-bit error-detection network is given in Fig. 3-24(b). These networks could be easily extended to accommodate any number of data bits. For odd parity, the same logic network could be used except that an inverter must be placed in the parity output of both the generator and detector.

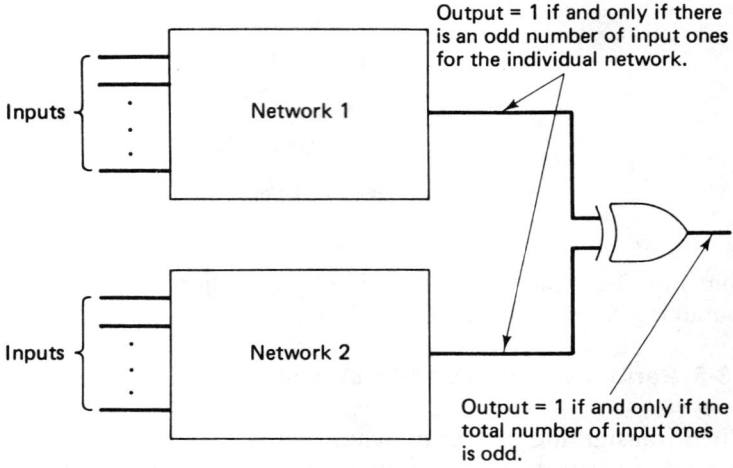

Figure 3-23 Relationship used in designing even and odd parity circuits.

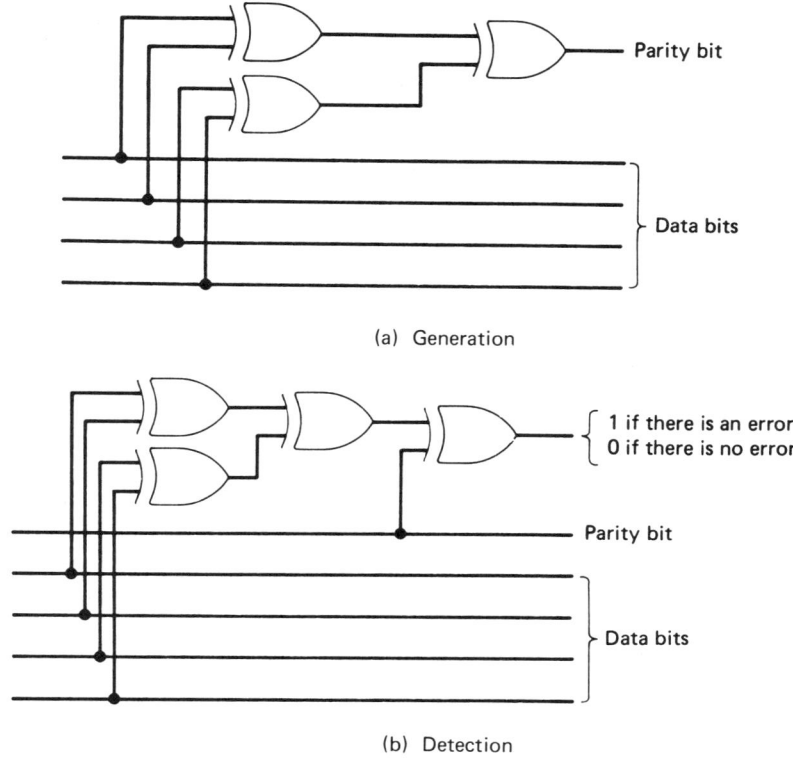

Figure 3-24 4-bit even parity generation and detection.

3-4 IMPORTANT SEQUENTIAL CIRCUITS

Combinational circuits have no memory, do not contain feedback, and are time-independent. Having these properties means that they cannot be used for storage, their outputs depend solely on their present inputs, and they have no intrinsic timing control. In contrast, sequential circuits have internal states that can be used to store information and modify their inputs. They also have triggering mechanisms that permit timed control over state changes. The sequential circuits considered here provide counting, frequency division, storage, time-related format conversions, addition, subtraction, multiplication, and division.

3-4-1 Counters and Frequency Dividers

A **binary counter** is used to count and store the number of pulses arriving at its input. If the pulses are evenly spaced with a known period, a counter can be used as a timer. Conversely, if the period is unknown but the total time over which the counting occurs is known, the counter can be used to measure an input's frequency. Figure 3-25(a) shows a 4-bit counter capable of counting from 0000 through 1111. The T flip-flops are negatively edge-triggered and therefore, the incrementing takes place on the trailing edge of the input pulses. Incrementing at the leading edge could be obtained by placing an inverter at the input to the first T flip-flop.

The Enable input provides a means of turning the counting process on and off, and the $\overline{\text{Reset}}$ input clears the counter. Note that the sixteenth pulse has the same effect as the $\overline{\text{Reset}}$ input: it will clear all four bits. However, if the output of the high order bit were used as an input to another 4-bit counter, the sixteenth pulse would cause the low order bit in the second counter to be set. Thus, counters having a small number of bits can easily be chained together to produce a counter with a larger number of bits.

A counter can also be used to produce a pulse train with a lower frequency. Figure 3-25(b) gives the timing diagram of the input and outputs of the four flip-flops. From this figure it is seen that the outputs of the first, second, third, and fourth flip-flops have respective frequencies that are one-half, one-fourth, one-

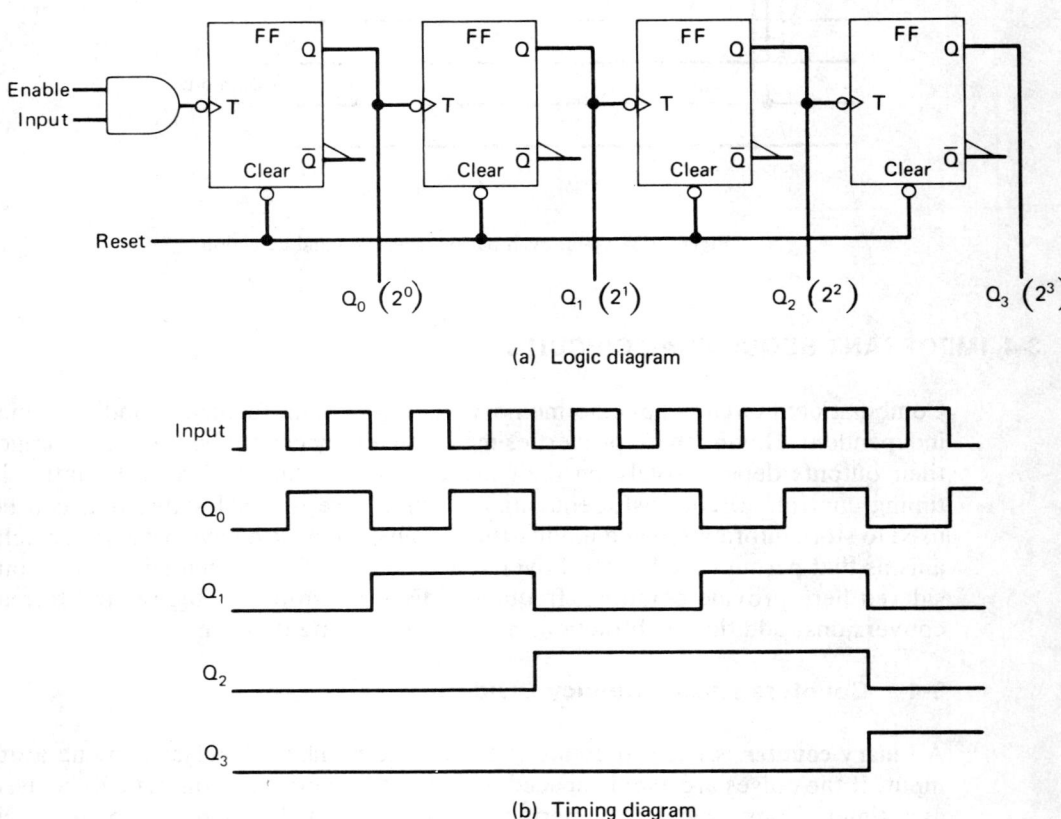

(a) Logic diagram

(b) Timing diagram

Figure 3-25 Ripple counter.

eighth, and one-sixteenth that of the input. By selecting one of these outputs, a clock with a frequency that is only a fraction of the input frequency is obtained. When a counter is used for this purpose, it is called a **frequency divider**.

The counter in Fig. 3-25(a) is referred to as a **ripple counter** because the final count may not be stable until the input signal ripples through all of the flip-flops. The time required to stabilize the signal is directly proportional to the number of bits and, if this number is large, a counter with extra look ahead logic, called a **synchronous counter**, may be required. A synchronous counter that causes all four flip-flops to react simultaneously is shown in Fig. 3-26.

A counter that performs 1-digit BCD counting, called a **decade counter**, is shown in Fig. 3-27. In this design, the triggering is at the positive edge and the two feedback paths cause the counter to be reset when an input pulse arrives and the counter contains 1001. Clearly, several decade counters could be chained to obtain a multiple-digit counter.

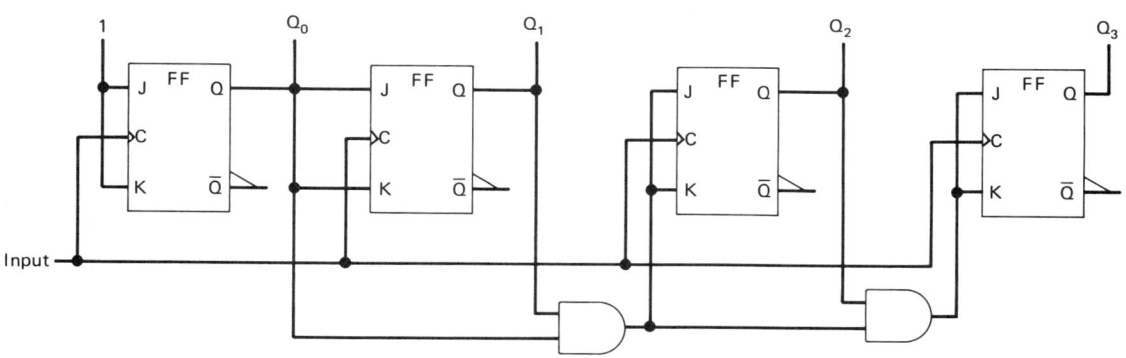

Figure 3-26 Synchronous counter.

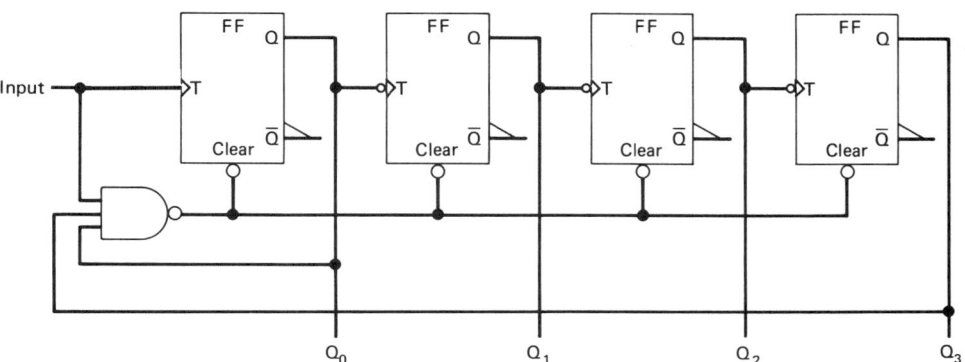

Figure 3-27 Decade counter.

Sec. 3-4   Important Sequential Circuits

3-4-2 Registers

Although information can be physically stored in many ways, the storage device that can be most rapidly accessed is one constructed of sequential logic. A **register** is a storage device that consists of flip-flops placed in parallel, with each flip-flop used for holding one bit. If n flip-flops are used, the register is said to have a **width** of n. A 4-bit register (i.e., a register of width 4) is shown in Fig. 3-28. The currently stored data are the current states of the flip-flops and can be monitored at the Q outputs. A pulse applied to the Load line causes the new contents of the register to become the signals applied to the D inputs.

In addition to being able to input, store, and output data, some registers must be able to rearrange their contents. In particular, **shift registers** are needed that can move their contents to the right or left. For example, if the flip-flops in an 8-bit shift register contain

01100101

and a 1-bit left shift operation is performed, the new contents of the register would be

11001010

After a 1-bit right shift the new contents would be

00110010

Note that for the left shift the leftmost bit is lost and a 0 is inserted on the right. Sometimes, the leftmost bit may be stored elsewhere and/or the bit on the right is not automatically cleared to 0 but is brought in from another location. If the leftmost bit is brought around and put in the right bit during a left shift, or the rightmost bit is put in the left bit during a right shift the operation is called a **rotate**.

Shift registers are used in:

1. Interfaces for changing the form of the data that are to be transmitted or are being received.

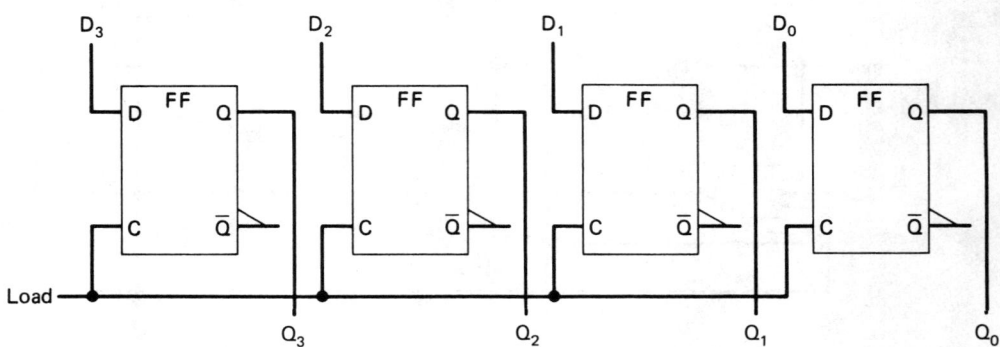

Figure 3-28 4-bit register.

2. Processing elements for performing packing, unpacking, bit searching, and arithmetic operations.

For the first case, consider the two ways binary data can be transmitted as 0-1 combinations. If n bits are to be transmitted, they could be sent simultaneously over n signal paths (e.g., wires) or they could be sent one after the other over one signal path. The former is known as **parallel transmission** and the latter as **serial transmission**.

If data are in serial form and need to be in parallel form, a shift register can be used to do the conversion as shown in Fig. 3-29(a). Assume that four bits arrive at intervals of T seconds and the clock input has a period of T. Approximately

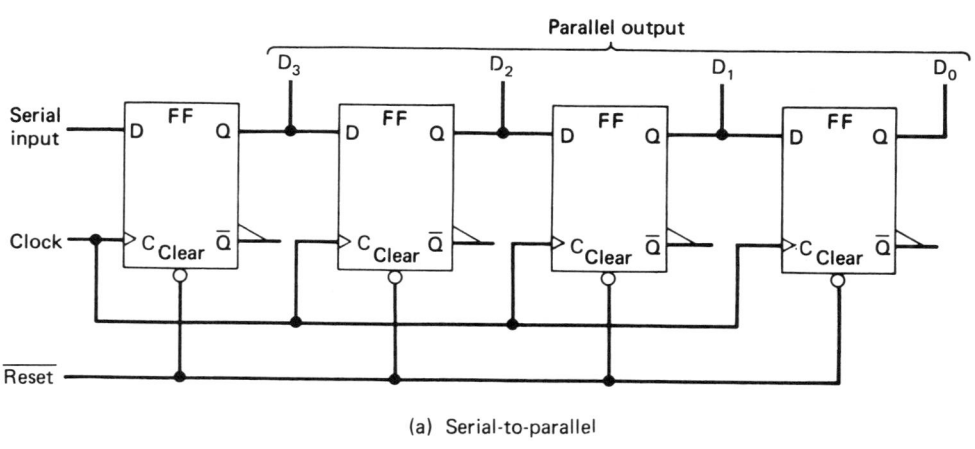

(a) Serial-to-parallel

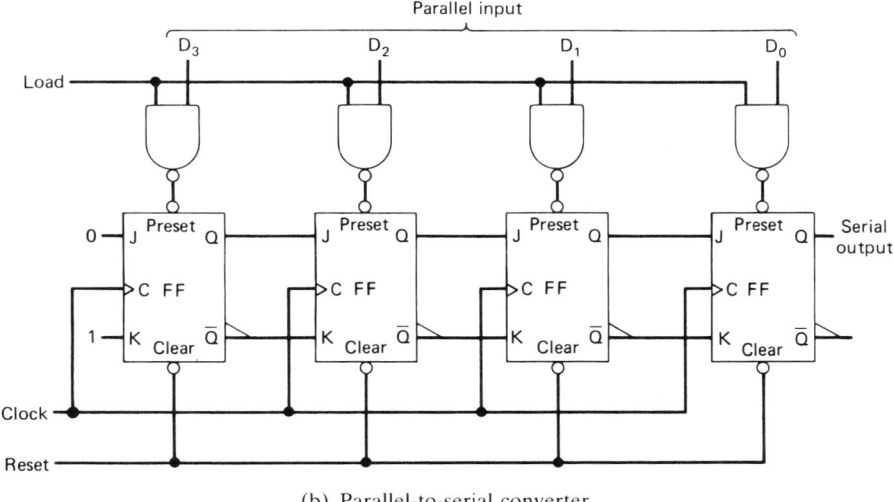

(b) Parallel-to-serial converter

Figure 3-29 Circuits for converting between parallel and serial transmission formats.

Sec. 3-4 Important Sequential Circuits

$T/2$ seconds after the first bit arrives, a clock pulse causes the first bit to become the contents of the leftmost flip-flop. After $T/2$ additional seconds the second bit arrives and then another clock pulse causes it to become the contents of the leftmost flip-flop. At the same time, the second clock pulse transfers the first input bit into the flip-flop that is second from the left. This transferring continues until all four bits have been brought into the shift register. The input data are then accessible from the Q outputs.

A 4-bit circuit that performs the reverse operation of converting from parallel to serial is shown in Fig. 3-29(b). The data are loaded by using a 1 pulse on the Load line to apply the data signals to the present inputs. After the data are loaded they are shifted out of the serial output by applying four clock pulses to the Clock line. If the clock period is T, the bits will occupy successive time intervals of length T. As bits are shifted out, the 0 applied to the D input of the leftmost flip-flop will cause 0s to be shifted into the flip-flops. In both of the circuits shown in Fig. 3-29, the $\overline{\text{Reset}}$ line can be used to clear the registers to 0.

The need for shift registers in processing elements is most evident because of the shifting included in the multiplication and division algorithms, although shifting may also be used to pack or unpack data or perform other bit oriented chores. A 4-bit register that can shift to either the right or left is shown in Fig. 3-30. It is loaded similarly to the parallel-to-serial converter in Fig. 3-29(b). The shifting is controlled by the Right and Left shift lines. Note the delay circuit inserted in the line that activates the C inputs. This delay guarantees that the shift signal has arrived at the D input before the positive edge arrives at the C inputs.

3-4-3 Serial Adders and Subtracters

The combinational logic adders and subtracters considered in Sec. 3-3-3 were **parallel** devices because they received all of the bits in their operands in parallel. It is possible to design **serial** arithmetic circuits that receive their operands one bit at a time, but because carries, borrows, and so on must be saved until the next bits arrive, these circuits must have memories and hence, be sequential. A serial adder is shown in Fig. 3-31. It is the full adder given in Fig. 3-17(b) with D flip-flops in the three input lines. The carry-out output is fed back into the carry-in flip-flop so that it will provide the carry-in for the next bit. Clearly, the flip-flops must be initially reset to 0 and the low order bits must be received first. A serial subtracter could be similarly constructed from a full subtracter (see Exercises 15 and 23). Serial multipliers and dividers could also be built, but would require more memory to hold intermediate results (see Exercise 24).

Serial arithmetic devices were used in the very early computers because they required so little logic and, at that time, logic circuits were very expensive. As the cost of logic circuits decreased, computers began to use parallel arithmetic to gain speed. However, interest has been renewed in serial arithmetic because, in special purpose applications where thousands of identical operations are done at once, it may require less logic and be faster to have thousands of serial circuits than a much smaller number of parallel circuits.

For example, consider an application for which 128-by-128 matrices of 32-

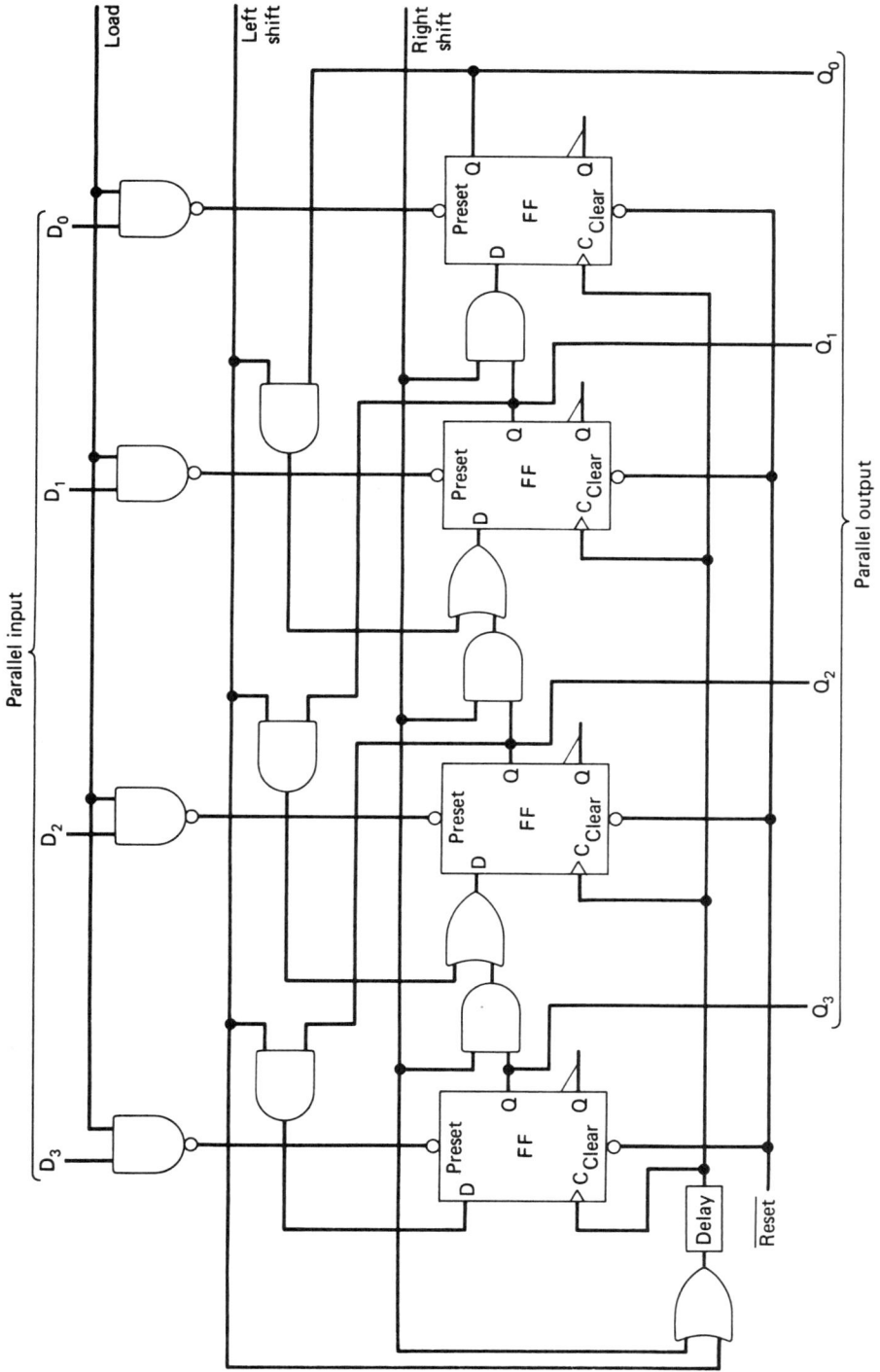

Figure 3-30 Register that can shift either left or right.

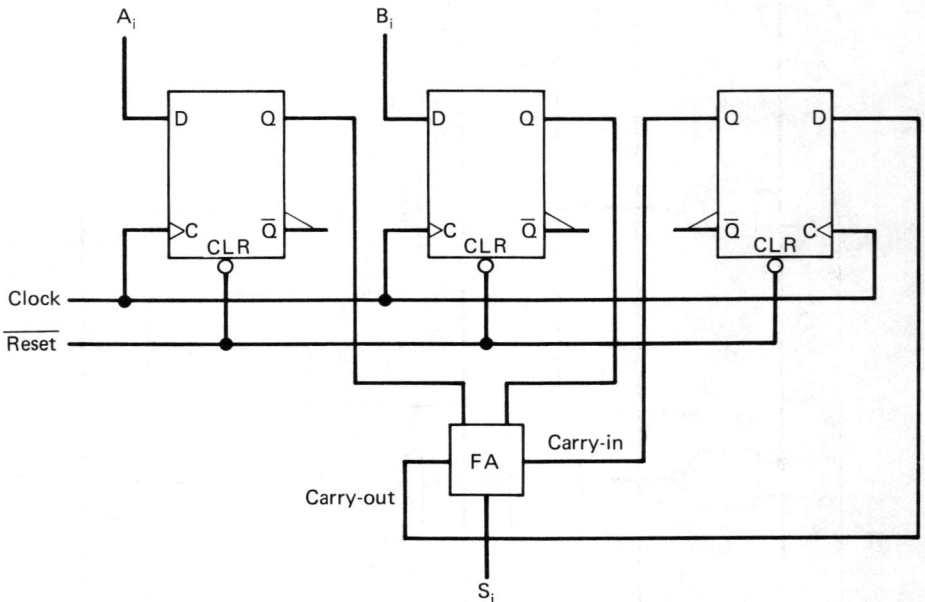

Figure 3-31 Serial adder.

bit integers must be repeatedly added. With today's technology it is not inconceivable to use 16,384 serial adders instead of, say, 2048 parallel ripple carry adders. Assuming that it takes four times as much electronics to make a flip-flop as it does a gate, and that five gates are needed for a full adder, then serial adders would require

$$16384 \times (3 \times 4 + 5) = 278{,}528 \text{ gates}$$

versus

$$2048 \times 5 \times 32 = 327{,}680 \text{ gates}$$

required for the parallel adders. If the clocking rate on the serial adder is 30 nS and the gate delay is 10 nS, the approximate times for performing each matrix addition on the serial and parallel adders would be

$$30 \times 32 = 960 \text{ nS}$$

and

$$32 \times 3 \times 10 \times (16384/2048) = 7680 \text{ nS}$$

respectively. Parallel addition could be done faster with look ahead carry adders, but they would require more gates.

The key to this example is the application's requirement for frequent simultaneous additions of thousands of numbers. This situation is very special and so, for general purpose computers, parallel arithmetic is almost always used.

3-4-4 Multipliers and Dividers

Although a detailed discussion of multipliers and dividers is beyond the scope of this book, Figs. 3-32 and 3-33 provide examples of how n-bit unsigned multiplication and division could be implemented. These examples are straightforward designs that follow directly from the algorithms introduced in Sec. 2-2.

The multiplier in Fig. 3-32 contains registers for holding and shifting the multiplicand and multiplier and holding the result. The sequencing is:

1. Reset all registers to 0.
2. Load the multiplier into its register and the multiplicand into the lower n bits of its register.

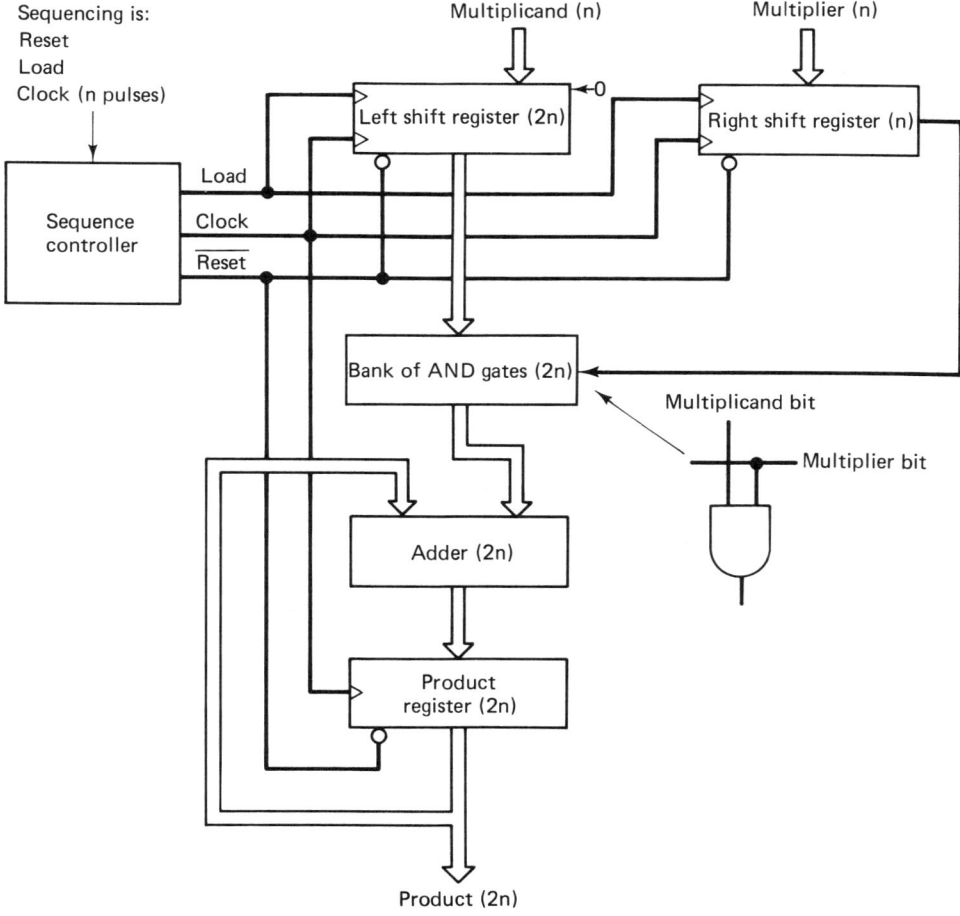

Figure 3-32 Multiplier.

Sec. 3-4 Important Sequential Circuits

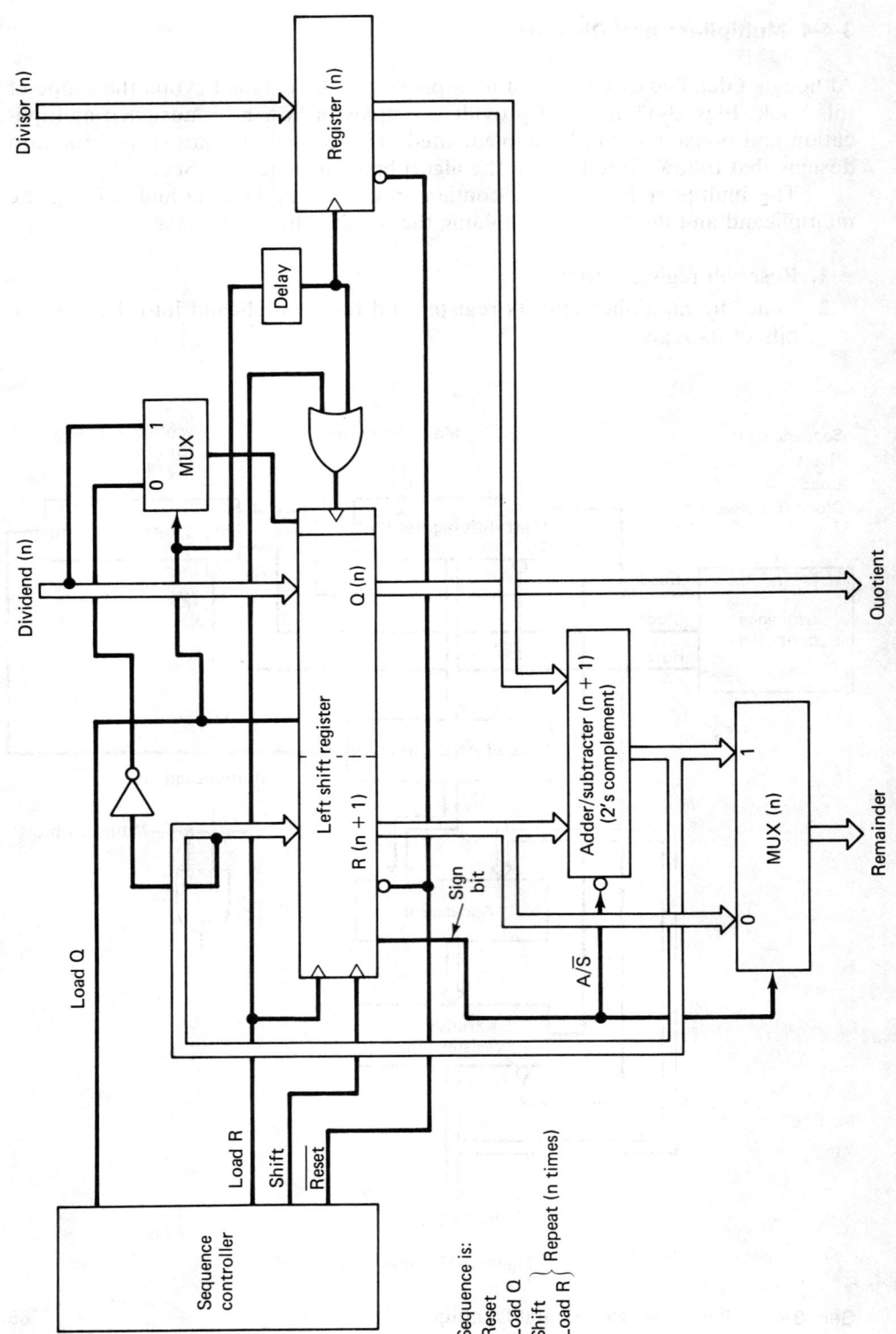

Figure 3-33 Nonrestoring divider.

3. Send a clock pulse that causes the product register to input the adder's output and the multiplier and multiplicand registers to shift. Repeat this step n times.

Just prior to each clock pulse, the output of the adder is either the contents of the product register or the sum of the shifted multiplicand and the contents of the product register, depending on whether the low order bit of the shifted multiplier is 0 or 1, respectively.

The divider in Fig. 3-33 is based on the nonrestoring division algorithm. It contains an n-bit register for holding the divisor and a $2n + 1$-bit left shift register. The latter has three parts that are loaded by separate signals but are shifted simultaneously during the division process. The parts are:

  (1) the low order bit,
  (2) the next $n - 1$ bits, and
  (3) the remaining $n + 1$ bits.

The sequencing is:

1. Reset both registers to 0.
2. Load the dividend into the lower n bits of the shift register and the divisor into its register by applying a Load Q signal.
3. Alternately apply a Shift signal to move the entire contents of the shift register to the left by one bit and a Load R signal to load the upper part of the shift register with its contents plus or minus the divisor. The Load R also loads the complement of the high order bit of the shift register into the low order bit. Repeat this step n times.

In the latter step, addition is performed if the high order bit is 0 and subtraction is performed if it is 1. Addition and subtraction are done using the 2's complement format even though the dividend, divisor, quotient and remainder are unsigned. The extra bit keeps track of the sign and is not passed through to the remainder. The n-bit multiplexer selects the output of the adder to be the remainder if the final sign bit is 1; otherwise, the remainder is taken directly from the upper part of the shift register.

3-5 LINK CONNECTIONS

If all the gates and flip-flops within a logic circuit have the same electrical characteristics (in particular, they use the same voltage levels for 0 and 1), no conversion electronics are needed to connect gates and flip-flops together. However, when joining distinct logic circuits together with a link, it may be necessary to:

- Convert from voltage signals to current signals or vice versa, or convert one pair of levels for representing 0 and 1 to a different pair.

- Increase the power of the signals.
- Electrically disconnect a logic circuit from the link.
- Connect several logic circuits to the same set of conductors.

The first two of these problems are resolved by using special circuits that are generally referred to as **drivers**. A driver that is on the receiving end of a transmission is usually called a **receiver**, and combinations that both transmit and receive are called **transceivers**. The design of drivers will not be discussed, but they will appear in some of the figures. The symbols that represent drivers in these diagrams are given in Fig. 3-34(a). When the triangular shape is used, the triangle points in the direction of the signal.

The third problem is resolved by a **tristate driver** or **tristate gate**, whose output may be 0, 1, or a high impedance state. As shown in Fig. 3-34(b), a tristate driver has two inputs—a data input and control input. When the control input is 1, the output is the same as the input (or the complement of the input if the driver is also an inverter), but when the control input is 0 the input is essentially disconnected from the output.

The situation related to the fourth problem is illustrated in Fig. 3-35. Output circuits cannot be ordinary gates because, if the outputs of such gates are connected together, then excessive currents may be produced that damage the gates' output transistors. One possibility is to let the output circuits be tristate drivers and design the logic circuits so that only one logic circuit at a time can activate its tristate outputs. If a tristate output is connected to a bus conductor used by several logic circuits and the control input to the tristate driver is 0, then the driver appears to be disconnected from the signals on the conductor.

A second possibility is to use specially designed gate circuits whose outputs can be connected together. The **wire-ORed gate**, or **open-collector gate**, is such a

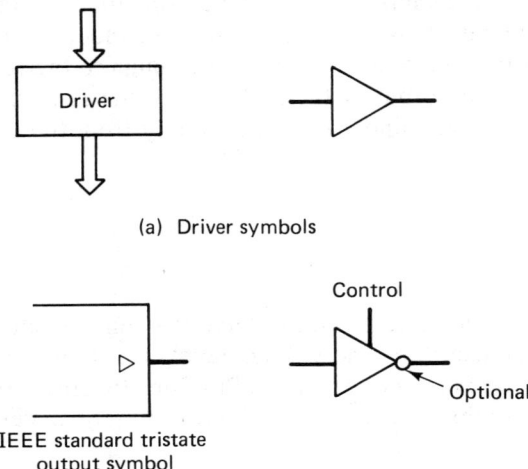

Figure 3-34 Drivers.

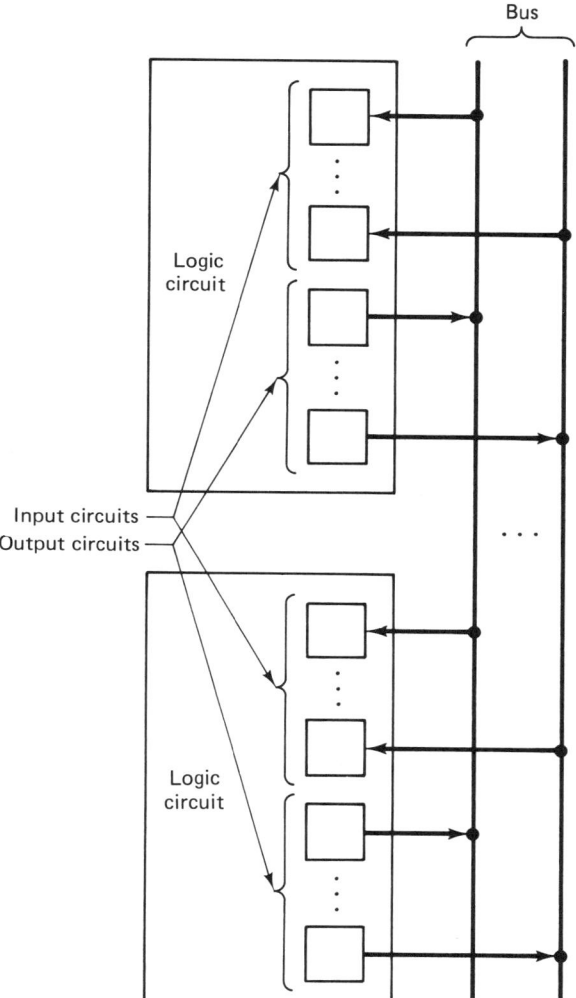

Figure 3-35 Common bus connections.

design and is such that the signal on the common output conductor is 1 if and only if all of the wire-ORed gates connected to the conductor are attempting to output a 1. Normally, the signals being put on and taken from the conductor are inverted as shown in Fig. 3-36. If the inputs are $A_1, \ldots, A_n$, then the conductor is 1 if and only if $A_1 = \ldots = A_n = 0$ and, therefore, the output X is 0 if and only if all of the inputs are 0. Wire-ORed gates could be assumed any time outputs are connected together, but for clarity, an OR symbol is sometimes placed over such connection where the signal is being taken from the conductor. One disadvantage of the wire-ORed arrangement is that the output transistors of the gates being connected must be supplied from a common source. This arrangement is accomplished by connecting the output conductor to the supply voltage through a resistor, referred to as a **pull-up resistor**, as shown in Fig. 3-36.

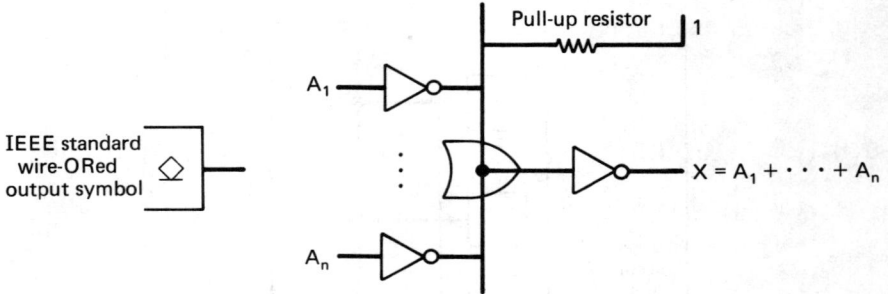

Figure 3-36 Wire-ORed connection.

Either wire-ORed gates or tristate drivers could be used as the output circuits shown in Fig. 3-35 but, unlike the tristate connections for which only one driver at a time can apply a signal to the conductor, all wire-ORed connections output signals and their signals are ORed. If all but one of the logic circuits puts 0s on the inputs of its wire-ORed gates, then the remaining logic circuit could communicate over the bus just as with tristate connections. But in some situations, the unique ORing property of a wire-ORed connection is needed. For example, consider the configuration shown in Fig. 3-37 in which one of the logic circuits is **master** and is to control the system and perform certain activities for the other **slave** logic circuits. Suppose that the $\overline{\text{Request}}$ line is to allow any slave to request the master to perform a specific activity S. If the $\overline{\text{Request}}$ line is implemented as a wire-ORed connection, any slave or combination of slaves could request activity S by pulling the $\overline{\text{Request}}$ line, which is normally 1, to 0. For example, in single

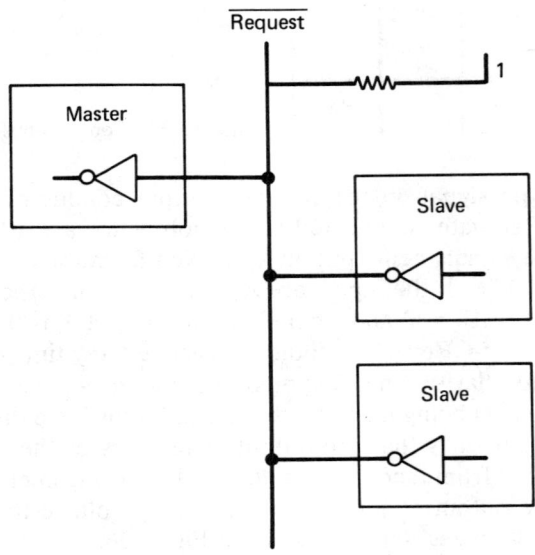

Figure 3-37 Use of the ORing property in making a request.

processor, single bus computer design, the processing element is normally the master and the other elements connected to the bus are slaves, and wire-ORing is used by the slaves to request use of the bus (see Chaps. 6 and 8).

3-6 INTEGRATED CIRCUITS AND TECHNOLOGIES

Modern digital logic circuits are constructed onto the surfaces of thin slices of a base material such as silicon. The resulting products are **integrated circuits (ICs)**, which are normally from 0.1 cm^2 to 1 cm^2 in area, but may contain hundreds of thousands of logic gates. There are many advantages to fabricating circuits containing large numbers of gates into a small area using an automated process.

- The small transistors used to make the gates use very little power.
- The capacitances are small so that the switching speeds are high.
- The distances are short so that propagation delays are small.
- The number of soldered connections is limited to the relatively low number of connections to the circuitry outside the IC.

The disadvantages are:

- Because of the small size of the IC's transistors, the amount of power that an IC can output may be small.
- Because of the small surface area, special means may be needed to dissipate the heat generated by the IC.

Ideally, one would like to put all of a computer's circuitry into a single IC, but the amount of circuitry that can be fabricated into such a circuit is limited because

- Current fabrication techniques and heat dissipation requirements limit the density of the transistors in a circuit.
- An IC's physical size is limited.

With regard to the first restriction, the reliability of an IC depends on its temperature and the materials used to make the IC. For an IC to be functional, its temperature must be kept below a limit that is a characteristic of the materials. Because the temperature rises with the amount of power that must be dissipated per unit area, for a given transistor configuration a maximum is placed on both the transistor density and average switching frequency, which determine the IC's operational speed. (Recall from Sec. 3-1-2 that the power dissipated is proportional to the frequency of discrete changes.) Special cooling may be used to keep the temperature down, thereby allowing the density or speed of the IC to be increased. For some very fast computers, called supercomputers, the processing element's circuitry is submerged in liquid nitrogen.

Technology	TTL	STTL	ECL	I²L	NMOS	HMOS	CMOS	GaAs MESFET
Fan-out	12	12	16	12	12	12	12	6
Power Dissipation	10mW	19mW	25mW	0.1 μW	1mW	0.5mW	0.01 μW	0.1mW
Switching Time	9nS	3nS	2nS	50nS	50nS	25nS	25nS	0.1nS

Figure 3-38 Typical per gate characteristics of the more common technologies.

The second restriction is due to the fact that flaws occurring during IC manufacturing cannot be corrected and therefore, any flaw would cause an entire IC to be worthless. The probability of a manufacturing flaw increases as the area of an IC's surface increases, thus causing the percentage of rejects to be directly related to the size of the IC. The ratio of good ICs to the total produced is called the **yield**. Clearly, the lower the yield, the more expensive it is to manufacture an IC.

A method for constructing an IC is called a **technology**. A technology is determined by both the geometry of a transistor and the materials used. Some of the characteristics of more commonly used technologies are summarized in Fig. 3-38 (see Chirlian [7]). They are the Transistor-Transistor Logic (TTL), Schotky Transistor-Transistor Logic (STTL), Emitter-Coupled Logic (ECL), Integrated Injection Logic (I²L), N-channel Metal Oxide Semiconductor (NMOS), complementary metal oxide semiconductor (CMOS), and Galium Arsenide Metal Semiconductor Field Effect Transistor (GaAs MESFET) technologies. Note that there are considerable ranges in power dissipation per gate and switching times. Those technologies with both low power dissipation and low switching times tend to either have low densities, be more expensive to make, or both. In addition to having a low fan out, the GaAs technology has a low fan in capacity.

3-7 DESIGN REMARKS

This chapter has dwelled a great deal on the tradeoff between the number of gates or gate inputs as a measure of initial cost and power consumption, and the time delays, as a measure of speed. However, as a circuit or system of circuits becomes increasingly complicated, the problems go beyond those that are simply related to cost, power, and speed. Designing a circuit with thousands, or possibly millions, of gates, flip-flops, and feedback paths is extremely difficult and the probability of design errors occurring, particularly errors associated with timing, is high. A typical example of the type of situation that can arise is demonstrated by the circuit in Fig. 3-39. If $A = X = 0$, $B = C = 1$, and A then changes to 1, X may remain at 0 or become 1 depending on the relative gate delays of the two AND gates. If the lower gate is faster, a constant 1 is maintained at the T input and X does not change; but, if the upper gate is faster, the T input may go low for a sufficient length of time to cause the flip-flop to switch.

In general, such timing problems are classified as races and hazards. It would take far too much space to discuss these problems and the way to avoid them in

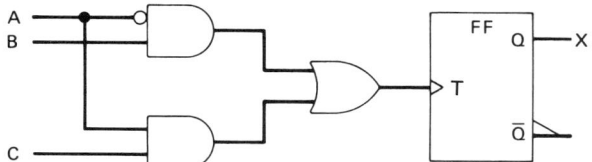
Figure 3-39 Potential timing problem.

this book. Instead, design discussions relating to races and hazards are left to books on logic design, such as Hill and Peterson [3]. Suffice it to say, for complex circuits, the potential for race and hazard type errors is considerable and special design techniques are needed to find and resolve time-related problems.

Complexity also reduces reliability. Reliability depends on many factors, some of which are:

Electrical design: There are usually several design possibilities and normally some of them tend to reduce the chances of future faults.

Number of components: If component failures are independent and equally likely and the probability of one component failing within a specified period of time is p, then the probability of at least one of n components failing is

$$1 - (1 - p)^n$$

For small p, this value is approximately np (e.g., if $p = 10^{-8}$ for a time period of one day and $n = 10^5$, the chance of failure in a day is 1 in 1000, which for some applications may be much too large).

Number of connections: After a system is installed and working properly, the most likely failure is that of a connection. There are connections to ICs, IC packages, and PC boards. The IC connections are on the package and once they are made and the IC has been installed in its ceramic package, they are not very vulnerable. On the other hand, the connections to the IC packages and PC boards are either soldered or maintained by mechanical pressure and are quite easily affected by the environment (vibration, corrosion, and so on).

Electromagnetic noise: As signals are transmitted they are subject to being erroneously changed by noise. Noise can be reduced by surrounding the circuit or link to be protected with a conducting shield, but this protection will not guard against noise generated within the circuit or link itself.

Environmental conditions: These conditions include temperature, humidity, presence of gases or fluids, vibration, and so on. They must be dealt with on an individual basis.

Packaging design: This factor relates to physical layout. Among other things, it must negate undesirable environmental conditions, minimize the numbers of components and connections, and reduce noise.

Reliability and its importance are relative. Although high reliability is always an important goal, it is sometimes the premier criterion (e.g., as in the case of computers that control spacecraft or nuclear power plants).

With regard to links, the primary items of concern are:

Propagation delay—due to inductance and capacitance or perhaps, the speed of light.
Skew—the difference in propagation delays.
Distortion of pulse shape—due to capacitance.
Driving power—needed to transmit the signal from one end of the link to the other.
Noise—caused by extraneous electromagnetic signals.

In addition, all of the above effects increase with distance. Obviously, propagation delay and skew are proportional to distance, but line capacitance and resistance are also proportional to distance and they affect pulse distortion and driving power. If a link is shielded, externally generated noise may not significantly increase with length because exposure will not depend on length, but the shielding will increase the capacitance. Other effects on the total capacitance are the capacitance of the connecting pads and the internal capacitance of the driving circuits and loads.

The total amount of power that is needed is important because it affects the capacity of the power supply and amount of heat that must be dissipated. Power supplies are notable for causing computer failures and, although their design is not to be discussed here, any computer designer should be acutely aware of the necessity of an adequate and reliable power source. As for heat, it affects the temperature, which in turn affects the characteristics of electrical circuits. Just how serious the heat problem is depends on the operating temperature of the circuitry, but in any event, the power dissipated as heat must be balanced by an adequate cooling system. In most cases, the cooling system should be redundant so that the computer will not fail because a single cooling component fails (e.g., a single fan).

The voltages output by a power supply must be held constant at all of the points where they are needed. To help maintain constant voltages, capacitors are liberally scattered around the supply system. Capacitors (typically 0.1 microfarads in size) are often placed between the supply and ground pins of an IC package. In this case, the purpose of the capacitor is to filter out changes in the supply voltage due to noise pulses. Therefore, the capacitance should be large enough that the time constant of the supply circuit is large compared to the width of the noise pulse. For example, if $C = 10^{-7}$ farads, $R = 100$ ohms, and the maximum noise pulse width is approximately 10^{-7} seconds, then the time constant is approximately 100 noise pulse widths and the effect on the supply voltage is negligible.

REFERENCES

1. Hamacher, V. Carl, Zvonko G. Vranesic, and Safwat G. Zaky, *Computer Organization*, 2nd ed. (New York: McGraw-Hill Book Company, 1984).

2. Hwang, Kai and Faye A. Briggs, *Computer Architecture and Parallel Processing* (New York: McGraw-Hill Book Company, 1985).
3. Hill, Frederick J., and Gerald R. Peterson, *Switching Theory and Logical Design*, 3rd ed. (New York: John Wiley and Sons, Inc., 1981).
4. Gibson, Glenn A., and Yu-cheng Liu, *Microcomputers for Engineers and Scientists*, 2nd ed. (Englewood Cliffs, New Jersey: Prentice Hall, Inc., 1987).
5. Fortes, Jose, and Benjamin Wak, "Systolic Arrays—From Concept to Implementation," *Computer, 20,* no. 7 (July, 1987) 12–17.
6. Nilsson, James W., *Electric Circuits*, 2nd ed. (Reading, Massachusetts: Addison-Wesley Publishing Company, 1986).
7. Chirlian, Paul M., *Analysis and Design of Integrated Circuits*, 2nd ed. (New York: Harper and Row Publishers, 1987).

EXERCISES

1. The step response of the following circuit has the form $V_0(1 - e^{-t/RC})$

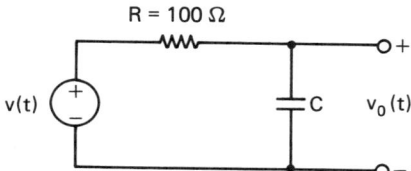

Given that $v(t)$ is a 5 V, 10 nS wide pulse, plot $v_0(t)$ for (a) $C = 10$ pF. (b) $C = 100$ pF. (c) $C = 1$ nF.

2. For the circuit in Exercise 1, what is the power dissipated by the resistor if the frequency of the pulses is 1 MHz, $C = 100$ pF, and the pulse width is 10 nS? The pulse width is 100 nS?

3. If a lossless transmission line has an inductance of 0.1 mH per meter and a capacitance of 100 pF per meter, what is the velocity with which a pulse will travel down the line? What fraction is this of the speed of light? Now assume a second line has the same inductance but the capacitance is 90 pF per meter and that both lines have a length of 100 m. How much sooner would a pulse arrive at the end of the second line?

4. Given the following Karnaugh map

		AB			
		00	01	11	10
	00	0	0	0	0
CD	01	0	1	0	0
	11	1	1	1	1
	10	0	0	0	0

X

(a) Draw a logic diagram of X that uses AND gates to get the minterms and then ORs the minterms.
(b) Draw a logic diagram using a minimized sum of products.
(c) Draw a logic diagram after factoring is used to reduce the number of gate inputs.
In each of the above cases, count the number of gate inputs and then, assuming a gate delay of 20 nS, determine the total delay for each design.

5. Use the decoder and encoder construction indicated in Fig. 3-10 and design a PLA that implements the outputs X, Y, and Z defined by

	AB			
CD	00	01	11	10
00	0	0	0	0
01	0	1	1	0
11	0	1	1	0
10	0	0	0	0

X

	AB			
CD	00	01	11	10
00	0	0	0	0
01	1	1	1	1
11	0	0	1	0
10	0	0	0	0

Y

	AB			
CD	00	01	11	10
00	0	0	0	0
01	1	0	0	1
11	0	1	1	0
10	1	0	0	1

Z

6. If the design approach of Fig. 3-12 is used, how many gate inputs would there be in a 2^n-to-1 multiplexer?
7. Design a 1-to-4 demultiplexer.
8. Design a quad 1-to-4 demultiplexer from simple 1-to-4 demultiplexers.
9. What changes would need to be made to convert an unsigned comparator into a 2's complement comparator?
10. Explain why the chaining of the $>$ comparators shown in Fig. 3-16 gives the correct $>$ output.
11. If XOR gates have a delay of 12 nS and AND and OR gates have a delay of 10 nS, what is the total delay for a 16-bit ripple carry adder? For a look ahead adder? For an adder that ripples the carry through four 4-bit look ahead adders?
12. Derive a formula that gives the total number of gate inputs needed to generate all of the carries in an n-bit look ahead adder assuming unlimited fan-in.
13. Adding 1 to a number is an important special case. Design a circuit, called an **incre-menter**, that will add 1 to the input, but requires much less circuitry than a complete adder. Compare the amount of circuitry needed for your incrementer with that of an adder.
14. Design a 1-digit packed BCD incrementer.
15. Design a **half subtracter** with borrow and difference outputs. Design a **full subtracter** with a borrow input and borrow and difference outputs. Show how they could be chained to form an n-bit subtracter.
16. Design a circuit that could be put in a 2's complement adder/subtracter and would output a 1 only if an overflow has occurred. (See Sec. 2-2-2.)
17. For the multiplier in Fig. 3-22, assume the full adder design in Fig. 3-17(b) and determine the total number of gate inputs and total delay before P_7 becomes stable. Assume that the total delay for each cell is 30 nS.

18. Design an odd parity generator and detector for a link that transmits eight data bits.
19. Assume the design shown in Fig. 3-27 and show how two decade counters could be connected to get a 2-digit counter.
20. Assume that the delay of a flip-flop is 15 nS and the delay of a gate is 10 nS. What is the total delay if a 32-bit counter is formed from eight 4-bit ripple counters? From eight 4-bit synchronous counters?
21. If the delay of a flip-flop is 40 nS and the time constant associated with the output is 5 nS, what is the maximum rate at which bits could be transmitted from a parallel to serial converter? (Assume 10 time constants are needed to produce a satisfactory wave shape.)
22. Modify the shift register in Fig. 3-30 to include left and right rotate operations.
23. Redesign the serial adder in Fig. 3-31 so that it can also perform serial subtraction.
24. Design a 4-bit serial multiplier.
25. Modify the design of the sequential multiplier in Fig. 3-32 so that it uses Booth's algorithm.
26. Determine the output of the following wire-ORed connection:

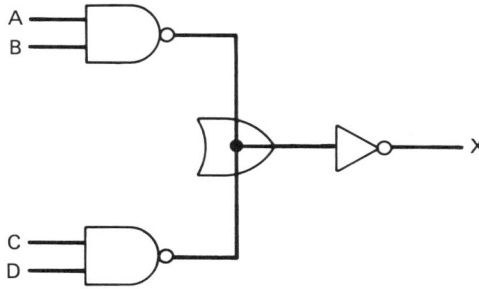

27. Suppose that A and B are connected to the D and C inputs, respectively, of a positive edge-triggered flip-flop using two long wires. If skew is not taken into account, what might happen? Give a possible remedy.
28. Assume the full adder design given in Fig. 3-17(b) and the data given in Fig. 3-38. If a 16-bit adder is constructed using only full adders and a ripple carry design, how much heat will the adder dissipate and what will be the overall propagation delay if the technology used is:
    (a) TTL
    (b) I^2L
    (c) NMOS
    (d) CMOS
    (e) GaAs MESFET
29. Repeat Exercise 28 for the 16 × 16 bit systolic array multiplier designed as shown in Fig. 3-22.
30. If the output resistance of a power supply is 50 ohms, the maximum expected noise pulse width is 0.5 microseconds, and a time constant four times the pulse width is judged to be sufficient to filter noise, what capacitance should be placed between the supply and ground pins of an IC.

4

Fundamental Computer Operations

The function of a processing element is to retrieve the data it is to operate on, operate on the data, and store the results. This chapter introduces the fundamental operations of processing elements and describes how they are told which operations to perform. The examples in this chapter will consist of short sequences of instructions that do simple, well-defined tasks. How to put such sequences together to form programs will be the subject of Chap. 5.

In this chapter we are concerned only with the simple configuration depicted in Fig. 4-1, which consists of a processing element, a single main memory element that contains all of the instructions and data that are needed by the processing element, and a bus that joins the processing and memory elements together. We are not concerned with how the instructions and data got into the memory element or what happens to the results after they are stored in the memory element. Our interests are restricted to the interaction between the processing and memory elements and the operations carried out by the processing element.

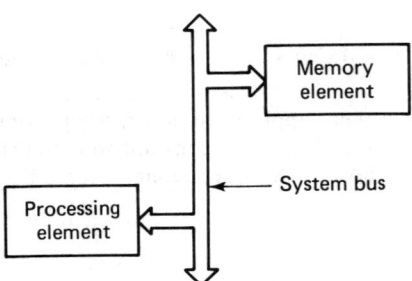

Figure 4-1 Processing configuration assumed in Chapter 4.

Figure 4-2(a) illustrates the cycle of activity that must be repeated while instructions are executed. This cycle consists of inputting, or **fetching**, the instruction from memory, executing the instruction (which may include fetching data from memory or storing results back into memory), and determining the location of the next instruction. The most important characteristic of a processing element is its speed, which is determined by the average time it takes to complete this cycle. Each of the cycle's three components takes time, but determining the location of the next instruction normally overlaps the execution of the present instruction. Thus, the cycle time is, for the most part, divided between the fetching and executing components and both have a direct bearing on a processing element's speed.

Processing elements are constructed so that the next instruction is taken from the next sequential memory location unless the present instruction indicates otherwise (i.e., the default location of the next instruction to be fetched is the one whose address sequentially follows that of the current instruction). Normally, only a few instructions can cause an instruction to be taken out of sequence. They are called **branch instructions** and may be **unconditional**, in which case the branch out of sequence is always taken, or **conditional**. For conditional branches the branch may or may not be taken depending on the state of the processing element at the time the branch decision is made. For branching purposes, this state is determined by the contents of a special set of flip-flops within the processing element that are referred to as **condition flags** (or **condition codes**). The condition flags are set or cleared according to the results of previous instructions (e.g., one of the flags may be set or cleared depending on whether the result of an arithmetic operation is zero or nonzero). It is conditional branch instructions that give a processing element its decision-making capability.

Shown in Fig. 4-2(b) are the principal components of the elements in Fig. 4-1. The memory is made up of groups bits, called **locations**, with each location being used to store a basic unit of information (e.g., a byte). Each location has associated with it a unique identifying number, called its **address**, which is used to put information into and take information from the location.

Included in the processing element are the bus control logic for interfacing to a system bus, the control unit that is responsible for decoding and executing the instructions, the arithmetic/logic unit (ALU) that performs the arithmetic and logical operations, and an internal memory consisting of a set of registers, called the **working registers**, which hold information that can be accessed quickly. The control unit also includes a set of registers. They hold instruction-related information that is needed during the execution of the instructions. The control unit's set of registers typically includes the:

Instruction register (IR): For holding the current instruction while it is being decoded and executed.

Program counter (PC): For holding the address of the next instruction.

Processor status word (PSW): A collection of flip-flops that includes the condition flags and other status information needed during the operation of the processing element.

(b) Major components

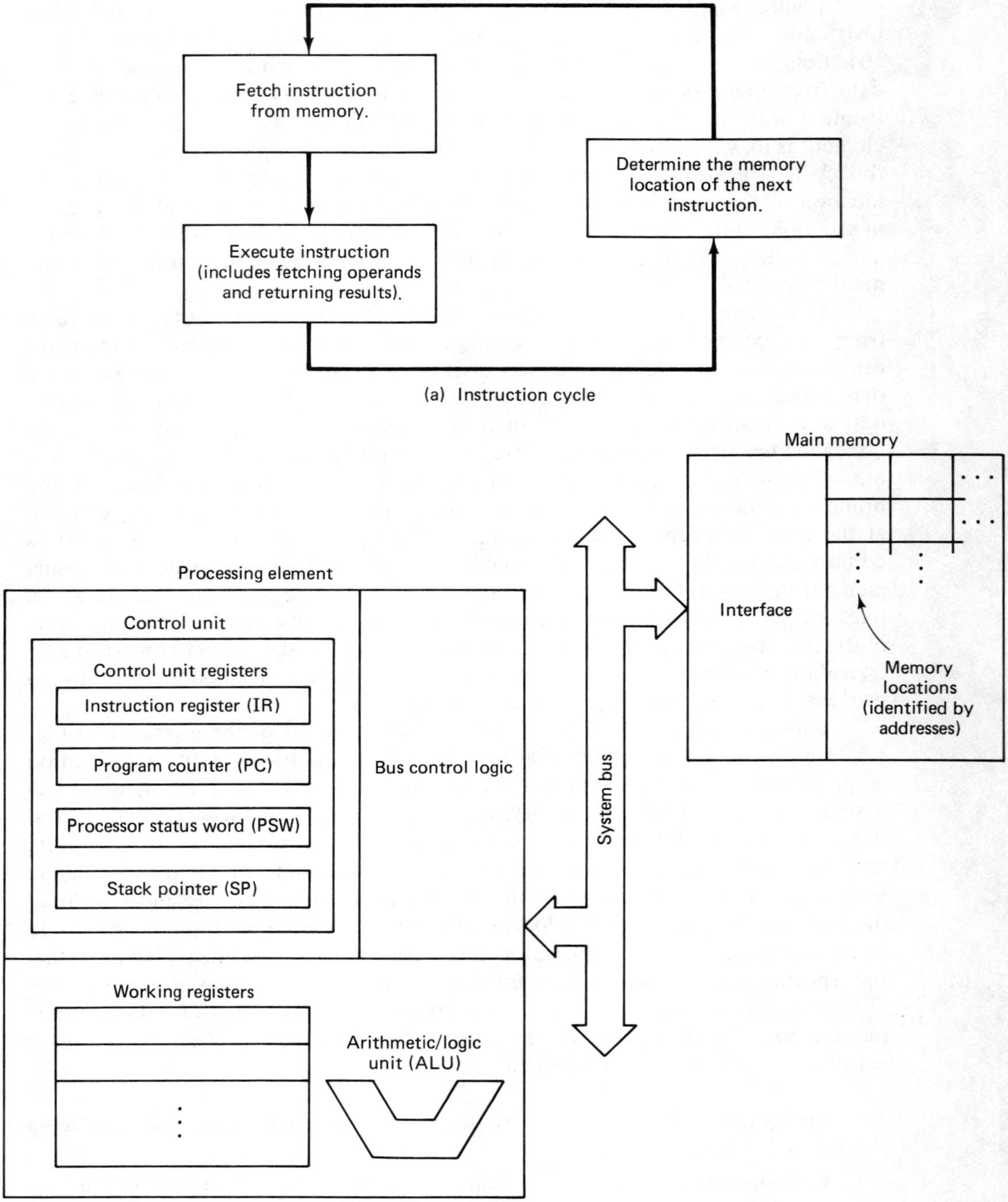

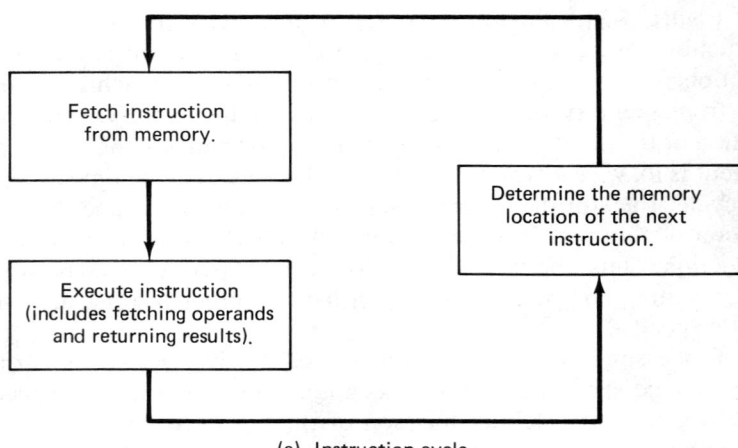

Figure 4-2 Processing operation and major components.

Stack pointer (SP): Used for accessing a special part of memory called a **stack**. (Stacks are discussed in Sec. 4-3.)

Figure 4-3 is a flowchart of the activity that takes place during the fetch and execution of an instruction. After the execution of an instruction is complete and the PC has been updated, the address of the next instruction is sent to the memory. The memory returns the instruction, which is then stored in the IR where it is decoded. If it is an unconditional branch instruction or a conditional branch whose

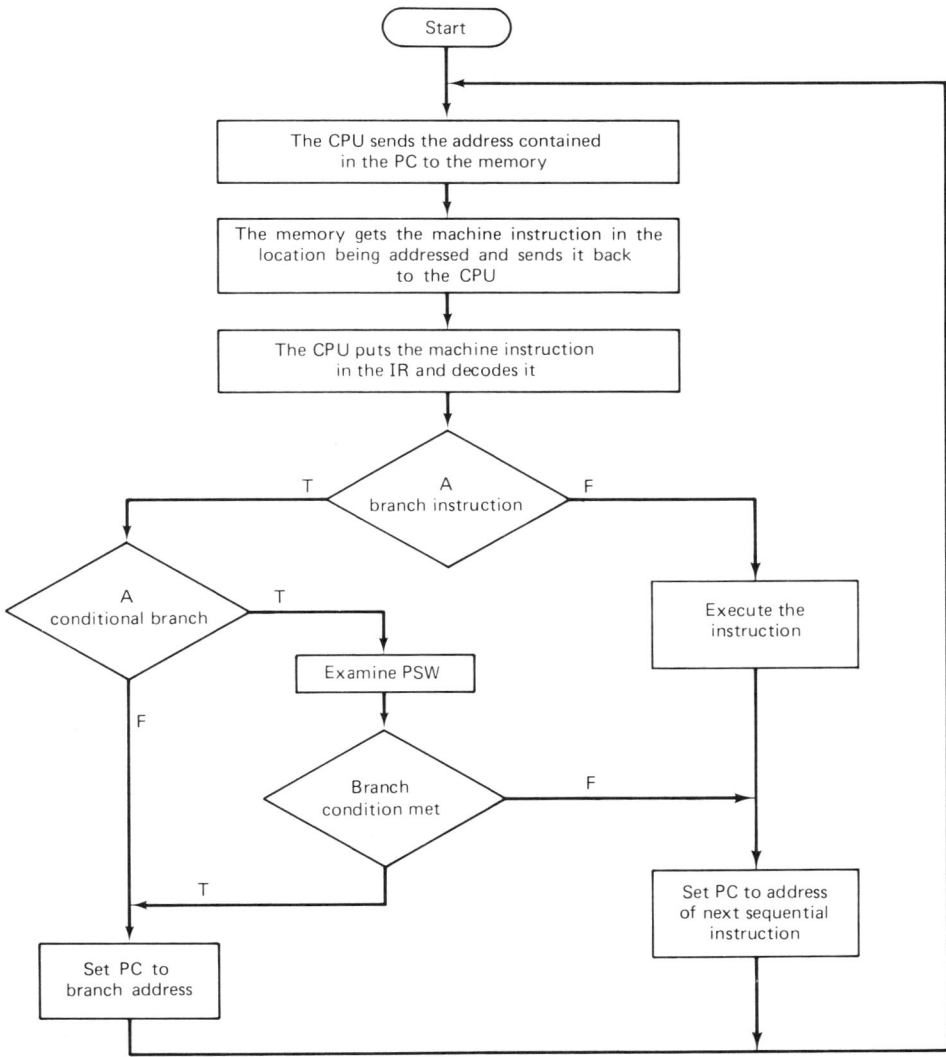

Figure 4-3 Flowchart of instruction execution activity.

Chap. 4   Fundamental Computer Operations

condition is satisfied, then the PC is filled with the address of the location that is to be branched to, an address indicated by the branch instruction. Otherwise, the next sequential address is put into the PC. In any event, after instruction execution is complete the new contents of the PC are sent to the memory and the cycle is repeated.

For a processing element to decode instructions, all instructions must be presented to it as combinations of 0s and 1s. As indicated in Chap. 1, such instructions are referred to as machine language instructions because they can be directly understood by the processing element's decode logic. However, because it is extremely tedious to write programs in machine language, almost all programs are written in an assembler or high-level language. The advantage is that meaningful strings of alphanumeric characters may be used to indicate what is to be done and to represent the quantities to be operated on. The programmer does not need to know the bit combinations that indicate the operations or that point to the operands. The disadvantage is that some means are needed to convert the statements that are easily understood by the programmer into the machine language instructions required by the processing element. This conversion is, of course, done by a translator program such as an assembler or compiler, the design of which is discussed in Chap. 5.

Although almost all programming is done using a high-level language, a computer designer is concerned with the details of the computer's logic and must think in terms of machine language instructions or their assembler language counterparts. Because this chapter primarily examines the fundamental operations of processing elements, its examples are given in terms of machine and assembler language instructions.

4-1 MACHINE LANGUAGE INSTRUCTIONS

While planning a processing element the question that must be answered first is: What operations must the processing element be able to do? Much of our attention in this section is given in response to this question. The broad categories of operations that instructions must perform are:

- Moving data
- Performing arithmetic and logical operations
- Decision-making
- Repeating
- Subdividing

The CPU of a general purpose computer is built to satisfy all five categories and, in terms of high-level languages, some of the first and all of the second of these categories are satisfied by assignment statements, the third by IF-THEN-ELSE statements, the fourth by looping, and the fifth by procedures, or subprograms.

4-1-1 Instruction Types and Formats

The machine language instruction types for executing the above operation types are summarized in Fig. 4-4. Transfer instructions move data around and, because only the simple configuration shown in Fig. 4-1 is considered in this chapter, only the first three types of transfer instructions are discussed. Transfers involving I/O or mass storage are considered in Chap. 6.

Arithmetic instructions perform comparisons as well as the standard arithmetic operations. Comparisons are normally used in conjunction with conditional branching. A comparison instruction sets the condition flags to indicate the results of relational operations ($=, \neq, >, \leq, <, \geq$) and then the conditional branch is made or not made according to the status of the condition flags. Compare/branch instruction combinations implement the high-level language IF-THEN-ELSE and looping control structures.

Bit manipulation instructions carry out operations at the bit level. Specifically, they perform testing, shifting, and rotating as well as the usual logical operations. Testing instructions are similar to compare instructions in that they are

Transfer:
    Register-register
    Register-memory
    Memory-memory
    Interface-register
    Interface-memory

Arithmetic:
    Negation
    Addition
    Subtraction
    Multiplication
    Division
    Comparison

Bit Manipulation:
    Complementation
    ANDing
    ORing
    XORing
    Testing
    Shifting
    Rotating

Branch:
    Unconditional
    Conditional
    Looping
    Procedure call
    Procedure return

Figure 4-4 Summary of machine language instruction types.

intended to be used with conditional branches. Instead of setting the condition flags to indicate relational results, the condition flags are set according to whether or not the bit patterns in the instruction's operands match. Shift and rotate instructions initiate operations performed by shift registers (see Sec. 3-4-2).

The decision-making, repeating, and subdividing requirements are all implemented by branch instructions. Unconditional branches are the machine language equivalents of high-level language GO TO statements. Although the use of GO TO statements is discouraged in high-level language programs, at the machine level, unconditional branches may appear frequently. This is because, in order to reduce the processing element's logic to a manageable level, machine language instructions are designed to do elementary operations and a simple instruction cannot both make a complex decision and execute a branch. A decision-making high-level language statement such as an IF-THEN-ELSE can perform many tasks at what seems to be the same time, and thereby avoids an explicit GO TO. However, when it is translated into machine language, the translation may include several unconditional branch instructions. As indicated above, conditional branch instructions are normally used with compare and test instructions and result from the translation of decision-making and looping high-level language statements. Procedure call and return branches are used for subdividing a program into small tasks by using procedures to perform these tasks.

As shown in Fig. 4-5, the bits that make up a machine language instruction are divided into subsets, or fields. One field is called the **operation code field**, or **opcode field**, and indicates what the instruction is to do. The others either contain the quantities or indicate the locations of the quantities to be operated on and are called **operand fields**. In a branch instruction, an operand field may contain the address of the location to be branched to or indicate the location of that address.

At this point, it should be noted that in many books and manuals confusion arises when discussing machine language instructions because of the ambiguous usage of the term "operand." To avoid this problem, when discussing *machine language instructions*, this book will use the word "operand" to indicate a quantity being operated on or a result, and the term "operand field" to mean any set of bits that make up an operand or whose purpose is to point to the location of an operand. A field that contains an operand is called an **immediate operand**.

The number of operand fields may vary from one instruction to the next. At one extreme are instructions, such as the one that halts the operation of a computer, which have no operand fields. On the other hand, an instruction may include several operands. For example, an instruction may include two quantities to be operated on, produce a result, and then branch to a specified address, thus requiring four operand fields.

Sometimes an instruction is such that an operand is not contained in or

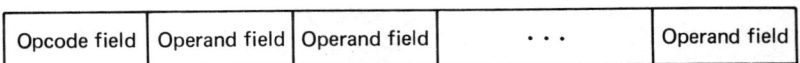

Figure 4-5 General format of a machine language instruction.

pointed to by an operand field, but the identity of the location of the operand is implied by the opcode. In such cases, the operand is called an **implicit operand**.

4-1-2 Operation Codes

The number of bits in the opcode field may vary from instruction to instruction. In addition to the bits needed to designate the basic instruction type, the opcode must include bits for specifying variations of the basic instructions, the length of the opcode, operand lengths, and so on. The design of a processing element's instruction set begins by dividing the instructions that must be available to the processing element into classes and determining a number of bits for the opcodes in each class. Then, keeping in mind that each instruction and variation must be uniquely identified by the processing element's decode logic, 0-1 combinations are assigned to the instructions and their variations. One design goal is to make these assignments so that the decode logic is minimized.

For example, consider a processing element that must be capable of performing the following operations on 8-bit (byte) operands or 16-bit (halfword) operands:

> Transfer, negation, addition (with or without carry), subtraction (with or without borrow), multiplication, division, comparison, complementation, ANDing, ORing, exclusive ORing (XORing), testing, shifting, and rotating.

and branches of the following types:

> Unconditional, conditional depending on 14 possible combinations of condition flag settings, procedure call, and procedure return.

The element is also to have a no operation instruction that does nothing (such as the FORTRAN CONTINUE statement) and a halt instruction for halting the element's execution.

Suppose that it has been decided to divide the instructions into four classes according to their opcode lengths of 4, 7, 10, and 16 bits. One possible assignment of 0-1 combinations is given in Fig. 4-6. This figure organizes the instructions into a tree-like structure with the main branches of the tree corresponding to:

- Miscellaneous instructions with 16-bit opcodes.
- Branch instructions with 10-bit opcodes.
- Shift and rotate instructions with 10-bit opcodes.
- Arithmetic and logic instructions with 7-bit opcodes.
- Arithmetic and transfer instructions with 4-bit opcodes.

The opcode bits are the leftmost bits in the instructions and their bit assignments are given in parentheses.

The 16-bit opcodes begin with at least nine 0s and the branch instructions, which have 10-bit opcodes, all begin with 000001. The other four bits in the opcode

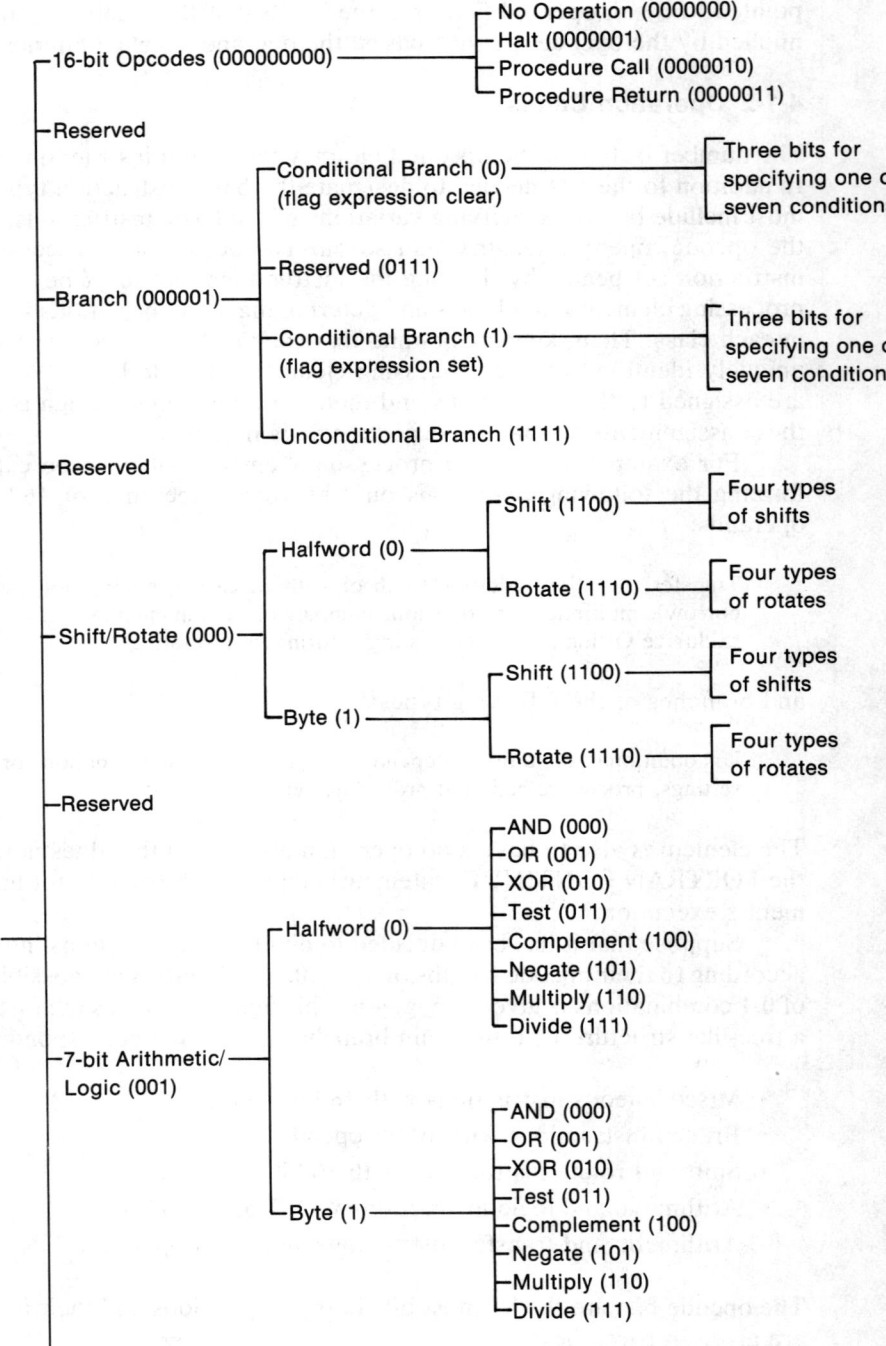

Figure 4-6 X16 machine language instruction bit assignments.

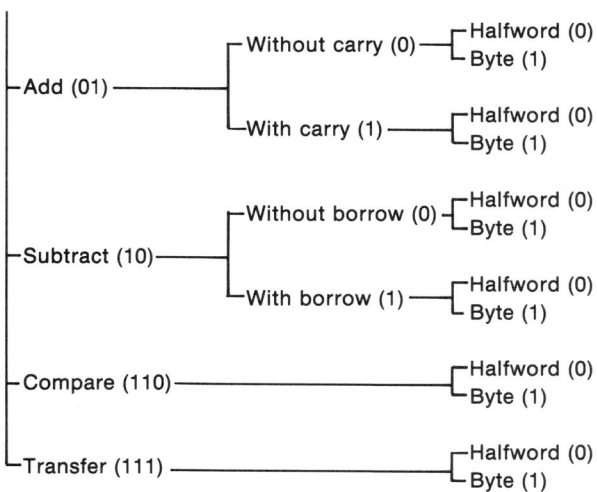

Figure 4-6 Continued

of a branch instruction designate whether the branch is conditional or unconditional and, if conditional, the condition under which the branch is to be taken. The shift instructions begin with 00001100 or 00011100 and the fourth bit indicates whether a halfword or a byte is being shifted. A 1 in the fourth bit indicates that the operand is one byte in length and a 0 indicates that the operand is a halfword. Similarly, rotate instructions begin with 00001110 or 00011110. In either case, the next two bits indicate the type of shift or rotate (see Sec. 4-2-6).

Four-bit and seven-bit opcodes are assigned to transfer, arithmetic, and logic instructions and, as with shift and rotate instructions, the fourth bit indicates the operand length. Seven-bit opcodes consist of 001 followed by the length bit and three bits that indicate the operation to be performed. Four-bit opcodes begin with 01, 10, or 11. For addition and subtraction, the third bit qualifies the basic operation by designating whether it is to be carried out with or without a carry/borrow. The reason for this distinction is discussed in Sec. 4-2-2.

The word "reserved" indicates ranges of bit combinations that have not yet been assigned. Some of these combinations may be used to add instructions later.

The above example begins the design of a processing element that will be referred to as the X16. The design will be expanded as this book progresses until it could be used as a complete general purpose processing element. A detailed summary of the X16 is given in Appendix C.

4-1-3 Operand Fields and Addressing Modes

Operand fields may also be of variable length and, as indicated in their definition, may contain an immediate operand or information that leads to the location of an operand. An operand field may consist of subfields, typically one to three subfields, with all but one of the subfields containing a constant, register address, or memory location address. The remaining subfield contains the **addressing mode**, which indicates how the other subfields are to be used to produce the location of the actual operand.

A wide variety of addressing modes is essential because it determines the flexibility with which data are accessed by instructions. As will be seen as we proceed, accessing different data types requires the use of different addressing modes. The absence of an appropriate addressing mode could make a data access cumbersome and inefficient.

The most common addressing modes are defined in Fig. 4-7 along with representative operand field formats that could be used with them. Each definition consists of a diagram in the right-most column that shows how the operand is obtained. The first is the immediate mode that is used to designate an immediate operand. This mode is illustrated in the defining diagram by showing the operand within the instruction. Because changing an immediate operand requires changing its instruction, the immediate mode is used for quantities that are constant throughout a program's execution.

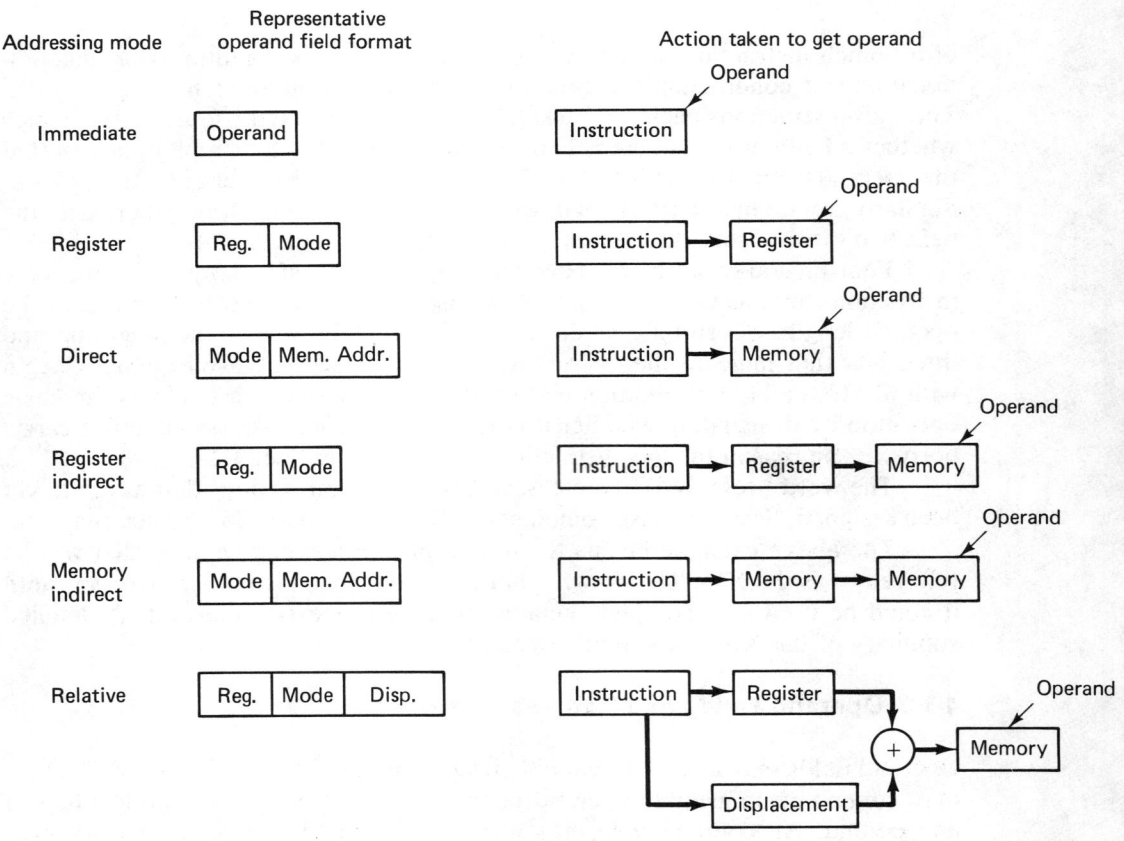

Figure 4-7 Principal addressing modes.

The **register** and **direct addressing modes** imply that the associated subfield contains the register or memory address of the operand. Both of these modes are used extensively but are limited in that the operand's address is contained in the instruction and is, therefore, constant throughout the execution of the program. However, unlike an immediate operand, the operand itself may vary.

An instruction that uses the immediate and direct addressing modes is:

Move the number 478 into the memory location whose address is 15A6.

(all addresses are given in hexadecimal). The first operand field contains a subfield that specifies the immediate mode and the number $478_{10} = 1DE_{16}$, and the second operand field contains a subfield that specifies the direct mode and the address 15A6. The format of this instruction might be:

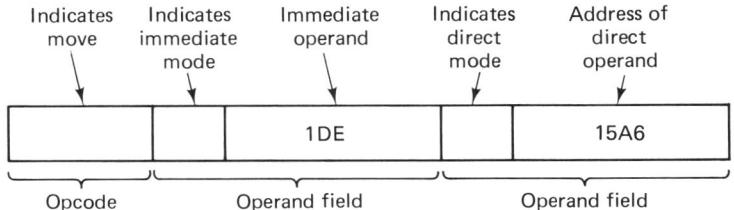

If X were associated with the memory location whose address is 15A6, then this instruction could be used to implement the Pascal statement:

$$X := 478;$$

For **register indirect addressing** the operand field contains the address of a register and the register contains the memory address of the location of the operand. Because the contents of a register can be changed, the register can refer to different memory locations and the operand does not always have to be in the same location. For example, the instruction

Add the contents of register R1 to the memory location whose address is in register R2.

which uses register addressing for the first operand and register indirect addressing for the second operand, would allow the contents of R1 to be added to different memory locations depending on the contents of R2.

Memory indirect addressing is similar to register indirect addressing except that the address of the operand is in a memory location. As with register indirect addressing, changing the contents of this memory location causes the location being operated on to change. Memory indirect addressing is not used as much as register indirect addressing, but it is convenient in some situations (e.g., referencing an operand via its pointer). Not all instruction sets include memory indirect addressing.

Relative addressing produces the address of an operand by adding the contents of a register to a constant, called the **displacement**, which is part of the operand field. As we will see, relative addressing serves many purposes, but the most apparent is related to working with arrays. An element of an array is normally referenced by adding the beginning address of the array to the element's index. This reference can be made automatically by letting the displacement be the beginning address and putting the index in the register. For example, an element of an array of bytes that begins at 2B00 could be referenced using relative addressing with a displacement of 2B00 and putting the index of the array element in a register. Referring to a different array element would simply involve changing the contents of the register.

Using relative addressing, but reversing the roles of the displacement and register contents so that the register contents are held constant is called **base addressing**. This type of addressing is used to randomly access a data structure in memory relative to a fixed base.

Relative addressing may be combined with indirect addressing so that the sum of the register contents and displacement point to a location that contains the address of the operand instead of the operand itself (e.g., this procedure could be used when accessing operands through an array of pointers).

If the register involved in relative addressing is the PC, the mode is referred to as **PC relative addressing**. This type of addressing is commonly used with branch instructions. The reasons for using the PC with relative addressing will be discussed in Chap. 5.

Let us now extend our X16 example by defining its register addresses, the formats of its operand fields, and its addressing modes. The internal configuration, or **programming model**, of the X16 is given in Fig. 4-8. All of the registers are 2 bytes wide and the X16 can input or output single bytes or halfwords. Each byte in memory has an address and, for halfwords, the low-order byte (which consists of the eight least significant bits) has the lower byte address and the high-order byte (which consists of the eight most significant bits) has the next higher address. A halfword is referenced using the address of its low order byte.

The relationship between halfwords and their addresses, along with the bit numbering convention that is assumed is given in Fig. 4-9. Any instruction that takes only one byte from a register or puts one byte into a register takes the byte from or puts it into the low-order byte of the register. The upper byte of the register is not changed.

The X16 has an IR, PC, PSW, SP, and six registers denoted R0 through R5. Except for the IR, which is not referred to by instructions, and the PSW, which is only implicitly referenced by opcodes, the addresses of the processing element's registers are given in Fig. 4-10(a). The immediate, register, direct, register indirect, and relative addressing modes are defined in Figure 4-10(b). The second column in this figure gives the 0-1 combinations that represent the modes and the third column lists the possible registers that can be associated with the modes. Figure 4-10(c) shows the overall format of X16 instructions. Opcode bits appear first, followed by the bits in the 0, 1, or 2 operand fields. The possible formats for the operand fields for the various addressing modes are given in Fig. 4-10(d). All X16

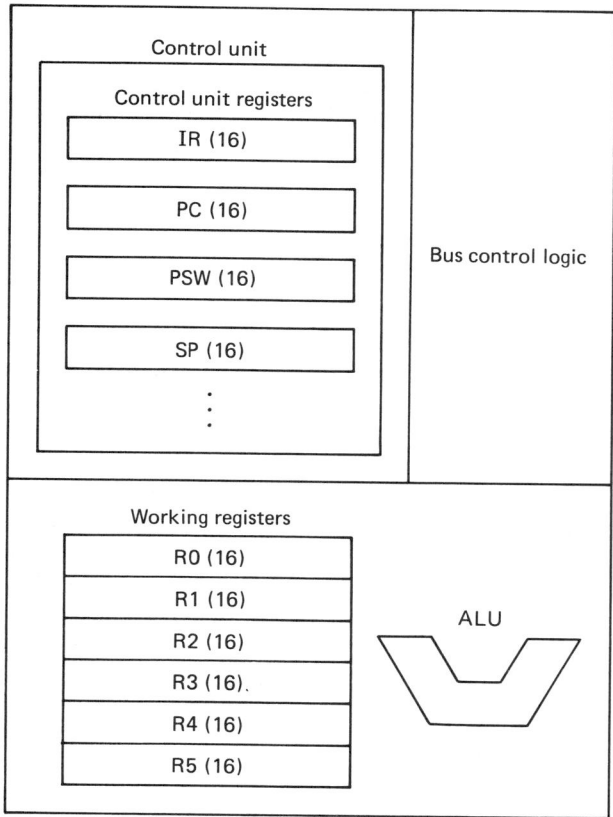

Figure 4-8 X16 programming model.

operand fields have either two or three subfields. The length of these subfields and what they contain depend on their instruction types as well as their addressing modes. In particular, the length of the first subfield may be 3 bits or 6 bits, depending on whether or not the instruction has a 7-bit opcode. For an instruction with a 7-bit opcode, if the first operand involves a register it is implicitly taken to be R0. Therefore, it does not need to be explicitly declared.

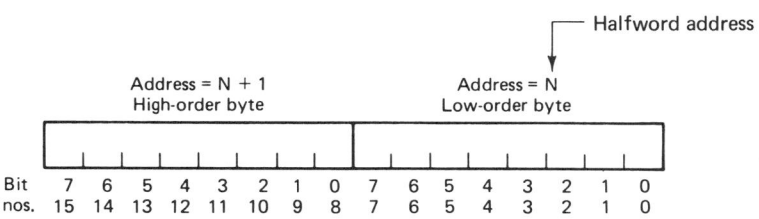

Figure 4-9 Addressing and bit numbering conventions for the X16.

4-1-4 Instruction and Instruction Set Design

Once the operations that a processing element is to perform have been decided upon, the instructions needed to carry out the operations and the 0-1 combinations that represent these instructions must be determined. These decisions must be made while attempting to:

1. Minimize the amount of logic in the processing element, particularly the instruction decode and ALU logic.
2. Make the processing element easy to program.
3. Make the processing element as fast as possible within the constraints imposed by (1) and (2) and the physical constraints due to other design decisions.

The number of instructions and the lengths of the opcodes most directly affect the complexity of the decode logic (see Chap. 7), but the uniformity of the arrangement of the bits throughout the entire instruction set is also important. Many factors and restrictions indirectly affect the decode logic design because they either affect the number of instructions or the opcode lengths. One restriction is that computers are designed to work with groups of bits, usually 8-bit bytes, and the instructions are constructed of multiples of these groups. The reason for making a special case for X16 instructions with 7-bit opcodes is so that for all

Symbol	Address
R0	000
R1	001
R2	010
R3	011
R4	100
R5	101
SP	110
PC	111

(a) Register addresses

Addressing mode	Representation	Possible registers
Immediate	010 or 111010	None
Register	000	R0–R5, SP
Direct	011 or 111011	None
Register indirect	001	R0–R5, SP
Relative	110	R0–R5, SP, PC

(b) Basic addressing modes

Figure 4-10 X16 operand field definitions.

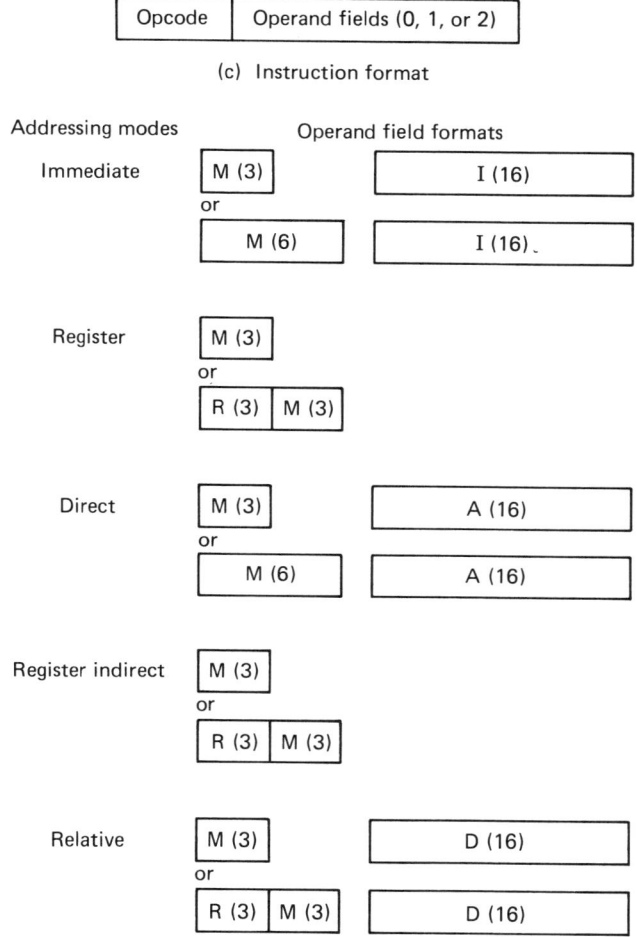

(c) Instruction format

(d) Operand field formats

In each pair of formats, the first format is for the first operand field in instructions with 7-bit opcodes. All other operand fields use the second format. The numbers of bits in the subfields are given in parentheses and the abbreviations are:

> R — register address
> M — addressing mode
> A — memory address
> D — displacement
> I — immediate operand

Figure 4-10 Continued

Sec. 4-1 Machine Language Instructions

instructions, the opcode, addressing modes, and register addresses will occupy exactly two bytes.

An important concept relating the amount of decode logic to instruction design is **orthogonality**. If two sets of instruction bits can be independently given values throughout a subset of instructions, they are said to be **orthogonal** with respect to the subset. For example, consider the subset of all X16 instructions with data operands and recall that for all such instructions the fourth bit specifies the operand length. Therefore, with respect to this subset, the fourth bit is orthogonal to the set of all other bits in these instructions. That is, the value of the fourth bit does not depend on the values of the other bits. This means that for instructions in the subset, the fourth bit can be decoded separately. The ideal situation would be to have an instruction set such that each bit could be decoded separately for all instructions, i.e., to have orthogonality between all bits with respect to the entire instruction set. Although this situation would minimize the amount of decode logic, it could be achieved only by assigning independent meanings that hold true for all instructions to all individual bits. This design is not realistic in most cases, but it is often possible to give independent meanings to subfields of bits and have those meanings apply to a set, or class, of instructions, e.g., a subfield may be reserved to specify an addressing mode for all instructions in a particular class.

The disadvantage of orthogonality is its tendency to increase instruction length. To demonstrate this point, consider the reservation of a 3-bit subfield for an addressing mode in all instructions, even though some of the instructions may not involve an operand or may have only one useful addressing mode. The tendency toward orthogonality is good, but must be weighed against having many more bits than are required to specify all of the instruction types and variations.

The amount of ALU logic that is needed depends to a large extent on the maximum number of bits that can be operated on by single arithmetic or logical instructions and the data types of the operands. The logic needed for performing floating point arithmetic is quite complex, and separate arithmetic units are usually included to perform the floating point operations. In general, integers are 16, 24, or 32 bits in length and the amount of logic needed to operate on them tends to be directly proportional to their length. As seen later, it is possible to emulate floating point arithmetic or arithmetic on integers of arbitrary lengths by using sequences of integer arithmetic instructions. For example, four instructions that perform 8-bit integer arithmetic could be used to carry out 32-bit integer operations. Although less ALU logic is required, the disadvantage of this approach is that it may take several instructions for each operation and therefore, more time to complete the operation. Thus, there is a tradeoff between speed and the amount of ALU logic.

The effects of instruction set design on speed are mainly due to instruction and operand lengths. The primary cause of these lengths adversely affecting processing speed is the fetch and store times required to transfer code and data between the processing element and memory. The overall length of an instruction is clearly the sum of the length of the opcode and the lengths of all operand fields. Some of the more common means of minimizing instruction lengths are:

- Keeping the number of instructions as small as possible, thereby minimizing the lengths of the opcodes.
- Reducing the number of operand fields by using some of them for more than one purpose. This is most often accomplished by storing an arithmetic or logical result back into the location occupied by one of the operands (e.g., replacing the augend with the sum).
- Reducing the number of operand fields by allowing branch instructions to perform only branches (e.g., a branch instruction that also performs an addition could require as many as four operands).
- Using register addresses in as many operand fields as possible because they are much shorter than memory addresses (e.g., use register indirect addressing).
- Allowing only transfer instructions to retrieve and store memory operands (all other operands would be in the working registers). Therefore, only register addresses are needed in all instructions other than transfer and branch instructions.
- Forcing all operands in an instruction to be of the same length; thus, only one operand length would need to be specified (e.g., the augend, addend, and sum operands of an addition instruction would all be of the same length).
- Using addressing modes (such as the relative addressing mode) that require only part of a memory address to be put in the operand field.

Many of these suggestions are aimed at reducing the number of direct memory references or the number of bits needed to specify a memory address. Such reductions must be taken because memory addresses are major contributors to instruction lengths. A memory containing 2^n locations requires n-bit memory addresses and, even for a memory containing only 64K locations, 16 bits are needed for each address. In contrast, because the number of registers is relatively small, only a few bits are needed to designate a register (e.g., only 3 bits are required to specify one of eight registers).

If a quantity is taken from a location, its associated operand field is referred to as a **source operand field**. If a quantity is deposited in a location, the associated field is called a **destination operand field**. Sometimes the same field is used to indicate both a source and a destination, in which case it is usually referred to as a destination field. Instructions are often classified by the number of operand fields they contain. A typical instruction set includes instructions with zero, one, two, or, perhaps, three operand fields, in which case the instructions are referred to as **no, single, double,** or **triple operand instructions**. For double and triple operand instructions the order is significant. For example, subtraction is not commutative and the decode logic must know from which field to get the minuend and from which to get the subtrahend.

Figure 4-11 gives the instruction formats for our X16 example. The X16 instructions may be 2, 4, or 6 bytes long and may be no, single, or double operand instructions. For double operand instructions the source operand field appears

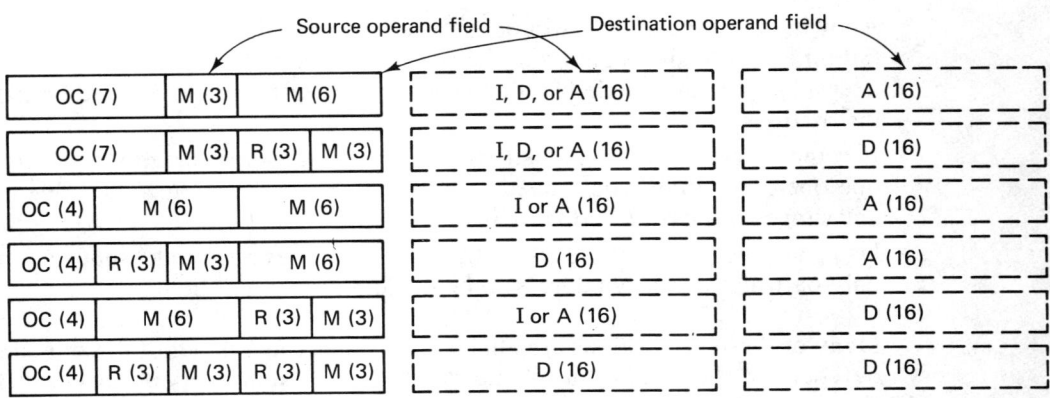

The byte/halfword represented by a dashed rectangle may or not be present. Whether or not it is present and what it represents depends on the mode. OC is the abbreviation for opcode, R, M, A, D, and I are as defined in Fig. 4-10(d).

Figure 4-11 X16 instruction formats.

first and the destination operand field second. To avoid 8-byte instructions, arithmetic and logic operations that have two source operands and produce a result are such that the second source operand is the augend, minuend, multiplicand, or dividend and the result replaces this operand. Therefore, the second source operand field is the same as the destination field. For example, for the subtract instruction, the subtrahend is associated with the source operand field, which appears first, and the minuend and difference are associated with the destination operand field, which appears second. *An immediate operand can only be a source operand.*

All instructions contain at least two bytes. No operation, halt, and procedure return instructions are two bytes long and procedure calls are four bytes long. For other instructions, the number of bytes depends on the addressing mode(s).

For the sake of orthogonality, it would be better if all double operand instructions had been given opcodes of equal length. Unfortunately, the decision to have two operand lengths, eight addressable registers, between four and eight addressing modes, and between eight and sixteen double operand instructions requires the double operand instructions to have

$$1 + 2(3 + 3) + 4 = 17 \text{ bits}$$

To reduce this bit count to 16 it was necessary to introduce 7-bit opcodes and eliminate the register subfield from the first operand field. In addition to decreasing orthogonality, the penalty we must pay is that the source operand register must now be implied by either the opcode or addressing mode—there is no longer complete flexibility in specifying the register. Therefore, for instructions with 7-bit opcodes, if the source operand includes a register, it must be R0. The decision to use 7-bit opcodes adversely impacts the decode logic design, but the alternatives would be to reduce the variety of double operand instructions or the number of addressing modes.

Six examples of X16 machine language instructions are given in Fig. 4-12. These examples were derived using the definitions in Figs. 4-6, 4-10, and 4-11. The instruction

Move the halfword in register R1 to register R2

can be broken down as follows:

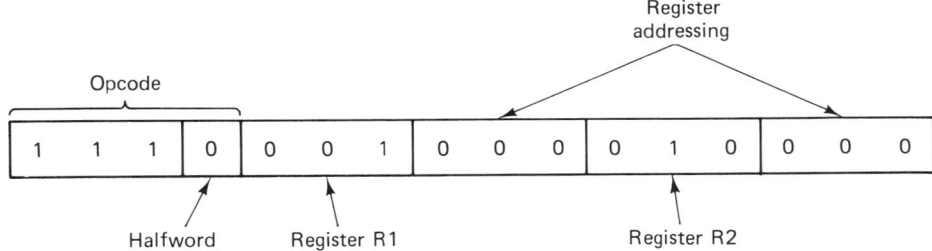

The overall format was determined from Fig. 4-11. The opcode was found in Fig. 4-6 to be 1110 and the register addresses 001 and 010 and the register mode representation 000 were taken from Fig. 4-10. Verification of the remainder of these examples is requested in Exercise 4.

4-1-5 Condition Flags and the PSW

All conditional branch decisions are made based upon the settings of condition flags. The number and types of these flags determine the decision-making versatility of a processing element. Almost all processing elements include the following condition flags in their PSWs:

Zero (Z) flag: Set to 1 if the result of an arithmetic/logic or shift/rotate operation is zero and clear to 0 if the result is nonzero.

Negative (N) flag: Set to equal the high-order bit of the result of an arithmetic/logic or shift/rotate operation.

No operation.

| 0 0 0 0 0 0 0 0 0 0 0 0 0 0 0 0 |

Procedure call to location 674B.

| 0 0 0 0 0 0 0 0 0 0 0 0 0 0 1 0 | | 0 1 1 0 0 1 1 1 0 1 0 0 1 0 1 1 |

Branch to the location 8 bytes beyond the current value of the PC.

| 0 0 0 0 0 1 1 1 1 1 1 1 1 1 1 0 | | 0 0 0 0 0 0 0 0 0 0 0 0 1 0 0 0 |

Move the halfword in register R1 to register R2.

| 1 1 1 0 0 0 1 0 0 0 0 1 0 0 0 0 |

Compare the hexadecimal number 10C2 with the contents of the halfword location whose address is in register SP.

| 1 1 0 0 1 1 1 0 1 0 1 1 0 0 0 1 | | 0 0 0 1 0 0 0 0 1 1 0 0 0 0 1 0 |

Add (without carry) 6 to the memory byte location 1B54.

| 0 1 0 1 1 1 0 1 0 1 1 1 0 1 1 | | 0 0 0 0 0 0 0 0 0 0 0 0 0 1 1 0 | | 0 0 0 1 1 0 1 1 0 1 0 1 0 1 0 0 |

Figure 4-12 Examples of X16 machine language instructions.

Carry (C) flag: For addition it is set to 1 if there is a carry from the high-order bit position and for subtraction it is set to 1 if a borrow is needed (i.e., the unsigned subtrahend is greater than the unsigned minuend).

Overflow (V) flag: Set to 1 if an arithmetic operation causes a signed overflow and clear to 0 if it does not cause a signed overflow.

The exact rules for setting and clearing these flags depend on the processing element, but the ones given above are representative. Transfer, branch, and most other instructions leave flags unchanged. The primary purpose of the flags is to reflect the results of arithmetic/logic operations so that conditional branches can be made according to these results.

The format of the PSW for the X16 is shown in Fig. 4-13(a). The condition flags are the Z, N, C, and V flags defined above. The interrupt and interrupt level bits will be discussed in Chaps. 6 and 7. The instructions for setting the carry flag and interrupt bits are given in Fig. 4-13(b). They are to be added to the instruction set indicated in Fig. 4-6. Their opcodes use some of the bit combinations that were previously "reserved."

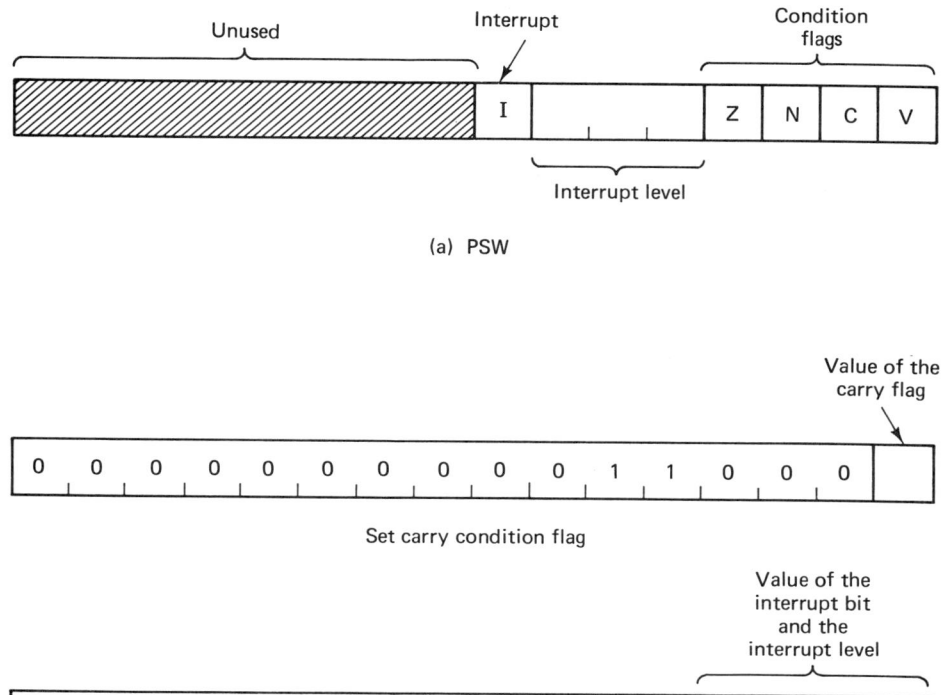

Figure 4-13 Definition of the X16's PSW and the instructions for setting PSW bits.

4-2 ASSEMBLER LANGUAGE INSTRUCTIONS

Assembler language statements fall into two categories, instructions and directives. Assembler languages are designed so that, with few exceptions, there is a one-to-one correspondence between their **instructions,** which are the statements that are actually executed while the program is being run, and the machine language instructions of the processing element. The purpose of an assembler language is to replace the 0-1 combinations that comprise machine language instructions with short but more readable character strings. It is the job of the **assembler** to convert these character strings into their 0-1 counterparts. An assembler language provides the programmer with the same control over the computer as the machine language while providing some of the convenience of high-level languages.

Directives are not executed, but serve only to give directions to the assembler. The more important directives reserve and label memory locations so that these locations can be referred to by symbolic names, but there are many others. We first consider instructions and their execution. The discussion of directives is delayed until Chap. 5. This section will present a number of examples of instruction sequences. These sequences will assume that the necessary directives for associating **labels**, or symbolic names, with memory locations are in the program, even though they are not shown.

An assembler language instruction must contain information sufficient to specify the opcode field and all of the operand fields of the corresponding machine language instruction, including the addressing modes, register addresses, memory addresses, operand lengths, instruction variations, and implicit operands. In addition, it must provide a means of labeling itself so that it can be referenced by other instructions via its label. Most assemblers have instructions with a format similar to the following:

>   *Label   Mnemonic   Operand, . . . , Operand   ;Remarks*

where each item in the format is a short character string and

>   *Label*—is associated with the memory address of the first byte of the instruction and is used by branch instructions to reference the labeled instruction. Labels are optional.
>   *Mnemonic*—specifies the opcode of the instruction.
>   *Operand*—provides the information needed to construct an operand field and point to an operand.
>   *Remarks*—permit the programmer to comment the program.

The semicolon indicates to the assembler that the *Remarks* that follow are not to be translated by the assembler, but are to be saved and output with the program listing. Blanks must follow the *Label* and *Mnemonic* and the *Operands* must be separated by commas. This assures that the assembler has a means of knowing when an item in the format ends.

The rules for constructing an *Operand* may vary considerably from one assembler to the next, but, regardless of the exact format of an *Operand*, the same types of items must be specified—addressing modes, registers, memory addresses, displacements, immediate operands, and so on. Many of these items are represented by character strings called **identifiers**. Typically an identifier is a string made up of letters, digits, and a few special characters, such as periods and underscore characters. The more important components of an *Operand* are:

>   **Constant:** A number or identifier that has been assigned to represent a number by a directive (discussed in Chap. 5). If it is a number, a suffix is normally used to indicate the base with "B" indicating binary, "H" hexadecimal, and the default is decimal (e.g., 01001001B, 6AB2H, and 529).
>   **String constant:** A character string or identifier that has been assigned to

represent a character string. If it is a character string, it is normally differentiated from an identifier by enclosing it in single quotes (e.g., 'ERROR').

Register ID: An identifier that represents a processing element register (e.g., R2 or PC).

Label: An identifier that represents or points to a location. A label appearing in an *Operand* must also appear in the label field of some instruction or directive so that the assembler will be able to identify the location that is being referenced (see Chap. 5).

Expression: A concatenation of constants, labels, and arithmetic/logic operation symbols (e.g., TABLE + 6).

In addition, an *Operand* may contain other identifiers and special symbols for specifying the addressing mode.

In the subsections that follow we will define an assembler language for the X16 processing element that is typical of assembler languages for actual processing elements. In the process, the reasons why the various instructions are needed and the advantages of the addressing modes are discussed. Although the X16 does not cover all possible features of processing elements, it encompasses several of the more important features and should provide the reader with a good feel for the types of instructions and addressing modes that should be present. In some cases, enhancements to the X16 are suggested, but the reader is reminded that such enhancements are usually accompanied by the cost of more complex decode logic. For easy reference, a summary of the X16 instruction set is provided in Appendix C.

The formats of the X16 assembler language *Operands* are summarized in Fig. 4-14. These formats will be assumed in the X16 examples that appear through-

Addressing Mode	Notation	Operand Examples
Immediate*	Label or constant expression preceded by #	#−25 #LAB #CONST
Register	Register ID	PC R3
Direct	Label, constant expression, or label ± constant expression	LAB CONST−2 LAB−CONST 2C4H
Register Indirect	Register ID enclosed in brackets	[R1]
Relative	Label, constant expression, or label ± constant expression followed by register ID enclosed in brackets	CONST[SP] LAB[PC] LAB+16H[R2] CONST[R1] 6[SP]

* When a label appears in an immediate operand, the address of the label is the value used.

Figure 4-14 X16 operand notation.

out the remainder of the book. When a label appears as an immediate operand, it is the address of the label that is used as the *Operand*. The *Operands* are to appear in the same order as the operand fields in the machine language instructions. An example of an X16 assembler language instruction is:

    POINT__A   ADDH   [R2],SUM   ;NEW ELEMENT IS ADDED TO SUM

The label POINT__A allows this instruction to be branched to by any branch instruction that has POINT__A as its *Operand* and the mnemonic ADDH indicates that halfwords are to be added. The *operands* indicate that the quantity whose address is in register R2 is to be added to the quantity in the location associated with the identifier SUM and the result is to be put back into SUM. The remark after the semicolon gives a brief explanation of the instruction.

    A second example is

    BRNN   POINT__A   ;IF NONNEGATIVE, GO TO POINT__A

which would branch to the instruction with the label POINT__A if the N condition flag is 0. Because this instruction does not have a label, it cannot be branched to.

4-2-1 Transfer Instructions

All X16 register-register, register-memory, and memory-memory transfers are accomplished by move instructions. The format of a move instruction is

    MOVB   *SRC,DST*

or

    MOVH   *SRC,DST*

depending on whether a byte or halfword is to be transferred. *SRC* and *DST* may represent any of the operand formats given in Fig. 4-14 except that *DST* cannot be immediate. No condition flag is affected by a move instruction. A move instruction copies the contents of *SRC* into *DST*, which is symbolically written

$$(SRC) \rightarrow (DST)$$

It is standard notation to use parentheses to mean "the contents of" and a right-pointing arrow to mean "replace." Therefore, the meaning of the above is:

    The contents of *SRC* replace the contents of *DST*.

Such abbreviated notation is often used when defining instructions and will be used as X16 instructions are introduced. Three examples of move instructions are given in Fig. 4-15 along with the actions taken when they are executed.

MOVB R1,R2   ;MOVES CONTENTS OF LOW ORDER BYTE OF R1 TO
              ;LOW ORDER BYTE OF R2

MOVH [R2],TOTAL   ;MOVES CONTENTS OF LOCATION POINTED TO BY R2 TO TOTAL

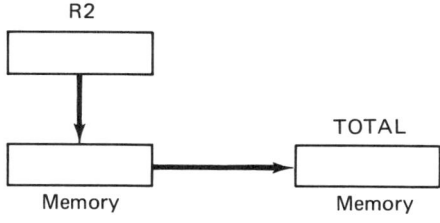

MOVB #5BH,X[R4]   ;MOVES 5B TO LOCATION X+(R4)

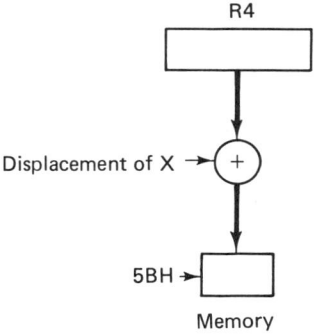

Figure 4-15 Examples of the move instruction.

An instruction sequence that interchanges (X) [i.e., the contents of memory location (X)] with (Y) is given in Fig. 4-16(a) and a diagram of the action taken is shown in Fig. 4-16(b). The first instruction brings (X) into register R0, the second transfers (Y) into location X and the third transfers (R0) into location Y. The Pascal equivalent of this sequence, which assumes X, Y, and TEMP are variables of type character, is:

TEMP: = X;
X: = Y;
Y: = TEMP;

Sec. 4-2   Assembler Language Instructions

```
      MOVB    X,R0        ;INTERCHANGE CONTENTS OF X AND Y
      MOVB    Y,X
      MOVB    R0,Y
```

(a) Instruction sequence

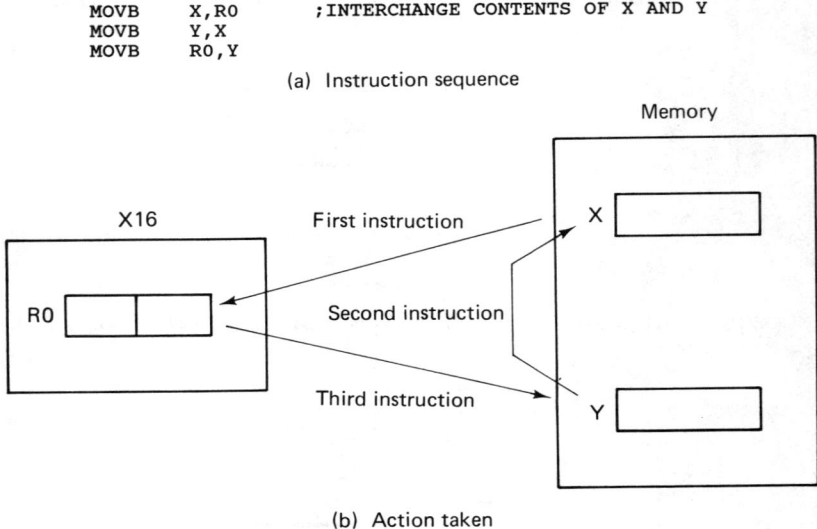

(b) Action taken

Figure 4-16 Example for interchanging two bytes located in memory.

Figure 4-17 gives the machine language code for the sequence in Fig. 4-16, assuming that the labels X and Y are associated with the locations whose addresses are 1440 and 1A00 and the beginning address of the instruction sequence is 12A4. (This code can be derived from the information in Figs. 4-6, 4-10, and 4-11—see Exercise 9.)

4-2-2 Arithmetic Instructions

The X16 performs negation, addition, subtraction, multiplication, and division on binary integers whose lengths are bytes or halfwords. Except for division, the ALU does not care whether operands are signed or unsigned. For division, operands are assumed to be unsigned and the ALU produces unsigned quotients and remainders. Signed integers are assumed to be in their 2's complement format. The X16 does not have BCD or floating point hardware; therefore, the arithmetic

```
Memory address          Machine language code

    12A4                    FEC0  ⎫
                                  ⎬  MOVB    X,R0
    12A6                    1440  ⎭

    12A8                    FEFB  ⎫
    12AA                    1A00  ⎬  MOVB    Y,X
    12AC                    1440  ⎭

    12AE                    F03B  ⎫
                                  ⎬  MOVB    R0,Y
    12B0                    1A00  ⎭
```

Figure 4-17 Machine language code for the interchange example.

operations on numbers in these formats must be emulated using instruction sequences involving integer instructions (see Sec. 4-2-6).

The negate, add, and subtract instructions affect the condition flags according to the definitions given in Sec. 4-1-5. If a register is associated with the source operand of a negate instruction, then it must be R0 because the negate instruction has a 7-bit opcode. An instruction sequence that assumes 16-bit integers and performs the same task as the following Pascal assignment statement is given in Fig. 4-18:

$$W := -(X + Y - 12);$$

Although X16 arithmetic instructions are limited to 16-bit operands (which means operands must be in the unsigned range 0 to 65535 or the signed range −32,768 to 32,767), multiple instructions can be used to add or subtract integers with larger magnitudes. Addition of 32-bit words could be achieved by adding low-order halfwords and then adding high-order halfwords; however, when adding the high-order halfwords, the contents of the carry condition flag must also be added to the result. Similarly, word subtraction could be accomplished using two subtract instructions with the second also subtracting the borrow, which is left in the carry condition flag by the first subtraction. Performing arithmetic on operands that are longer than can be handled by a single instruction is called **multiple-precision arithmetic**. Figure 4-19 gives an instruction sequence that performs the same computation on 32-bit words as was performed on halfwords in the example in Fig. 4-18. Negation is done by subtracting from 0 because there is no negate with borrow instruction. This double precision example assumes that low order halfwords are stored in the memory locations with lower addresses, i.e., the labeled halfwords. High-order halfwords are stored in the labeled halfwords plus 2. This example could be easily extended to perform a triple- or higher-precision computation (see Exercise 13).

```
        MOVH    X,R0        ;MOVE X TO R0
        ADDH    Y,R0        ;ADD Y TO X
        SUBH    #12,R0      ;THEN SUBTRACT 12 FROM THE SUM
        NEGH    R0,W        ;NEGATE DIFFERENCE AND STORE IN W
```

Figure 4-18 Example involving the negate, add, and subtract instructions.

```
        MOVH    X,R0        ;MOVE X INTO R1:R0
        MOVH    X+2,R1
        ADDH    Y,R0        ;ADD LOW-ORDER HALFWORD WITHOUT CARRY
        ADCH    Y+2,R1      ;ADD HIGH-ORDER HALFWORD WITH CARRY
        SUBH    #12,R0      ;SUBTRACT 12 FROM SUM, NO BORROW
        SBBH    #0,R1       ;WITH BORROW
        MOVH    #0,W        ;STORE NEGATIVE OF
        MOVH    #0,W+2      ;DIFFERENCE AT W
        SUBH    R0,W
        SBBH    R1,W+2
```

Figure 4-19 Double-precision version of example in Figure 4-18.

The *signed* multiply and divide instructions are:

MULB	SRC,DST	(DST)*(SRC)→(DST+1):(DST)
MULH	SRC,DST	(DST)*(SRC)→(DST+2):(DST)
DIVB	SRC,DST	Quotient of (DST+1:DST)/(SRC)→(DST)
		Remainder of (DST+1:DST)/(SRC)→(DST+1)
DIVH	SRC,DST	Quotient of (DST+2:DST)/(SRC)→(DST)
		Remainder of (DST+2:DST)/(SRC)→(DST+2)

As with the negate instruction, the corresponding machine language instructions have 7-bit opcodes and therefore, if a register is associated with the source operand, it must be R0. The multiplicand, multiplier, quotient, and remainder operands may be either bytes or halfwords.

However, as discussed in Sec. 2-2-2, forcing all multiplication or division operands to have the same length may not be the best arrangement because integer division produces both a quotient and remainder and a product may require twice as many bits as its factors. Therefore, for division, the dividend is twice the length of the divisor and, for halfwords, must be stored in two consecutive registers with the low-order halfword in the register with the lower address. The quotient and remainder replace the dividend with the quotient replacing the low-order part and the remainder replacing the high-order part. For multiplication, a product is twice as long as its factors and must be stored in consecutive registers with the low-order halfword in the register with the lower address. Figure 4-20 assumes X, Y, and Z are nonnegative and W is positive and gives the code needed to perform the same computation as the Pascal statements:

$$T := (X+Y)*Z;$$
$$U := T/W;$$
$$V := T \bmod W;$$

The importance of setting condition flags during multiplication or division is somewhat less than for addition and subtraction and the amount of logic needed to set the flags is somewhat more. As will be seen shortly, setting these flags is essential only for comparisons and it may be done for other arithmetic operations simply as a convenience. Therefore, as with many other processing elements, the X16 multiplication and division instructions leave the condition flags with no significant meanings.

Multiple-precision multiplication and division of signed operands could be done with shifts and adds. If the multiply instruction were *unsigned,*

```
        MOVH    X,R0
        ADDH    Y,R0            ;ADD Y TO X
        MULH    Z,R0            ;MULTIPLY SUM BY Z
        DIVH    W,R0            ;DIVIDE PRODUCT BY W
        MOVH    R0,U            ;STORE QUOTIENT IN U
        MOVH    R1,V            ;STORE REMAINDER IN V
```

Figure 4-20 Example involving multiplication and division.

Double-precision multiplication.

$$\begin{array}{r} a2^{16} + b \\ \times\ c2^{16} + d \\ \hline ad2^{16} + bd \\ ac2^{32} \quad\quad + bc2^{16} \quad\quad \\ \hline ac2^{32} + (ad + bc)2^{16} + bd \end{array}$$

where a and c are the high-order halfwords of the multiplicand and multiplier and b and d are the corresponding low-order halfwords. Care must be exercised when writing the code for this algorithm because all of the products are full words and addition with carry must sometimes be used. The final product is a doubleword (8 bytes). Figure 4-21 gives the X16 code for performing a double-precision multiplication. This code multiplies the word beginning at X by the word beginning at Y and stores the result beginning at W. Polynomial multiplication can also be used as a basis for triple- and higher-precision multiplication (see Exercise 16).

Multiple-precision division is even more difficult and quite often the divisor and dividend are not the same length. To develop an algorithm for performing an unsigned division of one halfword into three halfwords let us assume that

$$\text{Divisor} = a \qquad \text{Dividend} = b2^{32} + c2^{16} + d$$

where b, c, and d are the base 2^{16} "digits" of the dividend. Then the normal algorithm using base 2^{16} is:

$$\begin{array}{r} q_2 2^{32} + q_1 2^{16} + q_0 \\ a\ \overline{)\ b2^{32} + c2^{16} + d\ } \\ -\ aq_2 2^{32} \quad\quad\quad\quad \\ \hline r_2 2^{32} +\quad c2^{16} \quad\quad \\ -\ aq_1 2^{16} \quad\quad \\ \hline r_1 2^{16} + d \\ -\ aq_0 \\ \hline r_0 \end{array}$$

```
MOVH    #0,R2           ;ZERO REGISTERS R2 AND R3
MOVH    R2,R3
MOVH    X,R0            ;MULTIPLY LOW-ORDER PARTS
MUUH    Y,R0            ;OF X AND Y
MOVH    X+2,R4          ;MULTIPLY HIGH-ORDER PART OF X TIMES
MUUH    Y,R4            ;LOW-ORDER PART OF Y AND
ADDH    R4,R1           ;ADD PRODUCT TO HIGH-ORDER
ADCH    R5,R2           ;PART OF PREVIOUS PRODUCT
MOVH    X,R4            ;MULTIPLY LOW-ORDER PART OF X
MUUH    Y+2,R4          ;TIMES HIGH-ORDER PART OF Y
ADDH    R4,R1           ;ADD TO HIGH-ORDER PART OF
ADCH    R5,R2           ;PREVIOUS RESULT
MOVH    X+2,R4          ;MULTIPLY HIGH-ORDER PARTS
MUUH    Y+2,R4          ;OF X AND Y
ADDH    R4,R2           ;ADD TO FORM HIGH-ORDER
ADCH    R5,R3           ;WORD OF FINAL RESULT
MOVH    R0,W            ;STORE RESULT
MOVH    R1,W+2
MOVH    R2,W+4
MOVH    R3,W+6
```

Figure 4-21 Double-precision multiplication.

where q_2 and r_2 are the quotient and remainder resulting from b/a; q_1 and r_1 are the quotient and remainder resulting from $(r_2 2^{16} + c)/a$; and q_0 and r_0 are the quotient and remainder resulting from $(r_1 2^{16} + d)/a$. The code needed to implement this algorithm is requested in Exercise 17. A method that uses shifting and rotating to divide a word into a word is discussed in Sec. 4-2-6.

The compare instructions are:

```
CMPB    SRC1,SRC2        (SRC2)-(SRC1)
CMPH    SRC1,SRC2        (SRC2)-(SRC1)
```

They are arithmetic instructions because they perform subtraction, however they do not store the difference. They only set the condition flags to the same values as subtract instructions. Their purpose is to provide a means for implementing the high-level language relational operators $=, \neq, >, \leq, <,$ and $\geq$. The truth value of a relational expression depends on a comparison of two quantities and a compare instruction causes the condition flags to be set according to a comparison of two quantities. Therefore, following a comparison of the two sides of a relational expression, the truth value of the expression can be determined by examining the condition flags.

The correspondences between relational operators and condition flag combinations are listed in Fig. 4-22. This list includes correspondences for both signed and unsigned cases. For equality and inequality it does not matter whether the quantities are signed or unsigned; in either case the Z condition flag will indicate whether or not the quantities are identical. (Verification of the correspondences in Fig. 4-22 is requested in Exercise 20.)

A sequence of instructions for determining the truth value of the relational expression:

$$X + Y < W - 3$$

is given in Fig. 4-23. First $X + Y$ and $W - 3$ are computed, then they are compared

Relational Operator	Condition Flag Combination
(SRC2) = (SRC1) (signed or unsigned)	Z = 1
(SRC2) ≠ (SRC1) (signed or unsigned)	Z = 0
(SRC2) > (SRC1) (unsigned)	C ∨ Z = 0
(SRC2) ≤ (SRC1) (unsigned)	C ∨ Z = 1
(SRC2) < (SRC1) (unsigned)	C = 1
(SRC2) ≥ (SRC1) (unsigned)	C = 0
(SRC2) > (SRC1) (signed)	(N ⊻ V) ∨ Z = 0
(SRC2) ≤ (SRC1) (signed)	(N ⊻ V) ∨ Z = 1
(SRC2) < (SRC1) (signed)	N ⊻ V = 1
(SRC2) ≥ (SRC1) (signed)	N ⊻ V = 0

∨ indicates a logical OR
⊻ indicates a logical exclusive OR

Figure 4-22 Correspondences between the relational operators and condition flag settings after executing a compare instruction.

```
MOVH    X,R2        ;ADD X AND Y
ADDH    Y,R2
MOVH    W,R3        ;SUBTRACT 3 FROM W
SUBH    #3,R3
CMPH    R3,R2       ;COMPARE THE RESULTS
```

Figure 4-23 Determining the truth value of a rational expression.

by subtracting $W - 3$ from $X + Y$. If X, Y, and W are signed integers and the compare instruction causes the exclusive OR of N and V to be 1, then the relational expression is true; otherwise, the expression is false.

4-2-3 Branch Instructions

Branch instructions provide the means for performing branches in the IF-THEN-ELSE, WHILE, UNTIL, and CASE control structures of high-level languages. For this reason it is important that a general purpose processing element be able to branch unconditionally or conditionally according to any one of the relational operators $=, \neq, >, \geq, <,$ or $\leq$.

The X16 branch instructions, other than those used to call and return from procedures (which are discussed in Sec. 4-4), are defined in Fig. 4-24. All of these instructions branch to the location indicated by OPR when the condition in the third column is true; otherwise the branch is not taken. For immediate addressing OPR represents the label of the branch address, for register indirect addressing it represents the register ID of the register that points to the location containing the branch address, and for relative addressing it represents the displacement. For relative addressing the register used is always the PC. The fourth column gives the contents of the instruction's condition field for each type of branch. As seen in Fig. 4-6, the condition field consists of bits 9 through 6 of the instruction.

An X16 assembler language equivalent of the Pascal statement

IF X+Y<W−3 THEN X:=0 ELSE Y:=0;

is the code in Fig. 4-25. The first branch instruction branches to the THEN case if the relational expression is true; otherwise, the ELSE case is executed and an unconditional branch is made to the beginning of the NEXT statement. In either case, execution continues with the instruction at location NEXT.

A more complex IF-THEN-ELSE statement is implemented in Fig. 4-26. It is code for performing the Pascal statement

```
IF ((X>0) AND (Y<3)) OR X+Y−W=0 THEN
    BEGIN
        X:=X+1;
        Y:=W;
    END
ELSE
    BEGIN
        X:=W;
        Y:=Y+1;
    END;
```

Name	Mnemonic and Format		Condition	Condition Field
Branch on equal	BREQ	OPR	$Z = 1$	1100
Branch on not equal	BRNE	OPR	$Z = 0$	0100
Branch on greater than (unsigned)	BUGT	OPR	$C \vee Z = 0$	0101
Branch on less than or equal (unsigned)	BULE	OPR	$C \vee Z = 1$	1101
Branch on less than (unsigned)	BULT	OPR	$C = 1$	1001
Branch on greater than or equal (unsigned)	BUGE	OPR	$C = 0$	0001
Branch on greater than (signed)	BSGT	OPR	$(N \veebar V) \vee Z = 0$	0110
Branch on less than or equal (signed)	BSLE	OPR	$(N \veebar V) \vee Z = 1$	1110
Branch on less than (signed)	BSLT	OPR	$N \veebar V = 1$	1011
Branch on greater than or equal (signed)	BSGE	OPR	$N \veebar V = 0$	0011
Branch on negative	BRNG	OPR	$N = 1$	1010
Branch on nonnegative	BRNN	OPR	$N = 0$	0010
Branch on overflow	BROV	OPR	$V = 1$	1000
Branch on no overflow	BRNV	OPR	$V = 0$	0000
Branch unconditional	BRUN	OPR	—	1111

Only immediate, register indirect, and PC relative addressing are possible. The branch address is the operand and OPR indicates its location. The format of OPR is:
    #LAB - immediate
    [R] - register indirect
    LAB - PC relative (the assembler determines the length of the displacement)

Figure 4-24 Branch instructions.

```
              MOVH    X,R2
              ADDH    Y,R2         ;ADD X AND Y
              MOVH    W,R3
              SUBH    #3,R3        ;SUBTRACT 3 FROM W
              CMPH    R3,R2        ;COMPARE THE RESULTS
              BSLT    XZERO        ;BRANCH TO THEN CASE IF LESS THAN
              MOVH    #0,Y         ;ELSE CASE -- SET Y TO 0
              BRUN    NEXT
      XZERO   MOVH    #0,X         ;THEN CASE -- SET X TO 0
      NEXT    .
              .
```

Figure 4-25 Assembler implementation of an IF-THEN-ELSE control structure.

Note that the instruction

        BRNE   ELSECASE

did not require a preceding compare statement because the subtract instruction set the Z flag according to whether or not $X + Y - W$ resulted in a 0.

```
                CMPH    #0,X            ;IF X>0 AND Y<3 EXECUTE
                BSLE    ORCASE          ;THE THEN CASE; OTHERWISE
                CMPH    #3,Y            ;CHECK THE ALTERNATIVE
                BSLT    THENCASE
    ORCASE      MOVH    X,R0            ;IF X+Y-W=0 THEN EXECUTE
                ADDH    Y,R0            ;THE THEN CASE; OTHERWISE
                SUBH    W,R0            ;GO TO THE ELSE CASE
                BRNE    ELSECASE
    THENCASE    ADDH    #1,X            ;PERFORM THEN CASE
                MOVH    W,Y             ;COMPUTATIONS AND BRANCH
                BRUN    NEXT            ;TO NEXT STATEMENT
    ELSECASE    MOVH    W,X             ;PERFORM ELSE CASE
                ADDH    #1,Y            ;COMPUTATIONS
    NEXT          .
                  .
                  .
```

Figure 4-26 A second example of an IF-THEN-ELSE control structure.

Another example that implements the Pascal statement:

```
        CASE SIZE OF
            1:  CH:='A';
            2:  CH:='B';
            3:  CH:='C'
        ELSE
            CH:=' '
        END;
```

is given in Fig. 4-27. This example assumes SIZE is a 16-bit integer and CH is a byte that contains an ASCII character. The notation #'character' in the move byte instructions indicates an immediate operand whose value is the ASCII code for the character within quotes.

Throughout the preceding discussions, the emphasis has been placed on performing a conditional branch by first doing a comparison to set the condition flags and then executing a conditional branch. The possibility exists of combining the comparison and branch into a single triple operand instruction in which the first two operands are compared and the third operand indicates the branch address. If compare/branch instructions were available on the X16, the code in Fig.

```
                CMPH    #1,SIZE         ;IF SIZE=1
                BRNE    SIZE2
                MOVB    #'A',CH         ;PUT 'A' IN CH
                BRUN    NEXT
    SIZE2       CMPH    #2,SIZE         ;IF SIZE=2
                BRNE    SIZE3
                MOVB    #'B',CH         ;PUT 'B' IN CH
                BRUN    NEXT
    SIZE3       CMPH    #3,SIZE         ;IF SIZE=3
                BRNE    ELSECASE
                MOVB    #'C',CH         ;PUT 'C' IN CH
                BRUN    NEXT
    ELSECASE    MOVB    #' ',CH         ;ELSE PUT SPACE IN CH
    NEXT          .
                  .
                  .
```

Figure 4-27 Assembler implementation of a case control structure.

4-27 could be rewritten as shown in Fig. 4-28. Each time a conditional branch appears, the amount of required code is reduced from two instructions to one instruction, but the total number of operands has remained at three.

By allowing condition flags to be set by other arithmetic instructions, conditional branches are not necessarily preceded by comparisons, e.g., the SUBH instruction in Fig. 4-26. However, it is always possible to set up a conditional branch using a comparison even though it may be less efficient in a few instances. Therefore, it would be possible to eliminate the instructions that perform only conditional branches. In fact, because condition flags are needed only to store the processor's state until a conditional branch has had a chance to act on that state, always combining comparison with branching could be used to eliminate the need for condition flags altogether. The primary disadvantage of compare/branch instructions is their requirement for three operands. Many processing elements are limited to two operand instructions. We will continue to assume that the X16 can have at most two operands and not define a set of X16 compare/branch instructions.

4-2-4 Looping

A loop is also constructed using branch instructions, but for a loop, the branch returns to a point earlier in the code (i.e., a backward branch) so that previously executed instructions may be executed again. Loops in an assembler language serve the same purpose as those in a high-level language. However, in assembler language the components of a loop need to be examined more closely. A high-level language looping statement does not reveal the details that must be considered by the assembler language programmer.

The two principal types of loops are the pretesting loops and post-testing loops flowcharted in Fig. 4-29. Both types include the same components: initialization, processing, modification, and testing. The initialization component contains the code needed to set up the parameters used by the loop, the processing component does the actual work, the modification component updates the parameters for the next repetition of the loop, and testing determines whether or not the loop is to be repeated.

The two principal loop types differ only in the placement of testing relative

```
                CSNEH     #1,SIZE,SIZE2         ;IF SIZE=1
                MOVB      #'A',CH               ;PUT 'A' IN CH
                BRUN      NEXT
    SIZE2       CSNEH     #2,SIZE,SIZE3         ;IF SIZE=2
                MOVB      #'B',CH               ;PUT 'B' IN CH
                BRUN      NEXT
    SIZE3       CSNEH     #3,SIZE,ELSECASE      ;IF SIZE=3
                MOVB      #'C',CH               ;PUT 'C' IN CH
                BRUN      NEXT
    ELSECASE    MOVB      #' ',CH               ;ELSE PUT SPACE IN CH
    NEXT        .
                .
                .
```

Figure 4-28 Use of instructions that perform both a compare and branch.

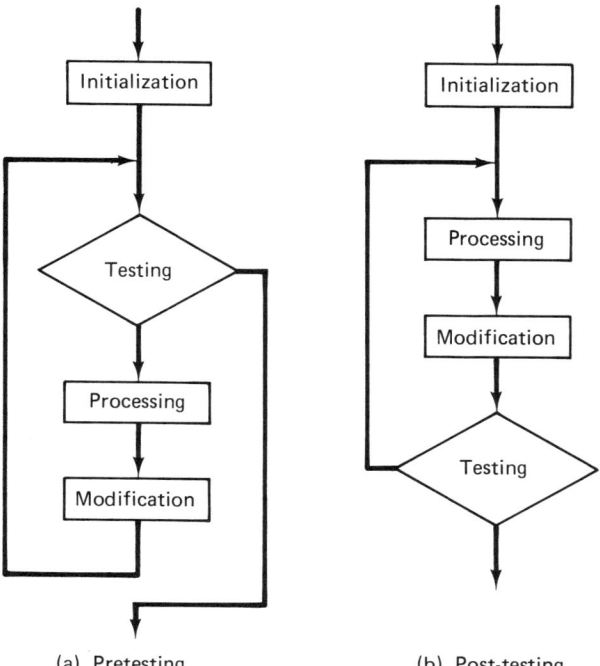

(a) Pretesting   (b) Post-testing   **Figure 4-29** Principal types of loops.

to the other components. In a pretest loop, testing is done at the beginning of the loop (as in a WHILE control structure) and the loop is executed as long as no branch is taken. If the test produces a branch the first time it is encountered, the loop is not executed at all. With a post-test loop, testing is done at the end (as in an UNTIL control structure) and the loop continues as long as the branch is made. The processing component of a post-test loop must be executed at least once.

The most common loop is one that is executed a predetermined number of times. It includes a parameter that counts the number of executions and when a limit is reached, the loop is exited. A variation of such a loop is one with a parameter that increments or decrements by a specified amount from one limit to another. In FORTRAN, such loops are known as DO loops and in Pascal, they are known as FOR loops. These loops are used primarily for performing the same operations on all elements of an array.

A loop that is equivalent to the Pascal statement

FOR I: = 1 TO 100 DO Y[I]: = X[I];

is given in Fig. 4-30. The initialization consists of putting the count and the beginning addresses of the two arrays into the registers R5, R0, and R1. The processing is the transfer of the integers from the X array to the Y array and modification consists of incrementing the addresses and decrementing the count. For

Sec. 4-2   Assembler Language Instructions

```
                MOVH    #100,R5   ⎫
                MOVH    #X,R0     ⎬   Initialization
                MOVH    #Y,R1     ⎭
        AGAIN   MOVH    [R0],[R1] >   Processing
                ADDH    #2,R0     ⎫
                ADDH    #2,R1     ⎬   Modification
                ADDH    #-1,R5    ⎭
                BRNE    AGAIN     >   Testing and branching
```

Figure 4-30 Transfer of an array using a loop.

this loop, because its repetition depends only on whether or not a single quantity has reached 0, testing and branching can be done with one instruction.

Because loops are so important to the operation of a computer, it is worthwhile to examine ways of making their implementation more efficient. It is most important to improve the efficiency within the loop (as opposed to the initialization component) because it may be repeated several times. This improvement is made by reducing the number of instructions in the modification, testing, and branching components of the loop. In the example in Fig. 4-30 four instructions were included in these components—two were for updating the addresses, one for decrementing the count, and one for testing and branching.

By far, the most prevalent use of loops is to operate on arrays in an orderly manner. This operation involves incrementing or decrementing the array indices by a fixed amount. One way of eliminating the extra instructions for modifying the indices would be to enhance the register indirect addressing mode so that the registers used for addressing are automatically incremented or decremented by the appropriate amount whenever they are accessed. Addressing modes that are derived from register indirect addressing in this way are called the **autoincrement** and **autodecrement addressing modes**.

Let us now extend the X16 to include autoincrement and autodecrement addressing modes by using two of the unused addressing mode bit combinations. The combinations 111 and 101 will be used for autodecrementing and autoincrementing, respectively. The assembler language notation for indicating these modes will be −[*Register*] for autodecrementing and [*Register*]+ for autoincrementing, e.g.,

    MOVB   [R1]+,−[R2]

The size of the increment or decrement will be one for byte operations and two for halfword operations. For autodecrementing the register is decremented first and then provides the address; but for autoincrementing, the register first provides the address. Therefore,

    MOV   [R1]+,R0

and

    MOV   R0,−[R1]

could be viewed as reciprocal operations. The value in this is most important when stacks are used and is discussed in Sec. 4-3.

With the availability of autoincrementing the example in Fig. 4-30 could be rewritten as shown in Fig. 4-31. Not only has the autoincrement mode reduced the number of instructions within the loop, but it has also reduced the number of instruction bytes that must be fetched during the execution of the loop. The code in Fig. 4-30 would require that

$$4+4+4+100(2+4+4+4+4) = 1812$$

bytes be fetched as opposed to

$$4+4+4+100(2+4+4) = 1012$$

for the code in Fig. 4-31.

A second way of reducing the modification component of a FOR loop is to eliminate the instruction for decrementing the loop count. This can be done by combining the decrementing instruction with the conditional branch instruction to form a **loop instruction**. Because the X16's branch instructions do not allow space to indicate the location of the count, this location must be implied. Let us suppose that the count must always be in register R5 when the loop instruction is executed. Assuming that the loop instruction's mnemonic is LOOP, the last two instructions in Fig. 4-31 could be replaced with

```
            LOOP    AGAIN
```

which would automatically decrement the count in R5 and repeat the loop if the result is nonzero. The number of instruction bytes that would then need to be fetched from memory during the execution of the loop and its initialization would be

$$4+4+4+100(2+4) = 612$$

Although loop instructions are very convenient, they may require a significant amount of decode logic. For the X16, one of the working registers would have to acquire a special meaning and, unlike the addition of autoincrementing and autodecrementing, this would tend to reduce the orthogonality of the instruc-

```
          MOVH    #100,R5        ;INITIALIZE COUNT AND
          MOVH    #X,R0          ;ADDRESS REGISTERS
          MOVH    #Y,R1
AGAIN     MOVH    [R0]+,[R1]+    ;MOVE INTEGER FROM X TO Y
          ADDH    #-1,R5         ;DECREMENT COUNT
          BRNE    AGAIN          ;REPEAT IF COUNT IS NONZERO
            .
            .
            .
```

Figure 4-31 Array transfer using autoincrementing.

```
        MOVH    #100,R5         ;INITIALIZE COUNT AND
        MOVH    #X,R0           ;ADDRESS REGISTERS
        MOVH    #Y,R1
        REPT                    ;SET REPEAT
        MOVH    [R0]+,[R1]+     ;MOVE INTEGERS FROM X TO Y
```

Figure 4-32 Sequence that uses a repeat instruction for summing the numbers in an array.

tion set. Therefore, we will not formally extend the X16 to include the loop instruction.

Another possibility is to not use a loop, but to repeat the move instruction 100 times. This repetition would reduce the number of instruction bytes fetched to 212. The obvious disadvantage is that the number of bytes of memory needed to store the code would be $4+4+2\times100=208$ versus $4+4+4+2+4+4=22$. A slightly less obvious, but equally serious, disadvantage to this approach is the loss of flexibility. Using several identical instructions in place of a loop could only be done if the number of times the operation is to be performed is known and fixed.

There is the possibility of eliminating the loop and simply having the control unit execute a single move instruction the required number of times. Instead of fetching the same instruction over and over, the processing element could fetch the instruction once and the control unit could hold it in its IR until it has executed, in the case of the present example, 100 times. To implement this approach, the count could, as shown in Fig. 4-32, be put in a register, say R5, and a special instruction, called a **repeat instruction**, could cause the control unit to suspend instruction fetches and re-execute the instruction in the IR until the count is 0. The count would be decremented by 1 each time the instruction is executed. This would reduce the total number of instruction bytes fetched during the loop's execution to two, but would require that a repeat instruction be added to the initialization code. The primary restriction to using a repeat instruction is that the total number of bytes in the processing and modification components of the loop be less than or equal to the number of bytes in the IR, which provides the only instruction storage in the processing element. A well known example that uses a repeat feature is the Intel 8086/8088 family of microprocessors. However, this approach will not be pursued further in this book.

4-2-5 Logical Instructions

The X16's logical byte instructions are:

NOTB	SRC,DST	$(\overline{SRC}) \rightarrow (DST)$
ANDB	SRC,DST	$(DST) \wedge (SRC) \rightarrow (DST)$
IORB	SRC,DST	$(DST) \vee (SRC) \rightarrow (DST)$
XORB	SRC,DST	$(DST) \veebar (SRC) \rightarrow (DST)$
TSTB	SRC1,SRC2	$(SRC1) \wedge (SRC2)$

where ∧, ∨, and ∀ indicate logical AND, OR, and exclusive OR, respectively. The mnemonics for the corresponding halfword instructions end with "H" instead of "B." Because these instructions have 7-bit opcodes, if a register is needed to determine the source operand, it must be the R0 register. They all perform bitwise operations on their operands. For the NOT instruction, each bit is complemented, and the other instructions operate on pairs of corresponding bits. For example, if the low-order byte of R0 contains 10101110 and the instruction

                NOTB   R0,R1

is executed, the new contents of the low-order byte of R1 are 01010001. Also, if the contents of the memory location TESTPAT are 01101001, then

                ANDB   R0,TESTPAT

would put 00101000 into TESTPAT,

                IORB   R0,TESTPAT

would put 11101111 into TESTPAT, and

                XORB   R0,TESTPAT

would put 11000111 into TESTPAT.

Logical instructions may be used in a variety of ways, but they are most frequently used to selectively set, clear, change, or test bits in the destination operand according to the bit pattern in the source operand. These selective operations are particularly useful for manipulating the bits in interface registers and data as they are being input or output. When they are applied in this way the source operand is called a **mask** and the operation is called a **masking operation**. Bits in a byte are selectively set by ORing as follows:

Because bits 1, 2, 4, and 6 of the mask are 1, they are also 1 in the result; but, because bits 0, 3, 5, and 7 of the mask are 0, these bits in the destination are not changed. Similarly, an XOR can be used to selectively change bits.

For selectively clearing bits, the bits in the mask that correspond to those to be cleared are set to 0 and all other bits in the mask are set to 1. Then the mask is ANDed with the destination as in the following example:

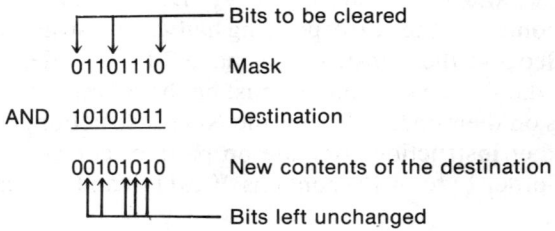

Bits 0, 4, and 7 are cleared and all other bits are left unchanged.

The test instruction is essentially an AND instruction that sets condition flags but does not store the result. It is the logical equivalent of the arithmetic compare instruction and is intended to be used in conjunction with a conditional branch. When used in a masking operation it tests to determine if any of the bits that are set in the mask are also set in the second source operand. If none of the corresponding bits are set in this operand, then $Z=1$; otherwise, $Z=0$. A subsequent conditional branch instruction could then branch or not branch according to the Z flag. A sequence that uses the test instruction to take the absolute value of the 16-bit integer in location X is:

```
         TSTH    #8000H,X
         BREQ    SKIP
         NEGH    X,X
SKIP:    .
         .
         .
```

Just as pairs of compare and branch instructions can be combined into single compare/branch instructions, so too can pairs of test and branch instructions be combined. The new test/branch instructions would have three operands and be very similar to the compare/branch instructions discussed in Sec. 4-2-3. The existence of such instructions would simplify conditional branching for logical computations just as the compare/branch instructions did for arithmetic computations, and together, the test/branch, compare/branch, and loop instructions could conveniently provide all conditional branching needs. However, they would cause a significant increase in the amount of decode logic.

4-2-6 Shift and Rotate Instructions

A shift instruction initiates an action of the same type performed by a shift register (see Sec. 3-4-2). For shifts, the C flag is normally treated as if it were an additional bit appended to the location being shifted. For a left shift, it would be as if the C flag were to the left of the location and 0s would be inserted at the right. For a right shift, it would be as if the C flag were to the right and 0s or, perhaps, 1s would be inserted at the left. There are two types of right shifts, logical and arithmetic. A logical right shift would always insert 0s on the left and an arithmetic right shift would insert 0s or 1s depending on whether the sign of the operand is nonnegative or negative, respectively (i.e., an arithmetic right shift retains the sign).

A rotate instruction is a shift instruction that does not insert 0s or 1s, but treats the operand, and perhaps the C flag, as circular registers. Some rotate instructions include the C flag in the rotation and others do not. Those that do not set the C flag in the same way as a similar shift instruction. The shift and rotate instructions for the X16 are defined in Fig. 4-33. For all of these instructions, the shift or rotate is by one-bit position. Examples of how these instructions would affect a one-byte operand and the C flag are given in Fig. 4-34.

Shifts and rotates are used for a variety of purposes, some of which are:

- Multiplying or dividing by a power of two.
- Using a bit pattern to control a program.
- Converting between unpacked BCD, packed BCD, and binary formats.
- Performing multiplication and division when these operations are not implemented in hardware (i.e., the multiply or divide instruction for the needed operand length does not exist).
- Performing floating point operations when there is no floating point hardware.

Name	Mnemonic and format		Description*
Shift logical left byte/halfword	SLLB SLLH	OPR OPR	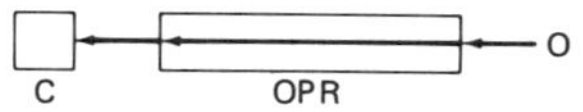
Shift arithmetic left byte/halfword	SALB SALH	OPR OPR	Same as shift logical left
Shift logical right byte/halfword	SLRB SLRH	OPR OPR	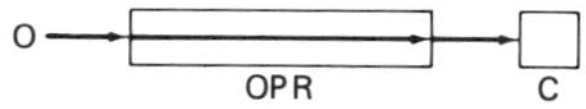
Shift arithmetic right byte/halfword	SARB SARH	OPR OPR	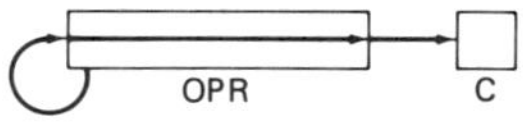
Rotate left byte/halfword	ROLB ROLH	OPR OPR	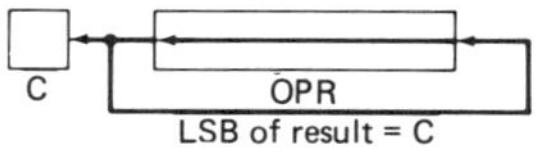 LSB of result = C
Rotate right byte/halfword	RORB RORH	OPR OPR	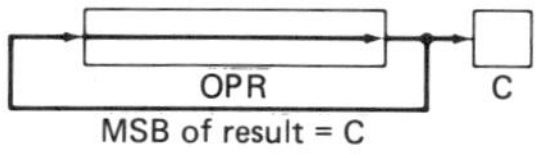 MSB of result = C
Rotate left through carry byte/halfword	RCLB RCLH	OPR OPR	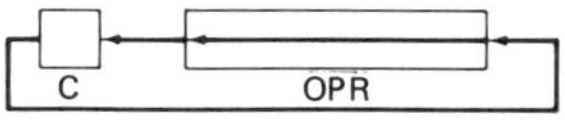
Rotate right through carry byte/halfword	RCRB RCRH	OPR OPR	

*All shifts and rotates are by one bit position.

Figure 4-33 Shift and rotate instructions.

Sec. 4-2 Assembler Language Instructions

```
Initially:   (OPR) = 11100010
             C = 0

Instruction                        Result in OPR

SLLB    OPR    C = 1               11000100
SALB    OPR    C = 1               11000100
SLRB    OPR                        01110001        C = 0
SARB    OPR                        11110001        C = 0
ROLB    OPR    C = 1               11000101
RORB    OPR                        01110001        C = 0
RCLB    OPR    C = 1               11000100
RCRB    OPR                        01110001        C = 0
```

Figure 4-34 Examples of the shift and rotate instructions.

The X16 could multiply (R3) by eight using the instructions

```
    SALH    R3
    SALH    R3
    SALH    R3
```

and divide (R3) by eight using the instructions

```
    SARB    R3
    SARB    R3
    SARB    R3
```

A sequence that scans the halfword in R0 from left to right and branches to Task 2 each time a 0 is encountered and executes Task 1 each time a 1 is encountered is given in Fig. 4-35.

Figure 4-36 provides the code for dividing a word into a word using the nonrestoring division algorithm introduced in Sec. 2-2-2 (an example is given in Fig. 2-7). The code assumes that the dividend is in the four bytes beginning at DEND and the divisor in the four bytes beginning at DIVSR. The remainder is

```
              MOVH   #16,R5        ;PUT NO. OF BITS IN R5
    BEGIN     ROLH   R0            ;ROTATE HIGH-ORDER BIT INTO C
              BUGE   TASK2         ;BRANCH ON C=0
                .                  ;EXECUTE TASK1
                .  } Task 1
                .
              BRUN   ENDLOOP
    TASK2       .                  ;EXECUTE TASK2
                .  } Task 2
                .
    ENDLOOP   ADDH   #-1,R5        ;REPEAT UNTIL COUNT IS 0
              BRNE   BEGIN
```

Figure 4-35 Program control using a rotate instruction.

```
              MOVH    #32,R5              ;PUT LOOP COUNT IN R5
              MOVH    DEND,R0             ;PUT DIVIDEND IN R1:R0
              MOVH    DEND+2,R1
              MOVH    #0,R2               ;AND ZERO R3:R2 TO
              MOVH    R2,R3               ;FORM 64-BIT DIVIDEND
BEGIN         SLLH    R0                  ;SHIFT DIVIDEND LEFT 1
              RCLH    R1
              RCLH    R2
              RCLH    R3
              BULT    ADDIT
              SUBH    DIVSR,R2            ;ADD DIVSR IF C=1
              SBBH    DIVSR+2,R3          ;OTHERWISE SUBTRACT DIVSR
              BULT    NEXT
              IORB    #1,R0               ;LOW-ORDER BIT=0 IF C=1
              BRUN    NEXT                ;OTHERWISE LOW-ORDER BIT=1
ADDIT         ADDH    DIVSR,R2
              ADCH    DIVSR+2,R3
              BUGE    NEXT                ;LOW-ORDER BIT=0 IF C=1
              IORB    #1,R0               ;OTHERWISE SET TO 1
NEXT          ADDH    #-1,R5
              BRNE    BEGIN
              CMPH    #0,R3               ;ADD DIVISOR TO
              BRNN    FINISH              ;REMAINDER IF NEGATIVE
              ADDH    DIVSR,R2            ;ADD DIVSR
              ADCH    DIVSR+2,R3
FINISH        .
              .
              .
```

Figure 4-36 Double-precision division.

left in R3:R2, i.e., the concatenation of R3 and R2, and the quotient is left in R1:R0.

A code segment for performing the floating point addition of two numbers in the IEEE single-precision floating point format is requested in Exercise 31. It takes over 100 X16 instructions to emulate floating point addition even if there is no checking for underflows or overflows and no algorithm for providing unbiased truncation. This is typical of floating point emulation and demonstrates the importance of floating point hardware. However, it takes complex hardware to replace this amount of software and the amount of logic in a floating point unit can approach the amount of logic in all of the remainder of a processing element. But if the processing element is to be used for applications that require many floating point operations the speed of floating point hardware may be required. Although a floating point instruction takes considerably longer to execute than other instructions, it takes much less time than the one hundred or so instructions it replaces (typically one tenth the time).

4-2-7 PSW Instructions

The mnemonics for the instructions given in Fig. 4-13(b), which set and clear the carry condition flag and put new values in the interrupt bit and interrupt level field of the PSW, are SETC, CLRC, and INTF, respectively. The SETC and CLRC instructions have no explicit operands, but the INTF instruction must be followed by a 4-bit constant that indicates the new values of the interrupt bit and level. The use of the INTF instruction is considered in Chap. 6.

4-3 STACKS

One method of accessing memory is used so often that it deserves special attention, and most processing elements include special hardware to facilitate these accesses. The method consists of sequentially storing information in memory and retrieving the information in reverse order. In other words, a portion of memory is implemented as a LIFO stack, which is frequently simply referred to as a **stack**.

As described in Sec. 2-2-5, one application of a stack is found in expression evaluation. The need for a stack arises because the amount of data that must be temporarily stored exceeds the number of registers. For example, the proposed X16 loop instruction discussed in Sec. 4-2-4 could use only R5 for counting the repetitions, but it is frequently necessary to nest loops. Figure 4-37 shows how a stack could be used to alleviate this problem. As the beginnings of the loops are encountered, the present (R5) are stored on the stack before the next loop count is put into R5, and as the loops are exited, the counts are retrieved. This procedure guarantees that the proper count is always in R5.

As indicated in Sec. 2-2-5, a stack is abstractly defined as a sequentially stored collection of information that is accessed in a last-in, first-out manner. This definition does not depend on where the information is stored or what hardware or instructions are used to put the information on or take information from the stack. However, normally a stack is stored in main memory and is accessed using register indirect autoincrementing and autodecrementing addressing through a **stack pointer (SP) register**. For most processing elements there is one SP and putting, or **pushing**, a datum onto the stack is done by decrementing the SP and

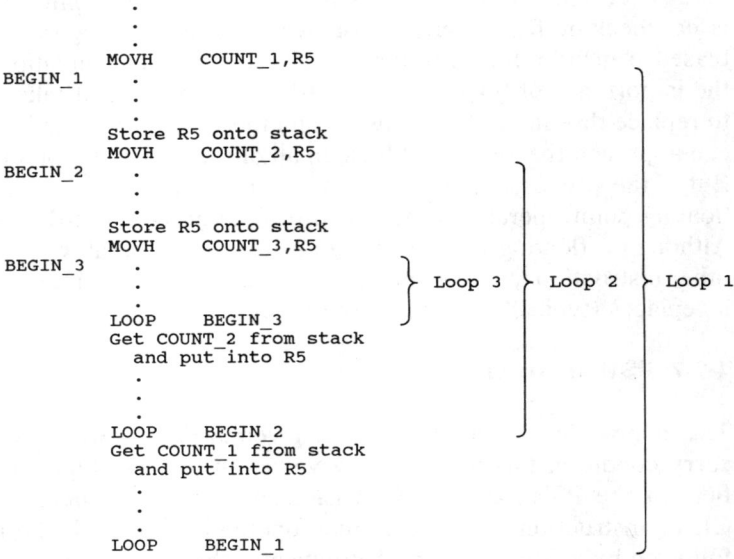

Figure 4-37 Application of stack storage to nesting loops.

then using the SP and register indirect addressing to store the datum. Retrieving, or **popping**, the datum is done by getting the datum using the SP and register indirect addressing and then incrementing the SP. This method implies that the SP will always point to the location of the last datum put onto the stack. This location is called the **top of the stack**. If a processor is specifically designed for handling more than one stack, then it may have an SP register for each stack.

Some processing elements allow register indirect addressing with autoincrementing and autodecrementing to be used only with an SP register and have special instructions for accessing the stack. Others, such as the X16, already have the necessary addressing modes and the stack operations are just a matter of using transfer instructions. But, even if register indirect addressing with autoincrementing and autodecrementing can be accomplished using any of the working registers, at least one special register is usually present whose sole purpose is to be an SP. The reason for this is that a stack is sometimes implicitly accessed and there is no explicit reference to a register; instead, the special SP register is assumed. We will see examples of this later.

Even though special transfer instructions may not be required, an assembler may include alternative mnemonics when a transfer is a push onto a stack or a pop from a stack. These mnemonics would make pushes and pops readily apparent to anyone reading a program. For the X16, these alternative mnemonics are:

Alternate mnemonic		Equivalent move instruction	
PSHB	SRC	MOVB	SRC, −[SP]
PSHH	SRC	MOVH	SRC, −[SP]
POPB	DST	MOVB	[SP]+,DST
POPH	DST	MOVH	[SP]+,DST

As will be seen in Sec. 4-4, it is often necessary to push and pop the PSW. Because the PSW has not been given an address, ordinary move instructions cannot be used for this purpose and we must add the PSHP and POPP instructions (no operands) to our X16 instruction set. (The machine code for these instructions is given in Appendix C.)

For the example in Fig. 4-37,

            PSHH   R5

would be used to replace "Store R5 onto stack" and

            POPH   R5

would replace "Get count from stack and put into R5." Fig. 4-38 shows the contents of the stack and the SP register as the counts are successively pushed onto and popped from the stack. In this figure it is assumed that the initial top of the stack is at 056E and COUNT__1 and COUNT__2 are 120H and 13AH, respectively. This example also shows that popping a stack does not change the

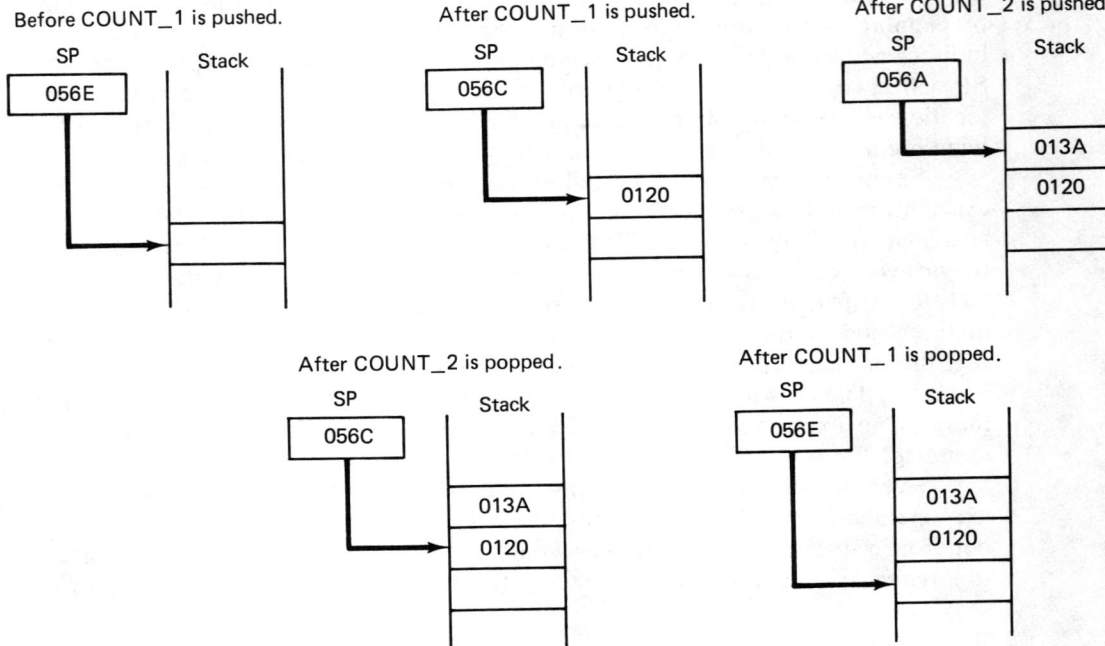

Figure 4-38 Stack activity as the loop counts in the example in Figure 4-37 are pushed and popped.

contents of the popped stack location. However, a succeeding push into the location does, of course, cause the location's contents to be replaced. Pushes and pops are no different from other memory transfers in this regard.

Another example of using a stack for temporary storage is given in Fig. 4-39. In this example, the double-precision inner product

$$X_1*Y_1 + X_2*Y_2$$

is computed. The stack is employed because there are only enough registers to hold one doubleword product. First, X_1*Y_1 is computed and left in R3:R2:R1:R0 using code similar to that of Fig. 4-21. Then, the result is pushed onto the stack

```
           .              ;COMPUTE X1*Y1 AND
           .              ;PUT IN R3:R2:R1:R0
           .              ;(SEE FIGURE 4-21)
    PSHH   R3
    PSHH   R2
    PSHH   R1
    PSHH   R0
           .              ;COMPUTE X2*Y2 AND
           .              ;PUT IN R3:R2:R1:R0
    ADDH   [SP]+,R0       ;ADD TO PREVIOUS PRODUCT
    ADCH   [SP]+,R1
    ADCH   [SP]+,R2
    ADCH   [SP]+,R3
```

Figure 4-39 Arithmetic example that uses the stack for temporary storage.

and X_2*Y_2 is computed using the same registers. After the second product has been computed, it is added to the first product.

4-4 PROCEDURES

Programs are usually subdivided into identifiable contiguous groups of instructions, called **modules**, that have clearly marked boundaries. Although the definition of a module is very broad, the subdivisions between modules are normally chosen so that each module is made up of a logically related set of instructions that serve a well-defined purpose. There are several reasons why the modular programming approach is used. The more important reasons are:

- When modules are defined so that they perform specific tasks, the overall program is easier to understand.
- While a program is being created, different modules can be assigned to different programmers.
- Debugging and testing can be done in a more orderly fashion.
- Documentation can be more easily understood.
- Modifications can be localized.
- Frequently used modules can be stored in mass storage files and used in several programs.

Although modules perform definite tasks, because they must communicate with each other and work together to perform an overall job, they are not independent of each other.

The principal tool for showing the organizational relationship of the modules is the **hierarchical diagram**. A typical hierarchical diagram is shown in Fig. 4-40. A hierarchical diagram shows subordination of the modules, i.e., the usage of modules by other modules. When discussing two modules that are connected in

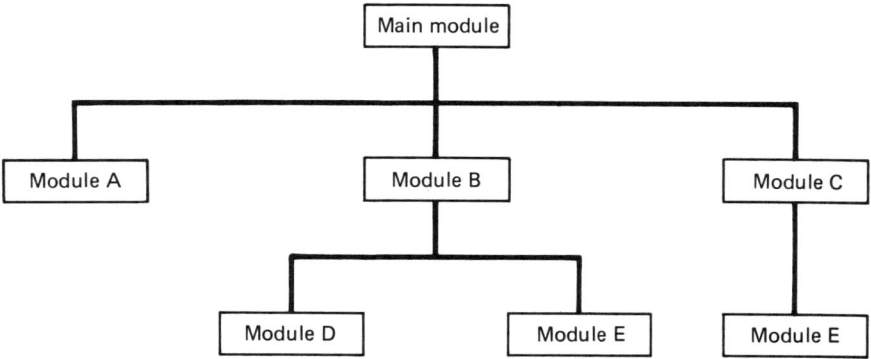

Figure 4-40 Typical hierarchical diagram.

a hierarchical diagram, the subordinate task is referred to as the **called molule** and the other is the **calling module**. For a called module to do useful work for a calling module it must be able to receive information from the calling module and pass results back to it.

4-4-1 Calls and Returns

The primary means of subdividing a program into modules is the use of **procedures**, or **subprograms**. A procedure is incorporated into an overall program by means of branch instructions referred to as **procedure calls** and **returns**. As shown in Fig. 4-41, a procedure call causes a branch to the beginning of a procedure and a return is a branch back to the point from which the call was made. The effect is as if the instructions in the procedure were inserted in the calling code. Because the task performed by a procedure may need to be called upon several times, the branch address of a return is not fixed. Therefore, a procedure call must be a branch with the unique feature that it anticipates a return to the instruction immediately following the call and stores the address of this instruction where the return branch can retrieve it. The return is a matter of getting this address, which is called the **return address**, and putting it into the PC.

The usual place to store a return address is to push it onto a stack, in which case the procedure call first pushes the return address onto the stack and then puts the address of the procedure into the PC. After the procedure has finished its work, the return instruction pops the return address from the stack and puts it into the PC. While executing the procedure, care must be taken to ensure that the number of pushes is the same as the number of pops so that when the return is executed the SP will be pointing to the return address. Otherwise, an erroneous address will be put into the PC and the return will not be to the proper point.

The stack is a natural choice for storing return addresses because procedures are frequently nested and, as with the loop example in Fig. 4-37, nesting retrieves stored quantities in reverse order. As an example, consider the sequence of calls and returns illustrated in Fig. 4-42, which may be listed as follows:

1. Main calls procedure A—the return address is 2600.
2. Procedure A calls procedure B—the return address is 3AB0.

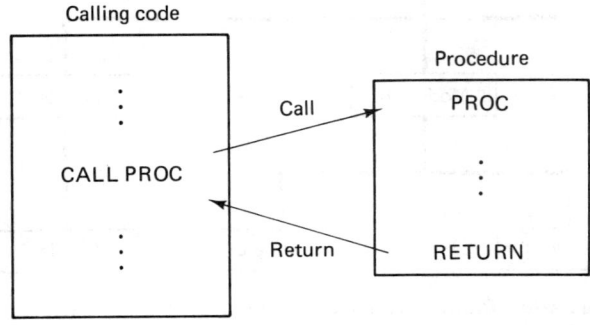

Figure 4-41 Calling and returning from a procedure.

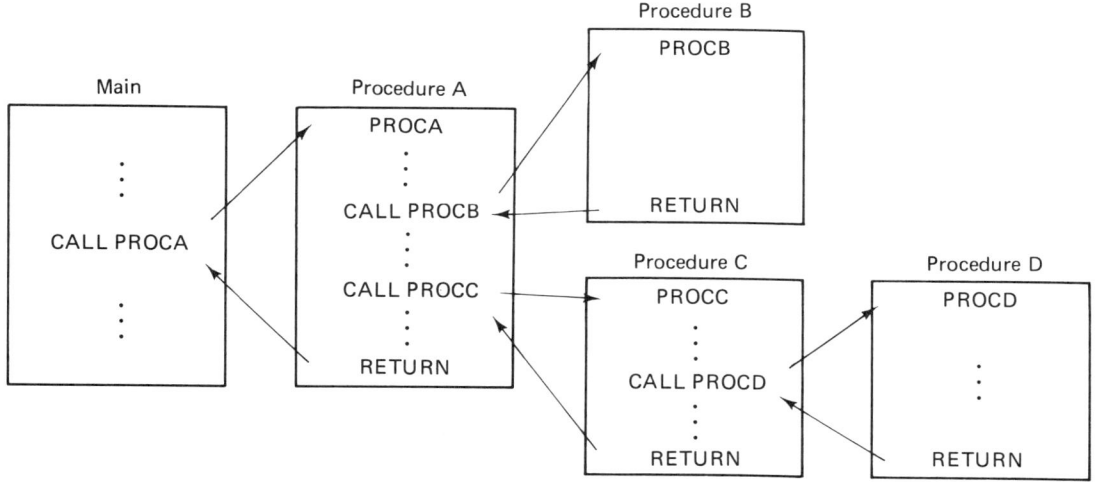

Figure 4-42 Nested procedures.

3. Procedure B returns to procedure A.
4. Procedure A calls procedure C—the return address is 3B12.
5. Procedure C calls procedure D—the return address is 5000.
6. Procedure D returns to procedure C.
7. Procedure C returns to procedure A.
8. Procedure A returns to main.

Figure 4-43 assumes that the original top of the stack is at 06C0 and shows the SP and stack after each call and return. If there is no other stack activity, a procedure can be entered only when it is called, a procedure can be exited only by executing a return, and if the returns are all eventually made, the stack will always produce the correct return address. This is true even if a procedure calls itself, a possibility considered later.

An important detail that we have been able to ignore, but must now consider, is the exact timing involved in determining the address of the next sequential instruction and, perhaps, placing this address in the PC. If the present instruction is a procedure call, this address is the return address. It has been vaguely mentioned that the address of the next instruction is found during the execution of the present instruction. Except when branches are taken, this address is the one needed for the next fetch and is already in the PC at the conclusion of the present instruction. Even for branch instructions, the PC is first incremented to point to the next instruction, and if the branch is to be taken, the branch address is computed and used to replace the incremented address in the PC. For a procedure call, this incremented address, which is the return address, is pushed onto the stack just prior to this replacement. Thus, a procedure call pushes the PC onto the stack after it has been updated to point to the next instruction and then puts the branch address in the PC.

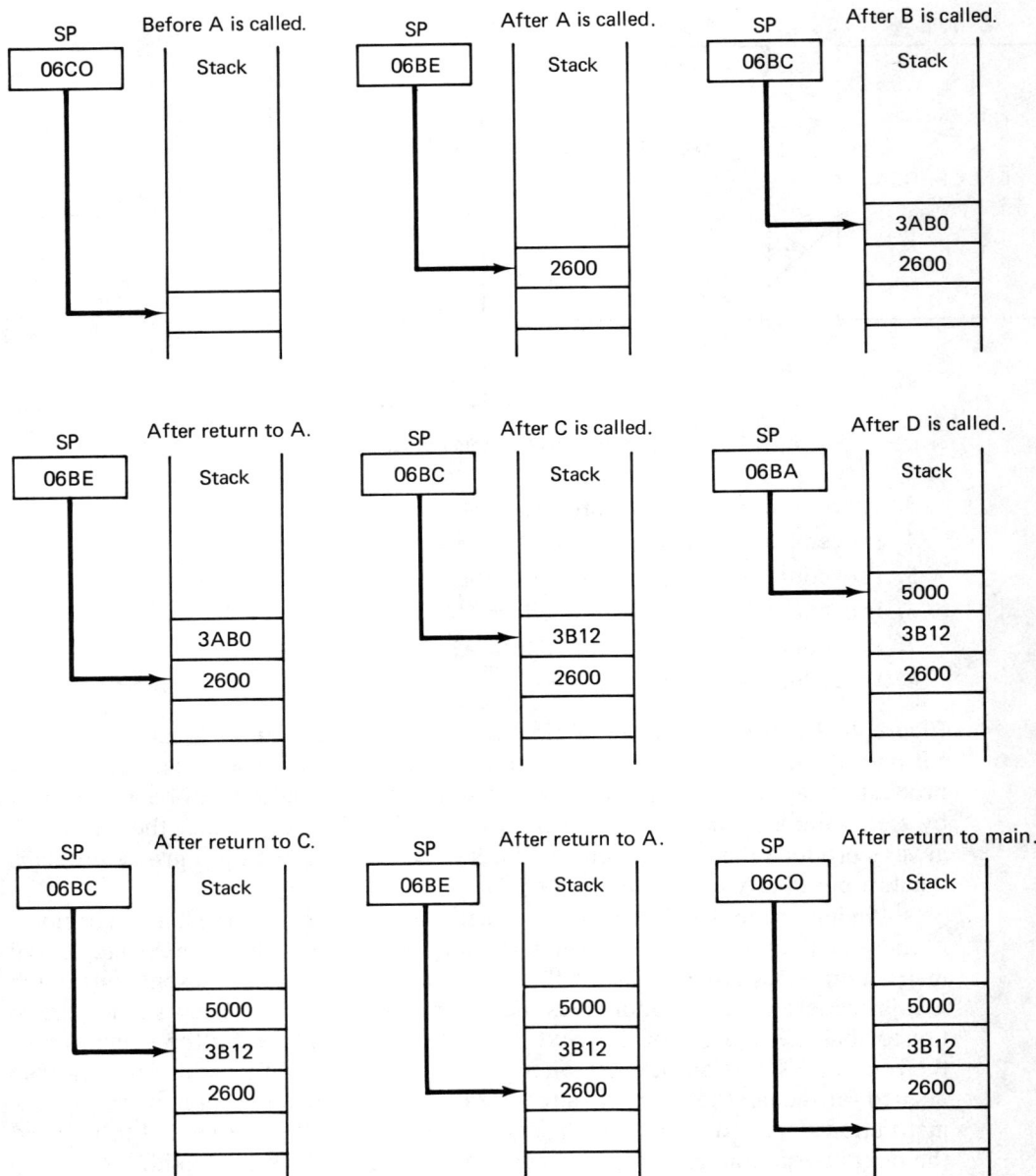

Figure 4-43 Stack activity resulting from the procedure nesting shown in Figure 4-42.

148   Fundamental Computer Operations   Chap. 4

The call and return instructions for the X16 are:

CALL   OPR

and

RETN

where OPR indicates the branch address that is contained in the second halfword of the instruction. The return address is pushed onto the stack by the CALL instruction and popped from the stack by the RETN instruction.

4-4-2 Parameter Passing and Side Effects

The purpose of the previous discussion has been to present the mechanics of calling and returning from a procedure. The emphasis was on the differences between the call and return instructions and other branch instructions. There is actually much more to calling a procedure than inserting a call instruction in an instruction sequence and a return instruction in the procedure.

A procedure may be used over and over within a program and may call other procedures or even call itself. Procedures are usually designed so that they can operate on and return results to different locations each time they are called. The first problem faced when designing a procedure is to decide how information is to be passed to and from a procedure. The individual pieces of information that are passed are referred to as **parameters**. There are two basic types of parameters, data and addresses of data. The first are called **call-by-value parameters** and the second **call-by-address parameters**. A single quantity can easily be passed as either a call-by-value parameter or call-by-address parameter, but in the case of an array, it would be impractical to pass the values of all of the array's elements. Therefore, the beginning address is passed as a call-by-address parameter and the procedure uses this address to compute the address of any other location in the array.

If there is a small number of parameters, it is possible to use the registers as the transfer vehicle. This is most often done for function-type procedures that receive one parameter, operate on it, and produce a single result. For the general case for which there may be numerous parameters, one of two methods is normally used. The first is to use the calling task to create a **parameter table** consisting of consecutive memory locations, put the parameters in the table, put the address of the table in a register, and then branch to the called procedure. The called procedure could retrieve the parameters by using either register indirect or relative addressing to access the parameter table. This method is illustrated in Fig. 4-44(a).

The second method is to push the parameters onto a stack, and then use the called procedure to retrieve them by popping the stack. This method is illustrated in Fig. 4-44(b). If the same stack is used to pass parameters and store return addresses or other information, it may be necessary to transfer the (SP) to another register after the parameters are pushed. The other register is then used to access the stack in the same way a register is used to access a parameter table. When

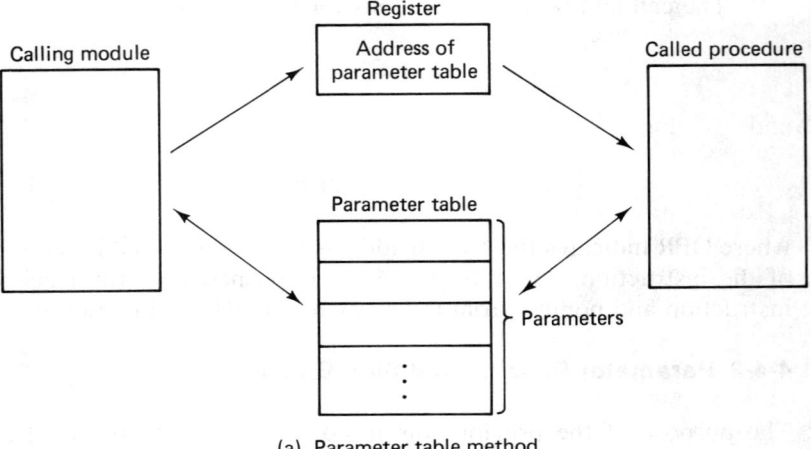

(a) Parameter table method

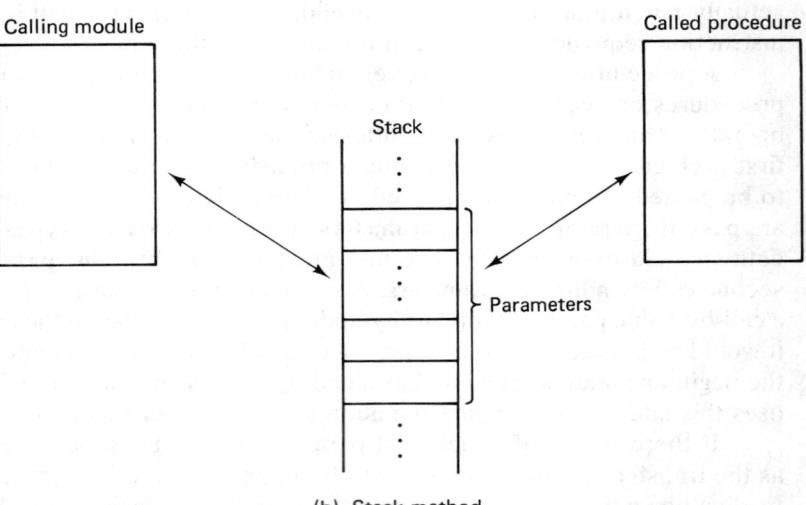

(b) Stack method

Figure 4-44 Methods of passing parameters.

a stack is used to pass parameters, after the return to the calling task, the SP must be returned to its original value, either by popping the parameters or simply adding to the SP an amount equal to the number of bytes occupied by the parameters.

With respect to a calling module, incidental changes that occur in the overall state of a program during the execution of a called procedure are called **side effects**. Side effects are due to the procedure changing:

- Parameter values other than results.

- Register contents.
- The PSW.

One of these changes could cause the calling task, after it has been returned to from the procedure, to use an unexpected quantity or condition flag setting. The first problem can be avoided only through judicious programming. The other two can be resolved by temporarily storing the contents of the PSW and the registers used by the procedure just after entering the procedure and then restoring their contents just before the return. A stack is normally used for this purpose and the necessary pushes and pops are inserted at the beginning and end of the procedure.

Collectively, code for storing parameters, calling a procedure, storing the registers and PSW, restoring the registers and PSW, returning to the calling task, and making parameter-related stack adjustments is referred to as **procedure linkage**. The procedure linkage most often used with the parameter table method of passing parameters is given in Fig. 4-45(a). When parameters are passed through the stack and there is only one stack being used, the linkage is as shown in Fig. 4-45(b).

For example, suppose that a procedure TOTAL is needed to add the first n elements of an array and return the sum. The Pascal code for defining and calling such a procedure is:

```
PROCEDURE TOTAL(N:INTEGER; VAR X:INTARRAY; VAR Y:INTEGER);
    BEGIN
        Y := 0;
        FOR I := 1 TO N DO Y := Y + X[I];
    END;
             .
             .
             .
    TOTAL (50, X_ARRAY, SUM);
```

For the assembler code a parameter table is to be used, the integer n is to be a call-by-value parameter, and the beginning address of the array and the address of the sum are to be call-by-address parameters. The desired procedure is given in Fig. 4-46(a), and a calling sequence that causes the procedure to add the first 50 elements of X_ARRAY and put the result into SUM is given in Fig. 4-46(b). Register R3 is used to pass the address of the parameter table. The contents of R3, the parameter table, and the stack after the call is made and the PSW and register contents have been pushed onto the stack, are shown in Fig. 4-47. The PROCEDURE and ENDP directives included in Fig. 4-46(a) indicate to the assembler the beginning and end of a procedure. One or more procedures may be contained in a single source unit, in which case, these directives would mark the beginnings and ends of the procedures.

Figure 4-48(a) gives calling linkage for the procedure TOTAL that passes the parameters through the same stack used by the other procedure linkage. Figure 4-48(b) shows the stack after the call is made and the PSW and registers have

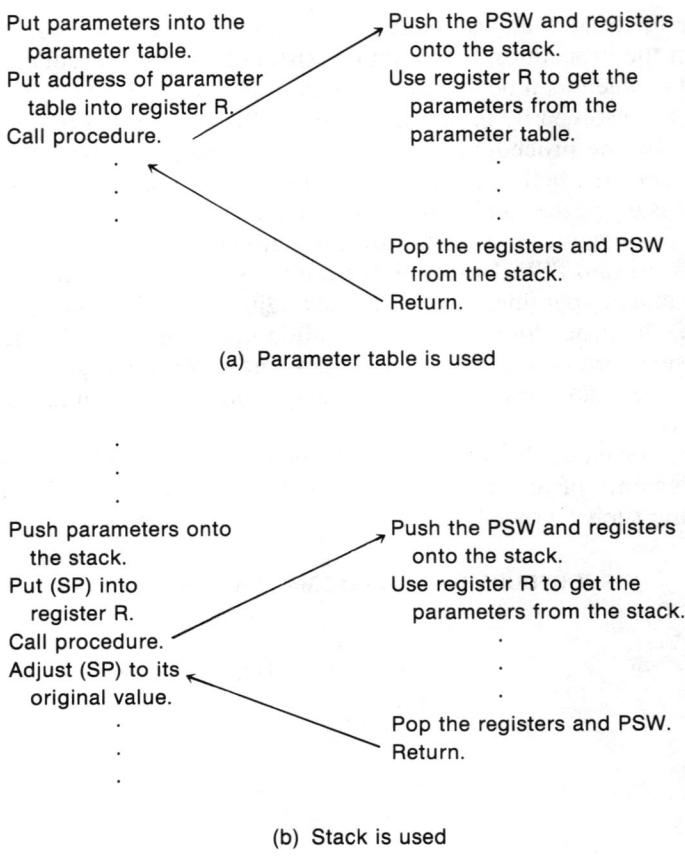

Figure 4-45 Typical procedure linkage.

been pushed. By transferring (SP) into R3 after pushing the parameters, the procedure itself would not require changing. Note the last instruction in the calling linkage. Its purpose is to readjust the stack so that the top of the stack is the same as it was before the calling sequence was entered. Some processors have return instructions that can re-adjust the stack as well as execute the return. If the X16 return instruction were given this feature, for the procedure TOTAL, the return instruction would be RETN 6 and the ADDH instruction following the call would be unnecessary.

The advantages of using a procedure as opposed to **inline code** (i.e., code that is inserted each time it is needed) are:

- At execution time, the procedure's machine code appears in memory only once instead of the number of times it is needed, thus saving memory space.

152 Fundamental Computer Operations Chap. 4

```
        PROCEDURE TOTAL
   TOTAL  PSHP                        ;SAVE PSW
          PSHH    R0                  ;AND REGISTERS
          PSHH    R1
          PSHH    R4
          MOVH    #0,R0               ;CLEAR R0 TO 0
          MOVH    [R3],R4             ;PUT NO. OF ELEMENTS IN R4
          MOVH    2[R3],R1            ;PUT ADDR OF ARRAY IN R1
   LP     ADDH    [R1]+,R0            ;ADD ELEMENTS OF THE ARRAY
          SUBH    #1,R4
          BRNE    LP
          MOVH    4[R3],R1            ;STORE THE RESULT
          MOVH    R0,[R1]
          POPH    R4                  ;RESTORE THE REGISTERS
          POPH    R1
          POPH    R0
          POPP                        ;AND PSW
          RETN                        ;RETURN
   ENDP
```

(a) Procedure

```
          MOVH    #50,P_TABLE         ;PUT PARAMETERS
          MOVH    #X_ARRAY,P_TABLE+2  ;IN P_TABLE AND
          MOVH    #SUM,P_TABLE+4      ;ADDR OF P_TABLE
          MOVH    #P_TABLE,R3         ;IN R3
          CALL    TOTAL               ;CALL PROCEDURE TOTAL
```

(b) Calling linkage

Figure 4-46 Representative procedure and its linkage.

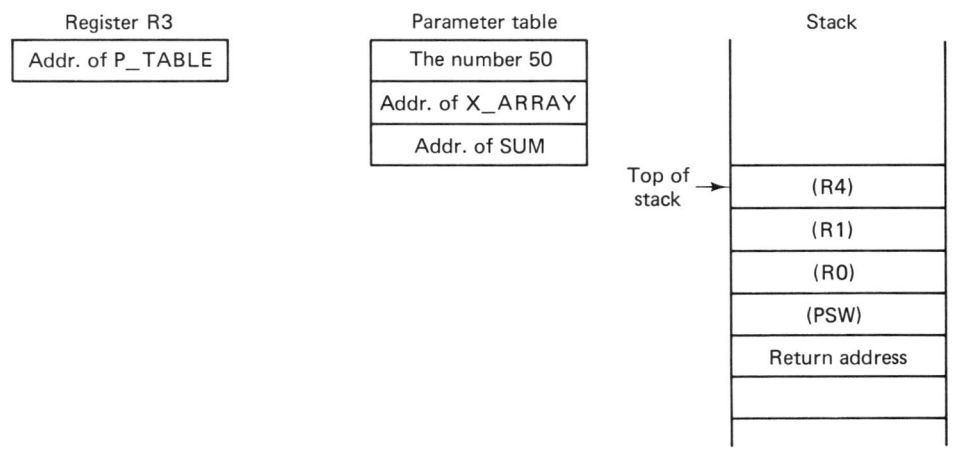

Figure 4-47 Contents of R3, the parameter table, and the stack after the linkage is executed for the procedure TOTAL.

```
PSHH      #SUM                    ;PUSH PARAMETERS
PSHH      #X_ARRAY                ;ONTO STACK
PSHH      #50
MOVH      SP,R3                   ;TRANSFER SP TO R3
CALL      TOTAL                   ;CALL PROCEDURE TOTAL
ADDH      #6,SP                   ;ADJUST STACK
  .
  .
```

(a) Calling linkage

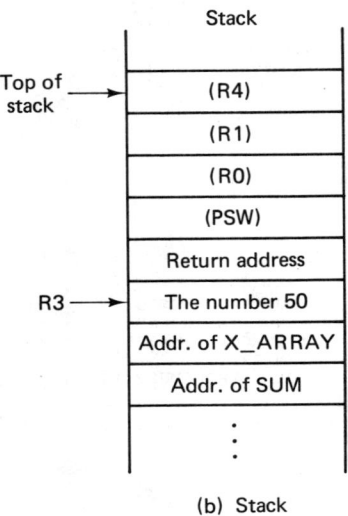

(b) Stack

Figure 4-48 Using the stack to pass parameters to the procedure TOTAL.

- The procedure's code needs to be written and tested only once.
- Procedures can be documented separately, and descriptions of their details would not have to be included in the description of the overall program.
- Procedures provide a good way of subdividing programs.
- A procedure, once it has been written, tested, and documented, can be kept in mass storage and joined with programs whenever it is needed.

The disadvantages are:

- The code for providing the procedure linkage would not be necessay if inline code were used.
- Execution of the linkage code takes time that could be saved by using inline code.

For example, the task performed by the code in Fig. 4-46 would require only 7 instructions and 26 bytes of memory if it were written as inline code. By using a procedure, these numbers, including the calling linkage, are increased to 22 and 70, respectively. Because the calling linkage requires 26 bytes and must be included with each call, the procedure TOTAL is too short to save memory space. However, if TOTAL is an important part of the program, the subdivision advantages of making it a separate task may outweigh the increased memory space and execution time.

The basic tradeoff is between good modularization and perhaps, reduced memory space versus increased execution time due to the linkage. The key factors that should be considered when deciding whether to use a procedure or inline code are the:

- Number of times the code is to be used.
- Percent increase in the execution time of the code.
- Modularization advantages.

The first two factors are similar to those affecting the decision as to whether or not a loop should be used, except that for loops, it is the number of repetitions and the execution time of the loop initialization that are important.

An important special case occurs when a procedure calls itself, in which case it is called a **recursive procedure**. Because the number of calls is indeterminate, the easiest way for a recursive procedure to pass parameters is through the stack. An example of a recursive procedure is one that determines the factorial of a parameter and is equivalent to the Pascal procedure

```
FUNCTION FACTOR (N:BYTE): BYTE;
  BEGIN
    IF N = 0 THEN FACTOR := 1 ELSE FACTOR := N * FACTOR(N – 1);
  END;
```

The assembler code for such a procedure is given in Fig. 4-49(a). The parameter whose factorial is to be determined is passed through the stack and leaves the result in R0. Figure 4-49(b) assumes the parameter is 3 at the time of the original call and shows the stack at the time of the innermost call. The block of information that is pushed onto the stack by a single call is referred to as a **frame**. Because a frame is added each time the procedure calls itself, the stack can become quite large. Stack size is a major problem with recursive programming.

Although the above example is trivial and there are easier ways to compute factorials, it does introduce the important concepts related to recursive procedures. The use of such procedures is very common in systems programs and some processing elements have special facilities for managing the frames generated by recursive programming. These facilities improve the processing element's ability to maintain and access the stack.

Both stack frames and parameter tables are examples of what are generally known as **activation records**. Each time a procedure is activated (i.e., called) an activation record is created to provide the communication between the calling procedure and called procedure. For recursive procedures, the facility for generating activation records must be dynamic because the depth of nesting is un-

```
PROCEDURE FACTOR
    FACTOR      PSHP
                MOVB    4[SP],R0
                CMPB    #0,R0
                BREQ    ZERO
                SUBB    #1,R0
                PSHB    R0
                CALL    FACTOR
                MULB    5[SP],R0
                ADDH    #1,SP
                BRUN    FINISHED
    ZERO        MOVB    #1,R0
    FINISHED    POPP
                RETN
ENDP
```

(a) Procedure

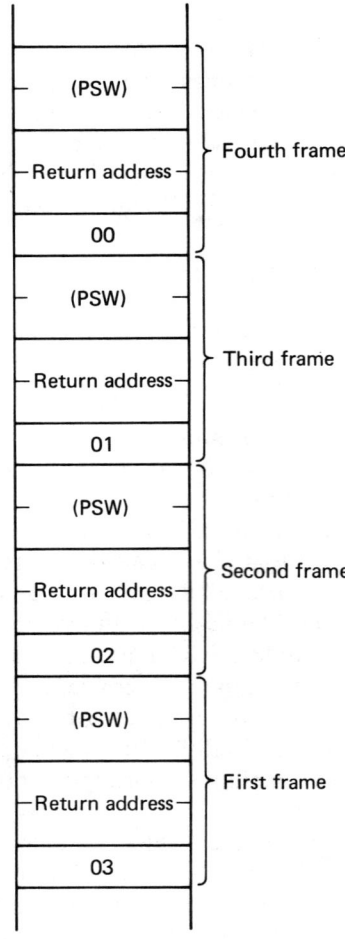

(b) Stack

Figure 4-49 Recursive procedure and the resulting stack activity.

known when the program is created. Therefore, the use of a stack for storing the activation records is a logical choice because a stack is open-ended and provides an easy means for determining where the record is to go. (For a more complete discussion of activation records see Calingaert [6].)

4-5 MACROS

Another way of separating the code needed to perform a specific task from the mainstream of assembler code is to write a macro. A **macro** is a sequence of assembler language code that serves as a template for inline code. After the template is defined, a code sequence corresponding to the template can be inserted in the program by putting a special statement known as a **macro call** at each point of insertion. Together, the template code and associated directives are called the **macro definition** and the insertions are referred to as **macro expansions**. The use of macro definitions, calls, and expansions is illustrated in Fig. 4-50.

The directives for delimiting macro definitions are MACRO and ENDM. The MACRO directive includes the *Macro name* that is used to call (i.e., cause an insertion of) the macro, the mnemonic MACRO, and a list of *Dummy arguments* that also appear in the template code. The format of a macro call is:

Label   Macro name   Argument, . . . , Argument

where *Label* is optional, *Macro name* is the name of the macro to be inserted, and each *Argument* is an identifier. When a macro call is made, each *Argument* is matched with a *Dummy argument* in the same way arguments and parameters are matched for high-level language procedure calls, i.e., the first *Argument* is

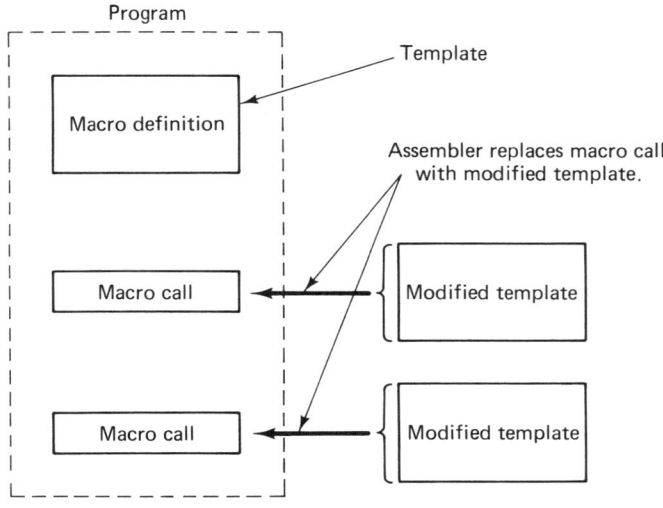

Figure 4-50 Definition and use of macros.

matched with the first *Dummy argument*, the second *Argument* with the second *Dummy argument*, and so on. When the assembler replaces a macro call with its expansion, each occurrence of a *Dummy argument* is replaced with the matching *Argument*.

A program that includes a macro definition and two macro calls is given in Fig. 4-51. The macro named DPADD adds double-precision integers. The macro expansions that replace the calls are shown on the right. Side effects were eliminated by pushing the PSW and popping the stack after the computation was completed. Not all macros are designed to eliminate side effects. In fact, such design may not always be desirable (e.g., the pop to the PSW would not be wanted if the macro call is to be followed by a conditional branch that causes a branch if the addition produces an overflow).

The discussion here is oversimplified and is meant only to introduce the concept of macros. Among the features that have not been considered are those that permit a variable number of dummy arguments and special automatic labeling of instructions. (When a label appears within a macro definition, in order to avoid an ambiguous label definition, it must be a different label each time the macro is called—see Exercise 43.)

In comparing macros to procedures, macros retain the advantage of requiring the programmer to write assembler code only once, but, because the code is repeated with each macro call, no memory space is saved. Limited modularity is attained, but code sequences defined as macros are not as independent and distinct as those implemented as procedures. On the positive side, macros do not require the complex linkage associated with procedures. Macros are primarily used to

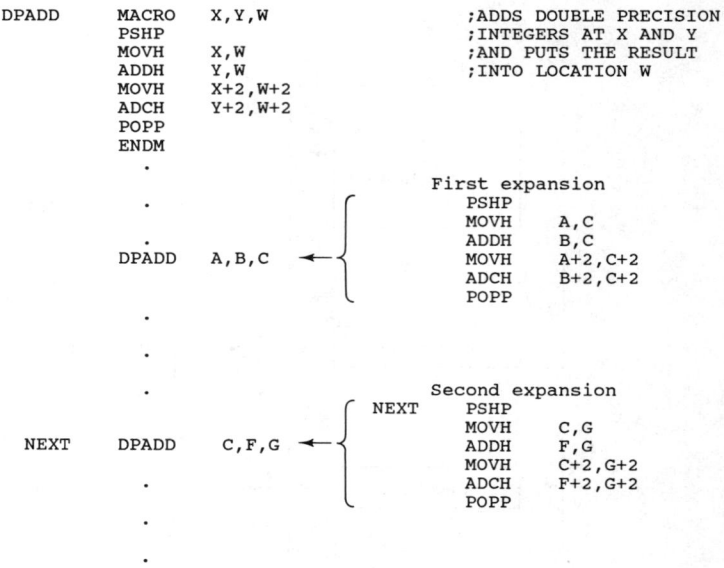

Figure 4-51 Example of macro usage.

replace short instruction sequences that perform a distinct task with single assembler language statements, thus making assembler code shorter and easier to understand.

4-6 INSTRUCTION EXECUTION TIME

The activity within a processing element is generally synchronously controlled by a clock that outputs one or more phases. Each clock pulse, and perhaps each phase, causes certain actions to occur during the fetch and execution of an instruction. Together these actions constitute an **instruction cycle**. A processing element's logic is designed to dictate which actions are caused by each pulse, or phase, and thereby determines the sequence of the actions in the instruction cycle.

We have seen that an instruction cycle primarily consists of fetching an instruction and then executing it and that, during the execution, one or more data operands may need to be fetched from or deposited in memory. A single instruction or datum may require more than one memory access. The number of bits of memory that can be accessed at one time is the basic information unit of the computer and depends on the designs of the link between processing and memory elements, the memory interfaces to this link, and the bus control logic. For most processing elements this basic unit ranges from 1 to 8 bytes, and for most microprocessors it is 1, 2, or 4 bytes. Typically, a transfer of one basic unit from memory to the processing element takes:

1. One clock period to send out the memory address.
2. One clock period for the memory to look up the basic unit.
3. One clock period for the memory to return the basic unit and inform the processing element that the basic unit is ready to be taken.

A transfer in the other direction usually requires:

1. One clock period to send out the address and basic unit.
2. One clock period for the memory to store the basic unit.
3. One clock period for the memory to inform the processing element that it has completed its work.

In either case, three clock periods are required for a single transfer. However, this time period is really a minimum, because normally, the memory element is designed separately from the processing element and Step 2 may take more than one clock period. In this event, the processing element must suspend its operation until the memory signals that it has finished its work. The clock periods over and above the one required are called **wait states**. The number of wait states is directly related to the speed of the memory element, and the most obvious way to increase the speed of a computer is to match the speeds of the processing and memory elements so that there are no wait states.

In addition to the clock periods needed to access memory, a few extra clock periods are required for an instruction's execution. For most instructions, this number of periods is fixed and is from 1 to 3, but for some instructions, this number may vary depending on the operands. For example, for a multiplication or division, the number of clock periods may depend on the bit patterns in the operands. As mentioned previously, there is the possibility of overlapping fetching and executing.

Suppose that the basic information unit for the X16 is one halfword and that all memory-memory operations, including simple transfers, require that the operands be brought into the X16 before the results are put into memory. If the control logic requires two clock periods in addition to the three required for accessing memory, then the instruction

                MOVH   R1,R2

would take 3 + 2 = 5 clock periods to complete (3 periods to fetch the instruction and 2 periods for the decode),

                MOVH   [R1],R2

would take 3 + 2 + 3 = 8 clock periods,

                MOVH   X,R2

would take 3 + 2 + 3 + 3 = 11 clock periods, and

                MOVH   X,Y

would take 3 + 2 + 3 + 3 + 3 + 3 = 17 clock periods. For a 10 MHz clock, the respective execution times would be 0.5, 0.8, 1.1, and 1.7 microseconds.

The advantage of keeping operands in the registers as much as possible is obvious. Assume that autoincrementing is overlapped with the operand access so that no extra periods would be needed for the autoincrement addressing mode. Then, the total execution time of the processing component of the following code (i.e., the first ADDH instruction):

```
           MOVH   #X,R0
           MOVH   #100,R1
           MOVH   #0,R2
AGAIN      ADDH   [R0]+,R2
           ADDH   #-1,R1
           BRNE   AGAIN
           MOVH   R2,SUM
```

would be 100(3 + 2 + 3) = 800 clock periods as opposed to 1400 clock periods if

$$\text{ADDH} \quad [\text{R0}]+,\text{SUM}$$

had been used.

Equally obvious is the loss of time spent fetching the bytes in the instructions. For the above code for adding a column of numbers, the time spent fetching the instructions would be

$$3[2+2+2+100(1+2+2)+2] = 1524$$

clock periods. The decode time and handling of the data operands would require approximately 800 clock periods. In other words, over 60% of the time would be needed to fetch the instructions, and a range of 20% to 50% is representative of the amount of time spent bringing in instructions, including their operand fields. This provides considerable incentive for using a repeat instruction or some type of fetch and execution overlapping.

For conditional branch instructions the execution time may depend on whether or not the branch is taken. If the PC is incremented to point to the next instruction during the execution of the current instruction as described in Sec. 4-4, then no time is required to set up the PC when the instructions are executed sequentially. However, for a conditional branch instruction, the incremented value of the PC may or may not be used as the address of the next instruction; thus, extra time may be needed to determine the branch address if the branch is taken.

4-7 DESIGN REMARKS

When creating code to perform a task, it is generally desirable to minimize:

- Execution time.
- Average instruction length.
- Number of instructions.

Although faster is not always better, the time needed to complete a task is generally a measure of performance and often the time must be less than some specified amount. The average instruction length and number of instructions determine the amount of memory needed to store the code and also, because of the instruction fetches, affects execution time. Also, the number of instructions is a general measure of the ease with which a task can be programmed.

When trying to match an instruction set to an application, it is important to examine the frequencies with which the various instructions occur in typical application code and the frequencies with which the instructions are executed. Because of branches and particularly, loops, these two frequencies may be entirely different. For frequency of occurrence, each instruction in the code counts only once. For frequency of execution, if an instruction is in a loop that is repeated 100 times, then that instruction is counted 100 times. Frequencies of occurrence and instruction lengths determine the amount of memory needed to store the code, while the frequencies of execution and instruction execution times determine the total execution time.

Before designing a processing element it is worthwhile to study the instruction frequencies closely—particularly for special purpose processing elements. The idea is to use these studies to determine which instructions are used most often and then focus the design so as to make these instructions more efficient (e.g., if floating point arithmetic is shown to consume a significant amount of execution time, then floating point hardware should be included).

Numerous studies have been made to obtain instruction frequency distributions for the more popular general purpose computers. For a general purpose computer, two types of studies are conducted, those that gather data on what the computer does while it is executing applications code, and those that gather data on systems code. For example, the operating system is responsible for directing the I/O, and compilers spend much of their time working with strings of characters. On the other hand, a system program would rarely use floating point arithmetic.

The types of instructions that a general purpose processing element is normally expected to perform were listed in Fig. 4-4, with the four major classifications being transfer, arithmetic, bit manipulation, and branch. Not all processing elements need to be general purpose and the instruction set of a special purpose processing element may, in fact, be quite limited. Some elements may be required to perform only arithmetic, or may even be restricted to a certain type of arithmetic. In a multiprocessor system, one of the processors could be specifically designed only to take inner products of integer vectors. Such a processor may not even decode its own instructions, but simply be passed the quantities that make up the inner product and signals indicating when the quantities are available. Although this chapter has been presented from the standpoint of what is needed by general purpose processing elements that must satisfy a variety of applications, there is a broad spectrum of processing elements. Some of these elements may use only a small subset of the instructions given in Fig. 4-4.

REFERENCES

1. Liu, Yu-cheng, and Glenn A. Gibson, *Microcomputer Systems: The 8086/8088 Family*, 2nd ed. (Englewood Cliffs, N.J.: Prentice Hall, Inc., 1986).
2. Cooper, Doug, and Michael Clancy, *Oh! Pascal!* (New York: W. W. Norton and Company, 1982).
3. Hamacher, V. Carl, Zvonko G. Vranesic, and Safwat G. Zaky, *Computer Organization*, 2nd ed. (New York: McGraw-Hill Book Company, 1984).
4. Gimarc, Charles E., and Veljko Milutinovic, "A Survey of RISC Processors and Computers of the Mid-1980s," *Computer, 20*, no. 9 (September, 1987), 59–69.

5. Gibson, Glenn A., and Yu-cheng Liu, *Microcomputers for Engineers and Scientists*, 2nd ed. (Englewood Cliffs, N.J.: Prentice Hall, Inc., 1987).
6. Calingaert, Peter, *Assemblers, Compilers, and Program Translation*, (Rockville, Maryland: Computer Science Press, Inc., 1979).

EXERCISES

1. Assume the following register and memory location contents and displacement:

    Program counter (PC) = 1A00
    Working register (WR) = 05C0
    Memory location 05C0 = 1200
    Displacement = A2

    For each addressing mode determine the location of the operand:
    (a) Register WR
    (b) Register indirect through WR
    (c) Indirect through location 05C0
    (d) Relative using WR
    (e) PC relative

2. Explain what is done by each of the following X16 machine language instructions (only the first halfword is shown and it is given in hexadecimal):
    (a) EE90 (b) 5220 (c) 07C1 (d) 85BB (e) 30BB

3. Re-design the branch, shift, and rotate instructions so that there can be branch instructions that use PC relative addressing with the second byte of the instruction containing the displacement. Discuss any problems that arise because of your changes.

4. Verify that the machine language code given in Fig. 4-12 is correct.

5. If, for the X16, (R2) = 0E40, what memory location would be accessed by the instruction E448?

6. What is done by the X16 instruction 0000?

7. For each of the following X16 addressing modes, assume that COST is a label and describe how the location of the operand is determined.
    (a) #2AH (b) 1B2AH (c) COST (d) COST + 4 (e) [R4] (f) COST[PC]
    (g) 4[R0]

8. Diagram what happens during the execution of each of the following move instructions (see Fig. 4-15):
    (a) MOVH R0, R5
    (b) MOVH R4, [R5]
    (c) MOVB STRING, [R3]
    (d) MOVB #'A', R0
    (e) MOVH X[PC], Y

9. Verify the code in Fig. 4-17 using Figs. 4-6 and 4-10.

10. Assume the labels TEXT and CHAR are associated with addresses 0BAE and 256A and give the machine language code for:
    (a) MOVH TEXT, CHAR
    (b) MOVB TEXT, CHAR
    (c) MOVB R0, [R1]
    (d) MOVH #123FH, TEXT
    (e) MOVH #TEXT, CHAR
    (f) MOVB [R0], [R1]

11. Write an X16 instruction sequence that will perform the same computation as the Pascal statement:
    (a) W := −X + (124 − Y) + 2;
    (b) W := (U + V) − (X − Y);
12. Repeat Exercise 11, but assume double-precision integers with the low-order halfwords having the lower addresses.
13. Rewrite the sequence in Fig. 4-18 for triple-precision integers.
14. Assume the labels X and Y are associated with the addresses 15A2 and 3000 and give the machine language code for:
    (a) ADDB X, R0   (b) SBBH Y, X   (c) SUBH [R0], [R1]   (d) MULB R0, R2
    (e) MULB #5, R2 (f) DIVH X[R0], R2
15. Write an X16 instruction sequence that performs the same single-precision computation as:
    (a) W := X∗Y − 15;
    (b) W := X∗(X − 2) + Y;
    (c) W := X/(Y − Z);
16. Assume that

$$X = a2^{32} + b2^{16} + c \qquad Y = f2^{32} + g2^{16} + h$$

and show how single-precision (2-byte) multiplication and addition could be used to carry out triple-precision multiplication. How many single-precision additions and multiplications would be needed?

17. Write an X16 instruction sequence that uses the algorithm discussed in Sec. 4-2-2 to divide a halfword X into a three-halfword dividend Y. Leave the quotient in R2:R1:R0 and the remainder in R4.

18. The division of a 32-bit word $c2^{16} + d$ by a 32-bit word $a2^{16} + b$ $(a > 0)$ can be carried out by using single-precision division to compute q and r so that

$$c = qa + r$$

and noting that

$$c2^{16} + d = qa2^{16} + r2^{16} + d$$
$$= q(a2^{16} + b) + r2^{16} + d - qb$$

where $r2^{16} + d - qb$ is the remainder of the original division. If this remainder is negative, repeatedly add $2^{16}a + b$ to it and decrement q until the remainder becomes positive. Use this algorithm to write an X16 instruction sequence to divide the word X into the word Y, store the quotient at U, and store the remainder at V.

19. Discuss the restrictions on the order in which the expression

$$(A∗B∗C)/(D∗E)$$

must be computed if A, B, C, D, and E are halfwords and the intermediate results cannot exceed 32 bits.

20. Verify that the correspondences in Fig. 4-22 are correct.
21. Let (X) = 10011010   (Y) = 11100111   (W) = 00011001
    (U) = 01101110   (V) = 00011001

and determine the flag settings after the following operations are performed:

(a) X − Y (b) X − U (c) W − V (d) U − V (e) Y − U (f) U − Y

Convert all of the operands and results to decimal numbers and compare the flag settings to those expected from Fig. 4-22.

22. Write an X16 instruction sequence that will set the flags according to the expression:
    (a) 2∗X > 0 (b) X + Y − 15 >= W + 2 (c) (W < 0) AND (X = Y)
    Also indicate what the flags would be after executing the sequence if X = 0, Y = 5, and W = −1.

23. Write an X16 instruction sequence that is equivalent to:

    (a) IF X>=Y THEN X:=1 ELSE X:=0;

    (b) IF ((X<0) OR (Y<=5)) AND (X+5=W) THEN U:=W+5
         ELSE V:=X−Y;

    (c) Rewrite the solution to Part (b) assuming there are compare/branch instructions such as those in Fig. 4-28.

24. Write an X16 instruction sequence that is equivalent to

    FOR I:=1 TO M DO A[I]:=I∗B[I]+C[I];

    Use a separate array for temporary storage and assume all results can be put into halfwords.
    (a) Assume there is neither a loop nor a repeat instruction.
    (b) Assume there is a loop instruction, but not a repeat instruction.
    (c) Assume there are both loop and repeat instructions.
    For each solution determine the total number of instruction bytes fetched if M = 50.

25. Write an X16 instruction sequence that is equivalent to:

    (a) COUNT:=0;
         FOR I:=1 TO N DO
             IF X[I]>0 THEN COUNT:=COUNT+1;

    (b) CASE ANSWER OF
             'A': FOR J:=1 TO 10 DO A[I]:=A[I]+B[I];
             'S': FOR J:=1 TO 10 DO A[I]:=A[I]−B[I];
         END;

26. Write an X16 instruction sequence that will clear bits 2 and 5 of X, set bits 1 and 7 of X, change bits 3 and 4 of X, and then branch to EXIT if none of the bits 1, 3, 5, or 7 is 1. Now modify the sequence so that a branch to EXIT is made if all of the bits 1, 3, 5, and 7 are 1. (Hint: Complement X before testing it.)

27. Write an X16 instruction sequence that will
    (a) Multiply the first 5 elements of an array X of 16-bit integers by 2^4.
    (b) Divide the first 4 elements of an array Y of 8-bit integers by 2.

28. Write an X16 instruction sequence for packing four consecutive ASCII decimal digits into a halfword. Assume that the low-order digit is in the first byte beginning at UPBD and the result is to be put in PBCD.

29. Write an X16 instruction sequence that will pack the eight 12-bit integers stored in

consecutive halfwords beginning at X into the six consecutive halfwords beginning at Y so that there will be two integers stored in each of the three bytes. Does it matter whether the integers are signed?

30. Write a sequence to unpack the integers that were packed in Exercise 28 assuming they are signed. Assuming they are unsigned.

31. Write an X16 instruction sequence that performs the floating point addition of two numbers in their IEEE single-precision floating point format. Assume that checking for overflows and underflows and providing for unbiased truncation is not necessary.

32. Assume that (SP) are initially 041C and show the contents of the SP and stack before and after each of the following stack operations:

   1. 152CH is pushed onto the stack.
   2. 0506H is pushed onto the stack.
   3. The stack is popped.
   4. 8A57H is pushed onto the stack.
   5. 0005H is pushed onto the stack.
   6. The stack is popped.
   7. The stack is popped.
   8. 1600H is pushed onto the stack.
   9. The stack is popped.
   10. The stack is popped.

33. Assume that the stack is used for storing the return address, (SP) are initially 092A, and the following procedure calls and returns are made. Show the contents of the SP and stack after each call and return:

   1. Main calls procedure A—return address is 1A00.
   2. Procedure A executes a return.
   3. Main calls procedure B—return address is 1B26.
   4. Procedure B calls procedure C—return address is 1C00.
   5. Procedure C calls procedure C—return address is 2C52.
   6. Procedure C executes a return.
   7. Procedure C executes a return.
   8. Procedure B executes a return.

34. Assume that the X16 has a stack, but does not have procedure call and return instructions. Show how procedure calls and returns could be accomplished with other X16 instructions.

35. Draw a hierarchical diagram of a program in which Main calls Task A, Task A calls Task B, Task B calls Task C and Task D, Main calls Task B, and Main calls Task E.

36. What are side effects and their primary causes?

37. List the important components of procedure linkage.

38. Write an X16 procedure that will subtract two 96-bit integers. The parameters are to be passed through a parameter table whose address is put in R3. Write a calling se-

quence that will subtract the integer beginning at COST from the integer beginning at TOTAL and store the difference beginning at NET. Show the contents of R3, the parameter table, and the stack after the procedure has been entered and the PSW and registers have been pushed onto the stack (see Fig. 4-47).

39. Repeat Exercise 38, but use the stack for passing the parameters. Show the stack after the call and the PSW and registers have been saved (see Fig. 4-48).

40. Write the following Pascal procedure using X16 code:

```
PROCEDURE MAXIMUM (VAR N:INTEGER; VAR XARRAY:INTARRAY;
    VAR MX:INTEGER);
  VAR I: INTEGER;
  BEGIN
    MX := XARRAY[1];
    FOR I := 2 TO N DO
      IF XARRAY[I] > MX THEN MX := XARRAY[I];
  END;
```

Assume that R3 points to the address of N at the time the procedure is entered and the address of N is followed by the beginning address of XARRAY and then the address of MX.

41. Write a recursive procedure that uses Horner's rule to evaluate an integer polynomial. When the procedure is entered the first time it assumes that the degree of the polynomial and the address of the low-order coefficient have been pushed onto the stack. The coefficients are to be in an array with the low-order coefficient in the first element. The independent variable is to be in R2 and the result is to be put into R0.

42. Write a macro NEGATE that negates a 32-bit integer and leaves the result in a pair of registers that are specified by arguments. Eliminating side effects is not necessary. (Normally, the replacement of dummy arguments by arguments is a matter of replacing character strings, e.g., "R2" for "REG"; therefore, a dummy argument can represent labels, constants, register identifiers, and even mnemonics.) Give a call that causes the integer beginning at X to be negated and the result to be put in R3:R2. Also, give the resulting expansion.

43. Write a macro ABS that replaces a 16-bit integer with its absolute value. Note that the label that appears in the template code must be listed as a dummy argument. An automatic labeling facility could be designed into the macro facility of the assembler that would allow the programmer to specify variable labels in the MACRO directive. A variable label would appear in a *Label* field in the template code and would automatically change with each call. It would not need to be listed as a dummy argument. State a set of rules for automatic labeling that assumes the template labels have digits appended to them that change with each call. Rewrite ABS using these rules.

44. Assume that the decode and execution time for all X16 instructions, except the multiply and divide instructions, is two clock cycles. For the multiply and divide instructions, the time is eight clock cycles for byte operands and 16 clock cycles for halfwords. Determine the total number of memory accesses (one halfword per access even for byte operands) and the total time in clock periods needed to execute the code in:
(a) Fig. 4-18 (b) Fig. 4-19
First assume that there are no wait states and then resolve the problem assuming two wait states per access.

45. Assume the X16 timing given in Exercise 44 and determine the total time in clock periods needed to execute the code in
   (a) Fig. 4-20   **(b)** Fig. 4-21

46. Assume the X16 timing given in Exercise 44 and the following frequencies of execution and average numbers of memory accesses:

Type of Instruction	Execution Frequency in Percentages	Average No. of Accesses
Transfer	32	3
Arithmetic		
Negation	4	3
Addition	12	4
Subtraction	8	4
Multiplication	5	3
Division	3	3
Branch	25	3
Logical	7	4
Shift and rotate	3	3
Other	1	2

For a 10 MHz clock, determine the average number of instructions fetched and executed per second.

5
Program Creation

Although it is possible to put machine language programs directly into memory, this would be done only for very special applications, such as when a computer is to be used as a simple controller. Machine language programming is far too meticulous and error prone to be used except when a program is extremely short. The usual procedure is of course, to write a program in an assembler or high-level language and then use a **translator** program to reduce the program's code to the machine level instructions of the computer. Assembler and high-level language programs are written as sequences of statements and it is the job of the translator and other systems programs to convert these statements into machine language instructions and prepare them for execution.

Two fundamental methods for preparing and executing a program are illustrated in Fig. 5-1. One uses a system program, called an **interpreter**, to input statements one by one, convert each statement to a sequence of machine language instructions, and then execute the machine language sequence. The other uses a system program, called an **assembler** or **compiler**, to convert all of the statements to machine language instructions and then uses other system programs, referred to as a **linker** and **loader**, to form the final machine language program and initiate its execution. Programs written in BASIC are normally interpreted and those written in C, Pascal, or FORTRAN are normally compiled.

Although there are several ways of implementing an interpretative or compilation system, as described in previous chapters, we will concentrate on a straightforward system that best illustrates the steps involved. We will primarily consider the compilation approach to program creation and execution because compilers produce more efficient code than interpreters and are more often used in professional settings. The process discussed in this chapter is the one used to assemble or compile and then execute programs (other than BASIC programs)

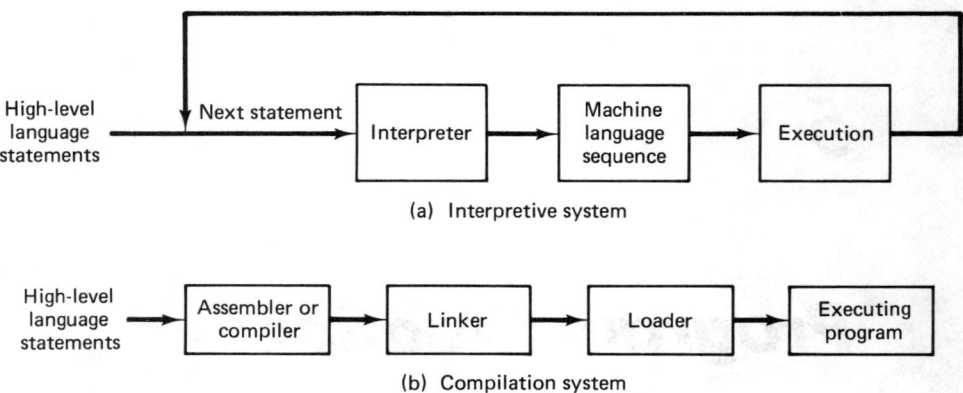

Figure 5-1 Program creation and execution.

on a personal computer but is fundamentally the same as that used on large computers. This discussion has been considerably simplified and is designed to emphasize only the major points. For a more detailed discussion of assemblers and compilers, refer to Calingaert [1] and Barron [2].

5-1 ASSEMBLERS

An assembler is a systems program that is run under the supervision of an operating system. Its execution is normally initiated by a system command just like any other program. A typical command for starting the execution of an assembler is of the form:

Assembler name   Source file name   Object file name

The input to the assembler is a **source file** that contains the code to be translated, and the output is to a file, called an **object file**. Both the source and object files may be subdivided into parts, called **units**. As depicted in Fig. 5-2, an execution of the assembler translates source units in the source file one by one and puts the corresponding object units that result from the assembly into the object file. For example, if the name of the assembler is ASMX16 then the command

ASMX16   PROG.ASM   PROG.OBJ

would translate the assembler source code in the file PROG.ASM and put the resulting object code in the file PROG.OBJ.

Keep in mind that an assembler is nothing more than a program that translates a language that closely corresponds to a computer's machine language into its machine language, and the definition of the assembler's syntax has nothing to do with the design of the hardware. Several different assemblers can be written for the same processing element and the syntax of each assembler is determined

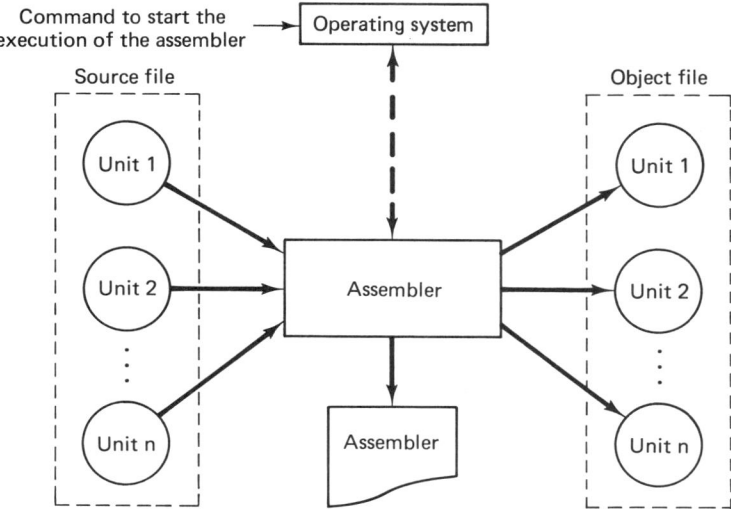

Figure 5-2 Execution of an assembler.

by the designer of the assembler. The rules for writing the assembler statements given in this section are for the X16 and are representative of assemblers in general, but one could write an assembler for the X16 that is much different from the one derived here. An assembler may be a **self-assembler**, which executes on the same processing element as the machine code it creates, or a **cross-assembler**, which executes on a different processing element. It may be written using any available language. It is not unusual for a microprocessor's assembler to be written in a high-level language, such as C or Pascal, and executed on a large computer or a specially designed computer-based development system.

Before continuing our discussion of the assembly process, it is necessary to consider the second type of assembler statements. Section 4-2 mentioned that there are two types of such statements—instructions and directives. Directives are nonexecutable statements whose purpose is to give directions to the assembler. Because directives are not related to the hardware they were not considered in Chap. 4, but they must be introduced at this point. Of immediate interest are directives that assign labels, allocate storage, and assign identifiers to constants. Other directives, such as those that delimit program modules and join the various parts of a program together, are introduced later.

5-1-1 Data-related Directives

In the assembler language examples in Chap. 4 identifying symbols were used to represent memory locations, but the code that was used to associate these identifiers with their memory locations was not included. The required code is analogous to the high-level language code that allocates memory areas, assigns names to the areas, and preassigns values to memory locations.

A typical assembler language format for a directive that allocates a memory area and assigns a label to the area is:

Label   Mnemonic   Size

where *Label* is an identifier, *Mnemonic* indicates the type of allocation, and *Size* is a numeric constant that specifies the size of the area being reserved. *Label* is optional and may not appear if the directive is needed for allocation only. A typical directive for reserving eight bytes and associating the symbol X with the first byte is

X   DB   8

where DB is the mnemonic for a define byte directive.

Assembler languages may allow storage to be allocated by units other than bytes (e.g., halfwords, words, and doublewords), but may or may not have directives for indicating data types. For example, the define word directive

Y   DW   1

reserves one 4-byte word and associates it with Y but does not specify the type of quantity to be stored at Y. This word may be used to store a 4-byte integer or a single-precision floating-point number. In contrast, most high-level language statements that allocate storage or assign symbols to storage areas indicate the data type associated with the area (e.g., the Pascal statement

VAR   Y: REAL;

specifies that Y is to be occupied by a floating-point quantity).

Although preassignment, as done by FORTRAN DATA statements, is not necessary, most assembler languages allow for it by making available directives that are typically of the form

Label   Mnemonic   Repeat (Constant, . . . , Constant)

where *Repeat* is a numeric constant and each *Constant* may represent either a numeric or string constant. *Repeat* specifies the number of times the pattern of constants inside the parentheses is to be repeated. (It serves the same purpose as a repeat factor in a FORTRAN DATA statement.) *Repeat* is usually optional, and if it is not present, it is assumed to be 1. For example, the directive

W   DH   (2,0,5)

would not only reserve three halfwords and associate the first halfword with W, but would also cause the halfwords at W, W + 2, and W + 4 to be filled with 2, 0, and 5 at the time the program is assembled, i.e., it would have the same effect as the FORTRAN statement

DATA   (W(I), I = 1,3)/2,0,5/

An example of a sequence of directives is given in Fig. 5-3(a). The first directive reserves three words and associates the first word with the label VECTOR. The second reserves four halfwords, associates the first halfword with the label FLAGS, and preassigns 0 to the first and third halfwords and 10 to the second and fourth halfwords. The third reserves five bytes, associates the first byte with the label MESSAGE, and preassigns the ASCII codes for "E," "R," "R," "O," and "R" to the bytes. The fourth reserves one doubleword but neither associates it with a label nor preassigns a value to it. Figure 5-3(b) illustrates the portion of memory allocated and preassigned by these directives. The preassigned values are shown in hexadecimal.

An important variation of the preassignment directive is one that permits the assembler to put addresses in memory locations. It normally has the form

Label   Mnemonic   Label

which causes the address associated with the second *Label* to be the preassigned value. As with the allocation directive, the *Label* to the left of the mnemonic in a preassignment directive is optional. This form of preassignment is needed to implement indirect addressing in which the instruction does not produce the operand address, but points to a memory location that contains the operand address. For example, the code

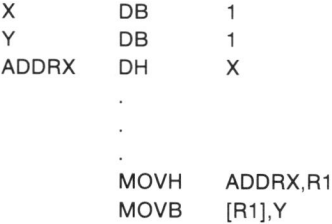

would cause the contents of X to be transferred to the location Y. The first two define byte directives, reserve bytes, and associate them with X and Y. The third directive preassigns the address of location X to the halfword associated with ADDRX. Later, during execution, the first move instruction puts the contents of ADDRX (i.e., the address of X) into R1 and the second move instruction copies the contents of X into location Y. The use of indirect addressing at the assembler level is similar to the use of pointers in Pascal. (Note that if memory indirect addressing were available, the two move instructions could be replaced by a single instruction.)

Some assemblers include directives for designating more complex data types and may even allow a programmer to specify the structure of a data type. In Pascal the structure of a data type can be defined by a TYPE-RECORD statement. A TYPE-RECORD statement does not allocate any memory nor designate a variable type; it describes a data type that is constructed from basic data types. For example, the Pascal statement

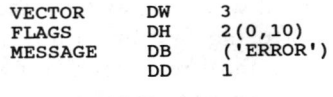

(a) Directives

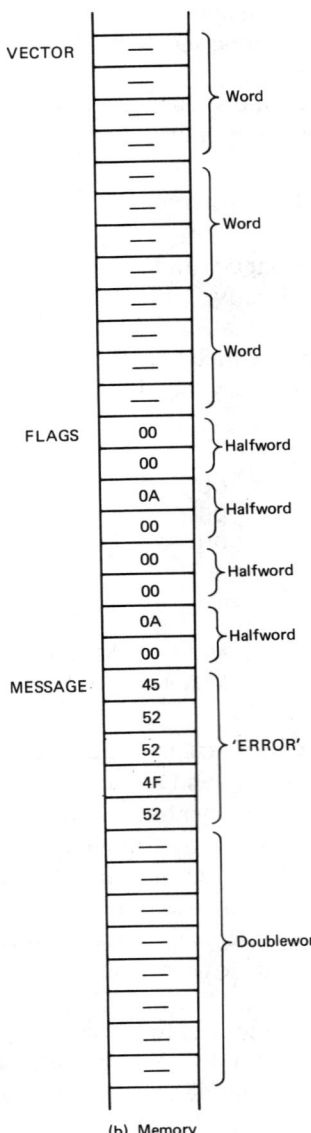

(b) Memory

Figure 5-3 Example directives and corresponding memory allocation.

```
TYPE PART = RECORD
              NUM: INTEGER;
              SIZE: CHAR;
              NAME: ARRAY[1. .5] OF CHAR;
            END;
```

only describes data type PART, which consists of an integer, a character, and an array of five characters. The Pascal statement

VAR INVENTORY: ARRAY [1..100] OF PART;

would then reserve space for 100 elements of the data type PART and give the beginning address of this space the variable name INVENTORY.

An assembler could be given a similar capability by including directives such as RECORD and ENDR as follows:

```
RECORD     PART
   NUM     DH    1
   SIZE    DB    1
   NAME    DB    5
ENDR
```

The sequence of directives would be equivalent to the above Pascal TYPE-RECORD statement. Once a record name appears in a RECORD directive it can be used as the mnemonic in an allocation directive to reserve the required space and assign a label to the beginning address of that space. Continuing our above example, the directive

INVENTORY   PART   100

would be equivalent to the above Pascal VAR statement.

If an assembler can define complex data types, it should also provide a special means of referencing the individual components of these data types by using compound identifiers. Often these identifiers are constructed of simple identifiers by using periods as separators (e.g., PART.SIZE would indicate the SIZE component of the record PART). The purpose of this labeling is to make assembler code easier to write and more readable when it is completed.

As with high-level languages, it is convenient to assign names to constants. Not only does this convenience provide a means of replacing constants with meaningful names, but it also gives a programmer a way of changing a constant value that appears several places by changing a single assignment directive. The latter is not just a convenience, but can also reduce errors caused by overlooking an occurrence of a constant. In Pascal, CONST statements are used to make such assignments. In assembler language, they are typically made by directives of the form:

Name   Mnemonic   Constant

```
Address   Machine              Assembler code
          code

 --        --       N      EQU      4           ;NUMBER OF AREAS
 --        --       LIMIT  EQU      500         ;LIMIT ON TOTAL AREA
                      .
                      .
                      .
116A       --       T_AREA DH       1           ;TOTAL AREA
116C       --       AREAS  DH       N           ;ARRAY OF AREAS
                      .
                      .
                      .
1210      EEAB              MOVH   #0,T_AREA    ;PUT 0 IN T_AREA
1212      0000
1214      116A
1216      EEA0              MOVH   #N,R4        ;NO. OF AREAS TO R4
1218      0004
121A      EE80              MOVH   #AREAS,R0    ;ADDR OF AREAS TO R0
121C      116C
121E      417B     AGAIN    ADDH   [R0]+,T_AREA ;SUM THE AREAS
1220      116A
1222      8EA0              SUBH   #1,R4
1224      0001
1226      053E              BRNE   AGAIN
1228      FFF4
122A      CEBB              CMPH   #LIMIT,T_AREA ;COMPARE TOTAL TO LIMIT
122C      01F4
122E      116A
1230      05BE              BSGT   CONTINUE     ;BRANCH TO CONTINUE
1232      004A
1234
                      .
                      .
                      .
```

Figure 5-4 Example that includes both instructions and directives.

where *Name* is the identifier used to represent the *Constant*. Assuming the mnemonic for the assembler directive for assigning a name to a constant is EQU, examples of assignment directives are:

SCALE   EQU   50

and

HEADING   EQU   'DESCRIPTION'

Figure 5-4 is a programming example that includes both directives and instructions. The code sums the four integers in the array AREAS, puts the result in T_AREA, and branches if the sum is greater than LIMIT. It is equivalent to the Pascal code:

```
CONST   N = 4;
        LIMIT = 500;
            .
            .
VAR     T_AREA: INTEGER;
        AREAS: ARRAY [1 .. N] OF INTEGER;
```

.
.
.
        T_AREA := 0;
        FOR I:=1 TO N DO T_AREA := T_AREA+AREA[I];
        IF T_AREA<=LIMIT THEN ... ;
.
.
.

It is assumed that the assembler has put the data and instructions in the memory locations indicated by the leftmost column. The machine language code is shown in the second column. The first two directives give the names N and LIMIT to the constants 4 and 500. There is no machine code corresponding to these directives because their only purpose is to tell the assembler to substitute 4 and 500 for N and LIMIT. The next directive reserves the halfword at address 116A and assigns it the label T_AREA, and the following directive reserves N = 4 halfwords beginning at 116C and associates the label AREAS with the address 116C. The instructions beginning at address 1210 add the four numbers in the halfwords beginning at AREAS and put the sum into T_AREA. They then compare the sum to LIMIT = 500 and branch to CONTINUE if the sum is greater than LIMIT.

5-1-2 The Assembly Process

The primary input to an assembler is **source code**, which consists of assembler language directives and instructions. The assembler's primary output is **object code**, which consists of machine language code intermixed with other information that may be needed by the system when it prepares the program for execution. As indicated earlier in Fig. 5-2, normally source code is taken from a source file that is kept in mass storage and object code is put into an object file in mass storage.

As the assembler draws text from the source file, it searches the text for a directive that indicates that it should begin its assembly. When this beginning directive is found, the assembler begins processing the text as source code until an end directive indicates the end of a complete set of source code. The code between the beginning and end directives constitutes a source unit and the resulting object code is the corresponding object unit. The assembler directives used here for delimiting a source unit are the UNIT and END directives. By placing a *Name* after the mnemonic UNIT, an identifying *Name* may be given to the unit.

Figure 5-5 gives a representative structure of an assembler source file. A command such as

        ASMX16   MATRIX.ASM   MATRIX.OBJ

would cause the assembler ASMX16 to be brought into memory and begin to run. ASMX16 would bring in the file MATRIX.ASM, assemble the source unit

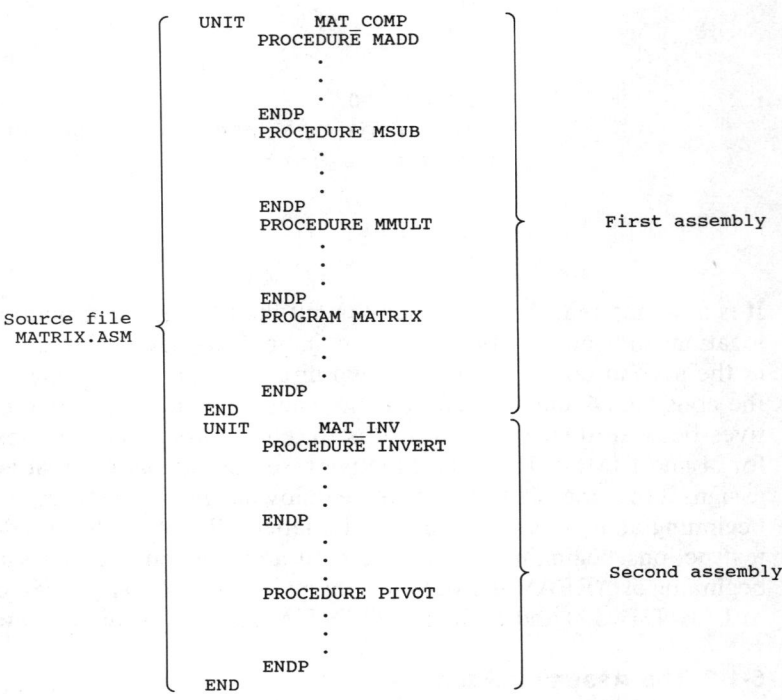

Figure 5-5 Typical structure of a source file.

MAT_COMP, produce an object unit MAT_COMP, assemble the source unit MAT_INV, produce an object unit MAT_INV, and store object units MAT_COMP and MAT_INV in a file MATRIX.OBJ. The PROGRAM directive denotes the beginning of a program and may include a program name. The ENDP directive denotes the end of a program as well as the end of a procedure.

The inclusion of procedures in the units is incidental to the assembly process. Procedures are simply translated into machine code along with the rest of the source code, but the PROCEDURE and ENDP directives are needed for readability. Frequently, a unit such as MAT_INV consists solely of a procedure or set of procedures.

Most assemblers are designed to scan the source unit twice and are called **two-pass assemblers**. The major components of a two-pass assembler are shown in Fig. 5-6. They are the symbol (or identifier) table, machine instruction table, directive table, and an integer variable known as the **location counter (LC)**. The machine instruction and directive tables contain the mnemonics for all of the machine language instructions and assembler directives and are used to identify the types of assembler statements. They also contain any length information that might be needed by the assembler. The machine instruction table includes the opcodes of the instructions. The LC increments as a unit is being assembled and

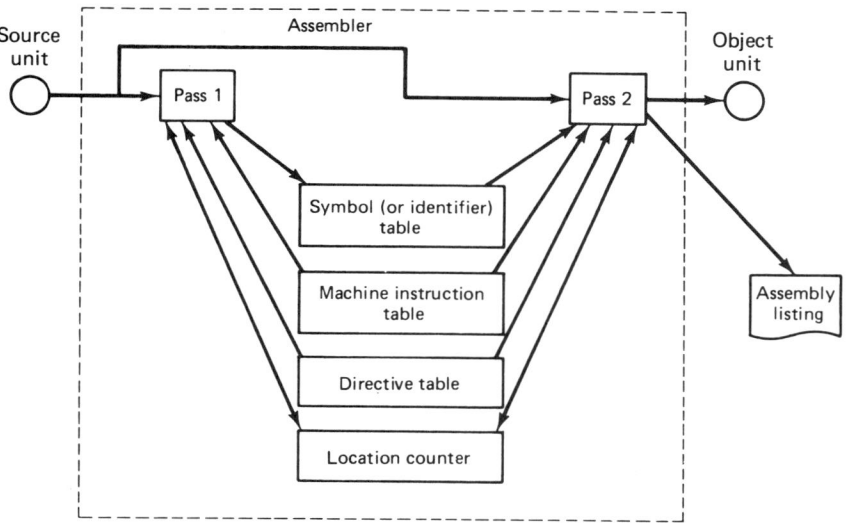

Figure 5-6 Major components of a two-pass assembler.

always points to the current position within the unit. It is used to note the relative positions of the labels within the unit.

As shown in Fig. 5-6, the first pass puts information into the symbol table and the second pass uses that information to determine the operand fields in the instructions. The primary purpose of the first pass is to determine the position of the labels relative to the beginning of the unit, but it may also note other information about the labels and other identifiers. The first pass scans the source unit looking for labels. Each time a label is found, it is stored in the symbol table along with its relative position within the unit and other important attributes. The symbol table may also contain, for each label, the location of all of the places where the label appears as an operand. The primary purpose of the second pass is to generate machine language instructions. It takes opcode and length information from the machine instruction table, length information from the directive table, and label and other identifier information from the symbol table.

A complete X16 program is given in Fig. 5-7(a). The code in this figure includes an origin (ORG) directive that gives the programmer a means for setting the LC. The LC is always initially set to 0000 and, if there is no ORG directive present, a unit is always assembled to begin at address 0000.

The two columns on the right in Fig. 5-7(a) give the value of the LC (in hexadecimal) at the time the assembler examines the corresponding statement and the length associated with the statement. Figure 5-7(b) shows the symbol table entries created by the first pass. In addition to labels, the symbol table includes information about other identifiers.

When the UNIT directive is encountered, the assembler initializes the LC to 0000, puts the unit's name, EXAMPLE, in the symbol table, and begins the assembly. The PROGRAM directive causes the program's name, VECT_COMP,

Assembler code			LC	Length
UNIT EXAMPLE			0000	--
PROGRAM VECT_COMP			0000	--
	ORG	10	000A	--
M	EQU	3	000A	--
N	EQU	2	000A	--
A_ARRAY	DH	(2,-12,M)	000A	6
B_ARRAY	DH	(-3,4,2B1H)	0010	6
START	MOVH	#M,R5	0016	4
	MOVH	#A_ARRAY,R0	001A	4
	MOVH	#B_ARRAY,R1	001E	4
LP	ADDH	[R0]+,[R1]	0022	2
	SUBH	#N,[R1]+	0024	4
	SUBH	#1,R5	0028	4
	BRNE	#LP	002C	4
	HALT		0030	2
ENDP			0032	--
END				

(a) LC activity

Symbol	Type	Unit length	Association	Location	Occurrences
EXAMPLE	Unit name	---	Unit	---	---
VECT_COMP	Program name	---	Program	---	---
M	Constant name	---	3	---	---
N	Constant name	---	2	---	---
A_ARRAY	Label	Halfword	Directive	000A	001C
B_ARRAY	Label	Halfword	Directive	0010	0020
START	Label	---	Instruction	0016	---
LP	Label	---	Instruction	0022	002E

(b) Symbol table

Figure 5-7 Example showing the LC activity and symbol table created by the first pass.

to be put in the symbol table. The UNIT and PROGRAM directives have no effect on the LC, but the ORG directive sets the LC to 000A. Setting the origin to 000A causes the program to be assembled as if it were going to be put in memory beginning at address 000A, and all operand addresses are assigned accordingly. The EQU directives cause the assembler to put M and N in the symbol table along with the constants they represent. Because these directives do not call for any memory space to be reserved, they do not change the LC.

The first DH directive causes the assembler to put the label A_ARRAY into the symbol table along with the current value of the LC (000A) and other attributes associated with the label. Because it reserves space for three halfwords, it causes the LC to increment by 6 to 0010. Similarly, the second DH directive puts B_ARRAY and 0010 in the symbol table and increments the LC by 6 to 0016.

When the first MOVH instruction is scanned, the assembler puts START and its location (0016) in the symbol table and increments the LC by 4 (the length of the instruction—see Sec. 4-1-4) to 001A. When the assembler examines the next two instructions it notes that the addresses of A_ARRAY and B_ARRAY need to be put into the second halfwords, respectively, of these instructions. For each of these instructions, the LC is incremented by 4. For the ADDH instruction,

LP and 0022 are put into the symbol table and the LC is incremented by 2; for each SUBH the LC is incremented by 4; and for BRNE it is noted that the address of LP is needed in the second halfword of the instruction and the LC is incremented by 4.

As each statement is examined during the second pass of the assembler, the mnemonic is looked up in the machine instruction table or directive table. Using the attributes found in the table, the machine language code for the instruction or directive is formed. For directives, preassigned values are inserted in the required locations and, for instructions, the opcodes, immediate operands, addresses, and displacements are assembled to form each instruction. If names, addresses, or displacements are required, the necessary information is looked up in the symbol table. For example, during the second pass, the first DH directive causes 2, −12, and M = 3 (where 3 is determined from the symbol table) to be put into the halfwords at 000A, 000C, and 000E. The second MOVH instruction puts EE80 and 000A in the halfwords at 001A and 001C. The complete machine language code produced by the assembler is given in Fig. 5-8. This code could be executed by putting it into the memory beginning at 000A and putting 0016 into the processing element's PC. (Note that the addresses would be incorrect if the program were put elsewhere in memory.)

Figure 5-9 gives a simplified flowchart of a two-pass assembler. During the first pass, before inserting an identifier in the symbol table, the table is scanned to see if the identifier already exists. If so, then a name would be assigned twice or a label would be associated with two different locations. In either case, there would be an ambiguity that would cause an error to be recorded and included in the assembly listing. Other errors may be recorded because the mnemonic cannot be found in either the directive table or the machine instruction table or, during the second pass, an identifier not contained in the symbol table is found in an

Address	Machine code	Assembler code		
000A	0002	A_ARRAY	DH	(2,-12,M)
	FFF4			
	0003			
0010	FFFD	B_ARRAY	DH	(-3,4,2B1H)
	0004			
	02B1			
0016	EEA8	START	MOVH	#M,R5
	0003			
001A	EE80		MOVH	#A_ARRAY,R0
	000A			
001E	EE88		MOVH	#B_ARRAY,R1
	0010			
0022	4149	LP	ADDH	[R0]+,[R1]
0024	8E8D		SUBH	#N,[R1]+
	0002			
0028	8EA8		SUBH	#1,R5
	0001			
002C	053E		BRNE	LP
	FFF2			
0030	0001		HALT	

Figure 5-8 Machine language code produced by the assembler language code and symbol table given in Figure 5-7.

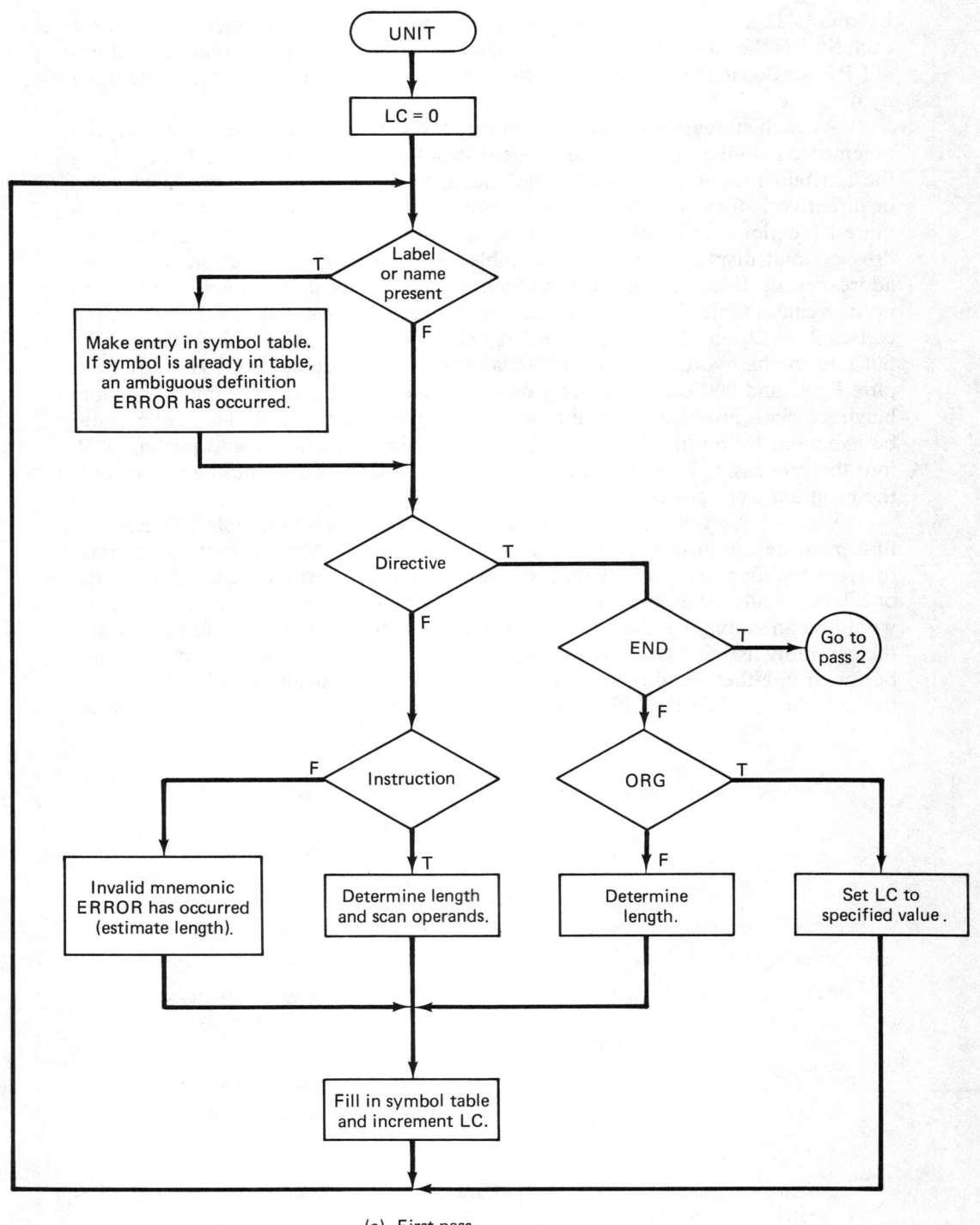

(a) First pass

Figure 5-9 Flowchart of a typical assembler.

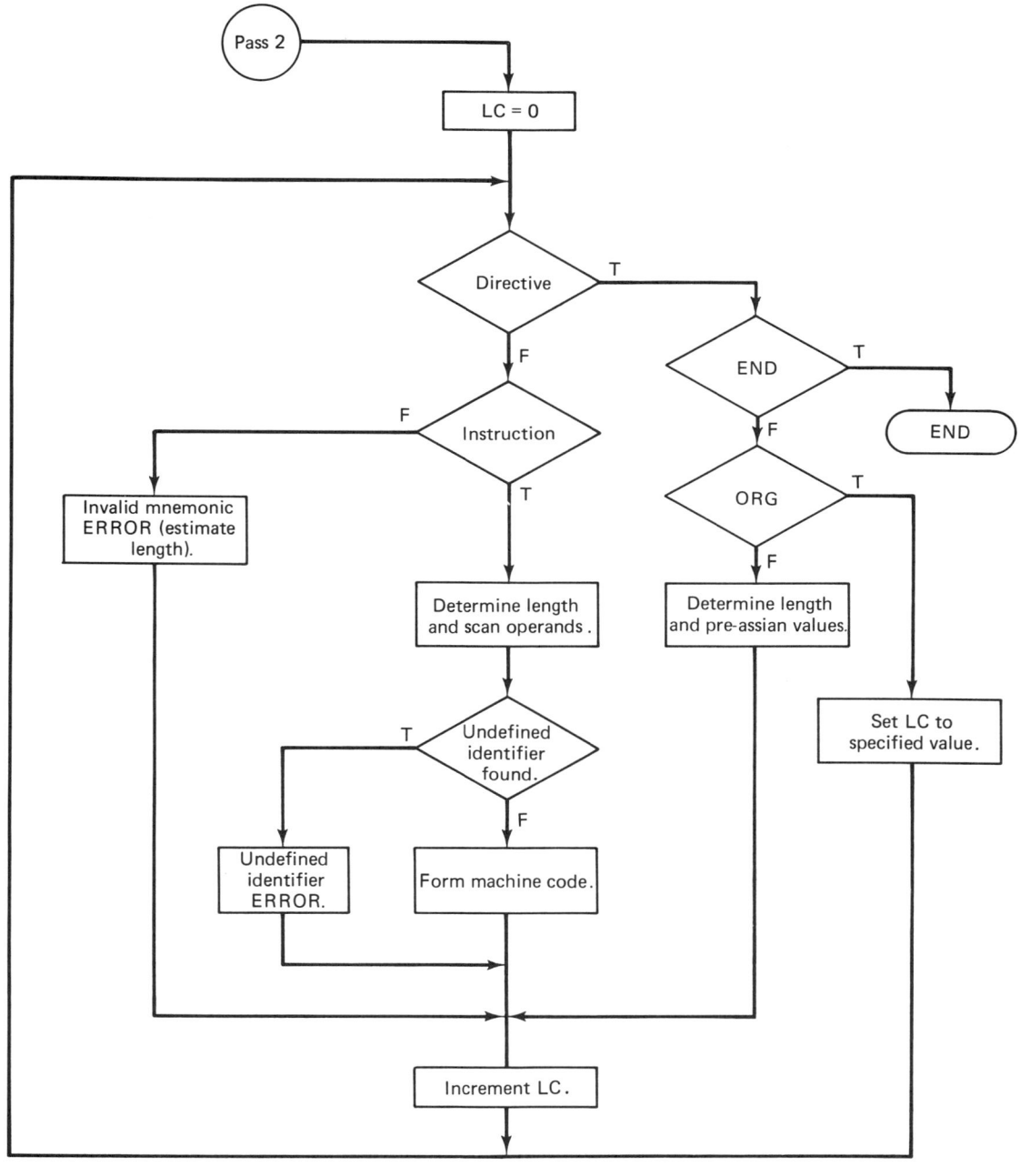

(b) Second pass

Figure 5-9 Continued

Sec. 5-1 Assemblers

operand. In the latter case, the identifier is said to be **undefined**. When the END directive is encountered during the second pass, it concludes the assembly of the source unit. The object unit would consist of the machine code and symbol table. As seen later, the symbol table may be needed when an object unit is joined with other object units.

Usually the facility that handles macros is incorporated into an assembler by inserting another pass, called a **prepass**, before pass 1. The prepass scans the code for macro calls and, each time a call is found, it inserts the template code with the *Dummy arguments* replaced by the *Arguments*. Then, when passes 1 and 2 scan the code, they see the macro expansions instead of the calls.

5-2 COMPILERS

A compilation is normally initiated in the same manner as an assembly, i.e., by giving a command of the form:

Compiler name   Source file name   Object file name

The action taken by the compiler indicated by *Compiler name* is the same as that of an assembler (see Fig. 5-2). The compiler simply converts a source file containing source units into an object file containing object units.

As with an assembler, a compiler translates source code that consists of character strings into object code that includes machine language instructions; but, unlike assembler statements there is not a close correspondence between the high-level language statements and machine language instructions. High-level language statements may be lengthy and quite complex and may translate into numerous machine language instructions. Because most assembler statements translate directly into machine instructions on a one-to-one basis, most assemblies are completed in two passes. However, a high-level language compilation may require several passes.

The tasks performed by a compiler may be broken down as follows:

- Lexical analysis.
- Syntax analysis.
- Semantic processing.
- General optimization and storage allocation.
- Machine code generation.
- Machine specific optimization.

Depending on the design of the compiler, some of these tasks may be distinct and executed in sequence while others are overlapped or executed together.

Lexical analysis breaks statements down according to the basic elements that make up the language, and syntactic analysis determines the structural relationships of these elements. All high-level languages have basic elements, or symbols, from which their statements must be constructed and a set of syntax rules, called a **grammar**, that govern how these elements must be put together. For example, for the Pascal statement

$$\text{FORCE} := \text{B}*(\text{C}+\text{D});$$

the basic symbols are "FORCE", ":=", "B", "*", "(", "C", "+", "D", ")", and ";". "FORCE", "B", "C", and "D" are recognized as variables (which are presumably included in VAR statements) and ":=", "*", "(", "+", ")", and ";" are key symbols reserved by the Pascal language. It is the grammar of Pascal that determines the meaning of this particular sequence of symbols and, in this case, indicates that the contents of FORCE are to be replaced by the product of B and the sum of C and D. The ";" marks the end of the statement. Although lexical analysis and syntax analysis are conceptually different, they are normally performed together.

Semantic processing is the interpretation of the results produced by the lexical and syntax analyses and its output is an intermediate code that is rigidly structured and can easily be used to complete the compilation process. Prior to obtaining the intermediate code the compiler's work is dependent solely on the high-level language. The work done after the intermediate code has been produced depends on the computer and its machine language. After the intermediate code has been formed, storage is allocated according to the storage declaration statements. Next, a general optimization of the intermediate code may be performed, the machine language code is generated, and then a final optimization may be performed that is specific to the architecture of the machine on which the code is to be executed.

Interspersed throughout Chap. 4 and Sec. 5-1-1 have been examples suggesting machine language code that might have resulted from various Pascal statements, such as assignment, decision, looping, procedure call, CONST, and VAR statements. However, the statements related to control flow (i.e., the sequencing of instructions) deserve additional attention. Most high-level language programs are written using the five elementary control structures given in Fig. 5-10. Their definitions are:

> **Simple sequence**—the successive performance of two or more actions. The state of the solution after the first step is completed is the state just prior to the execution of the second step and so on.
>
> **IF-THEN-ELSE**—a structure in which a condition is given; if the condition is true, one set of actions is taken, and, if the condition is false, a different set of actions is taken. Both paths return to a common point after the selected actions are completed.
>
> **WHILE**—a pretesting loop in which a given condition is tested; if it is true, specified actions are taken and the condition is tested again. The given actions are repeated as long as the condition is true. When the condition becomes false, the loop is exited. Clearly, the action in the loop must modify at least one of the variables in the condition; otherwise, the loop would be repeated ad infinitum.

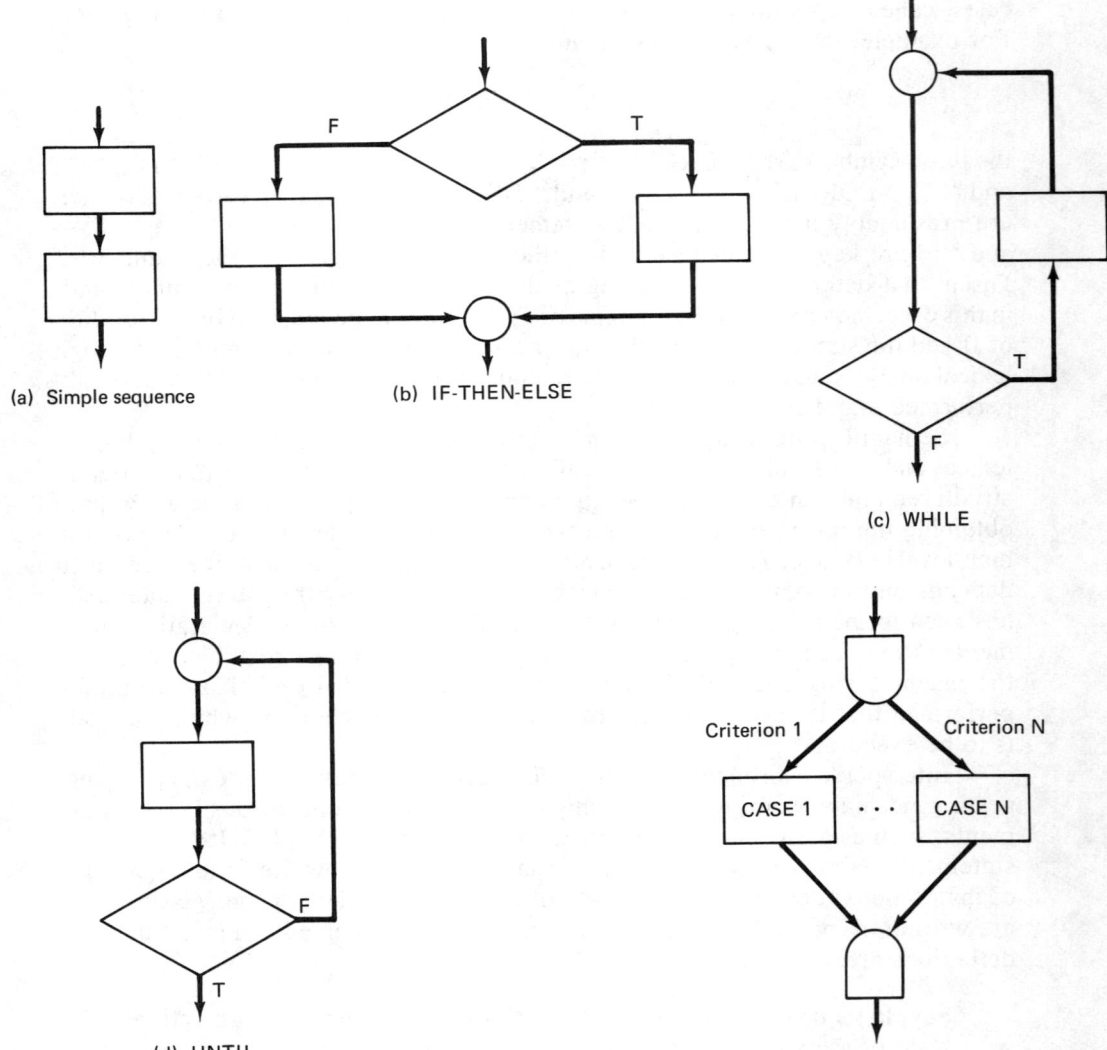

Figure 5-10 Elementary control structures.

UNTIL—similar to a WHILE structure except that it is a post-testing loop in which the actions are executed before the condition is tested; therefore, they are always executed at least once. The loop is repeated until the condition is true, at which time the loop is exited. Once again, at least one of the variables in the condition must be changed within the loop if exiting is to be possible.

CASE—a structure that includes a decision that may have more than two outcomes. Depending on the outcome of the decision, one of several actions is performed. Regardless of which action is executed, upon completion of the action, the program continues from a common point.

The action blocks represented by the rectangles in Fig. 5-10 may consist of one or more instructions and even include one or more elementary control structures. For example, Fig. 5-11 shows an UNTIL structure that includes an IF-THEN-ELSE structure and is itself part of a simple sequence.

Most high-level languages have statements for implementing the latter four control structures. For Pascal, these statements are the IF-THEN-ELSE, WHILE-DO, REPEAT-UNTIL, and CASE-OF statements, respectively. Because the control portions of these structures can be expressed by single high-level language statements, programs can be written that consist entirely of the elementary control structures. In contrast, assembler language instructions are capable of carrying out only machine-level actions and several such actions may be needed to make the computations and comparisons required in the decision-making condition of a high-level language statement. These actions normally include several branch statements, and it is impossible to construct assembler lan-

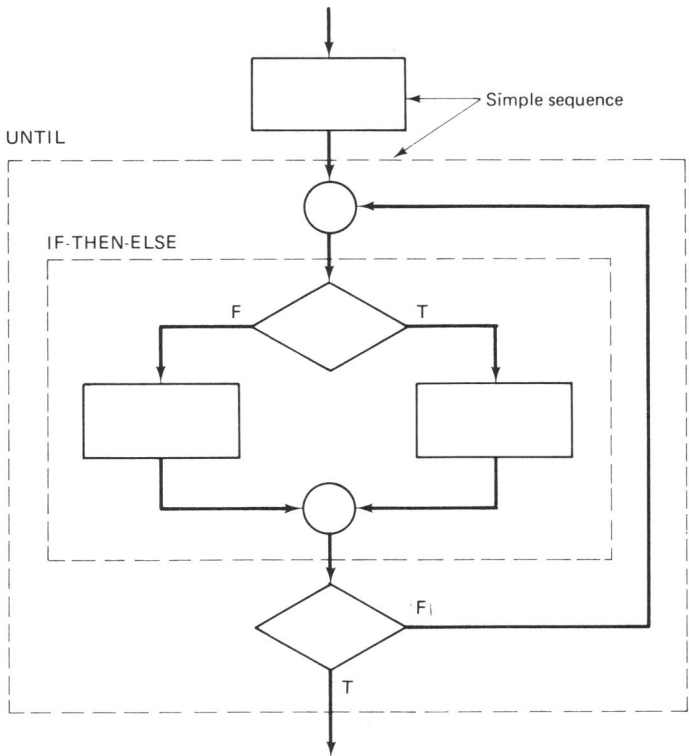

Figure 5-11 Example showing elementary control structures within elementary control structures.

guage programs with the same simplistic structures as their high-level language counterparts. During the compilation of high-level language statements, machine language patterns must be substituted for the elementary control structures. Representative patterns that could be used to simulate the IF-THEN-ELSE, WHILE, UNTIL, and CASE control structures are given in Fig. 5-12.

The code for computing the truth value of a condition and then branching

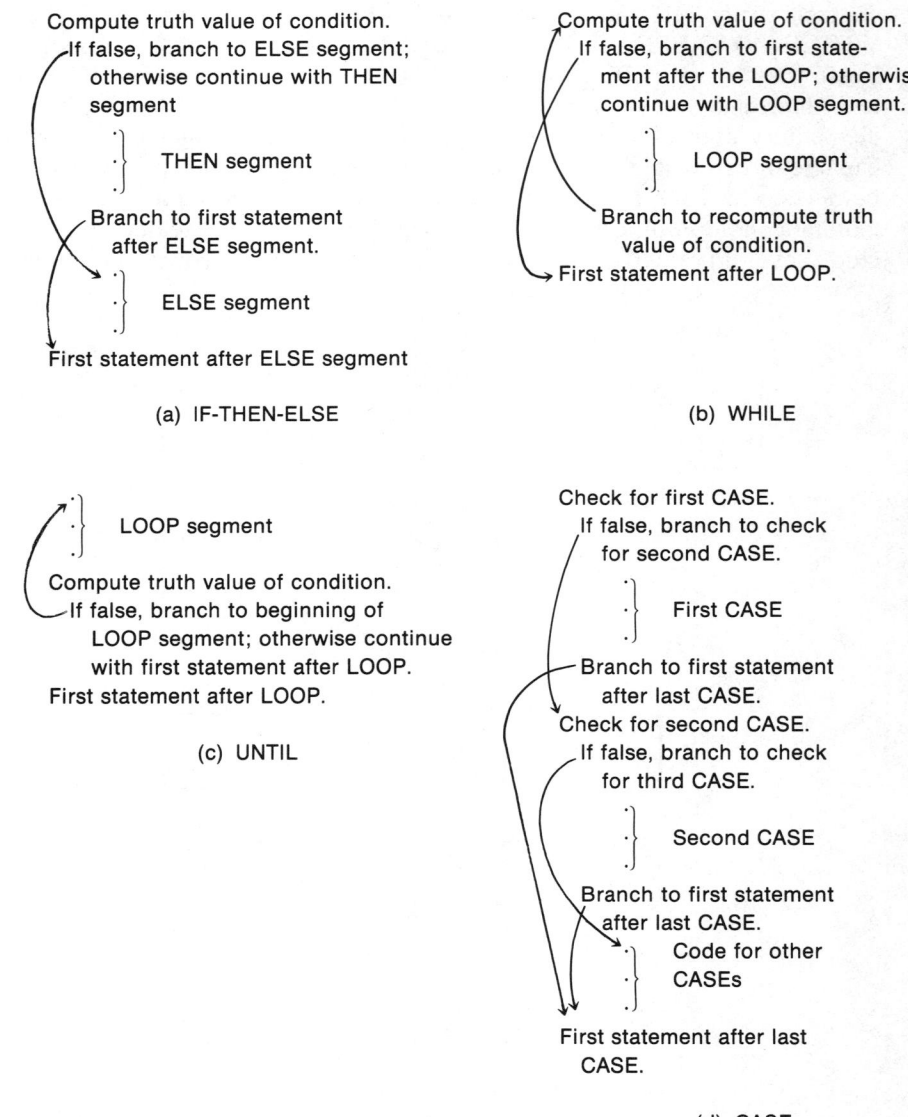

Figure 5-12 Patterns for simulating the elementary control structures in assembler language.

depends on the logical structure of the condition. An example is the condition

(A *R1* B AND C *R2* D) OR (E *R3* F AND G *R4* H)

where A through H are algebraic expressions and *R1* through *R4* represent relational operators. An implementation that branches to FALSE when the condition is false and to TRUE when it is true is given in Fig. 5-13. Note that if the condition is scanned from left to right and the relation *R1* is false, there is no need to test relation *R2*. Similarly, if relation *R3* is false, there is no need to test relation *R4*. On the other hand, if relations *R1* and *R2* are both true, then both relations *R3* and *R4* can be ignored. A Pascal statement with a condition such as the one described is:

IF (X+Y=1 AND Y<0) OR (Y=X+1 AND X<0) THEN Z=X ELSE Z=Y;

The X16 code that is equivalent to this statement is given in Fig. 5-14.

An important special case of the WHILE structure is the one for which the condition is the comparison of a count with a limit. This special case is implemented in Pascal with the FOR-DO statement and in FORTRAN with the DO statement. As discussed in Sec. 4-2-2, such loops occur so often that special loop instructions are usually included in the instruction set to make them more efficient.

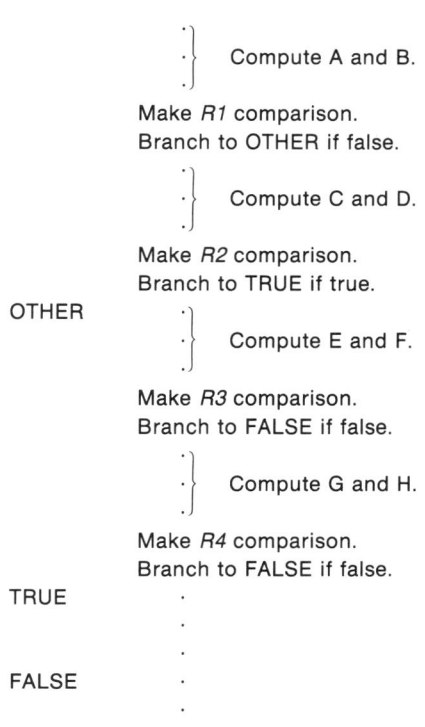

Figure 5-13 Implementation of a typical condition.

```
                MOVH    X,R0            ;DETERMINE THE TRUTH
                ADDH    Y,R0            ;VALUE OF X+Y=1
                CMPH    #1,R0           ;AND IF FALSE
                BRNE    OTHER           ;BRANCH TO OTHER
                CMPH    Y,#0            ;DETERMINE TRUTH OF Y<0 AND
                BSLT    TRUE            ;IF TRUE BRANCH TO TRUE
        OTHER   MOVH    X,R0            ;DETERMINE TRUTH VALUE
                ADDH    #1,R0           ;OF Y=X+1
                CMPH    Y,R0            ;AND IF FALSE
                BRNE    FALSE           ;BRANCH TO FALSE
                CMPH    X,#0            ;DETERMINE TRUTH OF X<0 AND
                BSGE    FALSE           ;IF FALSE BRANCH TO FALSE
        TRUE    MOVH    X,Z             ;EXECUTE THEN SEGMENT
                BRUN    EXIT            ;AND BRANCH TO EXIT
        FALSE   MOVH    Y,Z             ;EXECUTE ELSE SEGMENT
        EXIT     .
                 .
                 .
```

Figure 5-14 Implementation of a Pascal IF-THEN-ELSE statement whose condition has the same logical structure as the example depicted in Figure 5-13.

For the CASE structure, checking is usually just a matter of comparison (see Sec. 4-2-3). If the items being compared are not equal, then checking for the next CASE is conducted.

The conversion of the conditions in these control structures and of the structures as a whole clearly is a nontrivial task. This is why compilers require so many passes. Because of the one-to-one correspondence between most assembler statements and machine instructions, an assembler language programmer has precise control over which machine instructions are used and how they are sequenced. In contrast, a high-level language programmer can specify only high-level language statements and how they are used to form a program and must rely on the compiler to translate these statements into an efficient set of machine language code. To generate object code that is as efficient as or better than the code that results from a well-written assembler language program, a compiler must be sophisticated and include many (perhaps ten or more) passes. Such compilers are sometimes referred to as **optimizing compilers**.

For example, consider the Pascal statement

FOR T:=1 TO 10 DO X[I] := SIN(Y) + Z[I];

A simple compiler would not be capable of detecting that this statement, if taken explicitly, would cause the sine of Y to be computed ten times. An optimizing compiler would be able to recognize the multiple computation of the sine of Y and would produce object code that is the same as the following two Pascal statements:

TEMP := SIN(Y);
FOR I:=1 TO 10 DO X[I] := TEMP+Z[I];

This example is rather simple and a compiler capable of correcting this inefficiency would not be particularly complex, but there are compilers that can decipher very complicated and subtle situations and produce object code that is as good as that generated by the very best assembler language programmers. The basic tradeoff here is a complex compiler that takes a long time to execute and requires a great deal of memory, but yields efficient code, versus a simple compiler that is small and executes quickly, but yields object code that is comparatively slow.

Although our discussion of compilers has been extremely brief, compiler design is a very complex subject and requires much more space than is available in this book. For detailed information on compilers, refer to Calingaert [1] and Tremblay and Sorenson [8].

5-3 LINKING AND ADDRESS ADJUSTMENT

As indicated in the introduction to Sec. 5-1 (see Fig. 5-2), a program may consist of one unit or several units. It is the job of a second systems program, called a **linker** (or **linkage editor**), to join together the object units needed to form a program. A linker must bring in the required object units, decide how they are to be positioned relative to one another when they are loaded for execution, and then adjust the addresses according to this relative positioning.

The operation of a linker is illustrated in Fig. 5-15. Its inputs are the files containing the object units and its outputs are a **load unit** and a printed listing that provides information on how the object units have been linked together. The load unit contains the machine code for the entire program and other information that might be needed when the program is loaded for execution. As usual, execution of the linker would be initiated by giving a command that indicates the files that contain the object units, perhaps the names of the specific object units, and the load file. As an example, a linker command might be of the form

        LINKX16   *Object file (List)*, . . . , *Object file (List)*   *Load file*

where each *List* is a list of object unit names separated by commas.

Just as the assembler assumes each unit is to begin at 0000, the linker normally assumes the program is to begin at address 0000. Because only one of the object units can be positioned to begin at 0000 in the final program, the linker puts one unit at 0000 and puts the other units elsewhere. The addresses within these other units must be adjusted accordingly. The linker listing consists primarily of a **map** that indicates the assigned beginning addresses of the linked units.

Figure 5-16 shows three object units being linked to form a program. Unit 1 is assigned to begin at address 0000, unit 2 at address 1200, and unit 3 at address 1A00. The label X in unit 2 is assumed to have been associated with the address 04B8 by the assembler and so 04B8 was put in the second halfword of the instruction

        MOVB   X,R0

When the linker puts unit 2 at 1200, it must add 1200 to this halfword and the

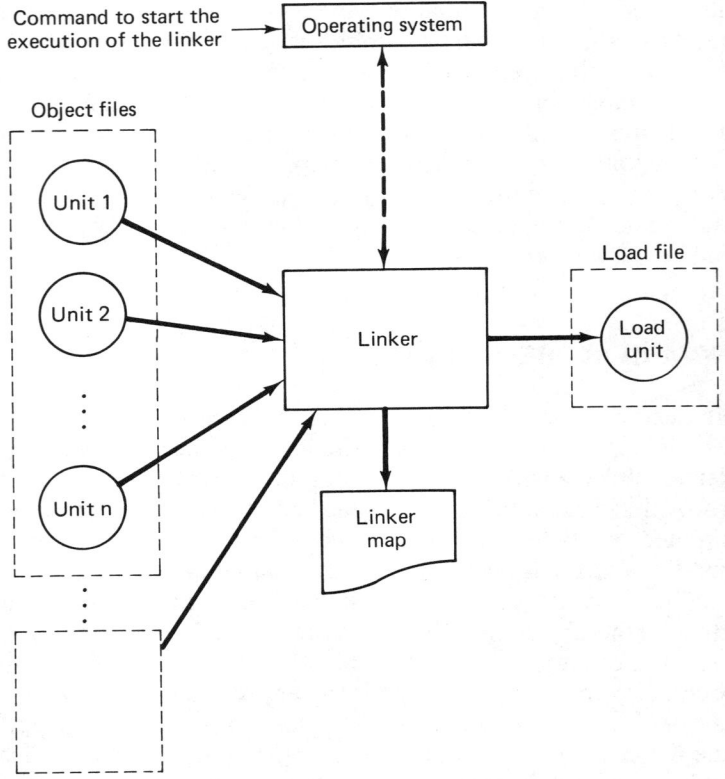

Figure 5-15 Execution of a linker.

other halfwords in unit 2 that contain addresses that originally corresponded to labels.

The number that is added to the addresses in a unit is called a **relocation factor**, and addresses that must be adjusted by adding a relocation factor are said to be **relocatable**. However, not all references are to addresses within the units; some are to specific locations in memory. For example,

                MOVH   2B84H,R0

would always move the contents of location 2B84 to R0, regardless of where this instruction is placed in memory. Such an address is said to be **absolute**. Any operand address that may change because of a label-address association is relocatable and any operand address that is purely a constant expression (which can be evaluated by the assembler) is absolute.

Several absolute and relocatable X16 operands are given in Fig. 5-17. These examples assume that the instructions and labels are within the same unit. As indicated by the first five examples in the figure, immediate operands or preas-

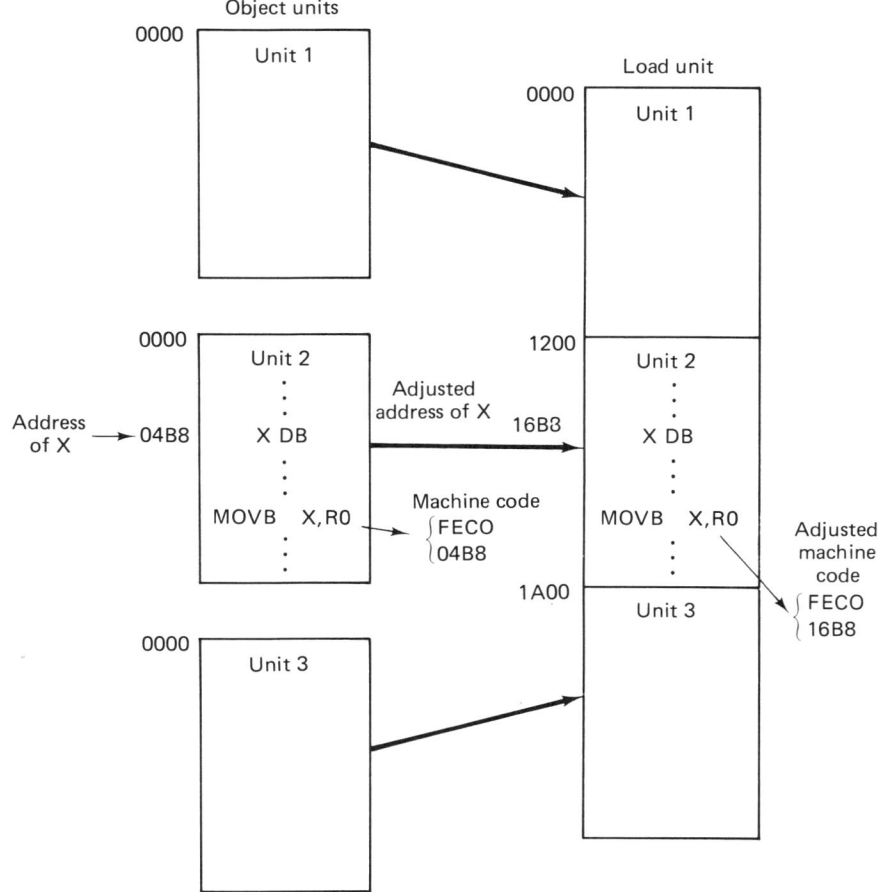

Figure 5-16 Linking object units and address adjustment.

signed values that are numeric or named constants do not require changing by the linker, but immediate operands that are labels require changes. Clearly, operands that involve only register identifiers, those that use register or register indirect addressing, do not need to be changed by the linker because the operand does not include a label. For direct addressing, if an operand is a constant, as in the eighth example, it need not be adjusted; but, if an operand is a label, as are the operands in the ninth example, then adjustment is necessary. Also the label that is preassigned by the directive in the tenth example must be adjusted. The operand in the eleventh example uses PC relative addressing and does not require changing. When a unit is executed, the PC always points to a location within the unit regardless of the position of the unit in memory. The displacement, which is the fixed difference between the PC and the location being referenced, is computed by the assembler. But relative addressing that uses any register other than the PC presents a problem. If the relative addressing is base addressing, as in the

Instruction or Directive*		Linker Adjustments
DB	(C)	No corrections.
MOVH	#C,R0	No corrections.
MOVH	#X,R0	Second halfword corrected.
BREQ	#X	Second halfword corrected.
ADDB	#15,Y	Third halfword corrected.
BREQ	[R2]	No corrections.
MOVH	[R0],[R1]+	No corrections.
XORH	57A2H,−[R3]	No corrections.
MOVB	X,Y	Second and third halfwords corrected.
DH	X	Halfword corrected.
BRUN	X	No corrections (PC relative addressing is used).
SUBH	X[R1],[R2]	Base addressing is intended - no corrections (assembler computes displacement).
SUBH	Y[R1],[R2]	Index addressing is intended - second halfword corrected.

* C is a constant and X and Y are labels defined within the source unit.

Figure 5-17 Examples of how operand fields are affected by the linker.

twelfth example, then the situation is the same as with the PC relative case because, when the instruction is encountered, the base register is presumed to point to a base location in the unit. On the other hand, for the index addressing used in the last example the *displacement* must be adjusted to point to a location in the unit. The assembler must be designed to differentiate between base and index addressing. (See Sec. 4-1-3.)

When joining units together, the linker must determine which locations to correct. This determination could be made by having the assembler put a list of these locations in the symbol table. An alternative could be to mark all points that require changes with a special bit combination. Then, the linker would simply scan the code for the special marks and add the relocation factor to the addresses and displacements following the markers. If all memory references in a unit are made using PC relative addressing, then all of the addressing responsibility would be given to the assembler and no linker adjustments would be required. Such units are said to consist of **position independent code**.

Until now we have not considered the possibility of one unit referencing a location in another unit. We have assumed that if a label appears in an operand but does not appear in the *Label* field of at least one statement, then it is undefined and an assembler error will result. But, it is often necessary for one unit to refer to labels in another unit. For example, if a main program is in one unit and one of its procedures, say a procedure that begins at COMPUTE, is in a different unit, then an instruction

                CALL   COMPUTE

in the main program would refer to the label COMPUTE, which is in the procedure unit. A problem arises because, during the assembly of the main program unit, the label COMPUTE is undefined and the assembler has no way of putting even a relative address into the second halfword of the call instruction. To solve this problem, a directive is needed at the beginning of the main program to warn the assembler of such labels. Although it is not necessary, some linkers also require that the unit containing the label give permission for other units to use the label. Typical directives for noting external labels and giving other units permission to use local labels are:

EXTERNAL Label, . . . ,Label

and

PUBLIC Label, . . . ,Label

Labels that are defined in units other than the one currently being assembled are called **external labels** and those defined in the current unit are called **internal** or **local labels**. Labels that appear in the external label directive are also put into the symbol table or perhaps, into a separate **external symbol table**. Because the operand fields corresponding to external labels cannot be filled by the assembler, they must be noted or marked and filled by the linker. If the linker is unable to match an external label, then the label will remain undefined and a linker error will occur.

5-4 LOADING AND ADDRESS ADJUSTMENT

After a program has been formed by linking its units together, it must be put into memory and readied for execution. This is done by a systems program called a **loader**. As shown in Fig. 5-18, when the proper command is given to the operating

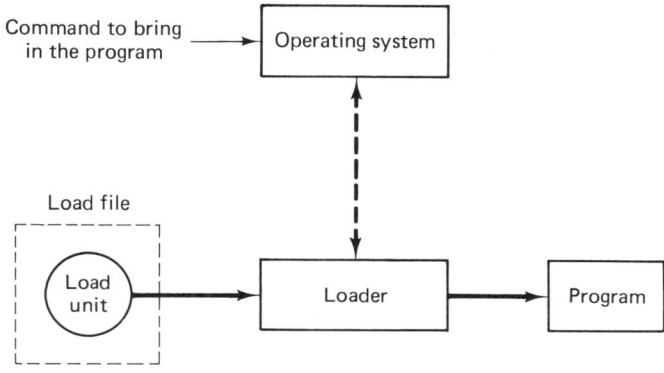

Figure 5-18 Loading a program for execution.

system, the operating system calls the loader to bring in the program and initiate its execution. A typical command for loading a program is:

Load file name   Location

where *Load file name* is the name of the file containing the program to be loaded and *Location* indicates where in memory the program is to be put. *Location* is optional and if it is not present the operating system will decide where the program is to be located.

Because the linker may assume a beginning address for the program that is different from the beginning address where the program is actually loaded, the loader may also need to adjust the addresses. Therefore, the symbol table information or address markers required to locate the operand fields that must be modified must also be included in the load unit. This information is used by the loader but is deleted from the final form of the machine language code. Execution begins when a branch is made to the program.

5-5 DESIGN REMARKS

The above description of how complete programs are created and executed was designed to emphasize the major steps and programs involved. The details differ from one system to the next and, in some cases, the steps may be combined (e.g., linking and loading may be done by one program, called a load and go program). Also, the commands for initiating the execution of the assembler, linker, and loader may be more complex. They may allow for a variety of defaults and options that make them more flexible.

An assembler must be designed to recognize and act upon directives as well as translate assembler language instructions into machine language instructions. The more important directives are to:

- Allocate memory space, assign labels, and preassign values to memory locations.
- Give names to constants.
- Delimit source units, programs, and procedures.
- Define macros.
- Provide information needed by the linking process.

Assemblers tend to be uncomplicated because of the one-to-one correspondence between assembler language statements and machine language instructions, but some assemblers are much more sophisticated than others and may include features for helping the programmer (e.g., a macro capability).

Compilers are much more complex than assemblers because their statements are oriented toward the way people speak and think, which may have little relationship to a computer's machine language. Like the use of abstract data types, a high-level language raises the level of abstraction and allows programmers to more easily conceptualize problems. Some compilers, such as those designed to teach students how to program, produce inefficient code but execute quickly. When teaching programming, it is more important that the compiling is fast because execution of the program is insignificant. Other compilers produce code that executes thousands or, perhaps, millions of times. In these cases it is important that the object code be made as efficient as possible because the time needed to execute the compiler is insignificant. Also, the amount of memory required by the compiler may be an important factor.

Programs comprised of more than one unit must be constructed with a linking process. This process must have a means of identifying and modifying relocatable addresses according to the order in which object units appear in the program. If linking and loading are separate processes, loading may also be required to modify relocatable addresses. The number of relocatable addresses can be reduced by using relative addressing. It is also possible to produce position-independent code that can be put anywhere in memory without being modified by the loader. Such code is often used for certain system program load units that must be quickly loaded into different areas of memory each time they are brought in to be executed (e.g., I/O drivers—see Chaps. 6 and 11). However, because the insertion of code or data between a referencing instruction and the instruction or data being referenced causes the displacement to change, code using relative addressing may be difficult to maintain. This case is particularly true if the referencing is between units.

REFERENCES

1. Calingaert, Peter, *Assemblers, Compilers, and Program Translation,* (Rockville, Maryland: Computer Science Press, 1979).
2. Barron, D. W., *Assemblers and Loaders,* 3rd ed. (New York: Elsevier North-Holland, Inc., 1978).
3. Tanenbaum, Andrew S., *Structured Computer Organization,* 2nd ed. (Englewood Cliffs, New Jersey: Prentice Hall, Inc., 1984).
4. Liu, Yu-cheng, and Glenn A. Gibson, *Microcomputer Systems: The 8086/8088 Family,* 2nd ed. (Englewood Cliffs, New Jersey: Prentice Hall, Inc., 1986).
5. Gibson, Glenn A., and James R. Young, *Introduction to Programming Using FORTRAN 77,* (Englewood Cliffs, New Jersey: Prentice Hall, Inc., 1982).
6. Cooper, Doug, and Michael Clancy, *Oh! Pascal!,* (New York: W. W. Norton and Company, 1982).
7. Hughes, Joan K., and Jay I. Michtom, *A Structured Approach To Programming,* (Englewood Cliffs, New Jersey: Prentice Hall, Inc., 1977).
8. Tremblay, Jean-Paul, and Paul G. Sorenson, *The Theory and Practice of Compiler Writing,* (New York: McGraw-Hill Publishing Company, 1985).

EXERCISES

1. Given the following X16 directives, illustrate how memory would be allocated and show the preassigned values—see Fig. 5-3(b):

M	EQU	6
X	DH	4
Y	DB	2(1,−1,M)
W	DB	('HELLO')
U	DD	2

2. Give a directive that assigns the:
    (a) Number 12DH to the name AUGEND.
    (b) String 'OVERFLOW' to the name WARNING.
3. Give the directives that should accompany the code in:
    (a) Fig. 4-19 (b) Fig. 4-27 (c) Fig. 4-35
4. Give a sequence of directives that preassigns the addresses associated with CASE1, CASE2, CASE3, and CASE4 to an array of halfwords beginning at CASE_TAB. Write a code sequence that uses these and other directives and implements the following Pascal statement:

    ```
    CASE NUMBER OF
        1:  A := 10;
        2:  B := 20;
        3:  C := 50;
        4:  D := 100;
    END;
    ```

    (Hint: Use the register indirect addressing mode for branching.)
5. Write a set of X16 code, including directives, that will search a 50-element byte array STRING for the character contained in ID and put a 1 in FLAG if a match is found and a 0 in FLAG if there is no match. Assume the addresses associated with STRING, ID, and FLAG are 2100, 2150, and 2151 and the first instruction is at 2200. Determine the corresponding machine language code. Use the format shown in Fig. 5-4.
6. Write a complete X16 program, including directives, that scans a 15-halfword array GRADES for negative integers and puts the number of negative integers found in the byte COUNT. Assign the number 15 to the name STUDENTS. Assume that the origin is initialized to 1000H and give the LC activity, statement lengths, and symbol table as in Fig. 5-7. Also, give the machine language code that would be output by the second pass of the assembler.
7. What happens when the same name or label occurs twice in a source unit? What is an undefined identifier?
8. Use the patterns in Fig. 5-12 to simulate the overall structure in Fig. 5-11.
9. Give X16 code that is equivalent to the following Pascal statements:

    (a) IF ((A+B>C+2) AND (C<0)) OR (5−C>B) THEN
            FLAG := 0
        ELSE
            FLAG := 1;

(b) WHILE (X>0) AND (X<10) DO X := 2*X+1;

(c) REPEAT
    X := X+1;
    Y := X*X;
UNTIL Y>=1000;

(d) CASE X OF
    1: Y := -1;
    2: Y := 2;
    3: Y := 0;
END;

10. Discuss the tradeoffs involved in compiler design.
11. Assuming all labels are defined within the unit being assembled, indicate the halfwords in the following instructions that may need to be adjusted by the linker:

    (a) MOVH   #1011B,R5

    (b) ANDB   [R1],[R2]

    (c) MOVH   X+2,[R0]+

    (d) MOVB   R1,Y-6

    (e) ADDH   A1,A2

    (f) SBCH   X[PC],Y

    (g) BRNE   #EXIT

    (h) BSGT   EXIT

    (i) BULE   [R1]

    (j) MOVH   X[R2],R0   (Assume base addressing)

6

Input/Output Programming

Until now, only transfers between processing and main memory elements have been considered. This chapter is concerned with transfers between I/O or mass storage elements and processing or main memory elements. More specifically, it is concerned with **I/O programming**, which is creating software to initiate and conduct these transfers. Although a mass storage element is a form of memory, it conducts transfers like an I/O element. This similarity justifies referring to the programming of these transfers as I/O programming.

The basic configuration assumed in this chapter is shown in Fig. 6-1. The I/O and mass storage elements are connected to the processing and main memory elements via the system bus and interfaces. The interfaces contain registers, called **I/O ports**, and the transfers to be discussed are between the I/O ports and the processing element's registers or the I/O ports and the memory locations. The I/O ports serve the following three purposes:

- Buffering data to and from the system bus.
- Holding control information that dictates how a transfer is to be conducted.
- Holding status information so that the processing element can monitor the activity of the interface and its associated I/O element.

Like memory locations, ports are accessed using addresses. These addresses may be in the same address space as the memory location addresses or in a separate space. If there are two address spaces, one is called the **memory space** and the other is called the **I/O space**. The two spaces are distinguished by a system bus Memory/IO ($M/\overline{IO}$) control line which is, for example, 1 when the transfer is with a memory location, and is otherwise 0. The instruction that is executed determines whether $M/\overline{IO}$ is 0 or 1. The instructions that cause $M/\overline{IO}$ to be 1 are

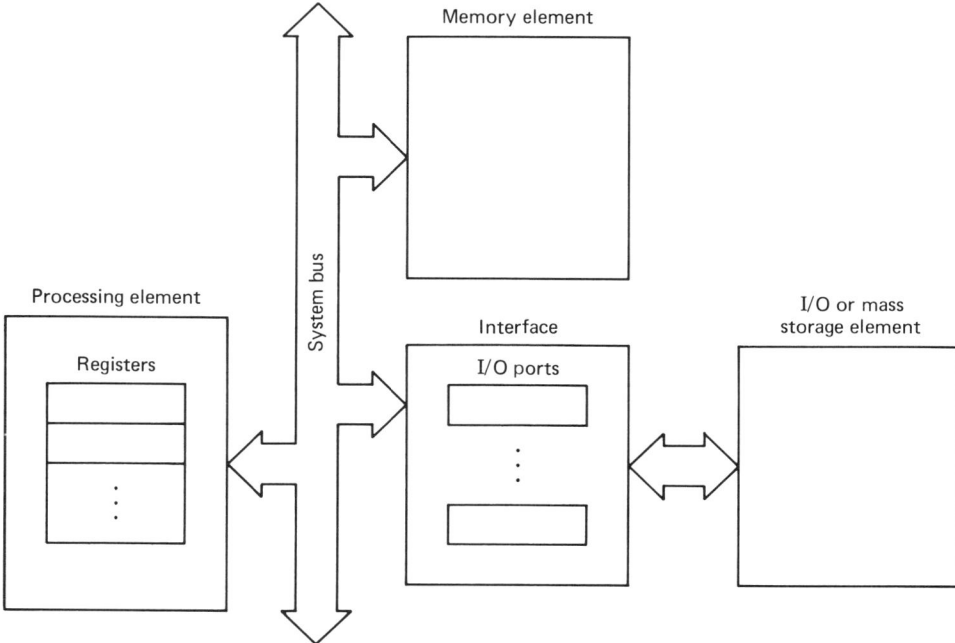

Figure 6-1 Configuration assumed in this chapter.

called **memory transfer instructions** and the other instructions that cause transfers external to the processing element are called **I/O instructions**. If there are two spaces, normally all of the I/O ports are in the I/O space and all of the memory locations are in the memory space. However, it will be shown later that this case does not always hold true.

I/O transfers may be classified according to the transfer rate or by the nature of the element with which the transfer is being made. With some elements, the time distribution of the transfer is aperiodic, and may be essentially random. An example of this type of element is a keyboard for which a transfer is made only when a key is struck. With other elements, once the transfer process begins, the transfers are periodic. For such elements, transfers are viewed as occurring in blocks and the transfer of all of the information in a block is called a **block transfer**. Examples of elements that perform block transfers are tape, disk, and diskette drives. Most elements that use block transfers are mass storage elements and, conversely, most mass storage elements perform block transfers. There are exceptions, such as analog to digital (A/D) and digital to analog (D/A) converters that may use block transfers when high data rates are essential or single datum transfers when the data rate is relatively low.

To perform an input or output, the processing element must be informed that there are data available in the interface or that the interface is ready to accept output. Then, a component capable of controlling the bus performs the transfer. If the processing element is to control the bus during the transfer, it could either interrogate the status of the interface to determine if the interface is ready to be involved in a transfer or the interface itself could notify the processing element when it is ready. In either case, instructions would then be used to carry out the transfer. If another component is to control the bus, when the processing element is informed of the interface's readiness it turns control of the bus over to the other component. Executing I/O by interrogating the interface, receiving notification from the interface, or passing control to another component corresponds to the three principal ways of performing I/O, which are:

- Programmed I/O
- Interrupt I/O
- Direct Memory Access (DMA)

Normally, the first two are associated with nonblock transfers and the third with block transfers. The first three sections of this chapter examine these programming approaches in order. The fourth section discusses the more important I/O elements.

6-1 PROGRAMMED I/O

Figure 6-2 shows a typical interface for making nonblock transfers. It includes a status register, a control register, a data-in buffer register, and a data-out buffer register. The buffer registers accommodate the timing differences between the

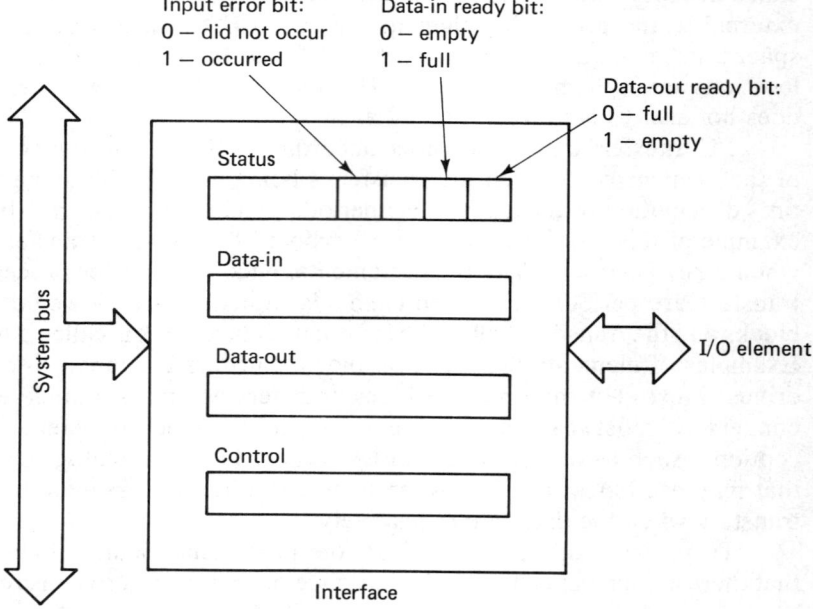

Figure 6-2 Typical interface for making nonblock transfers.

system bus and the I/O element connected to the interface. The data-in register passes data from the element to the bus and the data-out register buffers data in the opposite direction. The status register contains two bits that indicate the status of the buffer registers. When data are put into the data-in buffer, bit 1 is set to 1: when data are taken from this buffer, bit 1 is cleared to 0. For output, bit 0 is cleared to 0 or set to 1 when data are put into or taken from the data-out buffer, respectively. The status register also contains bits that indicate whether or not errors (such as parity errors) have occurred during a transfer between the interface and I/O element. In Fig. 6-2, bit 3 of the status register is set to 1 if a parity error was detected during the last input and is cleared to 0 if no parity error was detected.

Programmed I/O is performed by monitoring the status bits to determine when data are available for input or the data-out buffer can accept an output. A single input transfer could be conducted as flowcharted in Fig. 6-3. The data-in status flag is continuously tested until it becomes 1, indicating that the I/O element has put data into the input buffer. Then the data are brought in from the interface and the error bit is tested to determine if an error occurred during the transfer from the I/O element. If an error occurred, an error procedure is called. Output transfers could be similarly executed. The distinctive characteristic of pro-

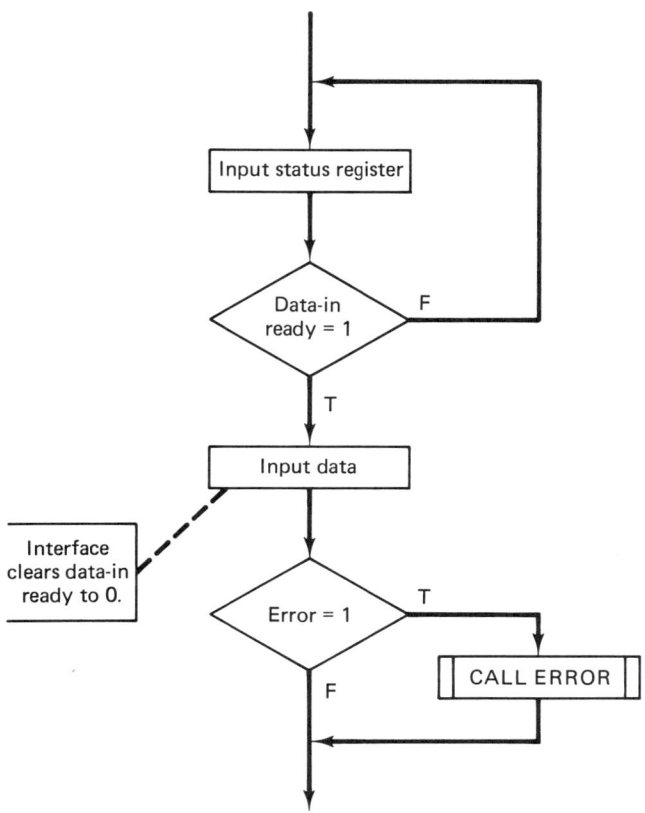

Figure 6-3 Flowchart of a programmed I/O input.

Sec. 6-1 Programmed I/O

grammed I/O is the use of status bits to determine when a transfer over the system bus is to be made.

Assume that the X16 has an M/$\overline{\text{IO}}$ line that is 1 when a transfer is initiated by a move instruction and is 0 when one of the following I/O instructions is executed:

INPB	PORT,DST	(PORT)→(DST)
INPH	PORT,DST	
OUTB	SRC,PORT	(SRC)→(PORT)
OUTH	SRC,PORT	

The machine language code for the in instruction is

1 1 1 X	0 0 0 0 1 1	Reg.	Mode

and for the out instruction is

1 1 1 X	Reg.	Mode	0 0 0 0 1 1

Recall from Sec. 4-1 that the fourth bit from the left indicates whether a byte or halfword is to be transferred. It is seen from Sec. 4-1 that the format of an in instruction is essentially the same as the move instruction that uses direct addressing to obtain the source, except that 000 appears in the source register field instead of 111. The destination mode can be any addressing mode except the immediate mode. For output, 000 appears in the destination register field and the source mode can be any mode. Neither an in nor out instruction affects the condition flags.

Figure 6-4(a) gives the X16 code for inputting n halfwords to a consecutive set of memory locations beginning at IODATA. This example assumes that:

- The port addresses of the status, data-in, and control registers are 0020, 0022, and 0026, respectively
- The status and control registers are one byte wide
- The buffer registers are one halfword wide
- The data-in ready bit is bit 1 of the status register.

The constant CONTROL is first put in the control register and then the address IODATA is put in R1 and n is taken from memory location COUNT and put into R5. (The contents of the control byte are not important at this point.) Next, a loop that implements the flowchart in Fig. 6-3 is entered and repeated n times.

A similar set of code for outputting the n halfwords beginning at IODATA is given in Fig. 6-5(b). It assumes that the address of the data-out register is 0024 and the data-out ready bit is bit 0 of the status register. It further assumes that the status register does not include an output error bit and therefore performs no output error checking. This omission is not unusual. Quite often the I/O element,

```
           CONTROL   EQU    00111011B        ;CONTROL REGISTER CONTENTS
           DIRDY     EQU    00000010B        ;READY AND ERROR BIT
           DORDY     EQU    00000001B        ;DEFINITIONS
           DIERR     EQU    00001000
           SREG      EQU    20H              ;I/O PORT ADDRESSES
           DIREG     EQU    22H
           DOREG     EQU    24H
           CREG      EQU    26H
                .
                .
                .
                     OUTB   #CONTROL,CREG    ;OUTPUT CONTROL BYTE
                     MOVH   #IODATA,R1       ;PUT DATA ADDR IN R1
                     MOVH   COUNT,R5         ;PUT COUNT IN R5
           INPUT     INPB   SREG,R0          ;LOOP UNTIL DATA IS
                     TSTB   #DIRDY,R0        ;AVAILABLE
                     BREQ   INPUT
                     INPH   DIREG,[R1]+      ;INPUT DATA
                     TSTB   #DIERR,R0        ;CALL ERROR IF AN
                     BREQ   NOERROR          ;INPUT ERROR HAS
                     CALL   ERROR            ;OCCURRED
           NOERROR   SUBH   #1,R5            ;DECREMENT COUNT
                     BRNE   INPUT            ;REPEAT UNTIL COUNT=0
                .
                .
                .
                            (a) Input



                .
                .
                .
                     MOVH   #IODATA,R1       ;PUT DATA ADDR IN R1
                     MOVH   COUNT,R5         ;PUT COUNT IN R5
                     OUTH   [R1]+,DOREG      ;OUTPUT FIRST DATUM
                     SUBH   #1,R5            ;DECREMENT COUNT
           OUTPUT    INPB   SREG,R0          ;LOOP UNTIL DATA-OUT
                     TSTB   #DORDY,R0        ;BUFFER IS READY
                     BREQ   OUTPUT
                     OUTH   [R1]+,DOREG      ;OUTPUT DATA
                     SUBH   #1,R5            ;DECREMENT COUNT
                     BRNE   OUTPUT           ;REPEAT UNTIL COUNT=0
                .
                .
                .
                            (b) Output
```

Figure 6-4 Inputting and outputting a set of data.

which must be responsible for checking for output errors, does not return an error signal. For example, a printer may have an indicator light that shows when an error has occurred, but would not return an error signal to the interface because the processing element has no way of correcting the error after it has already been printed.

It is significant that the first halfword is output without testing the ready bit. Whatever is in the data-out buffer will be replaced, but it is presumed that the data in the buffer are no longer important. Suppose that, for some reason, the I/O element had not taken the last datum in the previous set of transfers from the data-out buffer. Then, if the first transfer of the present set of transfers had to wait for the data-out buffer to become ready, it may have to wait indefinitely.

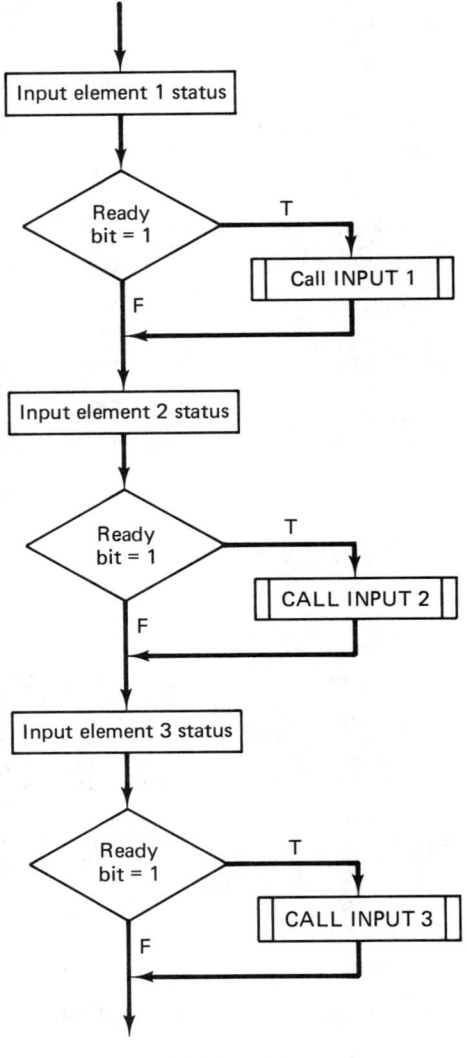

(a) Flowchart   **Figure 6-5** Polling example.

This phenomenon is not a problem when inputting, but it may be necessary to check the I/O element's status to ascertain that it is turned on and functioning properly before beginning to input.

Now, consider how several I/O elements could be managed. Suppose that a program is to check periodically the status of m input elements, numbered 1 through m, and input from the elements that have data available. The program is to test the data-in ready bit of each element in turn and, if needed, input the data. This technique for servicing multiple elements is called **polling**. A flowchart and instruction sequence for polling three I/O elements is given in Fig. 6-5. This se-

```
        DIRDY      EQU     00000010B       ;READY BIT DEFINITION
        SREG1      EQU     10H             ;STATUS REGISTER ADDRESSES
        SREG2      EQU     20H
        SREG3      EQU     30H
                    .
                    .
                    .
        ELEMENT1   INPB    SREG1,R0        ;TEST STATUS OF
                   TSTB    #DIRDY,R0       ;ELEMENT 1
                   BREQ    ELEMENT2
                   CALL    INPUT1          ;INPUT FROM ELEMENT 1
        ELEMENT2   INPB    SREG2,R0        ;TEST STATUS OF
                   TSTB    #DIRDY,R0       ;ELEMENT 2
                   BREQ    ELEMENT3
                   CALL    INPUT2          ;INPUT FROM ELEMENT 2
        ELEMENT3   INPB    SREG3,R0        ;TEST STATUS OF
                   TSTB    #DIRDY,R0       ;ELEMENT 3
                   BREQ    CONTINUE
                   CALL    INPUT3          ;INPUT FROM ELEMENT 3
        CONTINUE    .
                    .
                    .
```

(b) Code

Figure 6-5 Continued

quence includes no parameter passing to the procedures. If parameter passing is required it could be done as described in Chap. 4. The entire sequence could be put in a loop if more than one byte is to be input from one or more of the elements.

6-2 INTERRUPT I/O

If a processing element can do no other work while it is waiting for data to be input or output, then programmed I/O is a satisfactory method for performing I/O. However, it may be possible, from a computational standpoint, to continue processing while waiting for input data to become available or output data to be taken from the interface by the I/O element. If this is so, then the idle loops that continually check the status bits would be very inefficient. These loops tie up the processing element and prevent it from doing other work for indeterminate intervals of time. Instead of forcing the processing element to repeatedly poll the interface for its status, what is needed is a means by which the interface can notify the processing element that it needs to be serviced. The notification is called an **interrupt** and the facilities that provide the notification are called **interrupt facilities**. Although there are three types of interrupts—external, internal, and software interrupts—only external interrupts, which are used for I/O programming, are considered in this chapter. **Internal interrupts**, which are caused by events internal to the processing element, and **software interrupts**, which are initiated by special instructions, are considered in Chaps. 10 and 11. **External interrupts** are due to signals that originate from outside the processing element. A facility for supervising external interrupts includes:

- One or more interfaces capable of sending **interrupt requests** when they require servicing.

- A processing element capable of responding to interrupt requests.
- Lines in the system bus for relaying the requests and, perhaps, returning **interrupt acknowledgments** to the interfaces.

6-2-1 The Interrupt Process

When a processing element accepts an interrupt request it enters an **interrupt sequence**, which consists of the initial actions taken to service the requesting interface. These actions do not result from the execution of instructions, but are carried out automatically as soon as the request is recognized. Among other things, the interrupt sequence causes the processing element to branch to an **interrupt routine** and it is this routine that actually services the interface (e.g., inputs or outputs a datum). An interrupt routine is like a procedure, except that it is not entered because a procedure call has been executed but is entered in response to an interrupt request. Figure 6-6 illustrates the time relationship between a program and an interrupt routine. At each request the processing element switches from the program to the interrupt routine. Upon completion of the routine, a return is made back to the program. The return is similar to a procedure return because it returns to the instruction that immediately follows the last instruction executed before the branch to the routine. Note that no time is saved in servicing the interface. In fact, the interrupt sequence followed by the interrupt routine and the subsequent return takes more time than the inline code of programmed I/O. The savings is due to the elimination of the idle loops that may be executed over and over and do nothing but monitor the status.

There are some analogies between procedure calls and interrupt sequences, but there are also some important differences. As with a procedure call, an interrupt sequence must store the return address. Normally, the return address is pushed onto a stack and, for most designs, it is the same stack used by call instructions.

The PSW is almost always saved following or during a procedure call, but saving the PSW is not always necessary. Whether a procedure's changing of the

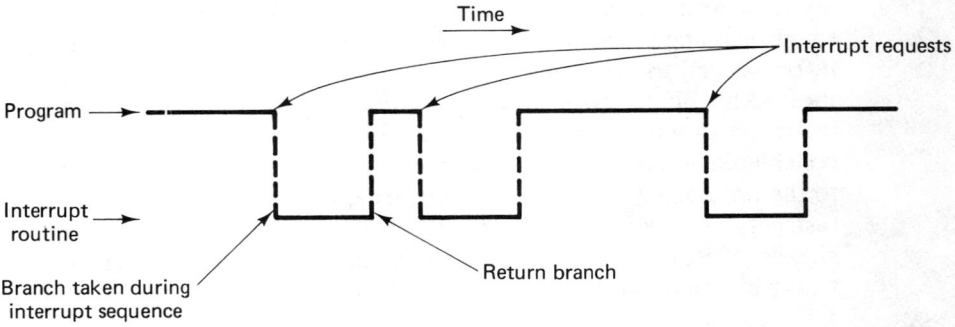

Figure 6-6 Alternating usage of a processing element by a program and an interrupt routine.

PSW will have adverse effects depends on the location of the call instruction. When an interrupt request is accepted it is mandatory that the PSW be saved because the point at which the interrupt occurs is unpredictable. External interrupt requests result from external events that have no time relationship to the program. Although the PSW could be saved by the beginning of the interrupt routine, many processing elements save it during the interrupt sequence and some even save the PSW and then load new contents into the PSW. The working registers that are used by the interrupt routine must also be saved and restored, but these tasks are usually done by the interrupt routine. If the return address is stored in the same way by both a procedure call and an interrupt sequence and no other registers are saved by the interrupt sequence, then the same return instruction can be used to both conclude an interrupt routine and return from a procedure. However, if there are any differences in the order or number of items stored, then there must be correspondingly different return instructions for interrupt and procedure returns.

The indeterminate nature of interrupts also makes it impossible to pass parameters. This implies that, for the program and interrupt routine to be able to communicate, there must be some memory locations that are known to both. Whether these locations are considered part of the program or part of the interrupt routine is not important. What is essential is that both the routine and the program are aware of the addresses of these locations.

Although a procedure's branch address is always determined by the call instruction, how the branch address of an interrupt routine is obtained depends on the design of the interrupt facility. The simplest design is one for which all external interrupts use the same branch address. This implies there is only one central interrupt routine, but it may call procedures to administer the various interfaces. The central routine would have to determine, perhaps by polling, which interface made the request and then call the appropriate procedure.

An approach that allows each interface to have its own branch address is one that has the interface provide the branch address during an interrupt sequence. If the address for each interface is unique, the need for polling would be eliminated. An even more flexible approach is to have the interface supply the beginning address of an area of memory called an **interrupt vector**. Among other information, the interrupt vector would contain the branch address. As shown in Fig. 6-7, after retrieving the address of the interrupt vector from the interface, the interrupt sequence would get the branch address from the interrupt vector. In addition to the branch address, other information related to the interrupt could be input from the interrupt vector. Most often this other information would be new contents for the PSW. Either of these approaches requires the processing element to return an interrupt acknowledge signal to the interface to prompt the interface to return the branch or interrupt vector address. The branch or interrupt vector address would be semipermanently determined by the interface's circuitry.

Interrupts also involve issues that are not related to procedure calls, issues such as when a request can be accepted and how to respond to multiple requests. It would be very difficult to design a processing element that would allow an external interrupt to be recognized in the middle of an instruction. This recognition

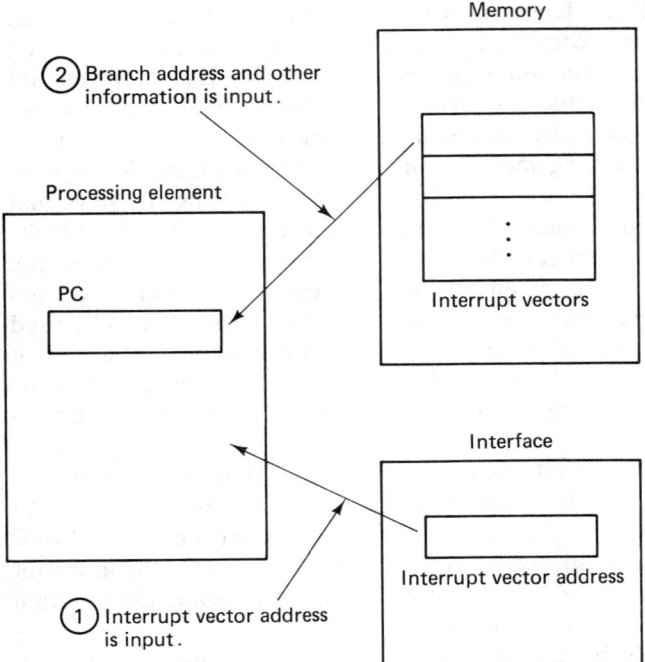

Figure 6-7 Interrupt sequence activity while retrieving the branch address in a facility that uses interrupt vectors.

would require the entire state of the processing element to be stored and then restored upon returning from the interrupt routine. Therefore, an external interrupt request is recognized only at the conclusion of the execution of an instruction. Once the execution of an instruction begins, it must be completed. For the same reason, an interrupt should not be accepted during an interrupt sequence, and it is sometimes undesirable to recognize an interrupt until at least some of an interrupt routine has been executed. Although an interrupt routine may be interrupted, the beginning of the routine may include critical processing that must be finished before a second interrupt is permitted. This suggests that there should be a programmable means of disabling and enabling the interrupt facility.

6-2-2 Interrupt Masking

Most processing elements accommodate two types of external interrupts, **nonmaskable interrupts**, which cannot be disabled, and maskable interrupts. For **maskable interrupts**, the processing element includes an interrupt bit that controls whether or not they are to be recognized. One of the actions taken by the interrupt sequence is to clear this bit, thereby disabling the maskable interrupts. An interrupt enable instruction is then used to set the interrupt bit once the critical processing at the beginning of the interrupt routine has been completed. Because reenabling the interrupts is frequently the last action taken by an interrupt routine, some return from interrupt instructions implicitly set the interrupt bit, thus eliminating the need for an explicit interrupt enable instruction. However, there is a general need for the programming ability to enable and disable interrupts. Thus, it is always necessary to have explicit instructions for setting and clearing the interrupt bit. The X16 interrupt bit, which is bit 7 in the PSW, can be set or cleared by the set interrupt field instruction (see Sec. 4-2-7).

Sometimes during processing that must satisfy strict timing requirements, stopping the processing to service an interface cannot be tolerated. In such situations, the critical sequence of code could be preceded by a disable interrupt instruction and followed by an enable interrupt instruction.

Nonmaskable interrupts are used sparingly. Normally, they are reserved for interfaces that must be responded to immediately. Typically, only one interface can make a nonmaskable request.

6-2-3 Interrupt Example

Before considering multiple interrupts, let us introduce a possible interrupt facility for the X16 and consider how it reacts to single requests. It is first assumed that the X16 uses interrupt vectors and responses to a request by outputting an interrupt acknowledgment. The interrupt sequence performs the following steps in order:

1. Pushes the PSW onto the stack.
2. Pushes the PC onto the stack.
3. Outputs an acknowledge.
4. Receives a 5-bit interrupt vector address with the two low-order bits set to 0.
5. Uses the interrupt vector address to input the new PSW contents.
6. Adds 2 to the address in Step 5 and uses the new address to input the branch address.

Because the interrupt bit is considered part of the PSW, whether interrupts are disabled depends on the new contents of the PSW brought in during Step 5. Steps 4, 5, and 6 show that the X16 uses interrupt vectors that occupy two consecutive halfwords each and that are located in the lower part of memory. The 16-bit address of an interrupt vector is formed by letting the 11 higher-order bits and two low-order bits be 0s. There can be up to eight vectors and each vector contains new contents for the PSW and PC. The organization of the lower part of memory is shown in Fig. 6-8.

The interrupt routine return instruction must differ from the procedure return instruction because an interrupt sequence pushes both the PSW and PC and a procedure call pushes only the PC. The mnemonic for this instruction is IRET. The instruction has no explicit operands, but implicitly pops the PC and PSW from the stack. The restoration of the original PSW by the interrupt return determines the value of the interrupt bit. (For maskable interrupts, this bit must have been set or the interrupt would not have been accepted.)

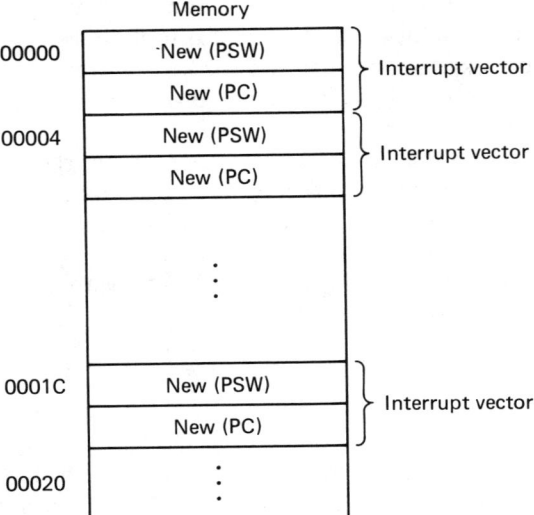

Figure 6-8 X16's interrupt vector organization.

A representative program and associated interrupt routine are shown in Fig. 6-9. When the program is ready to input from the interface corresponding to the interrupt routine, it performs some initialization and then enters a set of code that can be interrupted whenever the interface has input available. Each time an interrupt occurs, an interrupt sequence causes a branch to the interrupt routine that

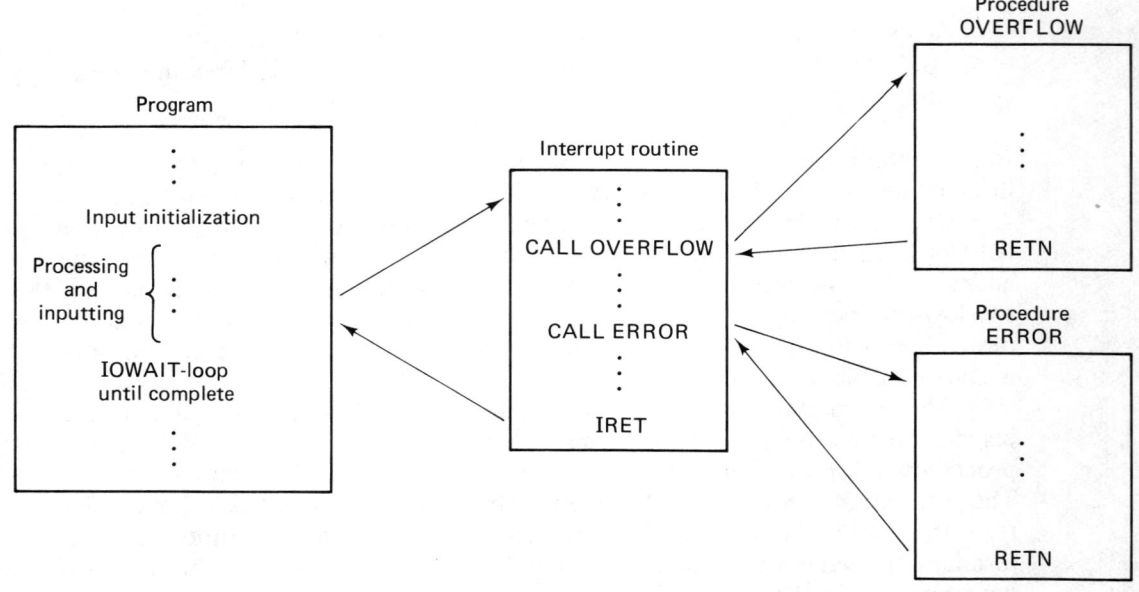

Figure 6-9 Interrupt I/O example.

inputs the data. The input is to an array in memory and, if the amount of input exceeds the size of the array, the interrupt routine calls the procedure OVERFLOW. If an input error is detected the procedure ERROR is called. It is assumed that the code following the IOWAIT loop needs to process the data and therefore must wait until all of the data have been input. If the input has not been completed before the IOWAIT loop is encountered, the program cycles in this loop until the reserved memory area has been filled.

Figure 6-10 gives the initialization and IOWAIT loop portions of the program and interrupt routine. The port addresses and data-in ready and error bits are assumed to be the same as in the programmed I/O example in Fig. 6-4. The beginning address of the memory array that is to receive the data is INDATA and the number of halfwords to be brought in is denoted by the constant AREA-

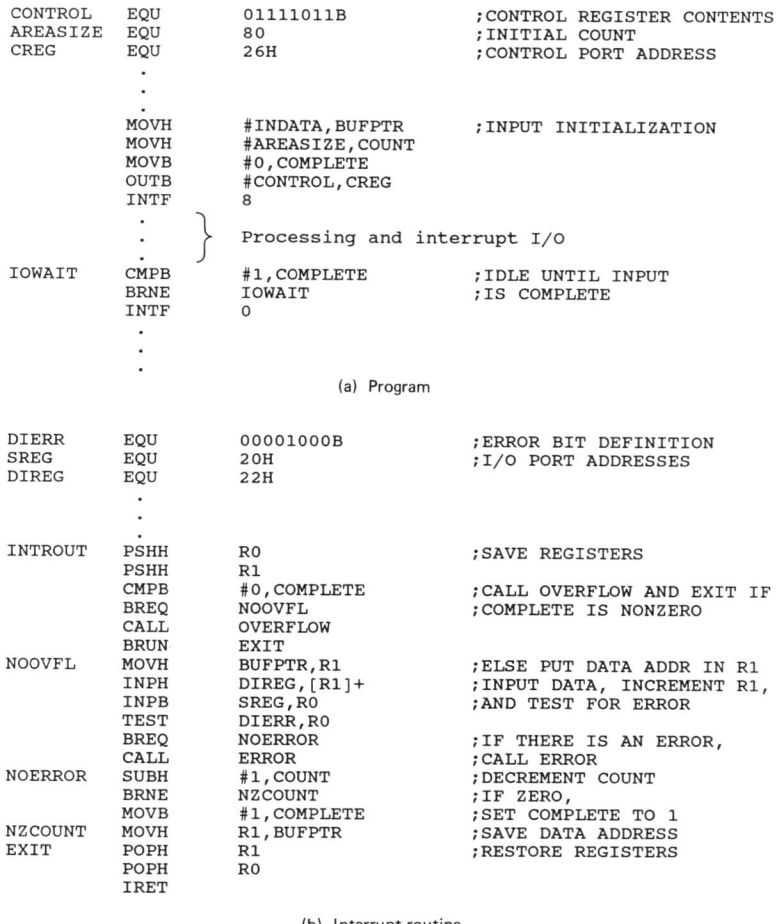

Figure 6-10 Interrupt I/O routine.

SIZE. The location COMPLETE indicates when the input of AREASIZE halfwords has been completed. Initialization consists of putting the address of INDATA into BUFPTR, AREASIZE into COUNT, 0 into COMPLETE, CONTROL into the interface's control register, and 8 into the interrupt field of the PSW (to enable interrupts). The IOWAIT loop does nothing but continually check COMPLETE until it becomes 1.

The interrupt routine first pushes the registers that it uses, R0 and R1, onto the stack and then checks the value of COMPLETE. If COMPLETE is not 0 then an interrupt has occurred after all of the intended data have been input and the procedure OVERFLOW is called. After returning from OVERFLOW, which may output a warning message or take some corrective action, a branch is made to EXIT without inputting the data. (Normally, the processing program would reach the IOWAIT loop before COMPLETE becomes 1, and interrupts would be disabled before too much data are input.) If COMPLETE is 0, the data are input to the location pointed to by BUFPTR and BUFPTR is incremented to point to the next halfword. An error check is made and, if there is an error, the procedure ERROR is called. Whether or not there is an error, the COUNT is decremented and, if its new value is 0, COMPLETE is set to 1. After the contents of R0 and R1 are restored, a return is executed that restores the original value of the PSW, including the interrupt bit, and puts the return address in the PC.

6-2-4 Interrupt Management

The control registers of most interfaces also include an interrupt enable bit. This bit controls whether the interface is to make interrupt requests. In the examples in both Figs. 6-4 and 6-10 the interrupt enable bit was assumed to be Bit 6. For the programmed I/O example in Fig. 6-4 it was cleared to 0 and for the interrupt I/O example it was set to 1. Together the interrupt bit in the PSW and the interrupt enable bit in the interface's control register provide a programmer with the means to either prevent interrupt requests from being made or allowing interrupt requests but controlling when they are recognized. The number and meanings of the other bits in the control register depend on the type of interface and are defined by the design of the interface.

If a system includes only one interface capable of making interrupt requests, then interrupts could be handled by simply sending request signals to the processing element and having the interrupt sequence branch to the routine for servicing the interface. If more than one such interface exists but only one can make a request at any given time, then all of the interfaces could share one interrupt request line and one interrupt acknowledge line. Upon receipt of a request, the interrupt sequence would return an acknowledge signal and the requesting interface would respond with an interrupt routine or vector address. Because there is only one requesting interface, only one interface would respond to the acknowledge signal. However, interrupts may be due to events that can occur at any time, events that occur regardless of whether interrupts are enabled or disabled or whether the processing element has just begun executing an instruction. Therefore, because I/O element interfaces act individually, it cannot be guaranteed that no more than one request will be pending at a given time. A practical interrupt facility must allow multiple requests to be made while an instruction is being executed or interrupts are disabled and must retain the requests until they are acted on.

One solution to this problem would be to use a request line that can be made active by any interface connected to it and then have some type of polling built into the interrupt sequence or programmed into a central interrupt routine. A primitive type of polling is to have one acknowledge line that passes through the interfaces in such a way that the first requesting interface receiving the signal blocks it from passing on to subsequent interfaces. The interface that intercepts the acknowledge responds to the acknowledge with the identifying information expected by the interrupt sequence. This type of polling is called **daisy chaining** and is considered further in Chap. 8. The disadvantage of any type of polling is that it is relatively slow. In general, interrupts should be responded to as quickly as possible.

Another solution would be to use pairs of request/acknowledge lines so that the interrupt sequence could identify the requesting line and respond on the corresponding acknowledge line. But, if individual request lines are used, a better approach would be to include in the processing element's bus control logic an **interrupt management facility** as shown in Fig. 6-11. This facility could be charged with retaining all requests and providing the interrupt sequences with the proper responses, thus eliminating the need for any acknowledge lines.

The interrupt management facility could be designed to be simple or complex depending on the degree of versatility desired. In addition to retaining requests until they are satisfied and supplying necessary identifying information, interrupt management may involve enabling/disabling and prioritizing requests. The management facility may permit requests to be disabled selectively, assigned to priority levels, and/or prioritized within levels. The levels may be used to selectively screen requests.

For example, suppose that instead of inputting from a single request line and replying via an acknowledge line, the X16 includes an interrupt management facility with eight interrupt request lines numbered 0 through 7. The interrupt level of the processing element is the binary value of the interrupt level bits, Bits 6-4 of the PSW, and the X16 responds only to those request lines whose numbers are greater than or equal to its interrupt level. By setting the interrupt level in the PSW to, say, 4 and the interrupt bit to 1, an interrupt may be accepted, but only if the request is received on one of the Lines 4 through 7. Requests on Lines 0 through 3 are retained until the X16's level is lowered to their levels. Clearly, a high priority interface should be connected to a request line with a high level. This allows lower priority requests to be blocked while permitting equal or higher priority requests to be recognized.

The X16 interrupt management facility is shown in Fig. 6-12(a). Requests are latched into a bank of edge-triggered flip-flops upon their arrival. The outputs of these flip-flops are fed into a priority encoder that encodes the number of the highest priority request into a 3-bit binary number that becomes Bits 4-2 of the interrupt vector address (all other bits are 0s). If the highest priority request has

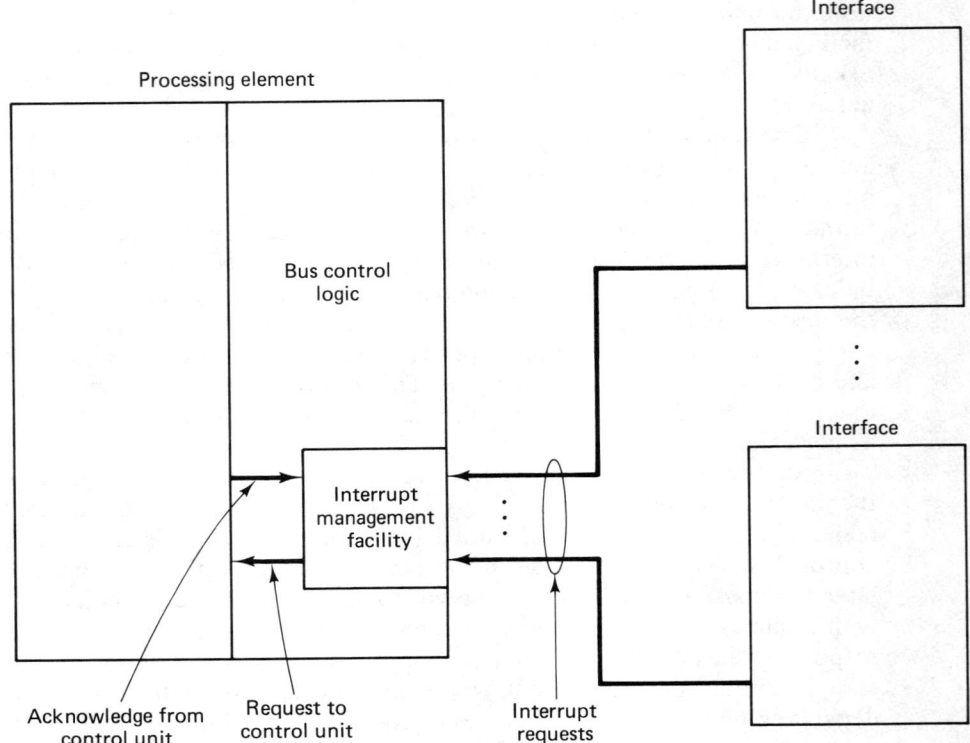

Figure 6-11 Use of an interrupt management facility.

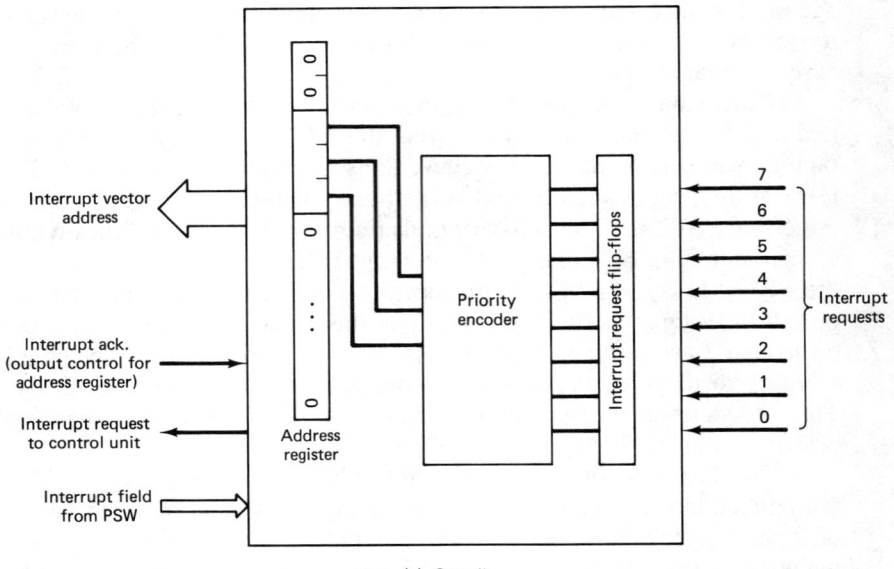

(a) Overall

Figure 6-12 X16's interrupt management facility.

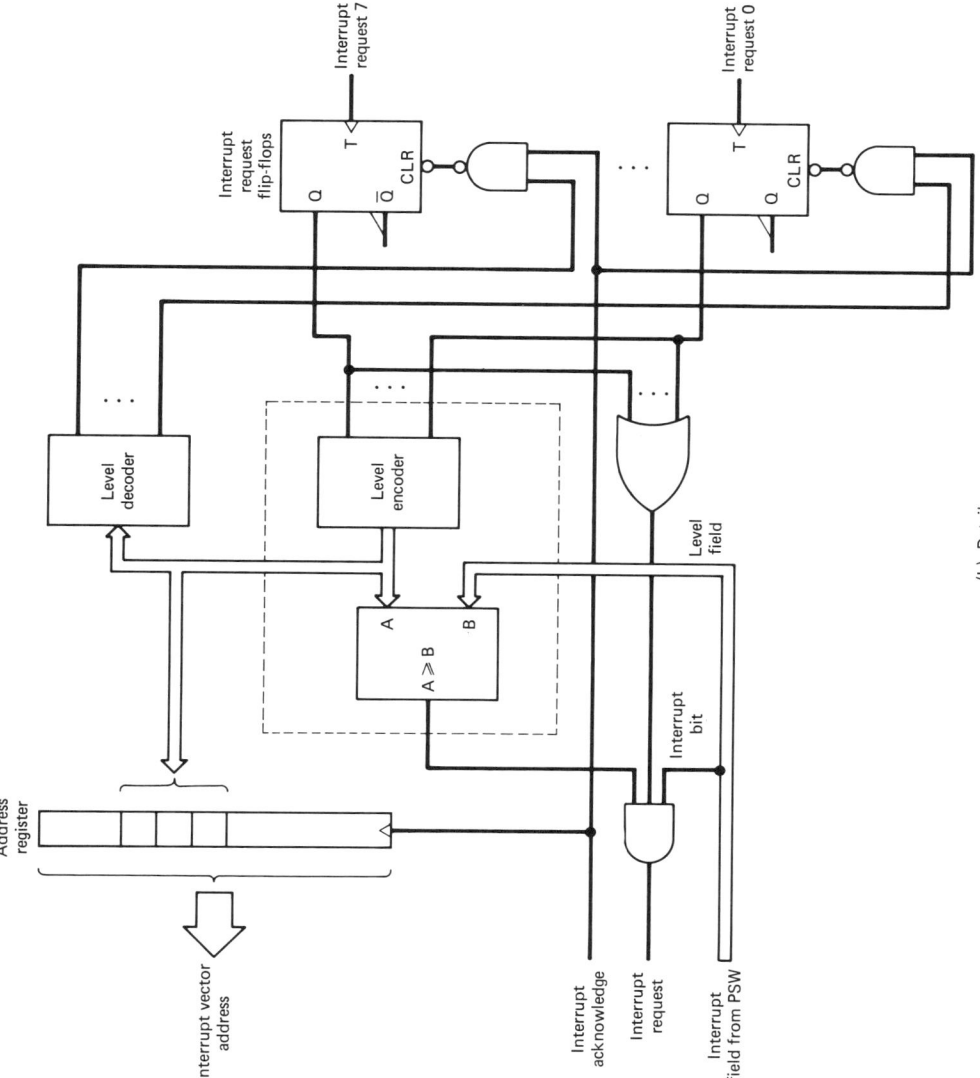

Figure 6-12 Continued

(b) Detail

a level greater than or equal to that of the processor and the PSW's interrupt bit is set, then an interrupt request is sent to the control unit. At the completion of the current instruction, the interrupt sequence is begun and an interrupt vector address output signal, which serves as an interrupt acknowledge, is returned. This signal latches the priority encoder output into the address register, enables the output of the address register, and clears the flip-flop corresponding to the request.

Figure 6-12(b) shows the interrupt management logic in greater detail. The priority decoder outputs clear the highest priority request when the interrupt acknowledge signal is returned. The only priority decoder output that is 1 is the output corresponding to the highest priority request and it is NANDed with the interrupt acknowledge signal to clear the interrupt request flip-flop with the highest priority.

Because (PSW) are replaced from the PSW portion of the interrupt vector during the interrupt sequence, the interrupt bit and level values at the time the interrupt routine is entered are determined by whatever was last put into the interrupt vector. Normally, the interrupt vectors would be set by an initialization routine when the computer is turned on and would not be changed.

Figure 6-13 demonstrates the effects of level on interrupt requests. Initially interrupts are disabled with an INTF 7H instruction. While the interrupts are disabled, requests at levels 0, 4, and 5 arrive. When the interrupts are enabled and the level is set at 3 by the INTF BH instruction, Request 5 (which is the highest priority request and has a priority greater than or equal to 3) is recognized. During the interrupt sequence, the interrupt field is set to 0 (disabling all interrupts) and Request 5 is cleared. Then, while Interrupt Routine 5 is executing, the interrupts are enabled and the level is set to 2 by INTF AH, thus allowing Request 4 to be recognized. Again the interrupt sequence disables the interrupts and clears the request.

Interrupt Routine 4 enables interrupts and lowers the level to 1, but still Request 0 cannot be accepted. The return to Interrupt Routine 5 resets the level to 2. Because there are no pending requests with a level of 2 or greater, Interrupt Routine 5 executes until the level is set to 0 by INTF 8H. At this time, Request 0 is accepted and the interrupt sequence disables interrupts and clears Request 0. During the execution of Interrupt Routine 0, a request arrives on Request 2 but is not recognized because interrupts are disabled. However, the return enables interrupts and Request 2 is immediately accepted and cleared. No more requests occur until after the return to Interrupt Routine 5 followed by the return to Program. The return to Program raises the level to 3 so that the subsequent Request 2 is not accepted until the level is lowered to 1 by the INTF 9H instruction in Program. (Although this example assumes that the interrupt fields in all new PSWs in the interrupt vectors disable interrupts and set the level to 0, this case may not always be true.)

There is a potentially serious problem with the design of the X16's interrupt management facility and that is the possibility of two or three very busy, high priority interfaces effectively blocking lower priority interfaces from being served. This phenomenon is referred to as **starvation** and can happen even if the level is kept at 0. Starvation is a problem in any priority-based system where there is

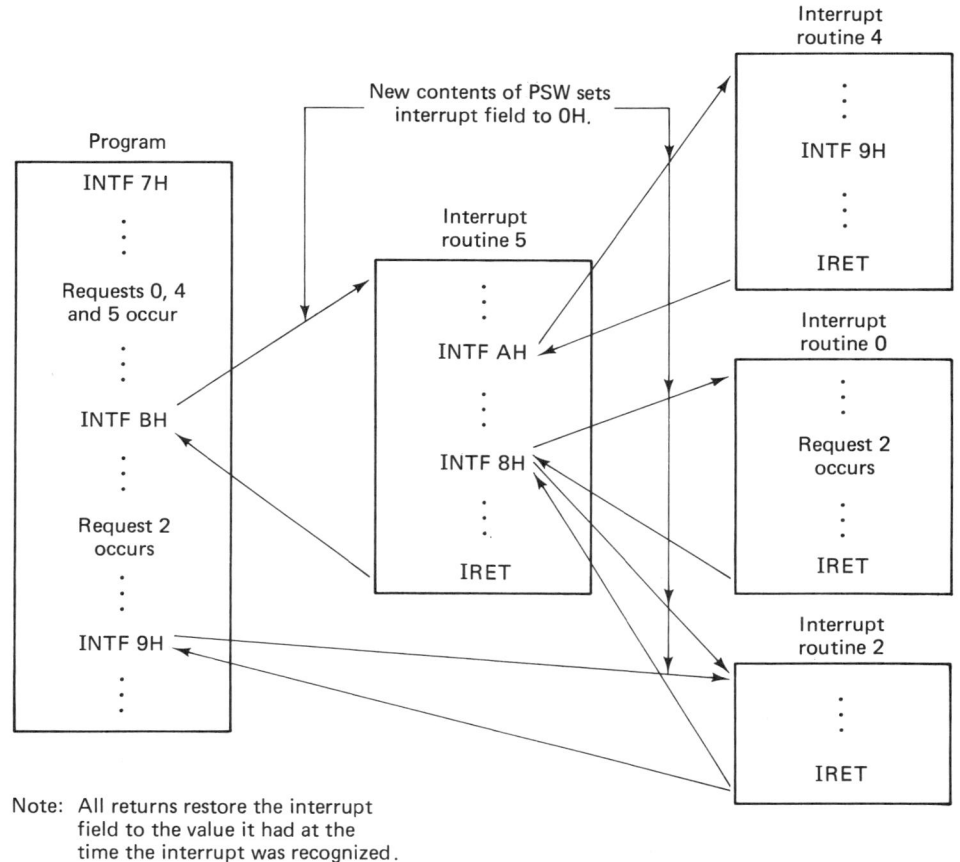

Figure 6-13 Example demonstrating the effects of level.

competition for limited resources and some elements in the system are constantly favored over other elements. It is also a problem in multiprocessor system design, which is considered in Chap. 12, and other situations that involve contention for available resources. One remedy is to not assign permanent priorities, but to allow them to change periodically. Instead of request line 7 always having the highest priority, the interrupt management facility could be designed so that the highest priority rotates from Line 7 to Line 6 to . . . to Line 0 to Line 7 and so on. The priorities could change each time a request is accepted.

In general, the use of interrupt I/O assumes that the average time between interrupts is much greater than the average time it takes to execute an interrupt routine. As the time for executing a routine approaches the average time between interrupts, input data may be lost because new data may arrive from the input element before the processing element has been able to take the previous data. Also, output may become erratic and not meet the timing requirements of an output element. If interrupts from all sources occur with relatively low frequency, then even bursts of interrupts can be processed in a timely fashion.

6-3 DIRECT MEMORY ACCESS

Programmed and interrupt I/O share the common problem of requiring one instruction to perform each transfer and other instructions to prepare for the transfer. For programmed I/O, only a few instructions are required, but, for interrupt I/O, an interrupt sequence and an entire interrupt routine must be executed. Using interrupt I/O, even a moderately fast processing element would take 20 µS to complete an interrupt routine and this amount of time would limit the transfer rate to 50 thousand transfers per second. Programmed I/O may increase this limit to 200 thousand, but some mass storage elements, such as disk drives, require transfer rates of over 1 million transfers per second. Also, such elements would not be able to tolerate the indeterminate delays caused by multiple interrupt requests arriving at essentially the same time.

Direct memory access (DMA) is achieved when an interface or logic associated with an interface is able to take control of the system bus and make a data transfer directly to or from memory. In this chapter the configuration shown in Fig. 6-14 is considered. The logic that controls the system bus during a DMA

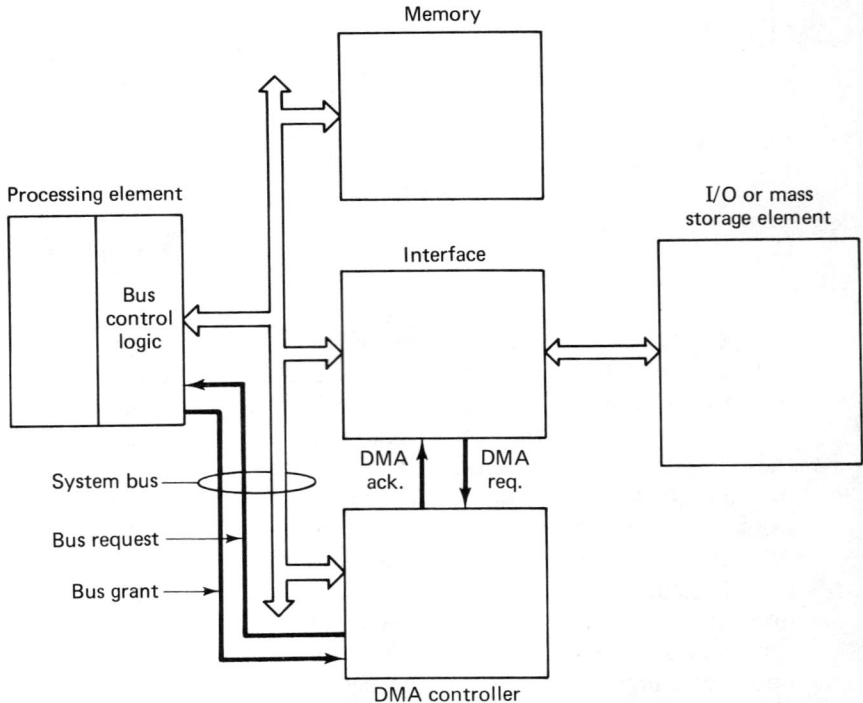

Figure 6-14 DMA configuration assumed in this section.

transfer is closely associated with the interface and is called a **DMA controller**. The processing element normally has control of the bus, but the DMA controller can gain control by sending a **bus request** to the processing element. After receiving the bus request and completing the current bus transfer (if one is in progress), the processing element turns supervision of the bus over to the DMA controller by sending the controller a **bus grant** signal. After the grant is received, the controller supervises a direct transfer between the memory and the interface. The act of taking control of the bus and performing a DMA transfer is called **cycle stealing**. If it takes 200nS to perform a bus transfer and memory access, then it would take at most 400nS to steal a cycle and execute the transfer. (The worst case would occur when a bus transfer has just started at the time the bus request is received by the processing element.) Therefore, the transfer rate could be as high as 2.5 million transfers per second.

6-3-1 Programming Block Transfers

As shown in Fig. 6-15, a DMA controller typically contains its own status and control registers and, in addition, a count register and memory address register. Like interface registers, these registers are I/O ports. A block transfer involves three distinct stages. They are the:

1. Initialization state that sets up the interface and DMA controller registers.

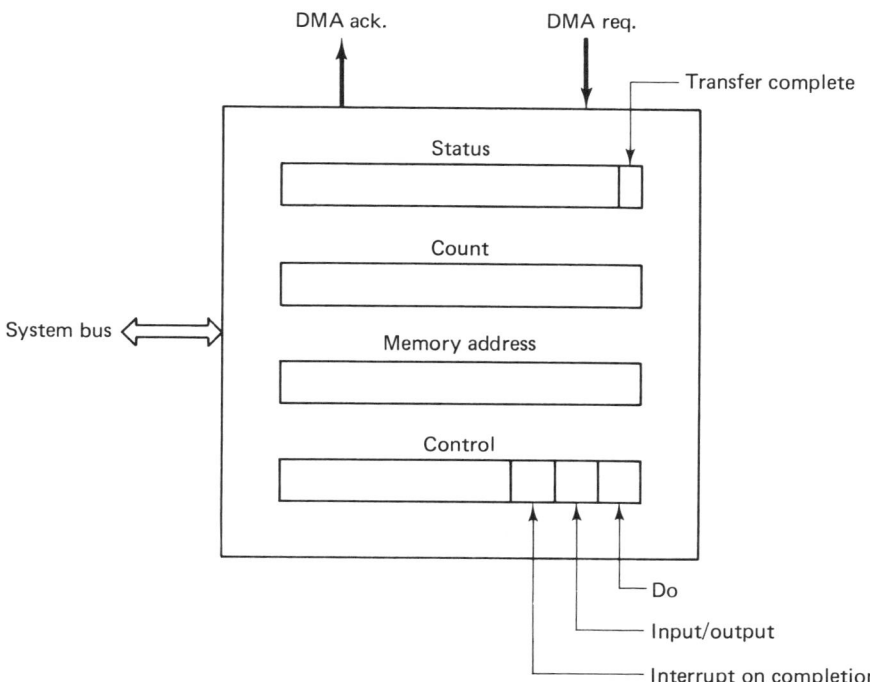

Figure 6-15 Major components of a DMA controller.

2. **Transfer state** that includes cycle stealing and carrying out the transfers while other processing may be taking place.
3. **Completion stage** that does error checking and other termination chores.

The initialization stage includes setting the:

1. Count register to the number of transfers to be made.
2. Memory address register to the beginning address of the memory array involved in the transfer.
3. Control register to the proper state so that the DMA controller can conduct the transfer.

One of the bits in the control register is the **Do** bit. This bit and a DMA enable bit in the interface must be set at the end of the initialization stage.

An input transfer proceeds as follows:

1. When the interface receives a datum from the input element it requests the DMA controller to conduct a transfer.
2. The DMA controller sends a bus request to the processing element.
3. The processing element completes the present system bus transfer and returns a bus grant to the DMA controller.
4. The DMA controller sends a DMA acknowledge to the interface (which causes the interface to drop its DMA request) and performs the transfer from the interface to the memory location whose address is in the memory address register.
5. The DMA controller increments the memory address register by the length of the datum (by 1 for a byte, 2 for a halfword, etc.) and decrements the count.
6. The DMA controller drops the bus request, thereby returning control of the bus to the processing element.
7. If the count is 0, the Transfer Complete bit in the status register is set and, if the Interrupt On Completion bit in the control register is set, an interrupt request is sent to the processing element. If the count is nonzero, steps 1 through 6 are repeated.

Output is similarly handled except the data flow direction is reversed.

Some DMA controllers include in their control registers a bit that controls whether or not Step 6 is performed. If Step 6 is not performed, the controller retains the bus until the count reaches 0 before dropping the request. Because the controller would not have to wait for grants between transfers, the overall transfer time would be the approximate time required for a single bus transfer and the transfer rate could be approximately doubled. If 200nS are needed for a transfer, then as many as 5 M transfers per second could be made. The cost of allowing the DMA controller to keep the bus until the entire block has been transferred is not letting the processing element continue its work (i.e., not allowing processing to be intermixed with data transfers), but a high transfer rate would allow little time for processing anyway. Having the DMA controller retain the bus between transfers would be done only if the I/O or mass storage element required the higher transfer rate.

If the Interrupt On Completion bit is not set, a program must test the Transfer Complete status bit to determine if the entire block transfer is complete. As with programmed I/O, the program could enter a loop that would test the Transfer Complete bit over and over until it is set. This loop would be placed so that as much processing as possible is done before the loop is encountered. Normally, the loop would be placed immediately before the code that must use the data in the block being input or the code that must rely on the block having been output. Once the loop has been entered, the processing element will be kept busy idling in the loop and no useful processing can be done (but transfers can continue to be made).

After it has been determined that the block transfer is finished, the completion stage is entered. The completion stage consists of the execution of a **completion routine**. What this routine does depends on the type of block transfer. One task that is common to completion routines is error checking. Unlike nonblock transfers, for which error bits are set and may be examined after each transfer, the error bits in the status register of a block transfer interface indicate whether or not an error has occurred during the transfer of the block as a whole. If a parity bit is appended to each datum, then the parity error bit in the status register would indicate only that at least one parity error has occurred. The datum or data that caused the error could not be identified. In addition to, or in place of, having a parity bit associated with each datum, it is common to have redundant information at the end of the block that can be used for error checking. This information is referred to as **block check characters (BCCs)**. How BCCs are generated will be discussed in Chap. 8. As with parity errors, the completion routine is responsible for checking the interface status bits set by errors in the BCCs and taking the appropriate action.

The format of a typical block is shown in Fig. 6-16. The header may contain identifying and descriptive information (e.g., the length of the block) that may be used by the completion routine. The block may also include a termination character and/or flags that mark its beginning and end. Which of these fields and characters are included in the block and what their formats are depends on the I/O or mass storage element.

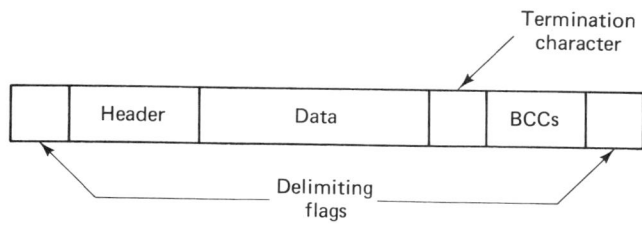

Figure 6-16 Typical block format.

6-3-2 Double and Triple Buffering

As an example, suppose that a program is needed to input and process a specified number of blocks. A flowchart of such a program is given in Fig. 6-17. It assumes the program has allocated two memory arrays, BUFFER1 and BUFFER2, and uses two locations, INPUTPTR and PROCPTR, to hold the beginning addresses of these arrays. The array that is currently being input to is pointed to by INPUTPTR and the array being processed is pointed to by PROCPTR. After the input element's interface and the DMA controller have been initialized, the addresses of BUFFER1 and BUFFER2 are put into INPUTPTR and PROCPTR, respectively; the number of blocks is put into BLKCOUNT; and 0 is put into FIRSTBLK. The program then enters a loop that continually inputs and processes the blocks until BLKCOUNT has decremented to 0, at which time the last block is processed and the program terminates. Within the loop, an input is initiated and, except for the first time through the loop, a call is made to the procedure PROCESS that processes the block of data that was last input. Upon returning from PROCESS, the program monitors the Transfer Complete bit and when it becomes set, the completion routine COMPLETE is called. Then, the addresses in INPUTPTR and PROCPTR are exchanged so that the arrays used for inputting and processing are interchanged.

The scheme used in this example is referred to as **double buffering**. When using double buffering, processing cannot begin until a block has been completely input. If the inputting of blocks is continuous (e.g., input from an A/D converter), the time it takes to process a block must be less than the time it takes to input the block. Otherwise, some input may be missed because a new block cannot be input until the processing is complete. If simultaneous inputting, processing, and outputting are required, then three arrays could be used to perform **triple buffering** by inputting to one array, processing it while inputting to the second array, outputting from the first array while processing the second array, and inputting to the third array. The three uses (inputting, processing, and outputting) of the three arrays could be rotated until the inputting is complete (see Exercise 13). For triple buffering, processing of a block cannot begin until the block has been completely input and outputting of a block cannot begin until the block has been completely processed.

6-3-3 Multichannel Controllers

If a single bus system has more than one DMA controller, many of the same problems arise as when a system contains more than one interface capable of making interrupt requests. The problems associated with priority apply as well as the physical design problem of deciding on the number of bus request and grant lines and exactly how these lines will be used. If two or more controllers make bus requests during a bus transfer, the processing element must somehow select which controller will be granted the bus for the next transfer. Preferably, the method for making this selection would avoid starvation of lower priority controllers.

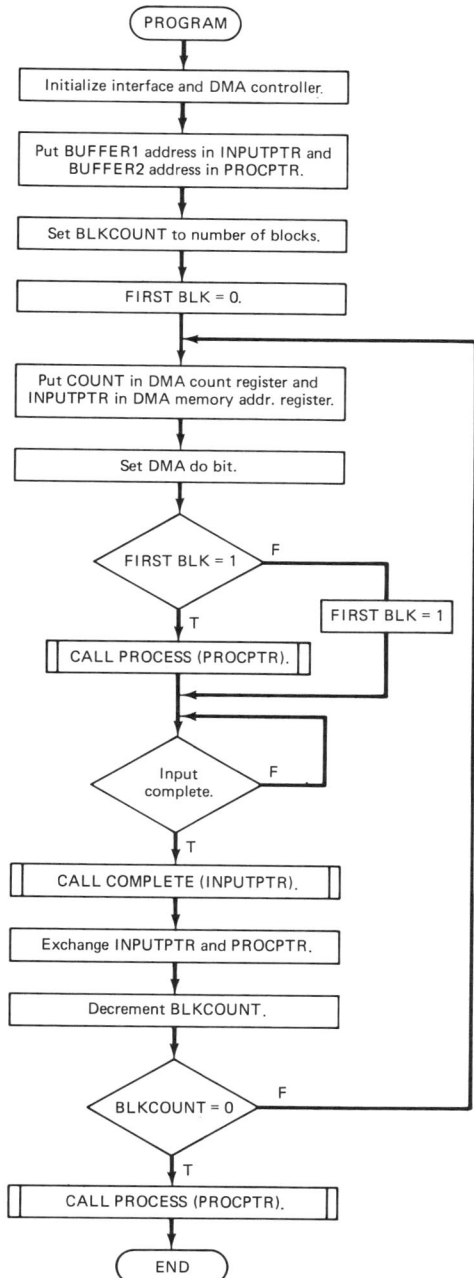

Figure 6-17 Double-buffering example.

Sec. 6-3 Direct Memory Access

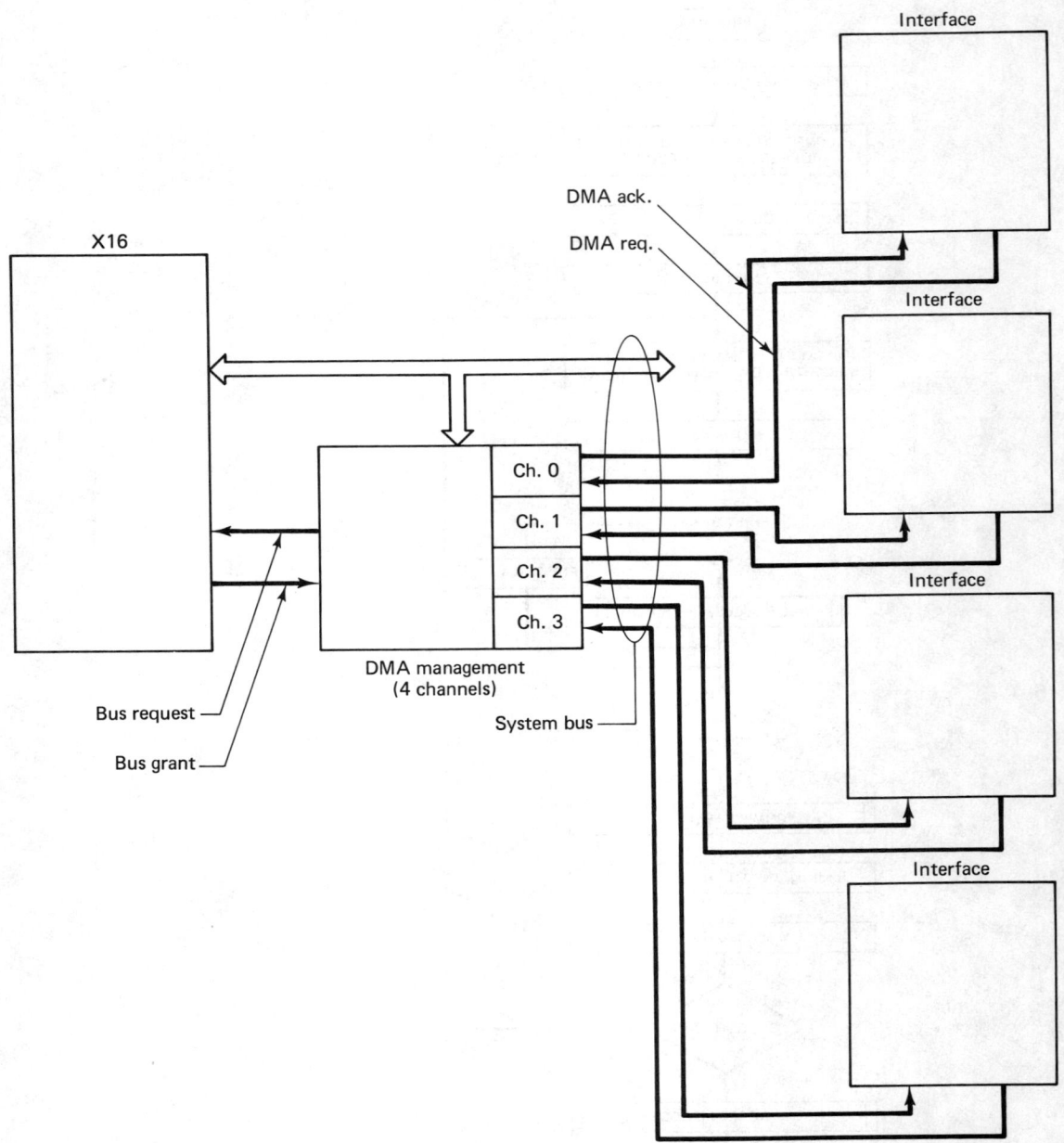

Figure 6-18 Use of a DMA management facility with an X16.

Physically, DMA controllers may be grouped together and not be adjacent to their corresponding interfaces. If this is the case, the controller may be located with and considered part of the processing element's bus control logic. Some microprocessors have DMA capability built into their ICs, thereby avoiding external communication with DMA registers. This internal design also avoids bus request and grant lines, but the DMA request and acknowledge lines must still extend from the DMA controllers, which are now part of the bus control logic, to the interfaces.

When DMA controllers are grouped together they are sometimes referred to as **DMA channels**. A group of channels would have associated logic for resolving questions of priority and other control functions that are central to all channels (e.g., sending requests and receiving grants). DMA channels and their surrounding logic are sometimes designed to be programmed to perform functions other than simple transfers. For example, a channel may be able to monitor the data it is inputting, detect special characters (such as end of file characters), and automatically cease its operation before the count has decremented to 0. Also, it may be capable of being programmed to input several blocks without being reinitialized between blocks.

The X16 is assumed to include only one bus request and one bus grant line. Therefore, if more than one interface requires DMA control, logic external to the X16 must be added to the system to manage bus requests. An X16 configuration for handling four DMA channels is shown in Fig. 6-18. The count, memory address, and control registers could be output to using out instructions and status registers could be examined using in instructions.

6-4 I/O ELEMENTS

Although I/O and mass storage elements are programmed similarly and use similar interfaces, only I/O elements are considered here. Mass storage elements are discussed in Chap. 9. There are numerous types of I/O elements and it would be impractical to consider a wide variety of them here. Therefore, this section examines only a few of the more important and broadly-used elements.

6-4-1 Keyboards and Monitors

The most familiar means of entering information into a computer is via a typewriter-like keyboard, which allows a person to enter information directly. When a key is pressed, the keyboard's electronics send a coded character (normally an ASCII coded character) to the interface where it is put into the data-in buffer register. Because even a fast typist cannot enter more than 10 characters per second, keyboards are considered slow input elements (e.g., a typical computer would execute more than 100 thousand instructions in the 100 mS it takes to enter a character). Therefore, either programmed I/O or interrupt I/O software would be used to carry out the input task.

The usual means of outputting a keyboard's input is a video monitor. There are many different types of video monitors, but the most popular are those that use cathode ray tubes (CRTs). An output to a terminal's monitor consists of the processing element outputting a character to the data-out buffer register in the interface and the monitor's electronics taking the character from the interface, converting it to the required electrical signals, and forming the display on the screen. A typical output transfer rate is 9600 characters per second. This rate is much higher than the input rate from a keyboard, but can still be easily accomplished using programmed or interrupt I/O. A keyboard and monitor may share the same interface.

Let us assume the configuration shown in Fig. 6-19. A program that uses programmed I/O for inputting a line of up to 80 characters plus a return character from a keyboard and echoing the characters back to the monitor as they arrive is given in Fig. 6-20. It is assumed that the control register has already been set and the port addresses and status bits have been defined as given in the previous examples (see Fig. 6-4). The data-in and data-out registers are one-byte registers and hold ASCII coded characters. The characters sent to the interface from the keyboard include a parity bit that causes bit 3 of the interface's status register to be set when a parity error has occurred. After putting the initial count of 81 into R5 and the beginning address of the array LINE into R1, the loop for inputting and echoing the characters is entered. In this loop, the input is checked for a parity error and procedure ERROR is called if an error is detected. Procedure ERROR is also called if the 81st character input is not a RETURN character (ASCII code 0D). Before calling ERROR, a code value of 1 is put into register R4 if there has been a parity error or a code value of 2 is put into R4 if there are too many characters in the line. The code is a parameter that allows ERROR to

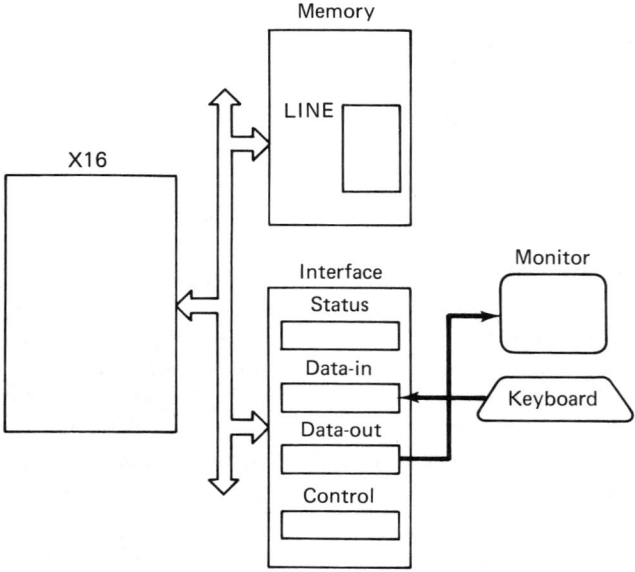

Figure 6-19 Connecting a keyboard/monitor to a computer.

```
                    .
                    .
                    .
                MOVB    #81,R5          ;SET CHAR COUNT TO 81
                MOVH    #LINE,R1        ;PUT LINE ADDRESS IN R1
    START       SUBB    #1,R5
    INPUT       INPB    SREG,R0         ;IDLE UNTIL INPUT
                TSTB    #DIRDY,R0       ;IS AVAILABLE
                BREQ    INPUT
                TSTB    #DIERR,R0       ;TEST FOR PARITY ERROR
                BREQ    NOERROR         ;IF THERE IS AN ERROR
                MOVB    #1,R4           ;SET ERROR CODE TO 1
                CALL    ERROR           ;CALL ERROR AND
                BRUN    EXIT            ;THEN EXIT
    NOERROR     INPB    DIREG,R2        ;ELSE INPUT DATA
                CMPH    #0,R5           ;IF 81ST CHARACTER
                BRNE    NOOVFL          ;AND IT IS NOT
                CMPB    #0DH,R2         ;A RETURN
                BREQ    NOOVFL
                MOVB    #2,R4           ;SET ERROR CODE TO 2
                CALL    ERROR           ;AND CALL ERROR
                BRUN    EXIT            ;THEN EXIT
    NOOVFL      MOVB    R2,[R1]+        ;ELSE STORE CHARACTER
                OUTB    R2,DOREG        ;AND OUTPUT
                CMPB    #0DH,R2         ;IF CHARACTER IS NOT A
                BRNE    START           ;RETURN, INPUT NEXT CHAR
    EXIT        .
                .
                .
```

Figure 6-20 Code for inputting from a keyboard and echoing to a monitor.

determine the type of error. After returning from ERROR, the code performing the input is exited. If there is no parity error or line overflow, then the character is stored in the array LINE and output to the monitor. If the character is a RETURN, inputting is terminated; otherwise, another character is input.

Most CRT monitors are of the raster scan type shown in Fig. 6-21. An electron beam whose intensity and direction are controlled by the electron gun continually scans the screen using a horizontal pattern of lines. As scanning takes place the intensity is varied and an image is formed on the screen. The color of the image is a property of phosphors and by using triplets of red, green, and blue (RGB) phosphors, a multicolored image can be produced. The clarity of the image

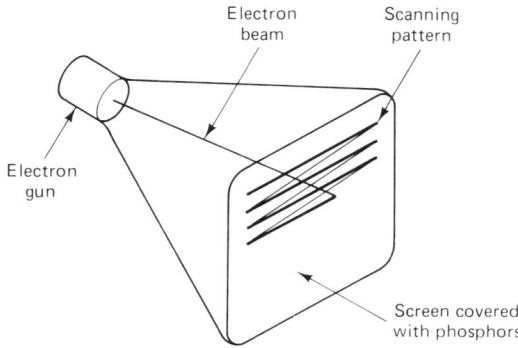

Figure 6-21 Raster scan monitor.

is determined by the number of lines and the analog bandwidth of the circuitry that drives the electron gun. The higher the bandwidth, the faster the electron gun can adjust the intensity, thereby producing a sharper image. A typical bandwidth, which permits the image to be updated 60 times per second, is 20 MHz. This value is approximately twice the bandwidth of most television sets.

The circuitry that controls the electron gun, called the **display generator**, views the screen as being divided into rows and columns of small areas, called **pixels**, and forms an image by either illuminating or not illuminating individual pixels. For multicolor monitors, the pixels include RGB triplets. A 20 MHz display generator is capable of forming 60 images, or **frames**, per second, each having 300 lines of 640 pixels (a total of 192,000 pixels).

A display generator gets the information it needs from a display memory contained in the terminal. If only characters are to be displayed, this memory would hold the coded forms of the characters. The display generator would group the pixels together to form rows and columns of pixel blocks and each block would be used to form a character. For example, if there are 300 lines of 640 pixels each and the pixels are grouped into 12 by 8 blocks, then a frame would consist of 25 rows of 80 characters each and the display memory would need a capacity of 2000 characters.

A monitor driven by a display generator and memory capable of controlling individual pixels, as opposed to blocks of pixels, is referred to as a **graphics monitor** because it can display detailed drawings and pictures as well as characters. Clearly, the display memory for a graphics monitor must include at least one bit per pixel or, if the monitor is multicolored, several bits per pixel. The display memory capacity for a graphics monitor would typically range from 20,000 to 500,000 bytes. Not only does the display memory need to be from 10 to 100 times as large as that of a monitor that displays only characters, but supplying the display memory at a sufficiently high rate is also a problem. For this reason, a graphics monitor is not connected to a computer through an I/O type of interface, but is interfaced through a memory element that is connected directly to the system bus as shown in Fig. 6-22. This allows data to be transferred to the display

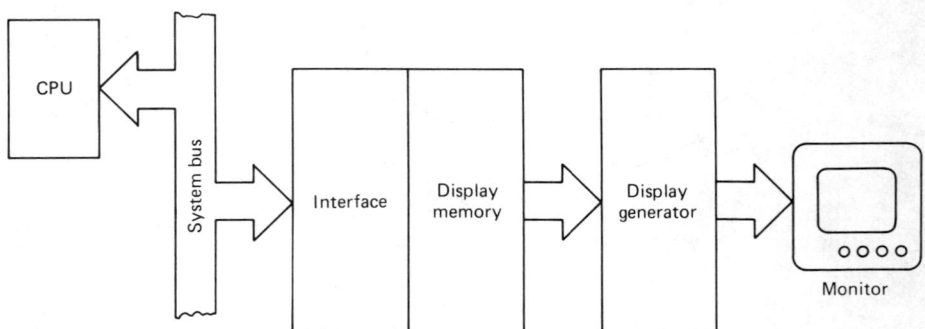

Figure 6-22 Graphics monitor configuration.

circuitry at a rate primarily determined by the memory access time, a rate which may be several million bytes per second.

There are also CRT graphics monitors that are not based on the raster scan technique. The electron beam does not scan the screen in a fixed pattern, but draws the image on the screen. The display circuitry is limited to directing the electron beam to draw straight lines between pairs of points on the screen. Therefore, all images are made up of straight line segments. The segments can be very short, thereby allowing curves to be approximated very closely. Using straight line segments to form images is called **vector graphics**. The advantages of vector graphics are the clarity of the lines, which are true lines and not constructed of dots (i.e., pixels), and the reduction in the amount of information needed to store the image. Instead of requiring values to be stored for all pixels, only the endpoints of the line segments must be stored. The size of the display memory is on the same order as that of a character display monitor and consequently, does not need to be directly connected to the system bus as a memory module. It may be communicated with via an I/O type of interface. There are even vector graphics monitors that do not need a display memory because they can maintain the image on the screen without repeatedly refreshing the screen. These monitors are constructed using **storage CRTs**.

The disadvantages of vector graphics are that the images must be formed from straight line segments, it may take several seconds to form a complex image, and coloring is difficult to achieve and is seldom available. For storage CRTs, an image cannot be changed; it must be erased and completely redrawn. This makes it impossible to achieve the illusion of motion.

6-4-2 Printers and Plotters

Printers and plotters serve the same purpose as monitors, but provide the visual display on hard copy. Because printers and plotters do not retain the information they output, they do not need display memories (although they may include a small buffer memory) and are connected to the computer via I/O type interfaces.

As with monitors, some printers can print only characters and others can output graphics. One way of classifying printers that print characters is by the number of characters they can print in a single action. A line printer prints an entire line at one time and a character printer prints only a character or part of a character at a time. A typical line printer can output over 1200 lines per minute, and each line consists of up to 132 characters. This feature provides a potential output rate of over 2600 characters per second as compared to 30 to 300 characters per second for character printers. A line printer includes some form of buffer memory to hold one line of characters. Because line printers tend to work with blocks of data (lines of print) and some line printers may output several thousand characters per second, a line printer interface is sometimes associated with a DMA controller. A character printer rarely uses a DMA controller.

There are three basic types of character printers: the **daisywheel printers** that use print mechanisms similar to those used by typewriters, **dot matrix printers** that form characters from dots, and **laser printers** that first imprint character images on a photographic drum and then transfer the pattern onto paper in the same manner as a copying machine. Daisywheel printers are known for their clarity, but are slow because of the mechanical motion involved in their print mechanisms. The print mechanism for a dot matrix printer is a print head containing a set of solenoid-driven wires that print dots by impacting a ribbon. The print head traverses the paper horizontally, printing the dots that form the characters as it moves. Then the paper is advanced a line and the action is repeated. Dot matrix printers are inexpensive, reliable, and faster than daisywheel printers, but their characters are formed from dots and may be irregular. Laser printers are relatively fast and provide well formed characters, but are more expensive than the other two types.

Figure 6-23 gives an X16 interrupt routine for outputting to a character printer. The main program outputs the first character to the interface and, after each character is taken by the printer, the interrupt sequence branches to the interrupt routine that outputs the next character. It is assumed that BUFPTR contains the address of the character to be output and DOREG is the port address of the data-out buffer register. There is no error checking. If a file separator character (ASCII code 1C) is detected, the location COMPLETE is set to 1 and no character is output. The text being output should appropriately include return and line feed characters (ASCII codes 0D and 0A).

Most dot matrix and laser printers can output graphics as well as characters. To provide graphics, a dot matrix printer must have solenoids that can be controlled individually by the software. A great deal of head movement is involved in using a dot matrix printer to form an image and it may take a minute or so to output a single page. A laser printer can provide graphics much more quickly because only the mechanical motion of the drum is required.

Plotters form their images using vector graphics. The plotter is given endpoints and draws line segments between the endpoints. The important characteristics of a plotter are the **resolution** with which it can locate the endpoints and its **linearity** (i.e., its ability to draw a straight line). Plotters tend to be slow, but provide inked lines with distinct edges. Some plotters can automatically select pens of different colors and thereby produce multicolored drawings.

6-4-3 Timer/Event Counters

The purpose of a timer/event counter is to provide a means of:

- Timing events within a computer.

```
          INTROUT    PSHH    R1                 ;SAVE R1
                     MOVH    BUFPTR,R1          ;PUT ADDR OF CHAR IN R1
                     CMPB    1CH,[R1]           ;IF CHAR IS FILE
                     BRNE    CONTINUE           ;SEPARATOR, SET
                     MOVB    #1,COMPLETE        ;COMPLETE TO 1
                     BRUN    EXIT               ;AND EXIT
          CONTINUE   OUTB    [R1]+,DOREG        ;ELSE OUTPUT CHAR,
                     MOVH    R1,BUFPTR          ;UPDATE BUFPTR, AND
          EXIT       POPH    R1                 ;RESTORE R1
                     IRET
```

Figure 6-23 Interrupt routine for character printer output.

- Sensing an external time standard.
- Sensing external events.
- Outputting timed pulses to control external activity.

A representative timer/event counter is shown in Fig. 6-24. In addition to the control and status registers, it contains count, initial count, and count-in registers. The initial count and count-in registers are I/O ports. The timer/event counter has two inputs and one output for communicating with the world outside the computer. The Clock/Event line allows an external clock or other device to apply pulses to the timer/event counter and the Enable line provides an external means for enabling and disabling the Clock/Event input. The Out line outputs pulses.

How the timer/event counter uses its registers and reacts to its inputs depends on its mode, which is determined by a set of bits in the control register. Typical modes are:

1. The initial count is transferred to the count register and then, while a 1 is applied to Enable, the count register is decremented each time a pulse arrives on the Clock/Event line. When the count register reaches 0, decrementing ceases, the Ready bit is set to 1, and, if the Interrupt Enable bit is set, an

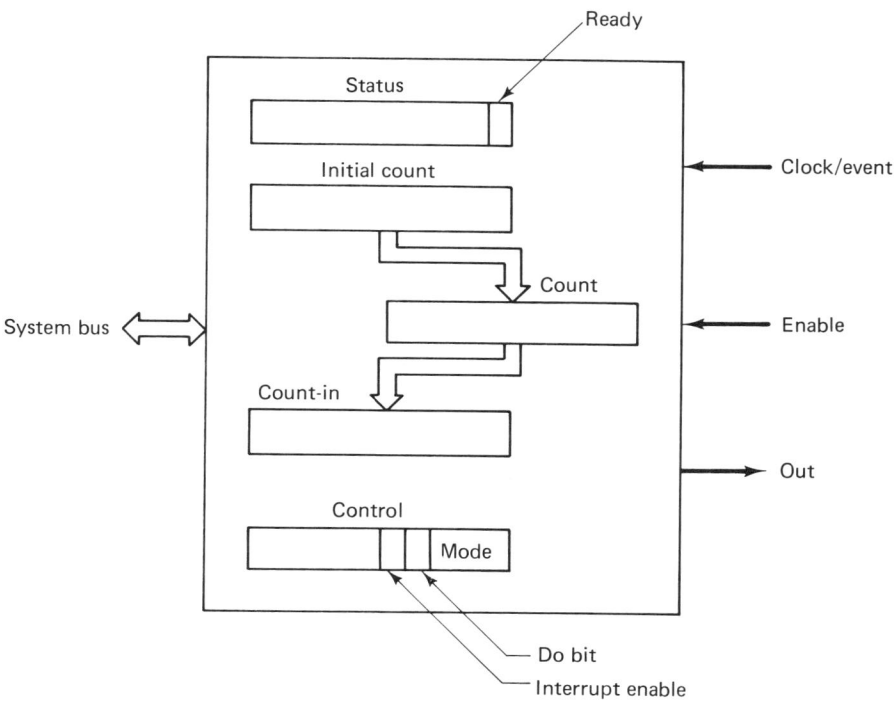

Figure 6-24 Representative timer/event counter.

Sec. 6-4 I/O Elements

interrupt request is made. The Ready bit is cleared following the status register being input by the computer.

2. Same as 1, except that when the count decrements to 0, the initial count is automatically loaded into the count register and the process is repeated.
3. Same as 1 except that instead of issuing an interrupt request, a pulse is output over the Out line.
4. Same as 3 except that when the count decrements to 0 the initial count is automatically loaded into the count register and the process is repeated.

To start any of the above actions, an initial count is output to the initial count register and the process begins when the Do bit is set. Each time the count register changes, its contents are transferred to the count-in register, which can be read by an in instruction. This transfer gives the computer a way of monitoring the count. Some timer/event counters include internal clocks and corresponding modes that cause internally generated pulses to be used in lieu of pulses on the Clock/Event line.

One important application of a timer/event counter is to produce evenly spaced interrupt requests that can be used by the computer to keep the time of day in its memory. By putting 1000 in the initial count register, applying a 1 kHz clock to the Clock/Event input, and putting the timer/event counter into mode 2 (described above), the timer/event counter could be used to provide an interrupt request once per second. The interrupt routine would update memory locations that are used to store the hour, minute, and second of the day. By inputting the count-in register, the computer could determine the time to the nearest millisecond. A timer/event counter used in this way is called a **real-time clock**. The interrupt requests from real-time clocks are normally connected to nonmaskable interrupt lines to insure that the time is updated promptly. In a time-shared system, a real-time clock produces the time slices that determine when program switches are to take place. (This is discussed further in Chap. 11.)

6-4-4 A/D and D/A Converters

An A/D converter converts a voltage level into a binary number. When used with sampling and timing circuits as shown in Fig. 6-25, it can convert a voltage signal into a sequence of binary numbers with the conversions being made at equally spaced points in time. The source of the voltage signal could be a tape player or a transducer that converts a physical quantity (such as temperature, pressure, displacement, and so on) into a voltage. A/D converters find a broad range of applications including monitoring and controlling physical processes and providing non-keyboard user inputs such as joystick and mouse inputs.

The configuration shown in Fig. 6-25 includes a programmable timer that allows the sample rate to be set by the program and sampling to be manually turned on and off. The program would initialize the interface and timer and then begin inputting the sampled data each time a datum is put into the interface's data-in register. Either programmed I/O or interrupt I/O could be used. Some

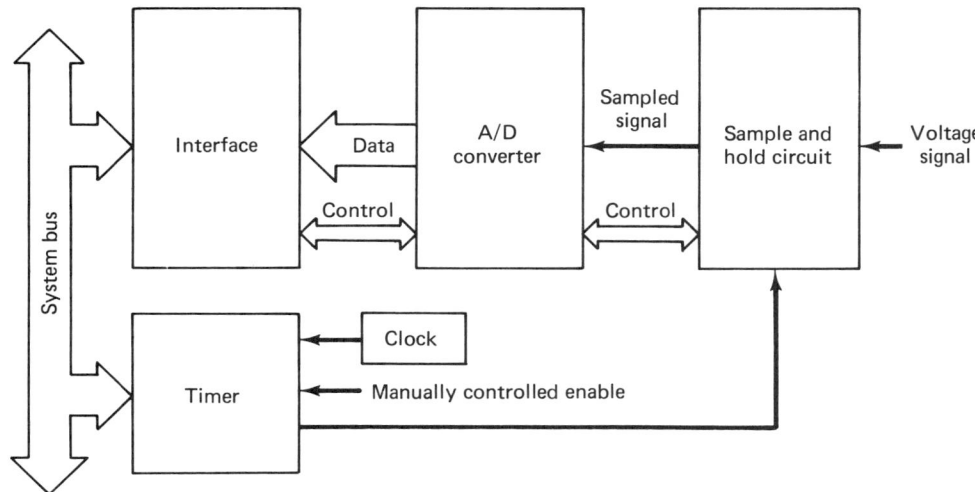

Figure 6-25 Interfacing an A/D converter to a computer.

A/D converter applications require a high rate of conversion and a DMA controller may need to be associated with the A/D converter's interface.

D/A converters perform the reverse operation and give a computer the means to output analog voltage signals. A timer could be used to measure the time intervals between digital outputs and a filter could be connected to the analog output to smooth out the voltage signal.

An application that requires both A/D and D/A converters is one in which a computer is used to control the speed of a motor. As shown in Fig. 6-26, a manual input from a keyboard supplies the desired speed and a transducer supplies the actual speed. Using these two speeds, the computer calculates an optimal output to the motor's speed controller and transmits this output through a D/A converter to the controller. For the construction of A/D and D/A converters, see Millman and Grabel [5] or Fletcher [6].

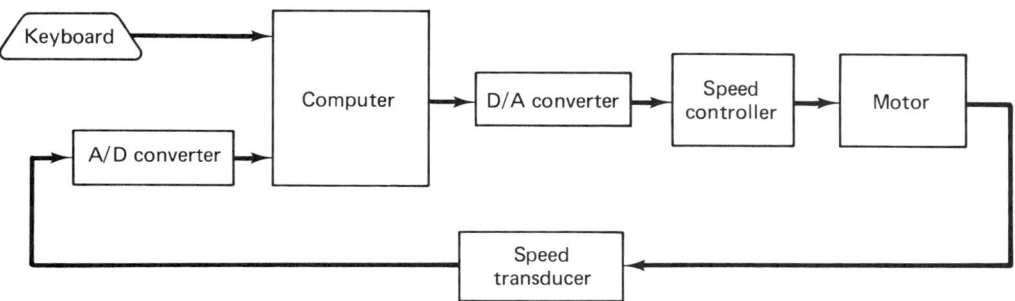

Figure 6-26 Application of A/D and D/A to a controller design.

6-5 DESIGN REMARKS

In deciding how to input from or output to an I/O or mass storage element it is important to account for the nature of the element. The more important attributes to be considered are the maximum transfer rate, whether the transfers are essentially periodic or essentially random, and whether the data are transferred individually or in blocks. For elements with low to medium transfer rates, either programmed or interrupt I/O can be used. For example, if there is an input once every millisecond and it takes 20 μS to perform a transfer, then only 2% of the processing element's time is required to execute the input-related instructions. However, as the transfer rate increases, the burden on the processing element may become too great or impossible.

Randomness tends to make interrupt I/O more appealing because interrupts avoid tying up the processing element in idle loops, but, if a system must wait anyway then there is no gain and the simplicity and faster response of programmed I/O may be preferred. The more periodic the transfers become, the better the I/O can be predicted and the easier it is to coordinate the I/O and processing.

Programmed I/O could be used for moderately high transfer rates. For the example in Fig. 6-4(a), if the average execution time of the instructions in the input loop were 1 μS and there were no errors, then eight instructions would be executed for each input (the loop's initialization is excluded) and the input rate could be as high as

$$\frac{1}{8 \times 10^{-6}} = 125{,}000 \text{ transfers per second}$$

Under the same assumptions, if the interrupt sequence takes 5 μS, then the maximum transfer rate using the interrupt routine in Fig. 6-10 would be

$$\frac{1}{(5 + 15) \times 10^{-6}} = 50{,}000 \text{ transfers per second}$$

For high transfer rates for which there is insufficient time to execute instructions, DMA is required and, if there is not enough time to steal individual cycles, the DMA controller would need to seize control of the bus throughout the entire block transfer. High transfer rates are normally associated with mass storage elements, but may be required of input from an A/D converter. The transfer rate is determined by the mass storage element or A/D conversion rate, and is often due to mechanical motion such as the rate at which the data pass a disk or tape head. The DMA controllers considered here perform block transfers for which the count is known in advance. Because most mass storage elements store their data in blocks of fixed size, this restriction is of little consequence. Some controllers, however, are able to monitor the input stream of data and terminate the input under conditions other than the count going to 0.

Double or triple buffering may be used for simultaneously inputting, processing, and perhaps outputting multiple blocks. However, if all three activities share the same bus and memory then each activity will be affected by the other two. The overall number of transfers per second cannot exceed the transfer capacity of the bus and memory configuration (see Chaps. 8 and 9). In particular, contention for the bus by inputting and outputting activities could be a problem. Another problem arises if the data rate is constant and must be maintained between blocks. Even if a completion routine is not needed, at least the buffer array pointers must be interchanged. If it takes 10 μS to switch the pointers and reinitialize the DMA controller(s), then the maximum transfer rate would be 100,000 transfers per second, even though the bus and memory may permit a much higher rate. This problem is most likely to occur when inputting from an A/D converter and there is not enough memory to store all of the data.

Care should be taken to include enough interrupt and bus request lines in a system. The X16's built-in interrupt management facility accommodates up to eight request lines. This capability would not be sufficient for many medium to large systems. Some interfaces may use more than one request line. For example, the interface in Fig. 6-19 that serves both a keyboard and monitor would use two lines, one for receiving data from the keyboard and one for sending data to the monitor. If there are too few interrupt request lines, they must be shared and the interrupt routines must include some form of polling.

The ultimate goal is to supply data to and output results from appropriate processing elements in a timely manner. The ideal would be to have the data immediately available to the processing elements when they are to be processed and the results automatically taken from the processing elements as soon as they are produced, without the processing elements being involved in the transfers. In practice, the finite times and coordination required for conducting transfers make this ideal unattainable. The processing element must be involved in the coordination effort and this, to some extent, detracts from its processing. For the examples and methods considered in this chapter, the processing element has supervised the coordination and, except for DMA, has even performed the transfers. This places a considerable burden on the processing element.

At the extreme, the primary I/O elements for the very early computers were teletype machines for which the I/O was performed one bit at a time. For input, the processing element was charged with inputting the individual bits, assembling them into characters, checking for parity, and performing other input tasks. Output was equally meticulous. Because interfaces were so primitive, the processing element had to do all of the work. This chapter assumed that the interface would detect errors and perform any required assembly or disassembly of the data. The processing element could input or output data in parallel and determine whether or not errors had occurred by examining the interface's status register.

Once initialized, a DMA controller further reduces the processing element's responsibility by supervising transfers of blocks of data. Even more complex interface/controllers exist that can communicate with several I/O or mass storage elements and, perhaps, execute their own programs. By executing their own programs they can perform complicated operations such as rewinding, searching, and reading a magnetic tape without intervention by the processing element.

Not only does the shift of responsibility to the interface make transfers more efficient, it also reduces the software executed by the processing element. The change from a simple interface that forces the processing element to form characters and check parity to an interface that performs these tasks itself was an exchange of more complicated hardware for a reduction in software. This exchange is representative of an important step in the evolution of interfaces and element control circuitry. At the other extreme, large mass storage systems may have one or more microprocessors embedded in them to simplify the software of the processing elements that use them. Although microprocessors must have software, this software is divorced from that of the system's central processing element and is the responsibility of the mass storage system designer. The programmer writing the software for the system's central processing element is concerned only with the rules that must be followed in communicating with the mass storage system as a whole; what makes up that system is not important. In large systems, the increased efficiency in the central processing element and the reduction in its software more than compensates for the added complexity of the mass storage hardware.

As noted in the introduction to this chapter, if there are two address spaces it is normal to have all memory locations associated with one space and all I/O ports associated with the other space. However, such an arrangement is not required. The type of transfer instruction being used determines the space being accessed. Although the M/$\overline{\text{IO}}$ control line may be set to 1 when a memory transfer instruction is executed and 0 when an I/O instruction is executed, there is nothing to prevent an I/O element interface from being designed to respond when M/$\overline{\text{IO}}$ is 1. Thus, memory transfer instructions must be used when communicating with the interface. The ports in such an interface are said to be **memory mapped**. Care must be exercised when using memory mapped ports to make sure that no memory element responds to the same addresses as those of the ports. When the ports in one or more I/O interfaces are memory mapped they are most often assigned to the highest addresses in the memory address space and the memory elements are blocked from using these addresses.

The advantage to employing memory mapped ports is that any instruction that can access memory can then be used to access I/O ports. For example, if FF1C is the address of an 8-bit port in an X16 system, not only could the port be accessed by a move instruction but it could also be modified by a logical instruction such as

                    ANDB   #FB,FF1C

which would clear bit 2 of the port. A typical address space assignment for an X16 system with memory mapped ports is shown in Fig. 6-27. The memory interfaces are designed so that they accept addresses only in the range 0 to 63K-1 and the addresses from 63K through 64K-1 are reserved for I/O ports.

It is similarly possible to have **I/O mapped memory**, i.e., memory elements designed to respond when M/$\overline{\text{IO}}$ is 0. This would mean that the locations in these memory elements could be accessed only by using I/O instructions. Although I/O mapped memory is not as prevalent as memory mapped ports, it may be designed into small controller systems that require very little memory for storing data. Controller systems tend to use input data immediately and then the data

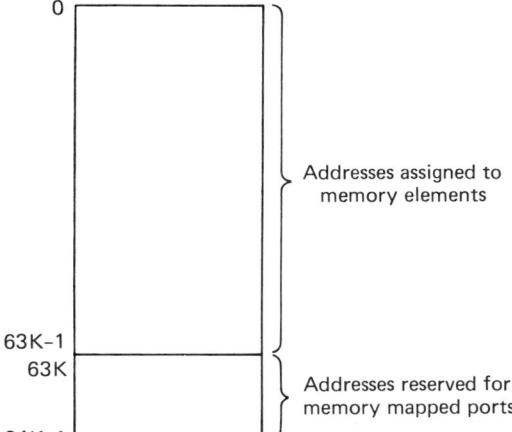

Figure 6-27 Address space assignment that reserves memory space for I/O ports.

may be discarded (e.g., the motor control computer in Fig. 6-26 would not need to retain the transducer output after it has computed the next output to the speed controller).

REFERENCES

1. Liu, Yu-cheng, and Glenn A. Gibson, *Microcomputer Systems: The 8086/8088 Family*, 2nd ed. (Englewood Cliffs, New Jersey: Prentice Hall, Inc., 1986).
2. Short, Kenneth L., *Microprocessors and Programmed Logic*, 2nd ed. (Englewood Cliffs, New Jersey: Prentice Hall, Inc., 1987).
3. Wiatronski, Claude A., and Charles H. House. *Logic Circuits and Microcomputer Systems* (New York: McGraw-Hill Book Company, 1980).
4. Gibson, Glenn A., and Mary L. Gibson, *Understanding and Selecting Small Business Computers* (Englewood Cliffs, New Jersey: Prentice Hall, Inc., 1986).
5. Millman, Jacob, and Arvin Grabel, *Microelectronics*, 2nd ed. (New York: McGraw-Hill Book Company, 1987).
6. Fletcher, William I., *An Engineering Approach to Digital Design* (Englewood Cliffs, New Jersey: Prentice Hall, Inc., 1980).

EXERCISES

1. What would be an important advantage to using separate address spaces for memory and I/O?
2. Write an X16 procedure that uses programmed I/O to output the message "AN ERROR HAS OCCURRED." Include in the procedure the directive needed to preassign the

message to an area in memory. Use the bit definitions and port addresses given in the EQU directives in Fig. 6-4.

3. If the I/O elements being polled in Fig. 6-5 were identical, a single procedure could be called and the identifying number of the element could be passed to the procedure as a parameter. However, the fact that the port addresses in the in and out instructions must be supplied using the direct address mode presents an inconvenience. Discuss this problem and how the procedure, as well as the polling sequence, could be shortened if register indirect addressing were used.

4. Suppose that 80 characters must be input, two seconds of processing (25 mS per character) must be done before the characters are used, and the average time between inputs is 50 mS. If a 0.1 mS interrupt routine is used and the processing and inputting can be overlapped, compare the approximate total time needed to perform the processing and inputting if interrupt I/O is used as opposed to programmed I/O (where the inputting is followed by the processing). Input using programmed I/O is to require 0.05 mS per transfer.

5. Write an X16 procedure that begins the output of the message "AN ERROR HAS OCCURRED" by outputting the first character, and then has interrupt I/O output the remaining characters. Also, write the interrupt routine. Assume the bit definitions and port addresses given in the example in Fig. 6-4.

6. In Exercise 5, why was it necessary to have the procedure output the first character?

7. Write an interrupt routine that will poll the status registers of three interfaces and service a requesting interface by branching to an appropriate procedure. Exactly one procedure is to be branched to each time the interrupt routine is entered.

8. In Exercise 7 what dictates the priorities of the interfaces? Rewrite the interrupt routine so that the priorities rotate (i.e., initially the priorities are 3-2-1, then 2-1-3, then 1-3-2, then 3-2-1, and so on).

9. Suppose that a fixed priority scheme is used in which interface 3 has highest priority, 2 has second priority, and 1 has lowest priority, and all three interrupt routines have an execution time of 0.5 mS and do not reenable interrupts until they are exited. If interfaces 2 and 3 perform four inputs each and the inputs occur every 0.9 mS, how much time will elapse before interface 1 is serviced? Assume that the initial requests from all three interfaces are made simultaneously.

10. Consider five input interfaces numbered 1 through 5 with 5 having the highest priority, 4 having the next highest priority, and so on. Assume that interrupts are disabled during the execution of the interrupt routines, all interrupt routines take 0.1 mS to execute, requests are made each time data arrive, and the data arrive at the interfaces as follows:

Interface	Times of Arrivals (in mS)					
5	0.6	2.3	4.3	5.5	6.3	6.8
4	0.5	0.8	2.1	4.0	4.7	6.5	7.2
3	0.1	1.6	1.7	2.5	3.0	4.5	6.5
2	1.1	1.5	1.9	2.8	2.9	5.1	6.6
1	1.7	3.6	5.0	6.2	6.6	6.9	7.2

Determine the order in which the interrupts are processed and how much data are missed. Resolve the problem assuming 0.2 mS is required to execute the interrupt routines.

11. Suppose that all bus transfers require 200 nS, bus requests are made every 450 nS, and a bus request arrives just after the fetch of the first halfword of the instruction MOVH X,Y. Discuss the bus activity during the execution of the instruction. Include the beginning times of all transfers in the discussion.

12. Write an X16 code sequence for initializing a DMA controller to input a block of 100 bytes to an array beginning at BUFFER. The port addresses of the count, memory address, and control registers are to be 32, 34, and 36, respectively, and the control bits are to be as defined in Fig. 6-15. In addition, Bit 3 of the control register must be set to 1 for byte transfers. Bit 1 of the control register must be 1 for input.

13. Draw a flowchart similar to the one in Fig. 6-17 that shows how triple buffering could be accomplished.

14. Give two reasons why a disk drive interface would need to be associated with a DMA controller. DMA bus requests are always recognized at the end of the current bus transfer. So, why must a DMA controller associated with a disk drive have priority over the processing element?

15. Consider the configuration in Fig. 6-18 and suppose that a bus transfer and memory access require 250 nS. If channel priorities are 3 (highest)-2-1-0 (lowest) and x is the transfer rate of all four elements connected to the channels, what is the maximum value of x?

16. Modify the code in Fig. 6-20 so that when a delete character (ASCII code 7FH) is detected it is not stored in the location pointed to by register R1 nor output to the monitor, but a backspace is output to the monitor and register R1 is decremented.

17. For the example in Fig. 6-20, discuss the possibility of using a stack to store characters as they arrive. Could the same stack that saves procedure and interrupt return addresses be used?

18. If a character monitor can display 400 rows of 720 pixels each and the character blocks are to be 16 pixels by 9 pixels, how many rows and columns of characters can be displayed?

19. If a graphics monitor can display 500 rows of 800 pixels each and each pixel can be not illuminated, illuminated at half intensity or illuminated at full intensity, what is the required capacity of the display memory in bits?

20. What is the major difference between a raster scan graphics monitor and a vector graphics monitor, and why does the raster scan monitor require more display memory?

21. A curve consists of connected line segments with segment endpoints that are superimposed (e.g., a curve with three line segments would include only four distinct endpoints). If it takes 50 mS to raise or lower the pen on a plotter and 5 mS/cm to move the pen, how long would it take to plot 40 curves averaging 30 segments per curve and 1 cm per segment? The average distance between the end of one curve and the beginning of the next curve is 20 cm.

22. Write an X16 interrupt routine that is entered each time there is an interrupt request from a timer/event counter. The routine is to keep the number of times it is entered, modulo 100, in a location CHANGE, and every time 0 is put into CHANGE, the routine is to branch to a procedure SWITCH.

23. Write an X16 instruction sequence that puts 500 in the initial count register of a timer/event counter, sets the mode in the control register (Bits 2-0) to 3, and sets the Do bit (Bit 3) to 1. Assume the port addresses of the initial count and control registers to be 42 and 44, respectively.

24. Assume an A/D configuration that includes a timer and DMA controller. Give a typical set of steps for initializing the interface, timer, and DMA controller.
25. Suppose that the execution time of each instruction is 2 µS and the interrupt sequence takes 6 µS. If all error and overflow checking were deleted from Figs. 6-4(a) and 6-10, what would be the maximum transfer rates corresponding to these sets of code?
26. Assume that there is no completion routine and that the execution time of each instruction is 1 µS. Use the flow-chart in Fig. 6-17 to estimate the maximum time it would take after completing the input of one block to begin inputting the next block.
27. Suppose that bit 11 of the X16's PSW is a serial input bit that is set or cleared according to bits arriving from an input element and that an interrupt occurs each time a bit arrives. Write an interrupt routine that assembles these bits into bytes (with the first bit received being the low-order bit) and stores the bytes into an array pointed to by BUFPTR until a RETURN character is detected. The RETURN character is to cause location FLAG, which is normally 0, to be set to 1. The last bit received in each byte is to indicate even parity. The interrupt routine is to branch to ERROR if a parity error occurs.

7
Processing Elements

This chapter discusses processing element design. Although the central example is simplified so that the main points can be emphasized, most of the principal design problems and associated tradeoffs are considered. Other more advanced concepts are studied in Chap. 12. For design purposes the processing element is not viewed in the same way as it is when programming. The programming model used in Chap. 4 (Fig. 4-8) shows the processing element resources that are available to the programmer and gives some insight into how the processing element operates. A hardware block diagram of a processing element shows not only the components a programmer must know about, but also the components needed by the hardware to perform its operations and the buses between these components.

A processing element is a set of logic capable of inputting instructions and data, temporarily storing data, operating on the data according to the instructions, and outputting results. The four major components that must be present in a processing element are shown in Fig. 7-1. They are: the Sequencing and Control Logic (SCL) for controlling the element's activity, the set of registers needed for storing the instructions and data that are used and operated on by the processing element, the logic for performing the processing, and the Bus Control Logic (BCL) for communicating with the outside world. A definition of these major components and the buses internal to the processing element that link them together constitute the **internal architecture** of a processing element. Two of the more obvious connection patterns used to form an internal architecture are given in Fig. 7-2. Although the one-bus configuration is simpler than the two-bus design, it does not allow information to flow as freely. An internal bus is a shared resource that allows only one piece of information to be communicated over it at a time. Therefore, the arrangement of the internal buses is of central importance when designing

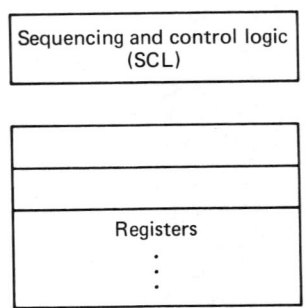
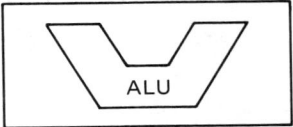

Figure 7-1 Major components of a processing element.

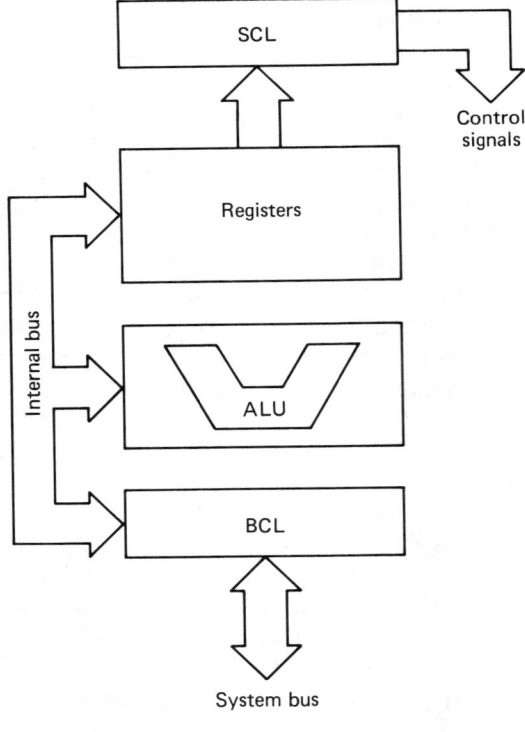

(a) One-bus

Figure 7-2 Configurations with one and two internal buses.

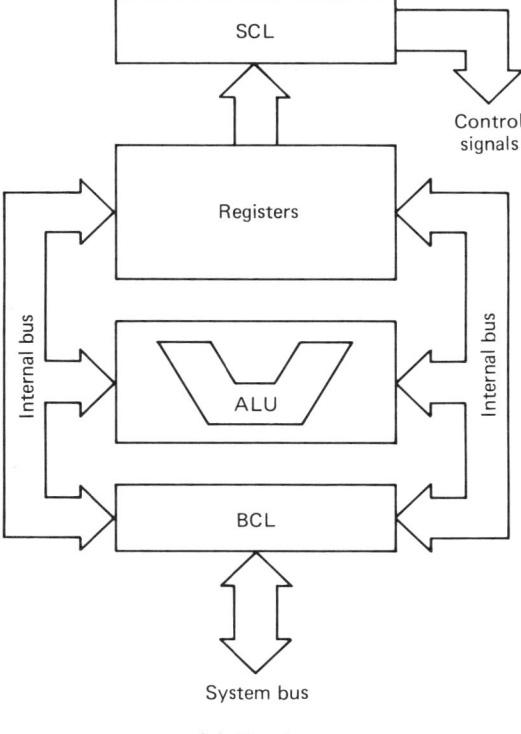

(b) Two-bus **Figure 7-2** Continued

a processing element, even though their arrangement is not important to a programmer.

The basic operation of a processing element is to repeatedly:

1. Fetch an instruction from main memory via the system bus.
2. Transfer the instruction over an internal bus to the IR.
3. Use the SCL to examine the IR and output the control signals needed to execute the instruction.

The control signals output by the SCL may not be output all at once. More often the signals are sequentially output in groups with each group consisting of a set of nonconflicting signals that avoid simultaneous usage of the shared resources such as the internal buses. Most of these signals are confined to the processing element and dictate the internal activity for performing the processing, but some of them may emanate out through the BCL and affect the system bus signals that control the other components of the computer.

In addition, the SCL contains the clock that regulates the timing within the processing element. This clock determines the times at which the successive groups of control signals are output. One group of signals is output during each clock period, but a clock cycle may be broken into phases and the exact time at which a signal is issued may be determined by the phase as well as the cycle. A group of signals output by the SCL during a single clock cycle is called a **microinstruction**. It may take the issuance of several microinstructions to complete the execution of a machine language instruction. The **microcontrol** that occurs during this execution is determined by these microinstructions. To clearly differentiate machine language instructions from microinstructions, in this chapter (and this chapter only), machine language instructions are referred to as **macroinstructions** instead of instructions.

7-1 MACROINSTRUCTION EXECUTION

Microinstructions are broken down into **microoperations**, which are the primitive actions that must be carried out during the execution of a macroinstruction (e.g., the transfer of data from one register to another or the initiation of an arithmetic operation). Hardware designers use abbreviated definitions of microoperations to describe them and the conditions under which they are performed. As a whole these definitions are referred to as a **hardware programming language**. Such a language can be used to concisely and completely define the internal operation of a processing element. Although hardware programming languages are not considered in this book (see Hill and Peterson [3]), a simplified hardware programming language is used to provide many of the examples in this chapter.

For the hardware programming language assumed here, each statement corresponds to a microinstruction—the activity performed during a single clock cycle—and has the format

$$\textit{Condition}: \quad \textit{Operation}, \ldots, \textit{Operation}$$

where *Operation* is the description of a microoperation and *Condition* is the condition under which the *Operations* are to be performed. Typical operations are

$$\text{Subtract} \rightarrow \text{ALU}$$

which indicates that a subtract signal is sent to the ALU that causes the ALU to perform a subtraction, and

$$R1 \rightarrow R2$$

which indicates a transfer from register R1 to register R2. A typical condition is

$$\text{Subtract reg. to reg. AND T3}$$

meaning that the *Operations* following the condition are to be performed if a register to register subtract instruction is being executed and the time during the instruction cycle is the clock period T3. Together, the symbolic form of the microinstruction is

$$\text{Subtract reg. to reg. AND T3:} \quad \text{R1} \to \text{R2, Subtract} \to \text{ALU}$$

To demonstrate the execution of macroinstructions in detail, let us assume the simplified one-bus design shown in Fig. 7-3. In addition to the control registers IR and PC, and the working registers R0 and R1, the BCL includes an external address register (XAR) for holding an address during a main memory access, an external data input (XDI) register for buffering data into the processing element, and an external data output (XDO) register for buffering data out of the processing element. XDI and XDO are needed to match the timing requirements of the internal data bus to the system bus. All instructions and data brought into or output from the processing element must pass through the XDI or XDO register. Also, the ALU includes an arithmetic/logic input (ALI) register and an arithmetic/logic output (ALO) register for temporarily storing a source operand and the output of the ALU. The ALI and ALO are needed because there is only one internal bus and only one source operand or result can use the bus at a time. Because the ALU increments the PC and other registers it is assumed that there is a control line for setting the ALI register to 1.

The microinstructions that fetch and execute a move from register R1 to register R0 macroinstruction are given in Fig. 7-4(a). The instruction fetch is performed during the first four clock cycles, T0 through T3, and, at the same time, the PC is incremented to point to the next sequential memory location. During T0, the (PC) are transferred to the XAR where they are used to address memory, and a Read signal is sent to BCL that causes the BCL to conduct a memory read. During T1 and T2, the (PC) are incremented by putting 1 in ALI, outputting the (PC) to the ALU and signaling the ALU to perform an addition, signaling the ALO to latch the result, and then transferring the (ALO) to the PC. After the PC has been incremented the activity in the processing element must be suspended until the macroinstruction has been returned to the BCL and placed in the XDI. Once the memory read is complete, the macroinstruction is transferred to the IR during T3. These four microinstructions are executed automatically at the beginning of each instruction cycle regardless of the macroinstruction to be executed.

After the macroinstruction has been put into the IR, it is decoded by the SCL and determines the remaining microinstructions. In the present case the macroinstruction is a register to register move with R1 and R0 specified as the source and destination, respectively. Therefore, during T4, the (R1) are transferred to R0. Finally, there is a time reset that causes the SCL to return to T0 and a new instruction cycle to begin.

Because the instruction fetch is always performed during the first four periods, the microinstructions executed during T0 through T3 are always the same. Therefore the only conditions given in these microinstructions are T0, T1, T2, and T3, respectively. What occurs during the later periods depends on the ma-

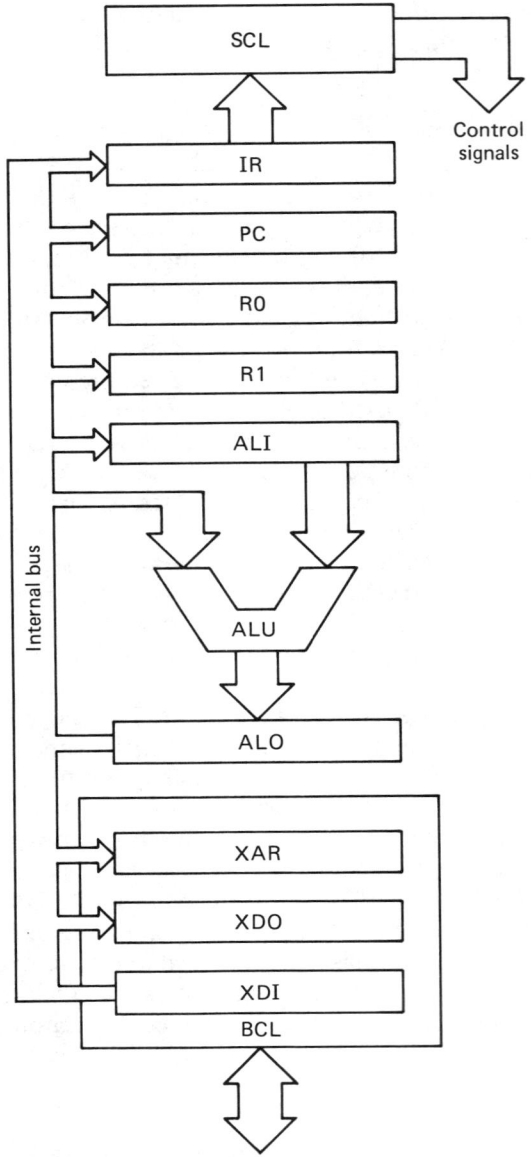

Figure 7-3 Example one-bus architecture.

croinstruction. For the example in Fig. 7-4(a), the macroinstruction type as well as the period identification appears in the periods T4 and T5. So, the microoperation R1 → R0 is to be performed if the macroinstruction is a register to register move *and* the period is the fifth period after a new instruction cycle has begun. A different macroinstruction may cause the action that occurs during the fifth period to be different.

                            T0: PC→XAR, Read→BCL
                            T1: 1→ALI, Add→ALU, PC→ALO
                            T2: ALO→PC, Suspend until ready
                            T3: XDI→IR
        Move reg. to reg. AND T4: R1→R0
                     "   T5: Time reset

                    (a) Move register to register

                                ·⎫
                                · ⎬ Instruction fetch
                                · ⎭

        Subtract imm. from reg. AND T4: PC→XAR, Read→BCL
                     "   T5: 1→ALI, Add→ALU, PC→ALO
                     "   T6: ALO→PC, Suspend until ready
                     "   T7: XDI→ALI
                     "   T8: Subtract→ALU, R1→ALO
                     "   T9: ALO→R1
                     "   T10: Time reset

                (b) Subtract immediate from register

          Figure 7-4 Example microinstruction sequences.

Figure 7-4(b) gives the microinstruction sequence for subtracting an immediate operand from register R1. The instruction fetch sequence is not shown because it is the same as in Fig. 7-4(a). In this example it is assumed that the macroinstruction occupies two locations in main memory with the opcode and register designation being in the first location and the immediate operand being in the second. After fetching the opcode, periods T4 through T7 are used to fetch the immediate operand and increment the PC to point to the next memory location. Subtraction is performed during T8 by applying a Subtract signal to the ALU and outputting the (R1), as the minuend, to the ALU. Then, during T9 and T10, the result is moved to R1 and a time reset is executed.

7-2 INTERNAL BUS TRANSFERS

It is apparent from the number of register to register transfers included in the examples in Fig. 7-4 that the entire operation of a processing element is heavily dependent on the ability of its buses to move information between its registers. This movement must be accomplished as quickly as possible using a simple means of control that can easily be generated by the SCL. Because it is the SCL's responsibility to decode the instruction in the IR, it is the SCL that must output the signals that control the transfers over the internal buses during the execution of that instruction.

One method for connecting the outputs of m registers to an internal bus is illustrated in Fig. 7-5. It uses m sets of n tristate gates each, with each set being used to output the contents of an n-bit register. Each set is controlled by a separate signal; thus, there are m control lines and a total of nm tristate gates. In designing the SCL, care must be taken to insure that only one set of gates is turned on at any given time. A second method for outputting from several registers to a common bus is to use a multiplexer. However, using a multiplexer requires a considerable number of interconnections and is not practical if the number of registers is large (see Exercise 2).

Input from an internal bus can be accomplished by applying a load signal to the register that is to receive the input. Unlike register output, several registers may input from the bus simultaneously. The input configuration shown in Fig. 7-6 assumes that the registers consist of n negative edge-triggered D flip-flops and loading is accomplished by applying a signal to the C inputs of the flip-flops.

Figure 7-7(a) shows how a transfer from one register to another could be

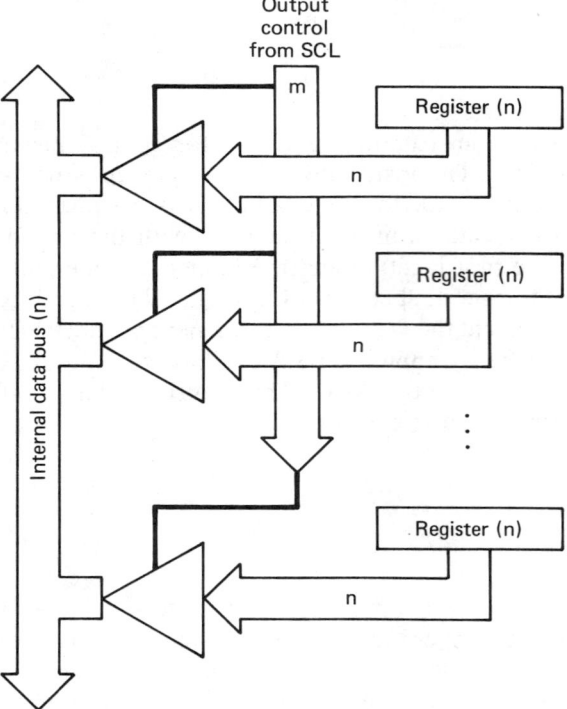

Figure 7-5 Outputting to a common bus.

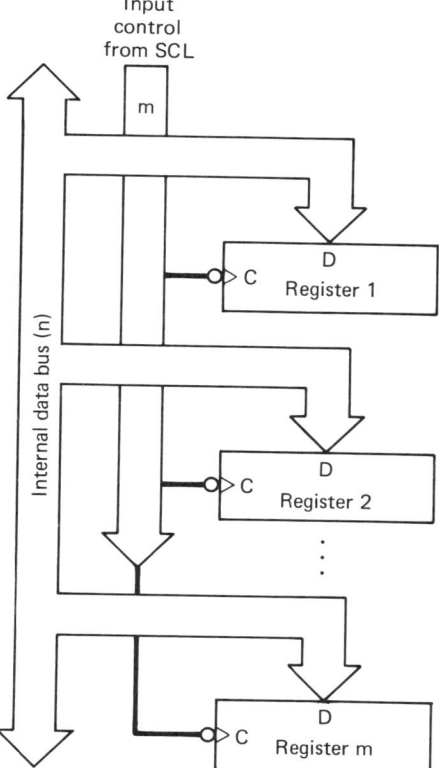

Figure 7-6 Inputting from a common bus.

conducted, and Fig. 7-7(b) gives the corresponding timing. The transfer proceeds by applying a pulse, Ri_{out}, to the output tristate gates associated with the register Ri. After waiting until the signals have propagated through the tristate gates and along the bus to the D inputs of the register Rj, and have stabilized at these inputs, the signals can be strobed into Rj by applying the negative edge of a pulse to the C inputs of the Rj register's flip-flops. Because Rj is negative edge-triggered, the leading edge of this pulse is not important, but the trailing edge must occur after all signals have arrived at the D inputs (i.e., skew has been taken into account) and have been maintained at the inputs long enough to be strobed into the flip-flops. The period during which the signals must be applied to the inputs is broken into two parts—the **setup time**, which is the amount of time the signals must be applied before the input pulse's negative edge arrives, and the **hold time**, which is the amount of time they must be maintained after this edge arrives. The trailing edge of the input pulse must occur slightly before that of the pulse controlling the tristate gate. If the signals must additionally pass through intervening logic (e.g., the ALU, as required by the arithmetic operations in Fig. 7-4), the propagational delay of the logic must be added to the delays shown.

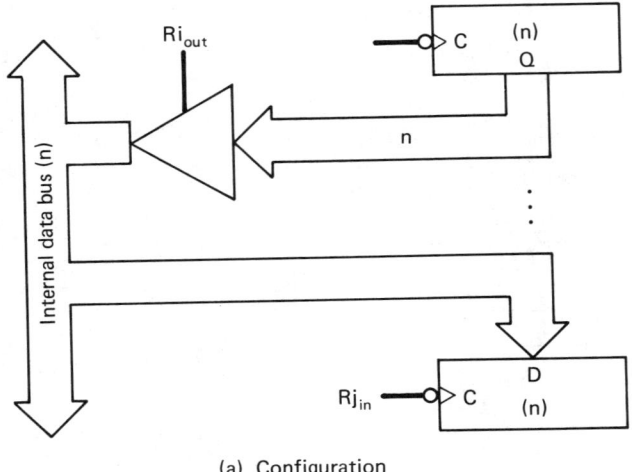

(a) Configuration

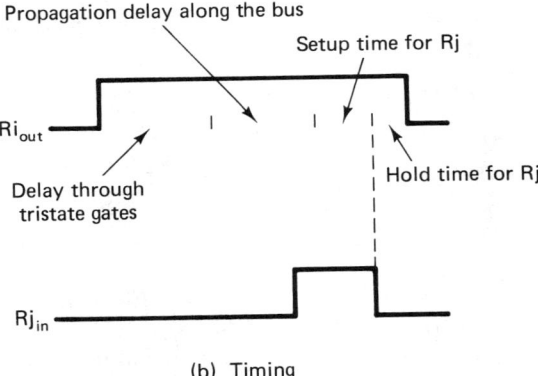

(b) Timing

Figure 7-7 Timing of a data transfer between two registers.

7-3 DETAILED INTERNAL ARCHITECTURE EXAMPLE

The above presentation was intended to serve as a very general introduction to the design and operation of processing elements. The fact is, the internal architectures of processing elements are extremely varied and, in order to consider design details, it is necessary to concentrate on a specific architecture and use it as a backdrop to discussing the design of the important components. The example architecture developed here is an implementation of the X16, whose machine and assembler languages were considered in Chaps. 4 through 6.

Although the presentation in this section concentrates on the X16, the concepts are generally applicable to the design of simple processing elements and the problems that arise are typical. To keep our presentation reasonably uncluttered, the following simplifications are assumed:

- Only halfword operands are permitted.
- The negate, multiply, and divide macroinstructions are eliminated.
- The only addressing modes for accessing data are the immediate, register, direct, and register indirect modes.

Several of the exercises at the end of this chapter are concerned with the effects of removing these restrictions.

The internal architecture of the X16 is given in Fig. 7-8. It includes the control registers IR, PC, PSW, and SP; working registers R0 through R5; six registers (ALI, TMP, IVR, XDI, XDO, and XAR) that are needed for various purposes but cannot be explicitly referenced by macroinstructions; and two internal buses. The ALI register is used to temporarily store one of the operands during double operand arithmetic/logic operations. As in the example in Sec. 7-1, the XDI and XDO registers buffer data between the processing element and the other elements in the system, and the XAR holds the address used to make an external access.

The IR is connected to Data Bus 2 so that it can directly receive instructions via the XDI. The PC is connected to Data Bus 1 so that it can be updated or modified using the ALU, and is connected to Data Bus 2 so that it can provide an address to the XAR. Also, the SP, TMP, and all of the working registers must be capable of outputting to and/or inputting from the internal data buses.

7-3-1 Macroinstruction Execution

As with the example in Sec. 7-1, the execution of an X16 macroinstruction involves the sequential execution of several microinstructions, each of which includes microoperations. Assuming the internal architecture given in Fig. 7-8, the microinstructions for executing the X16's macroinstruction ADDH R1, R2 is shown in Fig. 7-9. The first two microinstructions fetch the macroinstruction and increment the PC, and the last three perform the move and terminate the macroinstruction.

The first microinstruction causes a pulse to be sent to the PC's output tristate gates, a signal that causes (ALI) to be set to 2 to be sent to the ALI's controlling logic, an Add (no carry) signal to be sent to the ALU, a Read signal to be sent to the BCL, and pulses to be applied to the C inputs of XAR and PC. The pulse sent to the PC's tristate gates allows the PC's outputs to be applied to Data Bus 2. Putting 2 in the ALI and signaling the ALU to perform an add causes the sum of the signals on Data Bus 2 and (ALI) [i.e., (PC) + 2] to be output from the ALU to Data Bus 1. (Recall that the opcode portion of an X16 macroinstruction is 2 bytes long.) The trailing edges of the pulses sent to the XAR and PC cause them to latch their inputs, thus completing the transfer of (PC) to the XAR and (PC) + 2 to the PC. The Read signal prompts the BCL to initiate an input from memory using the address just latched into the XAR. The BCL returns a Ready = 0 signal to inform the SCL that it is busy.

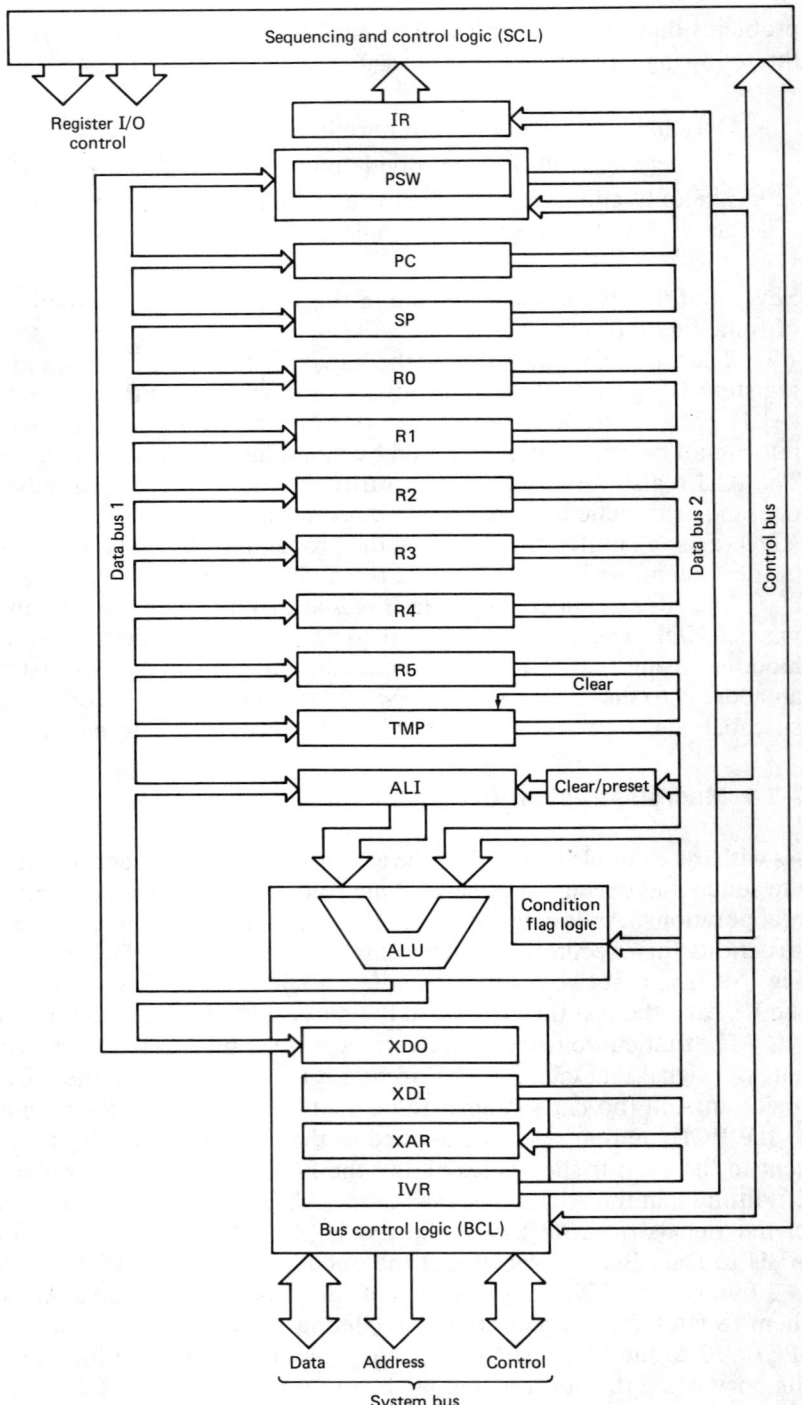

Figure 7-8 X16's internal architecture.

```
                    T0:  PC→XAR and PC, 2→ALI, Add (no carry)→ALU,
                         Read→BCL, Suspend until Ready = 1
                    T1:  XDI→IR
Add reg. to reg. AND T2: R1→ALI, Move→ALU
     "              T3:  R2→R2, Add (no carry)→ALU,
                         Cond. Flags Strobe→PSW
     "              T4:  Time reset
```

Figure 7-9 Sequencing for an X16 ADDH R1, R2 macroinstruction.

The Suspend microoperation causes the SCL to suspend its operation until it detects a 1 on the Ready control line. The BCL places a 1 on the Ready line after it has received the addressed data (the macroinstruction) and latched them into the XDI. When the SCL resumes its operation, the second microinstruction opens the XDI's tristate gates and latches (XDI) into the IR, thus completing the instruction fetch.

The next microinstruction performs the data transfer from R1 to ALI by opening R1's tristate gates and latching (R1) into the ALI. This transfer is made through the ALU and the microoperation Move → ALU indicates to the ALU that only a move is being executed and (R1) are to pass through the ALU unaltered. The fourth microinstruction opens R2's tristate gates, adds (R2) to (ALI), latches the result into R2, and updates the PSW's condition flags. As before, the last microinstruction causes the SCL to reset its timing logic to T0 so that the next clock pulse will initiate the fetch of the next instruction.

Note that because of the two-bus construction, a register to temporarily hold the result (i.e., the ALO register) is not needed and the result can be put directly into the destination register. Not only does this direct action eliminate a register, but, because of the frequent use of the ALU, it significantly reduces the number of periods needed to fetch and execute a macroinstruction—compare the sequence in this example to those in Fig. 7-4.

The example in Fig. 7-10(a) is the microinstruction sequence needed to perform an unconditional branch using PC-relative addressing. Because an instruction fetch is always performed during T0 and T1 and is always the same as indicated in Fig. 7-9, the microoperations occurring during these intervals are not shown. During T2 and T3 the (PC) are incremented by 2, the displacement is brought in from the two bytes following the macroinstruction, and the incremented (PC) are transferred to ALI. During T4 the displacement is added to (ALI) and the sum, which is the branch address, is put into the PC. Then the SCL is reset to T0 and the new (PC) are used to fetch the next instruction.

Figure 7-10(b) shows the necessary microinstruction sequence for a branch conditioned on the Z flag being 1. Note that the (PC) are incremented to point to the location after the displacement even if the branch is not taken, but when the branch is not taken, the time reset occurs in T3 and the periods T4 through T6 are eliminated.

Another X16 example is the microinstruction sequence for the macroin-

```
                                ·⎫
                                ·⎬ Instruction fetch
                                ·⎭
Branch PC-relative AND T2:  PC→ XAR and PC, 2→ALI, Add (no carry)→ALU,
                                Read→BCL
           "          T3:   PC→ALI, Move→ALU, Suspend until Ready = 1
           "          T4:   XDI→PC, Add (no carry)→ALU
           "          T5:   Time reset
```

(a) Unconditional

```
                                ·⎫
                                ·⎬ Instruction fetch
                                ·⎭
Branch PC relative AND T2:       PC→XAR and PC, 2→ALI, Add (no carry)→ALU
Z = 0 AND branch PC rel. AND T3: Time reset
Z = 1 AND branch PC rel. AND T3: No action
Branch PC relative AND T4:       PC→ALI, Move→ALU, Read→BCL,
                                 Suspend until Ready = 1
           "               T5:   XDI→PC, Add (no carry)→ALU
           "               T6:   Time reset
```

(b) Conditioned on Z = 1

Figure 7-10 PC-relative branches.

struction

MOVH   X,Y

that is given in Fig. 7-11. Also shown in this figure is a map of the register and internal data bus usage by the microinstructions. To minimize the number of periods, as many microoperations as possible should be put into each microinstruction. However, care must be exercised to insure that a microinstruction does not attempt to use a hardware resource more than once during a clock cycle (e.g., does not require different outputs to the same bus or different inputs to the same register). Note that microinstructions that follow an external read or write operation may not cause a loss of time because they may be overlapped with the external access.

Although including more resources tends to reduce the average number of microinstructions per macroinstruction, the gain in speed must be balanced against the cost of these resources. The X16 could have been designed with only one bus, but the two-bus design improved the performance with a minimal increase in cost. Adding a bus is relatively inexpensive, provided there is adequate space on the IC's surface and the bus layout is not unduly complicated by the addition. When adding a register, however, a designer must keep in mind that additional

⋮ } Instruction fetch

Move memory-to-memory AND T2: PC→XAR and PC, 2→ALI, Add (no carry)→ALU,
                                Read→BCL, Suspend until Ready = 1
            "   T3: XDI→XAR, Read→BCL, Suspend until Ready = 1
            "   T4: PC→XAR and PC, 2→ALI, Add (no carry)→ALU,
                                Read→BCL
            "   T5: XDI→XDO, Move→ALU, Suspend until Ready = 1
            "   T6: XDI→XAR, Write→BCL, Suspend until Ready = 1
            "   T7: Time reset

(a) Sequencing

Time	IR	PC	SP	R0	R1	R2	R3	R4	R5	ALI	ALU	XDO	XDI	XAR	Bus 1	Bus 2
T0		X								X	X			X	X	X
T1	X												X			X
T2		X								X	X			X	X	X
T3													X	X		X
T4		X								X	X			X	X	X
T5											X	X	X		X	X
T6													X	X		X
T7																

(b) Resource usage

Figure 7-11 Sequencing and resource usage for an X16 MOVH X, Y macroinstruction.

gates and register I/O control logic and lines will be required as well as the flip-flops that make up the register.

The move memory to memory example also demonstrates the effect that the addressing mode has on timing. The fetch and execution of a register to register move requires four periods in addition to the periods lost while the SCL is suspended once [see Exercise 5(a)], but the memory to memory moving using direct addressing, requires eight periods and the SCL is suspended five times. Although being able to transfer information from one memory location to another with just one instruction may reduce the number of instructions, it may not reduce the execution time as much as it first seems.

7-3-2 ALU and PSW Design

The designs of the ALU and PSW portions of the processing element are rather straightforward. For the ALU, it is primarily a matter of deciding what operations the ALU is to perform and then designing the circuitry needed to perform each of them. Associated with this logic there must be selection logic for using the SCL outputs to choose which operation is to be carried out and condition flag logic for updating the PSW. The X16's ALU design is representative of relatively uncomplicated processing elements and is diagrammed in Fig. 7-12. It consists of:

- Condition flags logic for updating the condition flags according to ALU results.
- Banks of AND gates, OR gates, XOR gates, and inverters for providing logical results.
- Shift/rotate logic with two sets of outputs, one set for left shifts and rotates and one for right shifts and rotates.
- An adder/subtracter for performing additions and subtractions.
- A control multiplexer for selecting the output to Data Bus 1.

Banks of logic gates and inverters implement the AND, inclusive OR, exclusive OR, complement, and test macroinstructions. The direct connection of Data Bus 2 to the control MUX is for the move macroinstructions and permits the transfer of data from Data Bus 2 to Data Bus 1 in general. The shift/rotate logic is obviously for implementing the shift and rotate macroinstructions. In addition to implementing the add and subtract macroinstructions, the adder/subtracter is used for clearing, negating and comparing. (Note that multiplication and division could be performed by repetitive usage of the shift/rotate logic and the adder/subtracter.)

Because the control MUX has eight sets of inputs, it requires three control inputs to make its selection. The shift/rotate logic must input the carry flag and three control signals, one each for indicating shift or rotate, left or right, and logical or arithmetic. The adder/subtracter must receive the carry flag plus two signals indicating add or subtract and whether or not the carry/borrow is to be included in the operation.

The condition flags control logic is given in Fig. 7-13. The Z flag is determined by NORing all of the bits output by the control MUX and the N flag is determined by bit 15 of the control MUX output. The carry flag may be determined by the shift/rotate logic, the adder/subtracter, or a set carry instruction. Assuming the ALU Control MUX bits are 010 or 011 for shifts and rotates and 001 for adds and subtracts, the two left-most AND gates in the carry flag logic determine whether the carry is to come from the shift/rotate logic or the adder/subtracter. For all arithmetic/logic macroinstructions that use Control MUX inputs other than 001, 010, or 011, the carry flag output is to be 0. If a set carry macroinstruction is being executed, both AND gates are closed and the carry is determined by the C Flag Clear/set signal from the SCL (which is discussed below). The overflow flag, which is the exclusive OR of bits 14 and 15 of an arithmetic result, is important only when the adder/subtracter is being used, i.e., the ALU Control MUX input is 001. For all other cases this output is to be 0.

It is important to note that these flag outputs do not necessarily become the new contents of the PSW condition flags. As we shall see shortly, the SCL supplies separate signals for triggering the flip-flops that store flags. If the triggering signal is not applied, the flag signal generated by the ALU is ignored. For example, a

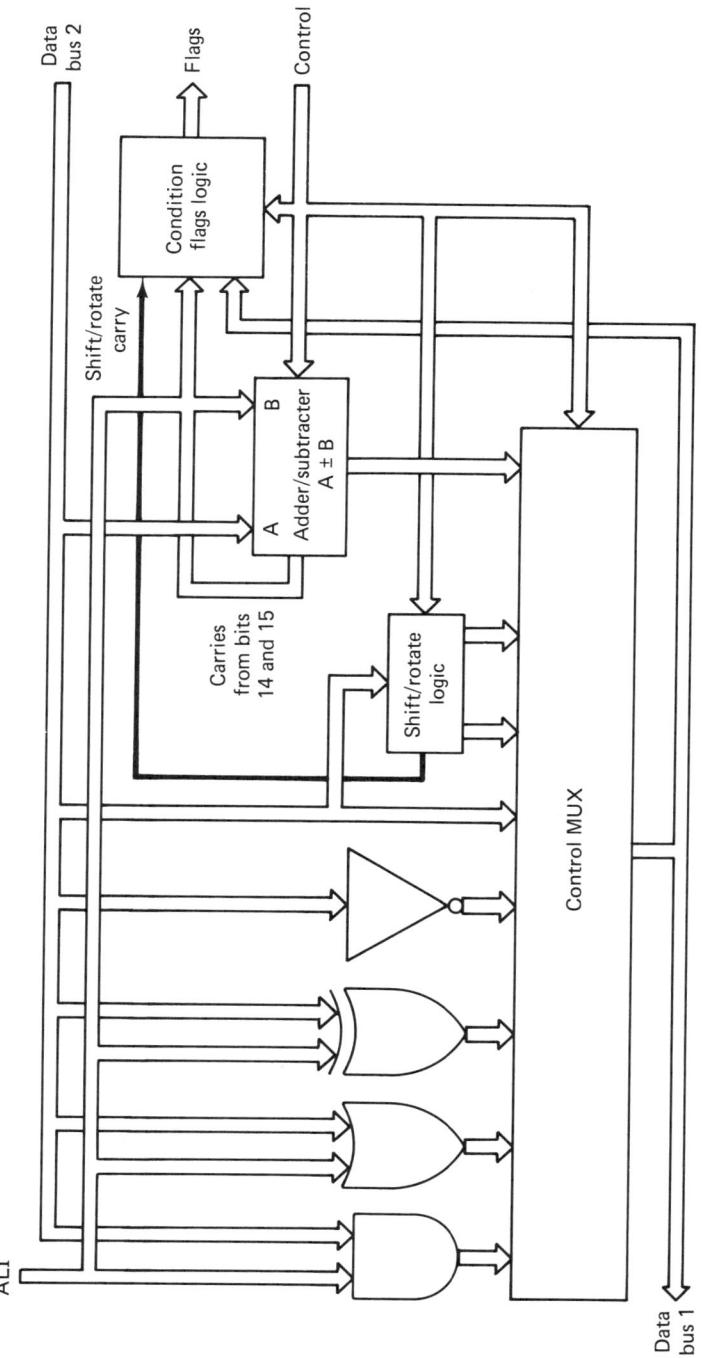

Figure 7-12 ALU design.

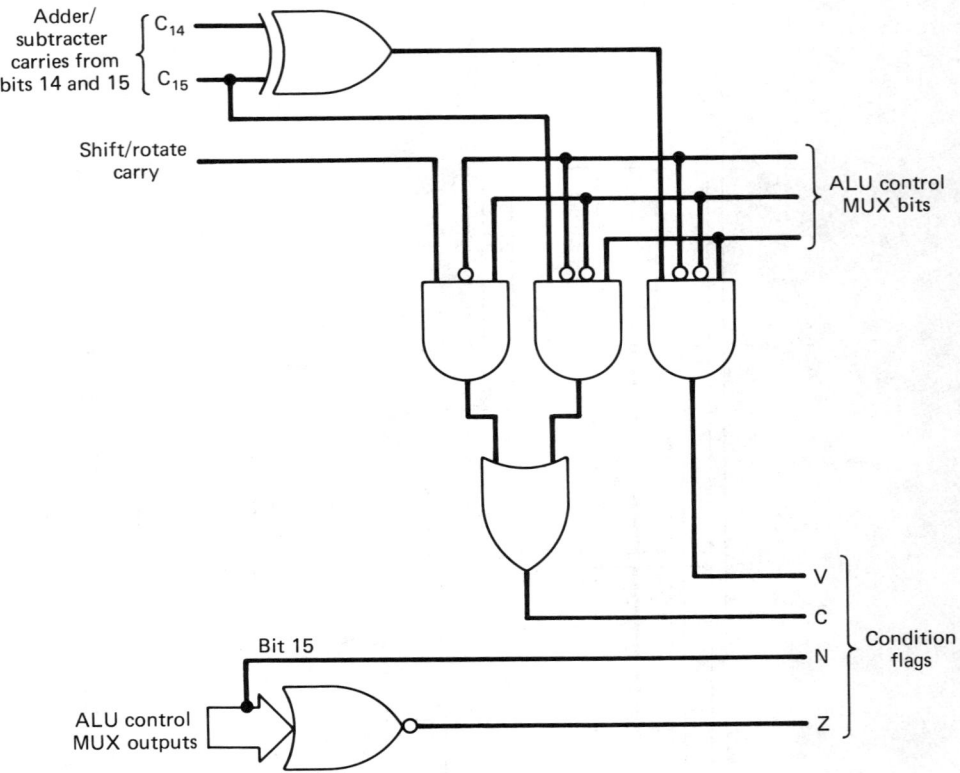

Figure 7-13 Condition Flags logic.

move instruction would cause a carry flag output of 0, but, because a move leaves all condition flags unchanged, the SCL would not issue a C Flag Strobe signal.

When the ALU requires two operands, one of them must come from the ALI register. Because the second operand must frequently be 0, 1, or 2, the clear/preset logic shown in Fig. 7-14 is associated with the ALI register. The clear/preset logic controls the clear and preset inputs of the flip-flops in the ALI register and allows the SCL to put 0, 1 or 2 into the ALI register. Being able to put 1 or 2 into this register permits the ALU to be used for incrementing and decrementing by 1 or 2. The clear and preset inputs are assumed to be inverted so that, when 00 is applied to the logic, a 0 is applied to all of the clear inputs and the (ALI) become 0. When 01 is applied, Bit 0 of the ALI register is set and all other bits are cleared, and when 10 is applied, Bit 1 is set and all other bits are cleared. An input of 11 leaves (ALI) unchanged.

The PSW design is shown in Fig. 7-15. It consists of D flip-flops and contains a 4-bit interrupt field in addition to condition flags. The bits in the PSW are changed by applying signals to the D inputs of the appropriate flip-flops and then instructing the SCL to apply pulses to the corresponding C inputs of the flip-flops. This is

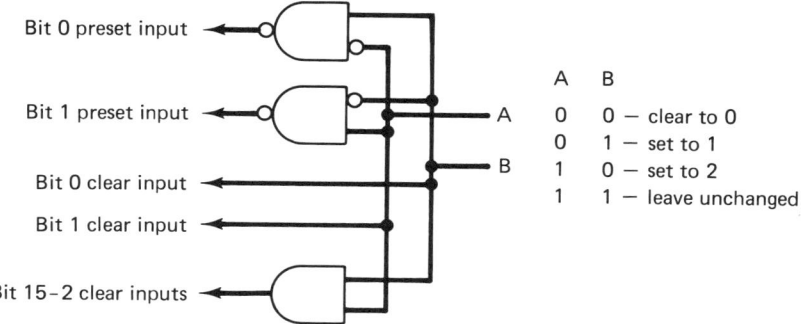

Figure 7-14 ALI Clear/Preset logic.

done by microoperations that result from the execution of the set interrupt field macroinstructions and any macroinstruction that affects the condition flags. Except during the execution of carry clear/set macroinstructions, the D inputs to the condition flags are supplied by the ALU, not the SCL. The SCL, however, supplies all of the strobing signals. Because the Z, N, V, and C flag outputs from the ALU are always input to the PSW at the same time, they share a common strobe signal. However, because the C flag can also be changed by the set carry and clear carry macroinstructions, it must additionally be connected to a separate C Flag Strobe line that is activated by only these macroinstructions. The logic for loading and outputting the contents of the PSW during push and pop operations is not shown—see Exercise 10.

7-3-3 BCL Logic

The BCL logic receives Read and Write signals that cause it to initiate external inputs and outputs. When it is busy performing an external transfer it outputs a Ready = 0, otherwise Ready = 1. A Ready = 0 in conjunction with a Suspend microoperation causes the SCL to suspend all processing element activity until Ready = 1.

The BCL also includes an interrupt vector register (IVR) and its associated interrupt management logic. Interrupt logic determines when an interrupt request is to be passed on to the SCL, which would then initiate an interrupt sequence (see Exercise 14). During the interrupt sequence, the IVR supplies the interrupt vector address (see Sec. 6-2-4). The details of the X16's BCL will be discussed in Chap. 8.

7-3-4 Control Bus

A summary of the control lines emanating from the SCL and the usage of these lines is given in Fig. 7-16. All of these lines and their purposes have been introduced in the macroinstruction and logic implementation discussions given pre-

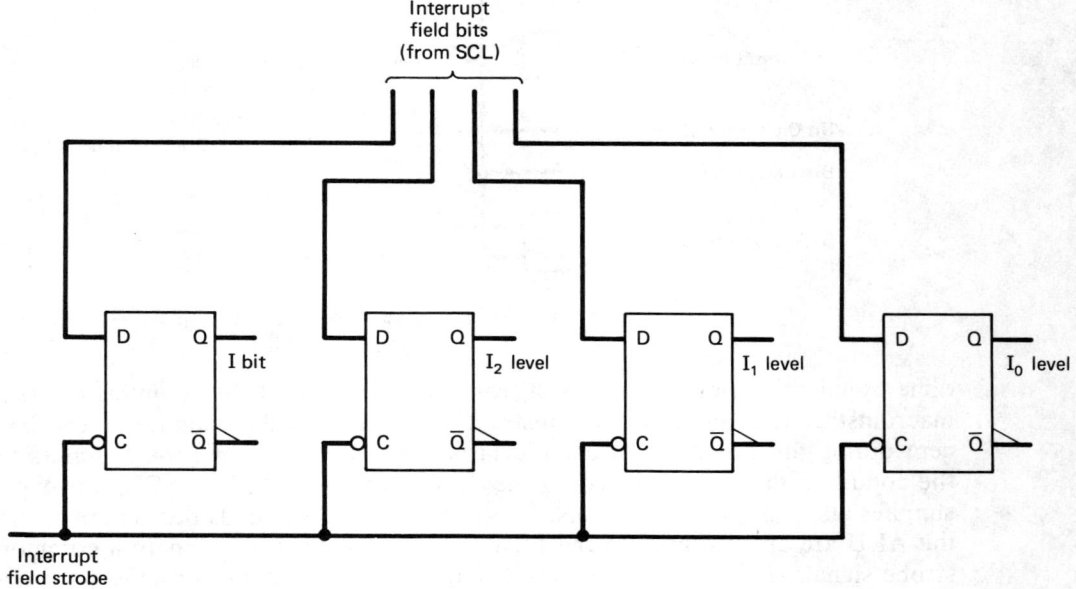
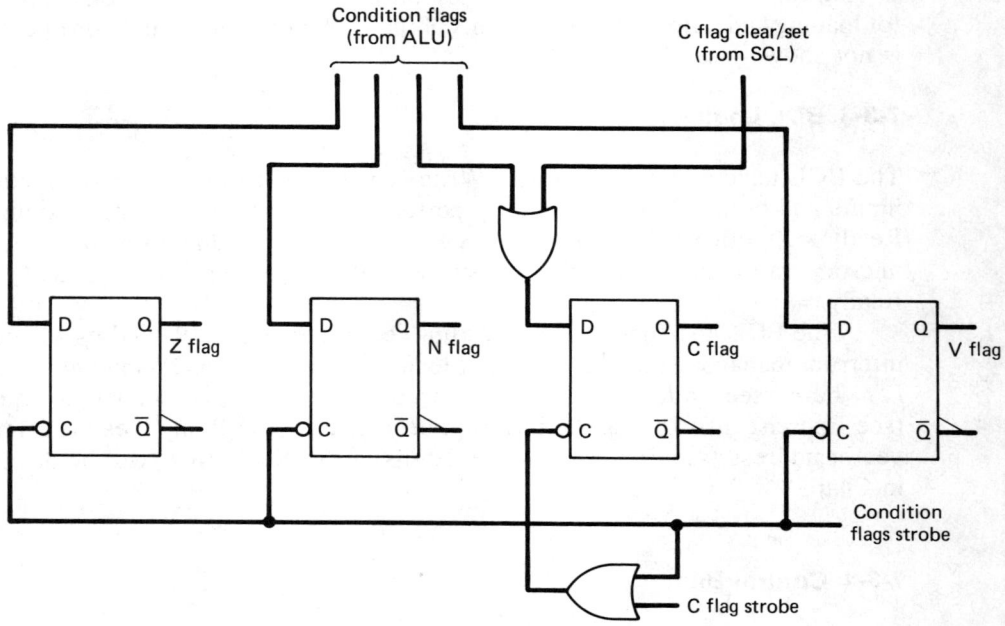

Figure 7-15 PSW design.

Name	No. of Lines	Destination	Description
Register Input Controls	14	All registers except XDI and IVR	Strobes bus data into register. One each for R0–R5, SP, PC, IR, PSW, TMP, ALI, XDO, and XAR.
Register Output Controls	12	All registers except ALI, IR, XDO, and XAR.	Opens output tristate gates. One each for R0–R5, SP, PC, PSW, TMP, XDI, and IVR.
Time Reset	1	SCL clock	Causes the SCL Time Generator to reset to T0.
ALI Clear/Preset Control Bits	2	ALI Clear/ Preset Control	Set ALI to 0, 1, or 2 as follows: 00 - 0 01 - 1 10 - 2 11 - ALI contents unchanged
Clear TMP	1	TMP	Clears TMP Register to 0.
Interrupt Field Bits	4	PSW Logic	Transfers new contents to interrupt field of the PSW.
Interrupt Field Strobe	1	PSW Logic	Strobes new contents into interrupt field.
Condition Flag Strobe	1	PSW Logic	Strobes new contents into Z, N, C, and V flags.
C Flag Clear/Set	1	PSW Logic	Transfers C Flag's new value to the PSW.
C Flag Strobe	1	PSW Logic	Strobes new value into C Flag.
Add/Subtract Control	2	ALU	Indicates add or subtract to ALU's Adder/Subtracter as follows: 00 - add (no carry) 01 - add (with carry) 10 - subtract (no borrow) 11 - subtract (with borrow)
ALU Control MUX Bits	3	ALU	Indicates to the ALU's Control MUX the selection it is to make as follows: 000 - move 001 - add/subtract 010 - left shift 011 - right shift 100 - complement 101 - OR 110 - XOR 111 - AND
Shift/Rotate Control	3	ALU	indicates to the ALU's Shift Logic the type of operation: shift/rotate, left/right, and arithmetic/logical.
Read	1	BCL	Signals an input is to be conducted using XDI and XAR.
Write	1	BCL	Signals an output is to be conducted using XDO and XAR.
Memory I/O	1	BCL	Indicates a memory (1) or I/O (0) access.
Suspend	1	SCL Clock	Goes to SCL Clock and causes it to suspend outputting pulses.

Figure 7-16 Definitions of the signals output by the X16's SCL Decode logic.

viously. Because there are 14 registers that can be input to and 12 that can be output from, there are 14 register input control lines and 12 register output control lines. There are 50 lines altogether and each microinstruction must apply a signal to all of them. For some of the signals it is the level (i.e., 0-1 value) that is important, but for others (those used for strobing) it is the transition at the trailing edge that is used. The signals resulting from the microinstructions that make up the

ADDH   R1,R2

macroinstruction (see Fig. 7-9) are given in Fig. 7-17. Dashes indicate that the value of the signal is not important.

Figure 7-18 contains a summary of the control signals that do not emanate from the SCL. Except for the Reset line, their uses have already been described. Note that the C flag output is connected to both the SCL and ALU. The C flag is the only condition flag that is used by the ALU.

The Reset line is included to provide a means for initializing the entire processing element. This line transmits a reset signal to all flip-flops and registers in the processing element. When power to the processing element is turned on, the processing element must enter a predetermined state. This state is arrived at by having the power supply voltage trigger a reset pulse that is sent to all components in the processing element. Normally, the reset pulse causes all condition flags and registers, except for the PC, to be cleared to 0 and the SCL's time generator to begin at T0. The value put into the PC is, of course, the address of the first

Time	Register Input Controls	Register Output Controls	Time Reset	ALI Clear/Preset Control	Clear TMP	Interrupt Field Bits	Interrupt Field Strobe	Condition Flags Strobe	C Flag Clear/Set	C Flag Strobe	Add/Subtract Control	ALU Control MUX Bits	Shift/Rotate Control	Read	Write	Memory I/O	Suspend
T0:	0041	010	0	2	0	–	0	0	–	0	0	1	–	1	0	1	1
T1:	0020	002	0	3	0	–	0	0	–	0	–	–	–	0	0	0	0
T2:	0004	400	0	3	0	–	0	0	–	0	–	0	–	0	0	0	0
T3:	0800	200	0	3	0	–	0	1	–	0	0	1	–	0	0	0	0
T4:	0000	000	1	3	0	–	0	0	–	0	–	–	–	0	0	0	0

Order of Register Input Controls: R0–R5, SP, PC, IR, PSW, TMP, ALI, XDO, XAR

Order of Register Output Controls: R0–R5, SP, PC, PSW, TMP, XDI, IVR

Entries are in hexadecimal, but the upper digit may represent less than four bits (e.g., there are only 2 ALI Clear/Preset Bits).

Figure 7-17 Control signals for the X16 macroinstruction ADDH R1, R2.

Name	From	To	Description
Interrupt Field	PSW	BCL	Transfers interrupt bit and interrupt level to BCL.
Z, N, and V Flags	PSW	SCL	Provides SCL with PSW's Z, N, and V flags.
C Flag	PSW	SCL and ALU	Provides the SCL and ALU with the C Flag.
Condition Flags	ALU	PSW	Transfers potential condition flags settings to the PSW.
Ready	BCL	SCL	Indicates to the SCL whether memory Read or Write is in progress: 0 - in progress 1 - not in progress
Interrupt	BCL	SCL	Indicates an interrupt sequence is to be initiated at next Time Reset.
Reset	BCL	All registers, flip-flops and SCL timing	Causes all registers and flip-flops to go to their startup states and the SCL timing to go to T0.

Figure 7-18 Control signals not generated by the SCL.

macroinstruction fetched from memory and is referred to as the **reset address**. Many computers also have an external switch or button that allows the user to initiate a reset without turning off the power. Some computers also have a macroinstruction that causes resets.

7-4 MICROCONTROL

Until now little has been said about how macroinstructions are decoded to produce the microcontrol provided by the SCL. The SCL can be designed independently from the design of the remainder of the processing element. There are two basic techniques for designing microcontrol logic. One is the **hardwired** approach, which consists of simply designing the combinational logic required to produce the SCL outputs. The other, called **microprogrammed control**, is to derive the SCL outputs from the contents of a ROM and have the ROM contents recalled according to the addresses applied to the ROM. The addresses are determined from the contents of the IR, the condition flags, and other signals that reflect the current state of the processing element.

7-4-1 Hardwired Control

The structure of a hardwired SCL is given in Fig. 7-19. It includes the circuitry for generating the clock pulses and timing signals T0, T1, ... ; the decode logic whose outputs are the SCL control signals discussed in the preceding sections; and other miscellaneous logic required to put the condition flags and other status information into the form needed by the decode logic.

A design for the time generator is shown in Fig. 7-20. It consists of a shift

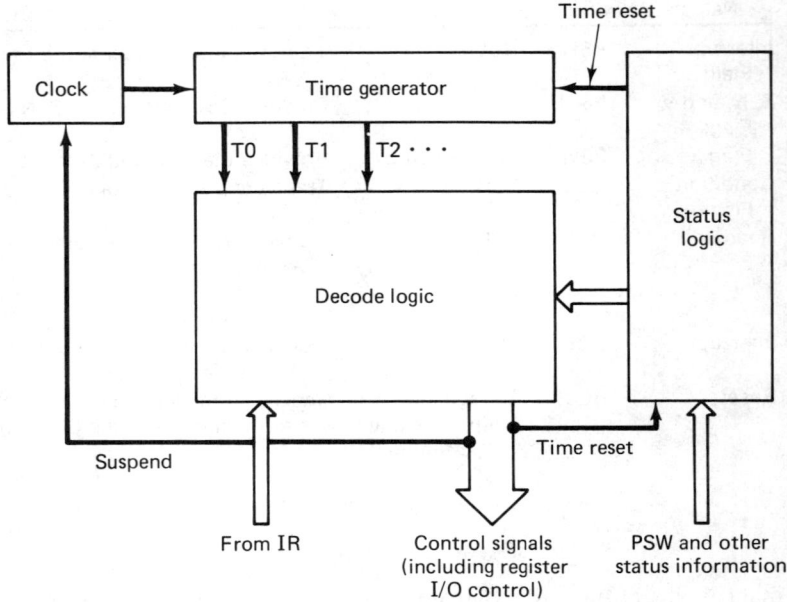

Figure 7-19 Major components of a hardwired SCL.

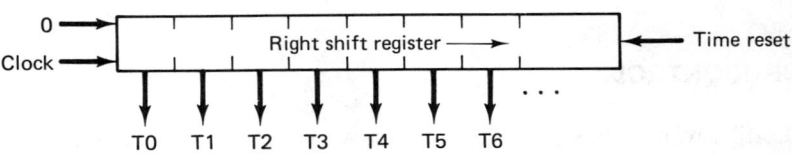

Figure 7-20 Time generator.

register that is initially filled by putting a 1 into its leftmost bit and 0s into the remaining bits. Each time a clock pulse is applied, a 0 is inserted at the left and the contents of the register are shifted to the right by 1. Therefore, at any given time, exactly one of the outputs T0, T1, . . . is 1. The incoming train of clock pulses can be disabled by the Suspend signal when the processing element is to suspend its activity. The number of bits in the shift register would be the maximum number of microinstructions taken over all macroinstructions.

Decode logic could be derived by simply determining, for each SCL output, all possible combinations that could cause the output to be 1 and then forming a Boolean expression for the output. The inputs to the decode logic would be (IR), the T0, T1, . . . signals, and status information derived from the condition flags and other status signals within the processing element. For example, the Boolean expression for the control signal applied to the PC's output tristate gates would be of the form

PC Output Control = T0 + T2·Move memory to memory
+ T4·Move memory to memory + . . .

A logic diagram corresponding to this expression is given in Fig. 7-21.

It is evident that these expressions could be very lengthy and the amount of logic, even after minimization, could be considerable. One approach to designing decode logic is to type the macroinstructions using the definitions in Chap. 4 (see Fig. 4-6) as a guide. Particular attention should be paid to the bit groupings and how the macroinstructions can be classified according to the source and destination operand fields. Such a classification is given in Fig. 7-22.

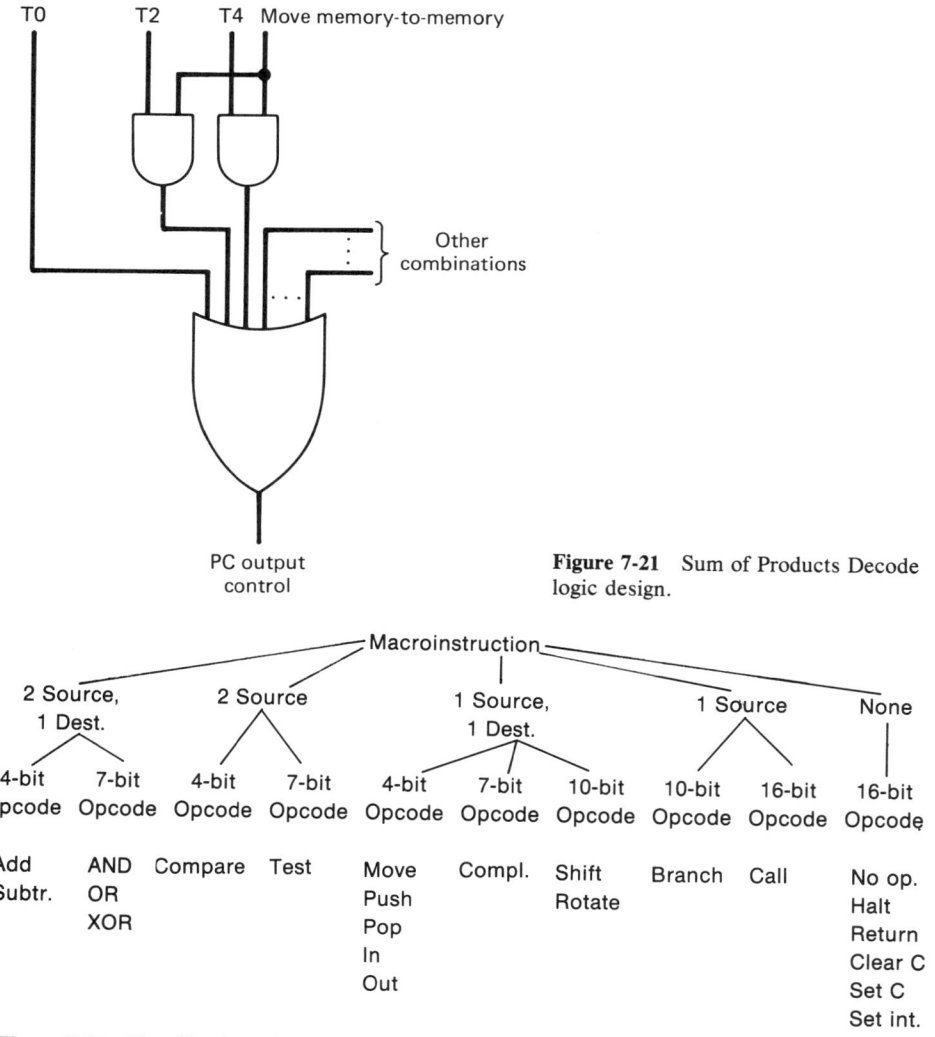

Figure 7-21 Sum of Products Decode logic design.

Figure 7-22 Classification of macroinstructions for the purpose of reducing decode logic.

Sec. 7-4 Microcontrol

For example, for the X16, the decode logic for the R0 through R5 input control signals could be arrived at by designing, for each macroinstruction, the logic needed to indicate when one of these registers is to receive an operand, ORing the outputs of these sets of logic, and then ANDing this output with the destination register address. Note that only the move, pop, in, complement, AND, OR, XOR, shift, rotate, add, and subtract instructions can put data into one of the registers R0 through R5 and all of them can deposit a result in any one of these registers. The microinstruction sequences for all possible moves into one of the R0 through R5 registers are given in Fig. 7-23. From these sequences and the machine language instruction definitions it is seen that a move causes an input into Rj when the address of Rj is the destination address and

$T3 \cdot$Immediate source addressing $+ T2 \cdot$Register source addressing

$+ T4 \cdot$Direct source addressing $+ T3 \cdot$Indirect source addressing

which is equivalent to the Boolean expression

$$b_{15}b_{14}b_{13}(T3 \cdot b_7\bar{b}_6 + T2 \cdot \bar{b}_7\bar{b}_6 + T4 \cdot b_7 b_6 + T3 \cdot \bar{b}_7 b_6)\bar{b}_2\bar{b}_1\bar{b}_0$$

where b_j denotes the jth bit of the IR.

Because an in, complement, shift, or rotate can be achieved by simply replacing the Move → ALU microoperation with the appropriate in, complement, shift, or rotate operation, the control of these macroinstructions over the inputs to R0 through R5 (i.e., the expression inside the parentheses) is the same as for a move. Therefore, the expression that controls whether a move, in, complement, shift, or rotate macroinstruction inputs to R0, . . . , or R5 is

$$(b_{15}b_{14}b_{13} + \bar{b}_{15}\bar{b}_{14}b_{13}b_{11}\bar{b}_{10}\bar{b}_9 + \bar{b}_{15}\bar{b}_{14}\bar{b}_{13}b_{11}b_{10})$$

$$\times (T3 \cdot b_7\bar{b}_6 + T2 \cdot \bar{b}_7\bar{b}_6 + T4 \cdot b_7 b_6 + T3 \cdot \bar{b}_7 b_6)\bar{b}_2\bar{b}_1\bar{b}_0$$

which can be implemented as shown in Fig. 7-24. The logic for the pop, AND, OR, XOR, add, and subtract macroinstructions can be similarly derived (see Exercise 19).

Regardless of the technique used to develop the decode logic, it is clear that the task is quite meticulous and a computer program is required to effectively complete and verify a decode logic design. It is apparent that uniformity of the macroinstruction bit meanings can be important to reducing the amount of logic needed. A PLA is often used to implement the decode logic because it provides a regular layout that permits the IC designer to achieve a high gate density. On the other hand, PLAs are restricted to one level of AND gates followed by one level of OR gates, i.e., sum of product implementations. Additional factoring of the sum of products expressions could considerably reduce the total number of gates (as seen by the design in Fig. 7-24 that required five levels of gates), but would result in an irregular layout. Normally a compromise is arrived at that uses a PLA for most of the decoding, but includes extra logic for accommodating exceptions.

An accounting of the time in a single clock period is given in Fig. 7-25. In addition to the time that the SCL outputs must be active, which includes data

```
                              ·⎫
                              ·⎬  Instruction Fetch
                              ·⎭
Move imm. to reg. AND  T2:  PC→XAR and PC, 2→ALI, Add (no carry)→ALU,
                              Read→BCL, Suspend until Ready = 1
           "          T3:  XDI→Rj, Move→ALU
           "          T4:  Time Reset
```

(a) Move immediate to register Rj

```
                              ·⎫
                              ·⎬  Instruction Fetch
                              ·⎭
Move reg. to reg. AND  T2:  Ri→Rj, Move→ALU
           "          T3:  Time Reset
```

(b) Move register Ri to Rj

```
                              ·⎫
                              ·⎬  Instruction Fetch
                              ·⎭
Move dir. to reg. AND  T2:  PC→XAR and PC, 2→ALI, Add (no carry)→ALU,
                              Read→BCL, Suspend until Ready = 1
           "          T3:  XDI→XAR, Read→BCL, Suspend until Ready = 1
           "          T4:  XDI→Rj, Move→ALU
           "          T5:  Time Reset
```

(c) Move direct to register Rj

```
                              ·⎫
                              ·⎬  Instruction Fetch
                              ·⎭
Move ind. to reg. AND  T2:  Ri→XAR, Read→BCL, Suspend until Ready = 1
           "          T3:  XDI→Rj, Move→ALU
           "          T4:  Time Reset
```

(d) Move indirect using Ri to Rj

Figure 7-23 Possible macroinstructions for moving data into one of the registers R0 through R5.

transfer time, a complete clock cycle must allow for the SCL decode time. The major advantage of hardwired designs is that the decode time tends to be less than that for microprogrammed SCLs because microinstructions are stored in a ROM and a memory access is included in the decode time. For hardwired designs that decode time is simply the propagation delay along the longest path through the decode logic. Note that the greater the number of gate levels, the longer the decode time.

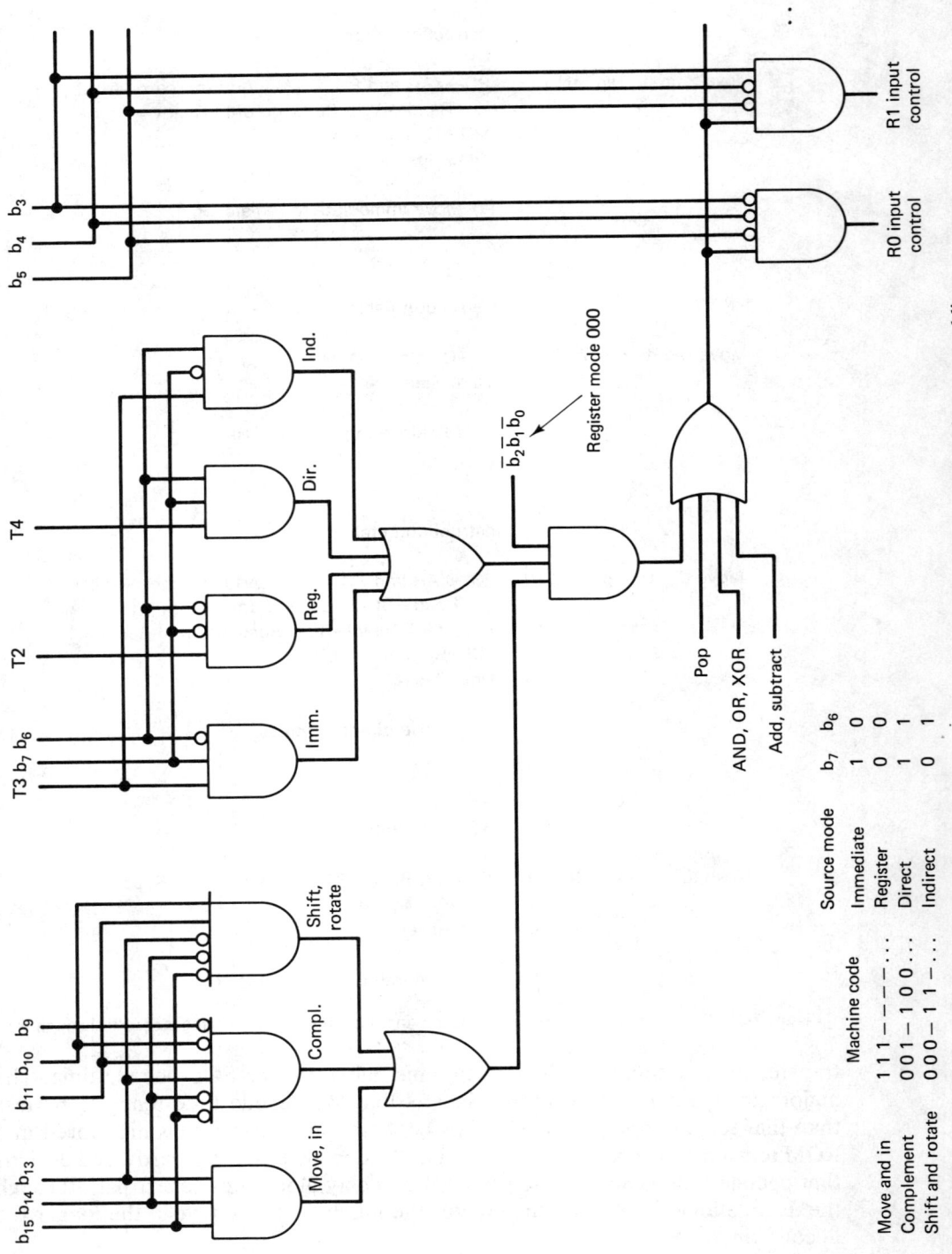

Figure 7-24 Logic needed to control the register R0 through R5 input control lines.

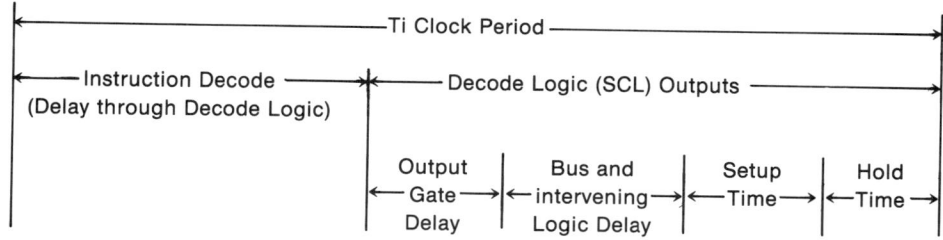

Figure 7-25 Breakdown of a single Ti period.

7-4-2 Microprogrammed Control

In a processing element that uses microprogrammed control, microinstructions are not generated by hardwired logic, but are permanently stored in a **control ROM**. During each clock cycle, an address is applied to the address inputs of the control ROM and the contents of the addressed location are output and used to control the activity in the processing element. Figure 7-26 is a block diagram that shows the major components of a microprogrammed SCL. The basic operation of a microprogrammed SCL is as follows:

1. The (IR), status information, and perhaps a portion of the current control output, generate a control ROM address.

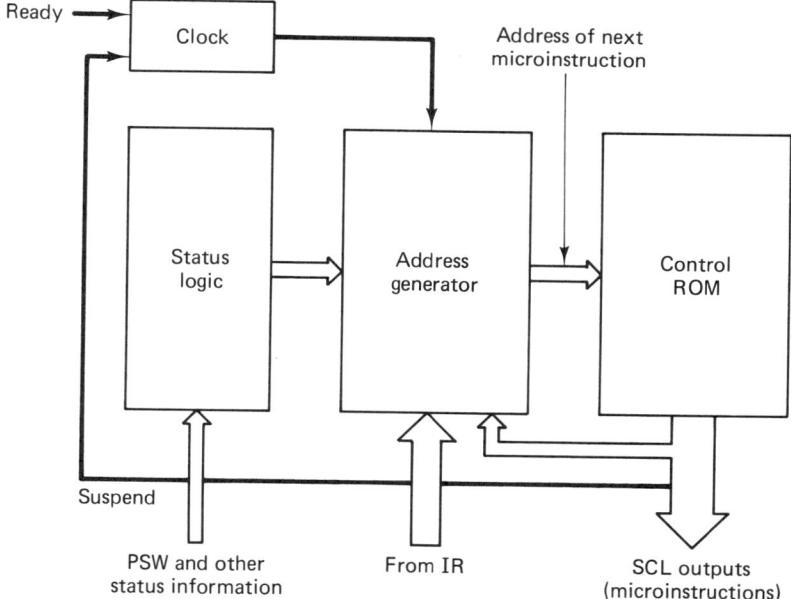

Figure 7-26 Block diagram of a microprogrammed SCL.

Sec. 7-4   Microcontrol

2. The clock signals when this address is to be passed to the control ROM.
3. When an address is received by the control ROM, the addressed microinstruction is output to the processing element's control bus.

As with a hardwired design, one of the control outputs could be used to suspend the clock output and thereby suspend the operation of the processing element.

The problem is that of arranging microinstructions in a logical pattern and generating addresses according to those patterns. In Sec. 7-3-1 it was seen that first the microinstructions for fetching the next macroinstruction must be executed and then a sequence of microinstructions determined by the macroinstruction must carry out the desired operation. This implies that the control memory must be structured as shown in Fig. 7-27. Here it is assumed that the fetch microinstructions are executed in sequence and are followed by a branch to the appropriate microinstruction sequence. The branch consists of a nonsequential change in the control ROM's address and the branch address is determined by the macroinstruction. After the microinstruction sequence corresponding to the macroinstruction has been executed, the address is reset to point to the beginning of the fetch sequence and the cycle is repeated.

The difficulty that arises when using the simplified scheme depicted in Fig. 7-27 for a large instruction set is apparent. A large instruction set would require a large control ROM whose access time is directly related to its size. Because

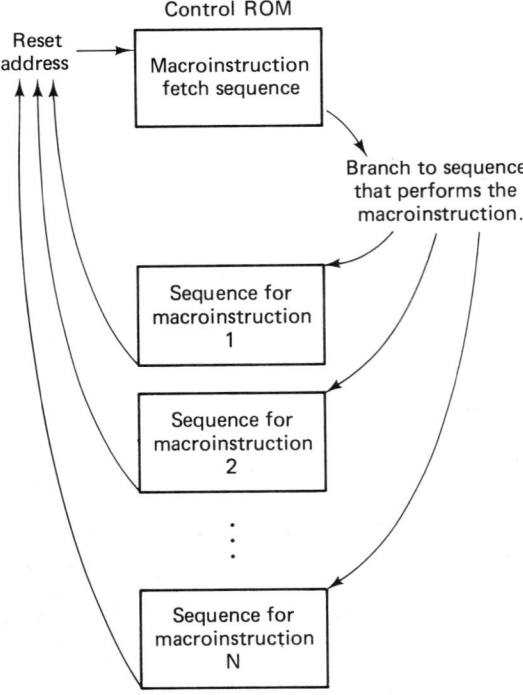

Figure 7-27 Simplified basic structure of a Control ROM.

each microinstruction must be retrieved from the control ROM, this access time determines the speed of the processing element. Also, it is often desirable to put the control ROM on the same IC as the remainder of the processing element's logic, but the area on an IC's surface is limited. To reduce the size of the control ROM it is necessary to reuse microinstructions whenever possible, but this requires a more sophisticated branching capability than that shown in Fig. 7-27. As a result, the branching scheme and circuitry needed to implement it are very important, and sometimes central, to the design of a microprogrammed SCL.

For example, let us assume that the SCL outputs are the same as defined in Fig. 7-16 and that a ROM address is 20 bits wide. Let us also assume that the reset address is 00000 and the (IR) are used directly as the upper 16 bits of the address output by the address decode logic after the fetch is completed. The lower four of these bits are 0s. The last microinstruction of the current macroinstruction would send an address reset to the address generator. This reset would cause the address generator to output 00000 to the control ROM and the fetch of the next instruction to begin. The microinstructions stored at 00000 and 00001 would fetch the next macroinstruction and then use the (IR) to generate the next address. If the fetched macroinstruction were ADDH R1, R2, the next address used to access the control ROM would be 42100 and the next sequence of microinstructions to be executed would begin at this address.

Because Fig. 7-16 includes 50 output bits and a 20-bit address implies 1M locations, the size of the control ROM needed in this example would be 50M bits. The reason that the ROM must be so large is that a separate microinstruction sequence is used for every possible bit combination in the first word of the macroinstruction and each macroinstruction points to a block of 16 microinstructions. (It is assumed that no macroinstruction requires more than 16 microinstructions.) Although this design provides a simple means of supplying SCL outputs and simplifies the branching and its associated address decode logic, it requires a ROM that is unrealistically large. The two ways of decreasing the size of the control ROM are: (1) reducing the number of bits in a microinstruction and (2) reducing the number of locations in the control ROM.

Reducing the Control ROM Width

First, let us consider how to reduce the number of bits in a microinstruction. In the case of the X16, note that several of the SCL outputs could be obtained directly from the macroinstruction. Because it does not matter what signals are applied to the PSW flip-flop inputs when they are not being strobed and the Interrupt Field Bits are strobed only by the interrupt set macroinstruction, these bits could be directly obtained from the lower four bits of the IR. Similarly, for the clear and set carry flag microinstructions, the C flag input could be connected to Bit 0 of the IR. Also, for the shift and rotate macroinstructions, the Shift/rotate Control Bits could be connected to Bits 9, 7, and 6 of the IR—see Fig. 4-6 and Exercise 22. Therefore, by using some of the IR bits to directly supply these outputs, the width of every location in the control ROM can be reduced by eight bits.

In addition, because the interrupt field set, clear carry, and set carry are the only macroinstructions that activate the Interrupt Field and C Flag strobes, by using the simple decode logic given in Fig. 7-28 these strobes can also be easily generated from the (IR). But, unlike the interrupt field and C flag inputs to the PSW, some logic, albeit simple, is required. This introduces the concept of combining the use of the control ROM with that of decode logic and requires that the diagram in Fig. 7-26 be modified as shown in Fig. 7-29.

In the case at hand, a trivial amount of decode logic allowed us to reduce the width of the locations in the control ROM by two more bits. If, as in Fig. 7-26, there is no decode logic between the control ROM and SCL outputs, the microinstructions directly supply the control signals and the design is said to be **horizontal**. Otherwise, as in Fig. 7-29, they must be decoded to produce the control signals and the design is said to be **vertical**. Actually, horizontal and vertical are not used in a black and white sense, but are used to indicate the tendency of a design. If a design uses very little decoding to produce its SCL outputs, then it tends to be horizontal, but if there is considerable decoding, it tends to be vertical.

The most significant gain through using vertical microcode is realized by eliminating some of the register I/O control bits from the microinstruction. For the X16's registers R0 through R5, this reduction could be made as shown in Fig. 7-30. Only three bits of the control ROM output, the Register In, Register Out, and Bit Group Select bits, are needed to indicate when a register is being input to or output from; which register is being accessed is indicated by the macroinstruction's register bits. Either Bits 9, 10, and 11 or Bits 3, 4, and 5 may be used to address a register that is being output from. The Bit Group Select signal de-

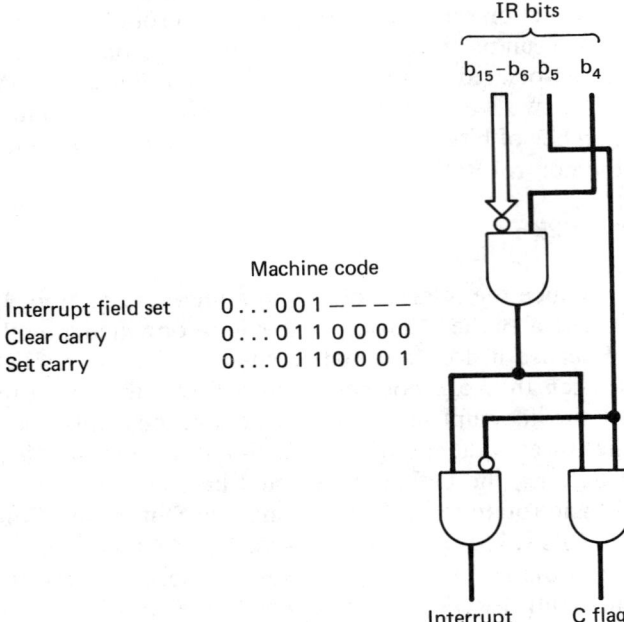

Figure 7-28 Logic for generating the Interrupt Field and C Flag strobes.

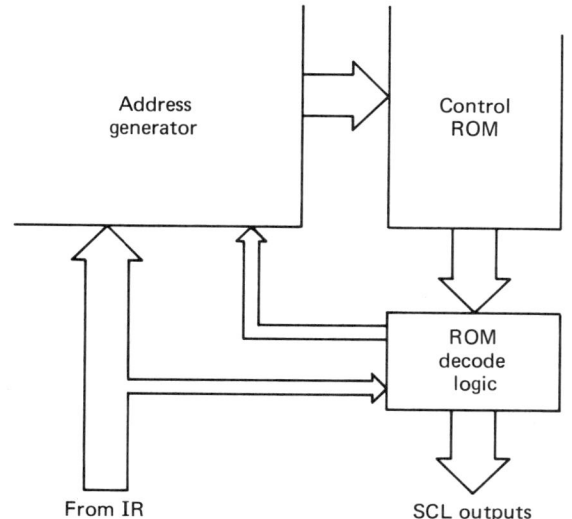

Figure 7-29 Addition of ROM Decode logic.

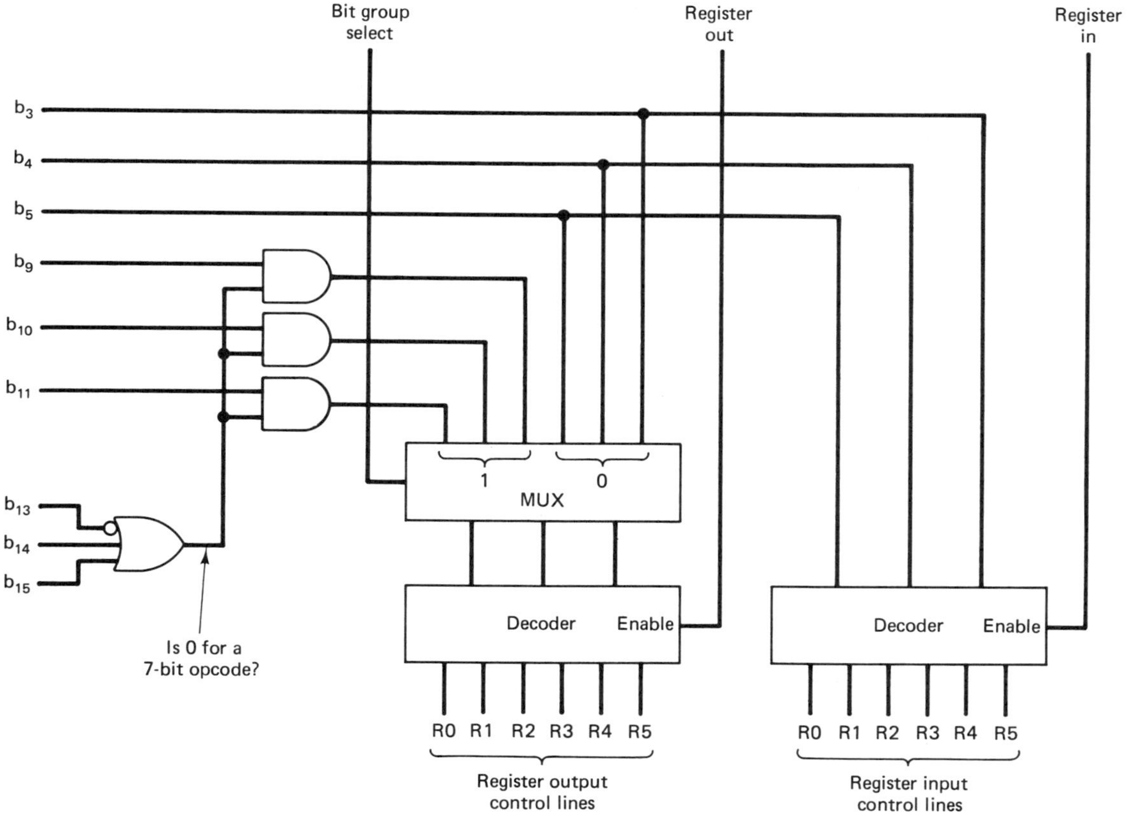

Figure 7-30 Logic for generating I/O control signals for registers R0 through R5.

Sec. 7-4   Microcontrol

termines which group is to be used. Only Bits 3, 4, and 5 can specify a register that is to receive input. For a macroinstruction with a 7-bit opcode (i.e., a macroinstruction whose three most significant bits are 001) the source register must be R0. This special case is accounted for by the OR and AND gates on the left.

Note that not only does this design approach reduce the number of bits in the control ROM, but it also allows control ROM outputs to be more generic by allowing them to access a register R0 through R5 without specifying which register. As will be seen later, this can reduce the number of microinstructions.

Because other register control signals may appear in microinstructions without being explicitly addressed by a macroinstruction, their addresses cannot be directly obtained from the macroinstruction. However, it may be possible to indicate their addresses by fields in the microinstructions instead of using one output bit and/or one input bit per register. For example, because only one of the six registers PSW, PC, SP, TMP, XDI, and IVR can be output from at a time, they can be indicated by a single 3-bit field. Then, a 3 to 6 decoder can be used to produce the register output controls as shown in Fig. 7-31. (Note that a problem arises if the same technique is applied to the register input control signals—see Exercises 23 and 24.)

The X16's microinstruction bits can now be summarized as shown in Fig. 7-32. In addition to the bits already considered is the IR Select bit, which has been included so that the ALU Control MUX bits and Add/subtract Control bits can sometimes be generated from macroinstruction bits. Although the use of this bit requires an increase in the amount of decode logic—see Exercise 27—as seen below it increases the flexibility of certain microinstructions and thereby reduces the total amount of microcode. The number of bits in a microinstruction has been reduced from the 50 bits indicated in Fig. 7-16 to 29 bits. This savings is significant but, to make the design practical, a reduction in the number of locations in the control ROM is also required.

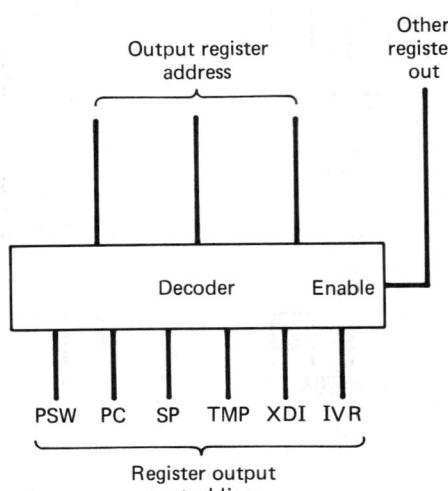

Figure 7-31 Logic for decoding the PSW, PC, SP, TMP, XDI, and IVR outputs.

Name	Register In	Other Reg. in Controls	Register Out	Output Reg. Address	Other Register Out
No. of Lines	1	8	1	3	1

Name	Bit Group Select	ALI Clear/ Preset	Clear TMP	Condition Flags Strobe
No. of Lines	1	2	1	1

Name	Add/Subtract Control	ALU Control MUX Bits	IR Select
No. of Lines	2	3	1

Name	Read	Write	Memory I/O	Suspend
No. of Lines	1	1	1	1

Figure 7-32 Summary of X16 microinstruction bits.

Reducing the Control ROM Length

The principal means of decreasing the number of control ROM locations is to permit branching within the microcode. This additional feature allows commonly used microinstruction sequences to appear only once, instead of being repeated for each macroinstruction and, perhaps, each addressing mode. There are basically two ways of adding branching capability at the microinstruction level. They are the same choices available at the macroinstruction level and are to:

- Use a separate set of instructions to perform branches.
- Extend the instructions to include the address of the next instruction to be executed.

For the former, an extra bit would be needed to indicate whether the instruction is to perform a branch. If so, the remaining bits would specify the condition under which the branch is to be taken and the branch address. These bits would replace those that generate SCL outputs. A typical branch microinstruction format is similar to that of a branch macroinstruction and is given in Fig. 7-33(a).

Using separate instructions for branching was chosen at the macroinstruction level because memory addresses tend to be quite long and concatenating an address to every instruction would lengthen instructions considerably. However, at the microinstruction level, the control ROM is relatively small and its addresses are correspondingly much shorter. On the other hand, the primary disadvantage

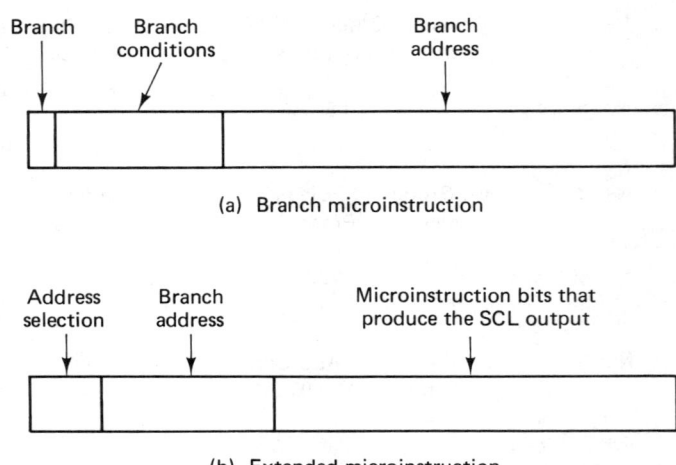

Figure 7-33 Methods for adding branching capability.

of having separate branch instructions is that they must be executed separately and therefore, add to the overall execution time. At the microinstruction level, the branch instructions directly add to the time it takes to complete the macroinstructions, thereby increasing the average execution time of the macroinstructions. As a result, extending every instruction to include the address of the next instruction as shown in Fig. 7-33(b) is more prevalent when designing microinstructions. It is this method of branching studied further below.

The address of the next microinstruction may be derived from either the macroinstruction or the microinstruction's address field (or perhaps, a combination of both). Fig. 7-26 has been modified and redrawn in Fig. 7-34 to reflect the use of branching.

The microinstruction format for a microprogrammed X16 is shown in Fig. 7-35. Three types of branches are used to select the next address:

- A conditional branch for which the branch is taken only if the condition specified by the branch macroinstruction is *false* according to the current settings of the condition flags. The branch address is obtained from the microinstruction and is normally 00. If true, execute in sequence.
- An unconditional branch to an address generated from a macroinstruction.
- The next address is unconditionally derived from the microinstruction's address field.

A conditional branch is indicated by the most significant microinstruction bit and the next bit differentiates between the two types of unconditional branches. The bit that is third from the left is used whenever an unconditional branch is made to an address partially determined by a macroinstruction. When it is active, bits

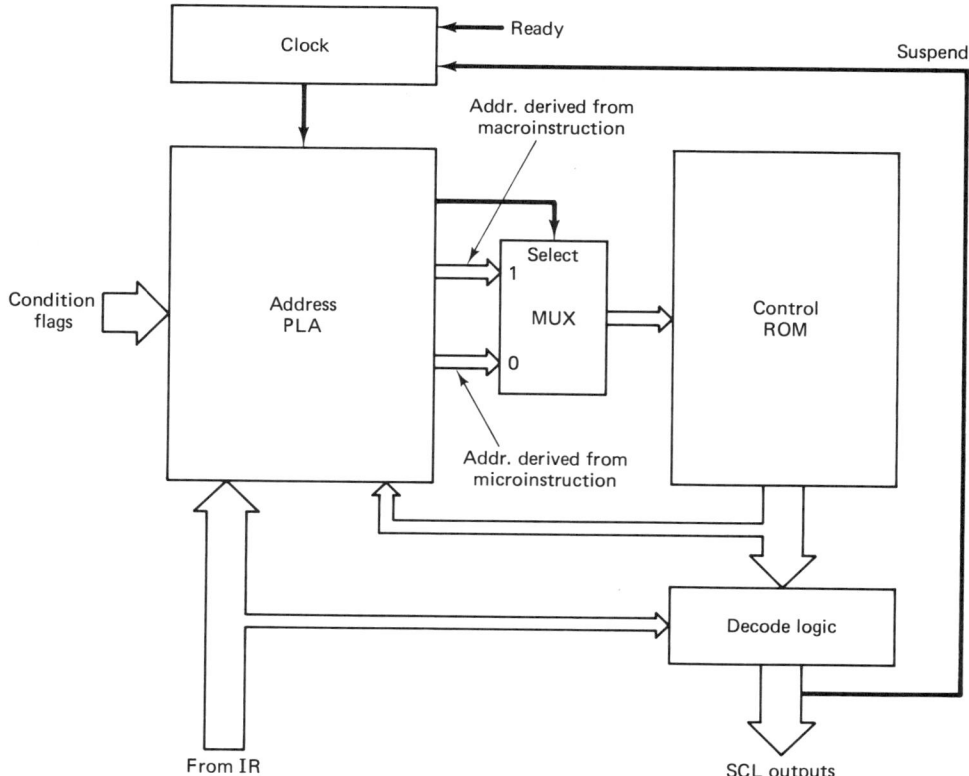

Figure 7-34 Microprogrammed SCL with branching capability.

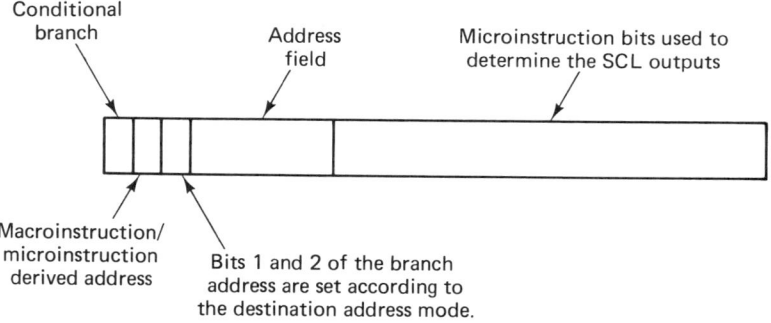

Figure 7-35 Format of an X16 microinstruction.

1 and 2 of the branch address are taken from bits 0 and 1 of the macroinstruction (i.e., the destination mode bits).

For example, consider some of the microcode for the X16. The first step toward recognizing instances of frequently occurring microcode is to classify ma-

Sec. 7-4   Microcontrol

croinstructions according to their source and destination operands as shown in Fig. 7-22. Note that the add, subtract, AND, OR, and XOR instructions all have two source operands and one destination operand. Thus, we can write the microcode for these instructions as in Fig. 7-36. The first column in the figure gives the control ROM address and the second either provides the next address or indicates how it is obtained.

The instruction fetch begins at address 00 and is essentially the same as in Fig. 7-9, except that the second microinstruction also uses (IR) to determine the next address. It is this microinstruction that uses the IR bits to point to the set of microcode corresponding to each basic macroinstruction type. It is assumed that for the group of macroinstructions being considered, the PLA produces the address 10 if the first operand's address mode is the register mode, 12, if it is the register indirect mode, 14 if it is the immediate mode, and 16 if it is the direct mode. The microinstructions from 10 to 17 put the first operand into the register TMP and those from 18 to 1F input the second operand, perform the desired operation, and store the result.

The key to being able to use the same sequence for five different macroinstructions is to decode the opcode bits and use the microoperation

Address	Next* Address	Microoperations
00	01	:PC→XAR and PC, 2→ALI, Add (nc)→ALU, Read→BCL, Suspend
01	IR	:XDI→IR
.		
.		
.		
10	18+	:Ri→TMP, Move→ALU
11	18+	:XDI→TMP, Move→ALU
12	13	:Ri→XAR, Read→BCL, Suspend
13	18+	:XDI→TMP, Move→ALU
14	15	:PC→XAR and PC, 2→ALI, Add (nc)→ALU, Read→BCL, Suspend
15	18+	:XDI→TMP, Move→ALU
16	17	:PC→XAR and PC, 2→ALI, Add (nc)→ALU, Read→BCL, Suspend
17	11	:XDI→XAR, Read→BCL, Suspend
18	19	:TMP→ALI, Move→ALU
19	00	:Rj→Rj, IR Select=1, Cond. Flags Strobe→PSW
1A	1B	:Rj→XAR, Read→BCL
1B	1C	:TMP→ALI, Move→ALU, Suspend
1C	00	:XDI→XDO, IR Select=1, Cond. Flags Strobe→PSW, Write→BCL, Suspend
1D	--	: --
1E	1F	:PC→XAR and PC, 2→ALI, Add (nc)→ALU, Read→BCL, Suspend
1F	1B	:XDI→XAR, Read→BCL

IR Bits Select = 1

* IR indicates that the next address is determined by the macroinstruction and a suffix "+" means that the address in the microinstruction is modified by the destination address mode.

Figure 7-36 Microcode for the add, subtract, AND, OR, and XOR macroinstructions.

in place of a microoperation that explicitly specifies the ALU Control MUX bits and Add/Subtract Control bits. Also, because register addresses are taken from the macroinstruction (see Fig. 7-30), it does not matter which registers are to be used in the microoperations involving the registers R0 through R5, e.g., the microoperation

$$R_i \rightarrow TMP$$

The entire microcode for the X16 could be put into less than 128 locations, which would imply a microinstruction address field width of 7 and a total control ROM width of

$$3 + 7 + 29 = 39 \text{ bits}$$

Therefore, the control ROM would require less than 5 K bits, which is far less than 50 M bits implied by the design originally considered. In fact, by providing a more sophisticated branching capability and restricting the push, pop, in, and out instructions to the registers R0 through R5 and the PSW, the microcode could be put into 64 locations, thus reducing the control ROM width to 38 bits and its capacity to less than 2.5 K bits.

Many different formats have been used to provide branching. There is no preferred format because the format is subject to the design philosophy. It is possible to design into the SCL a complex microinstruction set that includes microinstructions capable of branching on a variety of conditions, looping, and performing subroutine calls and returns. However, if this complexity is added the address generator must be replaced with a much more complicated **microprogram sequencer** that includes a means of storing and restoring return addresses and/or counting repetitions. We have been able to keep the X16's branching facility relatively simple by restricting its macroinstruction set. For a processing element with a complex macroinstruction set it may be necessary to resort to the microsequencer concept.

Just as an assembler can alleviate the error-prone and tedious task of writing machine language programs, a microprogram assembler could be developed to ease the production of microcode. A microprogram assembler could be designed to run on any machine and be written in an assembler or high-level language. The statements for a microprogram assembler would contain several operands because there are so many fields in a microinstruction that must be designated. Because of the widely varying contents and formats of microinstructions, the formats of a microprogram assembler's statements are heavily dependent on the design of the microinstruction set and the preferences of the assembler's designer.

Nanostore

Yet another technique for reducing the size of the control ROM is to divide the storage and control functions so that they use two separate ROMs as shown in Fig. 7-37. The control ROM does not contain the instructions that produce the SCL outputs, but contains only the addresses of these instructions within the second ROM, called the **nanostore**. The instructions that provide the SCL outputs

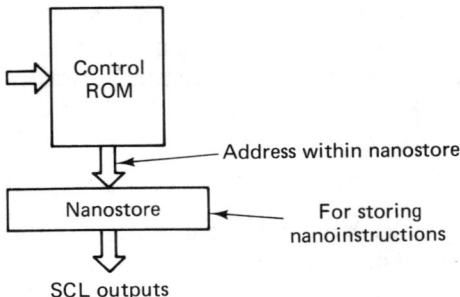

Figure 7-37 Use of nanostore.

(i.e., the contents of the nanostore) are called **nanoinstructions**. Nanostore takes advantage of the fact that there may be relatively few distinct nonbranch microinstructions in a processing element's microcode (e.g., in Fig. 7-36 there are only twelve distinct microinstructions and they would be frequently repeated in the microcode not shown). This limited number of microinstructions would mean that the nanostore would require only a few locations, and the width of each control ROM location could be reduced significantly. In addition, the decode logic used by vertical microinstructions could be reduced or eliminated. If the number of control ROM locations is n, the number of required nanostore locations is $m \leq 2^r$, and the number of bits in an SCL output is p, then the number of bits saved by using a nanostore would be $n(p - r) - mp$. For example, consider a complex processing element for which $n = 1$ K, $m = 100$, $r = 7$, and $p = 70$. Without the nanostore, $np = 70$ K bits would be required, and with the nanostore only $nr + mp = 14$ K bits would be needed, amounting to a savings of 80%.

The obvious disadvantage of using a nanostore is that two memory accesses are required per microinstruction, although one of the accesses would be to an extremely fast nanostore.

Advantages of the Microprogrammed Approach

One of the advantages of the microprogrammed approach to SCL design is the regularity of the ROM's pattern as opposed to the irregularity of the decode logic in a hardwired design. However, most advantages are due to the flexibility that microprogramming offers. It allows a designer to customize, and even optimize, the design of a processing element relative to the applications it is to satisfy. Through microprogramming, a processing element can be made to act like, or **emulate**, a processing element of a different design. Processing elements with quite limited capabilities can be microprogrammed to emulate more complex processing elements.

The person developing the microcode decides which microoperations are performed by each microinstruction and which microinstructions are executed by each macroinstruction. This gives the developer the power to determine the processing element's macroinstruction set. He or she is limited only by the element's internal architecture and the design of the microprogram sequencer. For example, if an X16 were to be used in an application that requires the frequent computation

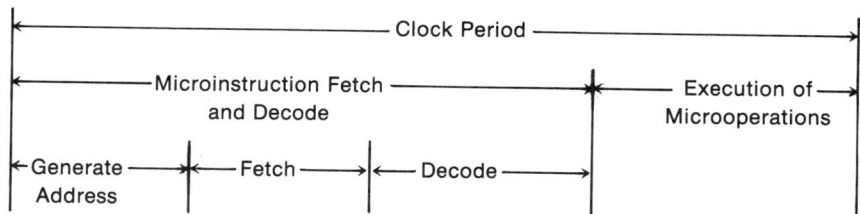

Figure 7-38 Breakdown of a clock period.

of inner products, a microinstruction routine could be written that would perform a multiplication followed by an addition. This routine could be initiated by a single macroinstruction so that evaluating the inner product

$$A_1B_1 + A_2B_2 + \cdots + A_nB_n$$

could be done by n macroinstructions. In fact, for a specialized application for which the dimension of the vectors is always the same, a microroutine could be developed that takes the entire inner product, thus allowing an inner product to be computed by a single macroinstruction. By writing a custom microroutine to perform the inner product, the calculation could be made more efficiently, only one macroinstruction would be fetched from memory, and there would be less wasted movement of the data operands. If a processing element does not have special hardware for performing floating point operations, an obvious application of microprogramming would be to microprogram these operations.

Unfortunately, many processing elements are manufactured into a single IC and the contents of the control ROM are permanently set by the original designer. If this is the case, only the original designer can take advantage of the flexibility microprogramming offers. Some processing elements, however, are constructed so that the control ROM is separate and can easily be replaced. If the control ROM is accessible, the manufacturer may market software to support microcode development.

Microprogram Timing

The primary disadvantage of the microprogrammed approach is the time it takes to produce the SCL outputs. For a hardwired SCL this time is the propagation delay of the decode logic. As shown in Fig. 7-38, a microprogrammed SCL needs time to generate an address, access the ROM, and, for vertical microinstructions, decode the microinstructions output by the ROM. Most of the time is spent accessing the ROM. The ROM's access time is a basic characteristic of the ROM's technology and can be shortened only by using a different type of ROM.

7-5 REDUCED INSTRUCTION SET COMPUTERS

Historically, early computers had small instruction sets because logic was extremely expensive. However, as the cost of logic became less, complex processing elements became more affordable and, with the introduction of microprogrammed control, expansion to very large instruction sets with numerous addressing modes became widespread. With microprogramming, a larger instruction set could be had by simply increasing the size of the control ROM. Many of the medium to large computers developed during the 1970s and 1980s are now referred to as **complex instruction set computers (CISCs)**.

However, in the early 1980s there was a renewed interest in designing computers with small instruction sets. In particular, this interest was centered on designs tending toward the following attributes (see Colwell et al [7] and Stallings [8]):

- Single-cycle operation for which a macroinstruction is executed during each clock cycle.
- Hardwired control.
- Fixed macroinstruction length and format.
- Relatively few macroinstructions and addressing modes.
- Load/store designs which allowed only load and store macroinstructions to access main memory.
- Large register set.
- More compile-time effort.

Computers resulting from these designs were referred to as **reduced instruction set computers (RISCs)**. The primary goal of a RISC design is not to have a small instruction set, but to achieve single-cycle operation. The remaining attributes follow from this primary goal.

Single-cycle operation is only a goal to strive toward; it cannot reasonably be accomplished in a general purpose computer. To execute a macroinstruction during each clock cycle, the next macroinstruction must be fetched while the current one is being executed. This overlapping of activity requires that the location of the next macroinstruction be known before the current one has executed, but for conditional branches this is not possible. Although there are ways of partially avoiding this problem there are no practical means for avoiding it altogether. (The overlapping of instruction fetching and execution is a form of pipelining, which is discussed in Chap. 12.)

A second problem impeding single-cycle operation is that some operations require much more time to execute than others, yet all operations must execute in one clock cycle. Therefore, the clock period must accommodate the worst case and this constraint places a severe restriction on the instruction set. Some RISCs do not include even a multiplication macroinstruction because of the expense of implementing a very fast multiplier. This omission means that several shift and add macroinstructions are required to perform a multiplication. This problem can be partially alleviated by using multiple sets of hardware to distribute the work (see Chap. 12), but this is practical only in special situations.

Another implication of single-cycle operation is, because all microoperations must be performed in one clock cycle, there is only one microinstruction for each macroinstruction and there is no point in using microprogramming. In addition to being slow, it would take as much decode logic to implement the addressing of the control ROM as it would to implement hardwired logic. But, to minimize hardwired decode logic the numbers of the instructions and addressing modes must be restricted and an instruction format that is easy to decipher must be used. The latter implies that the instruction set be highly orthogonal. Also, a uniform length for all macroinstructions in the instruction set is needed. Not only does a fixed instruction length reduce the amount of decode logic, but it is also needed to overlap fetches with execution so that the length is always known in advance.

To limit macroinstructions to a fixed length, it is necessary to severely restrict the use of memory addresses that tend to occupy a large portion of most instructions. This limitation is accomplished by allowing only special load and store instructions to load data from or store data into main memory. All other instructions would be permitted to operate on only the registers, and therefore would need to contain only register addresses. However, to reduce the number of load and store instructions, a large register set is required. The IC area for accommodating a large register set is primarily made available through the reduction in decode logic.

Finally, having a small instruction set with both limited addressing modes and limited access to main memory requires more macroinstructions to fulfill each task. This requirement implies that more macroinstructions be used to implement each high-level language statement and more work be done at compile-time. However, in a sense these implications are misleading in that using more macroinstructions does not necessarily imply a more complex compiler. In fact, attempting to make use of complex macroinstructions is often more difficult for a compiler than using several simple macroinstructions. In a RISC, what tends to complicate the compiler is optimizing the use of the register set, which may include special features (e.g., features for handling procedure linkage), and minimizing the number of main memory accesses.

Although very high performance machines still use CISC designs, several RISCs have been produced and have proved to be a very effective extension to the range of microcomputers. For single-IC processing elements, the RISC compromise between increasing the amount of SCL logic and the number of macroinstructions versus decreasing the time per macroinstruction and increasing the number of registers has been a good one. An argument has raged over the last several years as to the circumstances under which a RISC design is superior to a CISC design and vice versa. This controversy is not likely to be settled soon. Oddly enough, as technology improves and RISCs are better understood, the sizes of their instruction sets have tended to increase even though the central goal of single-cycle operation has been retained.

7-6 PACKAGING

There are several benefits to putting all of a processing element's circuitry on a single IC. This consolidation shortens the internal buses, minimizes capacitative effects that tend to slow down internal transfers, increases reliability because of the reduction of soldered connections, and decreases assembly costs. The primary deterrents to putting a processing element on one IC are the density limitations for the technology being used and the relationship between density and switching time. For a given technology there are only so many logic gates and conductors that can be packed onto the IC's surface and the more densely they are crowded together, the more difficult it is to maintain a satisfactory speed and operating temperature.

As discussed in Sec. 3-6, most technologies are such that, within the limitations of the technology, the product of the per gate power consumption and the gate switching time is approximately constant. Increasing the power supplied to the gate decreases the switching time, but increases the heat that must be dissipated. Therefore, for a given technology with given heat limitations, an increase in speed must be accompanied by a decrease in density. For a fixed IC surface area, this density decrease implies a decrease in the number of gates.

The overall conclusion is that there is a three-way tradeoff involving speed, the complexity of the processing element, and the number of ICs to be used to construct the processing element. If the requirements of a processing element are such that its construction is relatively simple, then all of its circuitry may be put on one IC even though high speed is needed. But a high-speed general purpose processing element with an extensive macroinstruction set may need to be constructed from more than one IC.

ICs are embedded in ceramic packages that protect them from the environment and are large enough to be easily worked with and mounted on PC boards. Normally, there is one IC per package, but it is possible to put several ICs in a single package. The advantage of putting more than one IC in a package is that the conductors between the ICs are kept short, thereby reducing the exposure to noise and the power needed to drive the conductors. The disadvantage of putting more than one IC in a package is that it is a delicate and expensive operation that is subject to a relatively high failure rate. Also, the package must be capable of dissipating the heat generated by all of the ICs.

When it is necessary to divide circuitry among several ICs, the divisions are made along the lines of the major components indicated in Fig. 7-1 (i.e., the SCL, set of registers, ALU, and BCL). For microprogrammed designs, the SCL may be separated into a microprogram sequencer and the control ROM. As mentioned in Sec. 7-4-2, having the control ROM on a separate IC allows the user to customize the microcode.

A commonly used approach to designing high speed processors is to use ICs that include several registers and an ALU, but are such that each register contains only a few bits and the ALU is capable of operating on only this limited number of bits. These ICs, which are called **bit-slices**, are connected in parallel to obtain a set of registers and an ALU that can store and operate on operands containing several bits. Figure 7-39(a) shows a single p-bit slice and the inputs and outputs needed to make the parallel connections. There are p data-in lines, p data-out lines, a set of address lines for controlling the internal data transfers, a set of control lines for directing the ALU operations, and the carry and shift inputs and outputs needed to connect the ALU sections together. When m bit slices are

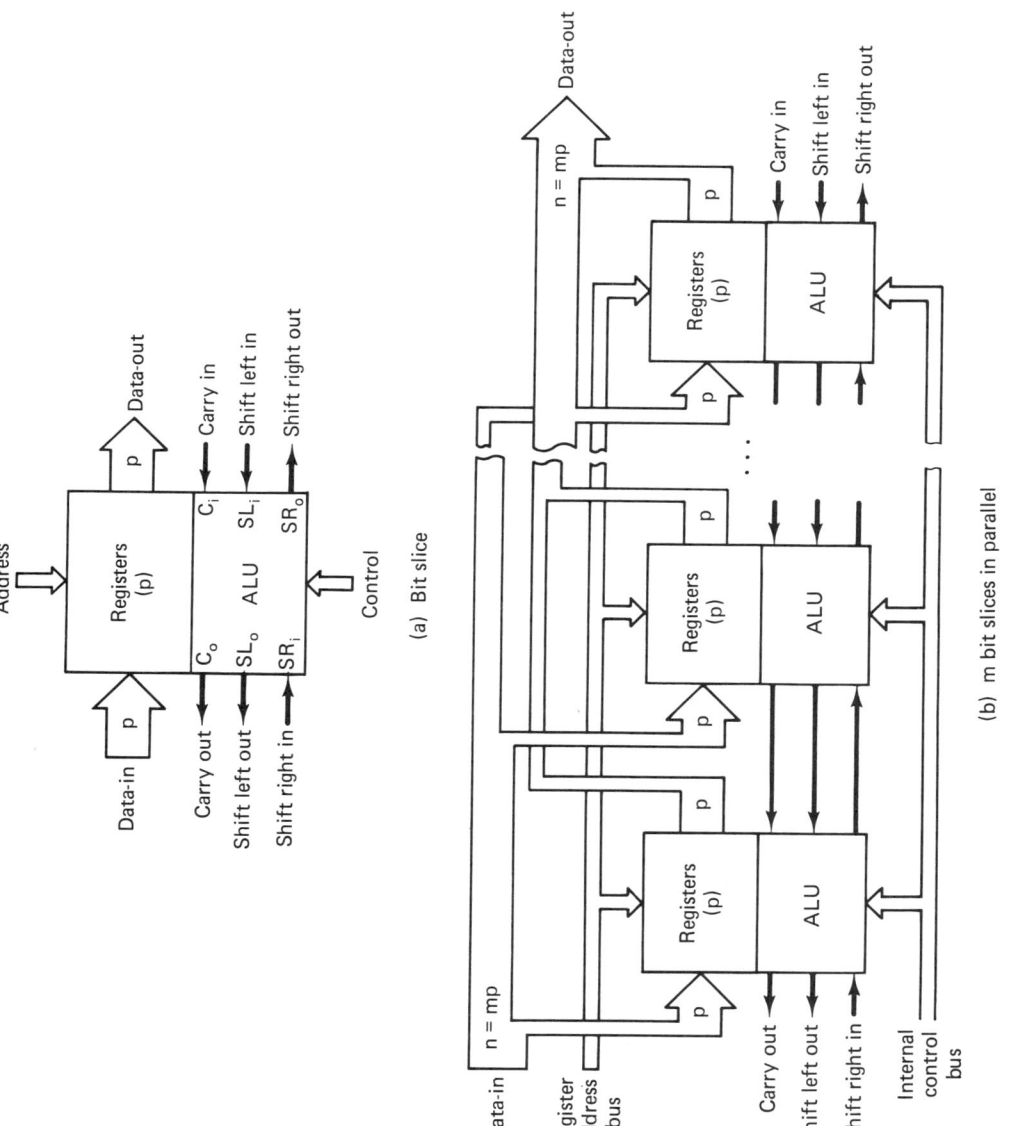

Figure 7-39 Bit slices connections.

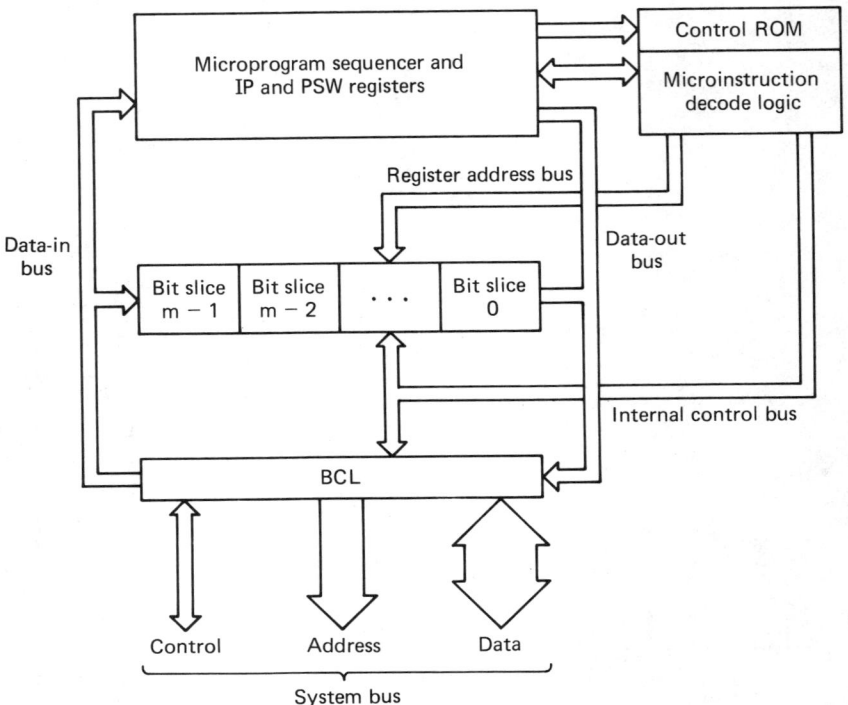

Figure 7-40 Typical microprogramming bit slice architecture.

placed in parallel as shown in Fig. 7-39(b), the total number of bits in the data-in and data-out buses is $n = mp$. Except for the left-most bit slice, the Carry Out and Shift Left Out outputs of a slice are connected to the Carry In and Shift Left In inputs of the next higher adjoining slice. Similarly, except for the right-most bit slice, the Shift Right Out output is connected to the Shift Right In input of the next lower adjoining slice. This connection allows the composite ALU, consisting of all the ALU sections, to perform n-bit add, subtract, shift, and rotate operations.

A microprogrammable bit slice processing element architecture is shown in Fig. 7-40. In addition to providing the versatility of microprogramming, this configuration offers its designer a means of adjusting maximum operand length. For example, using 4-bit bit slices a designer could include four slices if an application calls for only 16-bit operands or eight slices if 32-bit operands are required.

7-7 OTHER DESIGN REMARKS

This chapter has considered the design of general purpose processing elements whose activities are controlled by a single clock. We have seen that the basic components of such a processing element are the SCL, the ALU, the BCL, and a set of registers that includes the IR, PC, PSW, and SP as well as working registers.

The principal tradeoffs that must be considered when designing a processing element are listed in Fig. 7-41. Hardwired control logic reduces the time required to decode a macroinstruction and produce the SCL outputs, but a diverse macroinstruction set may require more logic than is practical. Also, unless a PLA is used, logic may tend to be irregular, which may increase the IC surface area. If the logic is implemented solely with a PLA, the PLA may need to be unacceptably large. A microprogrammed design may be slower, but a ROM large enough to implement a complex instruction set can be put into a relatively small area, particularly if vertical microinstructions or nanoinstructions are used. In addition, microprogramming provides flexibility in designing or redesigning a macroinstruction set.

A complex macroinstruction set offers a variety of addressing modes and operations and tends to reduce the number of macroinstructions needed to perform a task. It provides a programmer more options in writing code and may permit the programmer to write shorter and better structured programs. On the other hand, the cost of a CISC design is complex SCL and the need to use several clock cycles to execute each instruction. It may be unreasonable to use hardwired logic and may require vertical microinstructions or nanoinstructions to keep down the width of the microinstructions. In contrast, a RISC design simplifies the SCL and approaches single-cycle operation, but places severe restrictions on the instruction set and emphasizes the need to minimize the number of main memory accesses.

It is apparent from earlier chapters as well as the present chapter that the frequency of operand fetches has a strong impact on the overall speed of operation. Particularly for a RISC design, accessing external memory is time consuming compared to the internal speed of a processing element. The primary means of avoiding memory operand fetches is to keep as much data as possible inside the processing element. Registers, however, are costly in terms of IC area and, the greater the number of registers, the greater the number of bits needed to address them. An increased number of registers requires more SCL outputs and more SCL logic to generate these outputs. An alternative to having several registers is to include a small data memory in the processing element. This inclusion has been made in some special purpose processing elements, but, as will be seen in Chap. 9, even a small high-speed memory cannot be accessed as quickly as a register. For the examples considered here, outputting from a register is simply a matter of turning on tristate gates, and inputting is done by applying 1 to 0 transitions to the flip-flop's C inputs.

Hardwired control logic	vs.	Microprogrammed control
Complexity of the macroinstruction set	vs.	Amount of logic in SCL
Frequency of external operand fetches	vs.	Number of working registers
Versatility in making transfers	vs.	Number of buses

Figure 7-41 Tradeoffs related to processing element design.

Having an adequate number of buses for transferring instructions and data is essential to avoiding contention. If, as in a RISC, it is necessary to overlap instructions and data fetches with instruction execution, it is an absolute requirement that contention for the buses be minimized, if not eliminated. Overworked buses tend to be bottlenecks both inside and outside of processing elements. A bus is not expensive, but logic is needed to put information onto and receive information from a bus. If two buses both provide inputs to a register or other component, then a multiplexer must be present to select which bus is to supply the current input. Similarly, a demultiplexer or separate banks of tristate or wire ORed gates are required to output to separate buses. Also, there is a limit to the number of conductors that can be put onto an IC's surface, and the buses should be such that the number of bus crossings is minimized.

Processing elements basically serve two functions. They:

- Aid in moving data between points in the computer system.
- Perform arithmetic and logical operations.

General purpose processing elements attempt to do both functions reasonably well and compromises are made in their designs. If, however, a processing element is to serve a specific application, the design can be biased toward the application. Examples of applications oriented toward moving data are data logging, text processing, and simple controllers that require very little computation. For a processing element whose primary purpose is to transfer data the design emphasis would be on the BCL. This chapter has paid little attention to the BCL. It is discussed in depth in Chap. 8.

For applications that require a great deal of computation, the emphasis should clearly be on ALU design. Both the data types and lengths of the operands are important. Some applications may involve numbers that are from a relatively narrow range and integer arithmetic will suffice, while others may need the wide ranges provided by floating point formats. For example, data that are brought into a computer through an A/D converter are normally not more than 16 bits wide, and for many computational procedures there is no need to convert the data to a floating point or higher-precision format. If the data input rate is high, then a processing element is needed that can quickly process 16-bit quantities. On the other hand, an application that involves inverting large matrices or solving simultaneous partial differential equations would require high precision and the ability to work with a wide range of numbers. For this application, a floating point unit with high resolution would be needed.

Although this chapter has concentrated on computers that are capable of performing only one operation at a time, high-performance computers execute hundreds of millions or even billions of operations per second. Such computers must rely on the ability to execute several operations at the same time, i.e., in parallel. The more advanced concepts associated with parallel processing are introduced in Chap. 12.

REFERENCES

1. Hamacher, V. Carl, Zvanko G. Vranesic, and Safwat G. Zaky, *Computer Organization*, 2nd ed. (New York: McGraw-Hill Book Company, 1984).
2. Mano, Morris M., *Computer System Architecture*, 2nd ed. (Englewood Cliffs, New Jersey: Prentice Hall, Inc., 1982).
3. Hill, Frederick J., and Gerald R. Peterson, *Digital Systems: Hardware Organization and Design* (New York: John Wiley and Sons, Inc., 1973).
4. Tannenbaum, Andrew S., *Structured Computer Organization*, 2nd ed. (Englewood Cliffs, New Jersey: Prentice Hall, Inc., 1984).
5. Gibson, Glenn A., and Yu-cheng Liu, *Microcomputers for Engineers and Scientists*, 1st ed. (Englewood Cliffs, New Jersey: Prentice Hall, Inc., 1980).
6. Katzan, Harry, Jr., *Microprogramming Primer* (New York: McGraw-Hill Book Company, 1977).
7. Colwell, R., C. Hitchcock III, E. Jensen, H. Brinckley Sprunt, and C. Kollar, "Instruction Sets and Beyond: Computers, Complexity, and Controversy," *Computer*, Vol. 19, no. 9 (September, 1985) pp. 8–19.
8. Stallings, William, *Computer Organization and Architecture*, (New York: Macmillan Publishing Company, 1987).

EXERCISES

1. Assuming the example internal architecture given in Sec. 7-1 (see Fig. 7-3), give a microinstruction sequence that
   (a) Adds the (R0) to (R1).
   (b) Causes an unconditional branch. The instruction is to occupy two locations with the second location containing the branch address.
2. Assume that a processing element contains ten 16-bit registers and a multiplexer controls the outputs to a common bus. How many AND gates and OR gates would be required and how many inputs would there be to each gate? How many control lines would be needed? How many connections would be needed between the AND gates and OR gates? If only one level of OR gates is used, what would be their required fan-in capability?
3. If the multiplexer in Exercise 2 were replaced by tristate gates, how many tristate gates would be required and how many control lines would be needed?
4. Suppose that all gates have a 12 nS delay, the bus causes a 5 nS delay and the setup and hold times for all registers are 3 nS and 2 nS, respectively. How much time would be needed to perform a register-to-register transfer? Now suppose that the data width is 8 bits and the data path includes an 8-bit ripple carry adder. How much time would be required to transmit the operands to the adder, perform the addition and latch the sum into a destination register?
5. For the X16 architecture shown in Fig. 7-8, give a microinstruction sequence for implementing the following macroinstructions:
   (a) MOVH   R1,R2

(b) SUBH   #12,R2
(c) BRUN   #CONT

6. Give microinstruction sequences for implementing the following X16 macroinstructions:
   (a) XORH   X,R3
   (b) CMPH   [R1],X
   (c) BUGT   PLUS

7. First assume that only halfwords are shifted and design the ALU shift/rotate logic included in Fig. 7-12. Discuss the modifications that would be needed so that byte shifts and rotates could be implemented. Use the definitions of the X16's shift and rotate macroinstructions defined in Sec. 4-2-6.

8. Assume the X16 can perform register-to-register multiplication of bytes and give a microinstruction sequence for performing such an operation.

9. Give a step-by-step simulation of the answer to Exercise 8 by multiplying the signed binary integers 00110110 and 11101011.

10. Figure 7-15 does not show how the PSW could be loaded from Data Bus 1 or output to Data Bus 2 using register input and output signals. Discuss how this could be done and modify Fig. 7-15 accordingly. (Hint: For loading, use the preset inputs—see Fig. 3-29.)

11. Assume there is a byte/halfword signal to the condition flags logic and show how this logic must be modified to permit byte operations.

12. When a clear carry macroinstruction is being executed the ALU Control MUX bits must not be 001, 010, or 011. Why? How could this problem be avoided?

13. Using the format of Fig. 7-17, give the SCL outputs while the MOV X,Y macroinstruction in Fig. 7-11 is being executed.

14. Give the microinstruction sequence needed to implement an X16 interrupt sequence. Discuss the fact that the interrupt sequence is an exception to the rule that during T0 instruction fetches are begun.

15. Give X16 microinstruction sequences for the following macroinstructions:
    (a) Clear carry.
    (b) Set carry.
    (c) Set interrupt field.

16. Give a microinstruction sequence for implementing an unconditional branch that uses register indirect addressing.

17. If byte operands were permitted, what changes to the control lines summary in Fig. 7-16 would be required?

18. Using the microinstruction sequences derived in Exercise 15 and the macroinstruction formats given in Fig. 4-13, design decode logic for the interrupt field and C flag strobes.

19. Extend the design in Fig. 7-24 to include
    (a) A pop macroinstruction.
    (b) AND, OR, and XOR macroinstructions.
    Why can the in instruction be included as a move instruction? Why must the pop instruction be treated separately?

20. Assume hardwired control and design decode logic for the Interrupt Field Bits and the C Flag Clear/Set bit.

21. Assume hardwired control and design decode logic for the Shift/Rotate Control Lines.

22. In the microprogrammed design of the X16 discussed in Sec. 7-4-2, could the signals

on the Shift/Rotate Control lines be obtained directly from the IR if instructions other than the shift and rotate instructions (such as a multiply instruction) perform shifts and rotates? Explain.

23. Note that for the design shown in Fig. 7-30, one register can be output from while another is receiving an input, but there can be only one register being output from or receiving input at a time. Discuss why this situation is not a problem. Would this situation be a problem if the group of registers included all registers, not just R0 through R5?

24. By using a register input address field, further reduce the number of Other In Register Control lines indicated in Fig. 7-32. However, retain the ability to simultaneously input to more than one register from a selected set. You must choose the selected set.

25. Why must the Register Out and Other Registers Out lines in Figs. 7-30 and 7-31 be separate lines?

26. Modify the design in Fig. 7-30 so that byte operands can be used (see Exercise 17).

27. Design the decode logic needed to generate the ALU Control MUX and Add/Subtract Control Bits from the macroinstruction whenever the IR Select Bit given in Fig. 7-32 is active.

28. Design the portion of the Address PLA in Fig. 7-34 that is needed to produce the address $00010b_2b_10$ whenever an add, subtract, AND, OR, or XOR macroinstruction is executed. Bits b_2b_1 are to be 00 if the first source address mode is register, 01 if it is register indirect, 10 if it is immediate, and 11 if it is direct.

29. Design the portion of the Address PLA in Fig. 7-34 that is needed to branch to $00100b_2b_10$ whenever a branch macroinstruction is executed. Bits b_2b_1 are to be 01 if the address mode is register indirect, 10 if it is immediate, and 11 if it is PC relative.

30. Write the microcode corresponding to the branch macroinstructions assuming that it is branched to as indicated in Exercise 29. (Hint: Use a branch that causes a reset to address 00 if the macroinstruction branch condition is false; otherwise, the contents of the PC are to be replaced before continuing.)

31. If it takes 25 nS to generate a control ROM address, 40 nS to access the control ROM, 10 nS to decode the control ROM output, and 40 nS to perform the required operations, what would be the maximum clock frequency?

32. Discuss the possibility of overlapping the execution of operations with retrieving the next microinstruction. When could this not be done?

33. What was the impetus for developing RISCs and why do RISCs tend to have small instruction sets?

34. In Fig. 7-39 only data outputs and outputs needed to connect bit slices together were included. What other outputs would be useful?

35. How does the inclusion of two internal buses improve the performance of the X16?

36. For the X16 design, why is it so important that the adder/subtracter be made to execute as fast as possible?

37. What would be the primary advantage of including a small amount of code memory in a processing element?

38. Discuss the tradeoffs to be considered when designing a processing element that must perform arithmetic operations quickly as opposed to performing numerous I/O operations.

8

Links and Interfaces

Links and interfaces have a very strong effect on a computer's operating efficiency. It is the links and interfaces that provide for the communication of all instructions and data within the computer. This chapter examines the transfer of information within a computer system and concentrates on the hardware and steps needed to conduct a transfer. The instructions and general software for making transfers were discussed in Chap. 6.

As shown in Fig. 8-1(a), a link, or bus, is a path for transferring information between the elements of a computer system. It consists of the:

- Medium for transferring information.
- Medium for carrying the control signals needed to perform a transfer.
- Circuitry essential to conducting transfers. This circuitry may be physically located within the elements, even though it is considered part of the link.

The medium is represented by the large arrow and may consist of one or more signal paths, with each signal path being a conductor, fiber optic strand, or other physical means of transmitting a single signal. The signal paths must carry all information transmitted over the link, including both the data and the information needed to control the link. In some designs, the same signal paths are used for both data transmission and control and, in others, separate paths are used. A link that contains only one signal path for transferring data is called a **serial link**. It is possible for a serial link to include only one signal path, in which case, all data and control information is transferred over that path. A **parallel link** is one that contains more than one signal path for conveying data.

An **interface** is the circuitry that joins two links together or that joins a link

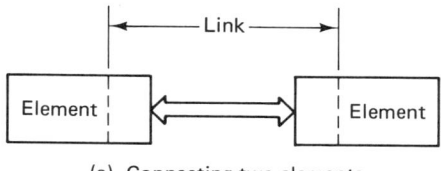

(a) Connecting two elements

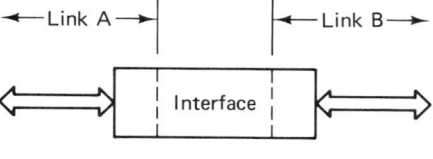

(b) Connecting two links

Figure 8-1 Basic connections.

to the internal logic of an element (e.g., a memory interface or the BCL of a processing element). Its purpose is to match the format and timing of the signals of the link to those of the element or other link. There is no precise physical division between an interface and a link and the circuitry associated with the end of a link may also be considered part of an interface. Figure 8-1(b) illustrates the connection of two links by an interface. Such an interface must include one set of circuitry for communicating with Link A and another set for communicating with Link B.

Links are often classified according to their relationship to a system's processing elements. The reason for this classification is that a link's characteristics are dependent upon where the link is situated relative to the processing element. Because the processing element is normally the fastest element in a system, its internal and adjoining links must be designed to accommodate this speed. There is no reason to have a high-speed processing element if there are no accompanying means of feeding it instructions and data at rates sufficient to utilize its quickness. On the other hand, a link that is remotely located relative to the processing elements may be able to operate much more slowly and have less stringent timing requirements.

For the discussions in this book, a link that is entirely contained in a processing element is called an **internal bus** and one that is connected to a processing element's BCL, but is not part of the processing element, is called a **system bus**. A link that is not connected to a processing element is called a **data link**. Interfaces are used to connect data links to system buses, thus allowing the elements and interfaces attached to data links to communicate with the system's processing elements. Data links that traverse long distances, particularly those that use telephone lines, are sometimes referred to as **communications links**.

This chapter first considers system buses, then interfaces, and concludes by discussing data links. Internal buses were considered in Chap. 7.

8-1 SYSTEM BUSES

The basic single-processing element configuration shown in Fig. 8-2 is the one that is assumed in this chapter. As with an internal bus, a system bus is almost always a parallel bus that is capable of the high transfer rates required by the processing element. A system bus is divided into three parts: the data bus, the address bus, and the control bus. The data bus conveys information (both instructions and data) and the address bus indicates the location that is to receive or supply the information. The control bus provides signals for controlling the current transfer, determining the next transfer, and communicating general control and timing information. The number of signal paths in the data bus is equal to the number of bits transferred at a time and the number of signal paths in the address bus determines the maximum number of memory locations and/or I/O ports that can be accessed by the bus.

During any given transfer, one of the elements connected to the system bus must control the transfer. That element is referred to as the **master** and the other element involved in the transfer is referred to as the **slave**. Normally, the processing element is the master, but a DMA controller becomes the master during a DMA transfer. However, while the instructions for initializing a DMA transfer are being executed (i.e., the count, beginning memory address, and control information are being loaded into the controller), the DMA controller is the slave.

There are two basic methods for controlling the transfer of data over a link. One uses a common clock signal to regulate the activity on the link and is called **synchronous transmission**. If a common clock is not used, the transmission is said to be **asynchronous**. For synchronous transmission, a basic unit of data is sent

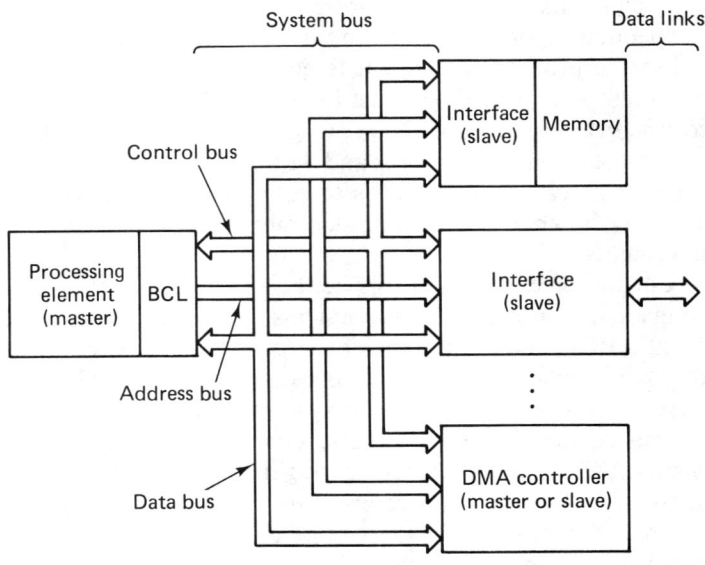

Figure 8-2 Single processor configuration assumed in this chapter.

during each clock period by having the transmitting element place the data on the link at the beginning of the clock period and the receiving element input the data before the end of the clock period. In contrast, an asynchronous transfer uses special handshaking signals to indicate when the data are available and when they have been accepted. As was seen in Chap. 7, internal buses begin a transfer at the beginning of a clock cycle and conclude the transfer just before the end of the clock cycle. Therefore, internal buses are synchronous. On the other hand, although some system buses are synchronous, most are asynchronous because the clock period for a synchronous link must be set according to the worst case propagation delays and element access times. This is satisfactory for internal buses because conductor lengths and connections to buses are fixed, but for system buses the lengths and connections may grow as new elements are added to the computer system.

A representative asynchronous control bus is shown in Fig. 8-3. In addition to the interrupt request/acknowledge and bus request/grant lines introduced in Chap. 6, and a reset line for initializing the system when it is turned on, it includes a:

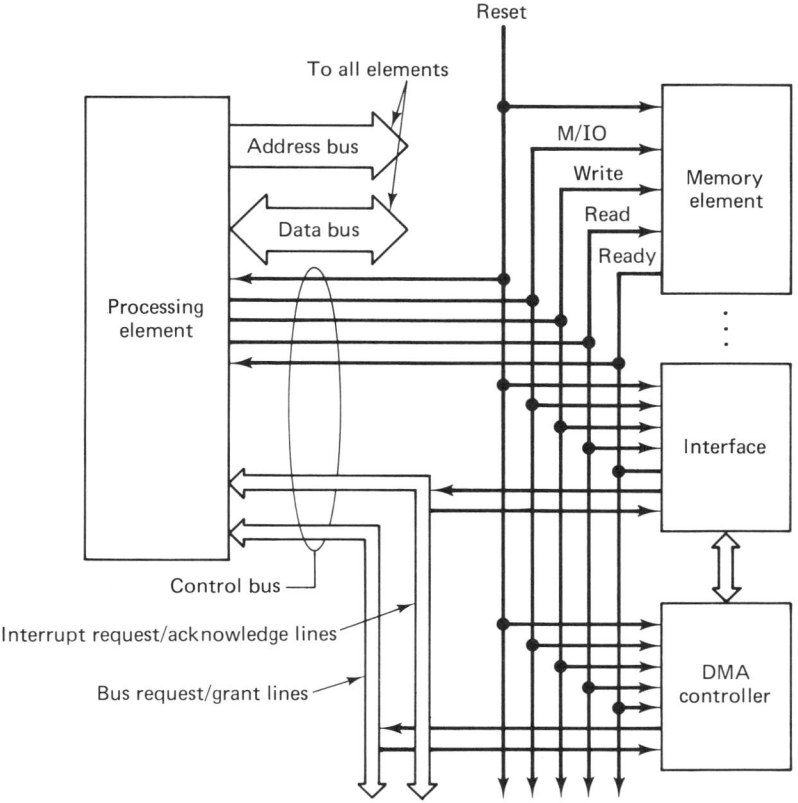

Figure 8-3 Typical control lines for an external bus.

Sec. 8-1 System Buses

- Memory/IO (M/IO) line for distinguishing between memory location and I/O port transfers.
- Write line to indicate that the information on the data bus is to be written into a memory location or I/O port.
- Read line to indicate that information is to be read from a memory location or I/O port and put onto the data bus.
- Ready line to signal that a memory element or interface has completed its part of a transfer.

To conduct a write, the signals on these lines are sequenced as follows:

1. The master outputs the data and address.
2. After allowing for skew, the master activates the Write Line.
3. Upon receipt of the Write Signal, the slave deactivates the Ready Line and inputs the data. The inactive Ready indicates to the master that the slave is busy and thus may cause the master to suspend its activity.
4. When the slave is no longer busy it activates the Ready Line.
5. Upon receipt of the active Ready Signal, the master drops the data and address, deactivates the Write Line, and resumes its activity.

For a read, the sequencing is:

1. The master outputs the address.
2. After allowing for skew, the master activates the Read Line.
3. Upon receipt of the Read Signal, the slave deactivates the Ready Line (which may cause the master to suspend its activity) and retrieves the data.
4. The slave outputs the data.
5. After allowing for skew, the slave activates the Ready Line.
6. Upon receipt of the active Ready Signal, the master inputs the data and deactivates the Read Line.
7. After allowing for skew, the master drops the address and, upon observing the deactivation of the Read Line, the slave drops the data.

The time required between bus cycles (i.e., the time between consecutive reads and writes) must be sufficient to allow all of the data and address signals to be dropped along the entire length of the bus. Therefore, the total time required to complete a read or write is three times the propagation delay along the bus plus the time that the slave is busy. The propagation delay is dependent on the properties of the bus and the busy time is determined by the access properties of the slave.

For a synchronous bus, the Ready Line is not needed and a write consists of outputting the address and data at the beginning of the clock cycle and assuming that the data has been accepted and the slave is no longer busy by the end of the cycle. A read is similarly conducted, except that the data must be retrieved by the slave and sent to the master by the end of the cycle. In either case, the clock period must be set according to the maximum time required taken over all propagation delays and busy times. This penalty can be considerable if the times for accessing the memory elements and interfaces vary significantly, because the same clock period must be used for all elements.

When a bus is controlled by a processing element, the element must synchronize external transfer activity with its internal activity. This synchronization is done by involving the processing element's clock in the external transfers, as shown by the timing diagrams in Fig. 8-4. Suppose that a transfer is to take place during the clock periods T_1, T_2, and T_3. For a write, the data and address are output at the beginning of T_1 and in the middle of T_1 the Write line is activated (thus, one half of a clock period is allowed for skew). When the Write signal arrives at the slave, the slave lowers the Ready line. Beginning with T_2, the processing element checks the Ready line at the clock cycle midpoint to see if it is high. If the Ready line is not high, then the processing element is considered to be in a wait state. During a wait state, a processing element's external activity is suspended. Clock periods that occur while a processing element is in a wait state are denoted by T_w. The first time Ready is high at the midpoint of a clock cycle (either T_2 or T_w), the processing element deactivates the Write line and the next clock cycle is T_3. At the beginning of T_3, the data and address outputs are terminated.

For a read, the address is applied at the beginning of T_1 and the Read line is made active at the midpoint of T_1. When the slave detects the active Read it deactivates the Ready signal and, as with a write, the processing element examines the Ready line at the midpoint of each succeeding clock cycle until it becomes high. If the Ready line is not high by the middle of T_2, wait states are inserted. After it goes high, at the next clock cycle midpoint, the processing element deactivates Read, inputs the data, and ceases entering wait states. At the beginning of T_3 the address is dropped and, when the slave detects that Read is inactive, it drops its output data. This sequencing assumes that the propagation delay along the entire bus is no more than one half of a clock period and allows a T_1 clock period to begin immediately following a T_3.

Relative to the discussion in Chap. 7, the processing element's internal activity may continue, even while the element is in a wait state. When internal activity must wait for the external transfer to finish, the processing element's Suspend signal is set to active by a Suspend microoperation and the processing element suspends its internal activity by blocking the clock pulses to its decode logic. When the external transfer is complete the internal Ready signal is raised and the Suspend is no longer enforced.

8-2 INTERFACES

Interfaces are the mortar for putting computer systems together. The primary responsibilities of an interface are to recognize whether it is being communicated with, provide the handshaking required by the links to which it is connected, and

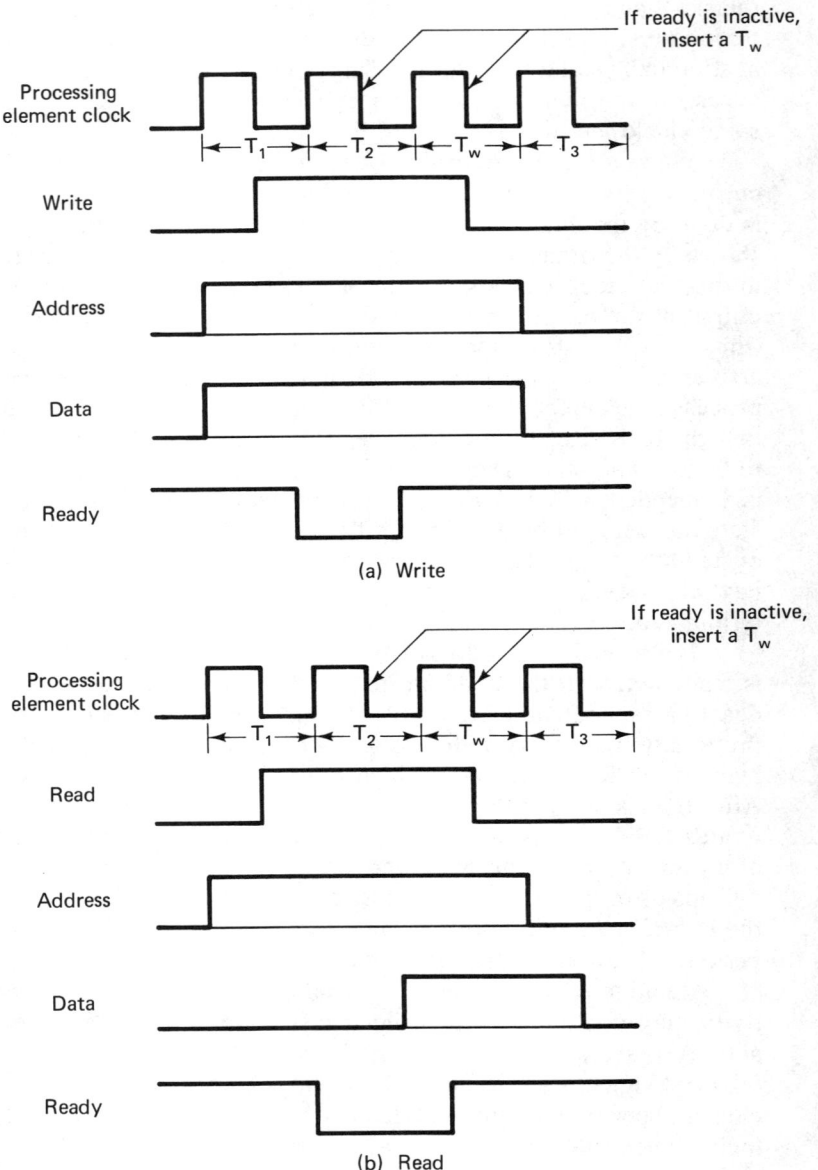

Figure 8-4 Typical processing element transfer timing.

buffer data. There are many different types of links, and the interfaces that join these links to elements or other links must serve diverse needs. Some interfaces are needed only to buffer data between two similar links and may be relatively simple, but others must provide the logic for interfacing to both a mass storage controller and a DMA controller and may be very complex. Because there is such a wide variety of interfaces, it would be impractical, and not particularly fruitful, to discuss even all of the major types of interfaces here. Therefore, the discussion in this section is limited to detailed examples of interfaces for connecting processing elements to system buses (i.e., bus control logic) and system buses to data links.

8-2-1 Bus Control Logic

The interfaces that must meet the most stringent requirements are the BCL portions of general purpose processing elements. The BCL of a processing element must interface the system bus to the internal buses of the processing element. The major components of a set of BCL are given in Fig. 8-5.

When the processing element is master of the system bus it must provide the address of the memory location or I/O port involved in a transfer. The address is derived from (PC) or the instruction currently being executed and is placed in a buffer register contained in the address logic. At the appropriate time, the address is applied to the address bus and is held there until the transfer is complete as shown in Fig. 8-4. Similarly, the data transfer logic contains buffer registers and, for an output (write) from the processing element, the data are placed in one

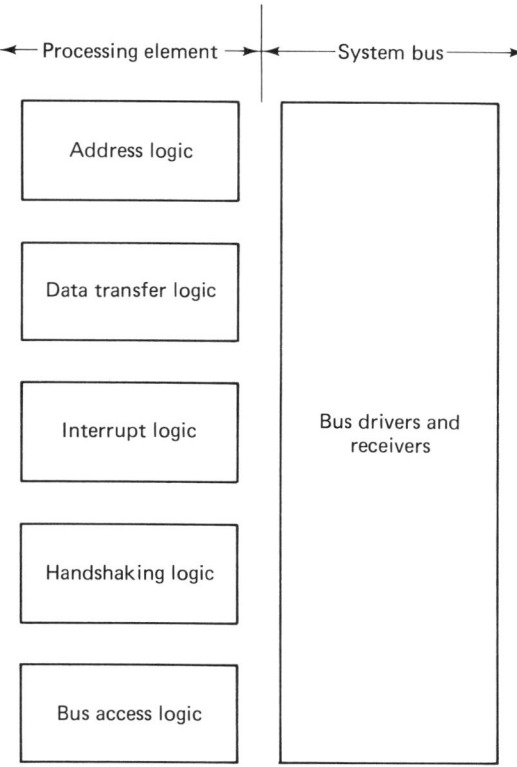

Figure 8-5 Major components of a typical BCL set.

of these registers by the current instruction and then placed on the system bus. For an input (read), the data are received from the system bus and put into one of the buffer registers until they are taken by the processing element. The handshaking logic, of course, coordinates these writes and reads and is responsible for the timing of the various signals. It must generate the signals that control the outputting of address signals and the outputting and inputting of the data signals as well as generate and receive the handshaking signals, such as the M/IO, Read, Write, and Ready signals introduced in Sec. 8-1 (see Fig. 8-3).

Normally, the address, data, handshaking, and, perhaps, other signals are not applied directly to the system bus but are output and input through a set of drivers and receivers. These drivers and receivers are tristate gates that can be turned off and on by control signals from the handshaking logic. This type of control allows the handshaking logic to determine the precise times at which the address and data signals are placed on or taken from the address and data buses. Also, they provide a means for disconnecting the system bus from the processing element when the processing element is not the bus master (e.g., during a DMA transfer) and for increasing the power of the signals output by the BCL.

Interrupt logic is for controlling interrupt related signals. It accepts requests, supplies acknowledgments, and generally carries out the interrupt sequence activities that involve the BCL or the computer external to the processing element. The interrupt logic may be designed to control a single request/acknowledge pair or may include interrupt management logic capable of prioritizing and responding to several interrupt requests. Similarly, the bus access logic handles bus requests and grants and may be the logic needed for a single request/grant pair or may manage several such pairs.

Detailed BCL Design Example

For example, consider the set of BCL for the X16 internal architecture described in Chap. 7 and given in Fig. 8-6. As in Chap. 7, it is assumed that the data bus is 16 bits wide and only halfword transfers are possible. (For an extension to byte transfers see Exercise 9.)

The address logic outputs an address to all interfaces on the system bus and each interface must use the high order bits to determine whether it is involved in the transfer. The address logic is shown in Fig. 8-7(a) and consists of the XAR and its connection to the system bus address drivers. New contents are put into the XAR via internal Data Bus 2 whenever a pulse is applied to the XAR Input Control line.

The corresponding data transfer logic is shown in Fig. 8-7(b). For a read, Fig. 8-4 shows that the data should be latched from the system data bus at the beginning of the next clock cycle if an active external Ready is received before the midpoint of the current clock cycle. After detecting an active external Ready, the handshaking logic sends a Synchronized Ready signal to the XDI register and raises the internal Ready signal to the SCL to 1. Then, the XDI register can be input by any microoperation that applies a pulse to the XDI Output Control line. For a write, the data on internal Data Bus 1 is simply latched into the XDO register

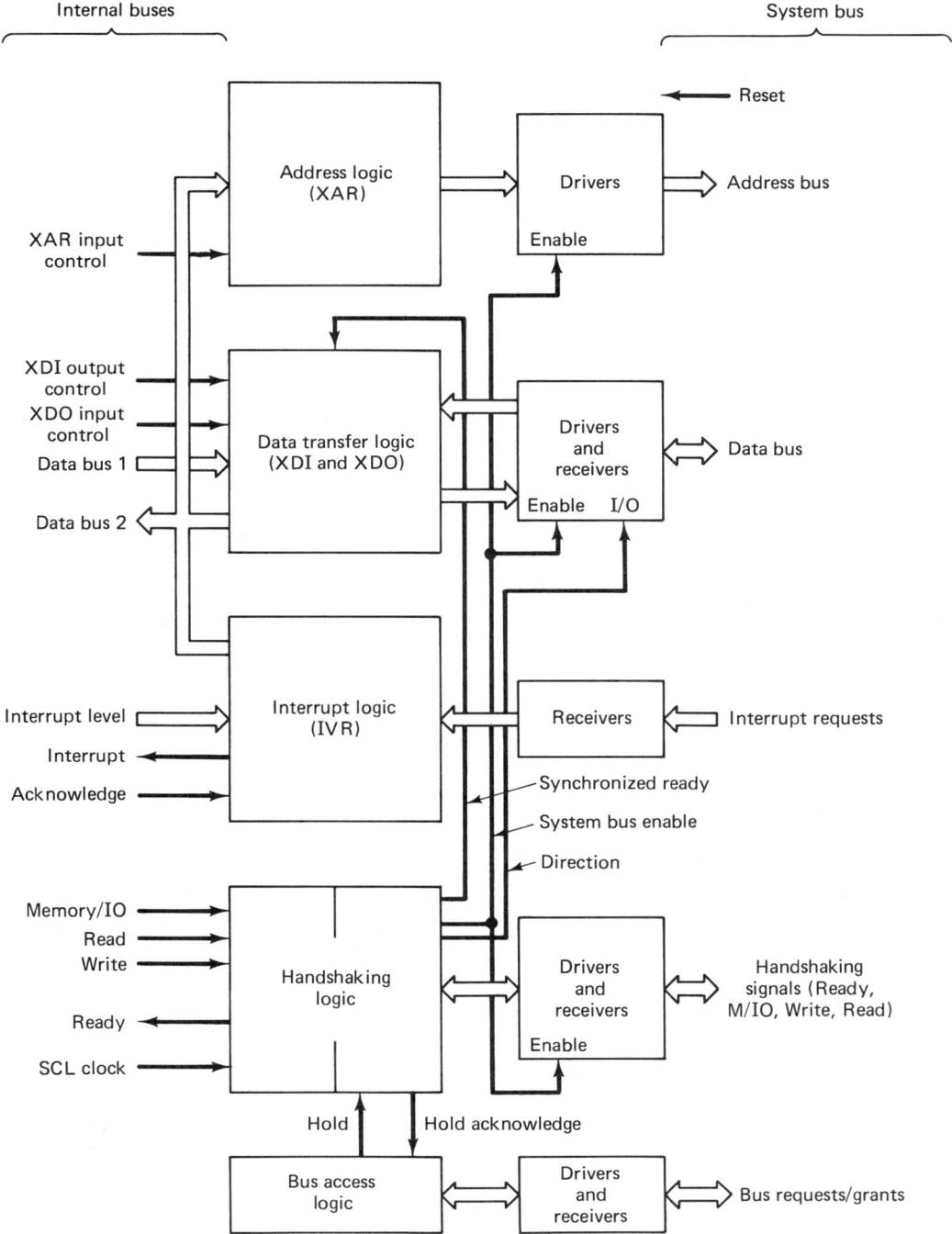

Figure 8-6 Typical Bus Control logic.

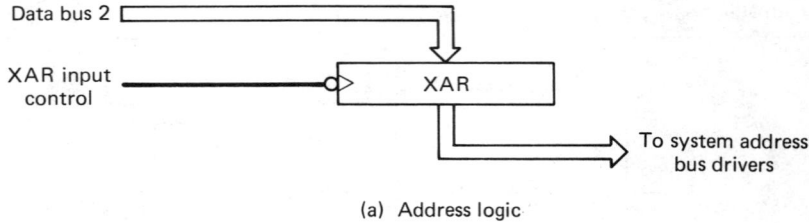

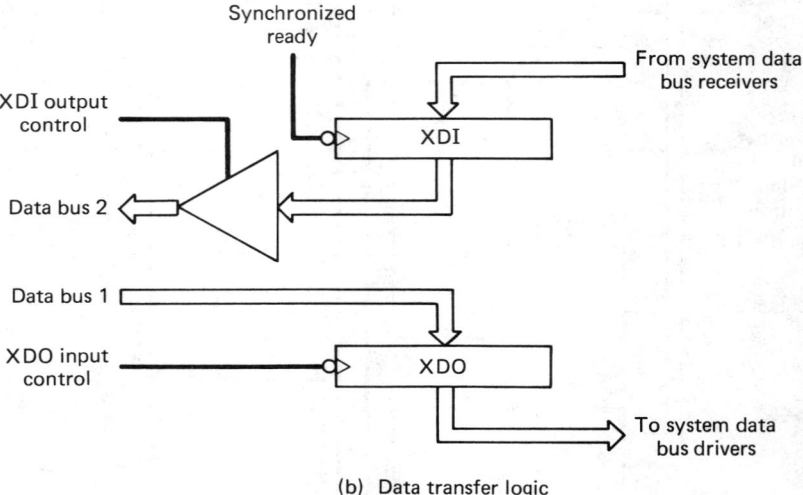

Figure 8-7 X16's Address and Data Transfer logic.

by having a microoperation pulse the XDO Input Control line. The output of the XDO register is connected to the system data bus drivers.

Signals are not actually received from or put onto the system address and data buses until the tristate gates that implement the drivers and receivers are enabled. This signal timing provides the precise timing needed to control the address and data signals on the system bus. Because the address bus is unidirectional, the address bus drivers can simply be a bank of tristate gates controlled by a single enable signal. However, it is seen from Figs. 8-6 and 8-7 that the set of data bus drivers and receivers must convert the bidirectional system data bus into two unidirectional buses and determine the direction of the transfer according to a separate Direction signal. This can be done with the logic shown in Fig. 8-8. If a write is to be conducted, an enable is applied to the drivers and, for a read, the enable is applied to the receivers. Otherwise, neither the drivers nor receivers are enabled.

Timing diagrams for both a memory write and memory read are given in Fig. 8-9. For a write, after microoperations have put the address and data into the XAR and XDO registers and set the internal Write and Memory/IO lines to 1, the handshaking logic enables the address and data bus drivers using the System

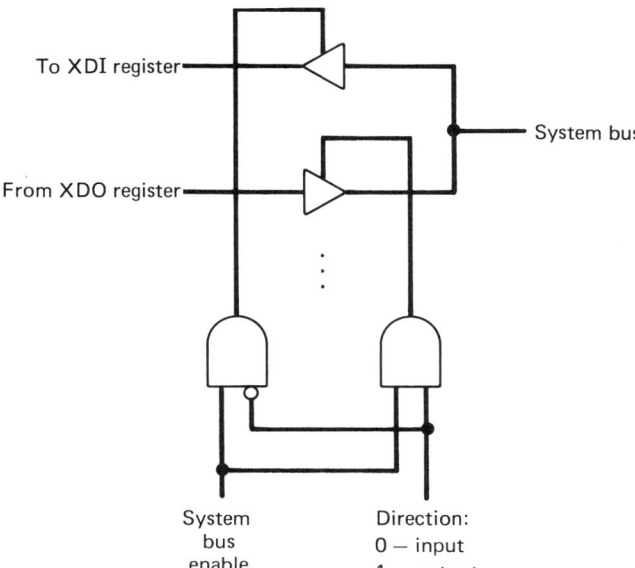

Figure 8-8 Drivers and receivers for Data Transfer logic.

Bus Enable and Direction lines, sets M/IO to 1, and clears the internal Ready line to 0. At the midpoint of T_1, the external Write line is raised to 1. When the memory interface receives the Write signal, it deactivates the external Ready and then reactivates it after it has accepted the data from the data bus. Once the external Ready returning to 1 has been sensed by the handshaking logic, it raises the internal Ready to 1 and then, at the beginning of T_3, it disables the address and data outputs and clears the M/IO and Direction signals. The Synchronized Ready line is not used.

For a memory read, microoperations put the address into the XAR and set the internal Read and Memory/IO signals to 1. At the beginning of T_1 the handshaking logic enables the address bus drivers and data bus receivers, sets M/IO to 1, and clears the internal Ready. A half cycle later, it sets the external Read and Synchronized Ready lines to 1 and, when the memory detects this transition, it clears the external Ready. After the memory puts the data on the data bus, it reactivates the external Ready line, thus causing the handshaking logic to clear the external Read and Synchronized Ready signals, raise the internal Ready signal, and latch the data into the XDI register by using the trailing edge of the Synchronized Ready signal. The address drivers and data receivers are disabled at the beginning of the next clock cycle.

The drivers and receivers for the system bus handshaking signals are also controlled by the System Bus Enable line; thus allowing the handshaking lines to be disconnected from the processing element during a DMA transfer. The drivers and receivers for interrupt requests and bus requests and grants do not need to be disabled during DMA transfers and therefore, do not need to be controlled by the handshaking logic.

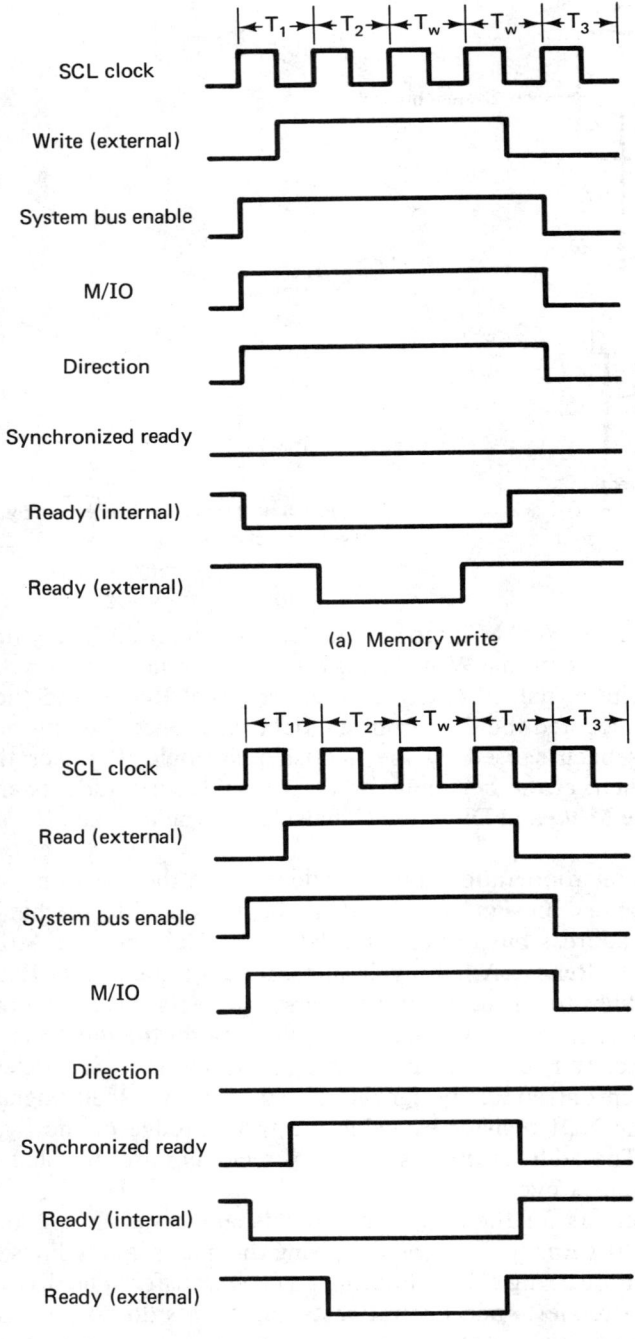

Figure 8-9 Timing of the X16's Handshaking logic.

The X16's interrupt management facility is shown in Fig. 8-10. By including an interrupt level that can be set by software, the X16 incorporates into its interrupt management the ability to selectively block interrupt requests. As discussed in Chap. 6, this gives interrupt routines the power to regulate the levels of requests that can interrupt them. The X16 has eight interrupt request lines, which are connected to eight positive edge-triggered flip-flops denoted IR0 through IR7. It is assumed that the interfaces connected to these lines will make requests by issuing pulses. The outputs of IR0 through IR7 are connected to a priority encoder that outputs a 3-bit binary number i if IRi is set but IRj is not set for all $j > i$. Thus, IR7 has the highest priority, IR6 has the next higher priority, and so on. If there is an interrupt pending, the priority encoder outputs a 1 on the Interrupt Pending line and provides one set of inputs to a comparator whose other set of inputs is the interrupt level stored in the PSW. The output of the comparator is 1 if the output of the priority encoder is greater than or equal to the interrupt level specified by the PSW. The output of the comparator is ANDed with the PSW's interrupt bit and the Interrupt Pending signal. Therefore, the AND gate's output Interrupt is 1 if and only if all three of the following conditions are met:

- An interrupt is pending.
- The interrupt bit is 1.
- The highest priority interrupt that is pending has a priority that is greater than or equal to the current interrupt level.

In addition, the output of the priority encoder puts the number of the highest priority interrupt into bits 4-2 of the IVR. The IVR's output is used as the interrupt vector address.

To cancel a request, the output of the priority encoder is decoded so that exactly one of eight lines is 1. The IVR output control is ANDed with each of these lines and the outputs of the AND gates are connected to the CLR inputs of the interrupt request flip-flops. The connections are made so that the highest priority request, the one being serviced, is cleared. All other requests remain intact and are serviced in order as permitted by the interrupt bit and interrupt level.

For the X16, requests are maintained in a set of interrupt request flip-flops and the priority of an interface is determined by the interrupt request line to which it is connected. Therefore, priorities are physically built into the connections and cannot be changed by instructions. Some systems have interrupt management facilities that allow request priorities to be dynamically changed by the software. There are also facilities that automatically change priorities after each interrupt. One common practice is to have the interrupt management logic rotate the priorities so that the interrupt requests take turns at having the highest priority. As discussed in Chap. 6, this rotation prevents one or two high priority interfaces that may be heavily used at certain times from starving the remaining interfaces.

An interrupt management facility can be built into a processing element and can communicate directly with the element's internal buses (as with the X16) or

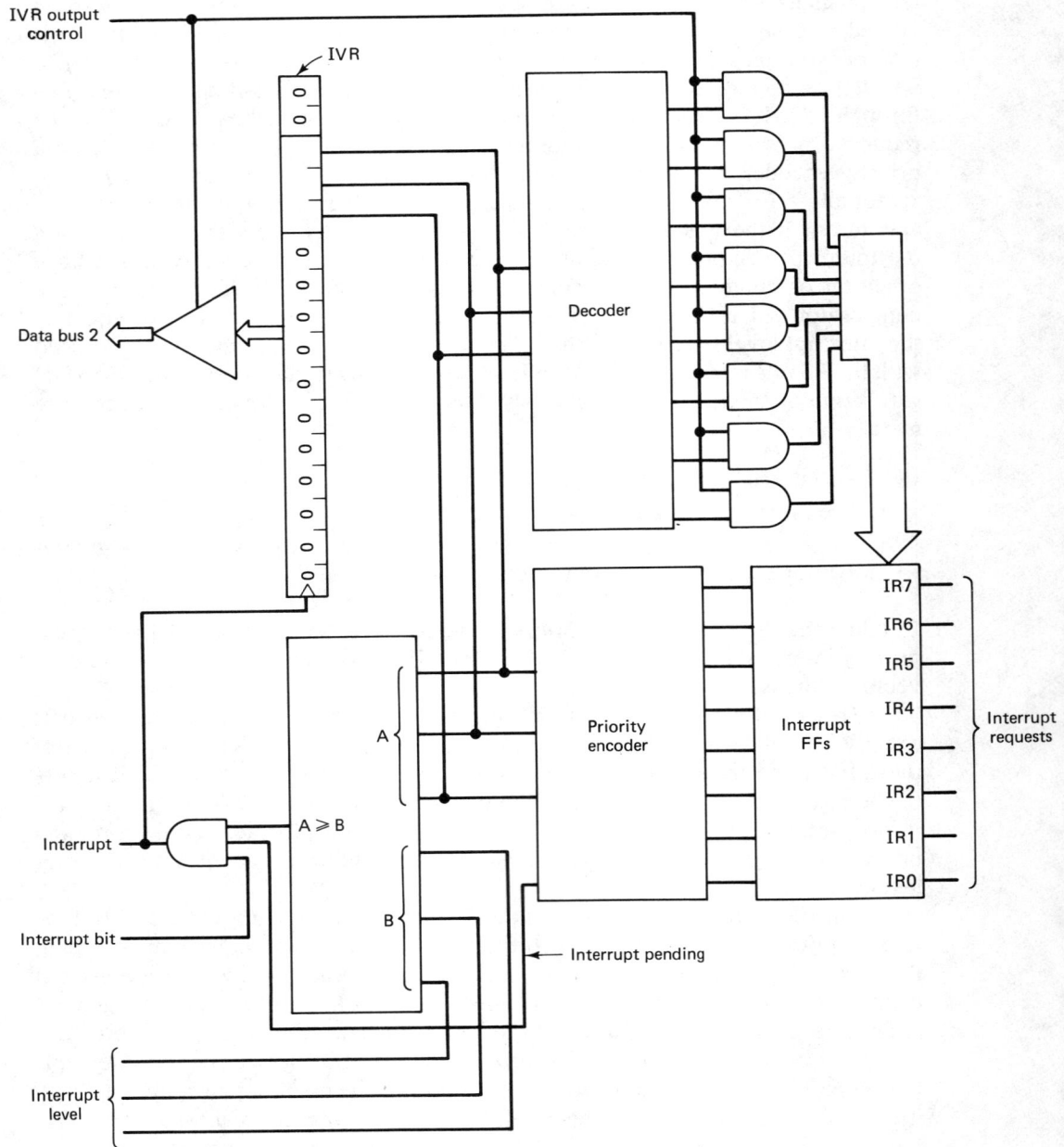

Figure 8-10 X16's Interrupt logic.

be such that it is programmed via the system bus. In the latter case, the facility's registers (which control the facility's priority, mode, etc.) would be addressed just like the registers in an interface. This would allow ordinary input and output instructions to control the interrupt management facility.

As with interrupt logic, the bus access logic may support only a single bus request/grant pair or several such pairs. Although we will not give the details of a specific design for the X16, many of the interrupt management comments regarding priority and programmable features also apply to bus access management. In Fig. 8-6, the bus access logic does show a Hold output to the handshaking logic and a Hold Acknowledge input from the handshaking logic. The Hold signal indicates to the handshaking logic that it is to disable the address, data, and handshaking drivers and receivers at the end of the current transfer, and the Hold Acknowledge verifies that the drivers and receivers have, in fact, been disabled.

Daisy Chain Arrangement

Either an interrupt facility with a single request/acknowledge pair or a bus access facility with a single request/grant pair can make use of a **daisy chain arrangement** such as the one shown in Fig. 8-11. Although an interrupt request/acknowledge pair is shown in the figure, it could just as well be a bus request/grant pair. The Interrupt Request line is wire-ORed and an interface signals a request by pulling the line low. If, or as soon as, the processing element's interrupt enable bit is set, the interrupt logic detects that there is at least one request and responds by sending out an Interrupt Acknowledge. The Interrupt Acknowledge is received first by the daisy chain logic of Interface 1. If Interface 1 has made a request it will accept the Interrupt Acknowledge signal and block it from propagating to other interfaces. What happens after the Interrupt Acknowledge has been accepted depends

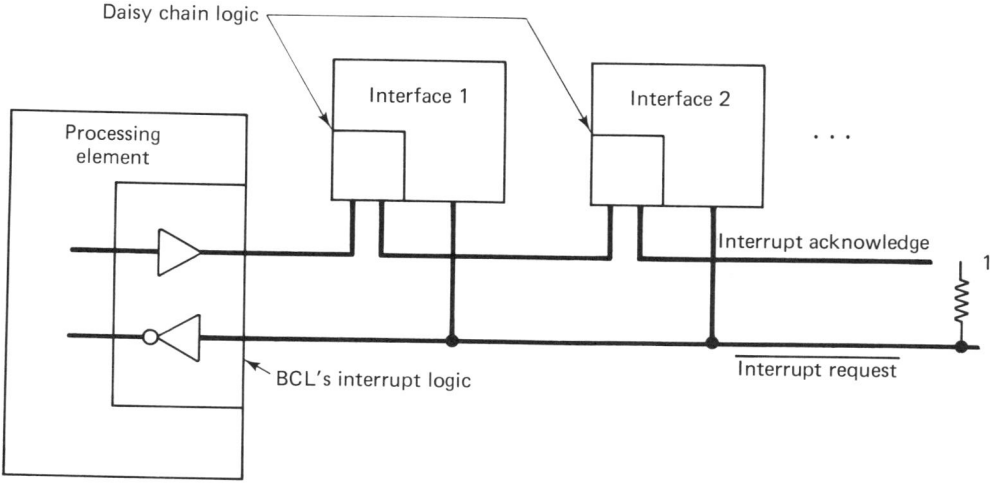

Figure 8-11 Typical daisy chain arrangement.

on the interrupt sequence designed into the processing element. If interrupt vectors are used, this sequence will initiate an input and expect the interface that accepted the Interrupt Acknowledge to return an interrupt vector or vector address over the data bus. When the interface returns the interrupt vector or vector address, it also drops its request. If Interface 1 has not made a request, it allows the Interrupt Acknowledge to be passed on to Interface 2. Upon receipt of the Interrupt Acknowledge, each interface either accepts it, if the interface has made a request, or passes it on to the next interface.

Note that, because the requests are wire-ORed, one interface dropping its request does not necessarily mean that the $\overline{\text{Interrupt Request}}$ line goes high. All requests must be satisfied before this line goes high. If an interface drops its request and $\overline{\text{Interrupt Request}}$ is still low, then the processing element will begin a new interrupt sequence as soon as interrupts are enabled. For example, if Interfaces 1 and 4 both make requests, and Interface 3 makes a request while the interrupt routine for Interface 4 is being executed, then the following sequence of events occurs:

1. The processing element enters an interrupt sequence and issues an Interrupt Acknowledge.
2. Interface 1 accepts the Interrupt Acknowledge, returns its interrupt vector, and drops its request.
3. When the interrupt routine enables interrupts, the processing element again enters an interrupt sequence and issues an Interrupt Acknowledge.
4. Interface 4 accepts the Interrupt Acknowledge, returns its interrupt vector, and drops its request.
5. When the interrupt routine enables interrupts and Interface 3 makes its request, the processing element again enters an interrupt sequence and issues an Interrupt Acknowledge.
6. Interface 3 accepts the Interrupt Acknowledge, returns its interrupt vector, and drops its request.

If no other requests are made, the $\overline{\text{Interrupt Request}}$ line will go high and, when the interrupt routine for Interface 3 reenables interrupts, another interrupt sequence will not take place.

A daisy chain arrangement maintains each request at the interface until the interface receives an acknowledgment, and the priority is set by the physical placement of the interfaces along the daisy chain. The interface that is closest to the processing element has the highest priority. The advantage of a daisy chain is its simplicity. Its drawbacks are that it has a built-in priority structure and, if there are several interfaces, the propagation delays through the sets of daisy chain logic can be excessive.

8-2-2 Link to Link Interfaces

Two sets of logic are included in a link to link interface, one set for each link. They may be quite different because each reflects the characteristics of its link. This section concentrates on interfaces for which one of the links is a system bus. A typical set of logic for connecting to a system bus is shown in Fig. 8-12. The driver and receiver circuitry could be of the same design as that given in Fig. 8-8.

The selection logic, which indicates to the interface that it has been selected, is typically designed as shown in Fig. 8-13. The high-order address bits are compared to an address that is determined by a set of switches that are included in

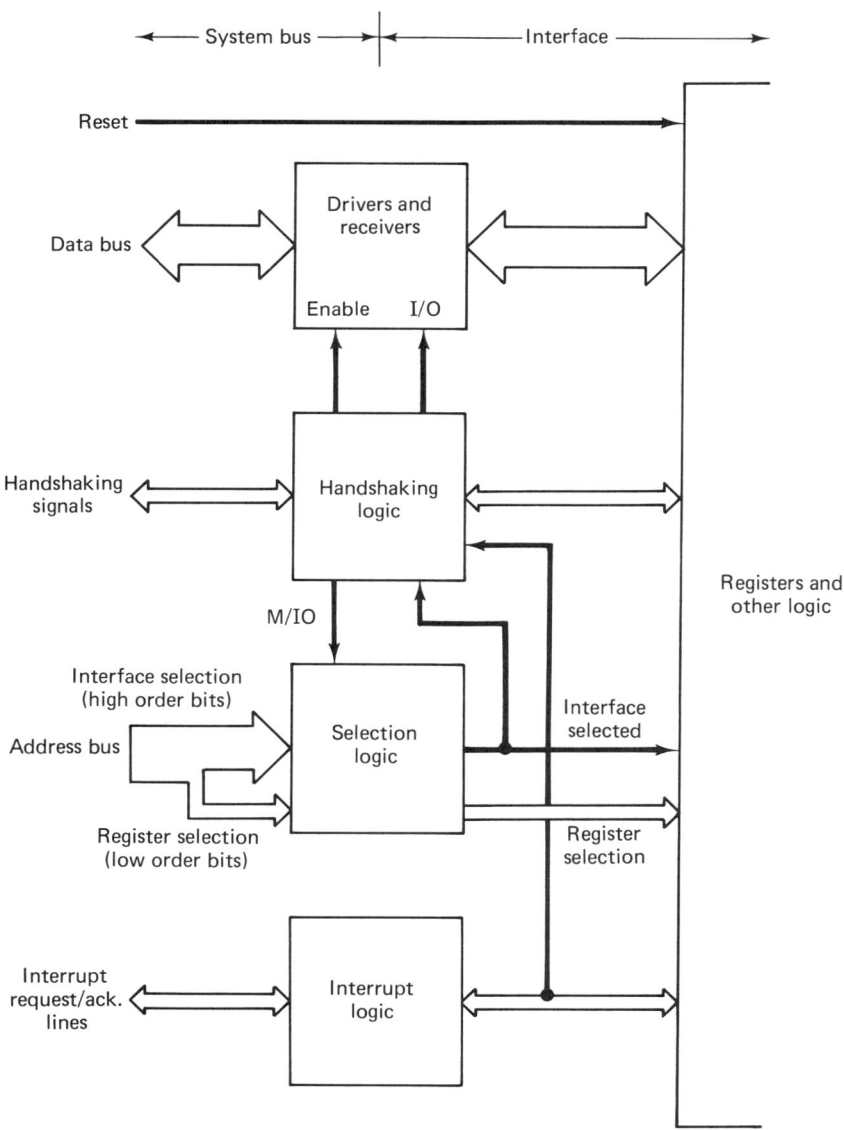

Figure 8-12 Logic for connecting an interface to a system bus.

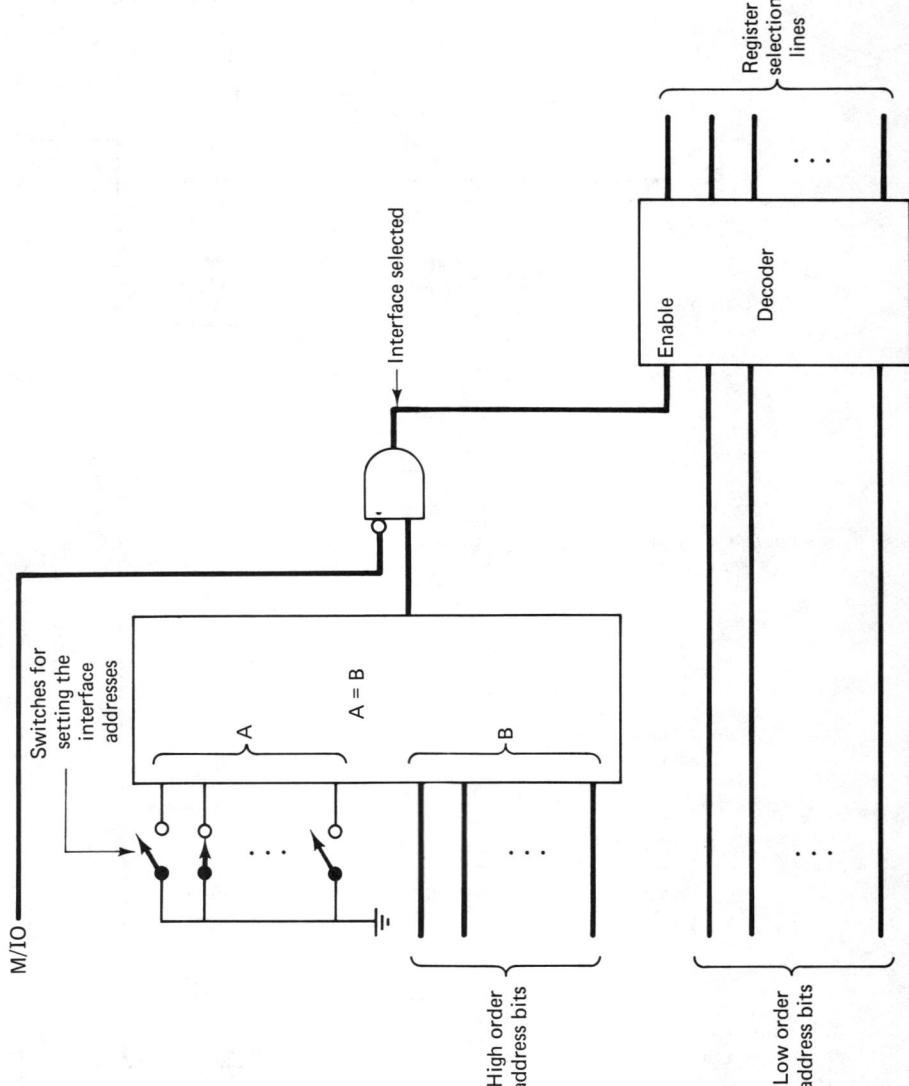

Figure 8-13 Logic for selecting an interface and a register within the interface.

the interface. If there is more than one address space, the output of the comparator is ANDed with address space signals, such as an M/IO signal. The Interface Selected output of the comparator and address space AND gate indicates whether the interface is to be involved in the transfer. The switches on the different interfaces must, of course, be set to different values. The low-order address bits are input to a decoder whose outputs are used to select the interface register (i.e., I/O port) that is to be accessed. The decoder is disabled when the interface is not selected.

Handshaking and interrupt logic obviously depend on the definitions of the handshaking lines in the system bus and the nature of the interrupt facilities. If daisy chaining is being used, the interrupt logic would primarily consist of daisy chain logic.

Figure 8-14 shows the logic needed to connect an interface to a system bus that is compatible with an X16. A Write signal causes the receivers to be enabled and a Read signal causes the drivers to be enabled. The Interface Selected signal produced by the selection logic is used to enable/disable the Read and Write signals. The X16's interrupt logic handles the interrupt acknowledgments and the return of the interrupt vector address; therefore, the interrupt logic consists of only the monostable multivibrators needed to generate the interrupt request pulses.

To illustrate the logic internal to an interface, Fig. 8-15 shows a set of registers and associated logic corresponding to the system bus connection logic given in Fig. 8-14. This figure assumes that the interface contains four registers—a status register, a data-in buffer register, a data-out buffer register, and a control register. The status and data-in buffer registers can be read from and the data-out buffer and control registers can be written into. Bit 1 of the status register indicates when the data-in buffer contains data that have not yet been read by the processing element and Bit 0 indicates when the last data put into the data-out buffer register were transmitted over the data link. Bit 5 of the control register is an interrupt enable bit and must be 1 for the interface to issue an interrupt request.

Because two of the registers can only be read from and two of them can only be written into, register selection differs from that shown in Fig. 8-13. By using the Read and Write signals as inputs to the decode logic, the only address bit that is needed is A_0. It is assumed that Read and Write are ANDed with the Interface Selected signal (as in Fig. 8-14) so that they can be active only if the interface has been selected. When the Read signal is active, the status is read if $A_0 = 0$ and the data-in buffer is read if $A_0 = 1$. When Write is active, the data-out buffer receives the output if $A_0 = 0$; otherwise the control register receives the output. The signal for reading from the data-in buffer also clears Bit 1 of the status register, thus indicating that the data in the buffer have been taken. When the buffer is refilled from the data link, this bit returns to 1 and, if interrupts are enabled, a receiver interrupt request pulse is output. Also, the signal that latches data into the data-out buffer clears Bit 0 of the status register and, when data are taken from this buffer, this bit is set to 1 and an interrupt may occur. A Ready signal is returned to the X16 when any one of the four registers is accessed but, for a read, the Ready signal is delayed to account for skew in the data signals.

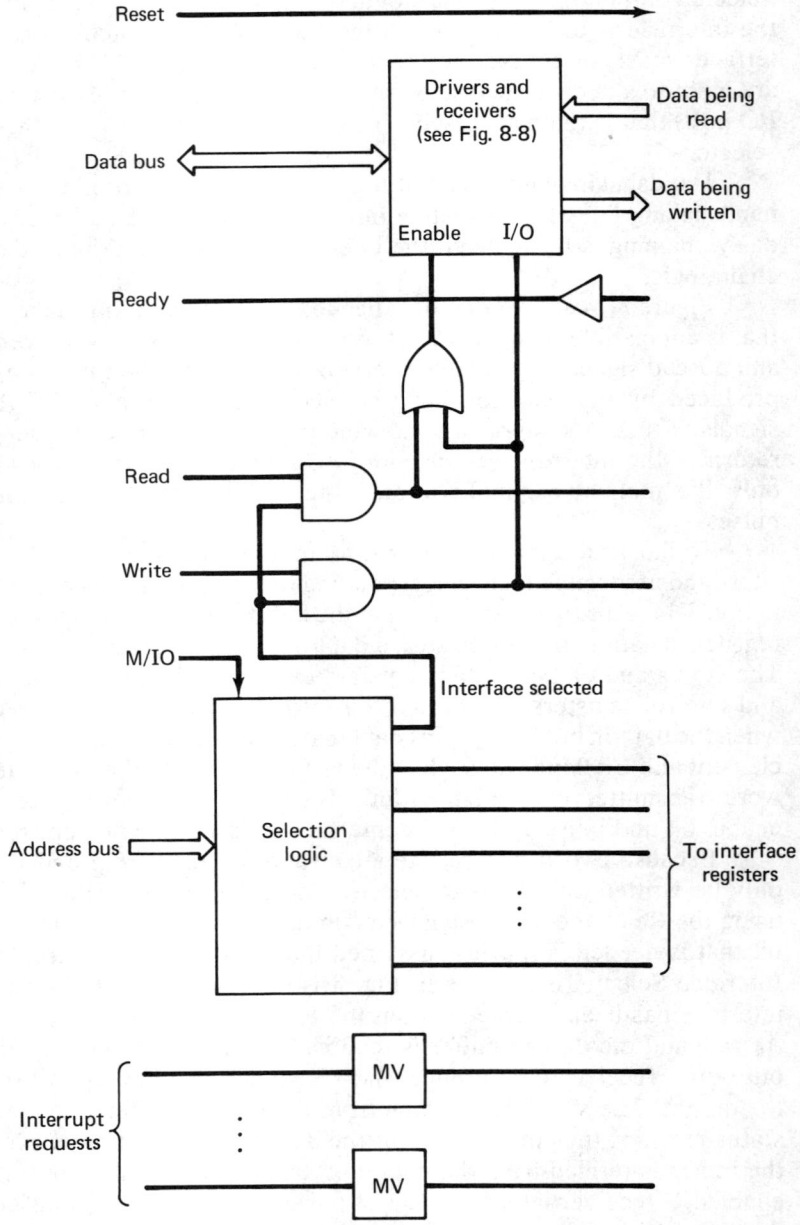

Figure 8-14 Logic needed to connect to an X16's system bus.

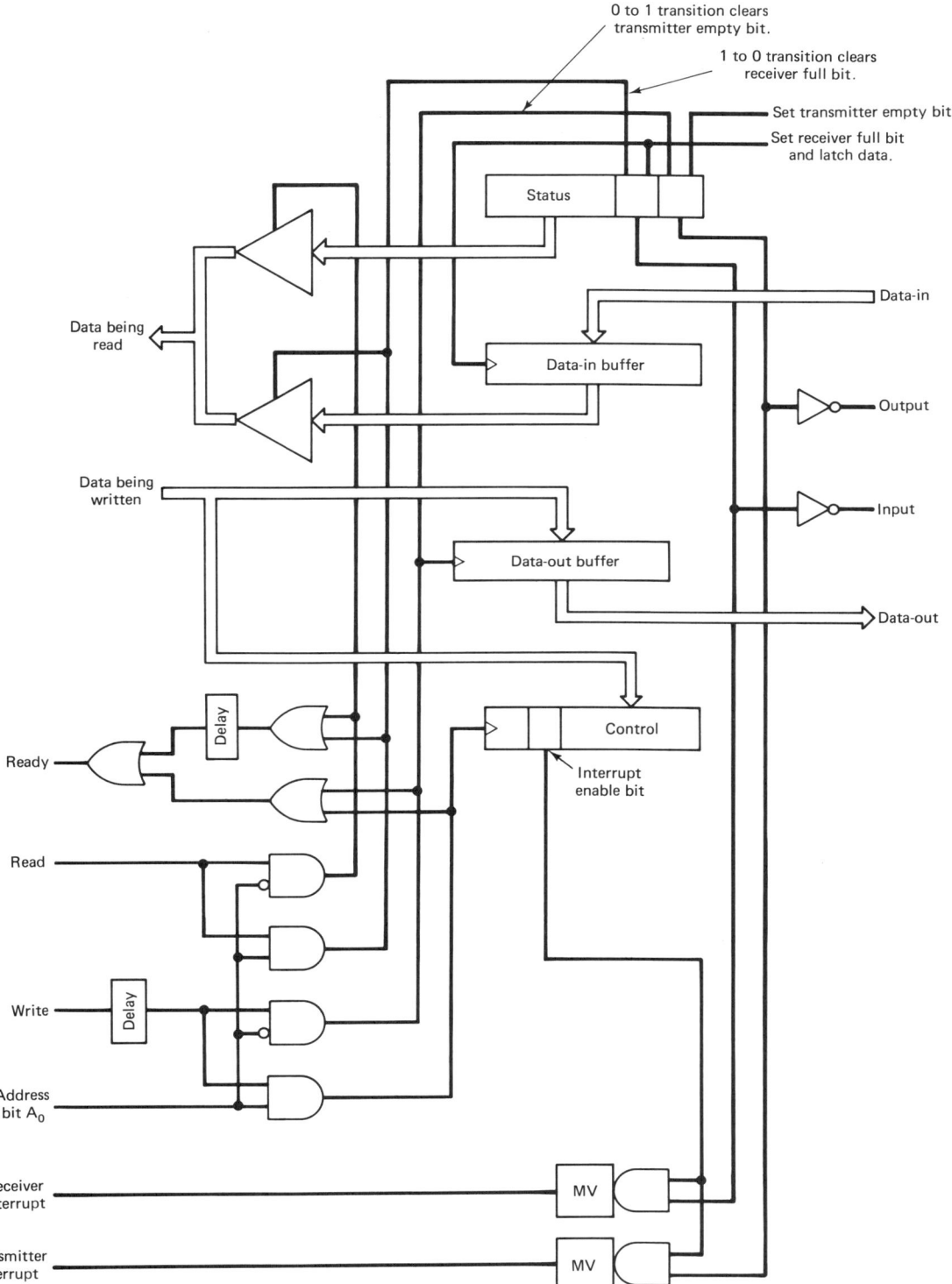

Figure 8-15 Typical X16 interface registers and associated logic.

The data link connected to the other side of the interface may be parallel or serial, or may be synchronous or asynchronous. A typical asynchronous parallel data link is shown in Fig. 8-16(a), with the corresponding sequencing being defined in Figs. 8-16(b) and 8-16(c). The logic for connecting the interface logic in Fig. 8-15 to this parallel data link is given in Fig. 8-17.

The Output and Input signals are the complements of Bits 0 and 1 of the status register, respectively, and Output enables the Data-out drivers and Input enables the Data-in receivers. Bit 1 of the status register is set by the AND of the Input and Input Acknowledge signals, and bit 0 is set by the AND of the Output and Output Acknowledge signals. The former indicates that the data-in buffer has just been filled and the latter indicates that data have just been taken from the data-out buffer. The AND of Input and Input Acknowledge is also used to latch the input data. The delay in the Output signal allows for skew in the output data.

Figure 8-18 outlines the data paths that are needed to connect to a serial data link. Shift registers provide the serial to parallel and parallel to serial conversions. The incoming data are shifted into a receiver shift register with the shift rate being determined by the receiver clock. The outgoing data are generated by the transmitter shift register using the transmitter clock. Normally, the frequencies of the receiver and transmitter clocks are the same, but this is not necessarily so. The circuitry for loading and enabling the various registers depends on whether the data link is synchronous or asynchronous and is not shown. Serial transmission is discussed further in Sec. 8-3.

Representative formats for the control and status registers are given in Fig. 8-19. Although it was not shown in the interface design given in Fig. 8-15, most interfaces are able to detect pertinent errors and store error indicators in their status registers. Parity error detection is the most common and interfaces to asynchronous links should include framing error detection, which is defined in Sec. 8-3. A third type of error, called an overrun error, occurs when new data replace the contents of a buffer register before those contents are passed on. For example, suppose that data are being transferred from a terminal keyboard to a processing element via a data link, interface, and system bus. An overrun error would occur at the interface if a character arrives from the keyboard before the previous character was taken from the data-in buffer by the processing element. Although the data link design in Fig. 8-17 would not allow an overrun, frequently the data link handshaking is incomplete and such an error can occur. Other bits in an interface's status registers provide information about the data link that may need to be monitored by the processing element.

The control register shown in Fig. 8-19(b) is for an interface to a serial data link. In addition to the interrupt enable bit, it includes bits for controlling the data link, designating the character format, and designating whether there is no parity bit, an even parity bit, or an odd parity bit. Control registers are used to allow a processing element a means of controlling the data link connected to the interface. There is a large assortment of possible control bits. Mass storage elements, in particular, must be provided a considerable amount of control information.

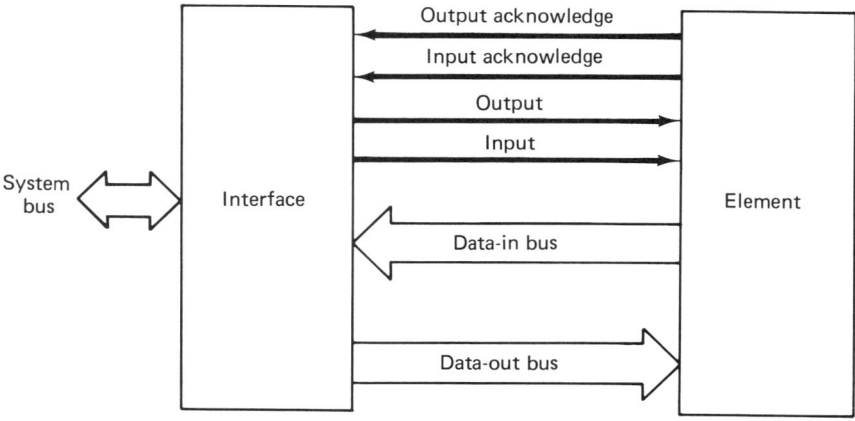

(a) Data link

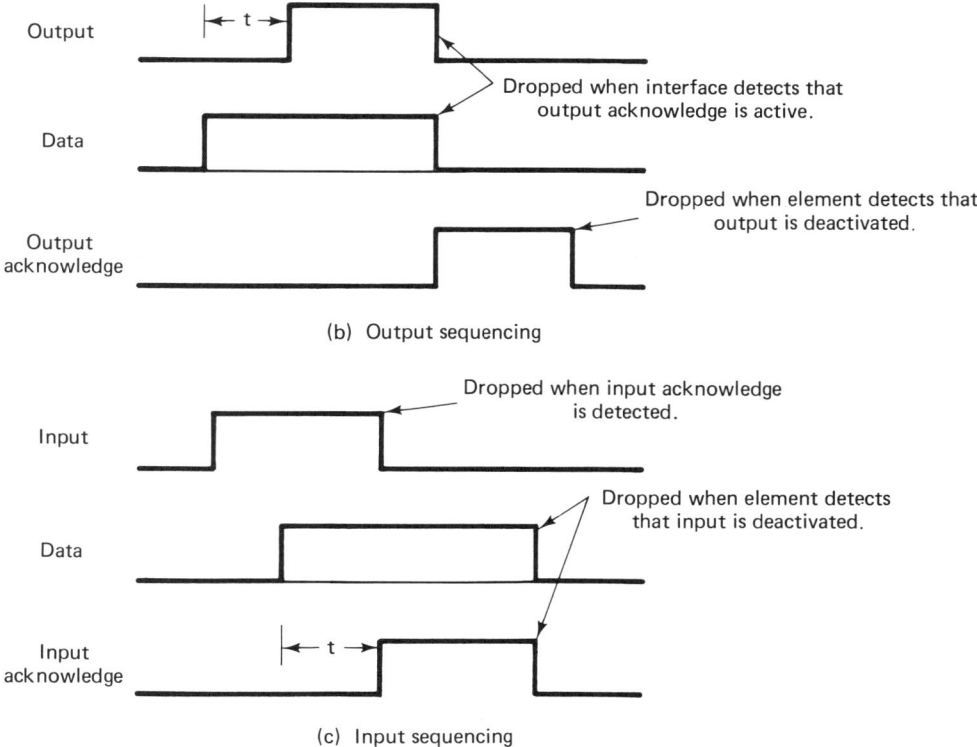

(b) Output sequencing

(c) Input sequencing

t = time sufficient to allow for skew

Figure 8-16 Typical parallel data link handshaking.

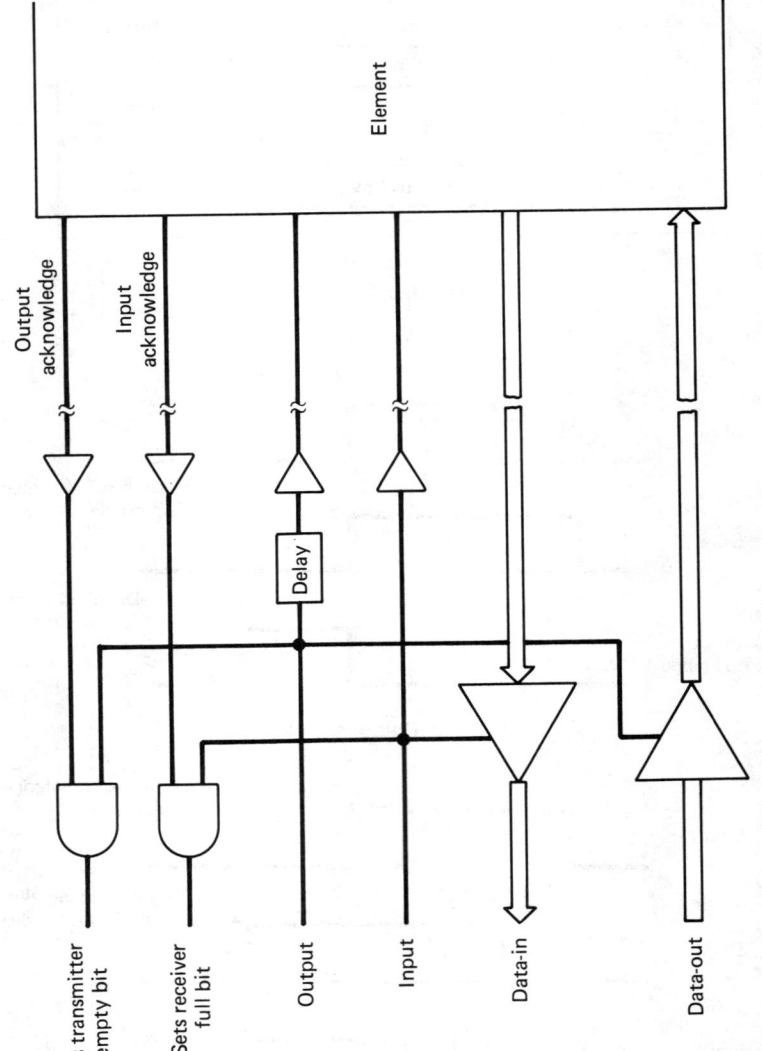

Figure 8-17 Interface to a parallel data link.

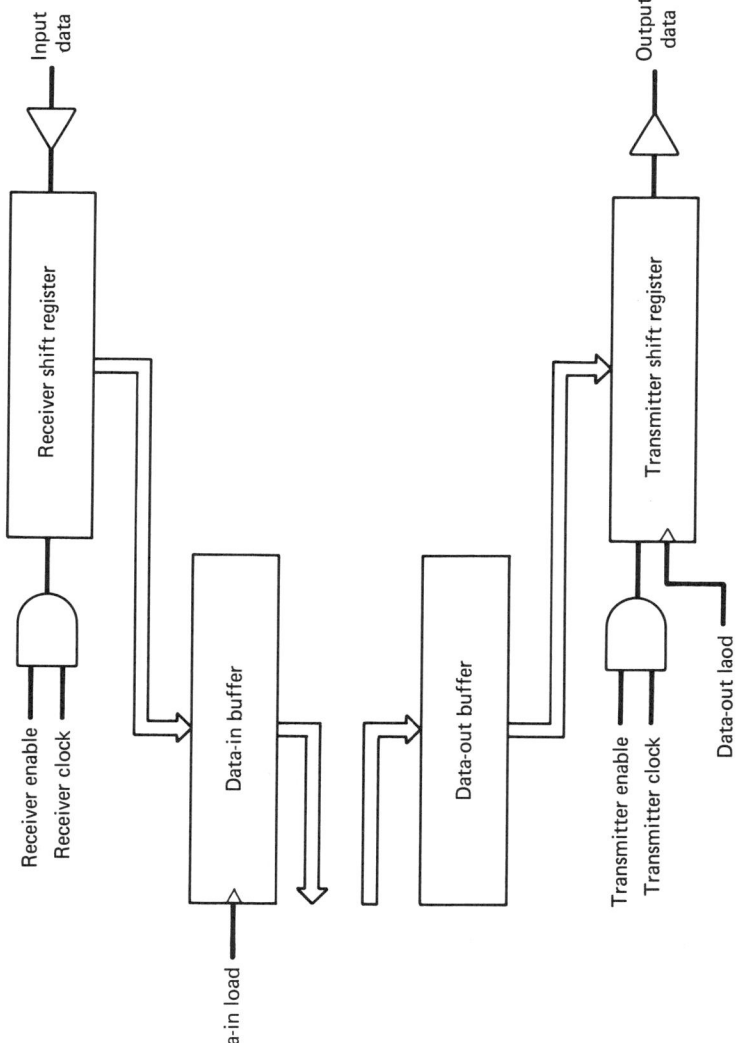

Figure 8-18 Data paths for a serial data link.

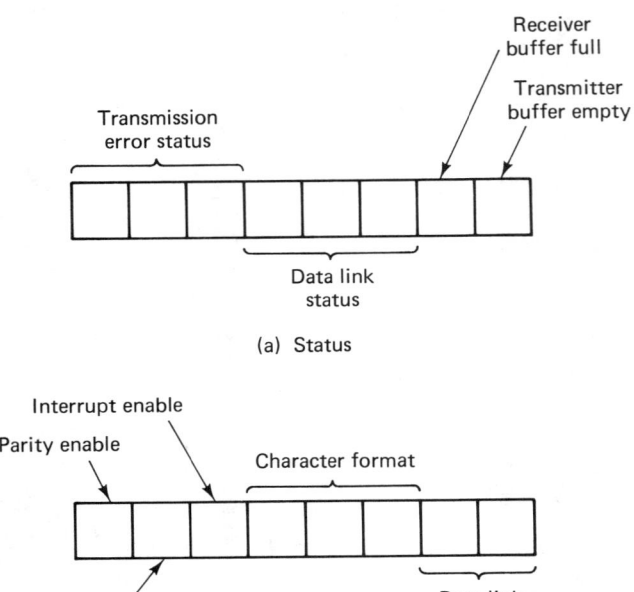

Figure 8-19 Representative status and control registers.

8-3 DATA LINKS

Although it would be impossible to give a thorough discussion of data links in one section, or even one book, it is felt that a brief introduction to them is in order. This section attempts to describe basically how data links operate and some of their characteristics, but, more importantly, it introduces some of the more common terminology related to data links. There are numerous books on data communications, some of which are Chou [1], [2], Meijer and Peeters [3], McNamara [4], Friend, Fike, Baker and Bellamy [5], and Tanenbaum [9].

Data links connect computers to their I/O and mass storage elements or to other computers. The characteristics of a data link depend on its use and physical requirements, and the length and required transmission rate of a data link strongly influence its design. A data link may be synchronous or asynchronous, serial or parallel, and its medium may be a set of wires, a coaxial cable, a fiber optic cable, or a set of microwave channels.

A data link provides a transfer path between an interface, usually an interface to a system bus, and an I/O element, a storage element, or another interface. If an element is locally situated relative to the computer to which it is connected, a simple data link such as the one shown in Fig. 8-20(a) is sufficient. A link to a remote location may need to be broken into parts as shown in Fig. 8-20(b). In this case, a local data link is used at each end to connect the system bus interface to a second interface, referred to as data communications equipment. The two

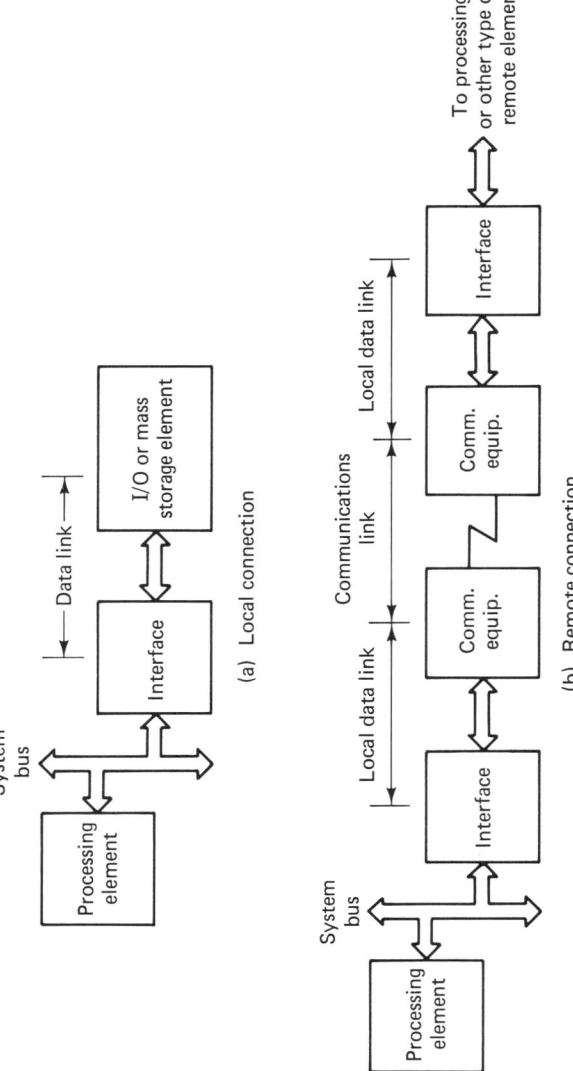

Figure 8-20 Links to local and remote locations.

sets of data communications equipment are then connected together by a communications link. A local data link is most often constructed of conductors, but may include a fiber optic cable. A communications link may be from a few hundred meters to several thousand kilometers in length and include several different types of media. A communications link frequently involves a telephone system.

The design of either a local data link or a communications link usually involves a tradeoff between transmission rate, measured in bits per second (bps), and cost. There are two ways to increase transmission rate. One is to increase the number of signal paths and the other is to increase the rate of a link's existing signal paths. If a link is relatively short (less than 100 m), then increasing the number of signal paths is a reasonable alternative; but, for long data links, particularly communication links, minimizing the number of paths is very important. For short links, an inexpensive cable of wires with relatively unsophisticated transmitter and receiver electronics can be used. For longer distances, not only is the cost of a given medium more (assuming cost is per unit length), but a higher quality medium and associated electronics are required just to maintain a specified transmission rate. The alternative to adding signal paths, which is increasing the rate of the existing signal paths, is also achieved by using a better medium and more complex transmitting and receiving equipment. However, the longer the link, the more likely that increasing the transmission rate of existing paths will be more cost effective. For communication links, a single signal path is almost always used.

Links can be classified in terms of signal direction as follows:

- **Simplex**—strictly unidirectional.
- **Half duplex**—bidirectional, but only in one direction at a time.
- **Full duplex**—bidirectional, in both directions simultaneously.

A simplex link has transmitters at one end of the link and receivers at the other end, while both half and full duplex links have both transmitters and receivers at both ends. Half duplex presents a problem because extra control is required to determine, for each transfer, which end is to transmit and which is to receive. When the direction changes between transfers, a turnaround occurs. A turnaround requires the circuitry at both ends to switch between transmitting and receiving. Unfortunately, turning a link around takes from a few milliseconds to over 100 milliseconds, which is a long time relative to other computer operations. As a result, the amount of data transferred between turnarounds should be fairly large. For example, if data are being communicated at 10 K bps and 20 mS is needed for a turnaround, 1800 bits must be transferred between turnarounds in order to utilize the link 90% of the time.

8-3-1 Signal Formats

Until now we have assumed that all computer information is transferred from one point to another using two levels, with one level representing 0 and the other representing 1. A signal that can take on only a finite number of levels (voltage, current, or light intensity levels) is called a **digital signal**. In contrast, one whose level varies continuously is an **analog signal**. Local data links normally use digital signals, and communication links, unless they are constructed of a fiber optic cable, use analog signals. Therefore, most data communications equipment must convert digital signals to analog signals and vice versa. An analog signal is normally derived from a digital signal by modifying a sinusoid, called the **carrier**, using a process called **modulation**. The reverse process is called **demodulation**. The portion of the data communications equipment that is responsible for performing modulation/demodulation is called the **modem**, and, if the communications equipment's primary purpose is to perform modulation/demodulation, then the communications equipment as a whole may be referred to as a modem.

Three of the more common digital signal formats are shown in Fig. 8-21. In each case the signal is always at one of two levels and is divided into time intervals of equal length, with one bit being transmitted during each interval. The number of time intervals per second is called the **Baud rate**, and for the formats in Fig. 8-21 the Baud rate is equal to the transmission rate in bps. The nonreturn-to-zero level (NRZ-L) format in Fig. 8-21(a) is the most straightforward. It represents a 0 by one level and a 1 by the other level and maintains the level throughout the interval. Transitions cannot occur during the intervals and may or may not occur between intervals. The format in Fig. 8-21(b) is called the biphase-level format (BI-L) or Manchester code. It defines a 0 as a low to high transition at the midpoint of an interval and a 1 as a midpoint high to low transition. The remaining example is the delay modulation-mark (DM-M) format or Miller code. For this code, a 1 is represented by a midpoint transition, 00 by a transition between the two intervals, and 10 by no transition between the two intervals.

The advantage of the NRZ-L format is its simplicity. As was seen in Fig. 8-18, simple shift registers can be used for transmitting and receiving a signal in this format. The problem with this format is that a succession of 0s or 1s may require a constant level to be maintained over a long period of time. If levels are represented by voltages (which is often the case), the transmitting amplifier must be able to hold its output constant indefinitely. This capability complicates transmitter design, but a potentially more serious problem occurs at the receiving end. If, as in asynchronous transmissions, there is no common clock signal to delimit the time intervals, then the receiver must estimate when each interval begins and ends. Level transitions can be used by the receiver to reestablish the beginning of an interval, but if there are no transitions, then the receiver's estimates will become progressively more inaccurate. Normally, there is a transition at the beginning of a character that allows the receiver to calibrate itself and, if it is possible for no further transitions to occur, then the length of a character is limited by the receiver's ability to estimate time intervals.

The Manchester code guarantees that there will be at least one transition every clock period. This eliminates the problem of maintaining a constant level and provides a receiver with a more than adequate means of updating its timing. In fact, even for synchronous transmissions, a receiver can reconstruct a clock signal from the data well enough to obviate the need for a separate clock signal (see

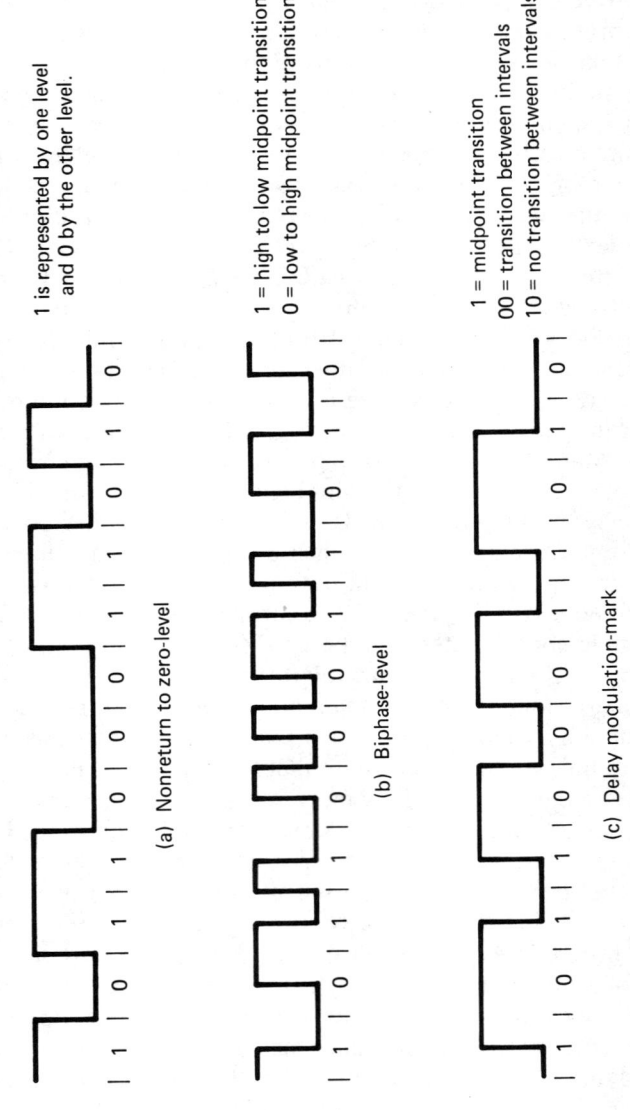

Figure 8-21 Digital signal formats.

Exercise 17). The main disadvantage of the Manchester code is that a succession of 0s or 1s causes two transitions per interval.

For digital signals, the maximum number of transitions between levels per second that can be sustained by a link or signal path is called the digital bandwidth of the link or path. Therefore, for the NRZ-L format, the digital bandwidth of the signal path could be the same as the Baud rate, but for the Manchester code, it must be twice the Baud rate. The Miller code provides a compromise. It guarantees a transition at least every other interval but cannot have more than one transition per interval, and the bandwidth can be the same as the Baud rate (see Exercise 18).

The format of an analog signal depends on the modulation type. The three basic types of modulation are amplitude, frequency, and phase modulation which, respectively, vary the amplitude, frequency, and phase of a carrier according to the digital signal. Fig. 8-22 gives examples of the three types of modulation along with the digital signal used to modulate the carrier. In Fig. 8-22(c), a phase change of 180 degrees represents a 1. Sometimes a group of bits is used to produce more than two amplitudes, frequencies, or phases. This allows the analog signal in a single time interval to represent more than one bit (e.g., phases of 45, 135, 225, and 315 degrees could represent the bit pairs 00, 01, 10, and 11). As a result, the transmission rate in bps may be more than the Baud rate. In addition, amplitude

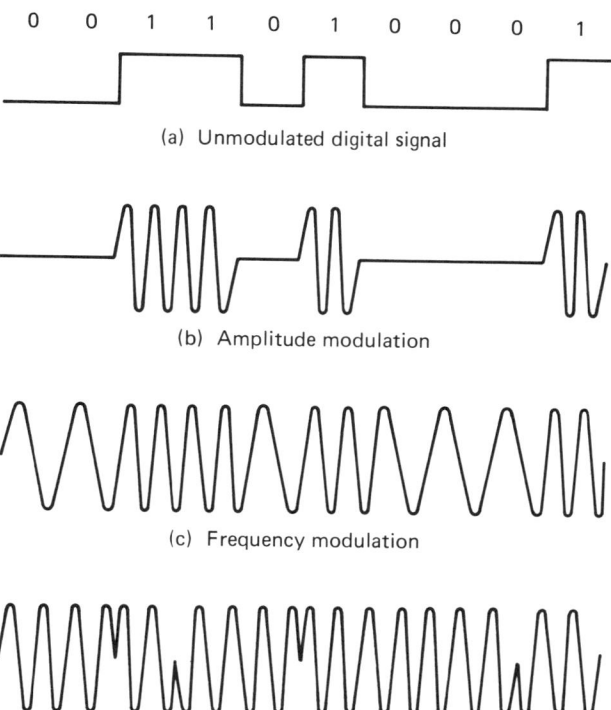

Figure 8-22 Types of modulation.

and phase modulation are sometimes combined. One standard method uses the amplitude and phase combinations shown in Fig. 8-23 to represent four bits per time interval.

8-3-2 Local Data Links

The usual format for serially sending an asynchronous signal over a local data link is shown in Fig. 8-24. Characters, such as ASCII characters, are not necessarily sent one after the other, but dead space is permitted between them. A 1, or mark, is maintained during the dead space and the beginning of a character is indicated by a 1 to 0 transition. The interval following this transition is called the start bit, and during this bit, a 0, or space, is maintained. The next n intervals, where n = 5, 6, 7, or 8, transmit the character. The 0s and 1s are represented by holding the signal at 0-level or 1-level throughout their intervals. A character may be followed by a parity bit and 1, 1½, or 2 stop bits. Stop bits are 1s and insure that the signal is held at the mark level from 1 to 2 intervals before the next character can begin.

A receiver uses the transition at the beginning of a start bit to adjust its clock. Its clock must then simulate the clock the transmitter used to generate the signal. The rates of the two clocks do not have to be exactly the same because of the readjustment at the beginning of each character, but their frequencies must be reasonably close or the received bits may be misinterpreted. If the receiver detects a 0 when it expects a stop bit, a **framing error** is said to occur. The start and stop bits mark the beginning and end of a character.

Synchronous transmission does not need to include start and stop bits, but

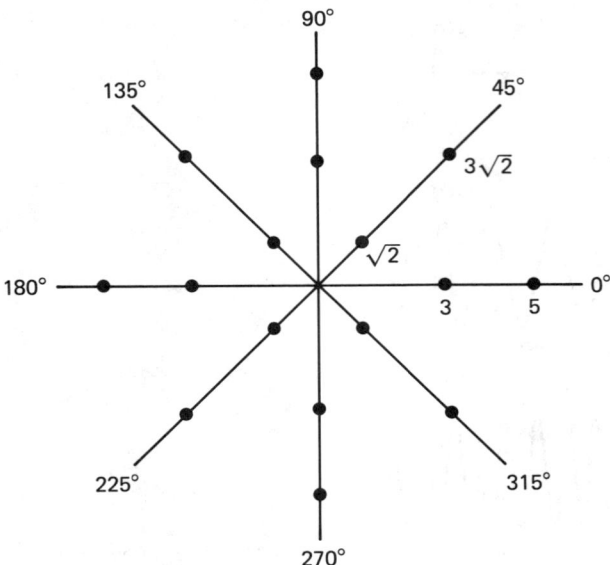

Figure 8-23 CCITT's V.29 standard set of amplitude/phase combinations used to modulate four bits per time interval.

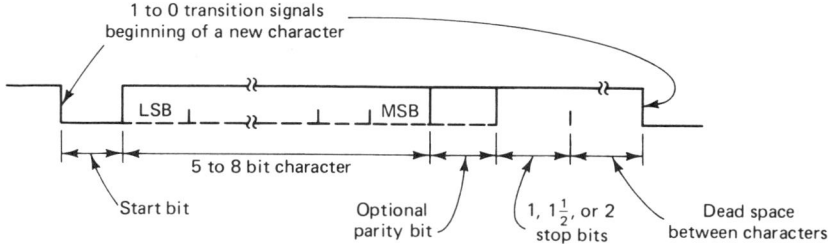

Figure 8-24 Format of a standard serial asynchronous character.

it also does not allow for dead space between characters. If a transmitter has no data characters to send, it must fill in with idle characters which, when the ASCII code is being used, are normally sync characters (hexadecimal 16). Dead space is allowed between groups of characters, but if the data link is allowed to go dead it must be restarted by sending a sequence of sync characters before sending the data. Sync characters are used by a receiver to lock into the character pattern and thereby recognize the first data character.

8-3-3 Data Link Standards

Because computers are often made from components purchased by several manufacturers and connected together by links, there is a need to standardize links for different applications. The four organizations that write most of these standards are: the Institute of Electrical and Electronics Engineers (IEEE), the Electrical Industry Association (EIA), the Comité Consultatif International Téléphonique et Télégraphique (CCITT), and the International Standards Organization (ISO). Standards typically include definitions of signal paths, electrical characteristics of signals and paths, and even mechanical properties of connectors. Once a standard has been established, manufacturers can design equipment to match the standard rather than the specifications set forth by other manufacturers. Standards provide a certain amount of order to the evolution of computer systems.

Some of the most accepted standards are the CCITT X series and V series standards and the EIA RS series standards. Many of the specifications in the X and V series parallel those in the RS series. The CCITT specification X.1 gives standard transmission rates in bps. They are 50, 100, 110, 134.5, 200, 300, 600, 2400, 4800, 9600, and 48000 bps. These rates are used by a wide variety of components from teletype machines to high speed, long distance data communications equipment.

As an example, let us consider a widely used standard for serial transmission, the EIA's RS-232 specification for connecting an interface to a modem. It includes both electrical requirements and signal path, or circuit, definitions. Typical electrical specifications consist of an equivalent circuit and a corresponding list of electrical limitations and requirements. The RS-232 equivalent circuit and a summary of its more important electrical properties are given in Fig. 8-25. The driver is the transmitter and the load is a combination of the transmission line and re-

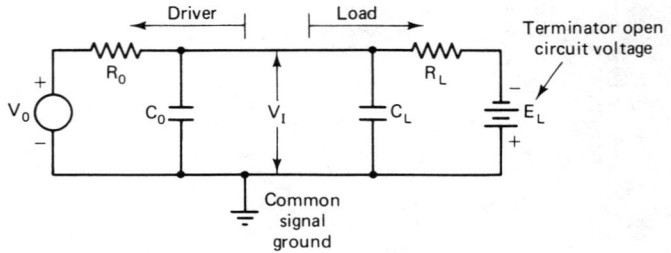

(a) Equivalent circuit

$V_O < 25$ V

Maximum short circuit current to any wire in cable -0.5 A

MARK signal at load < -3 V

SPACE signal at load $> +3$ V

MARK signal out of driver < -5 V and > -15 V

SPACE signal out of driver $> +5$V and $< +15$ V

$R_L < 7000$ ohms when measured with a voltage from 3 to 25 V, but > 3000 ohms

C_L including line capacitance < 2500 pF

When $E_L = 0$, 5 V $< V_I < 15$ V

$R_O > 300$ ohms under power off conditions

C_O is such that the slew rate of the driver's output voltage is < 30 V/microsecond, but the transition between -3 V and $+3$ V does not exceed the smaller of 1 mS or 4% of the bit time

(b) Requirements

Figure 8-25 RS-232 electrical specifications.

ceiver. A representative graph of the maximum length an RS-232 link can have versus its baud rate is given in Fig. 8-26. The dropoff in this graph is due to R_0, the internal resistance of the transmitter, and the parallel combination of C_0 and C_L, which represent the combined capacitance of the transmission line and receiver.

The more important RS-232 circuits are defined in Fig. 8-27 with the symbolic representation of each circuit appearing in the first column, its standard name in the second column, and its description in the third column. Only the first eight lines in Fig. 8-27 are needed for communicating over a direct asynchronous communications link. For transmitting, a Request to Send (CA) signal is sent to a modem by setting a bit in the control register and this signal is acknowledged by a Clear to Send (CB), which sets a bit in the status register. Then, transmission

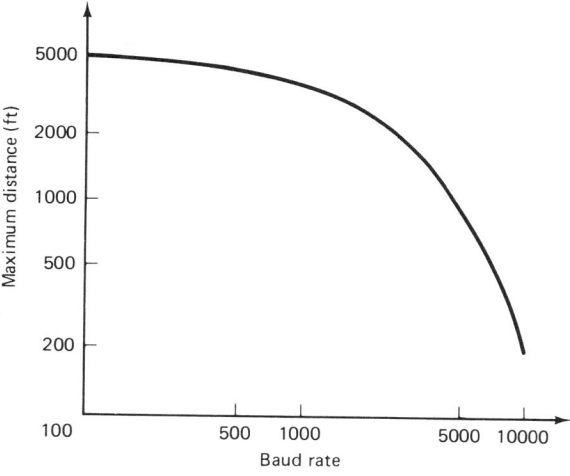

Figure 8-26 Representative graph of maximum distance versus baud rate for an RS-232 link.

may begin on the Transmitted Data (BA) line by outputting the data to a data-out buffer register.

For receiving, a Received Line Signal Detector (CF) line is activated by a modem to indicate that it is receiving a signal from a modem at the other end of the communications link. This signal sets a status bit and, perhaps, causes an

Symbol	Name	Description
AA	Protective Ground	Used as equipment ground
AB	Signal Ground	Used as common ground for all signals
BA	Transmitted Data	For outputting data to modem
BB	Received Data	For inputting data from modem
CA	Request to Send	To modem—to turn modem's transmitter on and off
CB	Clear to Send	From modem—indicates modem is ready to transmit
CC	Data Set Ready	From modem—indicates that modem power is on
CF	Received Line Signal Detector	From modem—indicates modem is receiving a signal from the modem at the other end of the link
CD	Data Terminal Ready	To modem—prepares modem to be connected to the communication link and begin transmitting
CE	Ring Indicator	From modem—indicates ringing signal is detected on link
DA	Transmitter Signal Element Timing (DTE Source)	To modem—provides modem transmitter with signal timing
DB	Transmitter Signal Element Timing (DCE Source)	From modem—provides interface or terminal with transmitter signal timing

Figure 8-27 The more important RS-232 circuit definitions.

Sec. 8-3   Data Links

interrupt request to be made. The Received Data (BB) line sends the received data from the modem to a data-in buffer register in the interface. The Data Set Ready (CC), which is also reflected by a bit in the status register, indicates that the modem is turned on and is in its data mode. This line must be active when either transmitting or receiving.

If a communication link is part of a switched telephone system, at least two more lines are required. By setting a control bit, a signal is sent to a modem over the Data Terminal Ready (CD) line, which causes the modem to establish a communication link. The Ring Indicator (CE) line is activated by the modem to indicate to the interface that the modem is receiving a ringing signal. The Ring Indicator signal would set a status bit and, to answer this signal, the computer would respond by setting a control bit to activate the Data Terminal Ready line. This response would cause the modem and its switching equipment to "answer the ringing phone."

Synchronous communication requires that timing information be communicated along with the data. There are two lines for providing this information. The DTE Source Timing (DA) line is used when the interface provides the clock signal and sends timing information from the interface to the modem. The DCE Source Timing (DB) line is used when the modem supplies the timing.

8-3-4 Packets

Most high-speed communications, particularly computer to computer communications, are carried out by using synchronous transmissions to send groups of bits called **packets**, or **messages**. The general format of a packet is given in Fig. 8-28. Delimiting flags mark the beginning and end of a packet and the header contains information such as the source address, destination address, packet type, packet length, whether the receiver is to respond, and information concerning previous packets. Termination characters primarily mark the end of the data but may indicate other information or may not be included.

The header format depends not only on the standard being used, but also on the type of packet. In addition to packets that transmit data, there are control packets for realizing a form of handshaking. Typically, control packets indicate the beginning of a sequence of packets, whether the last packet was correct or incorrect, whether the receiver is expected to respond, the end of a packet sequence, and so on.

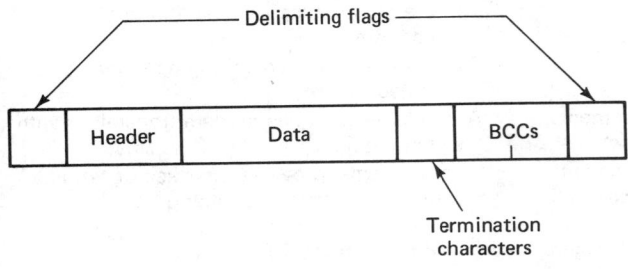

Figure 8-28 General packet format.

Although means for packet error detection could include attaching a parity bit to each character, all packet formats include Block Check Characters (BCCs) as a way of indicating whether there has been an error in the packet as a whole. The most widely used method for generating BCCs is to use a Cyclic Redundancy Check (CRC) generator such as the one shown in Fig. 8-29. A CRC generator consists of shift registers with feedback through exclusive OR gates that are inserted between the bits of the shift register. As a packet is being output, its bits are also sent to the transmitter's CRC generator. After the data have been transmitted, the BCCs are shifted out of the CRC generator and appended to the end of the packet. The receiver includes an identical CRC generator and, after receiving a packet, the received BCCs should match the BCCs in the receiver's CRC generator. If there is not a match, an error has occurred.

The placement of the exclusive OR gates is described by an expression, called a **generating polynomial**, that describes the positions of the exclusive OR gates. The generating polynomial corresponding to Fig. 8-29 is $X^{16} + X^{12} + X^5 + 1$, which is the one specified in many standards. Research has been performed on several generating polynomials to determine their error detection capabilities. It is always possible that an error has occurred even though the BCCs match, and the object of this research is to minimize the probability of this occurrence. The more prominently-used generating polynomials and the names that have been given to them are:

CCITT-CRC: $X^{16} + X^{12} + X^5 + 1$ (for 16-bit BCCs)
CRC-16: $X^{16} + X^{15} + X^2 + 1$ (for 16-bit BCCs)
CRC-12: $X^{12} + X^3 + X + 1$ (for 12-bit BCCs)

The inclusion of flags, headers, terminating characters, and BCCs adds overhead to data transmission. Clearly, for a fixed number of these extra bits, a longer packet means less overhead and a more efficient overall transmission. If there are m overhead bits and n data bits, the percentage efficiency would be

$$\frac{n}{m + n} \times 100\%$$

which goes to 100% as n goes to infinity. However, there is a tradeoff between packet length and the probability of an error occurring. When an error does occur,

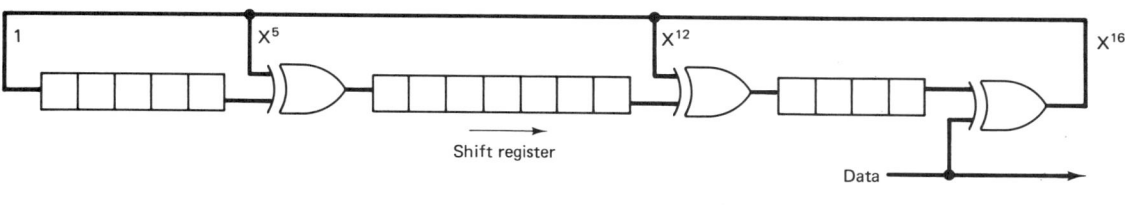

Generating polynomial = $X^{16} + X^{12} + X^5 + 1$

Figure 8-29 CRC generator.

the entire packet must be retransmitted and the longer the packet, the greater the time wasted. Also, it may be difficult to recover from an error because there is usually some error-related handshaking in addition to the retransmission of the packet. Thus, the recovery also generates overhead.

8-4 SUMMARY

Links and interfaces are used to communicate all information between the processing, memory, and I/O elements of a computer. Interfaces compensate for signal and timing differences between links and elements, and links conduct the actual transfer of information. The characteristics of an interface are dictated by the characteristics of the links and elements it is to join. Interfaces are simply designed to satisfy the requirements of the links and elements and may have very little in common. Buffer registers are needed to match different timing specifications and most interfaces contain status and control registers, but the widths and number of these registers and the purposes they must serve vary drastically from one interface to the next. The number of buffer registers primarily depends on the extent of the difference between the two sets of timing requirements—the greater this difference, the larger the required capacities of the buffers.

The principal attributes of links are summarized in Fig. 8-30. The primary property of a link is its maximum transfer rate, which indicates the link's capacity

```
Transfer Rate:
   Number of signal paths (serial or parallel)
   Bandwidth

Signal Direction:
   Simplex
   Half duplex (turnarounds)
   Full duplex

Signal Format:
   Digital (code—NRZ-L, etc.)
   Analog (modulation—amplitude, frequency, or phase)

Timing:
   Serial
      Asynchronous (start and stop bits)
      Synchronous (common clocking—data and clock pulses may be intermixed)
   Parallel
      Asynchronous (handshaking)
      Synchronous (worst case design)
```

Figure 8-30 Principal link characteristics.

to move information. Because a link's sole purpose is to move information, it is, in a sense, a necessary evil that decreases a computer's speed but does no useful work (i.e., processing). It is desirable that a link's speed exceed that of the elements to which it is connected so that it is not responsible for significantly decreasing the speed of the overall system. The speed of a link is determined by the number of its signal paths and the bandwidth of the signal paths in bps. If there are p paths in a link and each path is capable of transmitting at x bps, then the transfer rate is px. However, it may be that not all of the paths are used for data and not all of the bits sent over the paths are data bits. Some of the paths may be for timing or parity checking and some of the bits may be for error checking, framing, addressing, or link control. Therefore, the transfer rate of actual data may be somewhat less than px. For some links, particularly communications links, the true data transfer rate is further reduced by the retransmission of data when an error occurs, and the designer must have some indication of the error rates associated with the various design choices (e.g., the choices of transmission media).

Clearly, the obstacle to higher data rates and reliability is cost—the cost of the medium, drivers, receivers, and other electronics directly related to the link. As anyone who has purchased a high fidelity sound system can attest to, higher bandwidths cost more. Also, more reliability can be had only through better noise reduction (e.g., shielding the link) and higher quality electronics at the ends of the link.

REFERENCES

1. Chou, Wushow, *Computer Communications*, Vol. 1 (Englewood Cliffs, New Jersey: Prentice Hall, Inc., 1983).
2. Chou, Wushow, *Computer Communications*, Vol. 2 (Englewood Cliffs, New Jersey: Prentice Hall, Inc., 1985).
3. Meijer, Anton, and Paul Peeters, *Computer Network Architectures* (Rockville, Maryland: Computer Science Press, 1982).
4. McNamara, John E., *Technical Aspects of Data Communications* (Bedford, Mass.: Digital Equipment Corporation, 1978).
5. Friend, George E., John L. Fike, H. Charles Baker, and John C. Bellamy, *Understanding Data Communications* (Dallas, Texas: Texas Instruments, 1984).
6. Liu, Yu-cheng, and Glenn A. Gibson, *Microcomputer Systems: The 8086/8088 Family*, 2nd ed. (Englewood Cliffs, New Jersey: Prentice Hall, Inc., 1986).
7. Hall, Douglas V., *Microprocessors and Digital Systems* (New York: McGraw-Hill Book Company, 1980).
8. Short, Kenneth L., *Microprocessors and Programmed Logic*, 2nd ed. (Englewood Cliffs, New Jersey: Prentice Hall, Inc., 1987).
9. Tanenbaum, Andrew, *Computer Networks*, 2nd ed. (Englewood Cliffs, New Jersey: Prentice Hall, Inc., 1988).

EXERCISES

1. Why is a link sometimes classified according to its relationship to processing elements?
2. Why are system buses normally asynchronous?
3. Give a timing diagram that shows the order in which the data, address, and control lines shown in Fig. 8-3 are used while an instruction that stores a working register's contents to memory is fetched (first transfer) and executed (second transfer). See Fig. 8-4.
4. Suppose that a processing element is connected to three memory and I/O elements and the propagation delays along the system bus, times needed to read from the elements, and frequencies of the reads are:

	Propagation Delay	Access Time	Frequency of Reads
Element 1	5 nS	100 nS	60%
Element 2	7 nS	30 nS	15%
Element 3	10 nS	20 nS	25%

What is the average read time if the system bus is:
(a) Asynchronous?
(b) Synchronous?

5. Assume the instruction sequencing given in Chap. 7 (Figs. 7-9 and 7-11) and the bus sequencing in Fig. 8-4. Draw a timing diagram similar to those in Fig. 8-4 that shows the bus activity during the fetch and execution of:
   (a) MOVH X,Y
   (b) ADDH R1,R2
       MOVH R2,X

   Assume one wait state for each memory access and use T_I to denote those clock cycles for which the bus is idle.

6. Design the handshaking for a bidirectional bus that uses one direction line that is 0 for output and 1 for input. Give timing diagrams for typical outputs and inputs.

7. Suppose that an X16 is connected to a memory element via a bus that uses the timing defined in Fig. 8-4. If a clock period is 75 nS, it takes 30 nS for a signal to traverse the bus, and the memory takes 150 nS to put data on the bus after it receives a Read signal, how long would it take to fetch and execute the instruction MOVH X,R1? How many wait states would be included in the transfers?

8. Give the complete sequence of events that occur within the X16's address, data, and handshaking logic circuits (See Figs. 8-6 through 8-9) during the execution of the following instructions:
   (a) MOVH R1,X
   (b) MOVH X,R1

9. The address and data transfer logic given in Fig. 8-7 assumes a 16-bit data bus and only halfword transfers. If byte accesses were allowed as in the chapters prior to Chap. 7, the system bus as well as the internal control bus would have to include a byte/halfword control line. Discuss the extra burden that permitting byte transfers would place on the memory interface and the possibilities for distributing this burden between

the memory interface and the BCL. Consider both *reads and writes*. Recall that byte operations use only the lower bytes of the registers.

10. Suppose that an X16's interrupt level is 3, interrupts are enabled, and an interrupt request arrives at IR6. Use Fig. 8-10 to give a chronological description of the interrupt logic's signals that occur from the time the request arrives until it is cleared.

11. Suppose that the daisy chain arrangement in Fig. 8-11 is being used and Interfaces 1 and 3 simultaneously make interrupt requests. Interface 2 makes a request during the execution of the interrupt routine for Interface 1 and Interface 4 makes a request during the execution of the interrupt routine for Interface 3. Determine the order in which the interrupt routines are entered and exited assuming that interrupts are enabled:
    (a) As soon as the routines are entered.
    (b) By the interrupt return instructions.

12. Assume the design in Figs. 8-15 and 8-17 and give a chronological description of all handshaking and data signals as a byte is output from the system bus to the I/O element connected to the data link.

13. Design parity checking logic for the interface in Fig. 8-15. Bit 7 of the status register is to be set if Bit 7 of the control register is set and there is an even parity error in the input data. Reading the status register is to cause its Bit 7 to be cleared.

14. Use Figs. 8-18 and 8-24 to show how shift registers could be incorporated into Fig. 8-15 to obtain an asynchronous serial interface. Show how the receiver's shift register enable input and data-in register's load input could be controlled. Assume seven data bits, no parity bit, and one stop bit.

15. If 40 mS are required to perform a turnaround, the transmission rate is 9600 bits per second, and a turnaround occurs after the transmission of each 1200 bits, what is the percentage of time wasted by the turnarounds? If the transmission rate is 2400 bits per second?

16. Assume that a Manchester coded signal uses intervals of length T. Show that the signal can be derived from a NRZ-L signal by exclusive ORing the NRZ-L signal with a clock signal whose period is T. Also show that exclusive ORing the clock signal with the Manchester coded signal can be used to recover the NRZ-L signal.

17. Design a logic circuit that produces a clock signal from a Manchester coded signal.

18. Verify that the Miller code guarantees a transition at least every other interval, but cannot have more than one transition per interval.

19. If data are being transmitted at a Baud rate of 2400 using the amplitude/phase combinations shown in Fig. 8-23, what is the transmission rate in bps?

20. If an asynchronous transmission uses the format shown in Fig. 8-24 to send 7-bit ASCII characters followed by a parity bit and two stop bits and the link is capable of transmitting at 600 bps, what is the maximum transfer rate in characters per second?

21. If a packet containing 100 data characters is preceded by 1 flag and 5 header characters and followed by 2 BCC and 1 flag characters, and the link is capable of transmitting at 600 bps, what is the maximum average transfer rate in data characters per second? Compare this result with the one obtained for Exercise 20.

22. If an RS-232 data link is to be 1000 ft long, what is its approximate maximum Baud rate?

23. If a data sequence begins as follows and a CRC is used to obtain the BCCs:

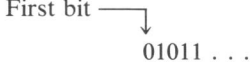

01011 . . .

show the contents of the CRC generator after the fifth bit is output assuming that the generating polynomial is:

(a) CCITT-CRC
(b) CRC-12

24. Suppose that a packet contains m overhead bits and n data bits and $e^{-(n+m)/50000}$ is the probability that an error will not occur during the transmission of the packet. What is the maximum value of n if $m = 20$ and 99.9% of the packets are to be transmitted without an error? If the percentage of error-free packets is to be 99.99%? In each case, what is the ratio of bad bits to good bits, where the bad bits include all bits that must be retransmitted?

9

Memory Hierarchy

Memory elements receive information, store it until it is needed, and then make it available to other elements in the computer. The act of putting information into or taking information from a memory element is called a **memory access**. For some memories, the time required to perform an access is essentially the same for all accesses and they are referred to as **random access memories**. For others, the time varies considerably. In either case, the access time, or the average access time, is an important property of the memory. The principal attributes of a memory element are its access time and its capacity, which is the total amount of information that can be stored in the element at any given time. Capacity is usually measured in bits or bytes.

Another important property is the number of bits transferred into or out of memory in a single access. If this number is n and the access time is T, then the access rate or **memory bandwidth**, in bits per second (bps) is n/T, which can be increased either by increasing n or by decreasing T. Other properties, whose significance depends on the application, are power consumption, supporting circuitry required, volatility, and removability. A **nonvolatile** memory can maintain its contents even when no power is applied to the memory's circuitry, but a **volatile** memory loses its contents when the power is turned off. The portion of memory that actually retains data (e.g., the circuitry, tape, or disk) is called the **medium**. If the medium is nonvolatile and can be taken out of the computer and kept in storage or inserted in another computer, then it is said to be **removable**.

A typical memory hierarchy is shown in Fig. 9-1. The number of memory levels and the memory types needed depend on the application. Small, special purpose computers may not include mass storage and only computers that require fast execution rates need to include the level labeled "buffer memory." The reason for the hierarchical arrangement of memory is the tendency for the cost per

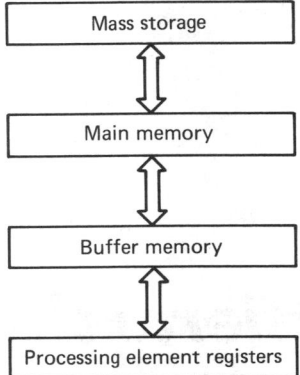

Figure 9-1 Typical memory hierarchy.

bit of a memory element to be inversely related to its access time. The greater the access time, the less a memory costs per bit of storage. Access times versus cost per bit relationships for common types of memory are shown in Fig. 9-2. Also, general purpose computers need at least some removable memory so that data can be copied and stored for safekeeping or transported between computers. Such memory is relatively slow and is normally included in the mass storage part of the memory hierarchy.

The purpose of the hierarchy is to provide an evenly matched flow of information from mass storage, where the information is kept, to the processing element, where it is used. This matched flow is at least partially attainable because

- Some of the information is used more than once and does not have to traverse the entire hierarchy each time it is needed. Therefore, even though mass

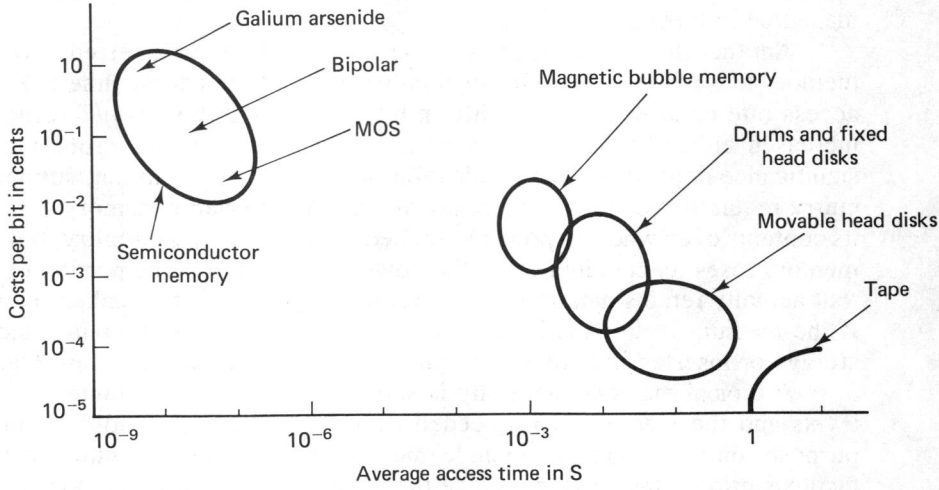

Figure 9-2 Cost vs. access time comparisons for common types of memory.

storage is slower than main memory, most information needs to be passed between mass storage and main memory only once regardless of the number of times it is used by the processing element (e.g., instructions within loops, constant data, and so on).

- It is possible to increase the access rate of a slower memory element by increasing the amount of information transferred per access. For example, if the access time for a memory element is T and it must supply information at x bps, the design must be such that the number of bits per access n satisfies the inequality $n \geq xT$.

Information flow demand is determined by the processing elements. From an efficiency standpoint, the ultimate goal is to supply the processing elements at rates sufficient to keep them busy 100% of the time.

Also important to the storage of information is the way in which the storage is viewed. The physical placement of information within the memory is called the **physical structure** of the memory and is determined by the construction of the medium and the hardware for accessing the medium. Nonrandom access memories often store information in physically contiguous areas on the medium, while random access memories store information in individually addressable locations, normally one byte in size. A second way of viewing memory is the way it appears to a program. A program works with memory using names, subnames, and numbers that may have dynamically changing associations with the physical locations in the memory. The organization of the names, subnames, and numbers (e.g., file names and record numbers or array names and indices) and their associated information is called the **logical structure** of the memory. The logical structure is used by program statements to refer to information and the physical structure determines the actual locations. Because information may be moved around within a memory the physical/logical association may change. Before an access can begin, the correspondence between the logical reference and the physical location must somehow be determined so that the hardware can be directed to the proper point in memory. For mass storage, this is usually done by the operating system and, for main memory, it may be done by the translation/linking/loading process, by hardware, or both (see Chap. 10).

9-1 MASS STORAGE

Mass storage can take on many forms, the more prevalent of which are tape drives, disk or diskette drives, drums, and magnetic bubble memories (MBMs). Tapes, disks, and drums all involve mechanical motion, which contributes significantly to their access times. MBMs do not require mechanical motion and have higher access rates, but are more expensive. The degrees of mechanical movement and the speed with which this movement can be accomplished have a marked influence on access time. None of these four types of mass storage is random access and their access times are specified as averages.

For nonrandom access memories there are two time quantities that are important. Blocks of information are contiguously located within memory and the average time needed to seek out and begin access of the first unit of information (bit, byte, etc.) is the **average access time**. Once the read/write mechanism has been positioned to begin the access, the successive elements in the block can be quickly read or written and the rate at which information is stored or retrieved is called the element's **transfer rate**. For example, the average access time may be 20 mS, but once the block transfer begins, the transfer rate might exceed one million n-bit units per second, i.e., each n-bit transfer may require less than one microsecond. For random access memories, the first access requires the same amount of time as all succeeding accesses even if information is contiguous.

Information is put into mass storage in related groups called **files**. Files may, in turn, be broken down into subgroupings, sub-subgroupings, and so on. The primary subgrouping is normally referred to as a **record**. To access a particular set of information, a program must establish communication with a file and then refer to the appropriate record using a record identifier. Normally, an entire record is read or written using a block transfer. The sub-subgroupings of information are logical entities called **fields** and **subfields**, which are used to access specific information after a record is input or before a record is output. For example, the logical structure of a file might be:

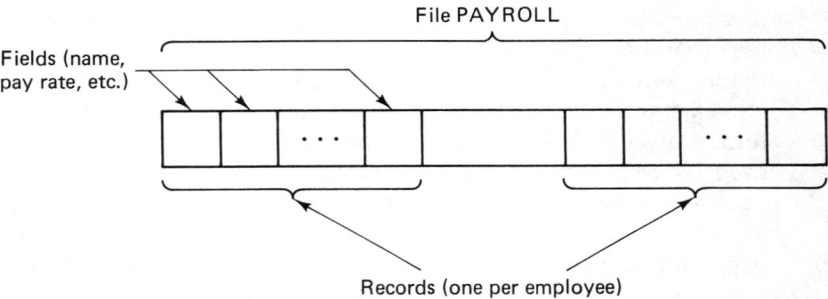

The data for an employee would be brought into main memory as a block and then the fields could be used to determine the employee's pay.

9-1-1 Magnetic Tape Units

For memory elements that use magnetic tape the medium is a long strip of mylar that is coated with a magnetically sensitive material and wound onto a reel. The most common type of magnetic tape is ½ inch wide and 2400 feet long and is wound onto a 10 inch diameter reel. Although cassettes or other kinds of tapes are also used, the discussion here concentrates on standard ½-inch wide, 10-inch reel tapes. For such tapes, the information is magnetically recorded by successively putting 8-bit bytes and one parity bit across the tape. Thus, these tapes are referred to as 9-track tapes. Both ends of the tape are marked by metal strips that can be detected by the tape drive unit. The magnetic patterns are maintained until

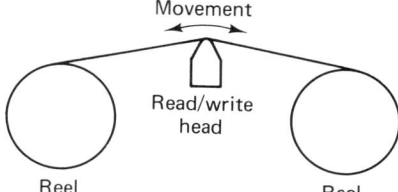

Figure 9-3 Basic operation of a magnetic tape unit.

they are purposely erased and therefore, magnetic tape is a form of nonvolatile memory.

As shown in Fig. 9-3, a tape drive transfers a tape from one reel to another while the tape is being accessed by a read/write head. There is one degree of mechanical motion and the reels must turn until the desired information passes over the read/write head. Typically, the tape passes over the read/write head at a rate of 45 to 300 inches per second (ips) while information is being read from or written onto the tape and 100 to 600 ips when the tape drive is in either its rewind or fast forward mode.

For example, if the read/write speed were 75 ips and the rewind speed were 200 ips, it would take 384 seconds to traverse an entire 2400 foot tape at the read/write speed and 144 seconds at the rewind speed. If a search is conducted by completely rewinding the tape and then searching at read/write speed in the forward direction, the average access time would be

$$144/2 + 384/2 = 264 \text{ S}$$

(On the average, half of the tape would be rewound and the forward search would be through half of the tape.) It is clear that this average access time is excessive and randomly accessing a tape is very slow. Therefore, information is usually stored on a tape in the order it is expected to be retrieved. This drastically reduces tape movement and thereby reduces average access time. Storing and retrieving information according to a fixed order is called **sequential access**, as opposed to **direct access**, which assumes no predetermined order.

Files and records are sequentially recorded on a tape with all of the records in the first file placed first, all of those in the second file placed second, and so on. As shown in Fig. 9-4, files are separated by **end of file (EOF)** markers, which are special patterns recorded on the tape at the time the file is recorded. Records

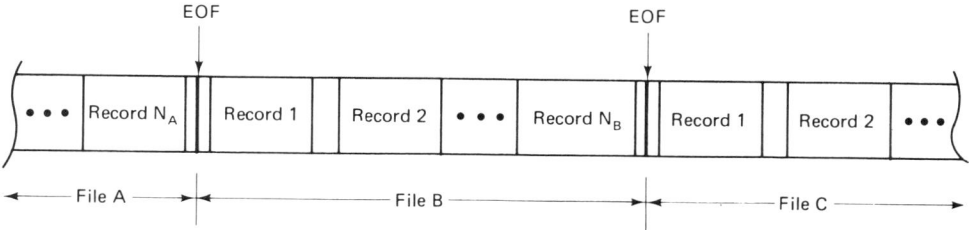

Figure 9-4 Format of a magnetic tape.

are separated by blank spaces called **record gaps**. The first record usually identifies the file and provides descriptive information about it.

Reading or writing is done by whole records. If the read/write head is arbitrarily positioned, then to search out a record, the tape is normally rewound and a forward search is conducted. However, if information is being accessed sequentially, then a search is made for the file, but after the file is found, the tape movement between accesses is only the movement across a record gap. Backing up to a previous record could be accomplished by backing up one record at a time, or **backspacing**. Restarting at the beginning of the current file could be accomplished by rewinding only to the beginning of the file. Rewinding to the beginning of the tape would be necessary only if a new file needs to be accessed.

After a tape has been positioned to read or write a record, the transfer rate is determined by the density of the information and the speed at which the tape moves. Typically, the information density is 800 to 6250 bits per inch (bpi). Because bytes are put laterally across the tape, 800 to 6250 bytes of information could be stored per inch and the transfer rate would be $800x$ to $6250x$, where x is the speed of the tape in ips. If the density is 1600 bpi and the speed is 75 ips, the transfer rate would be 120,000 bytes per second.

The maximum capacity of a single magnetic tape is the product of its density and its length. For a density of 1600 bpi and a length of $2400 \times 12 = 28,800$ inches, this maximum would be approximately 46 million bytes. But this maximum could be attained only for the unrealistic case in which there are no record gaps, i.e., the tape contains only one record. A record gap must be long enough so that the tape can be stopped and started between records. Depending on the lengths of the records, 10 to 50 percent of the tape may be needed for record gaps.

At any given time the capacity of a tape drive would be the capacity of a single tape, but tapes are almost always removable and there are robots capable of automatically loading and unloading tapes from a library. Although changing tapes would add to the access time (perhaps 15 to 50 seconds), having the ability to change tapes under program control could expand tape storage capacity indefinitely.

It is usually not possible to insert a new record in the middle of a tape because there may not be space available. Also, most magnetic tape drives have no way of precisely positioning a record on a tape and it is difficult to replace a record that is between existing records. A tape may be added to, but other modifications to the information on a tape must be accomplished by copying the tape and inserting the new or updated information during the copy operation. The problem of inserting information is typical of a sequentially accessed memory organization scheme and is a serious disadvantage of a memory element that must use sequential accessing. Copying from one tape to another requires either two tape drives or a very large amount of memory for temporarily holding the information to be copied.

Typical high-level language statements for manipulating sequentially accessed mass storage data are OPEN, CLOSE, REWIND, BACKSPACE, READ, WRITE, and ENDFILE. Retrieving information from a tape is done in two stages. The first stage positions the read/write head at the beginning of the indicated file and is initiated by the OPEN statement. The second stage searches out and reads the desired record. As flowcharted in Fig. 9-5, after the tape is rewound, the file identification in the first record of the first file is examined and if the file is not the one being sought, the remainder of the file is skipped. This continues until the indicated file is found or the end-of-tape marker is encountered. If the file is found and the nth record is desired, then the first $n-1$ records are skipped and the nth record is read and retained for processing.

The OPEN statement also indicates to the operating system that the file in

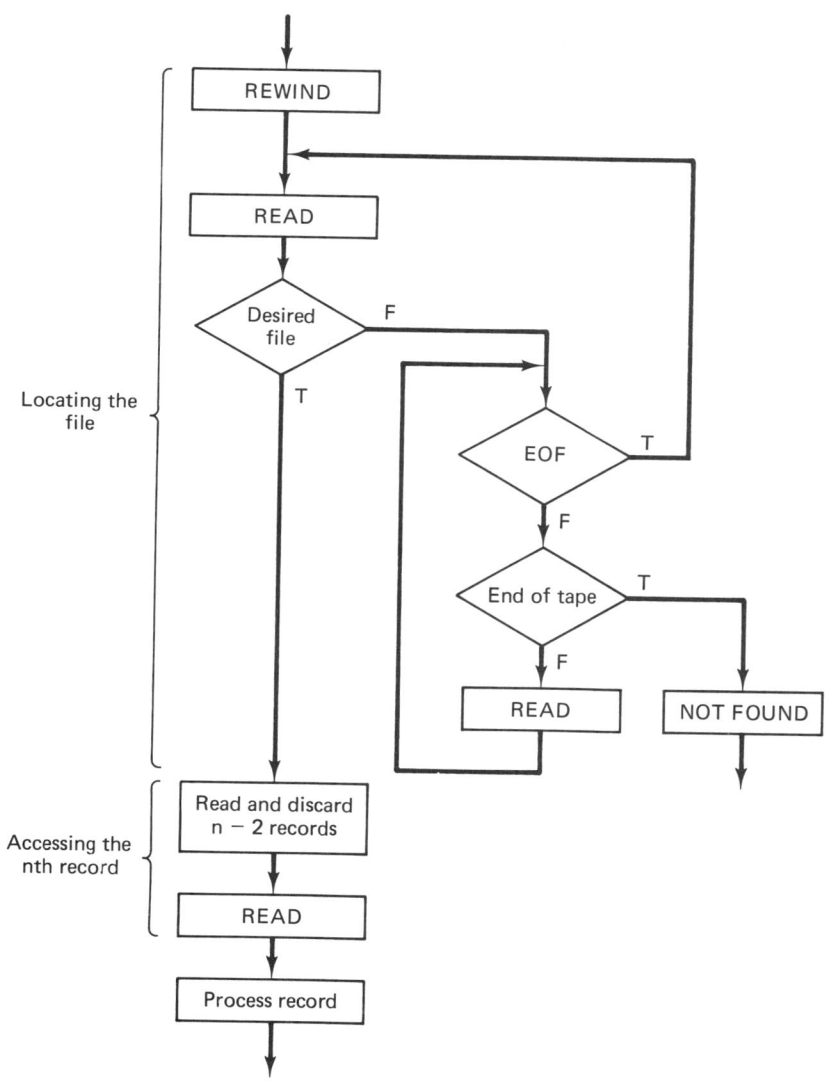

Figure 9-5 Retrieving information from sequentially accessed mass storage.

the OPEN statement is being accessed and assigns the file a logical unit number that the operating system uses when working with the file. The CLOSE statement informs the operating system that the file is no longer being accessed and deassigns the logical unit number. The ENDFILE statement causes an EOF marker to be written on the tape.

A REWIND statement is implemented by outputting bits to the tape unit interface's control registers that would cause the tape unit to rewind. A READ or WRITE is accomplished by setting up and then initiating a block transfer, and a BACKSPACE is most likely done by reading backward one record. The completion routine performed during a READ or WRITE would check the tape unit interface's status registers to determine whether errors occurred during the transfer and set the status parameters given in the READ or WRITE statement accordingly.

Updating a tape that contains a **master file** is done as shown in Fig. 9-6. Changes are assumed to be in a presorted **transaction file**. Records are sequentially read from the master file and then written to the new master file. When a change in a record is indicated by the transaction file, the change is made before the record is output. By presorting the transaction file, an entire update can be done in a single pass, thereby minimizing tape movement.

Sequential access is not suitable for applications that require frequent updating (e.g., an interactive airline reservation system), but can be used when changes are made as a group at specified intervals of time. A business that records its activity in a transaction file during the day and updates its records only at the end of the day could effectively use sequentially accessed files.

Another valuable application of magnetic tapes is to use them for backing up mass storage of all types. To prevent accidental loss of information, the information should be copied periodically and stored in a secure place. Because magnetic tapes are inexpensive, rugged, and easy to store and transport, they are frequently used for backing up other media. Special tape devices, called **streamer tape units**, specifically provide for fast backup operations.

Although standard ½-inch reel to reel tapes are most prevalent, there are many other types of magnetic tapes, and all of them share the same basic weaknesses. They all:

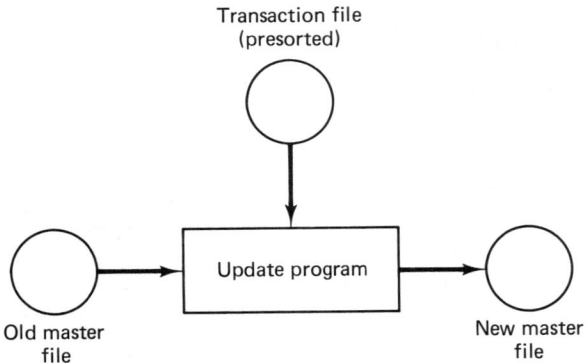

Figure 9-6 Updating a sequential file.

- Have long access times.
- Must use sequential access if they are to avoid excessive average access times.
- Tend to have low transfer rates.

9-1-2 Movable Head Disk and Diskette Units

As with magnetic tape, the medium for a disk or diskette unit is a coated surface capable of maintaining permanent magnetic fields. The magnetic patterns that represent the stored information are recorded and read by means of a read/write head. The medium is a disk or set of disks. From an operational standpoint, movable head disk and diskette units primarily differ from tape units in that they provide for two-dimensional accessing and involve two degrees of movement. As shown in Fig. 9-7(a) an access normally involves the in and out movement of a read/write head, or set of read/write heads mounted on a single assembly, and the rotation of the disk assembly under the head(s).

Information is recorded in concentric circles on the surfaces of a disk or set of disks (or platters) and is physically organized into cylinders, tracks, and sectors. The organization for a single-disk assembly is shown in Fig. 9-7(b). The information in a circle on a single surface is called a **track** and all tracks whose circles have the same diameter constitute a **cylinder**. Each track is subdivided into **sectors** and the sectors are identified by a cylinder number, a track number, and a sector number.

Cylinders are physically located according to their linear distances from the outer cylinder and a track is determined by the surface with which it is associated. All tracks begin at a fixed radial line whose position is determined by a hole, slot, or other marking on the disk assembly that can be detected by the electronics of the disk unit. Sometimes all sectors are similarly marked, in which case the disk assembly is said to be **hard-sectored**. The alternative is to mark the beginnings of the sectors by putting special sets of information at the beginning of each sector. New disks do not have these special records and these records must be written onto them before they can be used. This is called **formatting** the disk and it is done by a special program that writes formatting records onto the disk in a regular pattern. When formatting is used to mark the sectors, the disk is said to be **soft-sectored**.

To begin an access the read/write head must be placed over the proper track and the disk must then rotate until the beginning of the information is under the head. Average head movement times, or **seek** times, vary from 5 mS to 50 mS and rotational speeds range from 360 to 3600 revolutions per minute (rpm). If the average head movement time is 5 mS and the rotational speed is 3600 rpm, then the average access time would be

$$5 + \frac{1}{2} \times \frac{60}{3600} = 13.3 \text{ mS}$$

The factor ½ is due to the assumption that, on average, one half revolution is

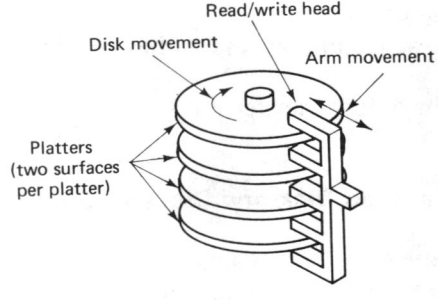

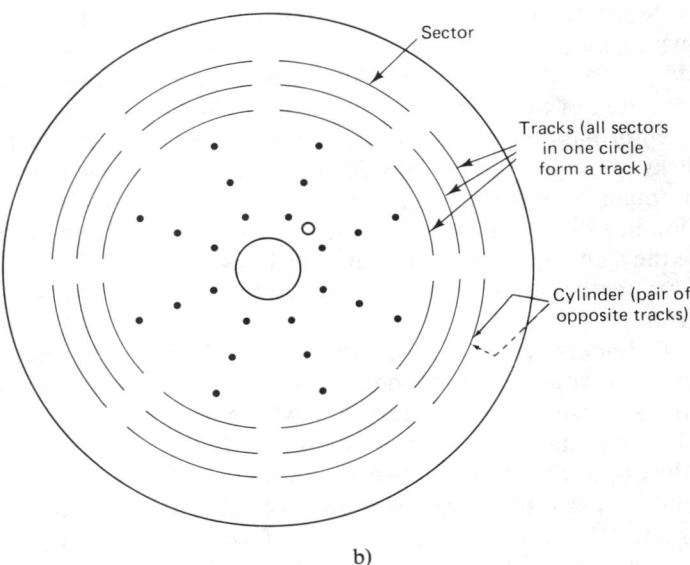

Figure 9-7 Disk unit.

required to bring the beginning of the information under the head. The delay due to the disk's rotation, is called the **latency time**.

Transfer rate is determined by the rotational speed and the number of bits per track, which may vary from 40 thousand bits for diskettes to over 1 million bits for high-speed disk units. If the rotational speed were 3600 rpm and there were 200 thousand bits per track, then the transfer rate would be approximately

$$\frac{3600}{60} \times \frac{200000}{8} = 1.5 \times 10^6 \text{ bytes/S}$$

All sectors contain the same number of bits and are accessed as a whole with each sector being accessed using a block transfer.

The information in a track is stored serially (one bit after the other) and timing information is normally intermixed with data. Timing is needed to synchronize the electronics while information is being retrieved. An alternative to intermixing the data and timing is to use a separate track, such as the outermost track, for storing the timing. For disk assemblies with several disks, one entire surface may be dedicated to timing so that each cylinder would contain its own timing track.

Unlike the magnetic tape arrangement of information, files may consist of records that are not contiguously located. Usually the records are placed in sectors, frequently one record per sector, and the sectors may be scattered around the surfaces of the disks. Figure 9-8 shows how a file of six sectors may be allocated. The advantage to allowing the sectors in a file to be put anywhere on the disk surfaces is that the available space is better utilized. Files are not of the same length and it is easier to add, delete, and modify files if length enters into the sector assignment algorithm only because it determines the total number of sectors required and there is no concern for having contiguous sectors. The disadvantage is that if a file contains m randomly placed sectors, it could take as many as m independent accesses to input or output a file and the total average access time would be mT, where T is the average access time of one randomly positioned sector. For example, if $T = 13.33$ mS and a file consists of eight independently positioned sectors, the average total access time would be $8 \times 13.33 = 106.67$ mS.

A compromise between the flexibility of being able to assign sectors arbitrarily and avoiding excessive head movement is to locate sectors in clusters. Clustered sectors are placed one after the other in the same cylinder so that after the first sector is accessed, the others in the cluster can be read or written without further head movement. The maximum number of sectors that could be in a cluster and still avoid head movement is, of course, the number of sectors in a cylinder. (The tradeoff between arbitrary sector assignment and head movement will be considered further in Chap. 11.)

Because files are not physically organized sequentially as they are on magnetic tape, there must be some method for determining the association between the cylinder/track/sector physical addresses of the sectors in a file and the file's logical records, which are referred to by the software. This association is maintained in **directories** stored on the disk. As shown in Fig. 9-9, each file has a directory entry that contains the correspondence between the logical identification of the file and the physical locations of its records. Exactly how the directory

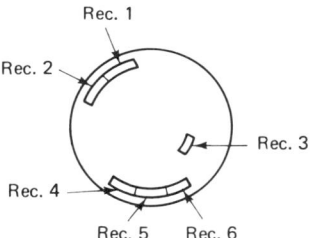

Figure 9-8 Typical allocation of a disk file.

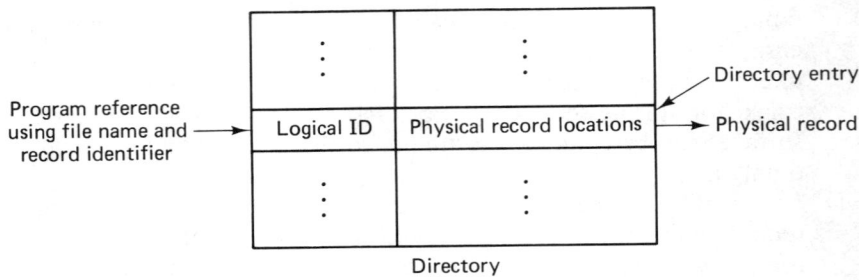

Figure 9-9 Use of a directory to establish a logical/physical association.

entries are organized depends on the system and is discussed further in Chap. 10. What is important here is that the directory's logical/physical associations are available to the operating system and other programs.

There may be several directories on a disk and there must be a key to them that is stored in a fixed location known to the operating system or other programs that need to access them. This key is often a special **root directory** that contains entries that point to physical beginning locations of other directories. Another possibility is to have only one directory in a fixed, known location. The organization of directories as a whole will also be discussed further in Chap. 10.

Although the records in a disk file may be accessed in a sequential manner, the two-dimensional property of a disk unit allows the more flexible direct accessing of records. Typical high-level language statements for working with direct access files are OPEN, CLOSE, READ, and WRITE. As with sequential files, an access is divided into two stages. An OPEN statement makes the logical/physical directory information related to the file readily available to the operating system and assigns a logical unit number to the file. Any record can then be read from or written to by specifying the logical unit and record numbers as parameters in the READ or WRITE statement. Once a record's physical position is found in the file's directory entry, the read/write head is moved *directly* to the appropriate sector. There is no rewinding to the beginning of a file or backspacing and no need for EOF markers. The CLOSE statement deassigns the logical unit number and cancels the file's recognition by the operating system. After a file has been closed it must be reopened by another OPEN statement before it can be used again.

An OPEN statement causes at least part of a file's directory entry to be brought into main memory so that the file's record locations can be quickly identified. Locating a directory entry may, itself, require that several directory records be read. A CLOSE statement does not involve accessing a disk, but simply cancels a file/logical unit number association and makes the memory area where the directory entry was stored available for other use.

In terms of assembler language, a read or write consists of outputting the proper byte count and memory buffer address to the DMA controller and proper control bits to the control registers in both the disk unit's interface and DMA controller. After the read or write, a completion routine does the necessary error and other processing.

There are many different types of disk assemblies. Large capacity disk units use assemblies with several disks and the cylinders include several tracks. Disk units with smaller capacities may contain only one disk and may use only one side of the disk. Disks may be rigid (hard) and made of metal or flexible (soft), as with diskettes, and made of mylar. In either case, the surface is coated with a material that can retain magnetic patterns indefinitely. A disk assembly may be removable or nonremovable. If a system is to be backed up, either a removable disk or magnetic tape unit is needed. For example, many personal computers include a fast, hard disk as their primary mass storage unit and a diskette unit so that the information on the hard disk can be backed up or transported to other systems.

For units that use hard disks, the read/write head is aerodynamically designed to ride on a cushion of air slightly above the surface of the disk. It is lowered near the surface when the power is turned on and retracted when it is turned off. This design allows the disk to revolve at a high speed without wearing the head or disk surface. The maximum bit density that can be achieved on the surface of a disk is closely related to the distance between the head and surface. The smaller the distance, the higher the maximum density. However, if the head is designed to ride too close to the surface, the probability of the surface being damaged by the head is increased. Such contact is most often caused by vibration or dust particles that have accumulated on the surface. Dust can be essentially eliminated by constructing sealed disk units called **Winchester disks.** A single two-surface Winchester disk may be able to store tens of millions of bytes. The disadvantage of Winchester disks is that their construction does not allow them to be removable and therefore, they cannot be transported from one system to another.

For diskettes, the head must be lowered onto the diskette's surface at the beginning of each access. This third degree of mechanical motion adds 8 to 16 mS to the access time of the first record. Hard disks revolve at up to 3600 rpm, but diskettes normally revolve at 360 rpm. Typical average load, positioning, and rotational delays for accessing an arbitrary record are 16, 200, and 80 mS, respectively. The transfer rate, which is approximated by multiplying the bytes per track by the rotational speed in revolutions per second, is

$$5000 \times 360/60 = 30,000 \text{ bytes/S}$$

for a diskette with 5000 bytes per track and a rotational speed of 360 rpm. In addition to increasing the access time by the amount of load time, the fact that the read/write head must be in contact with the diskette's surface causes the surface to wear and the heads to require periodic cleaning.

Diskettes are almost always soft-sectored and require formatting before they are used. The organization of a typical sector, including its formatting information is shown in Fig. 9-10. Format information begins with an index address mark and includes the cylinder, head (or track), and sector numbers. It also includes a two-byte Cyclic Redundancy Code (CRC) for error checking. The format field is fol-

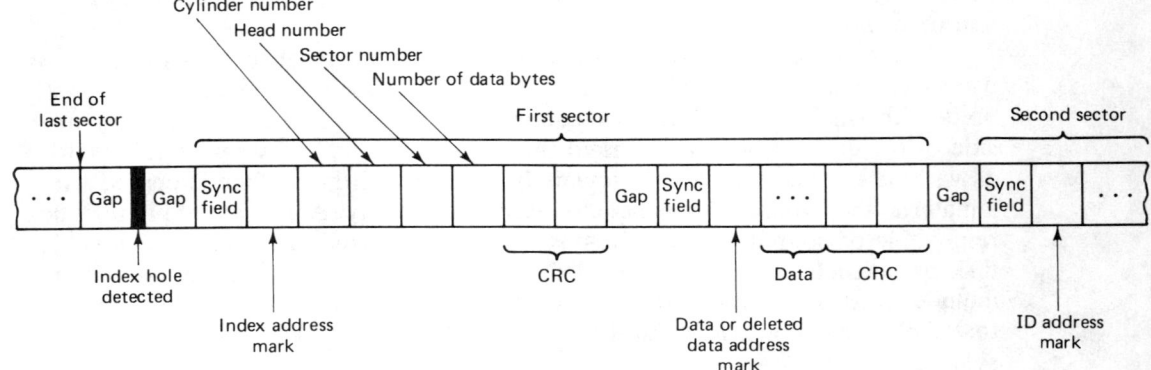

Figure 9-10 Typical sector format for a soft-sectored diskette.

lowed by a data field that may contain data. The data field begins with a data address mark that is set to a special value if no data are contained in the sector. None of the data fields on a newly formatted diskette contain information, but as the sectors are filled, their data address marks are changed to indicate that they are in use. Sync fields are needed by the diskette controller's electronics to synchronize the electronics with the signal from the read/write head before the format and data fields are accessed. Just as record gaps and file marks consume an appreciable amount of space on magnetic tape, format fields, sync fields, and gaps take up much of the space on a diskette.

9-1-3 Fixed Head Disks and Drums

The disk units discussed in the previous section were assumed to have heads that moved in and out over tracks. It is possible to construct disk units that have a separate head for each track. This design avoids one of the degrees of movement and correspondingly reduces access time, but considerably increases cost. Because the high cost must be justified by a lower average access time and higher transfer rate, fixed head disks tend to have high information densities and rotational speeds.

Drum units are similar to fixed head disks in that, as shown in Fig. 9-11, they have multiple heads and there is only one degree of mechanical motion. They differ in the physical shape of their storage surface. A drum has a cylindrical shape and the information is stored on the curved surface, not on the ends. This has the advantage of providing the same linear distance for each track. For a disk, this distance becomes shorter as the center of the disk is approached and the density limitation is determined by the inner track. Some drums are capable of storing billions of bytes. Fixed head disks and drums are not readily removable and are used only when a very fast form of mass storage is required.

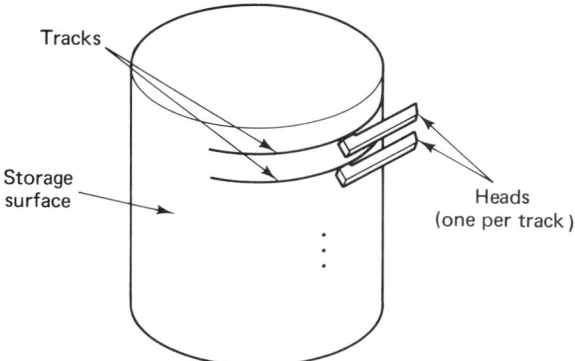

Figure 9-11 Construction of a drum storage unit.

9-1-4 Magnetic Bubble Memory

There are several materials that form a film that includes randomly distributed magnetic domains whose fields are perpendicular to the plane of the film. By applying an external magnetic field in the direction opposite to that of one of these domains, the domain can be reduced to what is called a **magnetic bubble**, or eliminated altogether. By applying a rotating magnetic field, whose direction is in the plane of the film, to the magnetic bubbles, the bubbles can be moved within the film. If a pattern is applied to the magnetic film, the bubbles can be forced to move along paths dictated by the pattern. Currents in a conducting network that is inserted between the film and pattern can be used to control the magnetic field so that individual bubbles can be generated, eliminated (annihilated), increased in size and split (replicated), or transferred from one path to another.

The basic interrelationships of the paths that guide the bubbles and the principal functions that must be performed within a magnetic bubble film are illustrated in Fig. 9-12. A 1 is indicated by the presence of a bubble and a 0 by its absence. Bubble-no bubble (1-0) combinations are continually rotated within minor loops

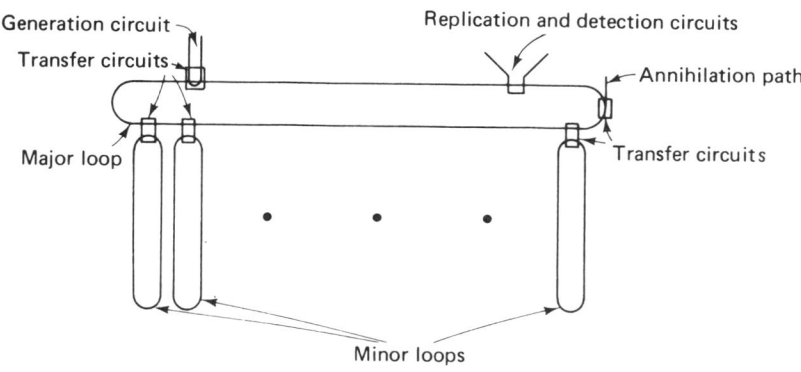

Figure 9-12 Typical path structure of an MBM.

Sec. 9-1   Mass Storage

by the rotating magnetic field. If there are n minor loops, information is stored in or retrieved from the minor loops n bits at a time as the desired information passes under the transfer circuitry (which is part of the conductive network that has been placed between the magnetic film and pattern). During a read operation, once a group of n bits, called a **page**, has been transferred to the major loop, it is circulated within the major loop. If a page is to be passed to external circuitry and then placed back into memory, it is replicated and the copy is directed to a detector while the original continues around the major loop and is transferred back into the minor loops at the same position from which it was taken. If the page is to be replaced by zeros, it is transferred to an annihilation path instead of being returned to the minor loops. A write into memory consists of applying signals to the generation circuitry at the proper time, circulating the generated bits around the major loop, and then transferring them (in parallel) into the minor loops.

The primary problem with magnetic bubble devices is the difficulty in fabricating a flawless film. To obtain reasonable manufacturing yields, more minor loops than are actually used are put onto an IC and defects in some of the minor loops are permitted. However, the positions of the bad loops must be known so they can be accounted for when writing into or reading from the memory. The bits being input must be interspersed with meaningless bits that are to be transferred into the defective minor loops. The bits in a page being read are not all useful and the positions of the bad bits must be known so that they can be eliminated from the output. This capability significantly complicates the external circuitry that must permanently store the pattern of the good and bad loops and control the insertion and deletion of the meaningless bits.

Theoretically MBMs with very large capacities could be produced, but practical considerations primarily due to flaws in the film limit the capacity of commercially available MBMs to less than 10 million bits. The advantages of MBMs are due to the lack of mechanical movement. This improves their reliability and reduces their access times, but their transfer rates are not particularly high. The transfer rate in bps is the same as the rotational frequency of the magnetic field that is parallel to the surface and this frequency is typically 100 to 200 kHz. The lack of mechanical motion makes MBMs relatively insensitive to vibration, which particularly restricts the use of hard disks. MBMs are also insensitive to other environmental conditions, but must be well shielded against electromagnetic noise. They are often used in mobile and airborne applications.

9-2 MAIN MEMORY

Access time is much more critical for main memory than mass storage because, in most computers, the memory hierarchy is such that processing elements must communicate directly with main memory. Therefore, the speed of a computer is heavily dependent upon the time it takes to input and output the instructions and data from and to main memory. Because speed is so important, main memory is constructed of semiconductor ICs. The capacities of these ICs range from 256 bits to 1 megabit.

Logically main memory consists of bit groupings, usually groups of 8-bit bytes, and each group is identified by a unique address in the memory address space. Physically, each group is considered a location whose bits are accessed in parallel, and the locations may be organized in several different ways. The most common way is to divide the memory into modules with the locations in each module being assigned consecutive addresses. If the number of locations in a module is a power of 2, then the high-order bits of an address could be used to select a module and the low-order-bits to select a location within the module. For example, if an address space is 0 to 2^{n-1} and there are 2^m locations in each module, then the high-order $n - m$ bits would select one of up to 2^{n-m} modules and the low-order m bits would specify the location. This example is illustrated in Fig. 9-13(a). Other ways of physically organizing memory modules will be discussed in Sec. 9-2-5.

Figure 9-13(b) shows the layout of a memory module. It basically consists of the interface to the system bus and an array of ICs that contain the circuitry for the memory locations. A module's interface must decode the high order address bits to determine whether it is the module being accessed and must transform the low order address bits into the Address and IC Enable signals needed to select a particular location from within the IC array. In addition, the interface must include the handshaking logic required for conducting bus transfers and any bus drivers and receivers that are needed. Although the organization of the IC array depends on the design of the ICs, normally these ICs would have separate pins for inputting and outputting. Therefore, the interface must provide the conversion between the system's bidirectional data bus and the two unidirectional sets of Data-in and Data-out lines that are connected to the ICs (although some memory ICs use bidirectional data lines). The system bus's memory read and write handshaking signals are used to set the IC array Read/Write signal.

The main memories in modern computers are designed so that all locations can be accessed in approximately the same amount of time and are, therefore, random access memories. The access time may not always be exactly the same because, as will be seen later, it may depend on how addresses involved in consecutive accesses are related (i.e., the differences between the addresses).

A diagram showing the major components of a memory IC is given in Fig. 9-14. These components are the:

Cell array which consists of rows and columns of groups of cells, called **memory words**, with each **cell** being the circuitry needed for storing one bit.

Row select logic, which selects the row of the memory word being accessed.

Column select and I/O control logic, which selects the column of the memory word being accessed and provides the circuitry for reading from and writing to the memory.

The connections to an IC consist of address lines, data-in lines, data-out lines, a Read/Write line, and an IC Enable line. The number of memory words

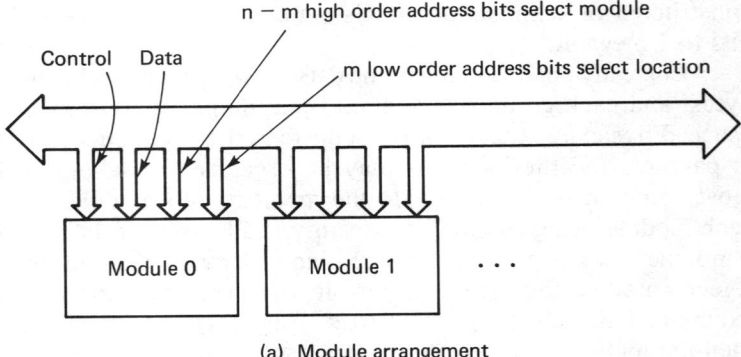

Figure 9-13 Typical main memory organization.

in the IC is 2^n, where n is the total number of address lines. Some of the address lines determine the row and the remaining lines determine the column. If the address lines connected to the row selection logic are A_{11} - A_5 and those connected to the column selection logic are $A_4 - A_0$, then there would be $2^7 = 128$ rows and $2^5 = 32$ columns of memory words, giving a total of 4096 words. If each memory word contains four cells, the cell array would provide storage for 16,384

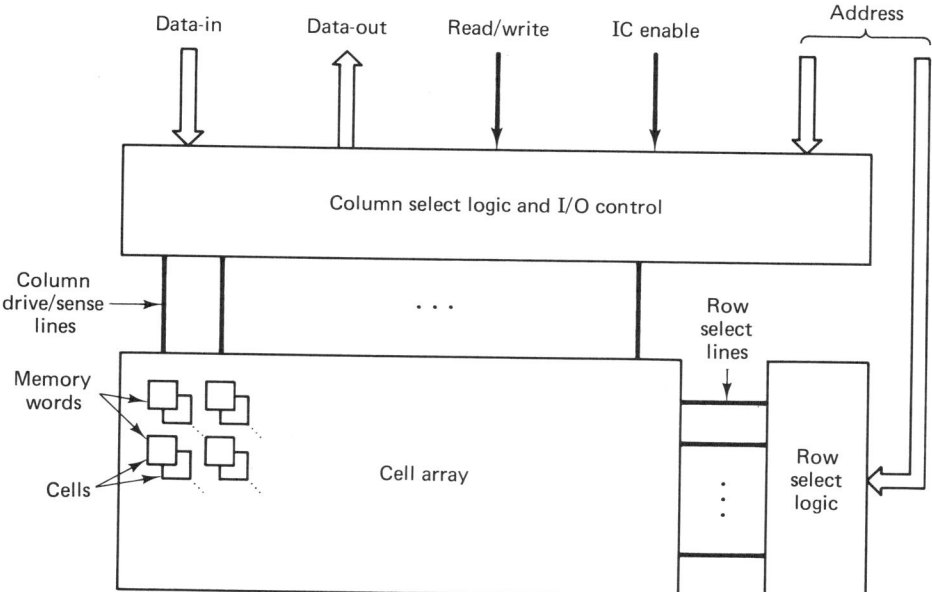

Figure 9-14 Major components of a memory IC.

bits. The number of data-in lines and data-out lines both equal the number of cells in a memory word and the bits in a word are accessed in parallel. The Read/Write line determines whether a selected word is being read from or written into and the IC Enable line indicates whether an IC is involved in the access.

The Row Select logic is simply a decoder that decodes the set of Row Address signals and activates exactly one Row Select line. The Column Select and I/O logic is much more complicated because it not only selects a column, but also performs a read or write. The lines between this logic and the cell array are used to sense the contents of a selected memory word or transmit data to a selected memory word. The number of these lines per column depends on the cell design and is one or two times the number of cells in a memory word. Figure 9-15 details the connections to a memory word. The Row Select line enables all of the cells in all of the words in a row, and the Column Drive/Sense lines (or pairs of lines) read from or write to all of the cells in the word in the selected column and the enabled row.

The width of a memory word may not be the same as the width of a memory location, which is the number of bits associated with a main memory address and is normally eight bits. A memory word width may be any integer that evenly divides the location width and may be one. If an IC contains 4K words of four bits each, it is said to be a **4K × 4 IC**. Such ICs could be used to form the IC array for a 16K byte memory module as shown in Fig. 9-16.

As an example, assume the module organization shown in Fig. 9-13 and that a 64K byte memory is to be constructed from four 16K modules, each of which

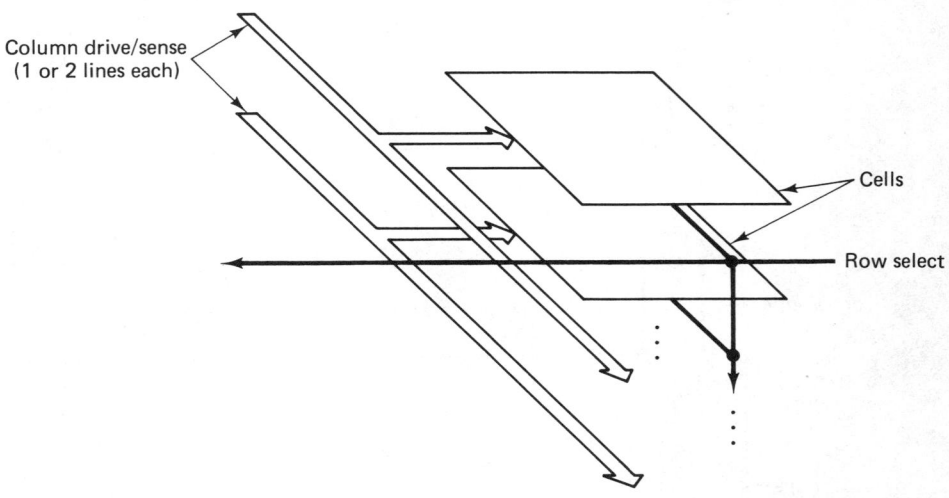

Figure 9-15 Memory word detail.

is constructed from 4K × 4 ICs as shown in Fig. 9-16. Then, 16-bit addresses would be required with bits 15 and 14 designating the module. Bits 13 and 12 are decoded to activate one of the IC Enable lines. The IC Enable line enables one row of ICs and thereby determines the 4K block of 8-bit locations to be accessed. The low-order address bits $A_{11} - A_0$ are connected to all of the ICs and make the memory word row/column selection. Also, the Read/Write signal is connected to all of the ICs. Referring to Fig. 9-16, each IC in the pair of enabled ICs contributes four bits to the 8-bit location being accessed.

A serious concern of a memory designer is power consumption. Of the electronic components in a computer system, it is the main memory that is likely to consume the most power and produce the most heat. Power consumption for semiconductor memory may be specified as a per IC or per bit (per cell) quantity. A 32K bit IC that consumes .05 mW per bit would consume a total of 1.6 W. A 1M byte memory constructed of these ICs would include

$$\frac{8 \times 2^{20}}{32 \times 2^{10}} = 256 \text{ ICs}$$

and dissipate 1.6 × 256 = 410 W of heat.

The circuitry needed in a memory interface depends on the type of ICs used. The principal memory IC types are summarized in Fig. 9-17. The primary types are read/write memory (RAM) and read only memory (ROM). (Originally, RAM was used to refer to random access memory, but later was used to distinguish between read/write memory and read only memory, even though read only memory may also be random access.) There are two types of RAM ICs and both are volatile. There are four types of ROM and they are nonvolatile.

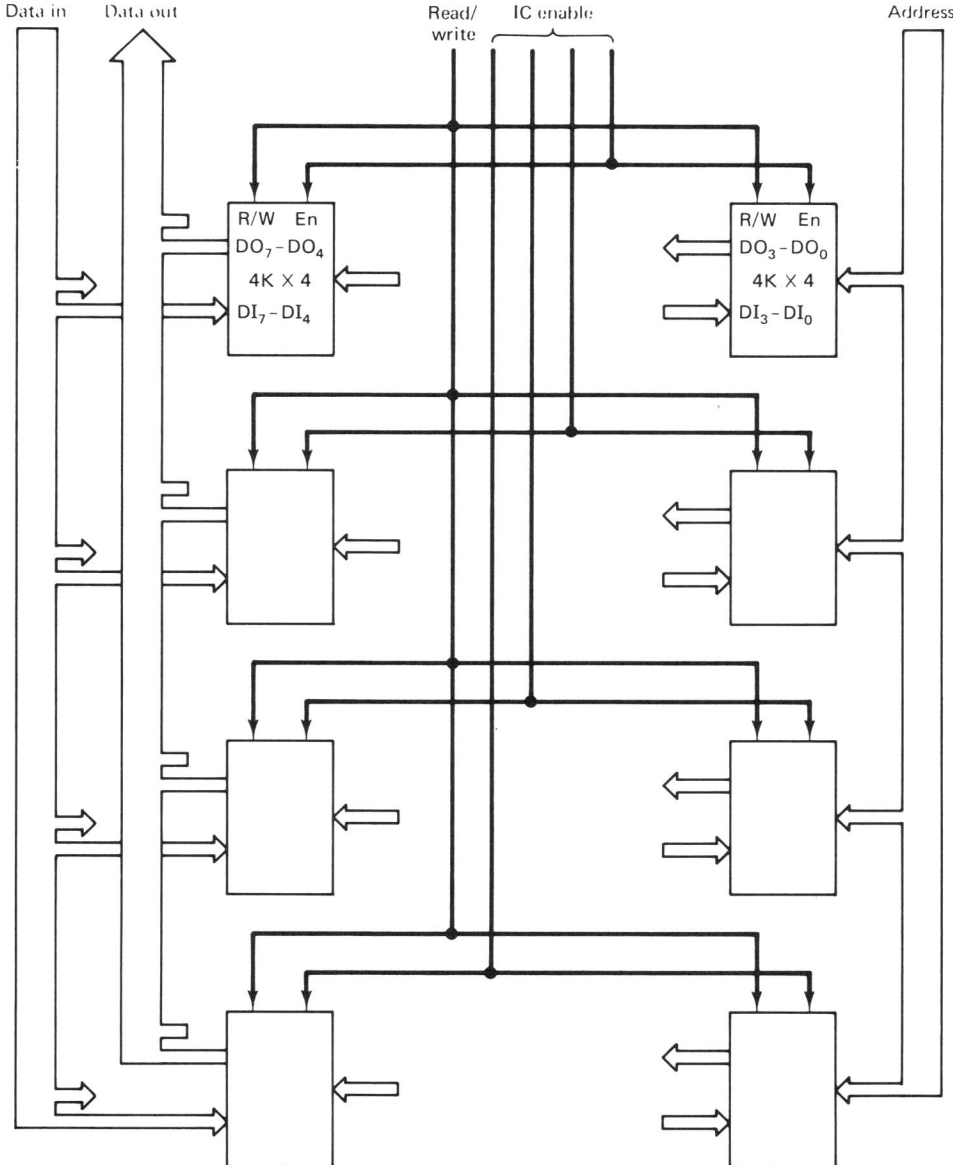

Figure 9-16 Representative IC array construction.

Sec. 9-2 Main Memory

Read/Write (RAM) - volatile

   Static RAM (SRAM)
   Dynamic RAM (DRAM)

Read Only Memory (ROM) - nonvolatile

   Masked ROM
   Programmable ROM (PROM)
   Erasable Programmable ROM (EPROM)
   Electrically Alterable Programmable ROM (EAPROM)

Figure 9-17 Types of memory ICs.

9-2-1 Static RAM

The connections to a static RAM cell are shown in Fig. 9-18. They consist of a Drive/Sense 0 line, a Drive/Sense 1 line, and a Select line. The cell is a bistable electronic circuit typically consisting of several interconnected electronic components. One of the states is assumed to represent a 0 and the other a 1. When the Select line, which is a Row Select line, is active, the cell can be accessed, i.e., the cell is enabled. When the cell is enabled its contents can be read by sensing the signals on the pair of Drive/Sense lines. If Drive/Sense 0 indicates a 1 and Drive/Sense 1 indicates a 0, then the cell is in its 0 state. On the other hand, if Drive/Sense 0 indicates 0 and Drive/Sense 1 indicates 1, then the cell is in its 1 state. An enabled cell is written into by applying signals to the Drive/Sense lines. A 0 is written into the cell if a pulse is applied to Drive/Sense 0 and a 1 is written if a pulse is applied to Drive/Sense 1.

    The IC's Column Select and I/O logic determine which Drive/Sense pair is to execute the read or write. The IC's address lines used to select the column determine which Drive/Sense pairs are used (one pair per cell in the memory word being accessed) and the remaining address lines select the row. The Read/Write

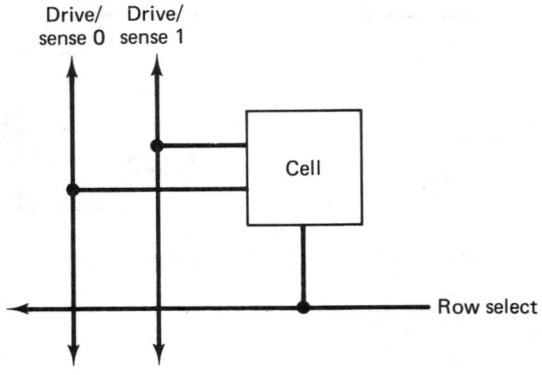

Figure 9-18 Static RAM cell connections.

line connected to the IC determines whether a read or write is to be conducted. A 0 or 1 value being read is transferred to the IC's Data-out line that corresponds to the cell, and a 0 or 1 value being written is taken from the Data-in line corresponding to the cell and causes the appropriate Drive/Sense line to be pulsed.

9-2-2 Dynamic RAM

The connections to a dynamic RAM cell are shown in Fig. 9-19. Each cell is connected to a Select line and a single Drive/Sense line, and consists of a transistor and a capacitor capable of storing a small amount of charge. The two states associated with a cell are determined by whether the capacitor is not charged (0) or charged (1). The transistor acts as a gate to the capacitor, which is opened or closed according to the signal on the Select line. To read the contents of a cell the gate is opened and, if the cell contains a 1, the charge drain from the capacitor is detected by the read circuitry connected to the Drive/Sense line. However, to avoid having a read operation change the state of a cell, if the charge is drained, it must be immediately replaced using a write operation. A write is a matter of opening the gate and using the Drive/Sense line to drain the capacitor if the cell is to contain a 0 or charge the capacitor if the cell is to contain a 1.

Because of the simplicity of its cell circuitry, cells in a dynamic RAM can be packed more densely than those in a static RAM. Thus, dynamic RAM ICs tend to have greater bit capacities than static RAM ICs, and fewer memory ICs are needed to make a memory with a given capacity. However, static RAM ICs, can be designed to have shorter access times than dynamic RAM ICs. Also, the use of a capacitor as a cell's storage medium introduces a problem. A capacitor loses its charge due to leakage current, which means that the contents of a dynamic RAM cell must be refreshed periodically. A refresh consists of reading the cell and immediately restoring its contents with a write. Any read will cause a cell to be refreshed, but it cannot be arbitrarily assumed that, during normal usage, every cell will be read often enough to prevent a loss of information.

There are two approaches to refreshing a dynamic RAM memory module. One is to build into each IC's Column Select and I/O logic the circuitry needed to guarantee an adequate refresh cycle. The other is to not put the refresh circuitry

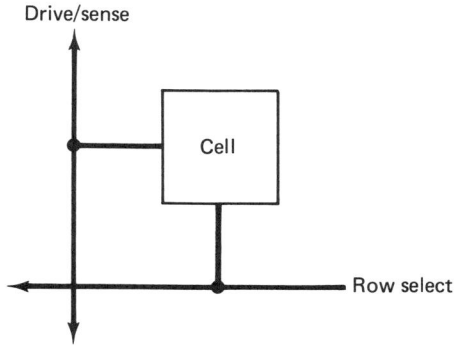

Figure 9-19 Dynamic RAM cell connections.

in the individual ICs, but put a set of common refresh circuitry in the module's interface that services all of the elements in the IC array. The advantage of having the refresh capability built into each IC is that the module level designer would not need to be concerned with it. The disadvantage is that the required circuitry would occupy space on each IC. If an IC must be externally refreshed, it would need a Refresh pin that, when activated, would block access to the IC during the refresh and initiate an internal read/write refresh cycle.

Refresh circuitry for servicing an entire IC array could be inserted in an interface as shown in Fig. 9-20. This figure assumes that the memory is to contain 16K bytes and the IC array consists of 4K × 4 ICs with each IC having 128 rows and 32 columns of cells. The refresh clock would output pulses at a rate that is sufficient to insure that no information is lost. The output of the refresh clock is applied to the Refresh pins of all of the memory ICs and is used to block the IC Enable signals. In addition, it causes a refresh counter to be incremented and the

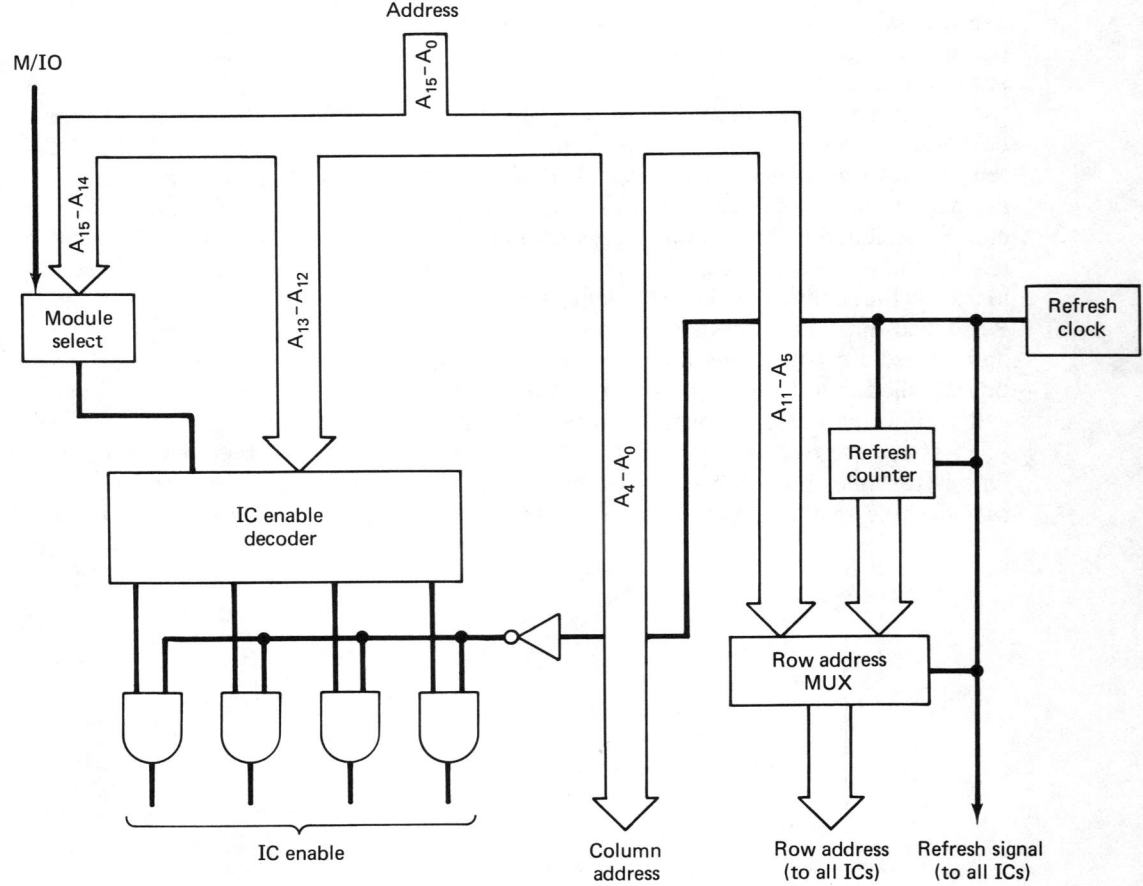

Figure 9-20 Dynamic RAM module interface Address and Refresh logic.

row address multiplexer to select the output of this counter as the row address to be used during the refresh cycle. Because the Refresh signal and the Row Address signals are connected to all elements in the IC array, a single refresh causes an entire row in all of the ICs to be refreshed simultaneously. If the cells must be refreshed every 2 mS, then the frequency of the refresh clock would have to be at least

$$\frac{128}{2 \times 10^{-3}} = 64,000 \text{ Hz}$$

Whether refreshes are done inside each IC or are executed on all ICs at the same time, the time for performing them represents a loss of available time for performing normal memory accesses. If a Read or Write request arrives at an IC, or the module, during a refresh then it must wait until the refresh is complete. If there are 128 rows, the time needed to perform a refresh is 400 nS, and a complete refresh must be done every 2 mS, then the percent of time that is not available for normal accesses is

$$\frac{128 \times 400 \times 10^{-9}}{2 \times 10^{-3}} \times 100\% = 2.56\%$$

Per bit power consumption for dynamic RAM is a small fraction of that required for static RAM. Therefore, it is possible to put more bits into an IC and allows dynamic RAM to be used in applications that require low power. Power consumption is typically 0.02 mW per bit for dynamic RAM and 0.1 mW per bit for static RAM; however, power consumption is very dependent on the technology used. Heat dissipation alone could limit the capacity of a static RAM. At 0.1 mW per bit, a 16K-bit IC would give off 1.6 W of heat. A 64K-bit dynamic RAM that dissipates 0.02 mW per bit would give off 1.28 W, which is less than the power consumed by a static RAM with one-fourth the capacity. In addition, when dynamic RAM is not being used but must retain its contents, it can be put in a standby state in which it consumes a much smaller amount of power. This capability is valuable when memory is used on board a spacecraft or must be supplied from a backup power source during a power failure.

9-2-3 Read Only Memory

The most obvious property of ROM memory is that it cannot be written into and therefore, its contents cannot be accidentally changed. But the most common reason for using ROM is its nonvolatility. To start up a computer of any type, regardless of its application, it must be able to store at least some instructions even when its power is off. It may also need to maintain critical data while the power is off. Although almost all forms of mass storage are nonvolatile, all modern computers draw their instructions from main memory and therefore, at least some nonvolatile main memory is needed.

The connections to a ROM cell are shown in Fig. 9-21. Because a cell cannot be written into, only a Sense line is required. The circuitry internal to a cell is extremely simple and may be a single diode or transistor. The binary state of the

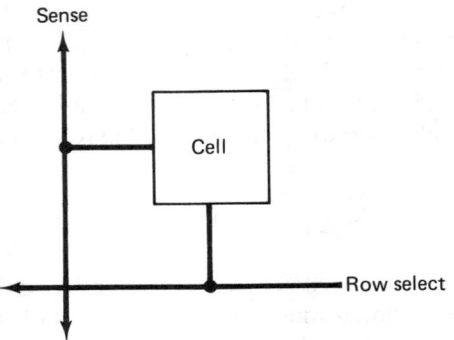

Figure 9-21 Connections to a ROM.

cell is defined by whether a signal on the Select line can be detected on the Sense line. As with RAM, a row is chosen by activating a Row Select line and the signal on this line is applied to all of the cells in the memory words in the row. The column and input logic determines which sense circuits are activated and, for a cell in the memory word at the intersection of the selected row and column, the signal on the Row Select line is either detected or not detected on the Sense lines according to the contents of the cells in the memory word.

As previously indicated in Fig. 9-17 there are four types of ROM. The contents of the cells in a masked ROM are permanently set during the ROM's manufacture. In contrast, a Programmable ROM (PROM) is manufactured so that the Sense line for a cell can always detect a signal on its Select line. The contents of the cells can then be set later using a special device called a **PROM programmer**. By applying voltage pulses to certain pins on the PROM IC, the PROM programmer can burn out connections in specified cells so that Select signals can no longer be felt on the Sense lines. Once a cell connection has been burned out it cannot be repaired, i.e., a connection can be made a disconnection but the reverse is not possible. For both masked ROMs and PROMs the cell circuitry may consist of a single diode that allows current to flow from the Select line to the Sense line. A cell is burned out by sending a current through it that is sufficient to destroy the diode.

The contents of a cell in an Erasable Programmable ROM (EPROM) are set, or **programmed**, by semipermanently putting or not putting a charge in the cell. This feature makes an EPROM cell similar to a dynamic RAM cell, but the cell charges in an EPROM are essentially immobile unless they are properly excited by a particular type of energy source. As with a PROM, a PROM programmer is used to set the contents of an EPROM. Unlike a PROM, an EPROM can be returned to its original state by redistributing the charge. This redistribution is usually done by shining an ultraviolet light directly on the surface of the IC. Therefore, an EPROM IC is covered with a thin slice of transparent quartz instead of being completely encased in ceramic material. A device that cancels the contents of an EPROM is called an **EPROM eraser**. Once the contents of an EPROM have been erased, a PROM programmer can put new contents into the EPROM (i.e., **reprogram** the EPROM).

Some EPROMs can be both programmed and erased electrically. They are called **Electrically Alterable PROMs** (EAPROMs) and are such that with the proper interfacing, they can be directly reprogrammed by a computer.

EPROMs are more expensive than masked ROMs and PROMs and are used primarily during the developmental stage of a design. After a system has been developed, EPROMs are replaced with ROMs with permanent contents. Because masked ROMs are customized, there is a high initial cost associated with them, but once in production, their cost per unit is very low. They are used when a system is to be mass produced.

Because of the simple construction of ROM cells, they can be packed very densely onto an IC surface. This simplicity also contributes to their speed, low power consumption, and low cost. A ROM cell has very little capacitance associated with it and this reduces the movement of charge which both slows the reaction of a cell and increases its power consumption. Not only are the cells inexpensive, but the lack of drive circuitry required for writing and the fact that so many cells can be put on a single IC make the per bit cost of a ROM IC much less than that of a RAM IC. Because ROM cells occupy such a small area, it is feasible to include relatively large ROMs on ICs that contain other logic. Their small size makes it possible to include a control ROM in a microprogrammed processing element design in the same IC as the processing, register, sequencing, and bus control logic.

Not being able to write to a ROM limits its application to storing static code and data. Because there is a limited amount of such code and data needed in a computer, ROM modules tend to have smaller capacities than RAM modules. This feature, coupled with the fact that each IC can contain so many bits, means that most ROM modules can be constructed with only a few ICs (often only one). The interface logic is correspondingly less complicated and, if data drivers are not required, could consist of just a few gates.

A ROM module comprised of two 128K $\times$ 8 ROM ICs is shown in Fig. 9-22. This example assumes a 20-line address bus with A_{19} and A_{18} being used to select the module and A_{17} being used to select which IC is to provide the output. The system bus is assumed to include a Memory Read line that, when active, always enables the ROM ICs. Data are not output from an IC unless they have been selected by $A_{19} - A_{17}$.

9-2-4 Memory IC Timing

The timing of the signals applied to a memory IC is shown in Fig. 9-23. For a read, the address setup time must be long enough to account for skew and allow the address to stabilize at the IC's address pins. Then, when the IC Enable signal arrives, the Row Select logic and Column Select and I/O logic cause a signal to be applied to the appropriate Row Select line, the data on the selected Drive/Sense line(s) to be sensed, and the data to be output through the IC's Data-out pins. The time for accomplishing this is the IC select to output delay. The IC Select signal must be maintained until the IC's Data-out lines have become stable and latched by the interface logic. The read recovery time is the length of time

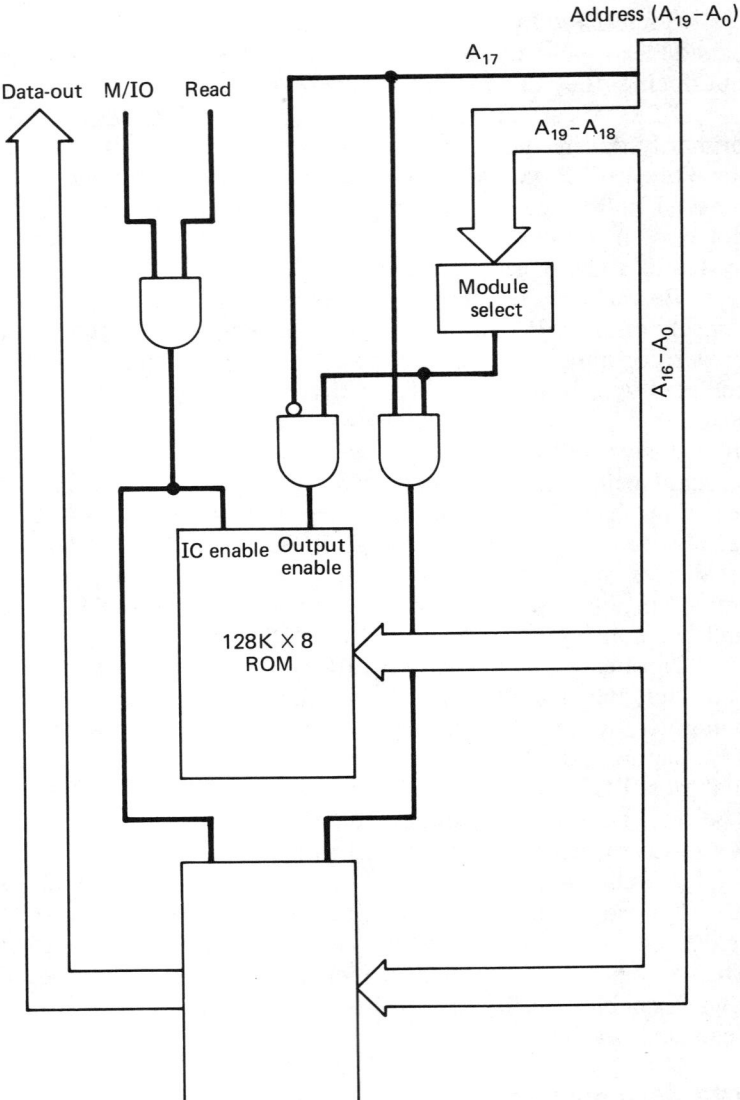

Figure 9-22 ROM module design.

the data-out may be present after the IC Select has been dropped. The total time required to complete a read is the IC's read access time. For dynamic RAM, the read access time must allow for the contents of the memory word to be restored.

For a write, both the address and data must be given time to set up before the write pulse is applied to the Read/Write line. The write pulse width must be such that the row and column can be selected and the data being written have

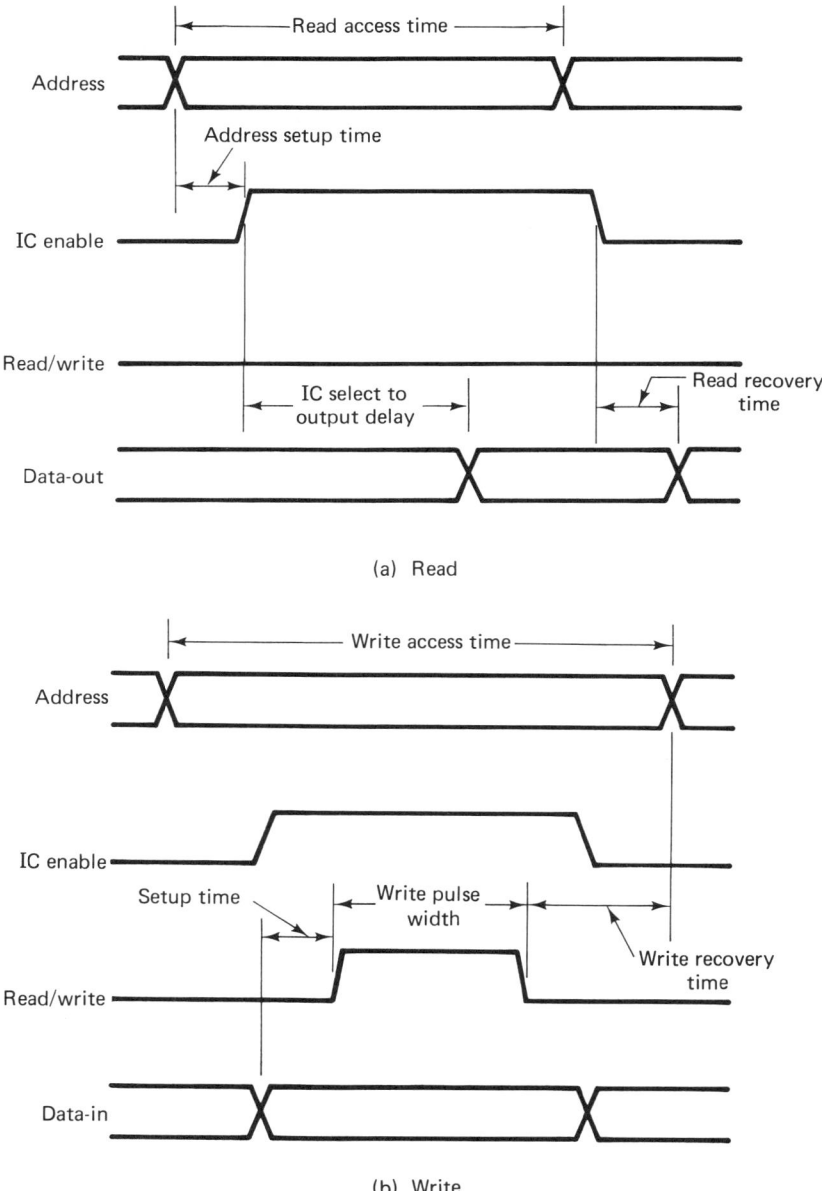

Figure 9-23 Memory IC read/write timing.

time to reach and be deposited in the memory word. As with a read, a recovery time is required after the write to allow the IC's internal logic to stabilize.

For both a read and write, the access time is dependent on the time it takes for the Row Select signal to propagate down the row of memory words and the contents of the selected word to propagate along the Drive/Sense lines. Because each cell has some capacitance associated with it, these delays are dependent on the numbers of cells in a row and in a column. As a result, the speed of a memory IC tends to have an inverse relationship to its capacity. These delays are small for ROM ICs and are the most significant for dynamic RAM. Also, each cell in a dynamic RAM contributes some noise on the Sense line, thus limiting the number of cells in a column.

9-2-5 Memory Module Interfacing

The above sections have concentrated on modules whose addresses are consecutive and whose locations are one byte wide. An interface for such a RAM module is shown in Fig. 9-24. The memory controller is assumed to contain

- Address receivers.
- Refresh logic, if dynamic RAM is used.
- A decoder for generating IC Enable signals.
- Logic for generating the Read/Write signal to the memory ICs and the Ready signal to the Bus Control logic.
- Logic to output the Enable, Strobe, and I/O Control signals to the Data-out register and data drivers and receivers.

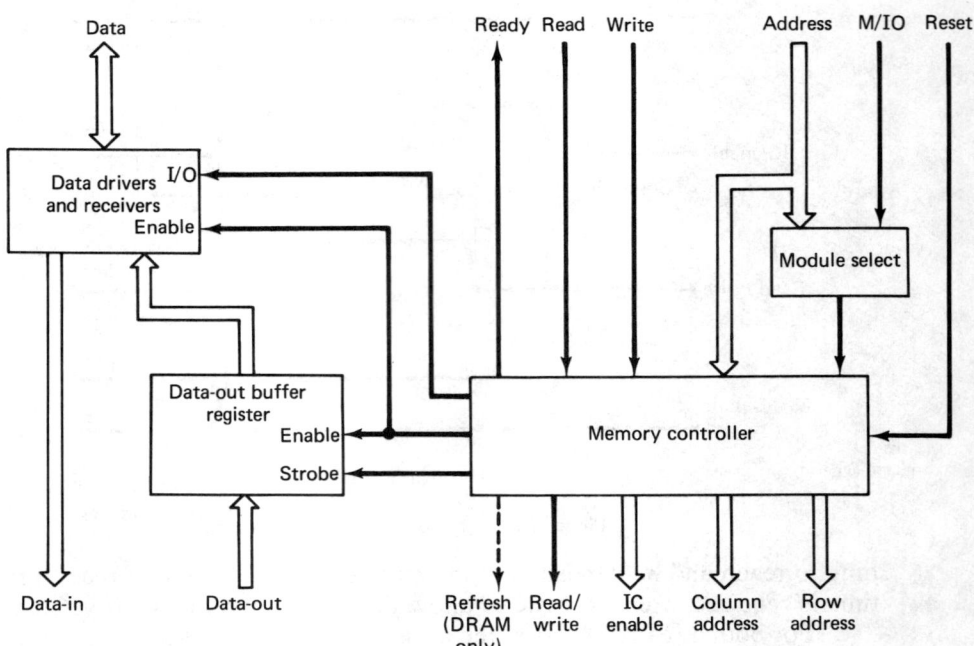

Figure 9-24 Memory module interface.

Module access time may be significantly more than the IC access time, but the time between the application of a Row Select signal and the detection of the cells' contents or the storing of data in the cells is still the primary contributor to the total access time. In addition to the IC access time, there is the latch time of the data-out buffer and the propagation delays through the module select, memory controller, and data drivers and receivers. Memory access times range from a few nanoseconds to 500 nanoseconds with the cost per bit being inversely related to access time. The capacity per IC is, in general, directly related to access time. Very fast memories are fabricated using materials such as galium arsenide for which the costs are high and the production yields are low. Also, the capacities obtained using the very fast technologies are low, usually less than 8K bits. Most memory modules have access times in the range of 50 nS to 500 nS, with memory modules for personal computers being in the 80 nS to 400 nS range. Higher access times permit larger capacity ICs so that large memories can be made from a few ICs, thus reducing assembly costs and conserving PC board space.

As discussed earlier, the rate at which information can be taken from or put into memory is n/T bps, where n is the number of bits involved in each access and T is the average access time. The only choices for increasing this rate are to increase n or decrease T. Decreasing T is, within limits, a straightforward tradeoff between cost, and perhaps power consumption, and speed, but when increasing n, the factors involved are not so clearly defined. The element that is using the stored information has a bearing on the amount of information involved in each access. The amount of information needed by a processing element could be constant for all accesses, but is more likely to be variable. A processing element may need only one bit or several bytes. Most processing elements compromise by having an 8-bit byte as their basic unit of information, although they sometimes operate on single bits and frequently operate on 2- to 4-byte integers or 4- to 8-byte floating point numbers.

It is always possible to make n large and access more information than necessary, but the true access rate would then be xn/T, where x is the average fraction of the n bits that are actually used. The value of xn would be

$$xn = P_1 \cdot 1 + P_2 \cdot 2 + \ldots + P_n \cdot n$$

where P_i is the probability that the number of useful bits is $i = 1, \ldots, n$. If P_n is almost 1, then $xn \approx n$ and the accessing process is efficient. Although a processing element may need less than a byte, the probability of this case is low and little is lost by accessing bytes in parallel. On the other hand, because character data is one byte wide and there may be 1-byte instructions, accessing more than one byte at a time may be such that xn is considerably less than n. The cost of increasing n is the cost of having more lines in the data bus and of adding extra drivers, receivers, latches, and other circuitry associated with a bus.

The above discussion is pessimistic because it assumes that if all n bits are not used immediately they will not be used at all. This is frequently not the case. In fact, when instructions are being fetched they are taken from memory in sequence, unless a branch is taken. Therefore, if the n bits included in the present fetch are from consecutive locations and only some of them are used, probably some of the remaining bits will be needed by the next fetch. In this case, the succeeding access may not need to access the memory IC array but may need to access only the data buffer register, which could be accomplished much more quickly. If t_M is the time required for a full memory access and t_B the time required to access the buffer, then the average access time would be

$$T = P_M t_M + (1 - P_M) t_B$$

where P_M is the probability of accessing the memory IC array. Sequential access of data may also occur (e.g., when operating on elements in an array). In either case, T is reduced by making n large and thereby reducing P_M. In the extreme, T would approach t_B.

As accesses become less sequential, T becomes increasingly greater than t_B. This relationship introduces the important concept of **locality of reference**. The closer the addresses of the information involved in a set of consecutive accesses, the more **local** it is said to be. Even though data are not sequentially accessed, if they are highly local, then having a large value of n may be advantageous.

When n is a multiple of the basic unit of the accessing element, accesses can be made from a set of separate modules as shown in Fig. 9-25. If a single access involves more than one module, high-order bits are used to indicate the location and low-order bits specify the module. During a read operation, the locations indicated by the high-order address bits are simultaneously accessed in all modules and the data from the module selected by the low order bits are put on the data bus. When consecutive reads tend to be made to the same addresses within different modules, the probability P_M becomes small and, for a large number of modules, the average read time would approach t_B. The use of the low-order address bits to select a module causes locations with consecutive addresses to be in different modules and the modules are said to be **interleaved**.

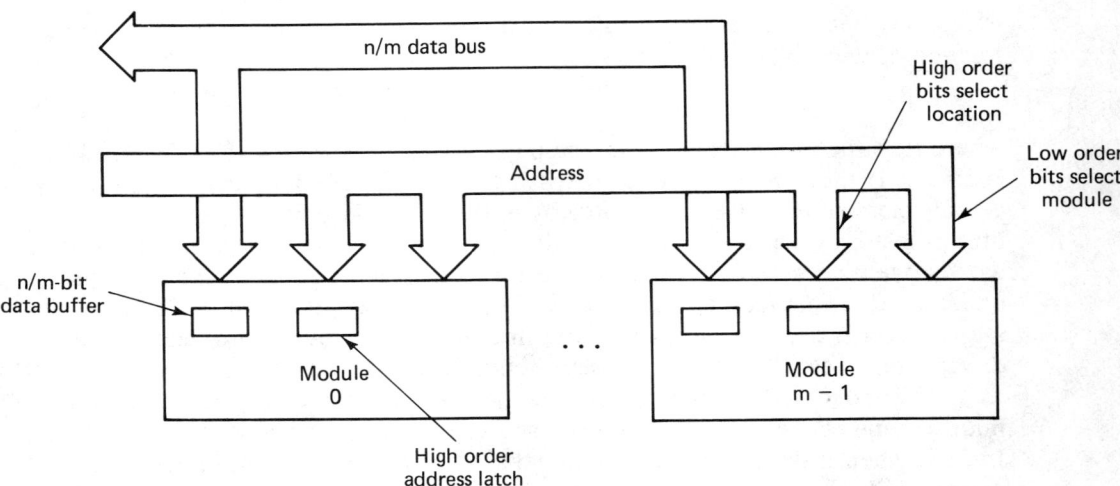

Figure 9-25 Interleaved memory configuration.

As will be discussed in Chap. 12, interleaving also permits the overlapping of accesses to consecutive elements in linear arrays. Because successive elements are in different modules, a succeeding access can begin before the previous access is complete.

Unfortunately, consecutive write operations cannot be done as efficiently as read operations. This is because memory is not changed by a read and transfers from memory to the data buffer registers can be made simultaneously in all modules, even though not all of the data are needed. For a write, the transfer to memory can be made in only the module for which the memory is to be changed. This is mostly offset however, by the fact that there are many more reads than writes (only 10 to 30 percent of memory accesses are writes - Mano [8]). Instructions are only fetched and, on the average, there are more source operands than results (e.g., a single register within a processing element would allow a whole column of numbers to be added before storing the single result).

9-3 MULTIPLE-PORT MEMORY

Some memories, called **multiple-port memories**, must be constructed so that they can be accessed from more than one bus. For example, as shown in Fig. 9-26, a bus separate from the system bus may be used to communicate between main

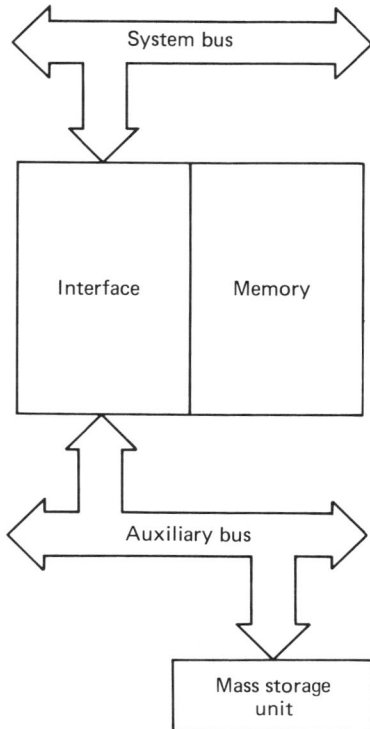

Figure 9-26 Module connected to two buses.

memory and a mass storage unit, thus allowing block transfers to be made without interfering with the activity on the system bus. As in this example, multiple-port memories allow communications to be divided among more than one bus and are primarily used to prevent a single bus from becoming a bottleneck. However, there is the danger of the memory then becoming the bottleneck. Another important application of multiple-port memories is to use them to pass information between subsystems in a multiprocessor system. This application will be considered further in Chap. 12.

The interface for a multiple-port memory must be capable of monitoring the Module Select bits of all buses connected to it and resolving any contention that may occur. The exact point at which there is contention depends on the design. Figure 9-27 shows a two-port design that assumes both buses are bidirectional. There are two sets of Module Select logic (one for each bus) and their outputs are to a set of Arbitration logic whose purpose is to prevent both buses from accessing memory simultaneously. Each bus has its own memory interface and the Arbitration logic enables only one interface at a time. While an interface is

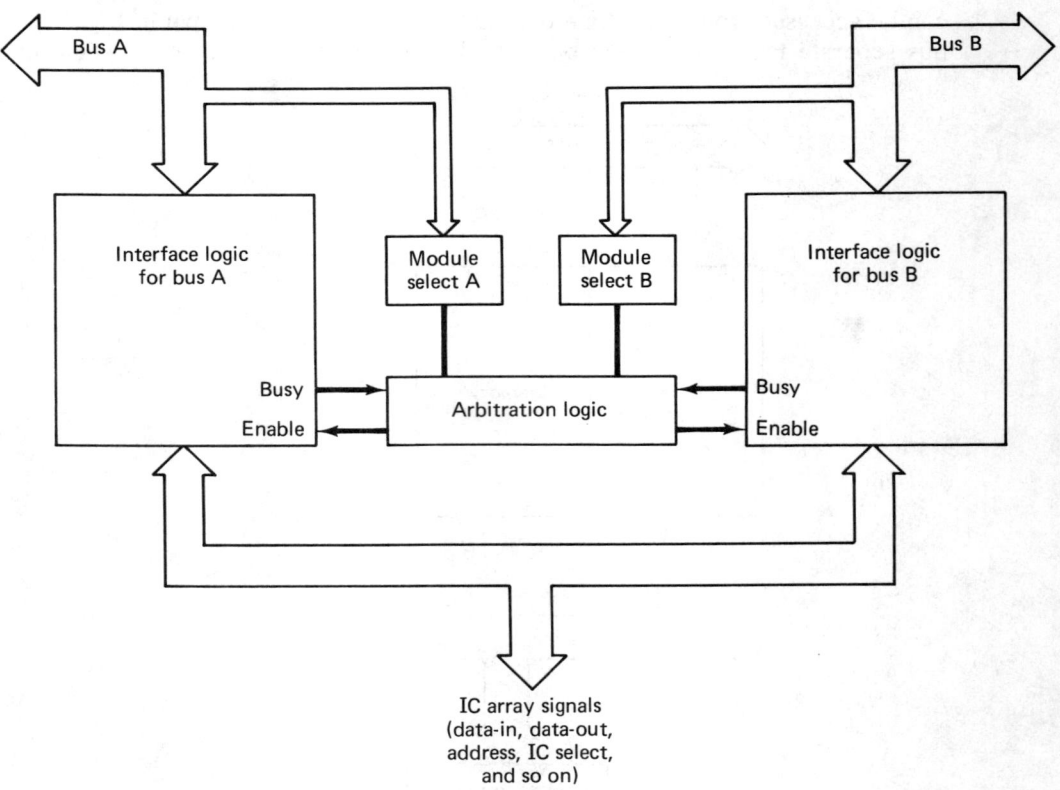

Figure 9-27 Two-port memory interface.

busy, the Arbitration logic cannot enable the other interface. This example assumes that the IC array and all of its associated circuitry are shared resources.

9-4 CACHE MEMORY

Most large, general purpose computers are designed to be multiprogrammed. During operation, they have an operating system and several applications and systems programs in their main memories at once, and the operating system regularly switches from one program to another in an attempt to maximally utilize the system. Traditionally, these computers have very fast processing elements and main memories with large capacities. Connecting a fast processing element to a large main memory is basically incompatible in that it is desirable to match the processing speed to that of memory accessing. Constructing a large memory whose access rate is approximately the rate at which a fast processor makes access requests is extremely complex and expensive. Therefore, the designers of such computers usually resort to inserting a very fast, but relatively small buffer memory between the main memory and the processing element as shown in Fig. 9-28. Such buffer memories are called **cache memories**.

In addition to access time and capacity, the important characteristics of a cache memory are its organization and the algorithms it uses to access main memory. The latter characteristic determines the efficiency with which a cache memory can provide information to and take information from the processing element.

If a location is addressed whose contents are currently in the cache, then a **hit** is said to occur; otherwise there is a **miss**. The average access time is

$$T = P_H t_C + (1 - P_H) t_M$$

where P_H is the probability of a hit and is called the **hit ratio**, t_C is the access time of the cache, and t_M is the access time of main memory. The quantity $1 - P_H$ is the probability of a miss and is called the **miss ratio**. It is assumed that t_C is much less than t_M and therefore, the objective is to decrease T by increasing the hit ratio. The organization and algorithms for accomplishing this objective depend on the pattern of the main memory accesses, which is determined by the use of the computer. (Strictly speaking, this equation is valid only for reading and certain methods of writing—for the more general case, see Exercise 25.)

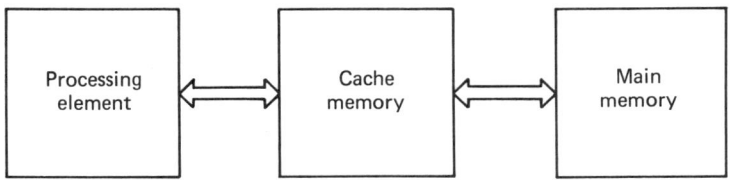

Figure 9-28 Configuration that uses a cache memory.

The way in which a cache memory views main memory is shown in Fig. 9-29(a). Main memory is divided into tag groups, or pages, which are subdivided into lines. Lines consist of one or more addressable locations (e.g., bytes) and each line in a tag group is also an element of a set. The ith set consists of all lines that occupy the ith positions within the tag groups. Note that the lines in a set are not sequentially located in main memory. The organization of the memory as seen by the cache is such that the memory is essentially treated as a 2-dimensional array in which the lines are the elements, the tag groups are the rows, and the sets are the columns. As shown in Fig. 9-29(b), the cache correspondingly treats memory addresses as if they are broken into three parts. The high-order P bits specify the tag group (the row), the next M bits specify the set (the column), and

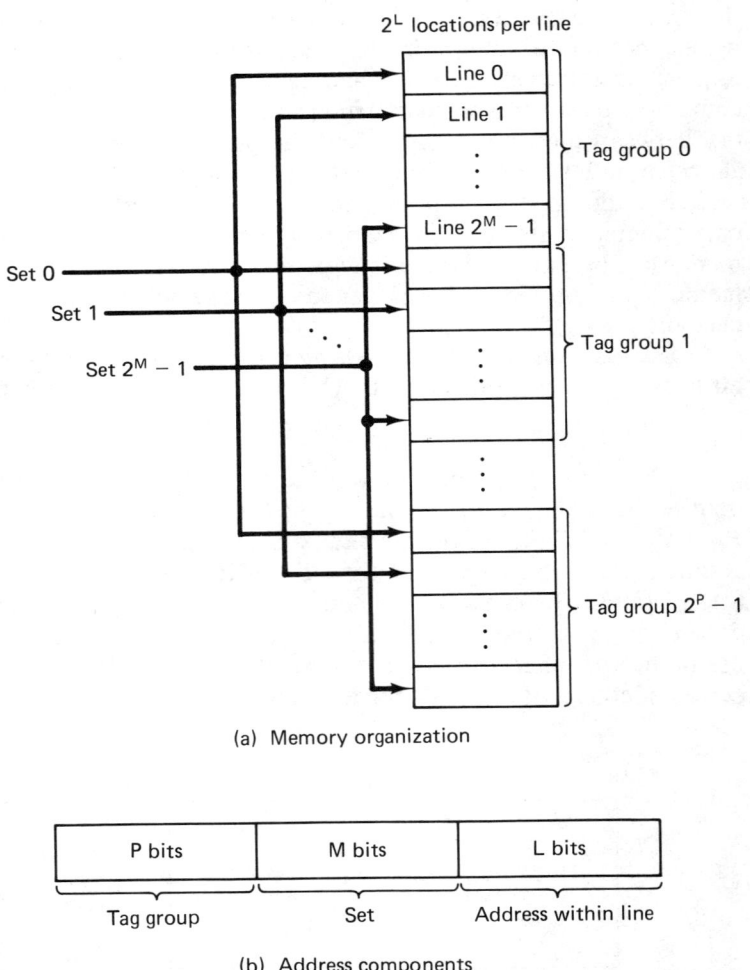

Figure 9-29 Main memory organization as viewed by the cache memory unit.

the L low-order bits point to the location within the line (the element). The total number of main memory locations is $N = 2^{P+M+L}$.

Because reading is more straightforward than writing, our initial discussion will be concerned only with reading. The concepts presented will then be extended to include writing.

The simplest way of organizing a cache is shown in Fig. 9-30. Such a cache is said to be **direct mapped** and is such that it can hold at most one line from each set (i.e., one element from each one column in the 2-dimensional array). Therefore, the capacity of a direct mapped cache is 2^{M+L}. All transfers between the main memory and cache are done by lines. The cache contains a:

Tag/Set register for holding the upper $P + M$ bits of the address.

Directory for storing the Tag fields (upper P bits) of the addresses of all of the main memory lines whose contents are currently stored in the cache. There are 2^M directory entries, one for each set.

Data memory for storing the 2^M lines of data that have been read into the cache. The lines and their associated directory entries are identified by Set numbers which range from 0 to $2^M - 1$.

A read operation begins by latching the upper $P + M$ bits of the address into the Tag/Set register. The Set portion of the address is then used to select one tag from the directory, which is then compared with the Tag portion of the address.

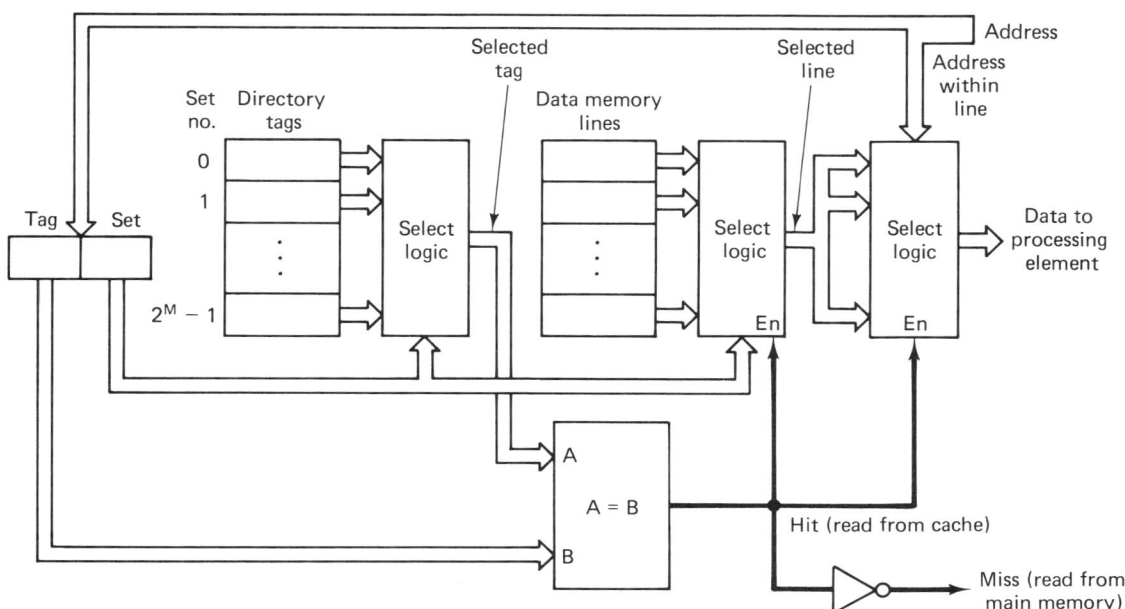

Figure 9-30 Reading from a direct mapped cache.

If the two are equal, a hit has occurred. The Set Address bits also designate the line being read and the lower L bits of the address select the location to be output to the processing element. If there is a miss, the line is read from main memory and put into the cache as well as being passed on to the processing element. When a line is put into the cache's data memory, its tag is put into the directory. Both the tag's location in the directory and the line's location in the cache's memory are determined by the M bits that indicate the set.

With direct mapping, when there is a miss, there is no choice as to which directory entry and line are replaced because the selection is dictated by the Set bits in the address. When a memory line is read whose Set bits are the same as those of a line that is currently in the cache but whose Tag bits are different from the cache line, the line being read replaces the cache line at that Set number.

For example, suppose that an address is 24 bits wide and $P = 8$, $M = 12$, and $L = 4$. Then, there are 256 tag groups, 4096 sets and 16 bytes per line. This implies that there are $2^{12+4} = 64K$ bytes in the cache's data memory, 4096 one-byte entries in the directory, and the capacity of main memory is 16M bytes. Fig. 9-31 illustrates a typical read from a direct mapped cache. If the address 4A2B02 is sent to the cache memory from the processing element, then the 4A and 2B0 are respectively put into the Tag and Set portions of the Tag/Set register and 2 is sent to the logic that selects a specific byte from a 16-byte line. The Set number 2B0 causes the 2B0th entry of the directory to be compared to the tag 4A and,

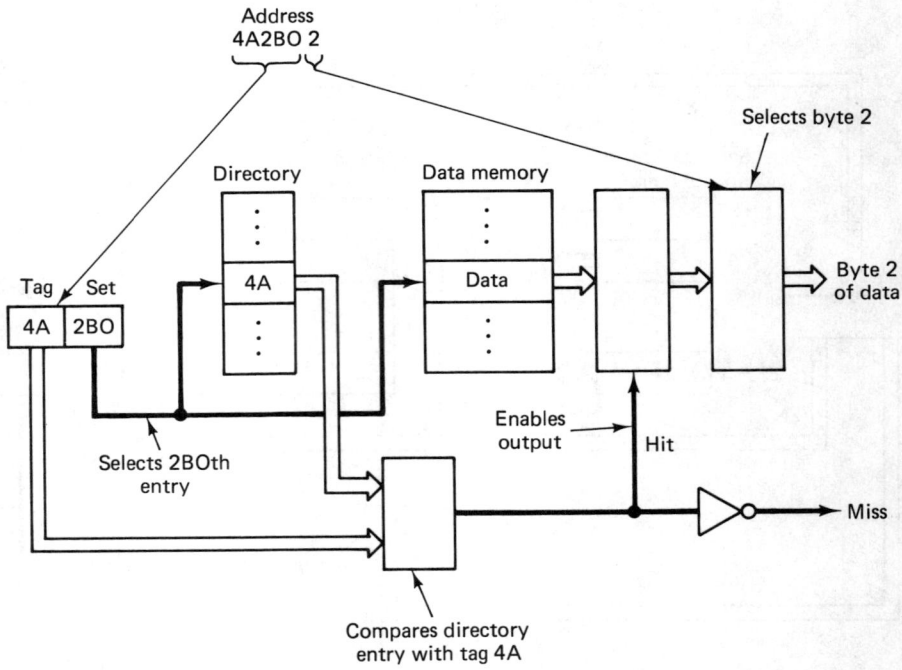

Figure 9-31 Direct mapped cache read example.

because there is a match for the example shown, there is a hit. The Set number also selects the 2B0th entry in the data memory and the Hit signal allows the line in this entry to be output to the Byte Select logic, which permits byte 2 of the line to be sent to the processing element.

If the 2B0th directory entry had not matched the tag, then there would have been a miss and a main memory access would have been required to retrieve the data, which would have then been put into the 2B0th entry of the cache's data memory. Also, the tag 4A would have replaced the contents of the 2B0th entry in the directory.

If the capacity of the cache were increased by a factor K, then its directory and data memory could be broken into K groups as shown in Fig. 9-32, with each group having a capacity of 2^{M+L}. The cache could store up to K lines from each set (i.e., from each column in the 2-dimensional array). By including a comparator with each group, the tags for all lines in the set indicated by the Set bits could be compared simultaneously and, if any one of them matched the Tag bits in the address, a hit would be indicated. When there is a hit, the line pointed to by the Set Address bits in the group having the matching tag would be output to a multiplexer that would select the location based on the lower L bits of the address.

This configuration is called a **K-way associative cache** and allows lines having the same Set numbers, but different tags, to be simultaneously stored in the cache. Up to K lines with the same Set number can now be stored. Again, consider the example illustrated in Fig. 9-31 and assume a 2-way associative cache. A read would cause the tag to be compared to two directory entries as shown in Fig. 9-33. The upper comparator indicates a hit and the bottom comparator indicates a miss. Therefore, there is an overall hit, and byte 2 of the 2B0th line in the associative group 1 is output to the processor.

If there is a miss and all K lines in the Set entries of a K-way associative cache are filled, then there is a choice as to which line is replaced. However, this introduces a problem because, any time a choice is offered, a decision must be made and the algorithm for making the decision must be specified. The algorithm for making a replacement decision in an associative cache is called a **replacement policy**. It can be proven that the optimal replacement policy is:

> Always replace the line that will be used furthest in the future.

The obvious fallacy with this replacement policy is that there is no way for a cache's logic to know which line will not be referenced for the longest time. Therefore, an algorithm that is likely to approximate this policy is needed. It so happens that the line that will be referenced furthest in the future is often the one that was referenced least recently; hence, the most popular replacement policy is the **Least Recently Used (LRU)** policy. To implement the LRU policy, ordinals are attached to lines to indicate their order of usage, and Logic for managing the ordinals is also required.

There has been considerable research into which replacement policy is the best and no absolute answer has been found. Modified forms of the LRU policy are most commonly used. For more information on LRU policies and replacement policies in general see Stone [1].

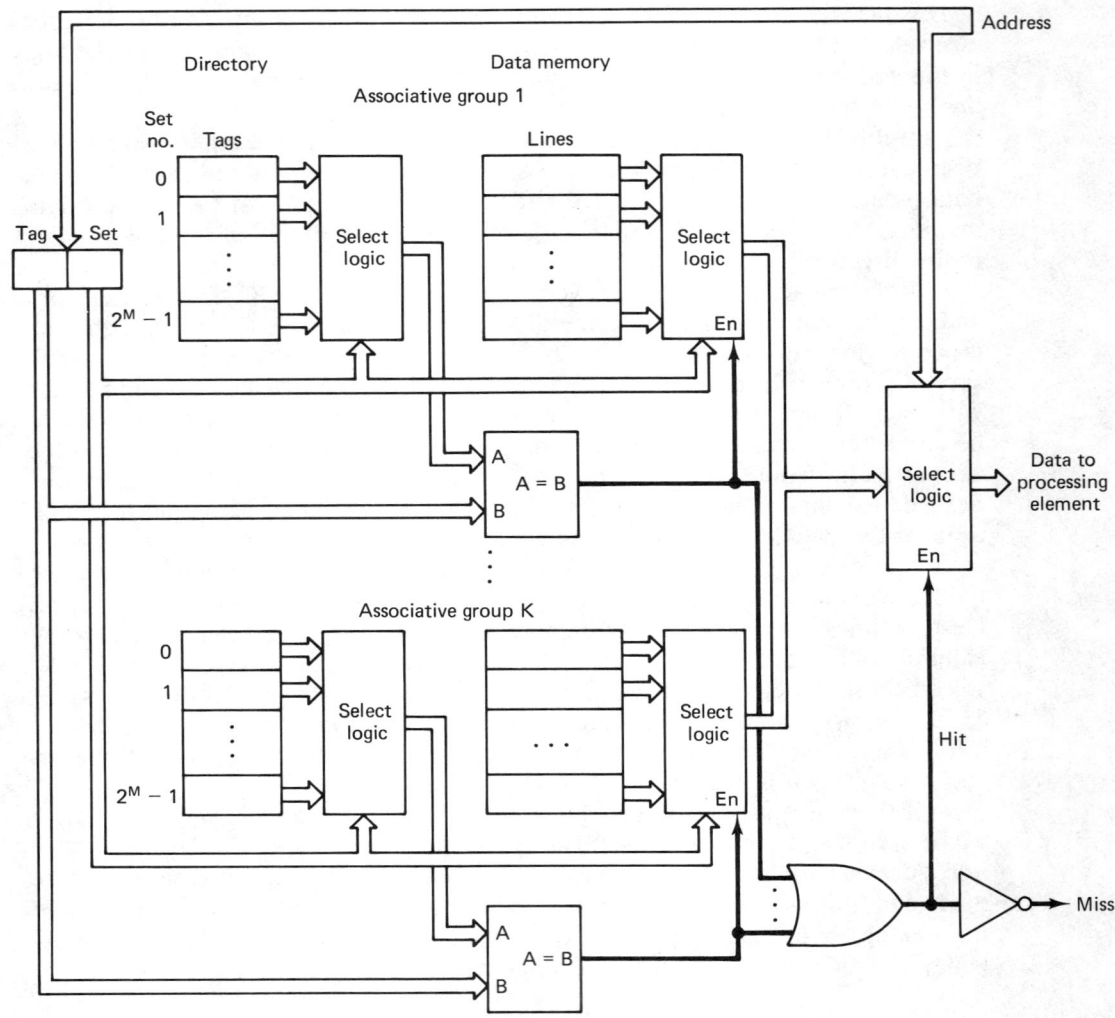

Figure 9-32 K-way associative cache.

Although the diagrams in both Figs. 9-30 and 9-32 show separate selection logic for the directory and data memory, this representation was done as an illustrative convenience. Selection logic could be built into the memory design as discussed in Sec. 9-2. Each location would include both a tag and a line and have a width of P + L. A K-way associative cache would require K separate memories, each having its own Selection logic.

A representative curve giving the hit ratio as a function of the capacity of a cache is shown in Fig. 9-34. The curve increases rapidly at first, but then reaches a point at which it must bend and asymptotically approach 1. Beyond this bend a large increase in capacity is needed to obtain a small gain in the hit ratio. Up

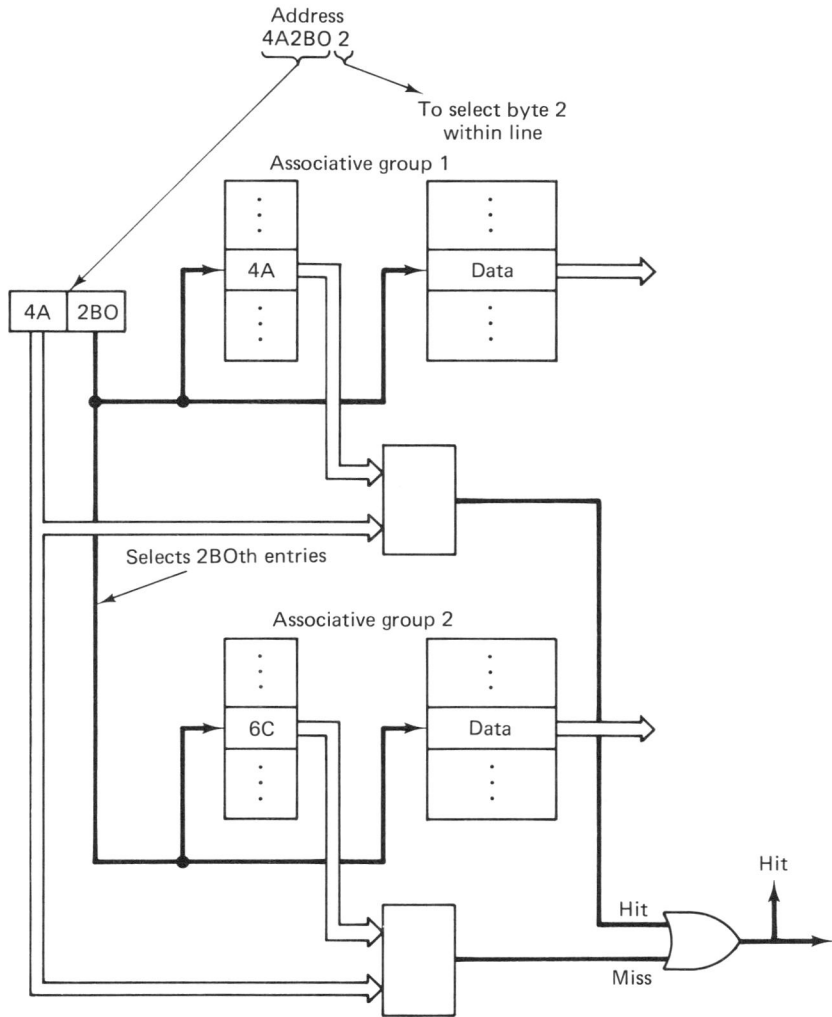

Figure 9-33 Typical read from a 2-way associative cache.

to a point the hit ratio improvement can be had by simply making the cache larger, but past that point it may be better to spend additional logic on making the cache associative or improving the replacement policy than to add more memory.

The number of main memory locations that can be stored in a K-way associative cache is $K \times 2^{M+L}$, which makes K, M, and L the primary design parameters. When $K = 1$ the cache is reduced to direct mapping. The other extreme occurs when $M = 0$ and there is only one set but more than one associative group. In this case the cache is said to be **fully associative**. For $K > 1$, K-way associativity requires K tag comparators plus the logic required to implement a replacement policy. The gains in using associativity are the ability to store

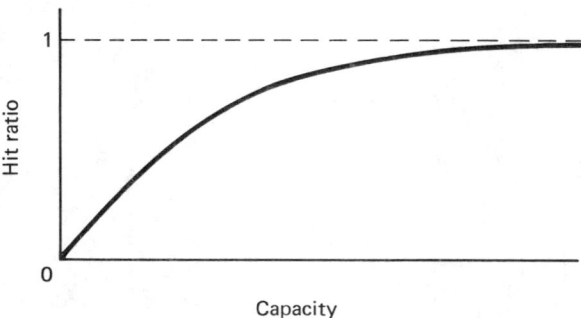

Figure 9-34 Hit ratio as a function of capacity.

lines that are identically placed within up to K different tag groups (i.e., being able to store more than one line per column) and the increased flexibility in choosing when a line is to be replaced. There is no definitive answer as to how much this flexibility is worth, but if associativity is used, K is usually small. Once the value of K has been chosen, the size of the cache is determined by M + L, where L is the number of memory locations involved in each transfer. Within the last few years the value of M + L has increased dramatically as the cost of fast memory has dropped.

Locality of reference is an important consideration when designing a cache memory. Note that the lines in a tag group are consecutive lines in memory and each line in a set must belong to a different tag group, i.e., the lines in a set are spaced at least 2^M lines apart. If each program's code and data could fit into a single tag group and only one program were to run at a time, then a direct mapped cache would be adequate. However, for a large program, a locality may occupy more than one tag group or, for a multiprogramming system, the tag group being accessed may change frequently. In either case, K-way associativity may be needed to reduce the miss ratio.

Because multiprogramming is normally used when main memory is large, for a given cache size the hit ratio tends to decrease as main memory size increases. This implies that larger main memories tend to require larger caches. Most caches can store the contents of from 2K to 64K bytes of main memory. For example, for a 4-way associative cache with 2K sets and 8 bytes per line, K = 4, M = 11, and L = 3 and the capacity of the cache is 64K bytes. If main memory has a capacity of 16M bytes, there are 1K tag groups and P = 10. (A thorough discussion of cache design in a multiprogramming environment is given in Stone [1].)

A problem with using two memories to store the same information is that of keeping both memories up to date or, alternatively, indicating which memory contains the valid data. If a cache is being used and new information is brought into main memory from the mass storage or I/O subsystem, then some of the information in the cache may not match the new information in main memory. To indicate whether the two memories have like or unlike information, an extra bit, called a **valid bit**, (not shown in Fig. 9-30 or 9-32) is associated with each cache line. When information is brought into main memory lines from the outside, the cache logic checks to determine whether the lines are in the cache. For those main memory lines that are also in the cache, the corresponding valid bits are cleared to indicate that the cache lines no longer match those in main memory. In order for a hit to occur, both the valid bit must be set and the tags must be matched. Because the contents of a memory are unpredictable when its power is turned on, all valid bits must be cleared during power up.

Now let us examine the transfer of results from a processing element to a cache. If a datum is written to the cache only, then there may be a temporary disagreement between the contents of a location in cache and the corresponding location in main memory. The danger in not insuring that the two memories have the same contents is that a transfer to an I/O or mass storage subsystem could result in a wrong value being output or permanently stored. This problem can be resolved by always writing to both cache and main memory. This is called the **write through** method and is depicted in Fig. 9-35(a). The disadvantage of the

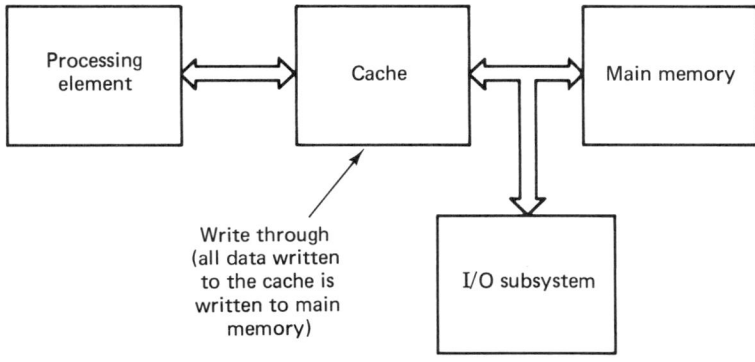

(a) Write through

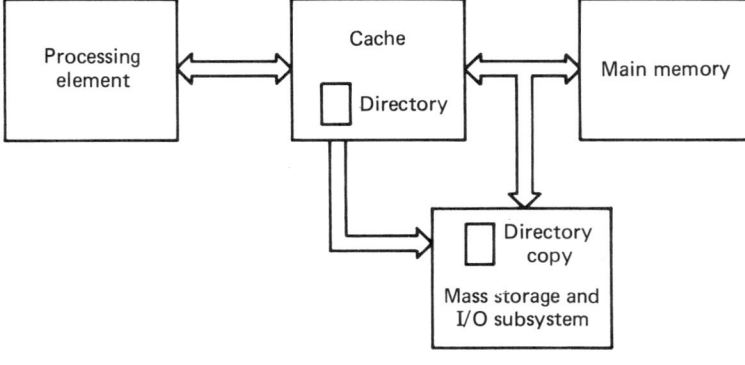

(b) Write back

Figure 9-35 Methods for handling write operations.

write through method is that it partially negates the purpose of using a high-speed cache by requiring that all writes also be made to main memory.

The alternative, called the **write back** method, does not immediately write a result output to the cache back into main memory, but transfers a line to main memory when there is a miss and subsequent replacement. This method leaves a short term disagreement between the memories, but this disagreement is overcome by making a copy of the cache's directory available to the I/O and mass storage subsystem as shown in Fig. 9-35(b). If the I/O and mass storage subsystem detects that a line is in the cache, it takes the line from the cache instead of main memory. The directory used by the I/O and mass storage subsystem needs to be updated only when there is a miss. The duplicate directory requires extra logic, but reduces the number of writes to main memory.

9-5 HIERARCHY DESIGN

As indicated previously the purpose of the memory hierarchy is to provide for buffering between the I/O and permanent storage areas of the computer and the logic that performs the processing. There may be from two to seven levels of memory in a hierarchy. A hierarchy may include the processing element registers, cache, a second intermediate cache, main memory, a fast form of mass storage such as a drum, a slower form of mass storage for permanently storing data, and buffer memory associated with mass storage. For a small controller application there may only be processing element registers and a small main memory. At the other extreme, a very large and fast multiprogrammed supercomputer may have two levels of cache memory, a fast form of temporary mass storage, and mass storage buffer memory in addition to the traditional three levels of memory.

As shown in Fig. 9-36, at each level, the memory closer to the processing

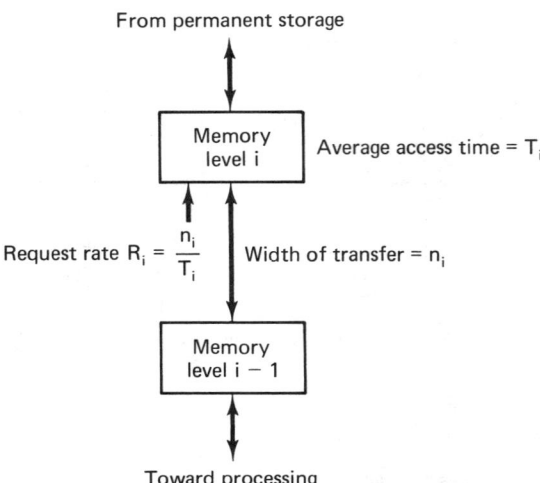

Figure 9-36 Matching information flow with information demand.

makes requests to the next higher level of memory, which is closer to the permanent storage and I/O. Ideally, at all levels the rate of requests should exactly match the transfer rate capability of the higher level memory. Assume that R_i is the rate of requests made to the ith level, n_i is the width of the data being transferred with each ith level access, and T_i is the average access time of the ith level; then $R_i = n_i/T_i$ should be true for all i. If the request rate attempts to be higher than the maximum transfer rate, the computer must operate below its processing capability. If the maximum transfer rate exceeds the request rate, the higher level memory is more expensive and complex than necessary.

If the request rates R_i and R_{i+1} are equal, then an attempt should be made to make

$$n_i/T_i = n_{i+1}/T_{i+1}$$

But, T_i would normally be much less than T_{i+1} and, therefore, n_{i+1} would need to be made much greater than n_i. If all levels have the same request rates, the mass storage level transfer may have to be extremely wide. Fortunately, the nature of computers is such that request rates increase as information is moved closer to the processing. As indicated previously, this situation occurs because both the instructions and data brought in from the higher levels may be used more than once by the lower levels.

For example, instructions embedded in loops or procedures may be fetched several times by a processing element even though they are transferred from mass storage only once. Also, a single set of data may be used in numerous operations after it has been brought near the processing element or may only be output to the intermediate levels of memory before it is used again. At a more remote distance from the processing element, in a multiprogrammed system, a drum may be used to shuffle program and data segments into and out of main memory, but the programs and data would be transferred from a permanent mass storage area only once.

To understand the inequality of the request rates better, let us extend the concept of hit ratio to memories in general. If h_i is the hit ratio of the ith level memory, then the information rate associated with the $i + 1$th level memory is

$$R_{i+1} = (1 - h_i)R_i \quad i = 1, \ldots, m$$

which implies that

$$\frac{n_{i+1}}{T_{i+1}} \geq \frac{n_i}{T_i}(1 - h_i) \quad i = 1, \ldots, m$$

where the inequalities would become equalities if optimal matching were attained at every level. However, because a system may serve a variety of applications, optimal matching over all applications is probably not possible.

Consider the memory arrangement depicted in Fig. 9-37 and suppose that the average memory access times are to be found. Then

$$T_1 \leq \frac{n_1}{R_1} = \frac{2}{32 \times 10^6} = 62.5 \text{ nS}$$

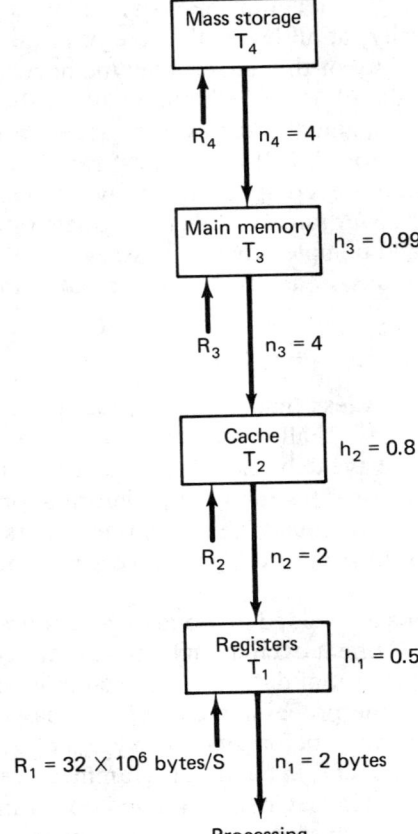

Figure 9-37 Access time matching example.

$$R_2 = (1 - h_1)R_1 = (1 - 0.5)\, 32 \times 10^6 = 16 \times 10^6 \text{ bytes/S}$$

$$T_2 \leq \frac{2}{16 \times 10^6} = 125 \text{ nS}$$

$$R_3 = (1 - 0.8)\, 16 \times 10^6 = 3.2 \times 10^6 \text{ bytes/S}$$

$$T_3 \leq \frac{4}{3.2 \times 10^6} = 1250 \text{ nS}$$

$$R_4 = (1 - 0.99)\, 3.2 \times 10^6 = 32 \times 10^3 \text{ bytes/S}$$

$$T_4 \leq \frac{4}{32 \times 10^3} = 125 \text{ }\mu\text{S}$$

The maximum access times for the register set, cache, and main memory (T_1, T_2, and T_3) could be easily attained by semiconductor technology, and the mass storage average access time could be achieved by a disk whose average time for

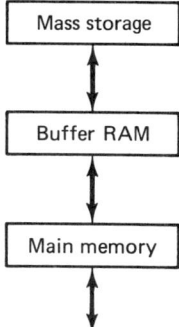

Figure 9-38 Mass storage buffer RAM.

accessing and transferring a 1024-byte sector is

$$\frac{1024}{4} \times 125 \times 10^{-6} = 32 \text{ mS}$$

The long and erratic access times of mass storage can seriously affect the efficiency with which data are moved to and from mass storage. As a result, high performance computers sometimes include a semiconductor RAM buffer memory in the mass storage subsystem as shown in Fig. 9-38. Because main memory sees only the buffer RAM, this configuration tends to provide a more even flow of information between mass storage and main memory. However, the even flow can be effectively maintained only if the mass storage system can anticipate which information will be requested next. For sequential access, guessing what will be needed in the near future is easy, but for direct access the mass storage subsystem must receive advance notice from the operating system or have some form of intelligence so that it can make predictions and act independently. It is important that the prediction algorithm have a reasonable success rate; otherwise the wasted mass storage activity would outweigh the gain of sometimes having the needed information available in RAM. The increased activity could cause contention for the storage medium and associated circuitry and this could actually increase the effective access time over what it would be without the RAM buffer. Such buffers are most useful in multiprogrammed systems. It will be seen in Chap. 11 that such systems queue mass storage and I/O accesses and arrange the accesses so that seek and latency times are minimized. In these cases, the order of near future accesses is known.

REFERENCES

1. Stone, Harold S., *High Performance Computer Architecture*, 2nd ed. (Reading, Massachusetts: Addison-Wesley Publishing Company, 1990).
2. Gibson, Glenn A., and Yu-cheng Liu, *Microcomputers for Engineers and Scientists*, 2nd ed. (Englewood Cliffs, N.J.: Prentice Hall, Inc., 1987).

3. Liu, Yu-cheng, and Glenn A. Gibson, *Microcomputer Systems: The 8086/8088 Family*, 2nd ed. (Englewood Cliffs, N.J.: Prentice Hall, Inc., 1986).
4. Hall, David V., *Microprocessors and Digital Systems* (New York: McGraw-Hill Book Company, 1980).
5. Short, Kenneth L., *Microprocessors and Programmed Logic*, 2nd ed. (Englewood Cliffs, N.J.: Prentice Hall, Inc., 1987).
6. Gibson, Glenn A. and James R. Young, *Introduction to Programming Using FORTRAN 77* (Englewood Cliffs, N.J.: Prentice Hall, Inc., 1982).
7. Hamacher, V. C., Z. G. Vranesic, and S. G. Zaky, *Computer Organization*, 2nd ed. (New York: McGraw-Hill Book Company, 1984).
8. Mano, M. Morris, *Computer System Architecture*, 2nd ed. (Englewood Cliffs, New Jersey: Prentice Hall, Inc., 1982).

EXERCISES

1. For a memory that is accessed 16 bits at a time, draw a graph that shows the memory's transfer rate in bps versus its access time as the access time varies from 50 nS to 5 mS. Both axes are to be logarithmically scaled.
2. Assume that a standard ½ inch, 9-track tape drive reads and writes at 100 ips, rewinds at 200 ips, and uses a density of 6250 bpi.
   (a) If the read/write head is arbitrarily positioned on a 2400-foot tape, what would be the average rewind time?
   (b) What would be the unit's transfer rate?
   (c) On the average, approximately how long would it take to rewind the tape from an arbitrary position and begin to read an arbitrarily positioned record?
3. Consider the tape unit described in Exercise 2. If the average length of a record is one inch, a record gap is 0.3 inches, the average number of records in a file is 50, and the end-of-file marker and gap between files is 3 inches:
   (a) What percentage of the tape would be filled with useful information?
   (b) How many bytes of information could be stored on the tape?
   (c) If records are sequentially copied from one tape to another one at a time, the tape must be started and stopped between records, and it requires 4 mS to start and stop the tape, approximately how long would it take to copy a tape that is completely filled with records?
4. Assume that a disk unit contains a 4-disk assembly, information is stored on both sides of all disks, there are 1024 tracks per surface and 128 sectors per track, there are 512 bytes of actual data stored in each sector, and the disk revolves at 1800 rpm.
   (a) How many tracks are in each cylinder?
   (b) How many bytes are stored in each track? Disk? Cylinder?
   (c) What is the capacity of the disk unit?
   (d) If 25% of each track does not contain actual data, what is the unit's transfer rate?
   (e) If the average seek time is 8 mS, what is the unit's average access time?
5. Consider the disk unit described in Exercise 4. How long would it take to input an entire file if the file consists of 10 randomly positioned sectors and 3 randomly positioned directory sectors must also be read?
6. If the average seek time of a diskette unit is 225 mS, its head load time is 16 mS, and

its rotational speed is 360 rpm, how long would it take, on the average, to begin reading a given sector?

7. If the design of a disk head and the quality of the disk's surface is such that the maximum bit density is 20,000 bpi, the minimum spacing between tracks is 0.005 inches, there are to be 14,000 bytes of storage per track, and only 70% of each track is occupied by actual data (the other 30% is formatting information and gaps):
   (a) What is the minimum diameter of the inner track?
   (b) What is the minimum diameter of the outer track assuming that the storage capacity of each surface is to be 10.5 million data bytes?

8. Suppose that an MBM has 270 minor loops, 14 of which are assumed to be flawed, each minor loop contains 2000 bits, there are 100 bit positions between the detection circuit and its closest minor loop, and a 200 kHz rotating magnetic field:
   (a) What is its capacity?
   (b) What is its transfer rate?
   (c) What is its average access time? (Assume that the needed page is arbitrarily positioned within the minor loops.)

9. Design a 64K byte memory IC array using 64K × 2 ICs. Using 8K × 8 ICs. In each case what is the total number of conductors connected to the array if:
   (a) Static RAM ICs are used?
   (b) Dynamic RAM ICs are used?
   (c) ROM is used.

10. If a 1 M byte memory module is constructed of 128K × 1 ICs, how many ICs would be needed?

11. Suppose that a 4 M-byte memory is to consist of eight modules with each module being constructed of 64K × 1 ICs whose cell arrays are made up of 256 rows and 256 columns. Give a possible breakdown of the use of the address bits.

12. Assume the design indicated by Exercise 11. If the per bit power consumption is 0.02 mW, what is the amount of heat given off by
    (a) Each IC. (b) Each module. (c) The entire memory.

13. Why does a dynamic RAM need to be refreshed?

14. Suppose that a 256K-byte dynamic RAM module is constructed of 128K × 1 ICs that have 512 rows and 256 columns of cells. If the cells must be refreshed every 3 mS and 600 nS are required to complete a refresh, what percentage of the available time is lost due to refreshing?

15. Design a ROM module that contains 4K 32-bit locations using 4K × 8 ICs.

16. If a memory IC has 128 rows and 64 columns of cells, the resistance associated with each Row Select line and each drive/sense line is 0.1 ohms, the capacitance per cell of each Row Select and Drive/Sense line is 5 nF, two time constants are needed for a cell's output to be selected, five time constants are needed for an output to be sensed, and the address setup time is 10 nS, what is the approximate read access time of the IC? Resolve the problem assuming 256 rows and 256 columns. (To calculate the time constants, refer to Sec. 3-1).

17. Why are PROMs used instead of masked ROMs when only a few identically programmed ICs are required?

18. Consider the interface design in Fig. 9-24. If the propagation delays through the Module Select logic, memory controller, Data-out buffer, and data drivers and receivers are 15, 25, 20, and 15 nS, respectively, and the IC write time is 150 nS, what is the total memory write access time?

19. Design the portion of the memory controller shown in Fig. 9-24 that is needed to produce the Read/Write and IC Enable signals.
20. Assume that a processing element always operates on one or more bytes and fetches data and instructions 4 bytes at a time. If the probabilities of the element using 1 byte, 2 bytes, 3 bytes, and 4 bytes are 0.3, 0.2, 0.1, and 0.4, respectively, and the average memory access time is 250 nS, what is the effective average access time in terms of useful information?
21. Consider the memory interface design in Fig. 9-25. If the time required for a complete memory access is 200 nS, 64 bits are accessed simultaneously, the data buffer register access time is 40 nS, and the probability that the data being accessed are already in the data buffer register is 0.4, what is the average access time of the memory?
22. Design the arbitration logic for the two-port memory interface shown in Fig. 9-27. Assume that Bus A always has higher priority.
23. Assume the definitions of P, M, L, and K given in Section 9-4 and the following contents of a 4-line direct mapped cache with 4 one-byte locations per line:

Directory	Lines			
42	1A	00	01	50
1A	2C	DE	F0	20
20	00	6B	E2	F7
1B	92	10	DE	1F

   (a) What are the values of P, M, L, and K and what is the capacity of main memory?
   (b) If the contents of location 20A are to be read, would there be a hit or a miss? If there is a hit, what value would be passed to the processing element?
   (c) Repeat Part (b) for location 42B.
24. Extend the cache in Exercise 23 to a 2-way cache for which the contents of Associative Group 1 are given in Exercise 23 and those for Associative Group 2 are:

Directory	Lines			
21	00	01	02	03
FA	9A	9B	9C	9D
40	12	14	41	42
6C	F1	F4	F5	10

   (a) If the contents of 20A are to be read, would there be a hit or a miss? If there is a hit, what value would be passed to the processing element?
   (b) Repeat Part (a) for location 40B.
   (c) Repeat Part (a) for location 50B.
   (d) Suppose that accesses are made in the order

       20B   423   1BF   FA6   409   40A   609

   and the LRU replacement policy is used. Which lines in the cache will be replaced?
25. If the access time for main memory is 300 nS, the access time for cache is 75 nS, the hit ratio is 0.9, and 80% of the accesses are reads, what is the average memory access time if write through is used? If write back is used?
26. Consider a 4-way associative cache memory with 2K 16-byte lines in each tag group. If multiprogramming is being used and all programs, including code and data, are 16K

bytes in length, what is the maximum number of programs that could be entirely in cache at one time? Suppose that the programs occupy contiguous areas in main memory. To attain this maximum, what would be the restrictions on the beginning addresses of the programs?

27. Assume that a cache memory supplies a processing element 2 bytes at a time, draws information from main memory 4 bytes at a time, and has the hit ratio versus capacity curve shown below:

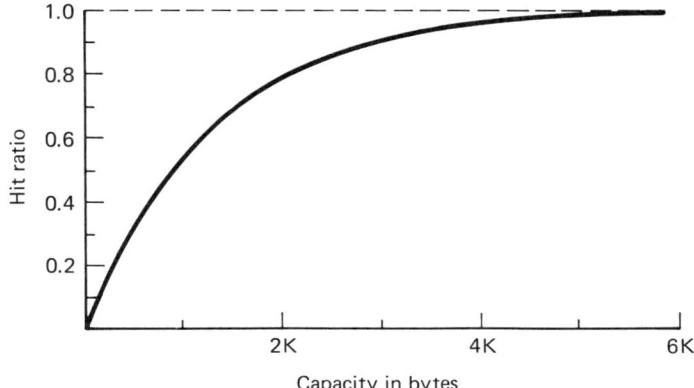

If the access times of the cache and main memories are 80 nS and 180 nS, respectively, write back is used, and the processor element's request rate is 20M bytes/S, what should be the approximate capacity of the cache?

10
Memory Management

Chapter 9 concentrated on the construction and physical attributes of different types of components in the memory hierarchy. Although there was some discussion of how information is stored and accessed by software, these discussions were limited to explaining why certain physical features are important or how the accessing method affects the physical attributes. Particular attention was paid to access time and capacity and the transfer of information from one element to another in the hierarchy. This chapter is concerned with the usage of the various types of memory elements. It examines how information is stored and accessed or, more generally, how it is managed and logically organized. Most of our attention is directed toward allocating, referencing, and protecting stored information.

The allocation of stored information is the assignment of the information to the addressable areas of a memory's storage medium. Any memory element has a fixed capacity associated with it that is determined by its number of addressable areas and the amount of storage in these areas. The goal is to make maximal use of the available space, but to do so in such a way that accessing requires as little effort and time as possible. Once an assignment has been made it must be logged so that the software can locate the information when it is needed. Equally important is to log unused space so that when a new assignment must be made, unused space can be found to complete the assignment.

Referencing is the act of accessing stored information. It concerns all aspects of the process whereby the software determines the required location(s) and then conducts the access. It is extremely dependent on the physical nature of a memory element. Mass storage, which is block structured and stores information in files, must use a completely different form of referencing than main memory, which has an address associated with each byte (or other addressable bit grouping).

Also, because of the large capacity of mass storage, referencing mass storage is primarily concerned with searching out information and then accessing it in an orderly fashion. Referencing main memory may be primarily concerned with the flexibility with which the references can be made. This flexibility is needed because of the frequent movement of the same information to and from main memory with different allocations being made as the information is shuffled in and out.

The third aspect of memory management that will be considered is protection, which provides the means for controlling the access of an information entity. For mass storage, protection may be assigned to individual files or to groups of files and controls who may use the files and how they may be used. For main memory, protection is needed to prevent accidental or unwanted access between programs or between code and data.

The extent to which memory must be managed is clearly a function of the complexity of a system. A small, dedicated system that has little or no mass storage would have very little to manage, but a large multiprogramming system with several levels in its memory hierarchy must be capable of keeping track of vast amounts of information, freely moving this information around within the memory hierarchy, and providing the protection required to prevent misuse of the information. It would be impossible to present all of the concepts related to memory management in a single chapter, but an attempt will be made to point out the concepts that are of central importance. The complexity of the systems assumed in our discussions will vary as appropriate to the topic being considered. The degree to which a memory element needs to be managed depends on the hardware associated with the element, but memory management of the memory system as a whole is a responsibility of the operating system.

10-1 MASS STORAGE MANAGEMENT

Because magnetic tapes must store information in a strictly sequential manner and changing the contents of a tape normally involves copying the tape, the management of tape storage is relatively simple and, for the most part, was already considered in Chap. 9. Therefore, our discussion here concentrates on the management of disk and drum storage, both of which are viewed as an array of numbered blocks. The facts that blocks are ultimately referenced using cylinder/track/sector identifiers and the translation between block numbers and their identifiers is required are unimportant. To simplify the presentation in this chapter and Chap. 11, it will be assumed that blocks with consecutive block numbers occupy areas on the storage medium that are contiguous.

A file consists of an integral number of blocks. Therefore, the last block in a file may not be full and some of the storage space may be wasted. This phenomenon is referred to as **internal fragmentation**. If there are m bytes in each block and n is the average number of blocks in a file, then the average amount of wasted space in a file is $m/2$ bytes and the average fractional amount of waste in a file due to internal fragmentation is

$$\frac{m/2}{mn} = \frac{1}{2n}$$

Clearly, for large n the waste is insignificant, but for small n it is a matter for concern. The allocation of space to a set of files and the effect of internal fragmentation is depicted in Fig. 10-1.

The blocks in a file may be physically grouped to form clusters, in which case the file would consist of an integral number of clusters. As indicated in Chap. 9, the purpose in using clusters is to reduce total access time when reading from or writing to a file by reducing head movement and rotational delays. The disadvantage to clustering is the increase in wasted space due to internal fragmentation. If the cluster size is p and n and m are as defined above, then, on the average, the wasted space per file is increased to $mp/2$ bytes and the average

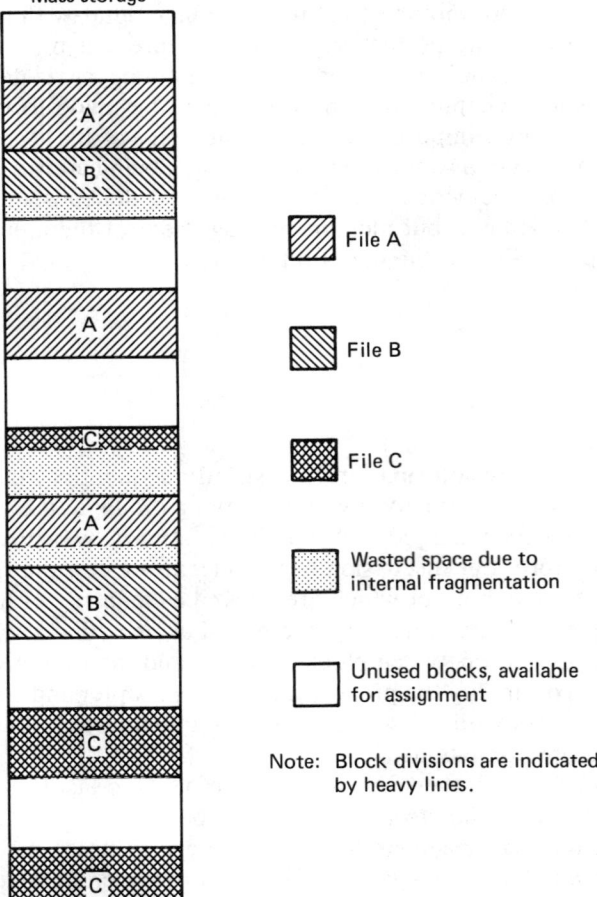

Figure 10-1 Internal fragmentation and the allocation of mass storage space.

fraction of wasted space for a file of n blocks becomes

$$\frac{mp/2}{mn} = \frac{1}{2(n/p)}$$

The unused space due to internal fragmentation is now insignificant only if n/p is large. Cluster size need not be fixed, but may vary from file to file. This variation permits users to optimize the cluster size tradeoff on a file by file basis. Most systems that allow the cluster size for each file to be selected also have a default size for each mass storage unit that tends to optimize the usage of the unit as a whole.

As indicated in the introduction to this chapter, an important part of managing any space is keeping track of unused areas. One way of tracking these areas for mass storage space is to maintain a **bit map**, which is a bit array that associates one bit with each block. When a block is currently part of a file, its corresponding bit is set to 1; otherwise the bit is 0. Maintaining a bit map is a matter of setting or clearing the appropriate bits as files are added, deleted, or changed in size. Although the approach is conceptually simple, for very large mass storage units with hundreds of thousands of blocks the bit map would be very large. A unit with one million blocks would require 125 thousand bytes just to store the bit map. Searching through the bit map for unused areas, which may include rotating bytes (or any other convenient bit grouping) through the carry flag, could be extremely time-consuming.

An alternative method is to provide a table whose entries define the unused areas, with each entry identifying the first block in an unused area and the number of blocks in the area. Typically, this table is organized as a **linked list**, which also includes in each entry a pointer to the next entry. An example of a linked list with five entries is given in Fig. 10-2. The table is an array that is indexed as shown in the column on the left and the pointers are given in the left-most column within the table. A 0 pointer indicates that a table element is not being used and

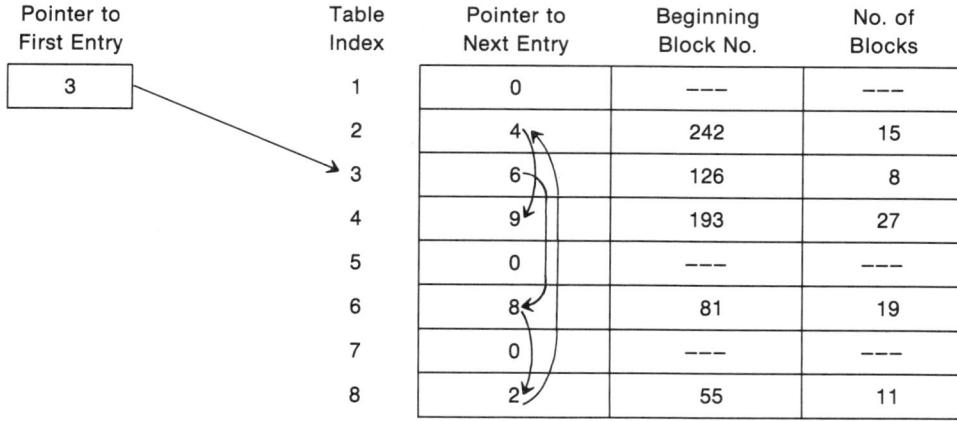

Figure 10-2 Linked list for recording the locations of unused areas.

a pointer equal to 9 signals the end of the linked list. In addition to the array there is a variable that points to the beginning of the list.

The advantage in using a linked list is the versatility with which entries may be added, deleted, or changed. An accounting of the unused areas must be dynamic and must change as files are added, deleted, or changed in size. An addition to the unused area linked list is needed when a file that has a subset of its blocks sandwiched between two blocks used by other files is deleted, as shown in Fig. 10-3(a), or when a file whose end block is adjacent to a used block is shortened. An addition is accomplished by:

1. Searching for an unused element in the array containing the linked list.
2. Filling the new entry with the required information (i. e., the block number of the first block in the unused area, the number of blocks in the unused area, and a 9 in the pointer field).

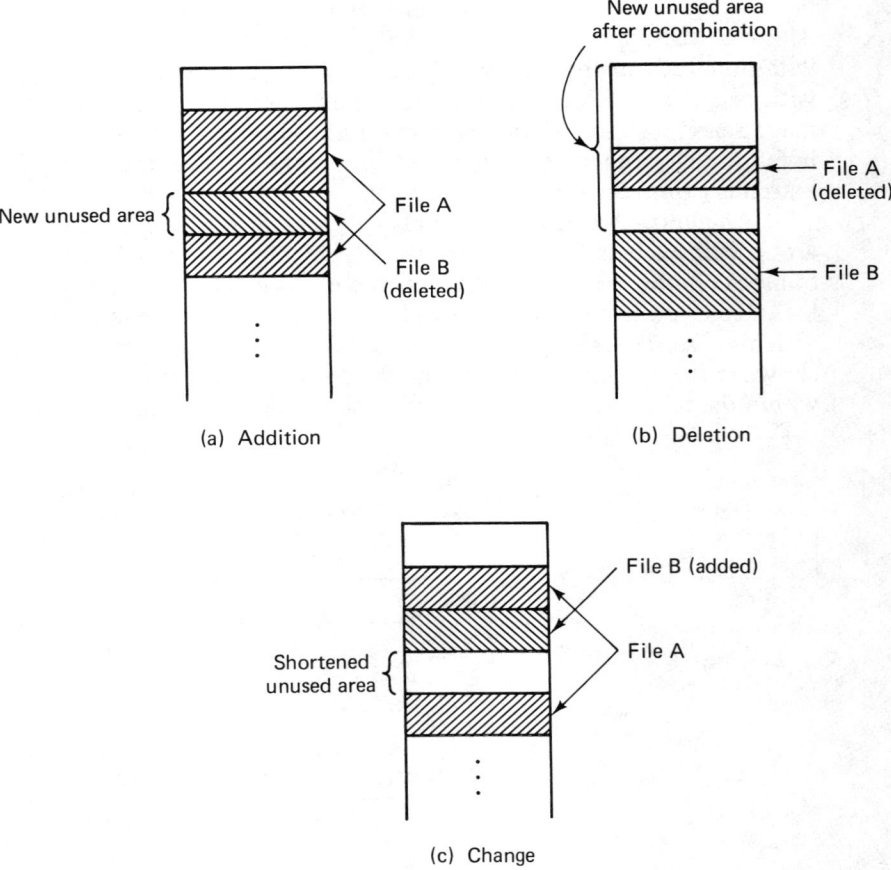

Figure 10-3 Examples of when changes are required in an unused linked list or its entries.

3. Searching the linked list to find its last entry.
4. Putting the index corresponding to the new last entry into the pointer field of the old last entry.

A deletion is needed when an unused area is completely filled by a new file that is added or an existing file that is expanded, or when a file that has a set of blocks that is sandwiched between two unused areas is deleted. An example of the latter, which causes unused areas to be combined, is given in Fig. 10-3(b). To perform a deletion:

1. Search through the list until the entry to be deleted is found.
2. Transfer its pointer to the pointer field of the previous element in the list.
3. Put a 0 in its pointer field.

An entry change must be made any time the beginning block or size of an unused area is changed due to a file addition, deletion, or change. An entry change requires the entry to be located by searching through the list for the beginning block number of the affected unused area and then making the necessary change.

As mentioned in Chap. 9, directories are used to keep an accounting of the used space on a mass storage unit. There are numerous techniques for organizing directories and these techniques range from simple to complex. The principal criteria for selecting an organizational technique are the amount of available space, the maximum number of files to be managed, and the flexibility required. Although the organizational structure of mass storage is a very important part of a computer system, space does not permit a lengthy discussion of these structures here. However, two examples are presented to introduce the central ideas related to file management. The file and directory structure is an integral part of an operating system and our first example is similar to the file and directory structure used by operating systems designed for early minicomputers. The second is a simplification of the structure used by the UNIX operating system. It is also similar to the Microsoft Disk Operating System (MS DOS) used on most personal computers.

Example 1:

In our first example, the directory is assumed to be of fixed length and to occupy a fixed area of mass storage space (e.g., the outer three tracks of the disk). The files are assumed to occupy blocks with consecutive block numbers (i.e., blocks that are physically contiguous). Each entry in the directory contains the block number of the first block in a file, the number of blocks in the file, and other information about the file that may be needed by the operating system. Because the files are made up of consecutive blocks, a simple way of noting unused areas would be to treat them as files and then indicate their true identities in their directory entries.

To the operating system, the directory would be a linear array. As files are added and deleted, unused array elements would become intermixed with the elements that are used to store directory entries. When a change in the file structure requires a new directory entry, a linear search could be performed to find an unused element.

The primary problem with this scheme for allocating space is the requirement that files must be made up of consecutive blocks. Although this structure permits files to be accessed more quickly by minimizing the number of directory references and the mechanical motion between block accesses, it introduces **external fragmentation** (also known as **checkerboarding** or the **Swiss cheese effect**). Figure 10-4 illustrates the development of external fragmentation as several files are added and deleted. Initially, files A through D are added in the order shown in Fig. 10-4(a). Then E is added and file B is deleted [Fig. 10-4(b)], file F is added and file D is deleted [Fig. 10-4(c)], and file A is deleted and G is added [Fig. 10-4(d)]. It is seen that as time progresses a number of small unused areas appear that could be used to store only very small files. Therefore, a large file may be refused storage even though the total unused space is large enough to hold the file. As far as the large file is concerned, the unused areas are wasted space. The adjective **external** is used to describe this kind of fragmentation because the wasted space is external to the files in the system as opposed to being internal to them (which is the case for internal fragmentation).

When a file is to be added, the choice of which unused area to put it in should be such that the effects of external fragmentation are minimized. There are basically two algorithms for making this choice. They are the **first fit algorithm**, which puts the file in the first unused area that is found to be large enough, and the **best fit algorithm**, which chooses the smallest unused area that is large enough to contain the file. The first fit algorithm is faster because the search for an unused area may

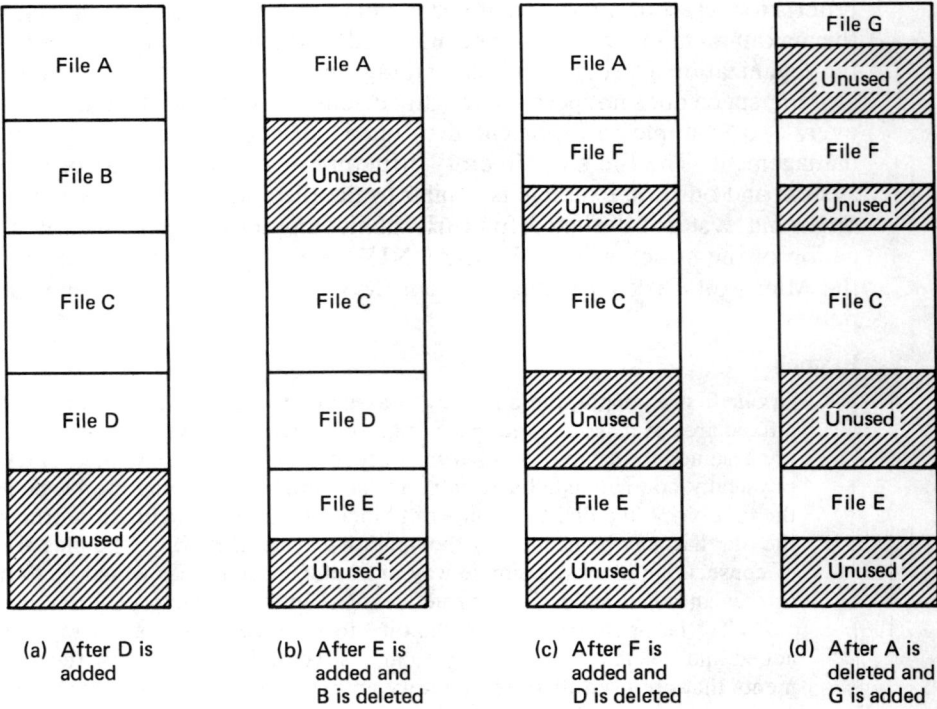

Figure 10-4 Development of external fragmentation.

cease when one that is large enough is found. It is also generally considered to be superior in reducing external fragmentation because the best fit algorithm tends to generate very small unused areas that are likely to remain "wasted space."

The ultimate solution to external fragmentation is **compaction** (or **garbage collection**). When a file is to be added, and it cannot fit into an existing unused area, the entire file structure could be compacted so that all files become contiguous and all unused areas are combined into one large area. The result of compacting the files in Fig. 10-4(d) is shown in Fig. 10-5. Although compaction must be done when a large enough space does not exist, it is a very time-consuming process that not only requires files to be moved but requires directory changes as well.

The file system in this example makes no distinction between users and therefore, provides no protection against unwanted usage of the file. It is primarily designed to fulfill the requirements of a system that is available to only a single user or a small group of users.

Example 2:

In this example, there may be several directories and they are treated as files. The files are logically structured in a treelike manner as shown in Fig. 10-6. At the top of the figure is a ROOT directory from which the remainder of the tree is derived. Within the ROOT directory there may be several files, some of which may be directories. Each of these directories may also contain directories and so on. Each file has a name and is associated with a path that extends from the ROOT directory to the file. All files in the path except the file of interest (i.e., the last file) must be a directory. The paths are also referred to by names, and these names consist of all of the names of the files in the path except for the name ROOT (which is implied because it must be in all paths). The names are listed in order and separated by slashes, e.g.,

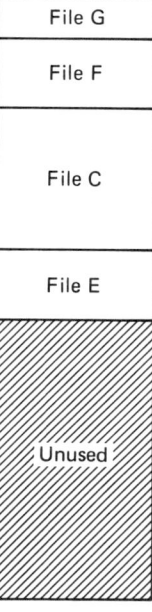

Figure 10-5 Compaction of the files in Figure 10-4(d).

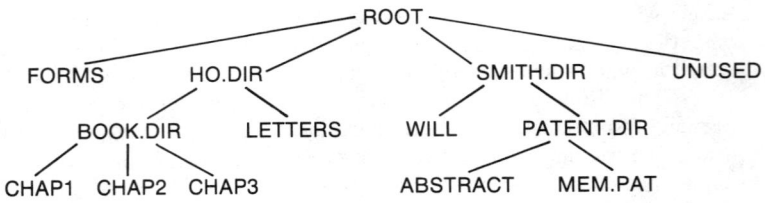

Figure 10-6 Example tree-like file structure.

/HO.DIR/BOOK.DIR/CHAP1

A file is always completely identified by its pathname (i.e., the operating system can always locate a file from its pathname).

Each file has associated with it a node and an entry in one of the directories in the tree. The directory entry contains the name of the file and a number that identifies the file's node. The node contains all of the descriptive information about the file that is needed by the operating system. In addition to the numbers of the file's blocks, the node may contain information such as the file's type and size, an indication of who may use the file and how they may use it, and a log of the file's recent usage. All of the nodes are contiguously stored in a set of fixed locations in mass storage and are organized in such a way that the operating system can easily compute the location of a node from the node's identifying number. The ROOT directory is also located in a fixed position that is known to the operating system. Therefore, given a pathname, the operating system can use the directory entries and nodes to thread through the directory structure until the node of the desired file is found. Then it can use this node to locate the blocks in the file.

For example, for the pathname

/HO.DIR/BOOK.DIR/CHAP1

the operating system could proceed as shown in Fig. 10-7. The ROOT directory would be scanned for the filename HO.DIR and then the corresponding node number would be used to access the node. From the contents of the node, HO.DIR could be retrieved and scanned for the BOOK.DIR entry, which would indicate the location of the node containing the block numbers of the blocks in BOOK.DIR. Finally, BOOK.DIR would be searched for the CHAP1 entry and this entry would point to the node from which the blocks in CHAP1 could be found.

Because some files contain a large number of blocks, it would be impractical to make the nodes, which are all the same size, large enough to include all of the block numbers for such files. This problem can be solved by having some of the block numbers in the node point to blocks that contain the remainder of the file's block numbers. UNIX, for example, provides for 13 block designations, with only the first 10 designating blocks in the file. The other three designate blocks for indirectly obtaining the remaining blocks in the file.

The log of unused areas is a linked list that is kept in a special file under the

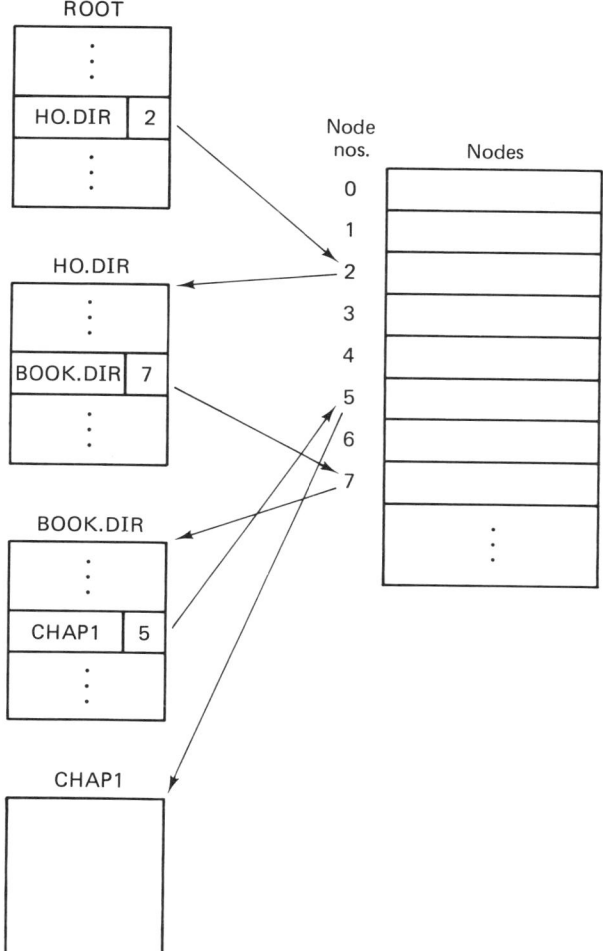

Figure 10-7 Following a path to find a file.

ROOT directory. For the primary mass storage unit, much, if not all, of this file would be maintained in memory while the system is running.

Except for clustering, the blocks in a file do not have to be contiguous, thus external fragmentation and the need for compaction are eliminated.

The principal advantages to the file structure in this example are the flexibility with which files can be added and deleted and the ability to subdivide files into protected groups. When creating a file, in addition to finding unused blocks in which to put the file, an unused node must be found and filled with the file's descriptive information and a directory entry must be posted in the proper directory. A file deletion would cause a node to become unused, an entry to be deleted from the directory containing the file, and entries to be added to the file of unused areas. Adding a file may call for the addition of a mass storage block to a directory, and the deletion of a file could conceivably cause a directory block to become unused.

However, for the latter, whether a directory block becomes unused would depend on the method for keeping order in the directories as files are dynamically added and deleted (see Exercise 11). An accounting of the unused nodes could be kept by simply marking the nodes not currently in use with a special pattern or by using a linked list (see Exercise 12).

A potential problem with a file structure such as the one in this example is the number of mass storage accesses that may be needed before a file is retrieved. In the example illustrated in Fig. 10-7, if no information were in memory when the search for CHAP1 begins, it would take at least five mass storage accesses to retrieve a block from CHAP1. The number of accesses would be even larger if one or more of the block numbers had to be obtained indirectly through the nodes or a directory were more than one block long. Fortunately, this problem is largely alleviated by storing some directory and node information in memory. Although it would require too much memory to store all of this information, by keeping the most recently used node and directory blocks in memory, the number of mass storage accesses could be reduced dramatically.

The treelike structure of this example allows users to not only create their own directories, but to also create their own file systems as subtrees of the overall tree. Because all references to a file must be made through the nodes in its path, protection from unwanted usage of the files can be provided by including protection information in the nodes. Typically, files are protected according to the category of the user and the type of access. Each file is assigned to a user, called the **owner** of the file, and a user group (which would include the owner). A file's protection may allow only the owner to access the file, allow only members of the owner's group to access the file, or allow anyone to use the file. Each category of user may be permitted different types of access, with the three possible types being read only, read/write, and execute only. For example, if a file is a program, it may be desirable to restrict program changes to the owner, but allow the owner's group to read or execute the program and anyone to execute the program.

The operating system must provide a means for setting protection bits in a node when a file is created and for changing these bits as the need arises. The owner of a file would be recorded in the node at the time the file is created and only the owner or the person who manages the system, sometimes called the **superuser**, would be permitted to set or change the file's protection bits.

Although the above discussion of two examples is incomplete, it should now be apparent that accounting for the space in a mass storage unit and dynamically updating a file structure as files are added, deleted, and changed is a nontrivial task. Simple file structures such as the one considered in the first example may be adequate for a single-user system, but do not provide the flexibility of creating multiple directories and the protection mechanisms of more complicated systems. They may also waste space and place restrictive limits on the number of entries in the directory, file lengths, and allocation of the mass storage space. In the second example, except for reserving specific space for nodes and the ROOT directory, complete freedom was allowed in allocating mass storage space and the only wasted space was due to the internal fragmentation within the final blocks (or clusters) of the files.

10-2 MAIN MEMORY MANAGEMENT

Although some of the overall concepts related to managing main memory are the same as those of mass storage, the management of main memory is significantly different. This difference is due to the way in which memory references are made and the fact that memory locations consisting of small groups of bits (usually 8-bit bytes) are referenced instead of blocks. Memory referencing is accomplished according to the addresses produced by the operand fields of the instructions, not by using block numbers (or their equivalent cylinder/track/sector designations) that must be sent to a mass storage interface. The directories required to manage and access mass storage are not needed.

A representative overall memory arrangement is shown in Fig. 10-8. The low part of memory is reserved for information needed by the operating system and normally contains the interrupt vectors and I/O-related information, and may include the stack used by the operating system. The operating system has been placed in the high part of memory. Adjacent to the operating system is an area for storing the I/O drivers that are needed by the programs currently residing in memory. Adjacent to these drivers is the area reserved for the buffers needed to buffer data between the executing program and the I/O and mass storage components of the system. The system and operating system areas are fixed in size, but the I/O driver and buffer areas may expand or recede according to the current demands on the system. The remainder of the memory is the user area.

Figure 10-9 shows a single program in the user area. The program consists of data areas interspersed with code areas that contain the main program and procedures. The data areas would be allocated according to VAR statements if the source program were written in Pascal or allocation directives if an assembler

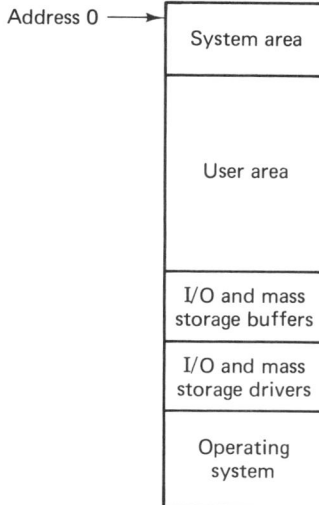

Figure 10-8 Representative allocation of main memory.

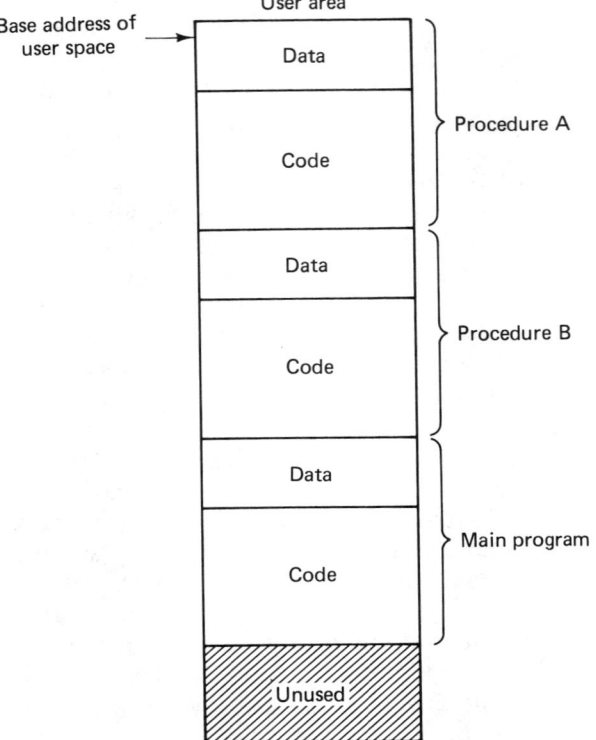

Figure 10-9 Organization of a typical program.

were used. If only one program is to be in memory at any given time and there is enough space to accommodate the program, very little memory management would be needed. A command to the operating system would cause the program to be loaded and the program would cause the operating system to retrieve the I/O drivers and reserve buffer areas as required.

Referencing in a single-program system is done by simply using the addresses supplied by instructions. However, if a program were compiled or assembled assuming that it is to start at Address 0, when the program is loaded, the base address of the user space would be used as the relocation factor and would be added to all of the relocatable addresses in the program. References to the operating system area are most likely absolute addresses and references to the I/O driver and buffer areas are made indirectly through the operating system.

Protection within main memory is to guard against accidental or unwanted accesses between

- User programs.
- The code and data sections within a user program.
- User programs and the operating system.

The first prevents a user program from interfering with other user programs and,

400   Memory Management   Chap. 10

obviously, such protection is not applicable to single-program systems. The second type of protection prevents code from being treated as data or data from being executed as code. The former can be disastrous if data are mistakenly written over a section of code. The latter can occur when a branch is accidentally taken into a data area (an error that is quite common if there is no protection against it). Small systems frequently do not provide such protection. But, because almost all processing elements, including microprocessors, output signals to distinguish between an instruction fetch and a data access, this type of protection could be built into most systems by separating the memory into a code memory and a data memory, each having its own address space. Other methods for affording this type of protection are considered later.

A means of protecting an operating system from a user program is often provided even in small systems. It can be implemented as shown in Fig. 10-10 by including a pair of limit registers that contain the lowest and highest possible addresses in the user's program. Addresses output by the user program are automatically compared to the limits, and addresses outside the limits are not normally passed on to memory but cause an internal interrupt. As introduced in Chap. 6, an internal interrupt is like an external interrupt in that it causes the interrupt sequence to be executed and an interrupt routine to be entered. The type of internal interrupt determines the beginning address of the interrupt vector or, perhaps, the interrupt routine. In the case at hand, the interrupt is a limits violation

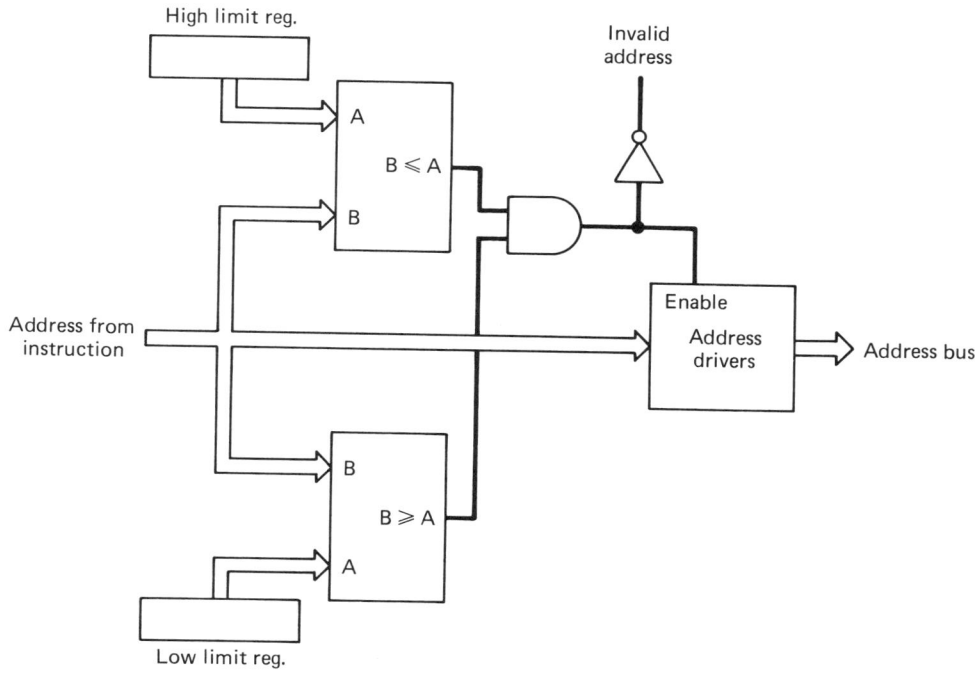

Figure 10-10 Implementation of limit registers.

interrupt and the interrupt routine, which is part of the operating system, would determine the action taken following a limits violation.

Because a user's program may need to employ some of the operating system's facilities (e.g., use the I/O drivers and buffers), exceptions must be allowed. The most common exception is to allow branches due to any type of interrupt, including software interrupts, to be to a point outside the limits. A software interrupt is simply a special instruction that causes the interrupt sequence to be initiated and an interrupt-type branch to be made to an address specified by the instruction. The branch is normally to a point within the operating system. If only interrupts can be used to enter the operating system, then all calls to the operating system would be made via software interrupts and subprogram calls could not be used for this purpose. This protection measure would make unintentional entry into the operating system highly unlikely.

Once an operating system has been entered, it must have complete control over all of memory. Therefore, a processing element would have two modes associated with it: a user mode and a supervisor mode. A mode could be indicated by a bit in the PSW that would automatically be set to 1 (indicating the supervisor mode) when the operating system is entered and cleared to 0 (indicating the user mode) when the operating system transfers control back to the user's program. Also, specific instructions that allow the mode bit to be set or cleared could be included in the instruction set.

In addition to restricting the accessible memory areas available to a user program, a mode may restrict the instructions that can be executed. There may be a substantial subset of instructions, called **privileged instructions**, that are allowed to be executed only when the processing element is in its supervisor mode. Because, in a general purpose computer, I/O is normally done by the operating system, many privileged instructions are related to I/O. Figure 10-11 depicts transfer between modes. The concept of having modes and privileged instructions is explored further in Sec. 10-3 and Chap. 11.

A slightly more sophisticated operating system would allow two programs to be in memory at the same time. Space permitting, the two programs could be placed one after the other in the user area. Such operating systems are called **foreground/background systems** and were used extensively by earlier minicomputers. They were primarily designed to allow a user to execute a program such as a text editor in the foreground, while a second, noninteractive program runs

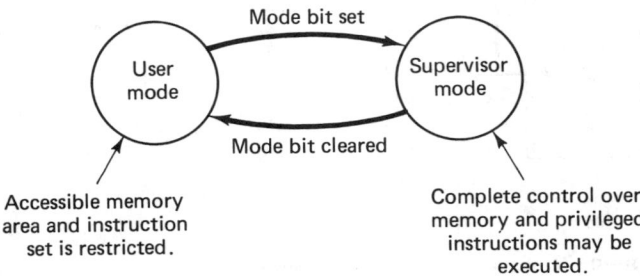

Figure 10-11 User and supervisor modes.

in the background. The background program executes whenever the foreground program is waiting for I/O (e.g., is waiting for a user to strike a key). As with single-program systems, if there is enough space to store both programs in memory the amount of memory management is minimal.

Referencing is done as in the single-program case, by simply using instruction addresses; but, when the second program is loaded, the relocation factor is the address immediately following the first program. Protection between the two programs could be provided by limit registers. A switch from one program to the other is done by the operating system (see Chap. 11) and the limit registers could be set during the switch according to the limits of the program that is to begin executing.

The reason for keeping two programs in memory at the same time is to utilize a system's processing element better by allowing the background program to execute while the foreground program is waiting for I/O. For large computers with expensive processing elements, the need to utilize the processing elements fully is even more pronounced. To accomplish this complete usage, multiprogramming operating systems capable of simultaneously managing several programs are used. As the number of programs that are concurrently in memory increases, there is a corresponding increase in the memory management that is needed. Multiprogramming systems must constantly juggle the various parts of the programs in and out of memory as they are being executed.

With the shuffling of programs in and out of memory, the same problems begin to arise in allocating main memory as those that were encountered in allocating file space in mass storage. Figure 10-12 shows what can happen as several programs are loaded, allowed to run until they are completed, and then replaced with other programs. Programs A, B, C, and D are loaded in order and the memory is allocated as shown in Fig. 10-12(a). Program E is then loaded and program B completes its execution. Memory is now utilized as shown in Fig. 10-12(b). Program F is then loaded and the execution of program D is completed [Fig. 10-12(c)]; finally, program A is completed and program G is loaded [Fig. 10-12(d)]. By comparing Figs. 10-4 and 10-12 it is apparent that external fragmentation develops in main memory while multiprogramming is in effect in the same way that it develops in mass storage as files are added and deleted. Also, the accounting for unused space becomes as necessary and complex as when working with mass storage.

Referencing may still be done by simply using the addresses supplied by instructions, but each time a program is loaded into memory, relocatable addresses must be adjusted according to the program's location. Although the example in Fig. 10-12 implies that once a program is loaded it remains in memory until its execution is complete, this is not normally the case. Most multiprogramming operating systems manage programs on a timeshared and/or priority basis. If a program is not due to run or has a low priority, it may temporarily be swapped out to mass storage and reloaded later. Each time a program is loaded it must have its relocatable addresses set according to the position in which it is to be placed. It is clear that as the loading of programs increases, so does the need to make the adjustment of addresses more efficient.

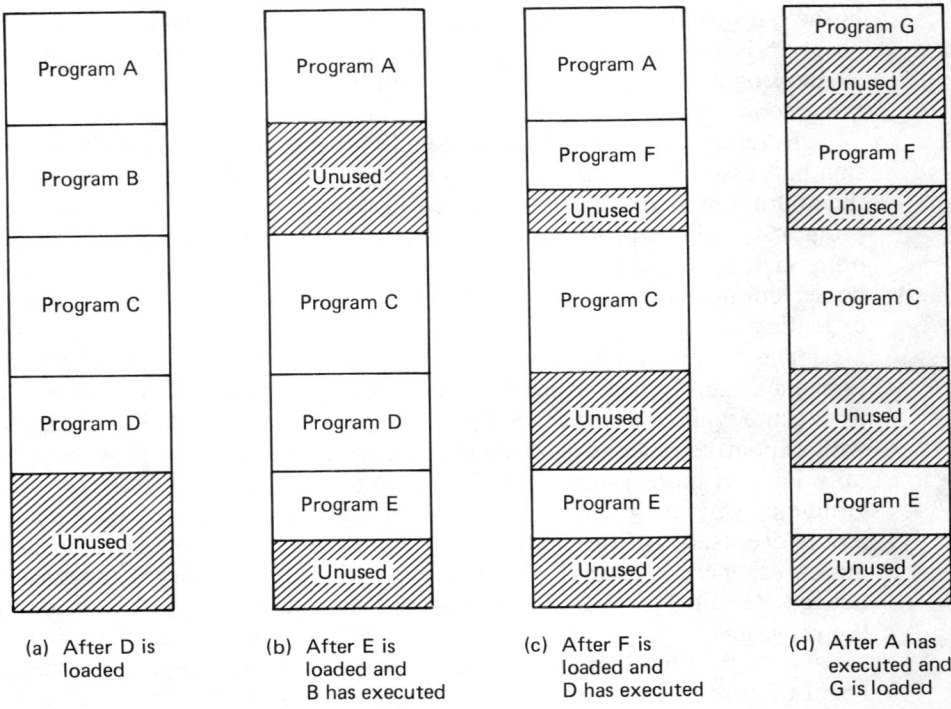

Figure 10-12 External fragmentation in a multiprogramming system.

It was indicated in Chap. 5 that the primary means of reducing the number of relocatable addresses is to use relative addressing. This approach could be facilitated by including in the processing element a program base register as shown in Fig. 10-13. When a program is loaded the operating system would also load the program base register with the program's beginning address. While the program is executing all branch addresses internal to the program and all data addresses other than system stack references would be added to the program base register. This process would allow a program that is compiled or assembled as if it were to be loaded at Address 0 to be put anywhere in memory without its internal references being changed.

In the above discussion it has been tacitly assumed that programs are loaded into contiguous areas of memory. By eliminating this restriction programs could

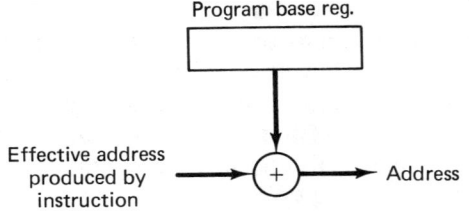

Figure 10-13 Use of a program base register.

be broken into parts which could fit into smaller unused areas, thereby reducing external fragmentation. This reduction is important in large computers that tend to run large programs. As the average size of a program increases it becomes more difficult to find sufficiently large unused areas, and working with programs as contiguous units can be very wasteful in terms of memory space. However, there are problems in allowing programs to be broken into pieces. Referencing is complicated by the fact that there must be a relocation factor for each piece and address adjustment becomes somewhat more complex. One solution is to include in the processing element more than one base register such as the program base register illustrated in Fig. 10-13.

For example, a typical processing element might contain four base registers, thereby allowing a program to be divided into four parts. One of the base registers could be dedicated to referencing a code area, another to a stack area, and two to nonstack data areas. Branch addresses could be added to the code base register, stack addresses to the stack base register, and nonstack data addresses to one of the data base registers. The program could then be divided into a code section, stack section, and two data sections. The base registers would need to be filled either by the operating system or by the code at the beginning of the program.

It is possible to combine the usage of base registers and limit registers by letting the lower limit register and the base register be the same. The second register could contain either the upper limit or the size of the area. When this combination strategy is used the area is called a **segment**. Extending the above example, a program could be divided into four segments, a code segment, a stack segment, and two data segments. Branches within the program could be made only to points within the code segment, stack accesses could be made only to the stack segment, and data accesses could reference only the data segments. All branches and data accesses would be made relative to the appropriate base (lower limit) registers. The base and upper limit registers would restrict all accesses to the currently executing program and thereby, provide protection between user programs and between the current user program and the operating system.

It is evident that as the activities of more and more programs or, perhaps, program segments must be monitored and supervised, an increasing burden is placed on the processing element and operating system. Therefore, there may come a point at which separate facilities are needed for managing memory, improving flexibility in making references, and providing the required protection.

10-3 MEMORY MANAGEMENT HARDWARE AND VIRTUAL MEMORY

Large multiprogramming systems normally include a Memory Management Unit (MMU) between the processing element and the address bus that supplies addresses to main memory. The placement of such a unit is shown in Fig. 10-14. The task of allocating memory space is still done by the operating system, but the MMU is designed to improve referencing and provide the protection mechanisms required on large computers.

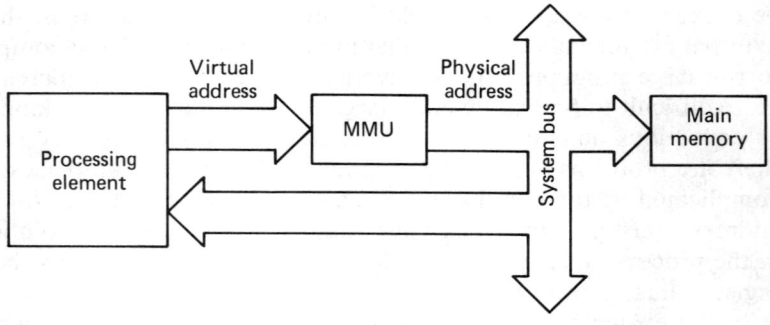

Figure 10-14 Placement of an MMU.

Improved referencing is attained by giving the MMU the ability to translate the **virtual addresses** output by the processing element (which are convenient to the program creation and loading processes) into the physical addresses used by memory interfaces. Not only does this translation allow the addresses used by a program to be independent from the actual memory addresses, but it also allows the virtual address space to be larger than the physical space. The advantage in having a large virtual space is that numerous load units, some of which may be quite large, can be prepared as if they are all to occupy space in a large virtual memory simultaneously. The fact that not all programs are actually in physical memory is compensated for by the MMU and operating system. If a switch is made to a program that is not in memory or a reference is made to a part of the currently executing program that is not in memory, a **memory fault** is said to occur. When a memory fault occurs the MMU causes the processing element to be interrupted and the needed program, or part of the program, to be transferred from mass storage into memory. As shown in Fig. 10-15, the transfer would be conducted by an interrupt routine that is part of the operating system.

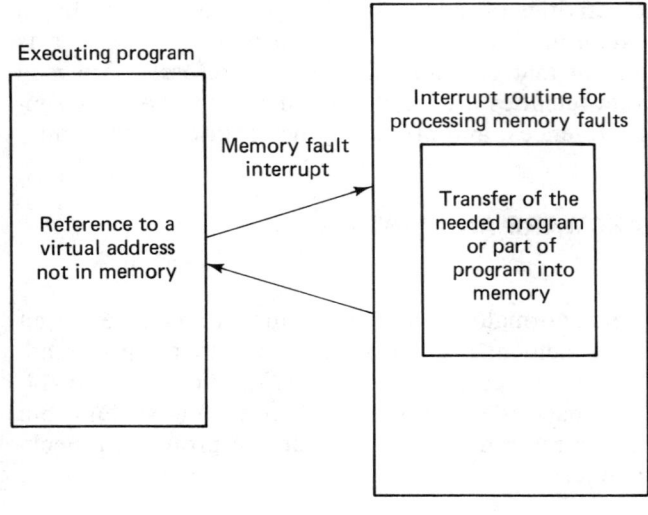

Figure 10-15 Processing a memory fault.

There are two quite different philosophies in designing MMUs, paging and segmentation. As seen in the subsection below, they fundamentally differ in the way they subdivide memory into parts.

10-3-1 Paging

Paging treats the virtual address space as if it were divided into subsets which have equal length and fixed boundaries. Both the subsets and the information contained in them are referred to as **pages**. The length of the pages is a power of 2 so that the high order bits in a virtual address indicate the page and the low order bits indicate the offset within the page. Pages are assigned to programs as a whole, and cannot be assigned to different programs at the same time. In this respect, the allocation of pages to programs is similar to the allocation of blocks to files, and memory space may be wasted due to internal fragmentation. The amount of wasted space is a function of page length and program length just as wasted mass storage space is a function of block length and file length (see Sec. 10-1). On the other hand, the MMU and operating system are designed so that the pages assigned to a program are not necessarily contiguous and external fragmentation is not a problem.

Physical memory is also divided into parts of equal length, called **page frames**, and the length of a page frame is the same as that of a page. It is the MMU's job to provide the necessary translation between pages and page frames. A representative breakdown of a virtual address space into pages and the physical memory into page frames is given in Fig. 10-16. This example assumes a page

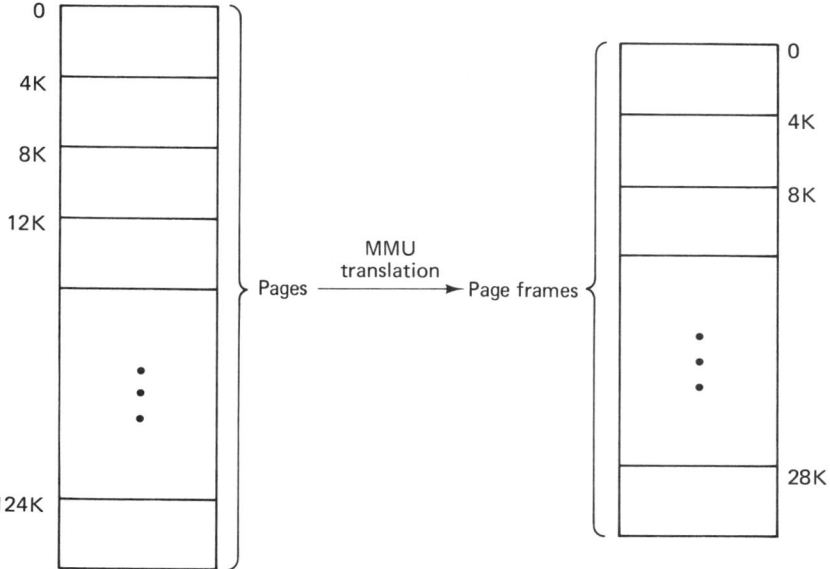

Figure 10-16 Representative virtual and physical address spaces in a paged system.

and page frame length of 4K and therefore, all pages and page frames begin on boundaries divisible by 4K. Note that the virtual address space is larger than the physical address space. There are 32 pages, but only 8 page frames.

The heart of the MMU in a paged system is the **page table**, which provides the address translation. The translation is done as shown in Fig. 10-17(a). An instruction in the currently executing program may use any of its addressing modes to construct a virtual address. The high order bits in the address index an entry in the page table and this entry provides a page frame number that gives the high order bits of the physical address. The low order bits in the physical address are the same as the low order bits in the virtual address. For the example given in Fig. 10-16, the page field in the virtual address is 5 bits long, the page table provides a 3-bit page frame field, and there is a 12-bit offset.

The format of a page table entry is shown in Fig. 10-17(b). All of the pages are stored in mass storage but, because there are more pages than page frames,

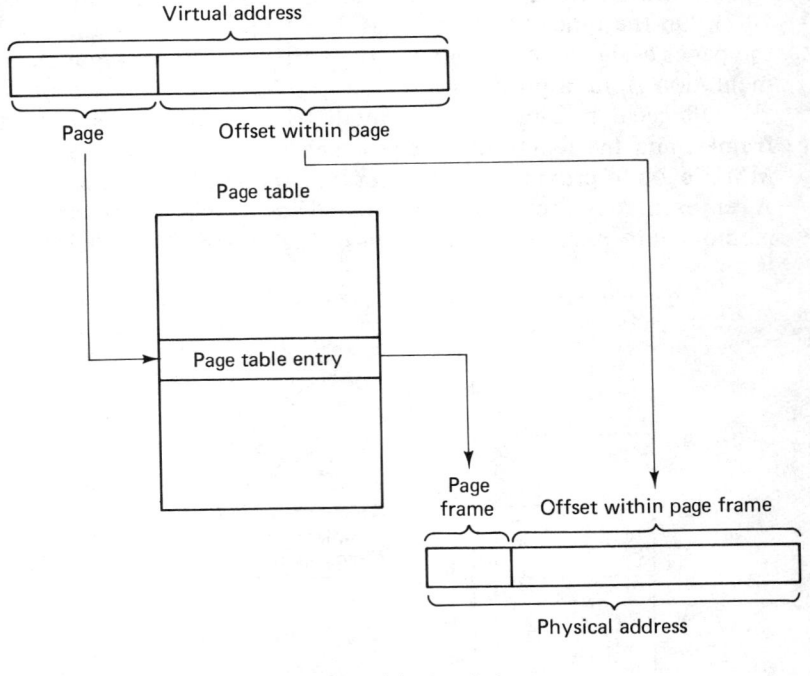

Figure 10-17 MMU translation in a paged system.

408 Memory Management Chap. 10

a page may not be in memory. If a page that is not in memory is referenced, a **page fault**, which is a form of memory fault, occurs. The page fault interrupt routine determines where in memory the page is to be put and then brings the page in from mass storage. The **presence bit** in a page table entry indicates whether the page is in memory. If it is not, the mass storage block number field specifies where it is stored and is used by the page fault interrupt routine to retrieve the page. If the page is in memory, the page frame field gives the page frame number that specifies its beginning physical memory address. The **dirty bit** indicates whether a page that is in memory has been changed since it was input. If the page frame occupied by a page is later needed by another page, it is necessary to output the page currently in memory to mass storage only if it has been changed; otherwise the original copy that is already in mass storage will suffice and the page fault routine will not need to perform a write to mass storage. For example, a page containing only code would not be changed and its dirty bit would always be 0.

When a page fault occurs the page fault routine has the task of determining which page frame in memory is to be used and then bringing in the page. As usual, an accounting of the unused memory space (i.e., unused page frames) must be maintained. If there are unused frames at the time a fault occurs, the fault routine merely selects an unused frame; but, if there is no unused frame, a page frame must be replaced. This replacement means that the page fault routine must include a replacement algorithm. The most commonly used replacement algorithm is the LRU algorithm introduced in the discussion of cache memory in Sec. 9-4. As with the replacement of lines in cache memory, the assumption is that the least recently used page is the one that is most likely not to be needed in the near future. Several other algorithms and modified forms of the LRU algorithm are also used but space does not permit a discussion of them here—see Tanenbaum [1] or Stone [2]. A flowchart summarizing a page fault routine's activity is given in Fig. 10-18.

The above discussion has assumed **demand paging**, which means that a page is not brought into memory until it is referenced. When a program first begins, none of its pages are in memory and there are numerous faults; but, as a program executes, it tends to cause fewer and fewer faults because most of its pages are already in memory. However, in a multiprogramming system there may not be enough page frames to store all of the programs simultaneously, and a program switch may cause a transient effect that includes several faults. In a timesharing system in which programs take turns, the next program to be executed may not have any of its pages in memory. If the total space needed by all programs is substantially larger than the existing memory, then each time there is a program switch, the new program may have to be completely reloaded and very little of the program's time slice would be left to execute the program's instructions. This and other cyclic situations can cause **thrashing**, which results anytime the pages being referenced are usually not in memory.

If P_h is the probability that the page being referenced is in memory (there is a page hit), t_h the time it takes to reference memory, and t_m the time it takes to retrieve a page from mass storage, then $1 - P_h$ is the probability that the page

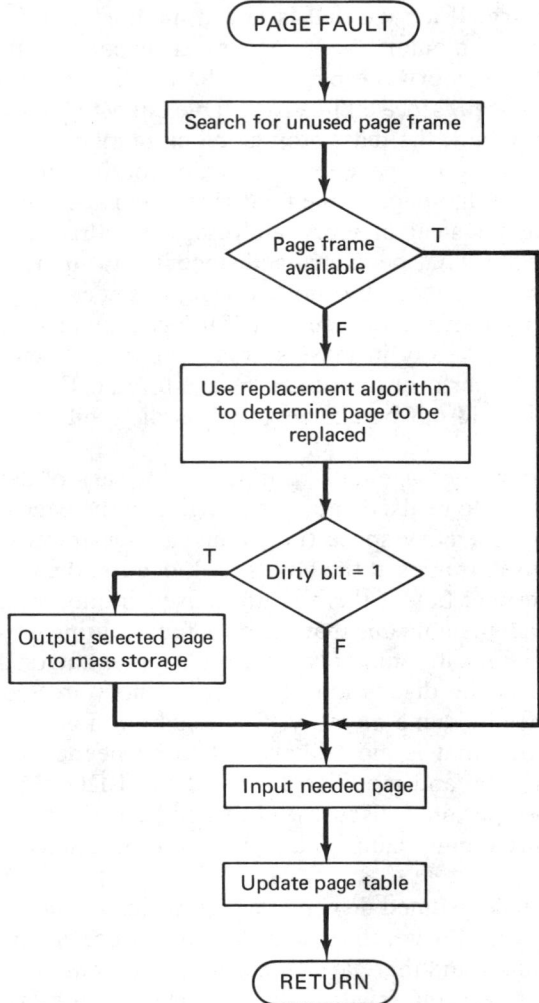

Figure 10-18 Flowchart of a page fault routine's activity.

is not in memory (there is a page miss) and the average reference time is

$$P_h t_h + (1 - P_h)(t_h + t_m) = -t_m P_h + t_h + t_m$$

This expression is a linear function of P_h that goes to t_h as P_h goes to 1, and goes to $t_h + t_m$ as P_h goes to 0. The time t_m is normally 10,000 to 200,000 times t_h. Thrashing occurs when a combination of the limited number of page frames and the sizes and other properties of the programs being run causes a sharp decline in P_h so that it approaches 0.

One way of avoiding thrashing is to not use demand paging, but to anticipate which pages will be needed next and, if they are not in memory, input them from mass storage in advance. This is not always possible, but for timesharing or other processing for which the order of page usage is predictable, it may be at least partially effective. A tradeoff arises because, if an anticipated page is input and then not used, the input effort is wasted and a page to be used in the near future may have been replaced. The tradeoff hinges on the probability that the anticipated page will be used. The question is: When it is known that a program is to be restarted, which of the program's pages should be input in advance? As a program proceeds, a record could be kept of the pages that it has used in the most recent k references. The resulting set of pages is called a **working set** and is a function of both k and time. (Note that k references may refer to $i \leq k$ pages.) The assumption is that, when a program is to be restarted, the pages it will need will be those it has most recently used, and so the pages to be brought in would be those in the working set. The MMU would be responsible for recording a working set for currently executing programs, and the operating system would store and retrieve working sets during program switches. The larger the value of k, the greater the number of pages to be input in advance and the fewer the number of page faults as programs restart. Unfortunately, as the sizes of working sets increase, so does the amount and complexity of MMU hardware. Using DMA, the working set for the next program can be brought in while the current program is executing. But, if a working set is too large, several pages that will not be used may be brought in and their input may have a significant adverse effect on system bus traffic.

Whether demand paging or the working set concept is used in retrieving pages, it is clear that if the locality of reference is small, the number of page faults will be correspondingly small as well. A small locality of reference implies that over relatively long periods of time only a few pages will be required or, from another standpoint, the working set will be relatively static.

The other major task assigned to the MMU is to provide protection. On a system that is paged, this protection may be somewhat limited because the page frames used by a program change dynamically and may be scattered throughout memory. Limit registers are not applicable to this situation but, because page frames are permanently assigned regions of memory, it is possible to use keys as a means of protecting these regions. This alternative could be implemented by extending each page table entry to include a protection key and assigning each program a protection key value. While a user's program is executing, each time a reference is made the program's assigned value is compared to the protection key in the referenced page table entry. If they do not match, a protection violation is detected and an interrupt signal is sent to the processing element. When a page fault occurs and a page table entry is added or replaced, the protection value associated with the new page is put into the new entry's protection key field.

The operating system, which must have access to all of memory, would be given a special value (e.g., zero) and would not be restricted by protection key matching. Any time an assigned value is the special value, the reference would be allowed to proceed regardless of the value of the protection key.

Ideally, an MMU is constructed of a very fast technology and contains the entire page table and the logic for implementing the replacement algorithm and protection scheme. A fast technology is required because every memory reference is delayed by the amount of time it takes for the MMU to do its work. Because the page table must be accessed with each reference, it is highly desirable that it be completely contained in the MMU and consist of a set of registers with a very fast access mechanism, e.g., a set that can be controlled by a decoder (see Sec. 7-1). But this is practical only if the number of page frames is relatively small. A large computer may contain over one hundred thousand page frames, in which case the amount of logic needed to implement the entire page table in the MMU would be unreasonably large.

Most large systems keep the entire page table in main memory but, to avoid two memory accesses with each reference, include a fast cache memory, called a **Translation Lookaside Buffer (TLB)**, in the MMU. The TLB is designed as discussed in Sec. 9-4 and may be fully associative. A memory reference is then performed as shown in Fig. 10-19. For each reference it is determined whether the needed page entry is in the TLB and, if it is, the reference proceeds as usual. Otherwise, the entry must be retrieved from the page table in main memory before

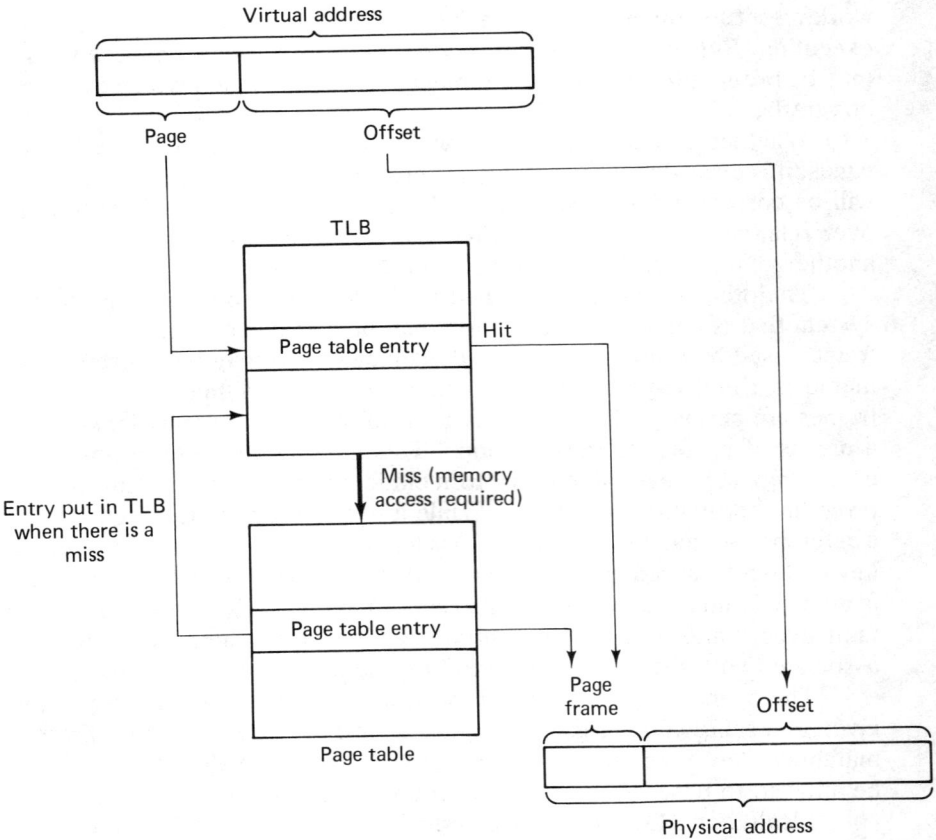

Figure 10-19 Use of a TLB.

the reference can be completed. To keep the most recently used table entries in the TLB, an entry that is brought in from main memory is also put into the TLB.

One important advantage of paging is that it is transparent to the user programmer. Paging is a service provided by the MMU and operating system and the user programmer does not even need to know of its existence. It will be reflected in the execution time of a program because the MMU will increase the main memory access time and the page faults will increase the average reference times and the amount of operating system overhead. The magnitudes of these increases depend on the frequency of the page faults and whether thrashing occurs.

10-3-2 Segmentation

The main drawback to paging is that pages bear no relationship to the logical divisions of programs, i.e., the procedures and the data and stack areas associated with the procedures. Pages, like blocks of mass storage, are simply units that can be easily manipulated in and out of a memory element. Segmentation, which was introduced with the definition of a segment in Sec. 10-2, solves this problem by dividing programs precisely along their logical boundaries. This division allows procedures, data areas, and stacks to be allocated memory areas as units and to be individually protected.

In a segmented system, addresses are in two parts, just as they are with paging. As shown in Fig. 10-20(a), one part is the index to the entry in a segment table that provides the beginning address of the segment, and the other part is the offset within the segment. The segment's beginning address is added to the offset to produce the physical address. Although Fig. 10-20(a) has somewhat the same appearance as Fig. 10-17(a) (the figure that describes the address translation for paging), segmentation is quite different from paging. The difference is revealed by comparing the format of a segment table entry, which is given in Fig. 10-20(b), to that of the page table entry provided in Fig. 10-17(b). Both formats include a presence bit and a dirty bit, but the segment table entry contains a beginning address that is added to the offset instead of a page frame number that is concatenated with the offset. In addition, a segment table entry contains a size, segment type, and set of protection bits that are not present in the page table entry.

Together, the beginning address and size specify the limits of a segment. Each segment can be viewed as having its own address space with the address within the space being specified by the offset. The addresses extend from 0 to the size of the segment minus 1. Thus, segmentation includes two-dimensional addressing, with the segment number indicating the address space and the offset indicating the relative address within the space. If, for a given segment, an offset is greater than or equal to the designated size, then there is a **segment limit fault** and an interrupt occurs.

Protection bits permit various kinds of protection to be assigned to each segment. The protection classifications most often used are for allowing or not allowing reading, writing, or executing. For example, one data segment may be protected so that it can only be read from and a second may be protected so that it can only be written into, and a code segment may allow only instruction fetches.

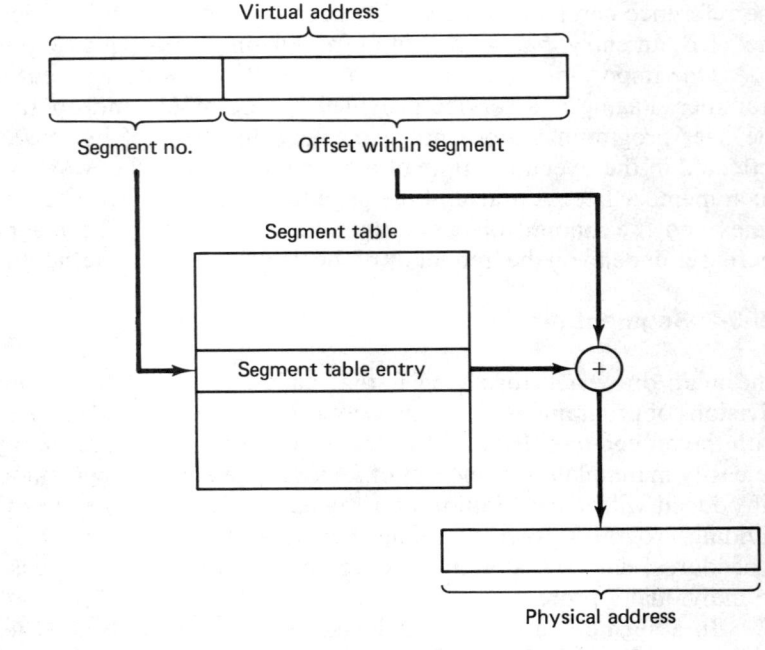

(a) Translation

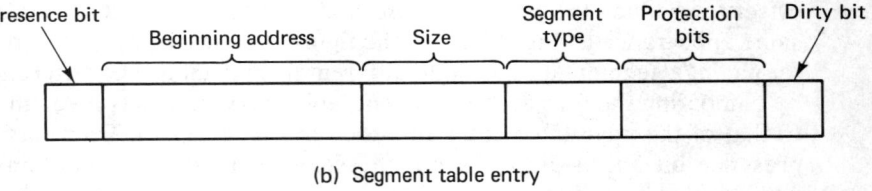

(b) Segment table entry

Figure 10-20 Translation and protection under segmentation.

In addition to being explicitly specified by protection bits, protection may implicitly depend on the segment type or whether the processing element is in its supervisor or user mode. Protection keys, such as those introduced in the discussion of paging, could be included to protect programs as a whole. With regard to protection however, the primary advantage of segmentation is the ability to isolate and protect the individual, logical parts of a program. With paging there is no reason for protecting individual pages because pages have no logical meaning.

Presence and dirty bits have the same meanings as described in the discussion of paging. When a referenced segment is not in memory, a **segment fault** occurs and the operating system inputs the segment from mass storage. Because a segment may occupy several noncontiguous blocks of mass storage, the locations of these blocks are kept by the operating system as opposed to being stored in a segment table entry.

From the above discussion it is seen that there are three types of interrupts associated with segmentation. They are due to:

- The upper address of a segment being exceeded.
- A protection violation.
- A segment fault.

Because segment sizes are variable, there is no internal fragmentation. But, for the same reason, there is external fragmentation and all of the problems associated with external fragmentation are present. Unused areas in physical memory must be noted by size as well as position. The segment fault routine would be responsible for maintaining the list of unused areas and allocating memory, and would include the algorithms for selecting unused memory areas and supervising replacements.

A segment table tends to be much smaller than a page table because the average length of a segment is usually much greater than the length of a page. It may be that only the segment information for the currently executing program is kept in the segment table in the MMU and the operating system may reload the segment table each time there is a program switch. One popular processing element, the Intel 80286, allows for only four segments at any given time and the equivalent of the segment table is contained in the processing element—see Liu and Gibson [3].

If segment entries are changed each time there is a program switch, it is useful to organize the segment entries so that each program has its own segment table. However, there is nothing to prevent two or more segment entries from pointing to the same segment, thus making it possible for programs to share segments. Figure 10-21 shows how three programs could have their private segments but yet be able to use some segments that are global in nature. This capability

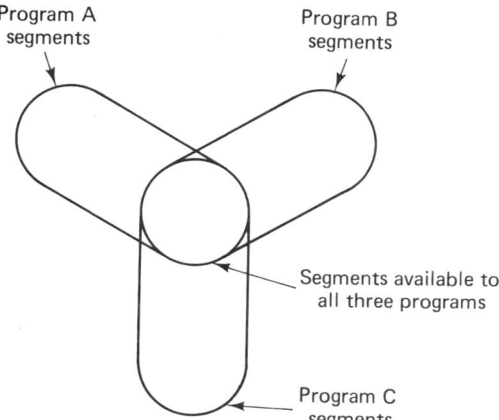

Figure 10-21 Shared segments.

allows important data and code segments, which may be used by a variety of programs, to be accessed by more than one program.

Associated with each program must be a set of information that provides for locating all of the program's segments and for the protection of those segments. For a user to have control over the assignment of protection and the use of a program's segments, some of this information would need to be supplied during a program's creation. While a program is being prepared to be recognized by the operating system as a **currently accessible** program (i.e., as a program that can share the use of the processing element), the operating system must put some of this information into main memory and the MMU. In particular, a segment table entry would need to be made for each segment in the program or a means would have to be provided for adding segment table entries as they are required. In addition, the segment fault interrupt routine would have to be given the location of the segments so that they could be brought in from mass storage as they are requested. Once all of a program's segment information has been properly situated, the operating system can freely access any part of the program. (How segment information is introduced to the operating system is discussed further in Chap. 11.)

Although the user must be conscious of the fact that segmentation is being used, the fact that the user must participate in the subdivision and protection associated with the segments gives the user some control over how memory is managed. This participation is often of value when optimizing the use of some programs or of the system as a whole. Some of the programming advantages to using segments are:

- The operating system can dynamically change the size of a segment while a program is executing.
- Because segments use a form of base addressing, a code segment may be added or changed without reassembling or recompiling an entire program. Also, linking is replaced by a process that structures the segment information.
- Both code and data segments can be easily shared by several programs.
- The programmer has a means of protecting the segments of a program from unwarranted use, either by other programs or by its own code segments.

10-3-3 Paging Versus Segmentation

Both paging and segmentation permit the virtual address space to be larger than the number of locations in the physical memory. Paging is done by using pages of information of fixed length that fit exactly into fixed partitions of physical memory. Because pages can be worked with as units, they can be easily manipulated. Handling the pages can be done by the MMU and operating system and is not of concern to the user programmer. Paging introduces internal fragmentation but eliminates external fragmentation. A large system may require a very large page table, some of which may have to be stored in main memory or mass storage.

On the other hand, segmentation works with the logical subdivision of programs and accommodates two-dimensional addressing by giving each segment its own address space. The resulting form of addressing complicates referencing (addition must be used instead of concatenation to form a physical address) and the allocation of available memory space, but allows for sophisticated protection of the logical segments. Internal fragmentation is eliminated, but external fragmentation is introduced. Segment tables tend to be much smaller than page tables and can be entirely contained in an MMU or, perhaps, in the processing element. In contrast, segments are larger than pages. For this reason, there are fewer segment faults than page faults, but bringing a segment in from mass storage may require several accesses (see Exercise 25) and replacement may be more complicated.

Some large systems are designed to use both paging and segmentation and thereby, take advantage of the good points of both approaches. These systems basically use segmentation so that logical segments can be maintained as separate entities, but then they break logical segments into pages so that blocks of information can be manipulated as units.

The translation process of a combined paging and segmentation system is given in Fig. 10-22. It includes a set of page tables as well as a segment table. Each segment would have a page table associated with it and a program's page tables may be kept in mass storage. A virtual address consists of a segment number, page number, and offset. The segment number indexes an entry in the segment table that indicates the protection of the segment and supplies the segment's page table number. The page number indexes an entry in the segment's page table, and this entry supplies a page frame number that is concatenated with the offset to form the physical address.

Because it is necessary to make two references (one to the segment table and one to the page table) before accessing the required data, it is apparent that the price of the flexibility gained by combining paging and segmentation is a significant increase in access time. Also, if either the required page table or page is not immediately available, a fault occurs and the page table or page must be loaded from the appropriate memory elements. Therefore, frequently changing either the segments or the locality of reference could cause thrashing and have dire consequences.

10-3-4 Memory Management Remarks

Although memory management increases the amount of circuitry and access times, its associated versatility is sorely needed in large multiuser systems. Both paging and segmentation allow a program to use more main memory than is actually present in a system. When a part of a program is needed that is not currently in main memory, a fault routine simply brings it in and then causes the program to continue executing. Segmentation has the advantage that it divides a program along its logical boundaries and thereby permits protection of each of a program's logical parts, but requires the programmer to become involved with segmentation decisions. Paging, on the other hand, is handled automatically by the operating system and is not the programmer's concern.

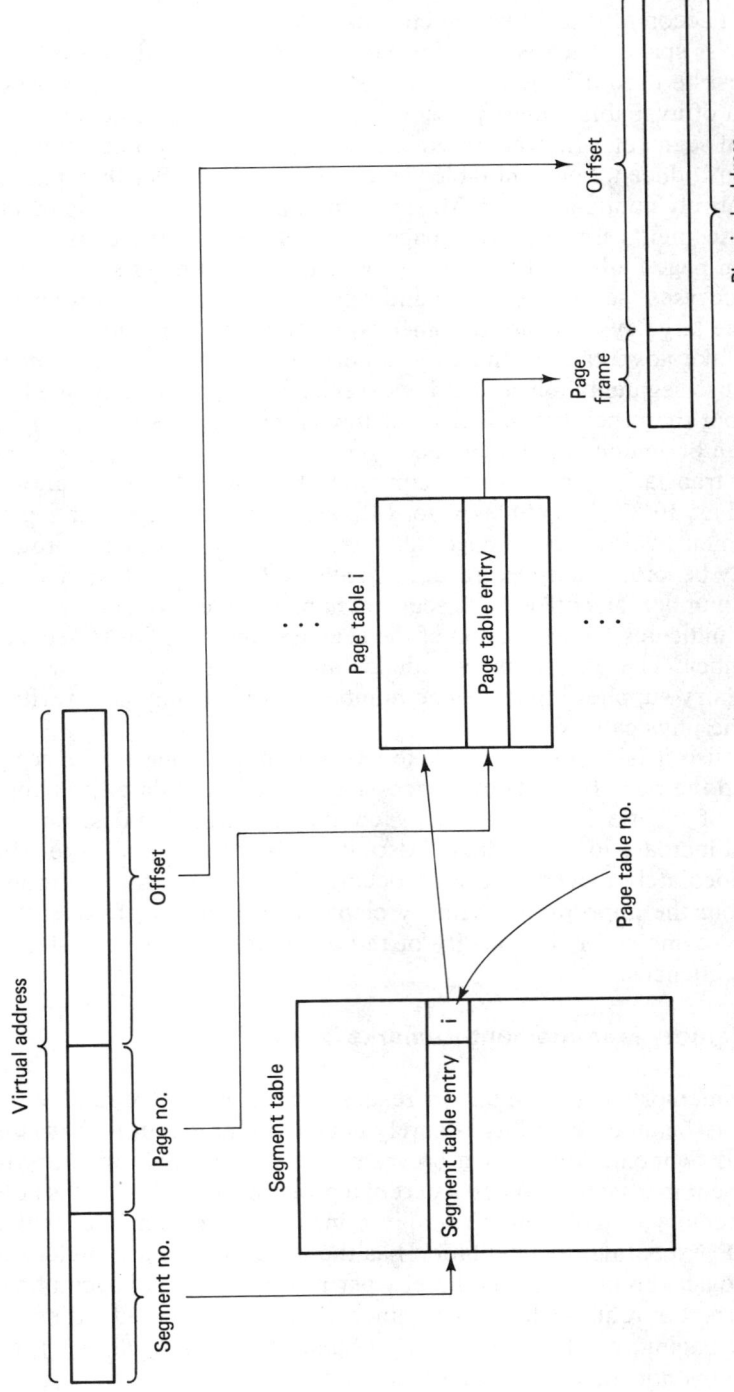

Figure 10-22 Translation in a combined paging and segmentation system.

Memory management involves not only the allocation of the available memory but also the movement of information from one memory element to another. It is desirable to remove the programmer from the memory management task as much as possible, but yet provide him or her with control over some aspects of memory management. It is essential that the overall memory management facility operates smoothly and with as little effort as possible, even though the vastly different timing requirements of the various types of memory elements make this task difficult. A good facility includes good hardware support and a well written operating system that makes maximum use of that support.

REFERENCES

1. Tanenbaum, Andrew S., *Structured Computer Organization*, 2nd ed. (Englewood Cliffs, N.J.: Prentice Hall, Inc., 1984).
2. Stone, Harold S., *High-Performance Computer Architecture*, 2nd ed. (Reading, Massachusetts: Addison-Wesley Publishing Company, 1990).
3. Liu, Yu-cheng, and Glenn A. Gibson, *Microcomputer Systems: The 8086/8088 Family*, 2nd ed. (Englewood Cliffs, N.J.: Prentice Hall, Inc., 1986).
4. Struble, George, *Assembler Language Programming: The IBM 360/370*, 3rd ed. (Reading, Massachusetts: Addison-Wesley Publishing Company, 1979).
5. Stallings, William, *Computer Organization and Architecture* (New York: Macmillan Publishing Company, 1987).
6. Peterson, James, and Abraham Silbershatz, *Operating Systems Concepts*, 2nd ed. (Reading, Massachusetts: Addison-Wesley Publishing Company, 1986).

EXERCISES

1. Draw a graph of the average fractional amount of wasted space in a file as a function of the average number of blocks in a file assuming a cluster size of 1; 2; 4.
2. Suppose that the length of a file (in blocks) may vary from 1 to 16 with each length being equally likely. What is the average fractional amount of wasted space in a file if the cluster size is 1? Is 2? Is 4?
3. Assume that unused blocks are noted as 0s in an array of 2^{16} bits. Write a set of pseudocode that will search out the number of unused blocks specified by BLOCKCOUNT and put the block numbers of the unused blocks in an array BLOCKNOS of halfwords. A block number is the same as its index within the bit array.
4. Write a set of pseudocode that, when a contiguous set of blocks in a file is deleted, will determine whether an entry in a linked list of unused areas must be changed or a new entry must be added. Assume that the block number of the first block is in BEGINAREA, the number of blocks is in AREASIZE, and FIRSTELEMENT contains the pointer to the first element in the linked list. ADDELEMENT is to be cleared to 0 if only a change is required and set to 1 if an element is to be added.

5. Extend the pseudocode in Exercise 4 to include the code needed to make the change or addition of the entry.
6. Modify the solution to Exercise 5 after assuming that a pointer to the last element in the linked list is kept in LASTELEMENT.
7. When using the file structure described in Example 1 of Sec. 10-1, the total space reserved for the directory may be exceeded even though the mass storage unit is not full. Discuss this problem and devise a means of extending the directory space when the need arises.
8. Assume an 80-block mass storage unit in which files are stored in contiguous blocks. Given the following file activity:

   File A (12 blocks) is added.
   File B (17 blocks) is added.
   File C (22 blocks) is added.
   File A is deleted.
   File D (20 blocks) is added.
   File E (10 blocks) is added.
   File B is deleted.
   File F (14 blocks) is added.
   File G (2 blocks) is added.
   File E is deleted.
   File H (4 blocks) is added.

   and that the first fit algorithm is used, show the assignment of mass storage during this activity (see Fig. 10-4).
9. Assume the best fit algorithm and repeat Exercise 8.
10. Why is the first fit algorithm generally considered better than the best fit algorithm?
11. Consider Example 2 in Sec. 10-1. Discuss the conditions under which a directory block might be deleted and describe how such a deletion could be handled.
12. Consider the directory and file structure in Example 2. Devise a scheme for linking unused node entries, i.e., marking unused entries in a special way and having the unused entries point to their succeeding unused entries as in a linked list.
13. Consider the file system described in Example 2 and suppose that a block can contain 128 block numbers and each node contains ten block numbers. The first eight block numbers in a node point to blocks in the file, the ninth points to a block that is used to store additional file block numbers, and the tenth points to a block that contains block numbers that point to blocks that are used to store additional file block numbers. What is the maximum number of blocks a file can contain? If no blocks are stored in memory and the blocks in a file are randomly accessed with equal probability, what is the average number of mass storage accesses needed to access a block in a file of maximum size in the ROOT directory? The ROOT directory is already in memory.
14. Sketch a system that has separate code and data memories and define a set of control lines for controlling the transfers between these memories and the processing element.
15. What does it mean for an instruction to be privileged?
16. What is the basic problem with having a user program fill its own base registers and how could this problem be solved?

17. Assume that compaction is used in a multiprogramming system to make space for new programs when the unused spaces are too small. Describe the compaction process if base registers are not used. Now, describe the process if base registers are used.

18. Consider a paged system whose pages and page frames are as defined in Fig. 10-16 and whose page table entry format is as shown in Fig. 10-17(a). If a block number occupies 11 bits and the fourteenth page table entry and the virtual address in hexadecimal are 800B and 0E024, respectively, is the needed page in memory? If it is, what is the physical address being accessed? Are the contents of the memory the same as those of the corresponding page in mass storage?

19. If a paged system uses pages of length 2K and 24-bit virtual addresses and has a physical memory with 2^{18} locations, how many pages and page frames are in the system?

20. Why is it that when demand paging is used, the page fault routine determines where a new page is to be put, but may not make this determination when a working set is used to anticipate a new page?

21. Draw a graph that gives the general shape of the function that relates the size of the working set to k, the number of references used to form the working set. Indicate what determines the working set's maximum size for a given program.

22. Suppose that demand paging is being used and a memory reference requires 0.5 microseconds. Draw a graph, with three curves, that gives the average reference time versus the probability of the referenced page being in memory (P_h) for mass storage units with average access times of 5, 20, and 50 milliseconds.

23. Consider a paged system with a TLB that stores the entire page table in main memory. Assume that

    P_{hh} = the probability that the page table entry is in the TLB and the page is in memory.

    P_{mh} = the probability that the page table entry is not in the TLB but the page is in memory.

    P_{hm} = the probability that the page table entry is in the TLB but the page is not in memory.

    t_h = the main memory access time.

    t_m = the average access time for mass storage.

    and give an expression for the average reference time.

24. Extend the solution of Exercise 23 to a system for which the entire page table may not be in main memory. Define any additional probabilities that are needed.

25. Consider a segmentation system for which

    P_h = the probability that the segment is in memory.

    t_h = the memory access time.

    t_m = the mass storage access time.

    r = the average number of mass storage accesses per segment fault.

    Give an expression for the average reference time.

26. For a combined segmentation and paged system that uses demand paging, outline a possible set of responsibilities assigned to the segment and page fault routines.

Chap. 10   Exercises

11

Operating Systems

An operating system is a program that controls the overall activity of the computer system in which it is installed. It provides services to the applications and systems programs that allow them to do their work in an efficient and coordinated manner. Computers that are used as simple controllers and perform only simple repetitive tasks may not need an operating system, but all general purpose computers and most special purpose computers should include some form of operating system. The operating system is charged with:

- Accepting commands from users.
- Loading programs for execution.
- Scheduling the use of the computer system's resources.
- Managing the memory hierarchy and allocating space within the various memory elements.
- Providing I/O and mass storage services and synchronizing the use of these services.

Any computer system that must perform more than one task would benefit from the centralized services of an operating system.

An operating system includes a **resident monitor** that is brought into a fixed area of memory when the computer is turned on and remains there until the computer is turned off. The resident monitor performs the services that are needed on a continual basis, services such as receiving and acting on user commands, allocating memory and mass storage space, updating the memory management system, and scheduling the use of the processing element and other resources.

An operating system also encompasses a set of routines for doing specific tasks for the resident monitor, systems programs, and applications programs on a demand basis. These routines would not need to be kept in memory all of the time but would be automatically brought into memory as required. They include routines for performing major reallocations of memory or mass storage (e.g., compaction), routines for performing initialization tasks while bringing up the system, and I/O drivers for transferring information to and from I/O and mass storage elements.

In addition to the operating system, there are systems programs that support the operating system. These programs are not executed automatically when they are needed, but may be initiated by user commands in the same manner as applications programs. They would perform systems related tasks such as:

- Formatting mass storage media.
- Manipulating files as a whole (copying, renaming, and deleting files).
- Initializing or making changes to the operating system so that it is customized according to the computer it must control.
- Performing backup operations.
- Creating source units and other text files.
- Translating source units into object units.
- Linking object units together to form load units.
- Debugging and changing machine language programs.

There are two broad categories of operating systems. There are **uniprogramming systems**, which can execute only one program at a time, and **multiprogramming systems**, which can simultaneously have two or more programs in execution. Most personal computers are uniprogramming systems and are designed for a single user to employ a single terminal to execute systems and applications programs one after the other. In contrast, multiprogramming systems may simultaneously accommodate several users and have several programs in progress at any given time. The reasons for using an operating system with multiprogramming capability are to allow resources to be shared and to increase the utilization of expensive system elements, such as a high performance processing element. This chapter first examines simple uniprogramming systems and then progresses to multiprogramming systems.

11-1 UNIPROGRAMMING SYSTEMS

The hardware assumed for the discussion in this section is shown in Fig. 11-1. It includes a processing element, ROM, main memory, terminal, printer, and mass storage element. Normally, the resident monitor is permanently stored in some fixed area in mass storage. Because most of main memory is volatile, the resident monitor cannot be stored in main memory and some means is needed to transfer the resident monitor from mass storage to main memory each time the computer is turned on. The purpose of the ROM is for permanently storing a small program,

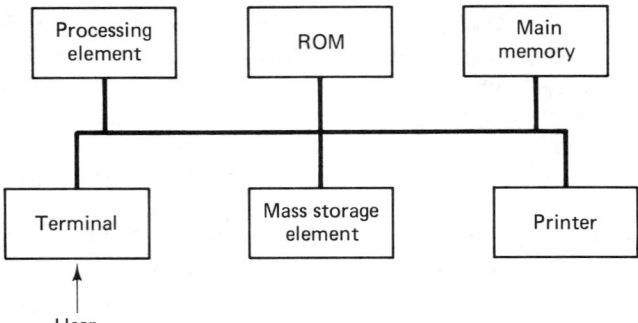

Figure 11-1 Hardware for a typical uniprogramming system.

called a **bootstrap loader**, to execute this transfer. The portion of the address space assigned to the ROM must include the initial, or **reset**, address (see Sec. 7-3-4) that is automatically put into the PC when power is applied to the processing element. The startup of the computer would then proceed as follows:

1. The reset address is put into the PC and execution begins.
2. The bootstrap loader inputs the resident monitor to main memory and then branches to it.
3. The resident monitor initializes the system by preparing it for general usage.

The initialization done by the resident monitor may include setting interrupt vectors, initializing the Interrupt Management logic, and putting the interfaces in their startup conditions.

Once the resident monitor has completed its initialization work, it awaits its first command. That portion of the resident monitor that receives and interprets commands is called the **command line interpreter (CLI)** and is flowcharted in Fig. 11-2. Each command contains the name of a program and it is the CLI's job to input this name, determine the location of the program, bring in the program from mass storage, and then begin its execution using a procedure call. After the program has completed its execution, control is returned to the CLI, which then waits for the next command. If a program cannot be found, the CLI outputs an error message to the user and then waits for the next command.

One way of describing the execution of an operating system is to use a state diagram. The state diagram for the uniprogramming system being considered is shown in Fig. 11-3. There are only two principal states in this system. One state represents the system in its waiting phase, while it is idly waiting for a new command, and the other represents the system's active phase, while it is executing a program. How fully a computer system is being utilized is primarily determined by the amount of time it spends in its executing state. However, uniprogramming systems are not designed to make maximal use of their resources. Such a system is usually inexpensive and its purpose is to provide a dedicated facility to a single user. The fact that most of the elements in the system are sitting idle while the user is typing commands or just thinking about what needs to be done next is not important.

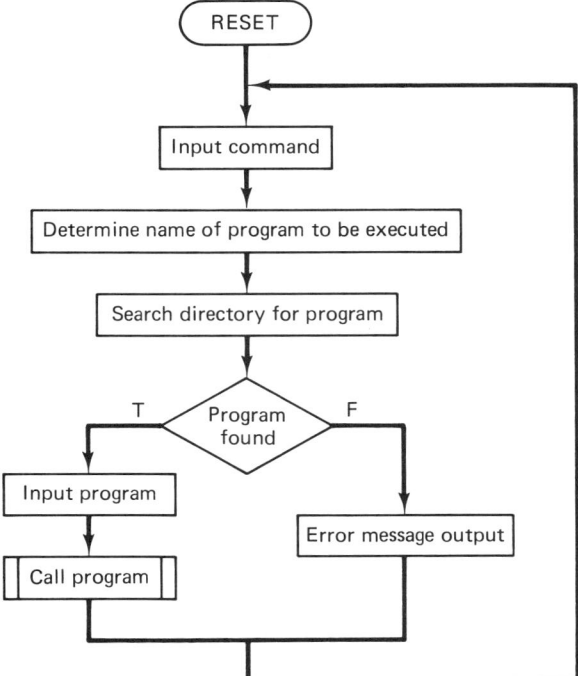

Figure 11-2 Flowchart of a uniprogramming system's command line interpreter.

A typical organization of main memory for a uniprogramming system is shown in Fig. 11-4. The low part of memory is reserved for interrupt vectors, system tables, and other memory areas that are needed by the operating system. It may also include the stack used by the operating system, the **system stack**. Adjacent to this area is that portion of the memory that is available to the user. It is here that programs are put when they appear in a command and are brought in from mass storage.

In this example it is assumed that the reset address is near the top of the address space and therefore, the ROM containing the bootstrap loader must occupy the high part of memory. The bootstrap loader puts the resident monitor in the area adjacent to the ROM, and between the user area and the resident monitor is an area reserved for I/O drivers and other system routines that are input from mass storage and executed as the need arises. This area may also include the memory space needed to buffer data as they are transferred between main memory

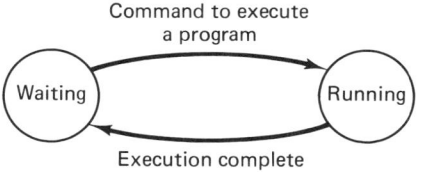

Figure 11-3 State diagram of a simple uniprogramming system.

Sec. 11-1   Uniprogramming Systems

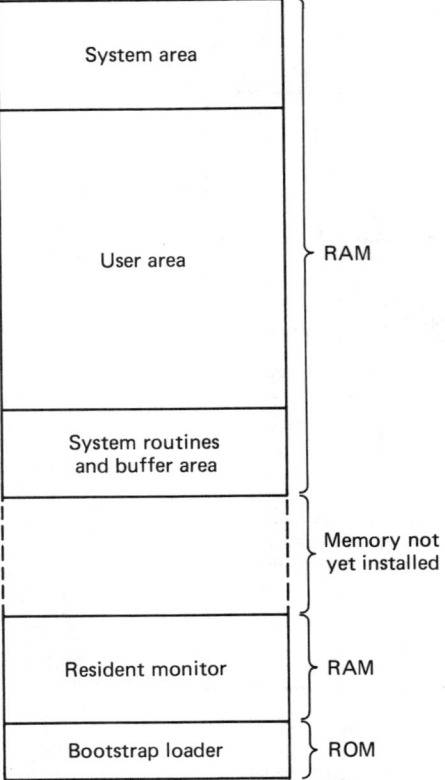

Figure 11-4 Typical memory organization for a uniprogramming system.

and the I/O and mass storage elements. The dashed lines indicate that not all of the address space is necessarily associated with memory that is physically present.

11-1-1 Memory and File Management

For a uniprogramming system there is very little to managing main memory. The user may be able to set the maximum size of the system stack and, if this stack is in the systems area, this size may be used to set the boundary between the systems area and the user's area. There should be some mechanism for preventing the system stack from overwriting the remainder of the systems area. Normally, this prevention would be accomplished by including in the hardware a stack limit register, and the stack pointer would not be permitted to decrement beyond the contents of the limit register. The only other variable in assigning memory would be the amount of space reserved for the system routines and buffers. Because the system routines are the parts of the operating system that may be shuffled in and out of memory and buffer area requirements may vary, the boundary between the user's area and the system routines/buffer area may be dynamically set by the operating system. It is assumed in the ensuing discussion that the entire program that is currently executing fits into the user's area.

The major components of a uniprogramming operating system are shown in Fig. 11-5. Unlike the main memory, the file system of the mass storage portion of the memory hierarchy would need to be managed. Each mass storage medium must include a directory, and managing the medium would require the operating system to access the directory when reading from or writing to a file or making changes in the directory. That portion of the operating system that must work with files is called the **file management system** and serves as an interface to the information in the mass storage subsystem. The file management system must be designed according to the structure of the mass storage elements and their directories. It simply provides the services needed to fully utilize the means for accessing the mass storage subsystem, which may include ways of protecting files from unwarranted use. The file management system may be called upon to:

- Retrieve a record from a specified file.
- Store a record in a specified file.
- Modify a directory by adding, changing, or deleting a directory entry. Changing a directory entry may involve changing a file's name or protection.
- Rearrange files to make room for a new file.
- Rearrange the directory to improve its usage.
- Use the directories to track unused mass storage areas.

11-1-2 Input/Output

Other than the CLI and file management system, there must be a collection of routines for handling I/O and mass storage transfers. This collection of routines is divided into the Basic I/O System (BIOS), which provides the CLI and file

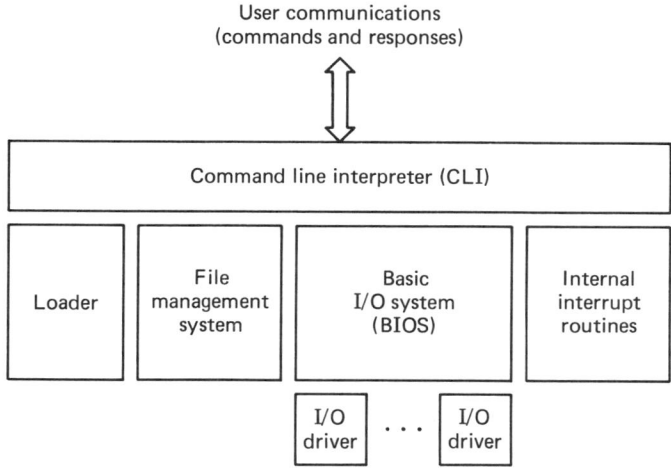

Figure 11-5 Major components of a uniprogramming operating system.

management system with the services needed to perform the transfers, and the I/O drivers that actually carry out the transfers.

The BIOS is designed to respond to and communicate with the operating system, and the I/O drivers are designed to communicate with the I/O and mass storage elements. Each driver is written to satisfy the requirements of a particular type of element (e.g., printer, terminal, or diskette unit). This allows the peculiarities of the various types of I/O or mass storage devices to be isolated from the remainder of the operating system. If a new type of I/O or mass storage device is added to the computer, then a new I/O driver must be written that can manage the new device and communicate with the BIOS, but the BIOS and other parts of the operating system can be left essentially unchanged.

Whenever the operating system, another systems program, or a user's program must communicate with mass storage or the external world it passes the necessary parameters to the BIOS and calls upon it to use the appropriate driver to perform the transfer. The parameters include a device identifier, the address of the main memory area to be input to or output from, and, in the case of mass storage, the physical locations of the records to be accessed.

To access a file, the operating system must first use the file management system to obtain the required directory entry from the appropriate directory. Normally the operating system keeps the most recently used portions of the directories in main memory, but, if the needed directory entry is not in memory, the BIOS and a driver must be used to bring in the directory record that includes the entry before the file can be accessed. If the directory is hierarchically structured or is scattered around the medium, several mass storage accesses may be required before the desired data transfer is made.

Typically, a high-level language user's program accesses a record in a file by first opening the file as indicated in Chap. 9, which causes a logical unit number to be associated with the file and the device on which the file is located. All such associations are stored in a table in the systems area of memory and subsequent READ and WRITE statements must refer to this table. Also, opening a file may cause a portion of the directory to be brought into main memory. After a file has been opened, a READ or WRITE would initiate a file access. During the access, the address of the main memory area to be used and the logical unit number would be passed to the operating system, which would use the logical/physical association and the file management system to locate the precise mass storage area to be communicated with.

As explained in Chap. 5, a program is brought into memory and begins executing whenever a user gives a load command. Giving a load command is normally a matter of typing in the name of the load unit to be executed. Some uniprogramming systems allow a user to specify the beginning address of the area at which the program is to be placed, but most often the operating system simply places it immediately following the system area in the low part of memory. Code is transferred into memory in the same manner as data, i.e., the program's location is found in the directory and then the BIOS and a driver perform the transfer. Once the code is in memory, it may be modified using a relocation factor. Then it is branched to from the resident monitor by using a procedure call. As indicated earlier (see Fig. 11-2), programs are normally concluded with a return branch to the CLI.

11-1-3 Operating System Services

Any part of the operating system or a user's program may make use of a service provided by the operating system by making a **system call**. If the service is provided by a procedure, the system call is a procedure call. However, such services are sometimes provided by interrupt routines. Most computers allow three types of interrupts: the external interrupts used by interrupt I/O and the DMA completions (see Chap. 6), software interrupts, and internal interrupts. It is the software and internal interrupts that are used to enter the interrupt routines that provide operating system services.

As indicated in Sec. 10-2, a software interrupt is initiated by an interrupt instruction that simply causes the processing element to enter its interrupt sequence. If the interrupt sequence requires a pointer to a vector address, then the interrupt instruction should include an operand that provides this pointer. A typical interrupt instruction might have the form:

    INTR *Operand*

where *Operand* is the pointer.

An internal interrupt occurs when the computer enters an unusual state. For example, such a state might result from:

- Attempting to divide by zero.
- Attempting to execute an instruction with an invalid op code.
- Attempting to access a portion of memory that is not physically present.
- Stack limit or other protection faults.
- A page or segment fault.

When one of these exceptional conditions occurs, the computer automatically begins an interrupt sequence. The pointer to the interrupt is determined by the exception type. As indicated in Fig. 11-5, the interrupt routines that are branched to are a permanent part of the operating system. An interrupt routine may attempt to recover from the condition and allow execution to continue (as in the case of a stack limit fault) or may cause an error message to be displayed and a return to be made to the CLI.

11-1-4 Systems Programs

In addition to the operating system and its routines, a general purpose computer system includes a number of systems programs for formatting mass storage media, changing the operating system, manipulating files, and performing a variety of other systems-related tasks. Included in this set of programs are programs for creating source units, translating or assembling source units, and linking object units (see Chap. 5). These programs would be loaded in the same way as user programs.

Text editors or word processing programs are used to create the text strings of assembler and high-level language programs. The data they operate on are character data and the source units they produce are text files. A translating program inputs this text as data and outputs the object units to object files, and a linker inputs the object files and outputs the load units to load files. To a translating program, linker, or loader, the code being operated on is treated as data.

11-1-5 Overlapping I/O and Processing

It was noted in Chap. 6 that when programmed I/O is used, I/O activity cannot be done simultaneously with processing because, when an input or output is to be conducted, the processing element is occupied with monitoring a status bit. Figure 11-6(a) illustrates the time relationship between the I/O and processing activities in such a system. In contrast, DMA transfers are used specifically to allow processing to continue while I/O is taking place. Figure 11-6(b) shows the possible overlap of processing and I/O activities while DMA transfers are being

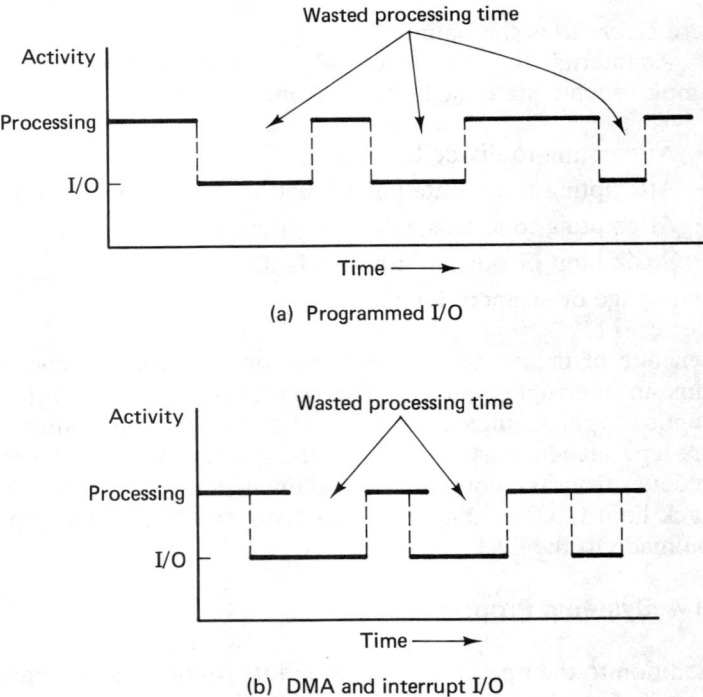

Figure 11-6 Time relationships between processing and I/O activities.

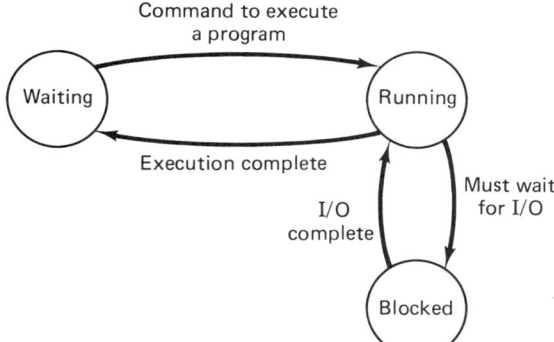

Figure 11-7 State diagram of a uniprogramming system with I/O being considered a separate activity.

made. In this case, once a transfer has been initiated, processing and the transfer continue in parallel until the processing must wait for the input or output to be completed (e.g., the processing must use the data being input).

Although interrupt I/O requires use of the processing element, it is similar to DMA in that processing can continue between the transfer of the individual pieces of data, thus allowing the processing and I/O to be intermixed without including wasted idle time. As with DMA, processing may reach a point where it must wait for the completion of a set of transfers (e.g., the input of a command).

Figure 11-7 is an expanded version of the state diagram in Fig. 11-3 which acknowledges the presence of I/O as a separate activity. As indicated by the figure, a program may be held up until an I/O activity has completed, at which time it would enter the blocked state. For programmed I/O, a program is in its blocked state whenever there is I/O, but for DMA or interrupt I/O, it may be processing and conducting I/O at the same time and enters the blocked state only when processing cannot continue.

A uniprogramming system can, at best, make only limited use of the overlapping of processing and I/O. This limitation is due to the close relationship between the computer and single user and the fact that the user is slow as compared to the computer. In such an environment, I/O is often initiated by a user action and this action is much slower than the time required to perform the I/O. A counterexample, however, is the continual inputting and/or outputting of blocks of data using double or triple buffering (see Sec. 6-3-2 and Exercise 13). Therefore, there are special applications that need to overlap processing and I/O even in a uniprogramming system.

11-2 MULTIPROGRAMMING SYSTEMS

The hardware configuration assumed in this section is shown in Fig. 11-8. Except for the inclusion of several terminals, it is the same as the uniprogramming configuration considered in Sec. 11-1. There may be a user at each terminal and a command may be given to the system via any of the terminals.

Before beginning our discussion of multiprogramming we must define the

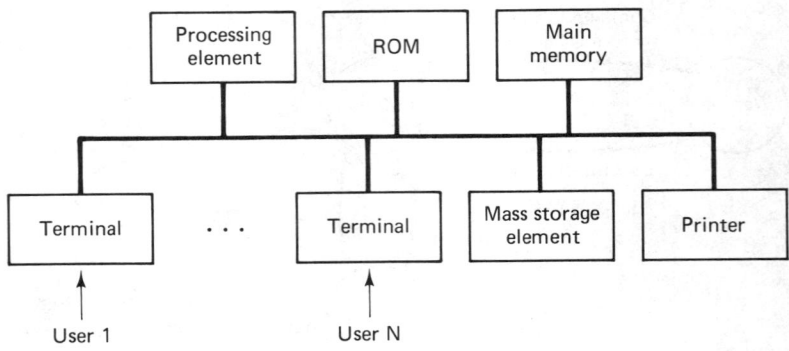

Figure 11-8 Hardware for a typical multiprogramming system.

entity that is central to multiprogramming. That entity is the process, which has been defined in a variety of ways with many definitions including a vague phrase such as "a program that is available for execution." The definition used here is quite specific:

> A **process** is a sequence of instructions that must be entered by a branch from the resident monitor and must exit using a branch to the resident monitor. The branch to the resident monitor may be due to an interrupt.

This definition does not exclude a process from being a part of the operating system (e.g., an I/O driver), although in most of our discussions it is helpful to view a process as a system or applications program that is separate from the operating system. Also, note that this definition does not imply that a process must be entered at its beginning nor exited from its end. In fact, we will see that most entries and exits are to and from various points within the process.

Figure 11-9 provides the basic state diagram for a multiprogramming system. Before a program can be executed it must become a process, which requires it to be properly introduced to the operating system. Such an introduction may result from a command by a user or a system call made by a program. In either case, the introduction consists of locating the program and providing the operating system a means of branching to it. When a program becomes a process, the process is said to be **created**.

A **multiprogramming system** is one that is capable of supervising two or more processes. At any given time, all processes must be in one of the three states shown in Fig. 11-9. When a process leaves the system of states shown in Fig. 11-9 it is said to be **deleted**. A process can delete itself, be deleted by the operating system, or with some operating systems, be deleted by another process.

The three states of the operating system depicted in Fig. 11-9 are the:

> **Ready state**—a process in this state is ready to execute and is waiting for the operating system to assign it to the processing element.

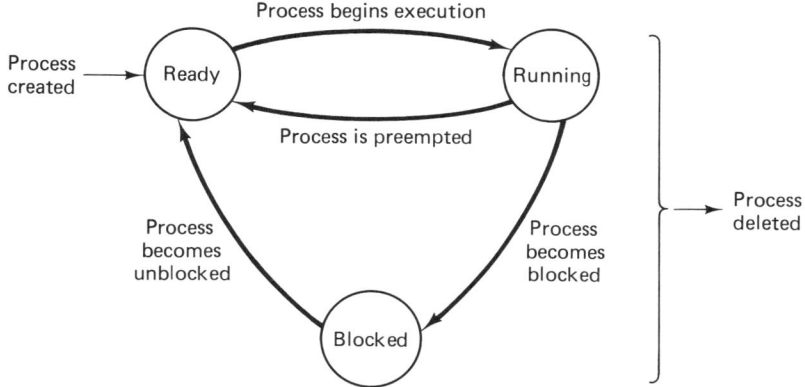

Figure 11-9 Basic state diagram for a multiprogramming system.

Running state—the process that has been assigned to the processing element is in this state and is the currently executing program. If there is only one processing element, only one process can be in this state.

Blocked state—a process is in this state when it cannot proceed until some specific set of conditions are satisfied (e.g., an I/O transfer requested by the process has been completed).

When a process is created it must first enter the ready state, but it may be deleted while residing in any of the three states. Switches between the states are managed by the operating system, which bases its decisions on the conditions surrounding the processes at the time the switch is made.

The chief advantages of a multiprogramming system are its ability to:

- Serve more than one user at a time.
- Better utilize the processing element.

The first can be achieved even when there is only one processing element by letting the processes being executed by users take turns occupying the running state, i.e., using the processing element. If the rules for choosing which process gets to enter the running state next are reasonably unbiased, then each user's process will be able to access the processing element frequently enough that the users may not even be aware that there are others on the system. This scenario is possible because human responses are slow compared to the speed of a computer. However, as the number of users grows, the total volume of commands and responses may approach the computer's processing capability and the existence of other users may become apparent. It is, therefore, important that the number of terminals, which determines the maximum number of users, does not exceed the overall workload capacity of the computer. Experience has shown

Sec. 11-2 Multiprogramming Systems 433

that as a multiprogramming system becomes overloaded it begins to degrade very rapidly.

Better utilizing the processing element, and thereby improving the interactive relationship between the system and its users, is realized by minimizing the time lost due to I/O. It was shown in Fig. 11-6(b) that processing and I/O can be overlapped by using interrupt I/O or DMA to reduce the time the processing element remains idle. Overlapping however, cannot eliminate the time wasted while waiting for I/O. Figure 11-10 demonstrates how additional time could be saved by switching back and forth between two processes. When one process is blocked from proceeding because it must wait for an I/O transfer to complete, the operating system switches to the other process. Although this switching does not eliminate the wasted processing element time entirely, having several processes in the system at a time can cause the amount of wasted time to approach zero. The only time the processing element would be idle is when all processes in the system are in the blocked state and therefore, no process is available to be put into the running state.

Although switching processes can utilize time that is otherwise wasted, it is not without cost. Switching is done by the operating system and the time spent executing the operating system also represents lost processing time to the users, even though the processing element is busy. The time lost while the operating system is executing is referred to as **overhead**. Normally, overhead is very small when compared to the time saved by switching processes, but as the frequency of switches increases so does the overhead. We will see later that activities other than process switches also contribute to a system's overhead and, as a system becomes overloaded, overhead can dominate the use of the processing element.

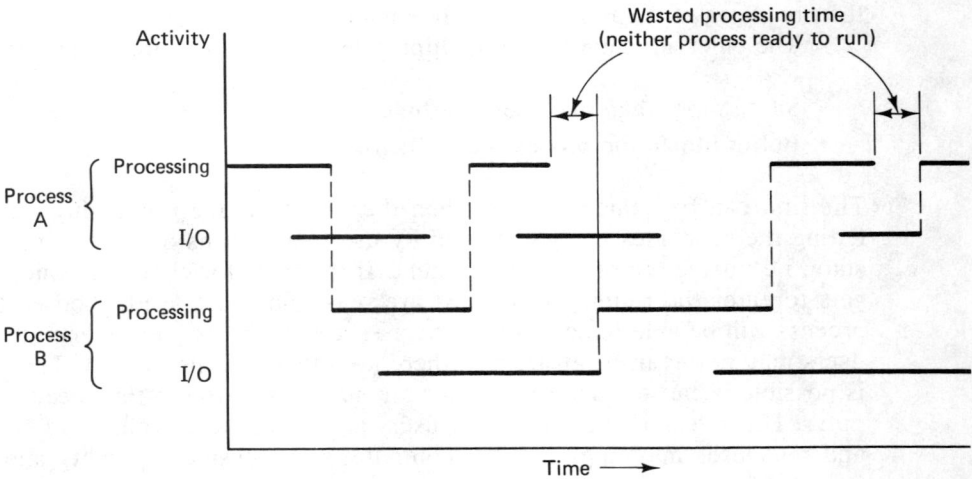

Figure 11-10 Time relationship between processing and I/O activities for two processes.

11-3 ORGANIZATION OF A MULTIPROGRAMMING SYSTEM

The principal components of a multiprogramming operating system are shown in Fig. 11-11. The CLI must be capable of responding to commands from and issuing results and messages to several users. Preferably, it should be able to communicate with the users in such a way that each seems to be the only one on the system. Commands are normally entered using interrupt I/O with a carriage return/line feed combination being used to trigger the execution of the completion routine. The completion routine would include the code from the CLI that would execute the command. Most, if not all, commands cause a process to be created.

11-3-1 Process Scheduling

The process scheduler, which appears at the left side of Fig. 11-11, determines which process in the ready state is to enter the running state next. The rules it uses to make this determination is key to a system's operation and is often used to classify a system. If all processes are treated equally and take turns on an equal basis, the operating system is said to be a **round robin** system. In contrast, some systems assign a priority to each process and then use these priorities to select which process is permitted to enter the running state next. They are called **priority-based** systems. Many operating systems use a combination that includes priority levels, but employs round robin (i.e., least recently used) selection within each level.

The operation of the process scheduler in a typical round robin system is depicted in Fig. 11-12. Because a process may exit the running state before it has completed its work, the entire environment surrounding the process at the time it leaves the running state, called the **process state vector**, must be saved. Then,

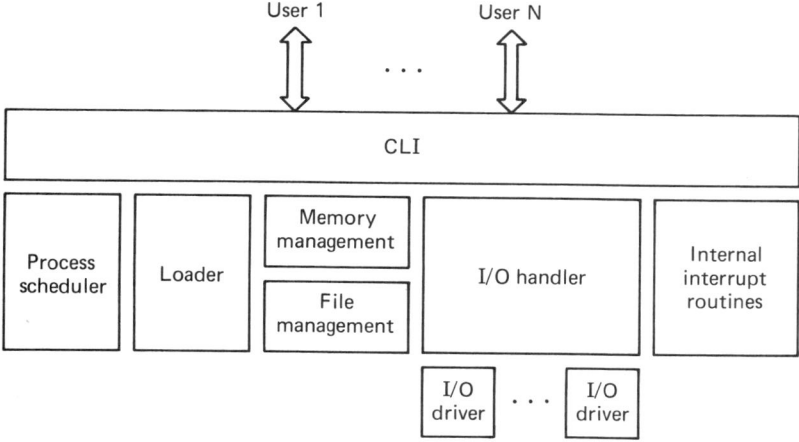

Figure 11-11 Principal components of a multiprogramming operating system.

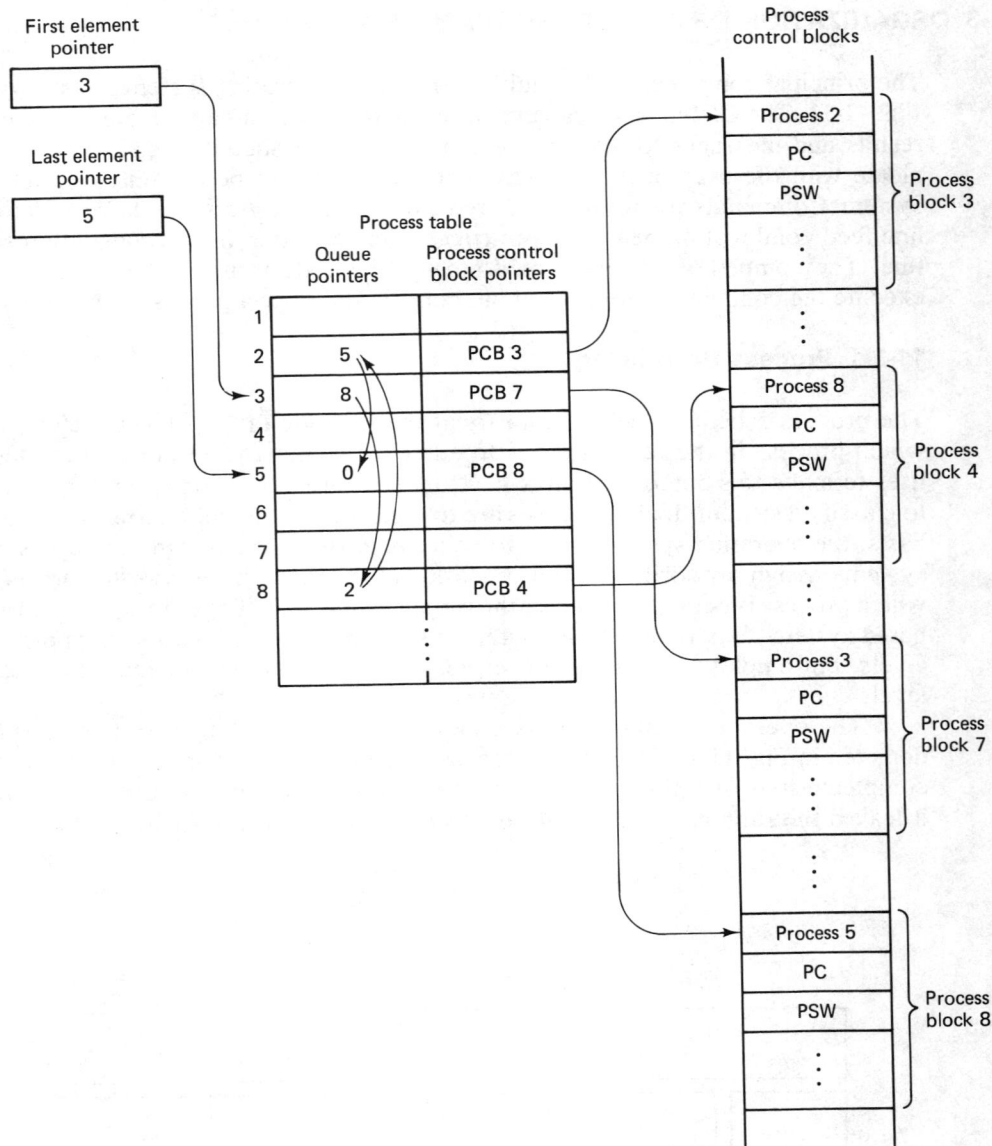

Figure 11-12 Operation of a process scheduler that uses a FIFO queue.

when the process returns to the running state, its state vector can be retrieved and the process can begin executing where it left off. The state vector must include the contents of the registers (the PC, PSW, SP, and working registers) and other important information pertaining to the process, such as the process's identification number. (When a process is created it is assigned an ID number that is used to track the process as it changes states.) Process state vectors are stored in process control blocks, which may be organized as an array or as a linked list that changes dynamically. The act of storing the state vector of a process into its process block and then retrieving the state vector of the process that is to run next is called a **context switch**.

At the heart of Fig. 11-12 is the process table, which contains an element for each process currently in the system. The process scheduler is responsible for maintaining this table and must keep an accounting of its unused elements. In the example shown in Fig. 11-12, the process table is an array and when a process is created it is assigned to an unused element in the table, and the element's index becomes the process's ID. Also, the newly created process is assigned a process control block and the beginning address of this block is put into the process's element in the process table. The initial contents of a process control block would include the beginning address of the process as the initial value of the PC. When a process is deleted from the system, both its element in the process table and its process control block are marked as unused.

Contained in the process table is the ready queue that consists of all of the processes that are currently in the ready state. In a round robin system the ready queue is simply a FIFO queue. In Fig. 11-12 the ready queue has been implemented as a linked list (see Sec. 10-1) with the entries in the Queue Pointer column of the process table pointing to the next entry in the linked list. The integer 0 is not used as an index and, when it appears, it marks the end of the linked list. The First Element Pointer points to the beginning of the ready queue and the element corresponding to the process to be selected to run next. The Last Element Pointer indicates the end of the queue. The Last Element Pointer is used to extend the queue when another process enters the ready state. As shown in Fig. 11-9, an existing process may enter the ready state from either the running or blocked state.

In summary, the process scheduler is responsible for:

- Maintaining a process table of all processes that are currently included in the system, adding entries to this table as processes are created, and deleting entries from the table as processes are deleted.
- Selecting the next process to be executed when the running state is vacated by the currently running process.
- Performing context switches by storing the state vector of the currently executing process when it leaves the running state and retrieving the state vector of the process to be run next.

This summary indicates that the process scheduler must be entered any time a process is added to or deleted from the system or the process in the running state is to be replaced. Adding or deleting a process may result from a request made by a user, the operating system, or by the currently running process. The rules for adding and deleting processes vary considerably from system to system.

The rules for replacing the process in the running state may also vary and are sometimes used to classify the operating system. All multiprogramming systems are such that the running process normally exits to the blocked state when it must wait for I/O; however, this is not the only reason for giving up use of the processing element. Other events that may cause the processing element to be relinquished are the need for the running process to wait for a specified time or until an event occurs in another process. In addition, a process may be forced to leave the running state due to a request by the operating system. Some systems limit the use of the processing element to some specific period of time called a **time slice**. In such systems, if a process has not exited the running state for some other reason before its time slice is up, it is forced to leave the running state and join the ready queue by the operating system. Such systems are said to be **timeshared**. The timing mechanism in a timeshared system is normally a timer/event counter, such as those discussed in Sec. 6-4-3, and it is the interrupt request from the timer/event counter that triggers the branch to the process scheduler.

In contrast, priority-based systems normally allow processes with a higher priority than the running process to force the running process to give up the processing element. Such systems are said to be **preemptive**. In priority-based systems, a process is not necessarily placed at the last of the ready queue, but its position is determined by its priority. In a preemptive system, a process's priority is also compared to that of the running process and, if its priority is higher, it will preempt the running process and cause the running process to join the ready queue.

11-3-2 Memory Management and Process Loading

Let us first suppose that when a process is created it is brought into memory and remains there until it is deleted. In this case, when a process is created, the memory management portion of the operating system is entered and is responsible for allocating sufficient space for the new process and then calling the loader to bring the process into memory. Depending on the memory management scheme, the loader may need to bias the addresses in the process according to the beginning address of the memory area where the process is placed (see Sec. 5-4).

If the process must occupy a contiguous section of memory as shown in Fig. 11-13(a), then the memory management software must search out an unused area that is large enough for the entire process. In the event that such an area cannot be found, either the entry of the new process into the system must be delayed or the processes already in memory must be rearranged. Because moving a process may require that its addresses be readjusted, moving a process may not be a matter of simply transferring the code from one area to another, but may require the process to be reloaded. Also, the process control block of the process would need to be updated to reflect the new position of the process. It is clear that requiring processes to remain intact introduces serious external fragmentation problems and may place a considerable burden on the memory management software and loader. In general, it is not recommended that existing processes be moved around. Therefore, the "contiguous" restriction would normally cause the introduction of new processes to be delayed until adequate space becomes available as existing processes are deleted. Such a requirement would cause programs

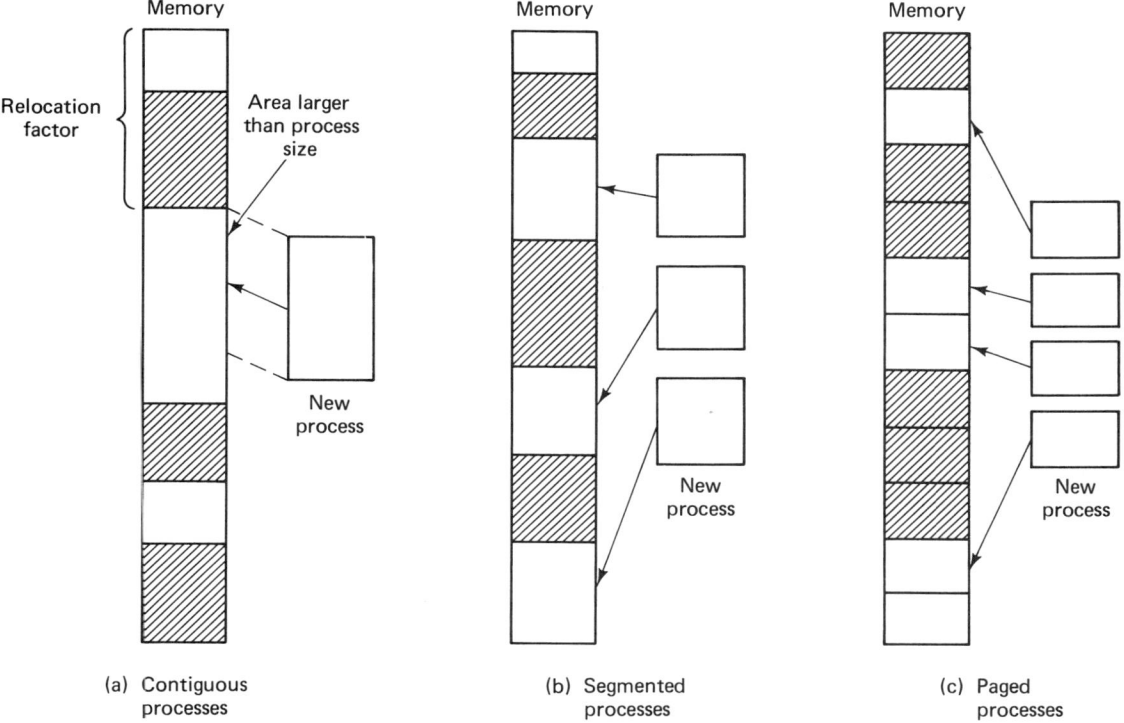

Figure 11-13 Allocation possibilities for newly created processes.

to be queued before they are allowed to become processes, which may not be a workable solution.

Alternatively, a process may be allowed to be broken into logical segments as shown in Fig. 11-13(b). This breakup would reduce the external fragmentation problem by allowing smaller areas to be used, but would not eliminate it. It is still possible for there to be a logical segment that is larger than the largest unused space. Also, allowing a process to be broken into segments should be accompanied by segment registers for biasing the addresses used by the process (see Sec. 10-2). Therefore, the memory management software must load the segment registers with the appropriate beginning addresses of the segments, but would reduce or, possibly, eliminate the need for the loader to perform address adjustments.

The other alternative is to use paging as shown in Fig. 11-13(c). Although paging must be supported by a substantial amount of paging hardware, it eliminates external fragmentation, and a new process is barred from entering the system only if the number of available pages is less than the number of pages in the new process. Addressing is done via the page table, and address adjustment during loading is avoided.

The above discussion has assumed that all of the processes in a system (i.e., all of the processes in the ready, running, or blocked state) must be in main memory. If we relax this requirement, then newly created processes can always be allowed to enter the system because existing processes, or parts of existing processes, can be temporarily removed from memory. When a process is temporarily removed, it is said to be **swapped out**. It can later be **swapped in** when it is to enter the running state. In a system that uses segmentation or paging, the swapping can be done on the basis of segments or pages instead of entire processes.

As the swapping traffic becomes appreciable, it may become necessary to insert a high speed mass storage element in the memory hierarchy as shown in Fig. 11-14. When a new process is created it would be transferred to the high-speed mass storage and then swapping would be used to bring it into memory as it is needed. If demand paging is used, pages would not be brought into memory until they are needed. In fact, pages would not normally be brought in until they are referenced by the operating system or the running program and a page fault occurs. As indicated in Chap. 10, a page fault is an internal interrupt that results from a branch to a code page or reference to a data page that is not currently in memory. The interrupt would cause the memory management portion of the operating system to be entered which, if necessary, would determine the page to be swapped out, determine the location where the new page is to be put, make the required page table adjustments, and call on the I/O software to load the new page. Similar statements could be made about a system based on segments.

11-3-3 I/O Handling

As indicated above, in a multiprogramming system, when the running process must perform input or output it is transferred to the blocked state until the input or output is complete. Then it is put into the ready queue until its turn comes up or its priority becomes high enough for it to be returned to the running state.

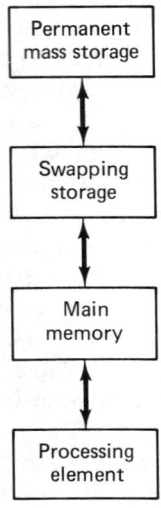

Figure 11-14 Use of swapping storage.

Because processes must share I/O and mass storage devices, an I/O operation may not be able to begin as soon as the blocked state is entered. If a needed device is already in use, the I/O operation would have to wait until the device becomes free.

If there are several processes in a system, many of them may call a device at more or less the same time and it becomes necessary to queue the I/O requests for each device as shown in Fig. 11-15. As with the ready queue, these queues may be organized as linked lists. When a running process must use an I/O or mass storage device it makes an I/O request by passing the necessary information to the overall control portion of the resident monitor and executing a branch to the monitor. During this transition the process's state vector is stored in the process control block for the process. The resident monitor constructs an I/O request

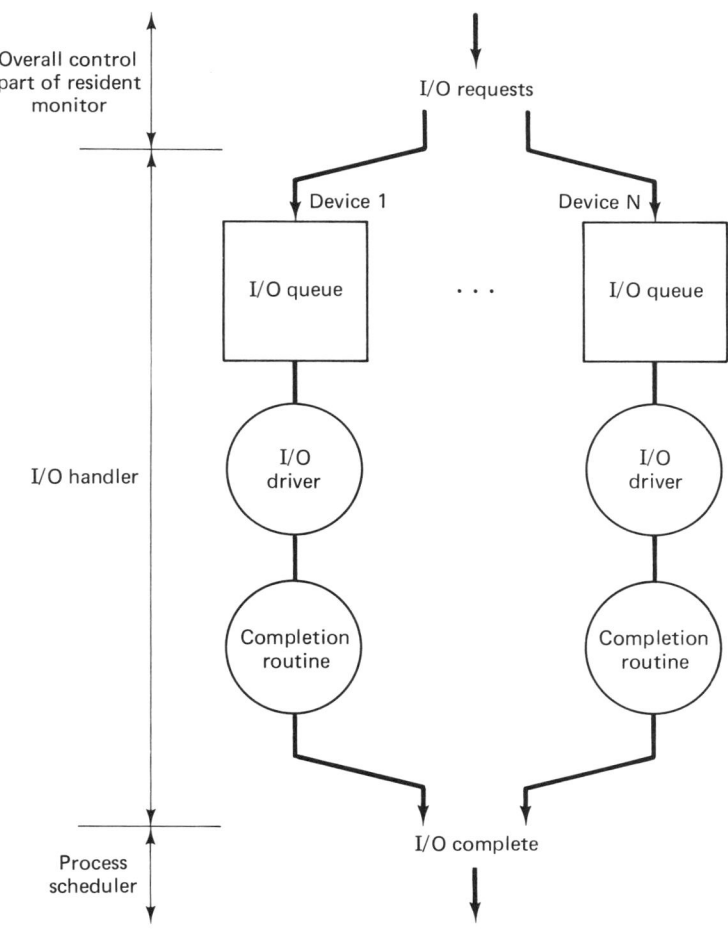

Figure 11-15 I/O queues.

block that it passes to the I/O handler, and the I/O handler puts the request block on the queue for the device that is to be used. A request block may include a priority that would allow a request to be placed at points other than at the end of the queue. After the I/O request block has been placed on its request queue, a branch is made to the process scheduler, which selects a process in the ready state to become the running process.

When a request reaches the head of the queue it is given the use of the device's I/O driver and the transfer is begun. Upon completion of the transfer, the completion routine is entered, normally as a result of an interrupt, and the transfer's completion tasks are performed (see Sec. 6-3). Then a branch is made to the process scheduler, which adds the process that was waiting for the I/O to the ready queue. In a preemptive system, the process scheduler would permit a higher priority process to immediately preempt the running process.

Because the code for the processes in a system and most of the data used by these processes comes from mass storage, disks and other mass storage devices are in particularly high demand and should be used efficiently. The primary means for efficiently utilizing a device that involves mechanical motion is to arrange its usage in such a way that the mechanical motion is reduced. This reduction is easily accomplished by not constructing the device's queue on a first come-first served basis, but by arranging requests in the queue according to the physical position of the needed information relative to the current position of the device's read/write mechanism.

For example, suppose that the I/O handler has received requests for accessing the disk sectors shown in Fig. 11-16. If the current position of the read/

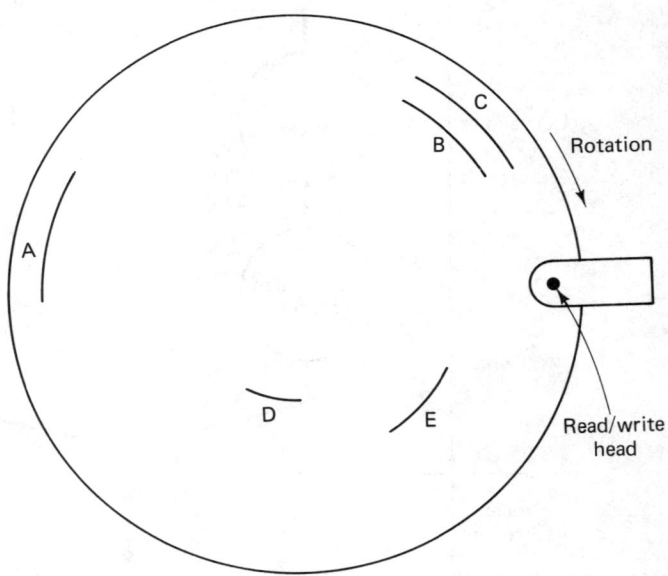

Figure 11-16 Typical distribution of sectors to be accessed.

write head is as indicated, a good strategy would be to access the sectors in the order C, A, B, E, and D, regardless of the sequence in which the requests were received. A typical way of arranging the requests in a disk's queue is to order them so that the read/write head continually sweeps in and out, accessing those sectors indicated by the outstanding requests in the order in which they pass under the head.

Normally, a multiprogramming system would not use programmed I/O because processing time would be wasted. A DMA request would be serviced when it reaches the front of the queue by initiating a block transfer, and the process scheduler would assign another process to the running state while the transfer is being made. Following the completion of the transfer an interrupt would result in a branch to the completion routine. Then the process scheduler would put the process that initiated the I/O into the ready queue and either return to the running process or replace it.

If interrupt I/O is to be performed, the input or output would be started in much the same way as a block transfer. However, most transfers would be conducted as an aside to normal processing. The running process would simply be interrupted, an interrupt routine would perform the transfer, and then a return would be made to the running process. But, even though individual items (e.g., characters) are being transferred as opposed to blocks, the items are normally input or output in groups and the last element of a group must be handled differently. After the last item in a group has been transferred, a completion routine similar to those used after block transfers may be entered. Also, the action following the execution of a completion routine is similar to that occurring after a block transfer.

For example, if a process is to output exactly one line of characters to a printer, its print request would be put on the printer's queue. When it reaches the front of the queue and the printer is free, the first character is sent to the printer. Then, the running process is allowed to continue. The interrupt routine for outputting characters to the printer will use the processing element whenever it needs it, but will always return control to the currently running process after it has finished outputting a character. (Note that the running process may be any process currently in the system and may even change while the line is being printed.) When the interrupt routine detects a carriage return/line feed combination, it does not return to the running process, but branches to the line completion routine instead. Then, the process scheduler is entered and, as usual, the process that caused the printing is put in the ready queue and a new running process may be selected.

11-4 SHARING RESOURCES

As noted in earlier chapters, a resource may be a piece of hardware, a set of software, or a collection of data. Regardless of the nature of a resource, if it is shared by two or more processes, then access to the resource must be somehow controlled to prevent more than one process from using it at the same time. For example, if one process were permitted to write to a file while another process is reading from the file, the information being read may be indeterminate depending on whether the various records in the file were written to first or read from first. As a second example, the output to a printer must be controlled so that the printed output of two or more processes does not become intermixed.

There are two important facets to sharing resources. First, mutual exclusion must be guaranteed to avoid the problems suggested by the above examples and secondly, mutual exclusion must be accomplished in such a way that deadlock does not occur. **Mutual exclusion** is giving a process exclusive use of a resource until the process is finished with the resource. At that time the process gives up all of its rights to the resource and another process is free to acquire those rights. **Deadlock** occurs when two or more processes want the same resource at the same time, but, even though none of the processes are able to acquire the resource, they succeed in blocking the other processes from using it. Deadlock causes the processes involved to become stalemated and may even cause the entire system to become inoperable. Providing mutual exclusion while avoiding deadlocks is possibly the most difficult challenge facing the designer of a multiprogramming operating system.

The fundamental means of achieving mutual exclusion while avoiding deadlock is illustrated in Fig. 11-17. Because all activity within a computer results from instructions being executed, the use of a shared resource results from two or more processes executing sections of code that use the resource. A section of code that utilizes a shared resource is referred to as a **critical section** of code. In Fig. 11-17 the critical section is preceded by a set of code that checks whether another process has entered its critical section. If not, the process must set an exclusion flag to indicate to the other processes that it has entered its critical

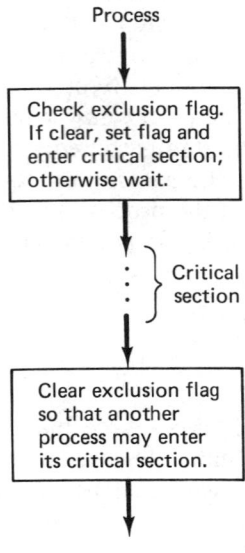

Figure 11-17 Controlling the entry into a critical section.

section; otherwise, the process must wait until the process using the shared resource leaves its critical section. Once a process has completed the execution of its critical section it clears the exclusion flag, thus allowing another process to enter its critical section. There must be a separate exclusion flag for each shared resource.

For mutual exclusion, the problem is that of checking the flag and then setting it if it is clear without permitting a process switch between the two actions. For example, consider the X16 code given in Fig. 11-18 for providing entry into the critical sections, for the same shared resource X, of the Processes A and B. This code is flawed in that if an event (e.g., the end of a time slice) should occur that causes a process switch between the testing and setting of X_FLAG it would be possible for both processes to enter their critical sections and therefore, access the shared resource at the same time (see Exercise 22).

Another attempt at regulating entry into the critical sections of Processes A and B is shown in Fig. 11-19. This time two flags are used for Resource X, one associated with Process A and the other with Process B. Although this code

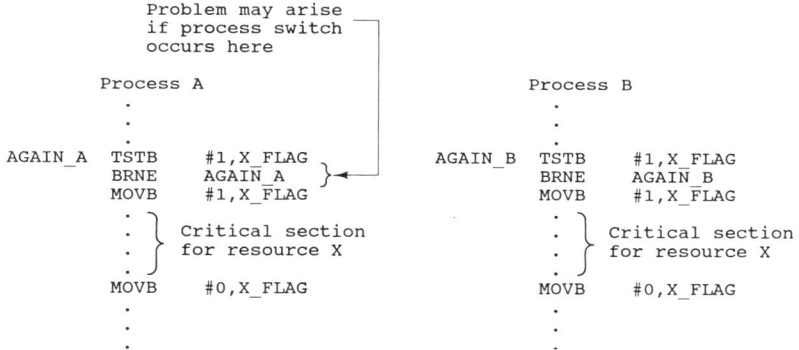

Figure 11-18 Flawed attempt at achieving mutual exclusion.

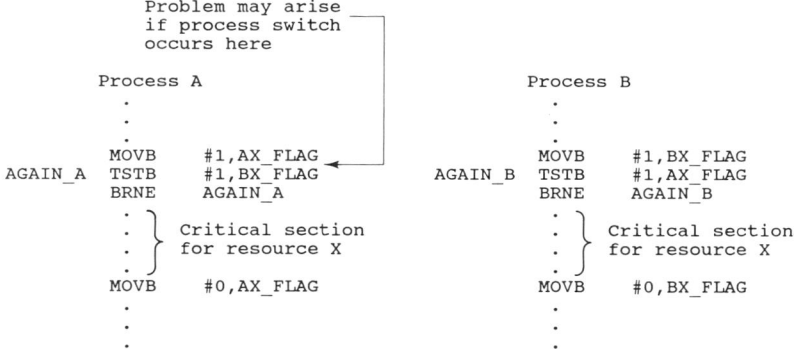

Figure 11-19 Critical section entry code that may produce a deadlock.

guarantees mutual exclusion, it opens the door to deadlock. If a process switch occurs after the flag for a process is set but before the flag for the other process is tested, both processes could have their flags set and the tests in both processes would always fail (see Exercise 23).

In both of the above examples, the problem arose because an interrupt could occur between certain instructions and the interrupt may result in a process switch. Because an interrupt cannot occur while an instruction is executing, what is needed is a **test and set** instruction that performs both the testing and setting. It would test the exclusion flag and then set both the Z condition flag and exclusion flag if the exclusion flag is clear, or clear the Z condition flag if the exclusion flag is set. By adding the test and set instruction TESB to the X16's instruction set, the following code could be used to provide mutual exclusion while avoiding deadlock (see Exercise 24):

```
        AGAIN   TESB    X_FLAG
                BRNE    AGAIN
                  .
                  .  }  Critical section
                  .     for resource X
                MOVB    #0,X_FLAG
                  .
```

Although a test and set instruction supplies satisfactory entry code, the entry code given above may not be suitable for all multiprogramming systems and is, at best, inefficient. In a priority-based system, this code does not provide a means for removing the highest priority process when it gets stuck in the test loop, and thereby allows an indirect form of deadlock. Because it has highest priority it cannot be preempted and therefore, the process currently tying up resource X

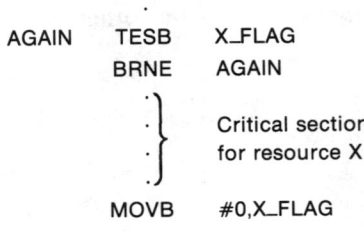

```
              .                           .
    AGAIN  TESB   X_FLAG                  BREQ    ACCESS
              .                           Put the process
              .                           into blocked state
              .                           BRUN    AGAIN
           ACCESS                         Critical section
              .                           for resource X
              .                           MOVB    #0,X_FLAG
              .                           Call the resident monitor in
    such      .                           a way that it unblocks those
              .                           processes blocked due to X_FLAG
```

Figure 11-20 Code for using a shared resource that puts a process waiting for the resource into its blocked state.

cannot become the running task. Even in a timeshared system in which the process using resource X would eventually be able to complete its critical section and release resource X by clearing X_FLAG, the system may spend a great deal of time unnecessarily idling in test loops. The solution is to expand the above code to that shown in Fig. 11-20, which causes a process that cannot enter its critical section to go into its blocked state. This solution forces a running process that must wait for a shared resource to give the use of the processing element to an unblocked process. When a process completes executing its critical section it must not only clear the exclusion flag, but must also remove from the blocked state those processes that are waiting on the flag.

11-5 AREAS FOR FURTHER STUDY

This chapter has progressed from considering uniprogramming systems that can manage only one program at a time to multiprogramming systems that juggle several programs in such a way that they can make maximum use of a single processing element. In the multiprogramming case it was tacitly assumed that programs, or processes, act independently and have no need to directly communicate with each other. Although the assumptions that there is only one processing element and the processes are independent are limiting, they permit a discussion of the major points related to operating system design. Operating systems may be very complex and their design is a complete area of study in itself. Unfortunately, space does not permit a full examination of operating systems, however, other books, such as Peterson and Silbershatz [1], provide more detail.

Four additional areas that particularly warrant further studies are:

Process synchronization, which is required when processes are not independent, but must communicate with each other in a coordinated manner. For example, one process may be unable to proceed until some event that is initiated by another process occurs. Most often the event is the transfer of information to the waiting process. Process synchronization involves the use of variables, called **semaphores**, that determine when processes must wait and when they may proceed (see Tanenbaum [2]).

Reentrant code, which allows more than one user or process to share a set of code. The shared code is a process, such as a compiler, that can be initiated by more than one user or, as shown in Fig. 11-21, a procedure that can be called by more than one process. In either case the shared code may simultaneously be part of more than one process and therefore, may be in several stages of execution at any given time. The name reentrant is derived from the fact that the code may be entered as part of one process and, because of possible intervening process switches, be *reentered* by other processes before it is exited. Reentrant code should not maintain local variables because, if X were a local variable that was set by Process A and then a process switch allowed Process B to change X, then X would contain an incorrect value when control was returned to Process A (see Liu and Gibson

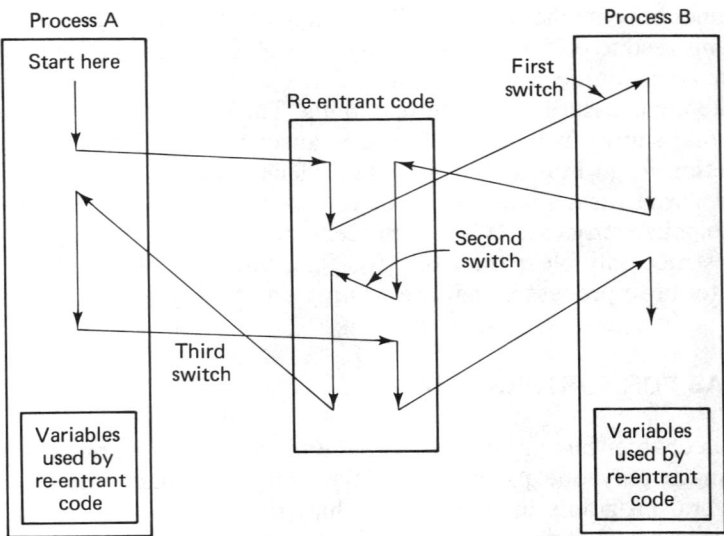

Figure 11-21 Typical usage of re-entrant code by two processes.

[3]). The purpose of reentrant code is to save memory space by allowing a large set of code to be brought into memory only once, even though it is being called by several users. Because reentrant code must appear exactly the same to all users, it is sometimes referred to as **pure code**.

Real-time executives, which are operating systems specifically designed to control a computer system that must respond to events as they occur in the external world, i.e., events that occur in *real time*. From the computer's standpoint, these events may appear to occur randomly (Intel [4]). Realtime executives are normally priority-based and preemptive so that some processes can have instant access to the computer's facilities. They are used in systems for monitoring and logging data, triggering alarms, and controlling industrial processes. Because they must respond to the external world, they are interrupt driven with the interrupts being generated by such things as realtime clocks, sensors, user activated or automatic switches, or control system transducers. A typical application of a realtime executive is the monitoring and alarm system used in a hospital's intensive care ward. As shown in Fig. 11-22, sensors could be used to send each patient's vital signs to a central nurses' station where they could be monitored and logged. In the event of an abnormal sign, an alarm could alert a nurse to take emergency action.

Multiprocessing operating systems relax the one processing element restriction that has been assumed in this chapter. The removal of this restriction significantly complicates the design of the operating system, especially in the areas of shared resources and process synchronization. With more than

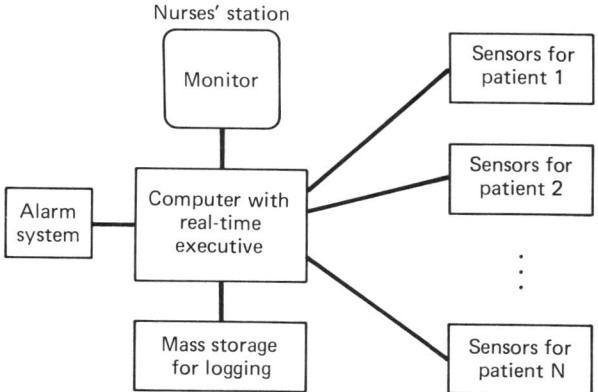

Figure 11-22 Typical application of a real-time executive.

one processing element, not only can several processes be in the system, but they can actually execute simultaneously. Therefore, the access to exclusion flags and semaphores must be rigorously controlled so that only one processing element may change a flag or semaphore at a time. For more information on multiprocessing operating systems, refer to Joseph, Prasad, and Naratajan [5].

It should be once again emphasized that an operating system is as important to a computer system as the system's hardware. An operating system should be designed to take maximal advantage of the hardware and, conversely, the hardware should be designed to support the operating system. Hardware that increases the efficiency of loading processes, managing the memory hierarchy, and performing context switching is often more important to a multiprogramming system than having very fast arithmetic hardware.

REFERENCES

1. Peterson, James L., and Abraham Silbershatz, *Operating System Concepts*, 2nd ed. (Reading, Massachusetts: Addison-Wesley Publishing Company, Inc., 1986).
2. Tanenbaum, Andrew S., *Structured Computer Organization*, 2nd ed. (Englewood Cliffs, N.J.: Prentice Hall, Inc., 1984).
3. Liu, Yu-cheng, and Glenn A. Gibson, *Microcomputer Systems: The 8086/8088 Family*, 2nd ed. (Englewood Cliffs, N.J.: Prentice Hall, Inc., 1986).
4. *Guide to Using the Distributed Control Modules* (Santa Clara, California: Intel Corporation, 1984).
5. Joseph, Mathai, V. R. Prasad, and N. Naratajan, *A Multiprocessor Operating System* (Englewood Cliffs, N.J.: Prentice Hall International, 1984).

EXERCISES

1. Discuss the services provided by an operating system and the differences between the principal types of operating systems.
2. Use X16 code to write a CLI for a uniprogramming system. Procedures may be used for inputting from and outputting to the terminal and to access mass storage. Although the procedures do not need to be written, define the procedures and the parameters passed between them and the CLI.
3. At what address does execution begin when a computer is turned on?
4. Redraw Fig. 11-1 and superimpose on the figure the movement of the code during startup.
5. What part of an operating system oversees the accessing of files?
6. Why is the I/O portion of a uniprogramming operating system divided into a BIOS and I/O drivers?
7. Assume a disk with 40 tracks and 128 sectors per track with each sector containing 256 bytes. Suppose that files are stored contiguously, the outer track is reserved for the directory, each directory entry is eight bytes long and contains the name of the file and the disk address of the beginning of the file, and the directory is searched linearly. The name of a file occupies six bytes and for an unused directory entry, the name field is filled with null characters. Assuming that the memory can hold only one sector of the directory at a time, flowchart the activity that occurs after a command is given to load a program into the user memory area shown in Fig. 11-4.
8. Repeat Exercise 7, but assume a file structure in which the directory and file records may be scattered around the disk, except that the first record of the directory must be in sector 0 of track 0. The last eight bytes of a sector are used to point to the next sector in the directory or file and are filled with 0s if the sector is the last sector in the directory or file.
9. In Exercise 7 or 8 no mention was made of how the file management system is to account for unused sectors. Discuss how a special file could be used for this purpose for the scheme in:
   (a) Exercise 7.
   (b) Exercise 8.
10. Referring to Exercise 9, if a single bit is used to indicate whether a sector is being used (1) or unused (0), flowchart a program that deletes a file from the file structure described in Exercise 7. Indicate in the flowchart the calls made to the file management system and describe what the file management system is to do when it is called. Discuss the difficulties that arise when deleting a file from the structure indicated in Exercise 8.
11. Discuss the two means for providing system services.
12. Assume that an invalid instruction causes an interrupt that results in the message

    INVALID INSTRUCTION−PROGRAM ABORTED

    being printed and the current program being terminated. Flowchart the actions taken by the invalid instruction interrupt routine and indicate its call to the BIOS. Describe the communication between the interrupt routine and the BIOS and what the BIOS is to do.

13. Draw a timing diagram that shows the I/O and processing activities in a uniprogramming system while triple buffering is used to simultaneously perform inputting, processing, and outputting.
14. Consider a multiprogramming system with a FIFO ready queue. Assuming that all processes cyclically process for 0.5 mS and are then blocked for I/O for 1 mS and a process switch requires 0.1 mS, draw a timing diagram that shows the activity of three processes through four process-I/O cycles. Determine the percentage of wasted time if all processes execute indefinitely and there are
    (a) Two processes.
    (b) Three processes.
    (c) Four processes.
15. Extend the ready queue shown in Fig. 11-12 to one that handles priority levels and uses round robin selection within each level.
16. Give a step-by-step accounting of what must be done during a context switch.
17. Assume all processes must be in memory, each process must occupy a contiguous area, and a process cannot be moved once it has been put into memory. Give a step-by-step description of the memory management's activities when a process is created. Describe the activities when a process is deleted.
18. Suppose that demand paging is being used and give a step-by-step description of what happens after the page routine is called.
19. Give at least two items that must be included in an I/O request block.
20. Devise a method for buffering sectors of information as they are transferred to and from a disk. Keep in mind that the space allocated within a program may be less than that needed for a sector.
21. Suppose that a printer is shared by several processes and describe a method for reserving the printer for a process until it has completed its printing. Describe how the method would affect the printer's I/O request queue.
22. Give a sequence of events that would allow the processes in Fig. 11-18 to be in their critical sections at the same time.
23. Give a sequence of events that would cause the processes in Fig. 11-19 to become deadlocked.
24. Prove that the test and set instruction can provide mutual exclusion while avoiding deadlock.
25. Give a scheme for putting processes that are waiting for shared resources into the blocked state and then later releasing them from the blocked state. Would the processes that are blocked need to be queued or simply noted in an array or list? If there are five shared resources and ten processes, how many queues, arrays, or lists would be required?
26. Use Fig. 11-21 to provide a sequence of events that would cause a local variable X in a set of reentrant code to have an incorrect value.

12

Parallel Processing

Until now our discussions have assumed computers with only one processing element which, in turn, have only one ALU. A typical processing element containing only one ALU was discussed at length in Chap. 7 and it was seen that the timing of such a processing element is dictated by the element's clock. The rate at which instructions are executed is ultimately determined by the clock's frequency.

From Chap. 3 it was seen that the maximum clock rate is determined by the switching time of the logic, and the switching time is determined by both the technology and power with which the logic is driven. Although logic fabricated from a given technology can be made faster by driving it with more power, the heat generated has an upper limit that cannot be exceeded. Also, as power increases, the IC's gate density must be decreased. The end result is that, even if one resorts to using several IC's (as in Sec. 7-6) and a high speed technology, there is an upper bound beyond which a single processing element, single ALU design cannot go. At some point a designer must consider using multiple sets of logic to decode the instructions and perform the arithmetic and logic operations.

In its most general sense, **parallel processing** is processing that uses more than one processing resource at a time. It may result from an attempt to obtain maximal utilization of the available hardware resources or the addition of resources for the specific purpose of allowing certain events to occur simultaneously. Parallel processing takes advantage of the fact that many of the activities that take place during the operation of a computer can be done concurrently. The two principal forms of parallel processing are multiprocessing and pipelining.

Multiprocessing is depicted is Fig. 12-1(a). It consists of using separate sets of computational logic capable of simultaneously performing a variety of operations. The source and destination storage areas may be separate (as shown in the

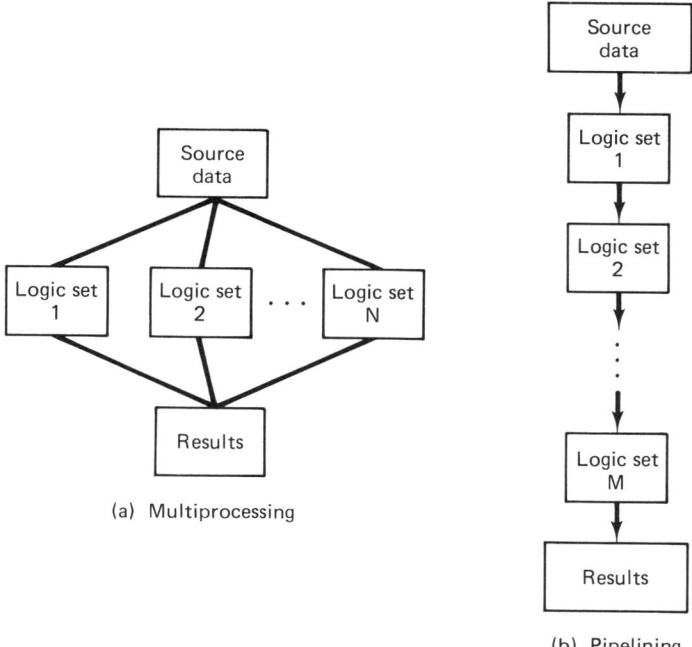

Figure 12-1 Basic types of parallel processing.

figure), combined into a single memory, or each consist of several diverse types of memories. Some of the sets of logic may be duplicates, while others may perform different operations. A multiprocessing configuration is analogous to a manufacturing plant in which there are several work stations, some producing the same products and others producing different products. In either case, the sets of logic or work stations increase the overall production by using facilities in parallel. As our discussion of multiprocessing systems proceeds, it will become apparent that a designer of such systems must pay particular attention to the:

- Overall control of the system.
- Synchronization of the work to be done.
- Communication of information within the system.

Pipelining, which sequentially uses more than one set of logic to accomplish a single overall operation, is illustrated in Fig. 12-1(b). Each set of logic performs a part of the operation and passes its partial result on to the succeeding set of logic until the last set of logic produces the final result. When a set of logic has finished its suboperation, it is free to begin another identical suboperation. Therefore, operations are overlapped in the same way the manufacture of identical products are overlapped using an assembly line. Each worker on an assembly line receives the partially completed product from the worker before him, adds something to the unfinished product, and passes it on to the next worker. The parallelism in a pipelined configuration is due to the fact that several sets of logic may be performing their suboperations simultaneously, even though they are different suboperations. Because pipelines satisfy very specific purposes and have a sequential nature, a designer's concerns for control, synchronization, and communication are somewhat diminished. The primary concern of a pipeline designer is that of guaranteeing that a set of logic has completed one suboperation before it is forced to begin another suboperation.

It is evident that multiprocessing can be used in conjunction with pipelining just as both parallel work stations and assembly lines can be incorporated into a single manufacturing plant. In fact, many analogies can be drawn between the design of a high performance computer and that of a large manufacturing facility, and much of the theory and procedures for studying these seemingly very different entities is the same.

12-1 MULTIPROCESSING

The configuration in Fig. 12-1(a) is designed to emphasize the parallelism involved in the computations made by the sets of logic. It is not intended to imply anything about the source data and result storage areas and does not rule out the possibility that the source data for one set of computational logic may come from a storage area associated with another set of computational logic. Indeed, multiprocessing systems are frequently constructed from complete simple computers, called **nodes**. A node may consist of only a processing element, a processing element and a memory element, or a processing element with a complete memory hierarchy and I/O subsystem. In addition to the nodes, a system may include shared memory and I/O elements.

The basic configuration of a multiprocessing system with respect to its nodes and the links interconnecting these nodes is referred to as the system's **topology**. Examples of the most commonly used topologies are given in Fig. 12-2. As will be discussed in Sec. 12-1-2, the topology to be used should be selected according to the classes of problems the system is to solve. If the spectrum of a system's applications is narrow, then the topology can be designed to optimize the system's performance relative to those specific applications. As the spectrum of applications broadens, the topology must be made more general, which implies more links must be included to allow greater freedom of movement of information between the nodes.

The most general purpose topology is the complete interconnection topology shown in Fig. 12-2(a). It permits every node to communicate directly with every other node and, thereby, optimally serves every possible communication pattern. However, an N-node complete interconnection topology requires $N(N-1)/2$ links and the addition of a node would require the addition of N links. For a few nodes the number of links is reasonable (e.g., for $N = 5$, the number of links is 10), but for a large number of nodes, the number of links becomes extremely large (e.g., for $N = 100$, the number of links is 4950). Some multiprocessing systems contain

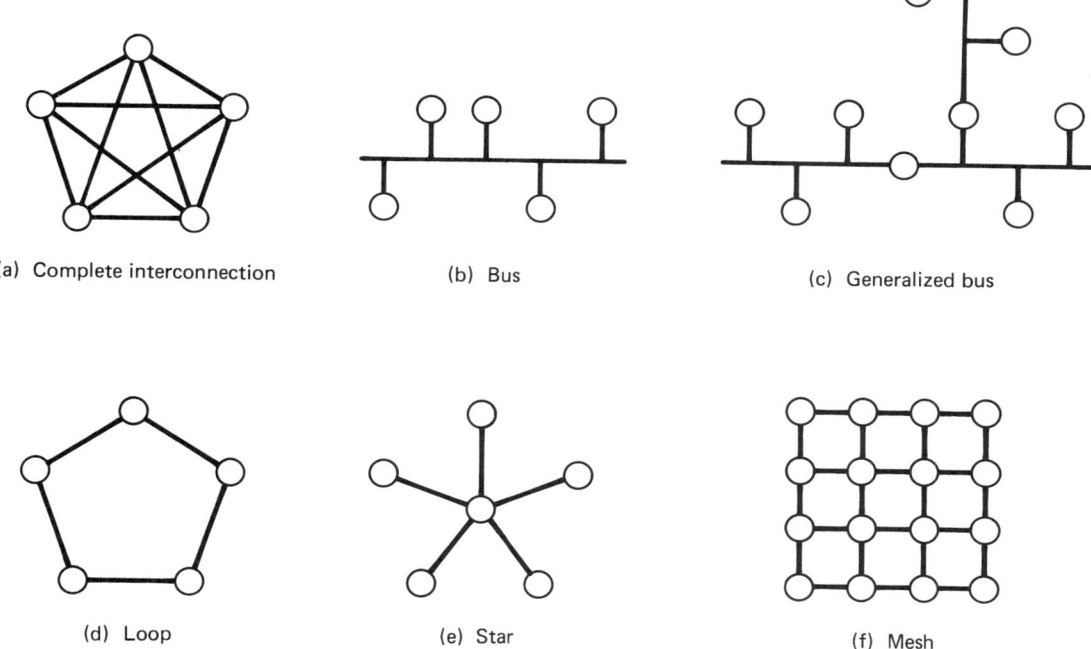

Figure 12-2 Principal topologies.

hundreds, or even thousands, of nodes. Also significant is the fact that the addition of a link not only involves the addition of the medium for implementing the link, but also requires the addition of interfacing logic at each end of the link.

If the number of nodes is large enough that a complete interconnection is impractical, a simpler topology must be chosen. Of the alternatives, the bus topology, shown in Fig. 12-2(b), or its generalized form, shown in Fig. 12-2(c), is the most common. A **bus** topology is the connection of several nodes to a single link and a **generalized bus** is obtained by joining two or more buses by using common nodes between the buses. Although a bus allows all of the nodes connected to it to communicate with each other directly, they must do so by sharing the bus. The use of a shared resource, of course, introduces the problem of contention and the associated requirement for arbitration. The addition of a node would require only the addition of the node's interface logic and an expansion of the arbitration system to include the new node.

A **loop** (or **ring**) topology, such as the one in Fig. 12-2(d), consists of elements connected by links that join only two nodes and are such that each node is directly connected to exactly two other nodes. This configuration limits direct communications to adjacent nodes and all other communications must pass through intervening nodes. The addition of a node would require the addition of a link and two interfaces for connecting the node to the new link and an existing link.

As seen from Fig. 12-2(e), a **star** is characterized by one central node being connected to all other nodes and all other nodes being connected to only the central node. A direct communication can be conducted only between the central node and one of the other nodes. Any two nodes can communicate with each other, but must do so through the central node. Quite often the sole task of the central node is to provide for communication among the other nodes, but the central node may also serve as a master for the entire system. The addition of a node would be a matter of adding a link and the two interfaces needed to connect the link to the central node and the new node.

The **mesh** topology shown in Fig. 12-2(f) is a rectangular mesh. A mesh can be drawn on a plane without any of the links crossing each other. Except for the nodes that lie along the boundary, a rectangular mesh is such that each node is connected to exactly four other nodes. Therefore, an interior node would be able to communicate directly with four other nodes. Rarely would only one node be added to a mesh. Rectangular meshes are extended by adding a whole row or column. The reason for this will become apparent in Sec. 12-1-2 in which mesh applications are considered. If a row or column of M nodes is added to a rectangular mesh, the number of new links would be $2M - 1$, or approximately two links per node.

Control of a multiprocessing system can be either **centralized**, in which the overall control of the system is assigned to one node, or **decentralized**. For a decentralized system, all nodes are considered of equal importance and no node has control over other nodes. In a decentralized system, nodes act independently. A bus topology may be either centralized or decentralized depending on whether one of the nodes has been assigned to be the controlling node. Likewise, a star topology may be either centralized or decentralized, but if it is centralized, the central node is the controlling node. If it is decentralized, the central node is normally just a switching node that directs the communications initiated by the other nodes. Loop and mesh topologies are almost always decentralized. However, most mesh systems include a controlling node that is not part of the mesh but is needed to initialize the mesh and output its results.

12-1-1 Bus Topologies

A simple bus configuration is shown in greater detail in Fig. 12-3. In addition to the subsystems that constitute the nodes and the central bus, the system must include the interfaces that connect the nodes to the bus and a means for arbitrating the use of the bus. The design of the bus itself must include a way for indicating when the bus is busy and a means for allowing the node interfaces to make requests and receive grants.

Two possible designs are shown in Fig. 12-4. The design in Fig. 12-4(a) uses a daisy chain to determine which node is to get access to the bus next. While the bus is making a transfer, the Busy line is active and when the Busy line becomes inactive, the bus becomes available to make another transfer. The daisy chain logic at each node is such that it outputs a 1 if the node is not making a request and its daisy chain input is 1; otherwise it outputs a 0. Therefore, the 1 signal

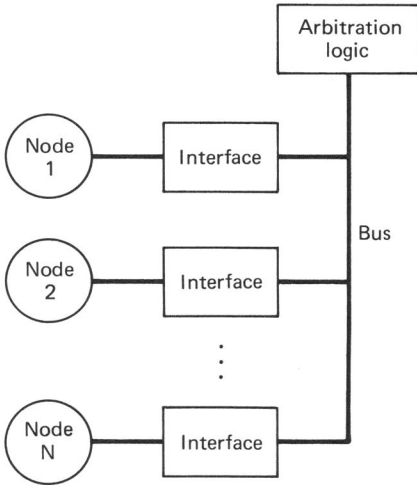

Figure 12-3 Simple bus.

applied to the highest priority interface propagates down the daisy chain until it encounters an interface that is making a request. The interface that intercepts this "grant" signal and blocks it from passing on to the next interface gets control of the bus by activating the Busy line and then proceeds to make its transfer.

This design includes the usual problems associated with daisy chaining (i.e., fixed priorities and the delay due to the propagation of the grant signal) and is not suitable for most multiprocessing applications. The propagation delay of the

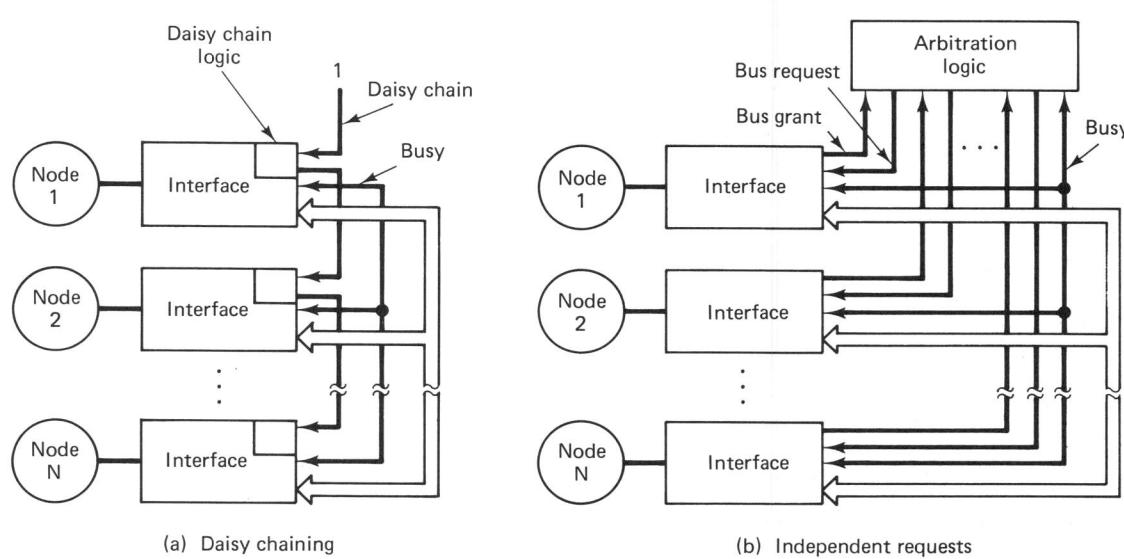

(a) Daisy chaining

(b) Independent requests

Figure 12-4 Representative bus designs.

grant signal is particularly troublesome because the bus is a shared resource and, for most applications, must have a very high transfer rate. Daisy chains are generally limited to systems with no more than three or four nodes.

The design given in Fig. 12-4(b) is much more flexible. Each interface has a request/grant pair associated with it that is also connected to the Arbitration logic. The Arbitration logic inputs the requests and outputs a grant to the interface currently having the highest priority. When the Busy line is deactivated, indicating the end of the current transfer, the interface receiving the grant reactivates the Busy line and proceeds with its transfer. The rules for determining the priorities of the requests could be programmed into the Arbitration logic and may be static until they are reprogrammed or dynamic so that they change with each request (e.g., the priorities may rotate as the requests are processed and thereby avoid starvation of any of the nodes).

Once an interface has been granted permission to use a bus it could conduct a transfer in the same manner as described in Sec. 8-1. After activating the Busy line it could apply an address to the address bus and signals to other control lines that indicate whether an input or output is to be performed and which address space is to be used. Each interface would have an address associated with it and contain Selection logic capable of identifying its address. After the addressed node has accepted the data, in the case of an output, or supplied the data, in the case of an input, it activates a Ready line. When the interface controlling the transfer detects the Ready signal, it drops its control, address, and, for an output, data signals and, after waiting for the bus to stabilize, deactivates the Busy line. A timing diagram for a typical output is given in Fig. 12-5.

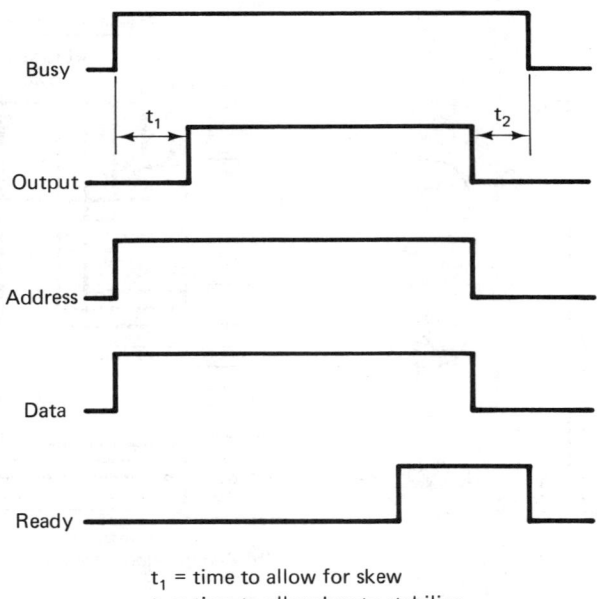

t_1 = time to allow for skew
t_2 = time to allow bus to stabilize

Figure 12-5 Timing diagram for an output transfer from one node to another.

One serious problem with this scheme is that the destination does not know in advance that it is to be communicated with and therefore, may not be able to receive or supply data immediately. When communicating with the memory or I/O interfaces considered in Chap. 8, the time needed for an interface to respond was known to be relatively short and predictable. However, this is not necessarily the case for a node interface. A node interface may be busy executing a completely unrelated task at the time it is signalled that it is needed to complete a bus transfer. At the time it receives notification of the transfer it may have to complete an operation before it is able to receive or transmit the required data.

This problem could be somewhat alleviated by installing buffer registers (or a buffer memory) in a node's interface, but if the node must supply data to the bus efficiently it must anticipate which data are needed next. Quite often the problem is resolved by not having nodes communicate directly with each other, but by having them communicate via a shared memory as shown in Fig. 12-6. Buffer areas within the memory are used to transfer data between nodes, and flags associated with the areas indicate when the areas have been filled or emptied. However, using a shared memory to provide buffering causes each transfer between nodes to require two bus transfers instead of one.

What is contained in the nodes of a multiprocessing system may vary according to the system requirements. Consider a system such as the one given in Fig. 12-7 and first assume that the nodes provide only processing and contain no

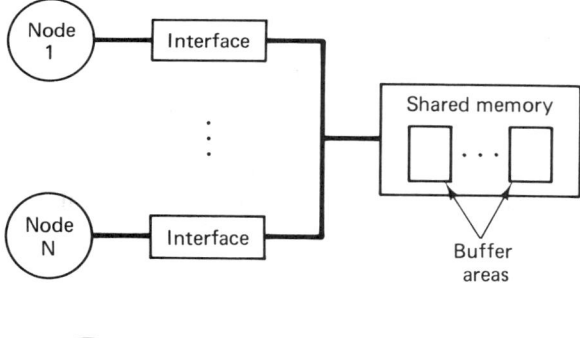

Figure 12-6 Buffered communication using a shared memory.

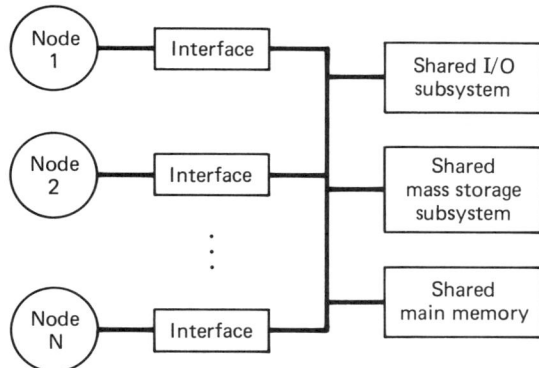

Figure 12-7 Multiprocessing system with shared memory, mass storage, and I/O elements.

main memory or I/O capability. Then, all instruction and data fetches must be made using the bus. If the bus bandwidth in transfers per second were B and, assuming no contention, the bus request rate for each of the N nodes were R, then a graph showing the bus transfers per second would have the form shown in Fig. 12-8. When NR is much less than B the graph is essentially a straight line of slope R (i.e., virtually all requests are honored immediately), but as N increases, wasted time due to contention and the randomness of the requests forces the bus usage by each node to drop below R. As N becomes large, the bus response to the nodes deteriorates and the overall bus transfer rate approaches, but cannot exceed, the bandwidth B.

As the product NR surpasses B by a significant amount, to further increase performance by increasing the number of nodes the designer must seek ways of reducing the traffic on the bus. The most obvious means for reducing this traffic is to include some memory in the nodes. A relatively small local node memory would considerably reduce or eliminate instruction fetches and, as discussed in previous chapters, these fetches frequently account for 30% to 50% of the traffic on a system bus. Larger local memories could be used to decrease data transfers as well, but the extent of the reduction would heavily depend on the application and the need for the nodes to share operands and results.

In addition to distributing memory elements among nodes it may be advantageous to give some nodes their own mass storage and I/O elements. If this is done, then each node becomes a system such as those considered in earlier chapters. The mass storage and I/O elements could be supplemented by shared elements, which may be expensive elements that are shared for reasons of cost or elements that must provide a central storage facility for shared data. It should be noted that there would be contention for the various elements in the shared I/O, mass storage, and main memory subsystems as well as the bus. However, these subsystems may contain several elements and properly designing them and their interfaces could minimize the effects of this contention.

One way to reduce bus contention and, at the same time, make it easier to access particularly important shared information is to use multiport memories. For example, a dual port memory could be connected to both the shared and local buses of a heavily used primary node. Then the designer could connect one port to the local bus of the primary node and the other port to the shared bus. This

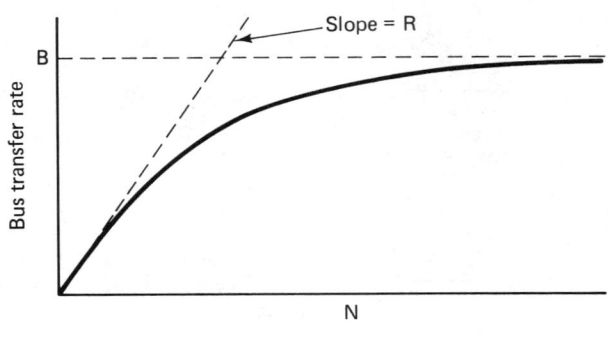

Figure 12-8 Bus utilization as a function of the number of nodes.

setup would allow the primary node access to the memory without contending for the shared bus and would still give the other nodes access to the memory without going through the primary node.

12-1-2 Non-bus Topologies

The common characteristic shared by strictly non-bus topologies, such as the loop, star, and mesh topologies, is that each link is connected to only two nodes, meaning that address lines are not needed for internode communications. For a simplex (unidirectional) link, the data could be output by one node and then, after allowing for skew, a single signal could be used to indicate that data are on the data bus. If the link is synchronous, the data are automatically dropped before the end of the clock cycle. For an asynchronous link, a Ready signal is used to indicate when the data have been accepted by the receiving node. A full duplex link could be constructed from two simplex links.

A half duplex link could be controlled as shown in Fig. 12-9. It is assumed that the nodes being linked are denoted A and B and the signal Data On Line (DOL) AB indicates an output from A to B and DOL BA indicates that the data are to be transferred in the opposite direction. When A wishes to output to B, it places a signal on DOL AB and waits slightly more than $2t_d$, where t_d is the

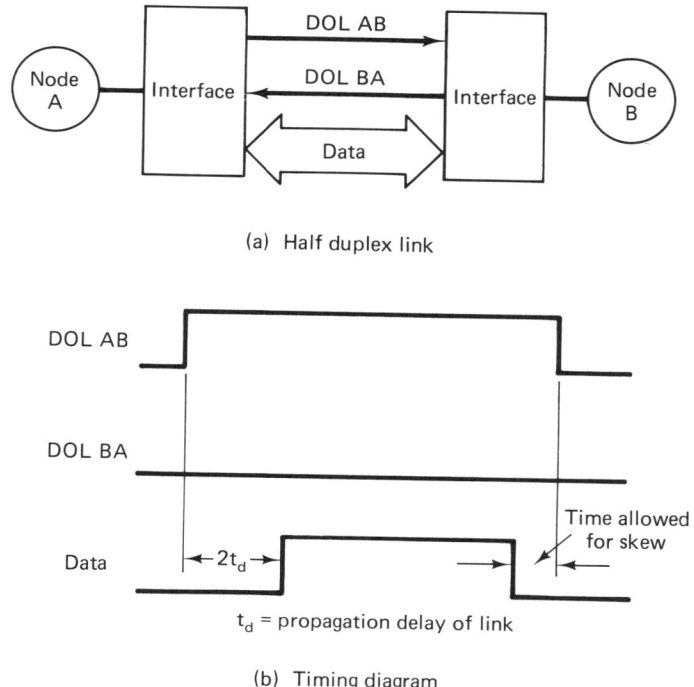

Figure 12-9 Communication between two nodes connected by a half duplex link.

propagation delay of the lines DOL AB and DOL BA. If, after $2t_d$ an active signal is not detected on DOL BA, then node A has control of the link and may put data on the data bus. Otherwise, node A waits a specified period of time and tries again. Communication from B to A is conducted in the same way except that the specified time for waiting before trying again must be different. The node having the shorter time would have priority over the other node. The link may be synchronous or asynchronous. If it is asynchronous, Ready signals are needed to indicate when data have been accepted.

In general, the links for a non-bus topology are much simpler than those of a bus. Not only has the need for address lines and arbitration been eliminated, but also handshaking is often simpler. This simplification is fortunate because there is normally a much greater number of links and link interfaces in a non-bus topology.

The topology of a multiprocessor system is often selected to satisfy a certain application or class of applications, particularly when multiprocessing is needed to provide solutions rapidly to a limited class of numerical algorithms, such as those for performing matrix operations or solving partial differential equations. There are two classes of applied mathematical problems that have been found to be basic to high performance computing; they are those described by

- Continuum models.
- Particle models.

A **continuum model** is one in which the activity at a point depends directly on only the points surrounding that point. Such models are mathematically described by partial differential equations involving space and time and concern the calculation of such variables as charge density or temperature. A **particle model** is one for which the effects at a point may be due to properties associated with distant points. For example, the motion of a particle at one point may depend on all other particles in a system. Typical physical variables in a particle model are velocity, displacement, and force.

Although space does not allow a thorough discussion of choosing a topology to match the problem(s) to be solved (see Stone [1]), it is worthwhile to study an example in detail. The equation describing a lossless transmission line is

$$\frac{\partial^2 V}{\partial x^2} = LC \frac{\partial^2 V}{\partial t^2}$$

where x is the distance from the reference end of the line, t is time, LC is the product of the distributed inductance and capacitance of the line, and V is the voltage difference as a function of x and t. Let us assume that the voltage function $v(t)$ is used to drive the line at one end, where $x = 0$, and the other end, at $x = x_n$, is shorted together so that

$$V(x_n, t) = 0$$

for all t. Let us also assume that $V(x, 0) = 0$.

To solve the problem using a digital computer, which has only a finite number of states, the problem must be put into a discrete form such as the one shown in Fig. 12-10. In the figure, both x and t have been reduced to a finite number of equally spaced points. The distance between the points in x is $\Delta x = x_n/n$ and in t it is $\Delta t = t_m/m$. Using the approximation

$$\frac{\partial^2 V}{\partial x^2} \approx \left(\frac{V_{i+1,j} - V_{ij}}{\Delta x} - \frac{V_{ij} - V_{i-1,j}}{\Delta x} \right) \Big/ \Delta x$$

and a similar approximation for $\frac{\partial^2 V}{\partial t^2}$, the above partial differential equation becomes

$$\frac{V_{i+1,j} - 2V_{ij} + V_{i-1,j}}{\Delta x^2} = LC \left(\frac{V_{i,j+1} - 2V_{ij} + V_{i,j-1}}{\Delta t^2} \right)$$

for all i and j such that $0 < i < n$ and $0 < j < m$. Solving for V_{ij} we get, for all interior points of the array shown in Fig. 12-10:

$$V_{ij} = aV_{i,j-1} - bV_{i+1,j} + aV_{i,j+1} - bV_{i-1,j}$$

where a and b are easily computed from L, C, Δx, and Δt (see Exercise 9). The values of the points on the perimeter of the array must satisfy the boundary conditions and are, therefore, known.

The problem is now one of solving $(n-1)(m-1)$ equations in an equal number of unknowns, where each equation gives V_{ij} as a weighted sum of the surrounding values of the voltage difference. It is known that such equations can be solved iteratively by assuming a set of values $V_{ij}^{(0)}$ and then letting

$$V_{ij}^{(k+1)} = aV_{i,j-1}^{(k)} - bV_{i+1,j}^{(k)} + aV_{i,j+1}^{(k)} - bV_{i-1,j}^{(k)}$$

Now suppose that a rectangular array of $(n-1)(m-1)$ processing elements, one for each value of V_{ij}, are used to solve the problem. During each iteration each processing element must obtain one value from each of its neighbors and

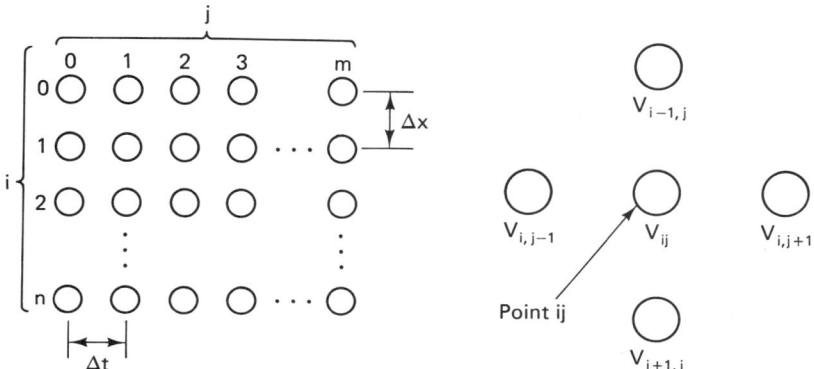

Figure 12-10 Reduction of a partial differential equation to a discrete form.

then evaluate a simple sum of products expression. The instruction sequence performed during each iteration by the processing element at the internal node ij is:

1. Zero an accumulator.
2. Input from node $i, j - 1$, multiply the input by a, and add the result to the accumulator.
3. Input from node $i + 1, j$, multiply the input by b, and subtract the result from the accumulator.
4. Input from node $i, j + 1$ and repeat the operations in Step 2.
5. Input from node $i - 1, j$ and repeat the operations in Step 3.

Iterations would continue until all new values differ by less than a specified amount from the corresponding current values.

Because there is a processing element assigned to each point, the iterations are computed very quickly, e.g., if an iteration requires 100 μS and there are 100 iterations, then only 10 mS would be required to obtain a solution.

The fallacy in this method is that a very large value of $(n - 1)(m - 1)$ is often needed to provide a sufficiently accurate solution. This value may be in the thousands or even millions. Therefore, solutions to partial differential equations, as well as other problems amenable to the use of multiprocessing, are often segmented into parts. For the above example, the array shown in Fig. 12-10 could be broken into subarrays according to the number of available processors. Then for each iteration, the new values would be found by sequentially determining new values for each subarray. However, if a processing element must be assigned to several points, it may become necessary to provide it with its own memory because the processing element's registers may no longer provide enough storage space.

12-1-3 Synchronization and Resource Sharing

In the continuum example, while performing iterations, all processing elements executed the same instructions and could execute them in a lock-step fashion. Therefore, synchronization could be maintained by a single clock connected to all processing elements.

In general, synchronization cannot be attained so easily. Frequently, there are several tasks that may be done in parallel and they are simply assigned to available processing elements. As tasks are completed, the processing elements may be assigned to other tasks and so on. However, the tasks are not normally independent because some tasks use the results of other tasks, which implies that there is an ordering among tasks and this ordering requires some form of synchronization. This synchronization is most often implemented using semaphores that determine when a task must wait and when it may proceed to be executed.

As with matching topologies to applications, space does not permit a thorough examination of task synchronization, but discussion of the more important problems related to synchronization and resource sharing is in order. In particular, we will briefly consider three examples that present three basic problems and offer possible solutions to these problems.

Example 1:

Let us first consider the task ordering shown in Fig. 12-11 and assume that three processing elements numbered 1, 2, and 3 are available. Processing element 1 could be used to execute task A and then tasks B, C, and D could be assigned to processing elements 1, 2, and 3, respectively. When tasks B and C are complete, processing element 1 could execute task E and when task E is finished, processing element 1 could be assigned task F. After both D and E have been completed, task G could be assigned to processing element 3. Finally, when tasks F and G are finished processing, element 1 could execute task H. When a task is complete it would activate its semaphore and when all of the required semaphores are active, the succeeding task(s) could begin. Because it may be necessary to reuse semaphores (e.g., the ordering shown in Fig. 12-11(a) may be inside a loop), the semaphores should be deactivated once they have been recognized and the next task is ready to begin.

Tasks may consist of single machine language instructions or entire programs. For a multiprocessing system to run efficiently, tasks should be more or less the same size; otherwise, there would be a tendency for many of the processing elements to be waiting for a relatively long task to complete. If the tasks are approximately the same size, this size represents the **granularity** of the system. A tendency toward small tasks is referred to as **fine granularity** and a tendency toward large tasks is called **coarse granularity**. In general, the finer the granularity the more difficult it is to achieve synchronization. Also, systems that use fine granularity tend to require more communication between processing elements (see Stone [1]).

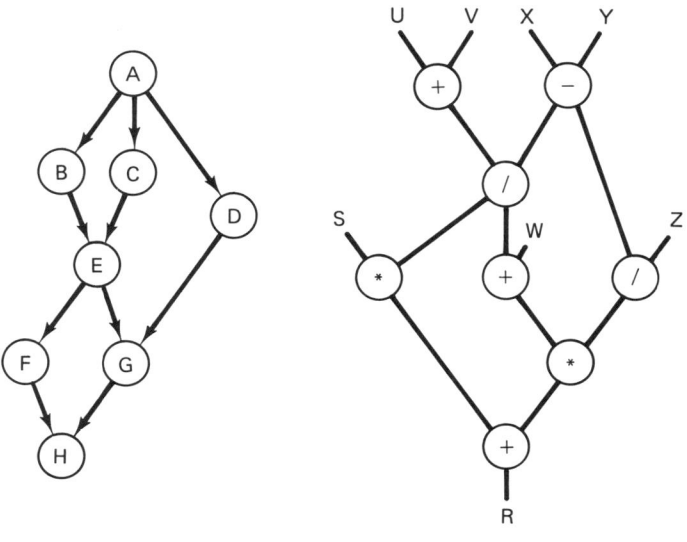

(a) Task of arbitrary size   (b) Instruction size tasks

Figure 12-11 Examples of task ordering.

Although it is more difficult to satisfy synchronization constraints for fine granularity, there is a class of computers, called **data flow computers**, whose members provide parallelism at the instruction level. Conventional computers, such as those discussed in this book, fetch and execute their instructions sequentially. Even though pipelining can be used to overlap the fetching and execution of successive instructions, the instruction fetched first must be executed first. In contrast, for a data flow computer, the order of execution of instructions is not determined by an a priori ordering of the instructions in memory, but by the order in which results are produced by the available processing elements.

For example, consider the following statement:

$$R := (((U+V)/(X-Y))*S) + ((((U+V)/(X-Y)) + W)*((X-Y)/Z));$$

A data flow graph showing the order in which the arithmetic operations are executed according to the parentheses is given in Fig. 12-11(b). There are eight operations to be performed and as many as three ALUs could be utilized. With three ALUs, the addition $U + V$ and subtraction $X - Y$ could be performed simultaneously, but the division $(U + V)/(X - Y)$ and the division $(X - Y)/Z$ would have to await their results. In turn, the addition of W would have to be delayed until after $(U + V)/(X - Y)$ has been computed and so on. If addition and subtraction require 400 nS and multiplication and division require 500 nS, then the delay along the longest path,

$$400 + 500 + 400 + 500 + 400 = 2200 \text{ nS}$$

determines the overall computation time, which is compared to the 3600 nS required to sequentially execute the eight operations.

The central idea behind a data flow computer is to execute operations sequentially only when it is necessary. Operations are performed as soon as their operands become available. Unfortunately, the implementation of this concept requires rather complicated hardware (see Hwang and Briggs [2]).

Example 2:

A second aspect of synchronization is the synchronization of the use of shared resources. In Sec. 11-4, the code

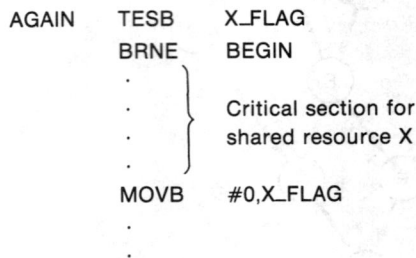

was used to provide mutual exclusion and avoid deadlock in a multiprogramming system. In a multiprocessing system an additional complication arises because the processes using the shared resource may be executing on different processing elements.

Consider the bus topology shown in Fig. 12-12 that includes a shared memory. In a multiprogramming environment, process switches are due to interrupts and can occur only between instructions. Therefore, by using a test and set instruction to both test and set the flag protecting the critical section of code, a switch could not occur between the test and set operations. However, in a multiprocessing environment such as the one in Fig. 12-12, access to the flag is made at the bus transfer level and instruction completion is not significant.

For example, suppose that the TESB instruction brings in the flag indicated by its operand, tests it, and then outputs the updated value. If both processing elements 1 and 2 begin executing the TESB instruction just prior to using the shared resource, processing element 1 uses the next bus transfer to input the flag, processing element 2 uses the succeeding bus transfer to input the flag, and both processing elements test the same flag value. If the flag is 0, then both processing elements will execute their critical sections of code and there is no mutual exclusion.

One way of avoiding this problem is to include a LOCK instruction that causes a Lock signal to be output to the processing element's bus interface throughout the execution of the next instruction. This signal could be used by the interface to hold the bus's Busy line active until the execution of the next instruction is complete. Therefore, the code

```
AGAIN   LOCK
        TESB    X_FLAG
        BRNE    AGAIN
          .
          .
          .
```

would cause the TESB instruction to be executed in its entirety before another processing element could have use of the bus. Therefore, the LOCK instruction prevents processing element 2 from using the bus until after processing element 1 has finished updating the flag and mutual exclusion is preserved.

Because of the need to synchronize both tasks and the use of shared resources, and the need to communicate both instructions and data between the elements in a system, it is impossible to fully utilize all of the elements in a system. Theoretically, a system containing N processing elements could be N times as fast as one with only one processing element. However, processing elements may sit idle while waiting for other tasks to complete or while waiting for instructions or data. The latter can

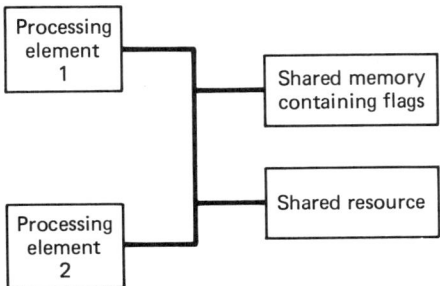

Figure 12-12 Use of a resource shared by several processing elements.

be alleviated by avoiding contention for heavily used resources (such as a shared bus) as much as possible, but the broader the application the more difficult it is to pinpoint these resources. Resource utilization may vary drastically with the tasks being performed. For multiprocessing systems that serve a wide variety of purposes it has been found that the average number of processing elements that are in use at a time typically does not exceed $N/\ln_2 N$ (see Hwang and Briggs [2]). For a specific application, such as the solution of partial differential equations, an appropriate hardware design could of course do much better.

Example 3:

For the third example, consider the configuration in Fig. 12-13. The memory element shown in this figure may be any element in the memory hierarchy, but the multiprocessing is more likely to be of fine granularity and the memory element is more likely to be a set of registers or a cache memory. Although two buses are shown, one for providing the processing elements with source data and the other for returning results, they are included only for the sake of clarity and a single bus would be adequate. The specific problem is that of allowing a sequence of instructions to be distributed to the processing elements and their execution to be overlapped in such a way that reading from and writing to the memory element is done in the correct order.

If instructions are drawn from a sequence and dispensed to the processing elements in order, a question arises as to when an instruction may proceed. It must certainly wait if it needs to use a processing element that is currently busy, but it must also wait if it must use results of instructions that precede it but have not yet been completed. Consider any two instructions, denoted A and B, that access the same location in the memory element. There are four possible access combinations. They are

```
READ/READ
READ/WRITE
WRITE/READ
WRITE/WRITE
```

where the first operation corresponds to instruction A and must be performed first and the second corresponds to instruction B.

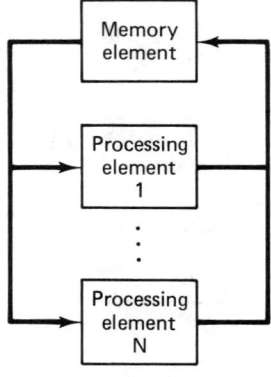

Figure 12-13 Example configuration for discussing the importance of access ordering.

The READ/READ combination is not important because the contents of the location are not changed by either operation, but the other three may require some interlocking mechanism to prevent accesses from occurring in the wrong order. If a READ by instruction A must occur before a WRITE by instruction B, an incorrect value may be read if the write by instruction B occurs first. A similar statement could be made regarding the WRITE/READ combination. For a WRITE/WRITE, instruction B must perform its WRITE last or the location may end up containing the wrong value. Consider the Pascal statements

$$X := Y + 2;$$
$$\text{IF } Y < 2 \text{ THEN } X := 1;$$

If the second statement is completed before the first statement and Y is 0, then the final value of X would be 2 instead of 1. (Also, a WRITE/WRITE problem may arise when the common location is the PSW—see Exercise 13.)

A simple way of guaranteeing correct access ordering is to associate with each memory location a valid bit that is cleared whenever a location is to be the destination of a result and set when the result arrives. The following rules can then be used to regulate instruction execution:

- A nonbranch instruction can continue to execute if and only if a reference does not attempt to access a location whose valid bit is cleared.
- A branch instruction includes the comparison that determines whether the branch is to be made.

This technique is referred to as **scoreboarding** and a proof that it does, in fact, ascertain proper ordering is requested in Exercise 14.

Although scoreboarding is relatively simple and permits some overlapping of instructions, more sophisticated schemes have been implemented that are less likely to cause an instruction to wait. Such schemes involve buffers for storing those instructions that must wait for results. Complications arise because instructions currently in a buffer may need to produce results for other instructions in the same buffer. As the buffer size grows, it becomes more difficult to implement the hardware. Note that as a buffer size goes to infinity the computer's operation approaches that of a data flow computer, whose instruction ordering is determined solely by the arrival of results (see Kain [4]). Because these extensions to scoreboarding usually require complex hardware to implement, the gain in speed may not be worth the cost. In any event, a design must be such that READ/WRITE, WRITE/READ, and WRITE/WRITE ordering cannot produce incorrect results or branching.

12-2 PIPELINING

Pipelining, which is the alternative method for simultaneously using processing resources, depends on the ability to break an operation into suboperations that are performed sequentially by **stages**. The hardware for a simple pipeline is shown in Fig. 12-14. For this configuration the output of each stage provides the input to the next stage and the buffers temporarily store outputs until they are needed. The operands for the operation are introduced at stage 1 and, when it completes

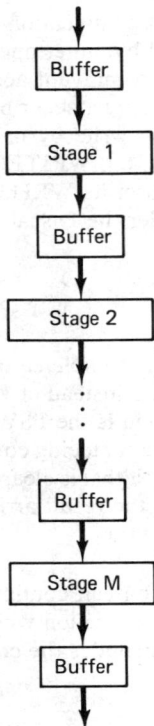

Figure 12-14 Block diagram of a simple pipeline.

its suboperation, it passes its result on to stage 2, which then begins its suboperation. At this time, stage 1 may accept operands for a second operation, even though the first operation is still in progress. After both stages 1 and 2 have completed their suboperations, stage 3 can begin operating on the output of stage 2, stage 2 can begin operating on the output of stage 1, and stage 1 can accept a third set of operands. This process can continue indefinitely.

The most commonly used method for illustrating the activity in a pipeline is shown in Fig. 12-15. Stages are indicated by the vertical axis and the numbers in the rectangles denote operations. Note that each operation is represented by a diagonal sequence of rectangles. The horizontal axis represents time and the

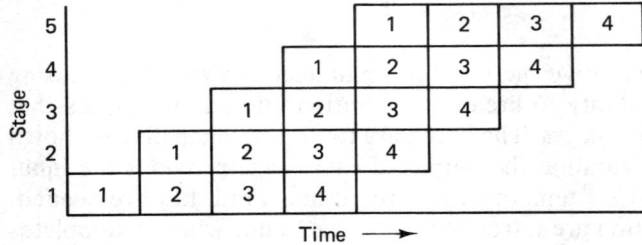

Figure 12-15 Graphical illustration of pipeline activity.

470   Parallel Processing   Chap. 12

overlapping of activities within the pipeline is indicated by the overlapping of the rows of rectangles.

A typical application of a pipeline is found in the design of floating point hardware. A pipelined floating point adder is shown in Fig. 12-16. The first stage subtracts the exponents and aligns the fractions and the second performs the addition. The third stage normalizes the results and the fourth uses the guard bits to round the normalized result to the proper number of bits. Figure 12-17 shows how N additions could be overlapped to obtain maximum use of the hardware. Note that only $N + 3$ time periods are required to complete N additions even though four time periods are needed for each operation.

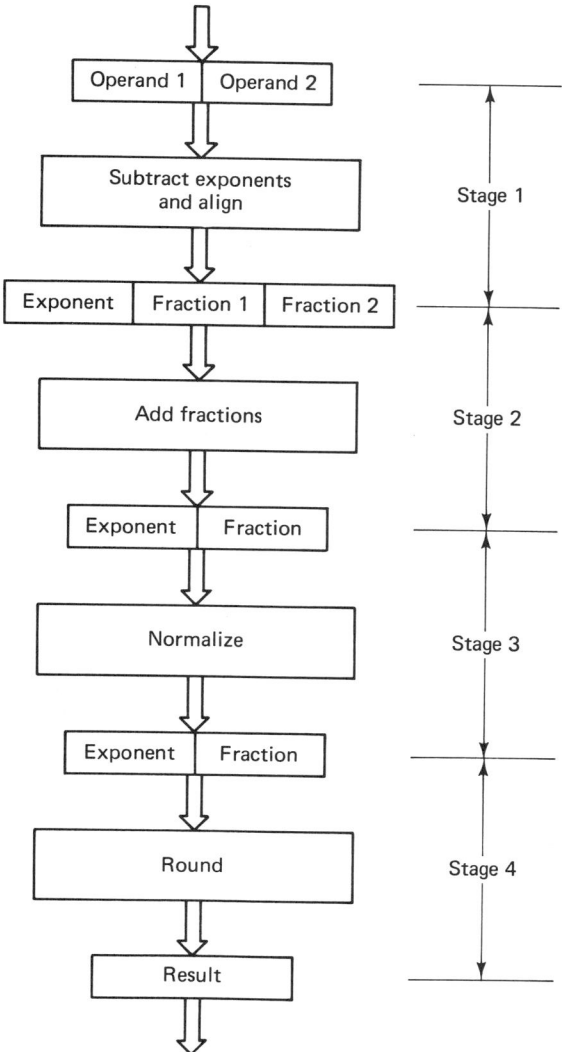

Figure 12-16 Pipelined floating point adder.

Sec. 12-2 Pipelining

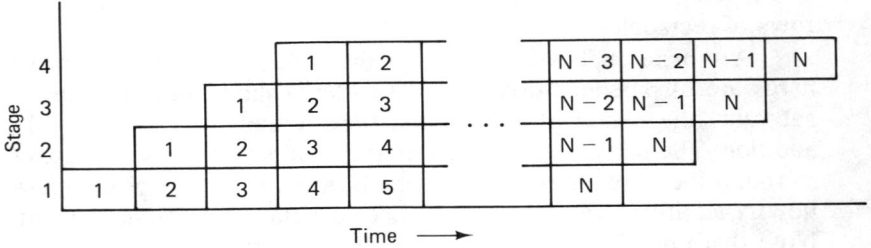

Figure 12-17 Activity of the floating point adder pipeline while performing N operations.

12-2-1 Pipeline Performance

The **speedup** of a pipeline is defined to be the number of times faster a pipelined component operates than a nonpipelined component that performs the same operation. If a component were not pipelined and M time units were needed to complete an operation, then it would take NM time units to complete N operations. In contrast, if the component were divided into M stages and each stage required one time unit then only $N + M - 1$ time units would be needed to complete the N operations. The speedup in this case is

$$\frac{NM}{N + M - 1}$$

which is a function of both the number of stages and the number of operations. As shown in Fig. 12-18, if M is held constant, the speedup as a function of N is 1 at $N = 1$ and asymptotically approaches M as N goes to infinity. For the pipeline described in Figs. 12-16 and 12-17, the speedup is $4N/(N + 3)$ which, for a large number of operations, is approximately 4.

Efficiency, on the other hand, measures the utilization of the stages. Consider the pipeline activity shown in Fig. 12-19(a). The shaded area represents the stages that are busy as operations are performed and the unshaded area inside the rectangle represents unused stages. The ratio of the shaded area (the total number of stage-periods that are used) to the area of the rectangle (the total number

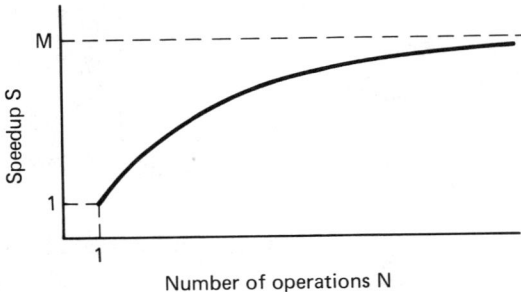

Figure 12-18 Pipeline speedup as a function of the number of operations.

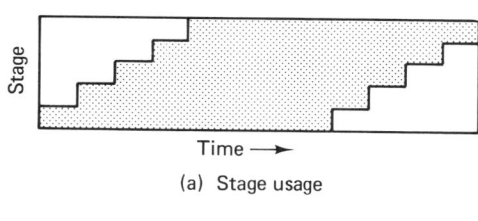

(a) Stage usage

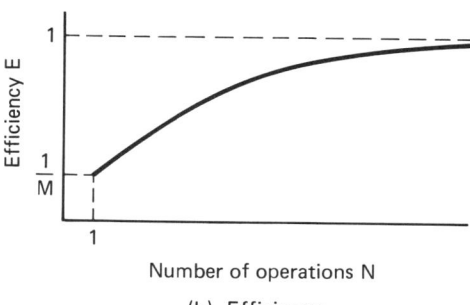

(b) Efficiency

Figure 12-19 Efficiency of a pipeline.

of available stage-periods during the overall time period) is the efficiency. If M is the number of stages and N the number of operations, then the efficiency is

$$\frac{NM}{(N + M - 1)M} = \frac{N}{N + M - 1}$$

A plot of efficiency as a function of N is given in Fig. 12-19(b). For $N = 1$, the efficiency is $1/M$ and as N goes to infinity the efficiency approaches 1. For the four-stage floating point example, the efficiency for a single addition is 0.25, but for 10 additions it is 0.77.

Note that the speedup tends to increase as M increases, because the greater number of stages permits a greater amount of overlapping and a nonpipelined component cannot take advantage of overlapping. However, increasing M does not increase efficiency and in fact, for a small number of operations, the efficiency is significantly decreased. This loss in efficiency is due to the increased time needed to start up a pipeline with a greater number of stages.

The above discussion of speedup and efficiency is slightly misleading in that it assumes that the total time for executing an operation is M times the time required to complete a stage, regardless of whether the component is pipelined. It has been tacitly assumed that all stages require the same amount of time and a nonpipelined component cannot be designed to do the same work in less time than the M stages. This case is not usually true however. To keep the pipeline fully utilized, it must work in a lock-step fashion with all stages using the same amount of time, and this time must be the maximum time taken over the set of all stages. If one stage requires less time to complete its work then the remaining time is wasted. As a result, it is important to design the stages so that they require approximately the same amount of time.

Sec. 12-2   Pipelining

A third measure of pipeline performance is **throughput,** which is the number of operations completed per unit time. For an M-stage pipeline that executes N operations, the throughput is

$$\frac{N}{(N + M - 1)T}$$

where T is the time needed to execute a stage. For given M and N, the throughput can be increased only by decreasing T. One way of decreasing T is to use duplicate hardware, as shown in Fig. 12-20(a), to implement those stages that require the most time. To see this, suppose that one stage takes twice as long as other stages. Then, that stage could be implemented by placing two sets of duplicate logic side by side and having them take turns performing the stage's suboperation. Thus, the stage would have two suboperations in progress at a time and would reduce the average time required by the stage to that required by the other stages.

An alternative is to reduce T by dividing those stages requiring the most time into more than one stage as shown in Fig. 12-20(b). This division increases the number of stages, but tends to decrease the denominator $(N + M - 1)T$. If, by adding P new stages, T is decreased by the factor $1/c$ $(c > 1)$, then the throughput becomes

$$\frac{N}{(N + M + P - 1)T} \cdot c$$

In particular, as N goes to infinity the throughput approaches c/T.

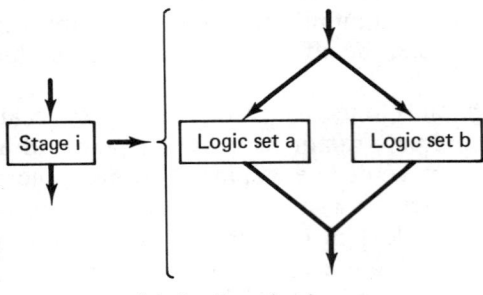

(a) Duplicate hardware

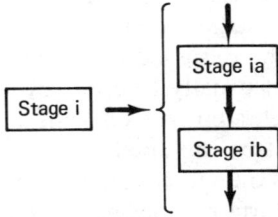

(b) Division into substages

Figure 12-20 Ways of decreasing stage execution time.

In all three of the performance criteria (speedup, efficiency, and throughput) the variable N was especially important. It is therefore worthwhile to briefly examine how N is determined. The variable N is the number of operations that can be executed consecutively while performing a task. For the floating point example, N could be the length of two vectors that are being added. The formulae for speedup, efficiency, and throughput presume that one vector addition must be finished before another can begin and therefore, the pipeline must be flushed and restarted each time vectors are added.

As a second example, consider the system in Fig. 12-21(a) and its pipeline for fetching and executing instructions given in Fig. 12-21(b). To avoid contention for the buses and memory, the instruction, source data, and result data streams have been separated. Also, an instruction can have at most one memory source operand. The first two stages fetch and decode the instruction and the second also makes any address calculation needed to fetch a source operand from memory. The third stage fetches a data operand from memory if one is needed; otherwise it does nothing. The fourth stage performs the specified operation and the fifth either stores a result in memory or does nothing. The pipeline can be kept full as long as the instructions are sequential, but must be flushed whenever there

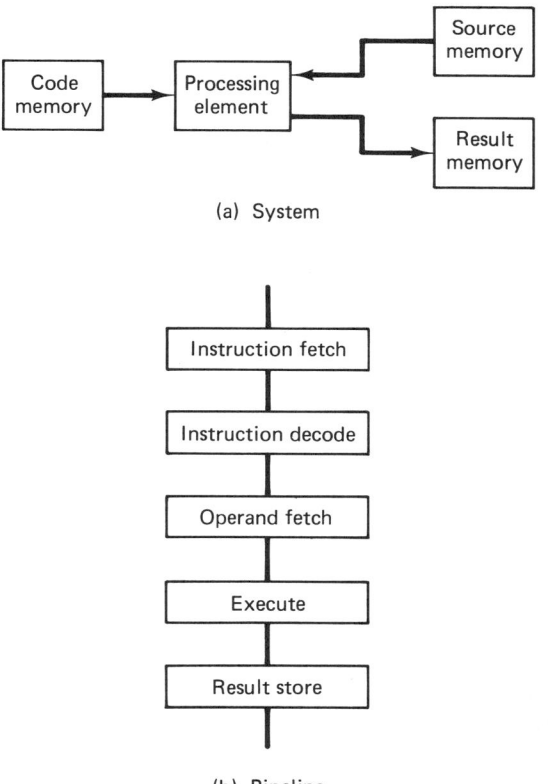

Figure 12-21 Pipelined fetch and execution of instructions.

is a branch out of sequence. For this example, N is the number of instructions executed between branches and therefore, may vary considerably as a program is executed.

The average value of N can be used to approximate the performance criteria and, if the average value of N equals 6, the approximate speedup and efficiency of the pipeline in Fig. 12-21 are 3 and 0.6, respectively. If $T = 100$ nS then the approximate throughput is 6 million instructions per second. Without pipelining, time would not need to be wasted when there is no source operand to be fetched or result to be stored, but the minimum execution time would still be 300 nS and the throughput would be between 2 and 3.33 million instructions per second.

12-2-2 Pipeline Design

The discussion until now has assumed pipelines for which the output of each stage is used as input to exactly one succeeding stage, thus causing the initial input to the pipeline to be modified once by each stage in an assembly line fashion. Also, the examples were such that contention for the resources used by the stages was avoided. The design of such a pipeline is straightforward and consists of simply breaking the overall operation into stages that require a small, and approximately the same, amount of time. However, more efficient use of the hardware can often be had by adding feedback to allow some stages to be reused and delays to avoid contention.

For example, in Fig. 12-21, three separate buses and memories were used to eliminate contention. If only a single bus and memory were used, as shown in Fig. 12-22(a), the memory accesses in the first, third, and fifth stages would disrupt the steady flow of the pipeline. A third instruction fetch could not be made two time periods after the first instruction fetch because the first instruction may be using the bus and memory to fetch a source operand.

To investigate conflicts such as the one in this example, reservation tables are used. The reservation table for the single memory, instruction fetch and execution example is shown in Fig. 12-22(b) and Fig. 12-22(c) gives a modified diagram of the pipeline that emphasizes the reuse of the bus and memory. The reservation table includes a row for each distinct set of hardware used by the pipeline and each row contains an entry for each stage. The ordering of the entries from left to right corresponds to time periods in which the stages are used. The leftmost entry corresponds to the stage used first and so on.

If one stage attempts to use a commonly used set of hardware at the same time as another stage, then a **collision** is said to occur. Collisions can be found by making a duplicate copy of the reservation table and pulling the copy across the original from left to right. When two Xs become superimposed, then a collision occurs corresponding to that displacement, where the displacement is actually a time delay. A record can be kept of the delays for which there are collisions by using a sequence of 0s and 1s. A 0 would indicate no collision and a 1 would indicate a collision. Such a sequence is called a **collision vector**. The collision vector for the pipeline in Fig. 12-22 is 0101. Note that there is one less entry in the collision vector than there are stages because there is one less possible delay

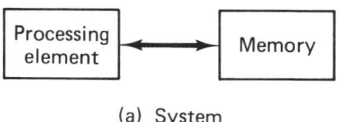

(a) System

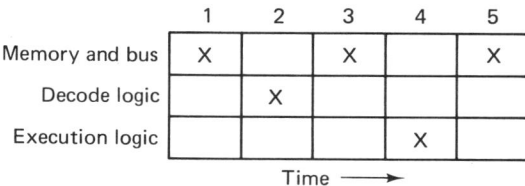

(b) Reservation table

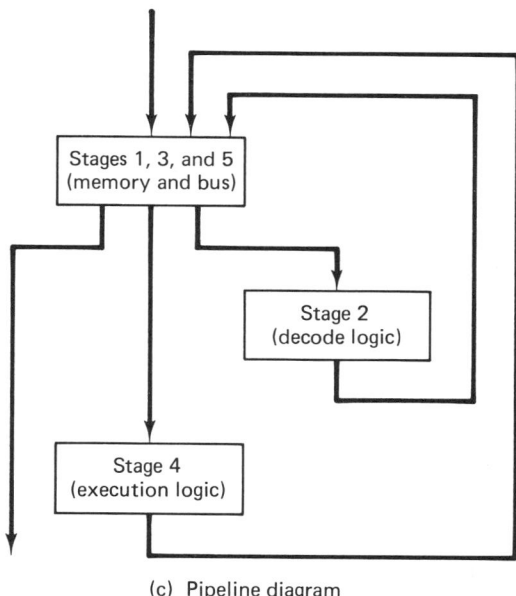

(c) Pipeline diagram

Figure 12-22 Single memory, instruction execution pipeline.

than there are stages. The collision vector 0101 means that another operation cannot begin either two or four time periods after an operation has begun.

Although a collision vector indicates delays that cannot be used it does not readily show which delay patterns can be used on a continual basis. The vector 0101 shows that a second operation can begin immediately after an operation has begun, but does not directly show when a third operation, which must take into account both previous operations, can begin. Because the resources used by both the first and second operations must be avoided by the third operation, to determine when a new operation can begin we must derive a new vector as follows:

$$\text{OR} \quad \frac{\begin{array}{cccc}0 & 1 & 0 & 1 \\ & 0 & 1 & 0 & 1\end{array}}{\begin{array}{cccc}1 & 1 & 1 & 1\end{array}}$$

The 0 on the left is ignored because the first stage of the first operation has already been executed by the time the second operation begins and does not need to be considered by the third operation. This new vector indicates that a third operation cannot begin for one, two, three, or four time periods after the second operation has begun. A new operation can always begin after five time periods because there are only five stages and after five time periods the pipeline would be flushed. Therefore, the pipeline allows operations to begin during the time periods 0, 1, 6, 7, 12, 13, . . . , which correspond to the delay pattern 1, 5, 1, 5, 1, 5, ... The average time between the initiations of successive operations is $(1 + 5)/2 = 3$ time periods.

This problem was rather easy to solve, but for more complex pipelines involving numerous resources the ideas presented above must be extended to a systematic approach. Before any operations have begun the pipeline is in its initial state. After the first operation is initiated the pipeline enters a new state and so on. Each new state is described by a vector obtained by ORing the vector of the current state with the collision vector displaced one to the left. The vector for a state indicates the possible displacements that can be used by the next operation. Each of these displacements can be used to generate new state vectors. Sooner or later the pipeline returns to its initial state. The diagram obtained by generating all possible distinct states is called a **reduced state diagram**.

The reduced state diagram for the pipeline in Fig. 12-22 is given in Fig. 12-23. In addition to the state whose vector is 1111 the diagram includes a state whose vector is 1101, which is entered by using a delay of 3 after the first operation

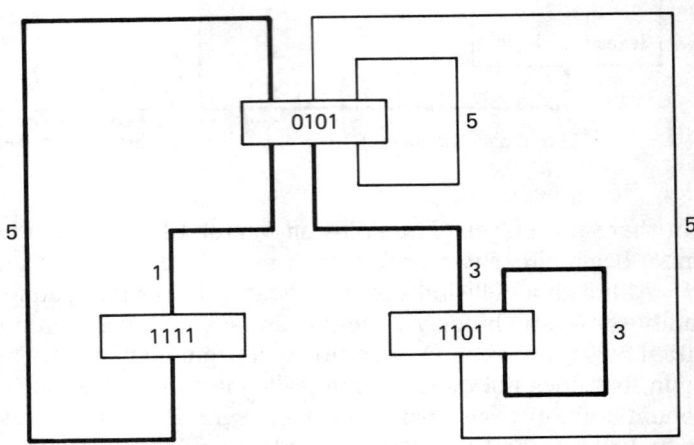

Figure 12-23 Reduced state diagram for the pipeline in Figure 12-22.

instead of a delay of 1. This vector results from

$$\text{OR} \quad \frac{\begin{array}{cccc} 0 & 1 & 0 & 1 \\ & 0 & 1 & 0 & 1 \end{array}}{\begin{array}{ccccc} 1 & 1 & 0 & 1 \end{array}}$$

The numbers next to the lines connecting the states indicate the delay causing the state change. Any complete loop within a reduced state diagram can be used to produce a delay pattern. The heavily lined loop on the left provides the 1, 5, 1, 5, . . . pattern arrived at above and the heavily lined loop on the right yields an alternate pattern 3, 3, 3, . . . , which corresponds to operations beginning at the time periods 0, 3, 6, . . . (every third time period). Two other possibilities are the patterns 3, 5, 3, 5, . . . and 5, 5, 5, . . . , but they would not allow new operations to begin as often.

In this example, the reduced state diagram was used to find patterns that allow the introduction of a new operation every third period, which is the same as, on the average, introducing $5/3$ operations every five periods. It is clear that this pattern is optimal because one of the rows in the reservation table contains three Xs and there are five stages. To do better would require more than the two unused entries that are available in that row. Although it was possible in this example to obtain an optimal pattern from the reduced state diagram without modifying the pipeline's design, this is not always the case.

Let us now consider the pipeline for the floating point adder given in Fig. 12-24(a). First, the exponents are subtracted and then the alignment is performed by a shifter. Because shifting takes twice as long as the other operations, shifting is done in two stages and the output of the shifter is shown to be fed back into the shifter. The fractions are then added and the shifter is used again to normalize the result. Finally, the result is rounded. The corresponding reservation table is given in Fig. 12-24(b). From the reservation table it is seen that the collision vector is 111100 and the reduced state diagram is as shown in Fig. 12-24(c). From the reduced state diagram, the best pattern of 5, 5, 5, . . . (or 0, 5, 10, . . .) is found. This pattern is less efficient than introducing, on the average, a new operation every four periods, which is the limitation imposed by the four Xs in the row for the shifter.

We now redesign the pipeline by inserting a delay after the fraction addition (stage 4) as shown in Fig. 12-25(a). This insertion produces the corresponding reservation table and reduced state diagram shown in Figs. 12-25(b) and 12-25(c). From the reduced state diagram it is seen that the optimal introduction pattern is 2, 6, 2, 6, . . . (or 0, 2, 8, 10, 16, 18, . . .), which yields an average introduction rate of one every four periods. It can be shown (see Stone [1]) that the maximum possible introduction rate determined by taking the maximum number of Xs taken over the rows in the reservation table can always be achieved by inserting delay stages. It is interesting that, although delay stages increase the number of stages and thereby increase the time needed to complete an operation, properly placed delay stages can also increase the throughput. Although the insertion of delay stages will not be discussed further in this book, descriptions of techniques for adding such stages can be found in Stone [1] and Hwang and Briggs [2].

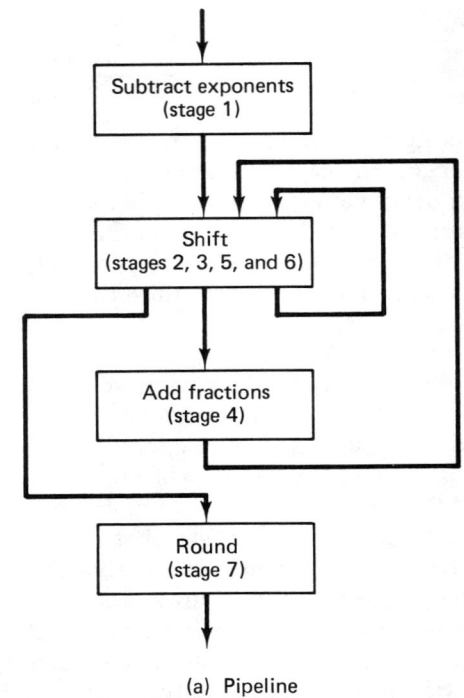

(a) Pipeline

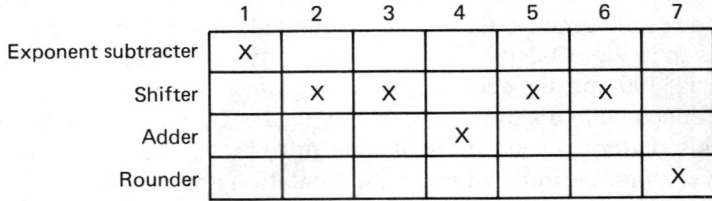

(b) Reservation table

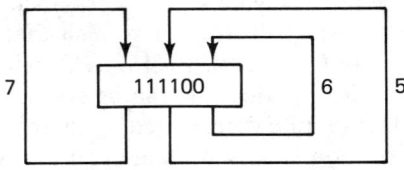

(c) Reduced state diagram

Figure 12-24 Design of a floating point adder pipeline.

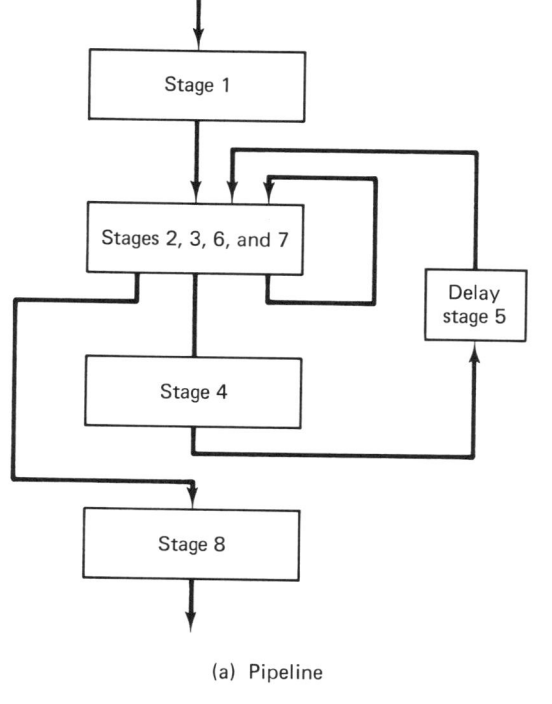

(a) Pipeline

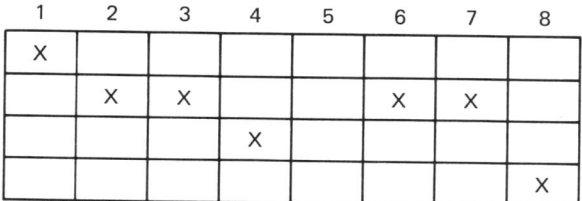

(b) Reservation table

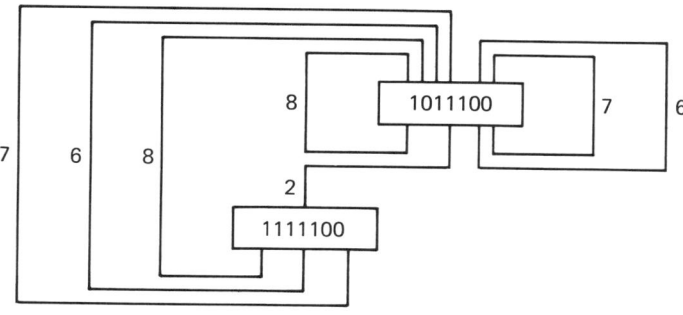

(c) Reduced state diagram

Figure 12-25 Modified floating point adder design using a delay.

Sec. 12-2 Pipelining

A second approach to improving the performance of the pipeline in Fig. 12-24 would be to duplicate the shifter hardware. From Exercise 21 it is seen that by using two shifters a new operation could be introduced every other period and by using four shifters an operation could be introduced every period. Note that addition of hardware to a pipeline requires that corresponding rows be added to the reservation table. The addition of the new rows causes the Xs to be divided among the new rows and existing rows, thereby reducing the number of Xs in the existing rows and the possibilities for collisions. Clearly, the places to add new hardware would be those places that would allow the Xs in those rows with the most Xs to be divided among two or more rows.

12-3 VECTOR AND MATRIX PROCESSING

Most applications that are so heavily computational that parallel processing is necessary include array processing in one form or another. The most prevalent arrays are one-dimensional arrays, vectors, and two-dimensional arrays, matrices. Although it is not possible to give a thorough discussion of vector and matrix processing here, a few examples are provided to introduce some of the concepts and problems related to using parallel processing to perform vector or matrix operations. For the most part, these examples assume ideal configurations that avoid memory and bus contention. Extensions to more realistic configurations are discussed in the references noted at the end of the chapter and are requested in the exercises.

12-3-1 Vector Addition

In a high-level language, vector addition is performed using a statement such as:

FOR I:=1 TO N DO C[I]:=A[I]+B[I];

This statement can easily be executed by parallel processing by using either pipelining or multiprocessing.

For pipelining, a configuration such as the one shown in Fig. 12-26(a) could be used. If the source and result memories can be accessed in one clock cycle and there are M stages in the pipeline, then $2 + M + N - 1 = M + N + 1$ clock cycles would be needed to add two N-dimensional vectors. If the execution time of a stage is much less than that for accessing memory, then a better design would be that given in Fig. 12-26(b). The memory modules are interleaved (i.e., successive elements are in different modules) so that accesses can be overlapped. Assuming that the clock period is shortened so that P cycles are needed for a memory access, the two vectors could be added in $P + M + N - 1 + P = 2P + M + N - 1$ clock cycles. Other, more practical, single-bus configurations are considered in Exercises 22 and 25.

A design for using multiprocessing to add vectors is given in Fig. 12-27. If M clock cycles are required to perform an addition and one clock cycle is needed

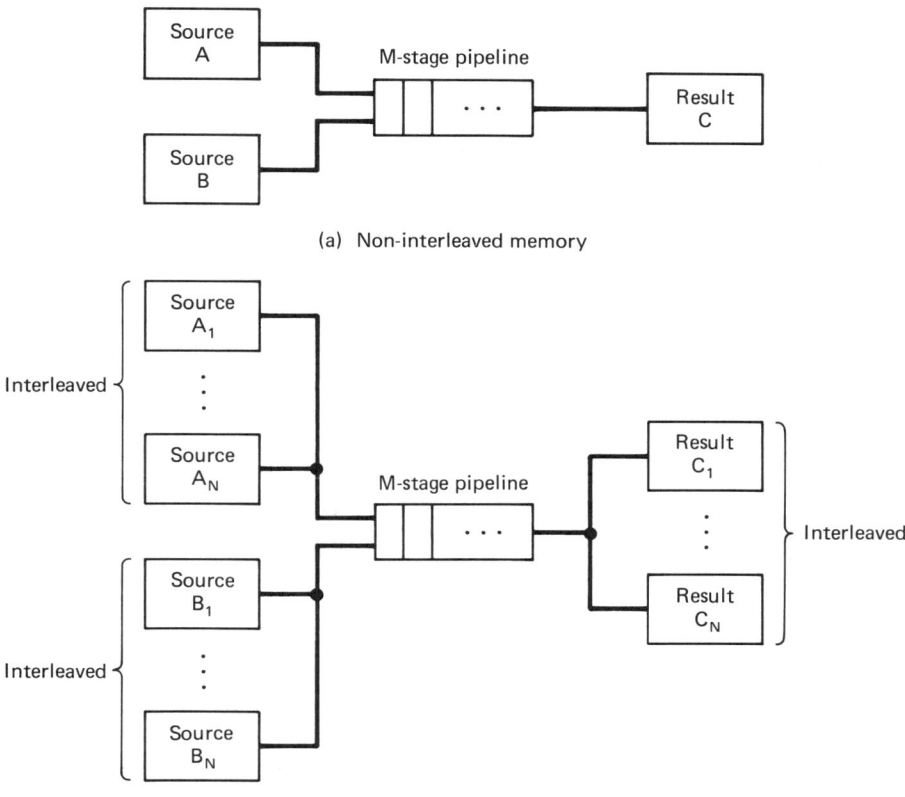

(a) Non-interleaved memory

(b) Interleaved memory

Figure 12-26 Pipelined vector addition designs.

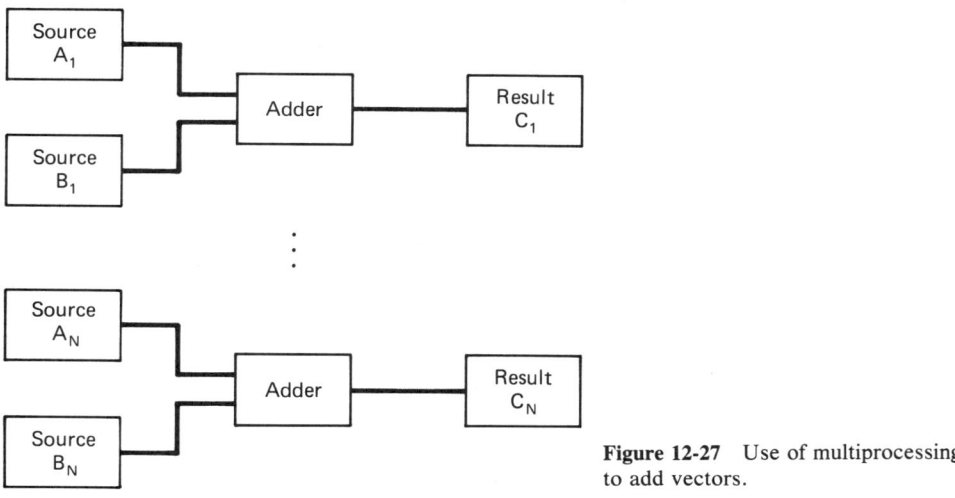

Figure 12-27 Use of multiprocessing to add vectors.

Sec. 12-3 Vector and Matrix Processing

for accessing memory, then the addition would require $M + 2$ cycles. At the expense of using N adders as opposed to one pipelined adder, $N - 1$ cycles could be saved.

12-3-2 Summing the Elements of a Vector

Typical statements for summing the elements of an N-dimensional vector A are

```
X := 0;
FOR I:=1 TO N DO X:=X+A[I];
```

This equation implies that addition is to be carried out sequentially according to the expression

$$(\ldots(((A_1 + A_2) + A_3) + A_4)\ldots) + A_N$$

But this ordering requires that each addition be finished before the next one begins, so neither pipelining nor multiprocessing can be used. However, if the operations are reordered as follows:

$$(((A_1 + A_2) + (A_3 + A_4)) + ((A_5 + A_6) + (A_7 + A_8))) + \ldots$$

then, either pipelining or multiprocessing is possible.

A 4-stage pipelined, single-bus configuration for adding numbers is given in Fig. 12-28(a). Assuming only one clock cycle is needed for each memory access, a diagram showing the pipeline activity while eight numbers are added is shown in Fig. 12-28(b). The figure shows that the total required time is 29 clock cycles. The gaps in the pipeline activity are due to the inability of the memory to perform more than one access at a time.

If multiprocessing were used to add the eight numbers, then four adders could simultaneously add the pairs. Two of the adders could then be used to add the quadruplets, and one adder could perform the final addition. How long it would take would depend on the memory and bus configuration. Assuming that memory accesses require one clock cycle, additions require four clock cycles, and the transfers of results between adders can be done at the same time and in one clock cycle, the total required time would be

$$1 + 4 + 1 + 4 + 1 + 4 + 1 = 16 \text{ clock cycles.}$$

In general, for adding N numbers $1 + 5 \log_2 N$ clock cycles would be required.

12-3-3 Inner Products

Example high-level language statements for evaluating an inner product are:

```
X := 0;
FOR I:=1 TO N DO X:=X+A[I]*B[I];
```

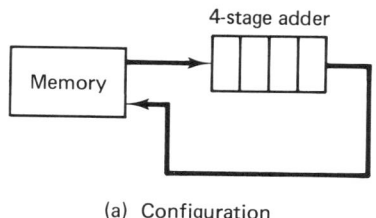

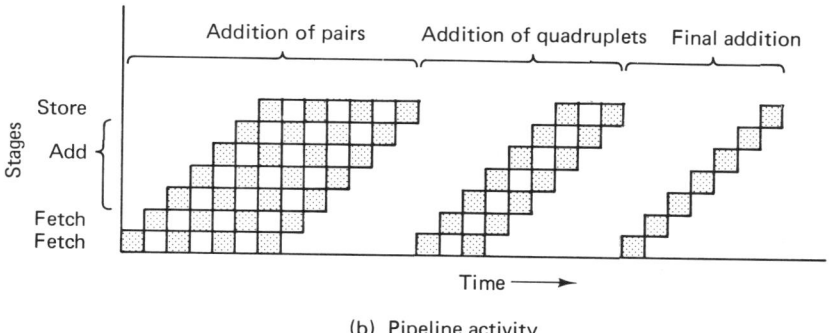

Figure 12-28 Pipeline for adding the elements of a vector.

By combining the multiplication and addition into a single multiply/add operation, this calculation is essentially the same as that of summing the elements in a vector. A pipeline that uses a 4-stage multiplier and 4-stage adder and assumes the ordering

$$(A_1B_1 + A_5B_5 + \ldots) + (A_2B_2 + A_6B_6 + \ldots) + (A_3B_3 + A_7B_7 + \ldots) + (A_4B_4 + A_8B_8 + \ldots)$$

is shown in Fig. 12-29. The buffer registers in the multiplier and adder are initialized to 0 and then the A_i and B_i pairs are brought in and multiplied at a rate of one pair per cycle. After five cycles (one cycle is needed for the initial fetch from memory), the products begin to be added to the output of the adder, which is 0 for the next four cycles. During the tenth cycle, the output of the adder is A_1B_1 and the addition $A_1B_1 + A_5B_5$ is begun. During the eleventh cycle the addition of $A_2B_2 + A_6B_6$ is begun and so on. This pattern continues until all products have been added into exactly one of the four partial products in the buffer registers of the adder. At that time, the output of the pipelined adder is fed into an adder that produces the final result. If this adder requires four cycles to perform each of the three final additions, then the inner product of two N-dimensional vectors could be computed in

$$1 + 4 + 4 + N - 4 + 3 \times 4 + 1 = N + 18 \text{ clock cycles.}$$

Sec. 12-3   Vector and Matrix Processing

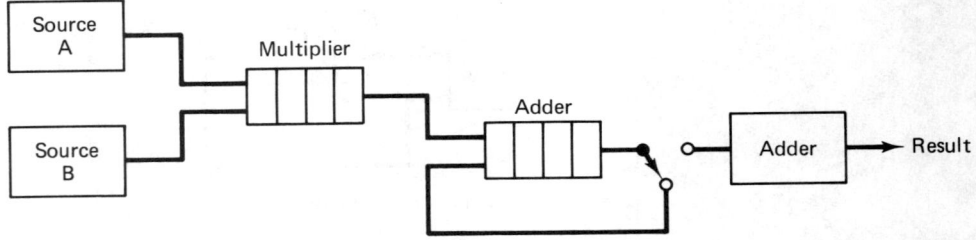

Figure 12-29 Pipelined configuration for taking an inner product.

As N becomes large, the number of clock cycles approaches N and the design is very efficient, but for small N the 18 clock cycles needed for startup, flushing the pipeline, and storing the result make the design somewhat less attractive. (Note that the same feedback concept could be used to sum the elements of a vector—see Exercise 27.)

A multiprocessing solution is to use N processing elements capable of performing both multiplication and addition. The N processing elements could simultaneously form the N products and then additions could be performed in the same manner as suggested in the above discussion of summing the elements of a vector. Under the same assumptions as those above, the time required is

$$1 + 4 + 5 \log_2 N + 1 = 6 + 5 \log_2 N \text{ clock cycles.}$$

12-3-4 Matrix Operations

Adding two $N \times N$ matrices is like adding N pairs of N-dimensional vectors. However, if a single pipeline such as the one in Fig. 12-26(a) is used, it would not need to be flushed between vector additions and the total time for performing the matrix addition using an M-stage adder would be $M + N^2 + 1$ cycles. For even moderately sized N, this value approaches N^2. If N pipelines were used, the time would be reduced to approximately N cycles.

The multiplication of an $N \times N$ matrix and a vector consists of N inner products. A total of N^2 multiply/add operations are required, which would take a single pipeline approximately N^2 cycles. As with the addition of $N \times N$ matrices, for N pipelines, approximately N cycles would be needed.

The multiplication of two $N \times N$ matrices consists of N^2 inner products or N^3 multiply/add operations. Because the number of operations involved is of the order of N^3, matrix multiplication is among the most computationally intense operations performed on a computer. Even with N multiply/add pipelines, more than N^2 cycles are required. Using N^2 multiply/add pipelines not only requires a tremendous amount of arithmetic logic, but also requires a complicated interconnection network to get the data into their right places at the right times.

One suggested network for performing matrix multiplication as well as other lengthy computations, such as fast Fourier transforms, is the hypercube connection. A 3-dimensional cube is shown in Fig. 12-30. A 4-dimensional hypercube is

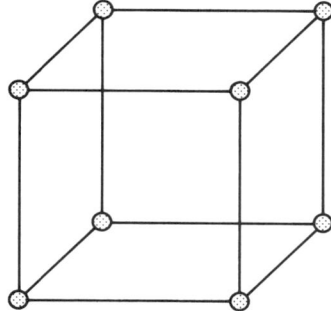

Figure 12-30 Connection pattern for a three-dimensional hypercube.

two cubes with the like corners connected together. Higher dimensional hypercubes are a generalization of this connection pattern. It can be shown (see Hwang and Briggs [2]) that if the rows of one $N \times N$ matrix are in a set of N strategically located nodes of an N-dimensional hypercube and the columns of a second $N \times N$ matrix in another set of N strategically located nodes, then $2N \log_2 N$ sets of simultaneous transfers could distribute the rows and columns to the required nodes. After the transfers are complete, the N^2 inner products could be conducted at the same time. Assuming one set of transfers per clock cycle and N cycles for performing an inner product, the total time required is $2N \log_2 N + N$.

12-4 HIGH PERFORMANCE COMPUTING SUMMARY

As our computing capabilities have increased, so has our desire to attack problems of increasing complexity involving more and more computations. These problems can be found in every facet of human endeavor. They include problems that involve partial differential equations for modeling fluid dynamics and electromagnetics; ordinary differential equations for modeling the motion of atomic particles or bodies in space; large systems of linear algebraic equations; complex multivariant statistical calculations that arise from studies in medicine, economics and social behavior; and signal and image processing that is used in space exploration, the military, and for identifying criminals.

To solve these problems in reasonable periods of time, some of which must be solved in realtime (i.e., as events are taking place in the real world), high performance computers capable of performing billions of operations per second are required. Because current technology limits the design of a single ALU to less than 100 million operations per second, it is necessary to resort to both multiprocessing and pipelining to attain the necessary computation rates. These two design approaches have been incorporated into single large computers in a variety of ways. The processing elements in a multiprocessing system may each be broken into stages and pipelined or a pipeline may be made up of stages where each includes a processing element. There is no optimal way of constructing a computer that uses parallel processing and, as already noted, the design of such a computer may depend on its intended applications. For a general purpose, high performance computer, a designer must rely on his experience, intuition, and imagination.

Figure 12-31 shows a typical arrangement in which several pipelined processing elements have been placed in parallel. Theoretically, if there are N processors, each with M stages, and each stage requires T seconds, then the throughput could approach NM/T operations per second as the number of operations in a task goes to infinity (e.g., if $N = 200$, $M = 5$, and $T = 50$ nS, then the throughput would approach 20 billion operations per second). However, as we have seen, providing the computational power to sustain a specified level of throughput does not mean that that level of throughput will actually be achieved. Processing elements must be initialized and pipelines require startup time, but the primary deterrents to attaining the maximum theoretical throughput are synchronization and communication. Losses due to synchronization can be lessened by properly choosing and optimizing the algorithms, but providing the links needed to communicate the instructions and data and then controlling those links may require a considerable amount of hardware.

Manufacturers often rate their computers by peak performance, which is normally computed by ignoring initialization, startup, synchronization, and communication and may even ignore the time used by nonarithmetic instructions. These ratings are measured in millions of operations per second (Mops) or millions of floating point operations per second (Mflops) depending on the computer's

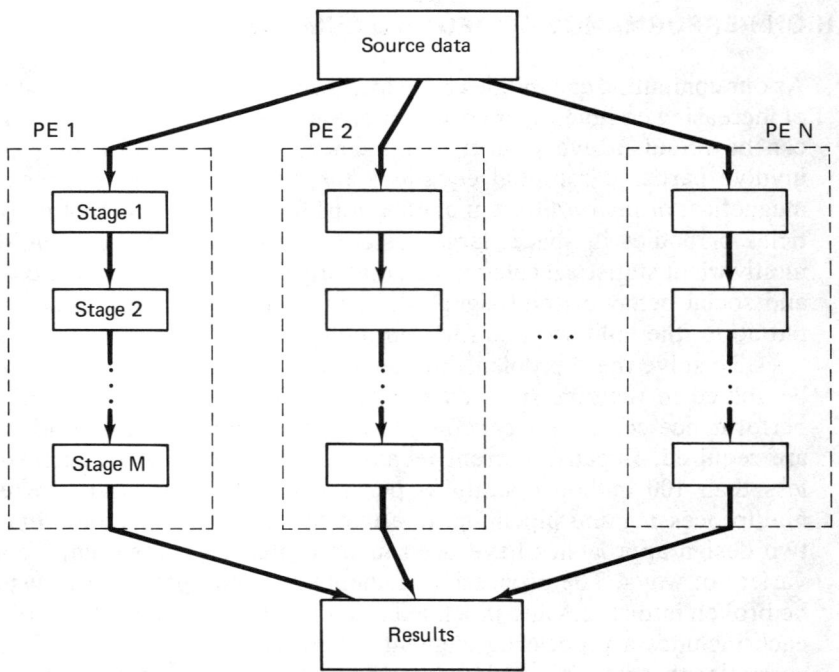

Figure 12-31 Typical pipelined multiprocessing arrangement.

intended application. Peak performance figures are very deceptive and actual performance is frequently only 10% to 20% of peak performance. For example, the peak performance of the Cray I is rated at 160 Mflops, but the actual performance has been estimated to be in the vicinity of 20 Mflops (Hwang and Briggs [2]).

The term "actual performance" is also deceptive because there is no standard procedure for measuring performance. A computer may do quite well for one application and poorly for another. It is virtually impossible to rate the performance of a computer by analytical means. Typically, performance is experimentally measured by executing a representative mix of the computations that the computer is expected to perform. An in-depth study of measuring the performance of very large computers, called **supercomputers**, is presented in Hockney and Jesshope [3].

During the design of a computer, simulations are the normal means of predicting how the computer will perform. These simulations are used not only to predict such criteria as efficiency and throughput, but also to determine the system's bottlenecks so that they can be eliminated before the computer is built. A simulation is run on an existing computer and attempts to model the architecture and activity of the computer being designed as a variety of "typical" tasks are performed. Because simulations are often very complex and each simulated instruction may require the execution of several instructions on the computer on which the simulation is being run, they tend to require huge quantities of processing time. Therefore, the simulations for designing new supercomputers must, themselves, be run on very large computers.

Although software has not been discussed in this chapter, providing software for fully utilizing the capabilities of a supercomputer has proven to be even more of a challenge than designing the hardware. The operating systems for computers with a large number of processing elements are extremely complex, and present day compilers only optimize parallel processing algorithms at a rudimentary level (e.g., optimize only innermost loops). It is very difficult to design a compiler that can arrange data so as to use a pipeline as efficiently as possible or to synchronize several processing elements. Although gains in technology will continue to improve the hardware in high performance computers, for the foreseeable future, it is the software designers that face the greater responsibilities in reaping the rewards of these gains. The design of software for computers that combine multiprocessing and pipelining has not yet been well formulated and is far beyond the scope of an introductory text.

REFERENCES

1. Stone, Harold S., *High-Performance Computer Architecture*, 2nd ed. (Reading, Massachusetts: Addison-Wesley Publishing Company, 1990).
2. Hwang, Kai, and Faye A. Briggs, *Computer Architecture and Parallel Processing* (New York: McGraw-Hill Book Company, 1985).

3. Hockney, R. W., and C. R. Jesshope, *Parallel Computers*, 2nd ed. (Bristol, Great Britain: IOP Publishing, Ltd., 1988).
4. Kain, Richard Y., *Computer Architecture: Software and Hardware*, Vol. 2 (Englewood Cliffs, N.J.: Prentice Hall, Inc., 1988).

EXERCISES

1. A barrel topology is formed by constructing a loop of 2^n nodes, numbering the nodes consecutively, and then adding connections to nodes that are $1, 2, 4, \ldots, 2^{n-1}$ nodes away from each node, i.e., node j is connected to nodes $j \pm 2^i$ for $i = 0, 1, \ldots, 2^{n-1}$. Give the number of links in a barrel topology as a function of n. Give, as a function of n, the maximum number of links that information must traverse when traveling between nodes.
2. Design the daisy chain logic needed in Fig. 12-4(a) in such a way that only one node can receive a grant. Discuss the timing of the grant with respect to the Busy signal.
3. Draw a timing diagram for a bus input that is similar to the one for output shown in Fig. 12-5.
4. Assume a bus topology with no shared memory and devise a scheme that uses buffer registers and separate bus lines to indicate when a node can accept data or has data to transmit.
5. Consider a bus topology in which two nodes communicate through buffers in a shared memory. When one node wishes to communicate with the other node it puts the information in a buffer and sets a flag that is associated with the buffer. Periodically each node checks the flags to determine whether it has buffer information it is to receive. There is a serious problem with this scheme. What is it and how could it be alleviated?
6. Suppose that an N-node bus topology is such that the no contention bus request rate for each node is 20 million requests per second and the overall bus transfer rate is

$$10^8(1 - e^{-0.2N})$$

Plot the average delay time for the bus requests made by the nodes as a function of N (i.e., the difference obtained by subtracting the time between requests when there is no contention and the actual average time between requests).
7. Consider the bus utilization graph given in Fig. 12-8. If the bandwidth B is 50 MHz and there are (for no contention) 2 million instruction fetches and 4 million data fetches per second for each node, what is the number of nodes at which the two dashed lines intersect? If each node were given a local code memory so that the instruction fetches on the shared bus were eliminated, what would be the number of nodes at which the intersect would occur?
8. In Fig. 12-9, the DOL AB line is held active for $2t_d$, where t_d is the propagation delay of the link, before the data are applied to the Data lines. Why is the factor 2 needed? The Data lines are held active for a period of time and then it is simply *assumed* the

data are taken. Discuss the design of the interfaces and the problems with this approach. Show the timing if a Ready line is used to indicate when the data are taken.

9. For the lossless transmission line example in Sec. 12-1-2, find the coefficients a and b as functions of L, C, Δx, and Δt. Write a program that will determine $V(x,t)$ for $L = 0.1$H, $C = 10\mu$F, $\Delta x = 0.1$m, $\Delta t = 0.1$ mS, $n = 10$, $m = 2000$, and

$$V(0,t) = \begin{cases} 100t & 0 \leq t < 0.1 \\ 0 & 0.1 < t \end{cases}$$

Use the iterative approach to solving the problem and iterate until the voltage difference (at any point) does not change between iterations by more than 0.01 volts.

10. Consider the task ordering indicated by Fig. 12-11(a) and assume that the tasks have the following execution times (in microseconds):

A	B	C	D	E	F	G	H
200	100	150	300	100	200	300	100

Determine the times at which each task begins. Determine the efficiency of the system (i.e., the fraction of total available processing time for all three processing elements that is actually used).

11. Give the data flow graph for the expression

$$((S+(T*(U-V)))*((X*Y)/Z)) + ((U-V)/(X*Y))$$

If additions and subtractions take 300 nS, multiplications take 700 nS, and divisions take 1000 nS, how long would it take to evaluate the expression on a data flow computer?

12. In light of Fig. 11-20 in Sec. 11-4, discuss the use of shared resources in a multiprocessing system in which the nodes may be multiprogrammed and two or more processes executing on a node may access the same shared resource.

13. Give an example and corresponding discussion that shows how two overlapped instructions that both affect a condition flag in the PSW could result in an incorrect branch.

14. Prove that the rules for scoreboarding given in Example 3 of Sec. 12-1-3 guarantee proper ordering with respect to the READ/WRITE, WRITE/READ, and WRITE/WRITE access combinations.

15. Graph the speedup and efficiency of an M-stage pipeline as a function of N (the number of operations) for $M = 3, 5,$ and 10.

16. Graph the speedup and efficiency of an M-stage pipeline as a function of M for $N = 10, 20,$ and 50, where N is the number of operations.

17. What is the throughput of a five-stage pipeline if $N = 100$ and the times required by the stages are 100, 200, 100, 300, and 200 nS, respectively? What would the throughput be if duplicate logic sets could be used in stages 2, 4, and 5? What would the throughput be if stage 4 could be replaced with two 150 nS stages but all other stages must remain the same?

18. Compute the speedup and efficiency for the three cases described in Exercise 17.

19. Give the reservation table for the following design of a pipelined floating point multiplier:

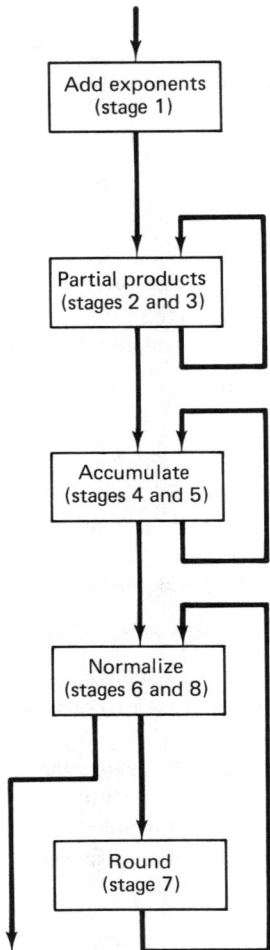

Use the reservation table to obtain the corresponding collision vector and reduced state diagram. From the reduced state diagram determine the delay patterns that produce the greatest throughput.

20. Given the following reservation table:

	1	2	3	4	5	6	7
Resource A	X				X		
Resource B		X	X				
Resource C				X			
Resource D						X	X

determine the corresponding collision vector and reduced state diagram. From the reduced state diagram find the delay patterns that produce the greatest throughput.

21. Show that by using two shifters in the pipeline design given in Fig. 12-24 a new operation could be introduced every other period and by using four shifters a new operation could be introduced every period.

22. Assume the following configuration for adding vectors:

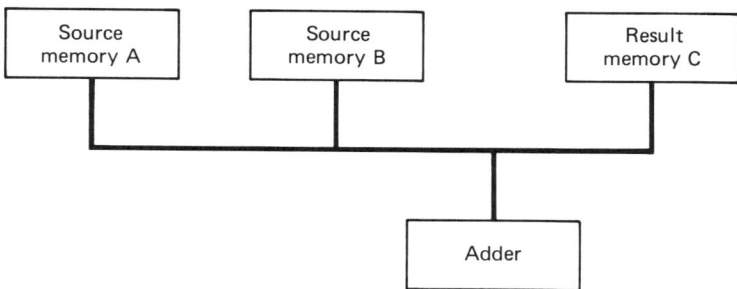

and that:

- A memory read consists of one period to send the address, one period to get the data, and one period to return the data over the bus.
- A memory write consists of one period to send the address and data and one period to store the data.
- An add requires two consecutive periods.
- The bus is free while a memory retrieves or stores data.

Determine the reservation table, collision vector, reduced state diagram, and a best delay pattern for the pipeline.

23. Use delay stages to modify the pipeline in Exercise 22 so that it attains its maximum theoretical throughput.

24. Assume a memory access takes two periods and rework Exercise 22. Rework again assuming a memory access requires three periods.

25. Design a single-bus, pipelined system for adding N-dimensional vectors that uses interleaved memory modules. Assume a three-stage adder and that four clock cycles are needed to access memory. One clock cycle is required for a bus transfer.

26. Assume the configuration in Fig. 12-28(a) and that reads and writes to memory can be simultaneous. Redraw the pipeline activity diagram in Fig. 12-28(b) accordingly.

27. Design a pipeline for summing the elements of a vector that uses the feedback concept shown in Fig. 12-29. Given that the adder has M stages and one clock cycle is needed per memory access, determine the number of clock cycles required to sum N numbers. For $M = 4$ and $N = 8$, compare this result to the one for the design in Fig. 12-28.

28. Suppose that the multiplier and adder in Fig. 12-29 have M stages each and that one clock cycle is needed per memory access. Determine the time required to take the inner product of two N-dimensional vectors as a function of N and M.

29. Assume that the pipelined adder in Fig. 12-29 has only three stages and alter the design so that the timing is correct. Repeat for a 5-stage adder.

30. Assuming one set of transfers per clock cycle and N clock cycles for performing an inner product, how long would it take to multiply two 16×16 matrices using a hypercube containing 256 nodes?

A

Number Systems and Conversions

Numbers are abstract entities that are defined by axioms and are not at all dependent on the symbols used to represent them. The internationally accepted standard for representing nonnegative integers is the Arabic system. It includes ten symbols, called **digits**, (0, 1, 2, 3, 4, 5, 6, 7, 8, and 9), and relies on the fact that any positive integer can be expressed as follows:

$$a_n 10^n + \cdots + a_2 10^2 + a_1 10 + a_0$$

where $a_n, \ldots, a_0$ represent digits. The rule for writing a positive integer is to use this format, but to omit the powers of ten and the plus signs, i.e., write it as $a_n \ldots a_2 a_1 a_0$.

There is nothing special about the number 10, except that it is convenient for counting because we have 10 fingers. The same scheme could be used with powers of any positive number $x > 1$, so long as x distinct symbols are used to represent the digits. The number x is called the **base**. The Arabic system has a base of 10 and is also referred to as the **decimal system**. When the base is 2, 8, or 16, the same method for representing positive integers is called the **binary**, **octal**, or **hexidecimal system**, respectively. The symbols used in the binary, octal, decimal, and hexadecimal systems are given in Fig. A-1.

Because computers work with bits, which can only be 0 or 1, it is natural for computers to use the binary system to represent positive integers. For example, inside a computer, the bit combination 01100101 would represent

$$0 \times 2^7 + 1 \times 2^6 + 1 \times 2^5 + 0 \times 2^4 + 0 \times 2^3 + 1 \times 2^2 + 0 \times 2 + 1$$

which in the decimal system is the integer

$$64 + 32 + 4 + 1 = 101_{10}$$

(Subscripting a number with its base is used to eliminate ambiguity.) Also shown in Fig. A-1 are the octal, decimal, and hexadecimal digits expressed in binary.

Binary (Base 2)	Octal (Base 8)	Decimal (Base 10)	Hexadecimal (Base 16)
0	0 (000)	0 (0000)	0 (0000)
1	1 (001)	1 (0001)	1 (0001)
	2 (010)	2 (0010)	2 (0010)
	3 (011)	3 (0011)	3 (0011)
	4 (100)	4 (0100)	4 (0100)
	5 (101)	5 (0101)	5 (0101)
	6 (110)	6 (0110)	6 (0110)
	7 (111)	7 (0111)	7 (0111)
		8 (1000)	8 (1000)
		9 (1001)	9 (1001)
			A (1010)
			B (1011)
			C (1100)
			D (1101)
			E (1110)
			F (1111)

Note: Binary equivalents are given in parentheses.

Figure A-1

Because we think in decimal terms and the computer works with binary numbers, it is frequently necessary to convert integers between these two systems. The conversion from binary to decimal was done in the above example by using decimal arithmetic to add the powers of 2 that have coefficients of 1. A second method is to use **Horner's Rule**, which is:

$$a_n x^n + a_{n-1} x^{n-1} + \cdots + a_1 + a_0 = (\ldots(a_n x + a_{n-1})x + \ldots)x + a_0$$

Using Horner's Rule, the above calculation becomes

$$\underbrace{0\ 1\ 1\ 0\ 0\ 1\ 0\ 1}$$
$$((((((0 \times 2 + 1) \times 2 + 1) \times 2 + 0) \times 2 + 0) \times 2 + 1) \times 2 + 0) \times 2 + 1 = 101_{10}$$

For conversion from decimal to binary, note that

$$((((\ldots(a_n x^n + a_{n-1})\ldots)x + a_2)x + a_1)x + a_0)/x$$

has a quotient of $((\ldots(a_n x + a_{n-1})\ldots)x + a_2)x + a_1$ and a remainder of a_0. In turn, this quotient divided by x has a quotient of $(\ldots(a_n x + a_{n-1})\ldots)x + a_2$ and a remainder of a_1, and so on. Thus, the reverse conversion can be accomplished by successive division and retention of the remainder as follows:

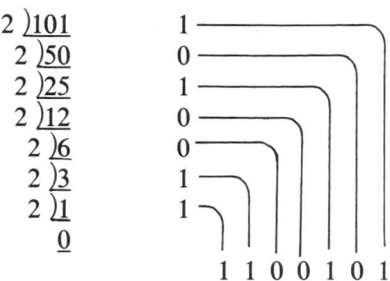

App. A   Number Systems and Conversions

Because only small integers can be written with a few bits, integers are normally expressed using 16 or more bits. But writing so many bits can be rather laborious. To reduce the number of symbols needed to write a large binary number, computer manuals and texts often use the octal and hexadecimal numbering systems. Because 8 to a power is equal to 2 to three times that power, and any octal digit can be expressed in the form

$$a_2 2^2 + a_1 2 + a_0$$

where a_2, a_1, and a_0 are binary bits, conversion from octal to binary is a matter of replacing each octal digit with its binary equivalent. For example:

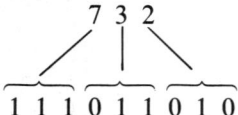

The reverse operation is to group the bits, beginning from the right, by threes and replace each group with its octal equivalent as follows:

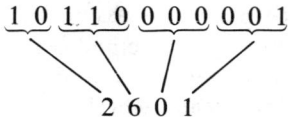

Conversions from hexadecimal to binary and vice versa are similar except that the groupings contain four bits, e.g.,

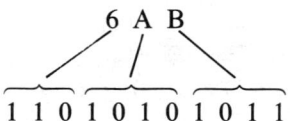

and

$$\underbrace{1\ 0\ 0\ 0}\ \underbrace{1\ 1\ 0\ 0}\ \underbrace{1\ 1\ 1\ 0}$$
$$8\quad C\quad E$$

The powers of 2 from 0 through 10 are given in Fig. A-2. Because of the closeness of 2^{10} to one thousand, which is associated with the prefix kilo (k), $2^{10} = 1024$ is referred to as one K. Also, because 1024 K is approximately one million, it is referred to as one M. The approximation $2^{10} \approx 10^3$ and the powers of 2 from 0 to 9 are useful in estimating large powers of 2, e.g.,

$$2^{32} = 2^2 (2^{10})^3 \approx 4(10^3)^3 = 4 \times 10^9 = 4 \text{ billion}$$

It can easily be shown that any real number can be approximated to within any tolerance, no matter how small, by an expression of the form

$$a_n 10^n + \cdots + a_1 10 + a_0 + a_{-1} 10^{-1} + \cdots + a_{-m} 10^{-m}$$

$$2^0 = 1$$
$$2^1 = 2$$
$$2^2 = 4$$
$$2^3 = 8$$
$$2^4 = 16$$
$$2^5 = 32$$
$$2^6 = 64$$
$$2^7 = 128$$
$$2^8 = 256$$
$$2^9 = 512$$
$$2^{10} = 1024$$

Figure A-2

where $a_n, \ldots, a_{-m}$ are decimal digits and n and m are integers. As when writing positive integers, the powers of 10 and the plus signs can be deleted. However, the beginning of the fraction must be marked and this marking is done with a period, which is called the **decimal point**. For example:

$$6 \times 10^2 + 2 \times 10 + 1 + 7 \times 10^{-1} + 5 \times 10^{-2}$$

is written as 621.75.

As before, there is nothing special about the base 10; a base of 2 could be used as well. Any real number could also be estimated arbitrarily closely by an expression of the form

$$a_n 2^n + \cdots + a_1 2 + a_0 + a_{-1} 2^{-1} + \cdots + a_{-m} 2^{-m}$$

where $a_n, \ldots, a_{-m}$ are bits and n and m are integers. The number

$$1 \times 2 + 0 + 1 \times 2^{-1} + 0 \times 2^{-2} + 1 \times 2^{-3}$$

is 10.101. Converting the integer portion of such a number to its decimal equivalent could be done as described above. Converting the fraction could be done by expressing it in the form

$$0.5(a_{-1} + 0.5(\ldots(a_{-m+1} + 0.5a_{-m})\ldots))$$

For example, the fraction 0.0101 in decimal would be

$$0.5(0 + 0.5(1 + 0.5(0 + 0.5 \times 1))) = 0.3125$$

and 1101.0101 would be 13.3125.

For the reverse conversion, note that

$$2 \times 0.a_{-1}\ldots a_{-m} = a_{-1}.a_{-2}\ldots a_{-m}$$
$$2 \times 0.a_{-2}\ldots a_{-m} = a_{-2}.a_{-3}\ldots a_{-m}$$

and so on. Therefore, the binary equivalent of 0.3125 could be found as follows:

```
 0.3125    0.625    0.25    0.5
 × 2       × 2      × 2     × 2
 0.625     1.25     0.5     1.0
```

0.0101

App. A   Number Systems and Conversions

EXERCISES

1. Convert the following binary numbers to decimal numbers; octal numbers; hexadecimal numbers.
   (a) 1010   (b) 110111   (c) 101101   (d) 101110001
2. Convert the following decimal numbers to binary:
   (a) 11   (b) 23   (c) 121   (d) 629
3. Convert the following octal numbers to binary:
   (a) 11   (b) 762   (c) 5761   (d) 52554
4. Convert the following hexadecimal numbers to binary:
   (a) 9   (b) AB   (c) 16CA   (d) 7BF0A
5. Show that any octal number can be expressed in binary by simply finding the binary equivalent of each octal digit and then placing the equivalents side by side. (Hint: Proceed by expressing the polynomial form for the octal number in the polynomial form for the equivalent binary number.)
6. Show how a decimal number could be converted to its hexadecimal equivalent by successively dividing by 16 and expressing the remainders as hexadecimal digits.
7. Convert the decimal numbers in Exercise 2 to hexadecimal.
8. Use Horner's Rule to convert the hexadecimal numbers in Exercise 4 to decimal.
9. Convert the following binary numbers to decimal:
   (a) 11.011   (b) 10110.1001   (c) 1011.1001101
10. Convert the following decimal numbers to binary:
    (a) 3.25   (b) 23.625   (c) 0.1 to seven significant bits

B*

Logic Level Design

The activity inside a computer consists of accessing, operating on, transmitting, and storing what are abstractly referred to as 0s and 1s. The physical representations of the 0s and 1s vary, even within a given computer. For storage, the 0 or 1 state is normally determined by the current flows or magnetic fields within the element used for storing the 0 or 1; operating on 0s and 1s is almost always a matter of receiving the 0s and 1s as voltages and converting the voltages to those of the results; and 0s and 1s are normally transmitted as voltages, currents, or light intensities. The exact representations of 0s and 1s are important to the designer who implements the electronic circuitry by interconnecting transistors, diodes, and so on, but there are two levels of digital electronics design. The higher of the two levels is concerned only with the 0s and 1s and not with how they are represented; it is called the **logic level**. It is this level with which this book is primarily concerned.

At the logic level, computer circuits, or networks, can be viewed as boxes with a set of 0-1 inputs and a set of 0-1 outputs as shown in Fig. B-1. They may be combinational or sequential. A **combinational circuit** is one whose 0-1 outputs are completely defined by its inputs. For a **sequential circuit**, its outputs depend on its current internal states as well as on its inputs. This appendix first introduces elementary combinational circuits and discusses combinational logic design, and then introduces elementary sequential circuits.

* Much of the material in this appendix was taken, by permission, from Chap. 3 of Gibson and Liu [2].

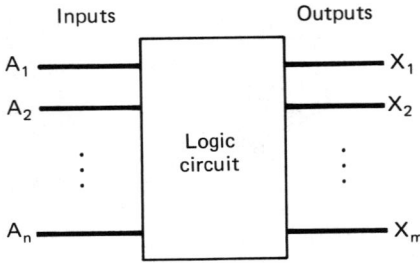

Each input or output is a 0 or 1.

Figure B-1 Arbitrary logic circuit with n inputs and m outputs.

B-1 ELEMENTARY LOGIC GATES

A combinational circuit with only one output is called a **logic gate**. All combinational circuits can be constructed from the elementary gates as defined in Fig. B-2. Because a combinational circuit is completely described by giving the value of each output for all possible inputs, it can be defined by simply listing the outputs for the various inputs in an organized tabular form, called a **truth table**. (The term "truth table" comes from the similarity between two-value true/false logic, which

A	$\bar{A}$
0	1
1	0

(a) Inverter

A	B	AB
0	0	0
0	1	0
1	0	0
1	1	1

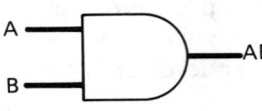

(b) AND gate

A	B	A + B
0	0	0
0	1	1
1	0	1
1	1	1

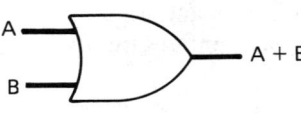

(c) OR gate

Figure B-2 Elementary logic gates.

is part of mathematics, and the 0-1 nature of logical circuits.) The truth tables that define the elementary logic gates are given at the left side of Fig. B-2 and the corresponding symbols used to represent these gates are at the right side. For an inverter, the output is always the reverse of the input A and is denoted $\overline{A}$. The AND gate output is denoted AB and is 1 if and only if both input A and input B are 1. The OR gate is denoted $A + B$ and is 1 if and only if input A is 1, or input B is 1, or both.

The impetus for using the term "gate" for AND and OR circuits is seen by viewing one of the inputs, say A, as the gate control. For an AND gate, if $A = 0$ the gate is closed and the output is 0 regardless of the B input. If $A = 1$, the gate is open and the B input is able to pass and become the output. For an OR gate, the situation is reversed; when $A = 0$ the B input is the same as the output and when $A = 1$ the output is always 1.

Figure B-3(a) demonstrates how elementary logic gates can be connected

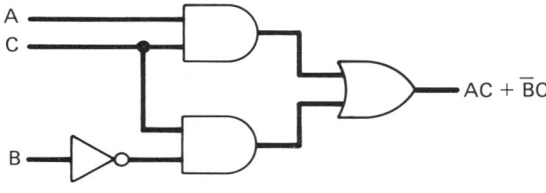

(a) Original circuit

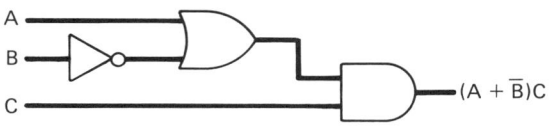

(b) Equivalent circuit

A	B	C	AC	$\overline{B}$	$\overline{B}C$	$AC + \overline{B}C$	$A + \overline{B}$	$(A + \overline{B})C$
0	0	0	0	1	0	0	1	0
0	0	1	0	1	1	1	1	1
0	1	0	0	0	0	0	0	0
0	1	1	0	0	0	0	0	0
1	0	0	0	1	0	0	1	0
1	0	1	1	1	1	1	1	1
1	1	0	0	0	0	0	1	0
1	1	1	1	0	0	1	1	1

Same

(c) Truth table showing equivalence

Figure B-3 Logic circuits containing more than one gate and their equivalences.

Sec. B-1   Elementary Logic Gates

to form more complex logic circuits. A graphic illustration of a logic circuit such as the one in Fig. B-3(a) is called a **logic diagram**.

Two logic circuits are said to be *equivalent* if they have exactly the same input/output relationships. One way to prove equivalence is to compare the truth table outputs of the two logic circuits. The circuit in Fig. B-3(b) is equivalent to the one in Fig. B-3(a) because the seventh and ninth columns of the truth table in Fig. B-3(c) are identical. The other columns in the truth table show the step-by-step development of the expressions $AC + \overline{B}C$ and $(A + \overline{B})C$ using the definitions in Fig. B-2.

As output expressions become more complex, a need arises for a mathematical system that permits an organized means of working with expressions. The mathematical system for serving this purpose is **Boolean algebra**, whose set consists of 0 and 1 and whose operations are complementation, multiplication, and addition. The defining tables for these operations are the same as the truth tables for the inverter, AND gate, and OR gate, respectively, and the same notation is used to represent the results of Boolean operations as is used for the outputs of these gates. An inverter can be viewed as the logic implementation of Boolean complementation, an AND gate as the implementation of Boolean multiplication, and an OR gate as the implementation of Boolean addition. Logic circuit output expressions, such as those in Fig. B-3, are the same as the Boolean expressions obtained by assuming the inverters, AND gates, and OR gates represent Boolean complementation, multiplication, and addition, respectively.

As with all mathematical systems, once the underlying definitions of the system have been established, other basic facts, or theorems, can be derived. The most fundamental theorems for Boolean algebra are given in Fig. B-4. These theorems, which are all equivalences, can be proved either by deriving identical columns in truth tables or by using previously proven theorems. For example, the truth table in Fig. B-5 proves the left distributive law, and the left distributive law and the commutativity of multiplication is used to prove the right distributive law as follows:

$$(B + C)A = A(B + C) = AB + AC = BA + CA$$

The proofs of the remaining equivalences in Fig. B-4 are left to the reader (see Exercise 3).

The value in these equivalences is their use in reducing Boolean expressions. For example,

$$\begin{aligned}
\overline{A}\overline{B}C + BC + AB &= (\overline{A}\overline{B} + B)C + AB \\
&= (\overline{A} + B)C + AB \\
&= \overline{A}C + BC + AB \\
&= \overline{A}C + (\overline{A} + A)BC + AB \\
&= \overline{A}C + \overline{A}BC + ABC + AB \\
&= \overline{A}C(1 + B) + AB(C + 1) \\
&= \overline{A}C + AB
\end{aligned}$$

$$A = \overline{\overline{A}}$$
$$AA = A$$
$$A + A = A$$
$$A \cdot 0 = 0$$
$$A + 0 = A$$
$$A \cdot 1 = A$$
$$A + 1 = 1$$
$$A \cdot \overline{A} = 0$$
$$A + \overline{A} = 1$$
$$AB = BA \quad \text{Commutative law for multiplication}$$
$$A + B = B + A \quad \text{Commutative law for addition}$$
$$(AB)C = A(BC) \quad \text{Associative law for multiplication}$$
$$A + (B + C) = (A + B) + C \quad \text{Associative law for addition}$$
$$A(B + C) = AB + AC \quad \text{Left distributive law}$$
$$(B + C)A = BA + CA \quad \text{Right distributive law}$$
$$\overline{A + B} = \overline{A}\,\overline{B}$$
$$\overline{AB} = \overline{A} + \overline{B}$$
$$\left.\begin{array}{c}\end{array}\right\} \text{De Morgan's laws.}$$
$$AB + A\overline{B} = A$$
$$A + AB = A$$
$$(A + \overline{B})B = AB$$
$$(A + B)(A + \overline{B}) = A$$
$$(A + B)(A + C) = A + BC$$
$$A(A + B) = A$$
$$A\overline{B} + B = A + B$$
$$\overline{A}B + A\overline{B} = A \oplus B$$
$$\overline{AB}(A + B) = A \oplus B$$

Figure B-4 Some of the equivalences most frequently used in reducing Boolean expressions.

Note that
$$A + B = \overline{\overline{A + B}} = \overline{\overline{A}\,\overline{B}}$$
which shows that addition can be expressed in terms of complementation and multiplication. Thus, addition is not an independent operation, and in terms of logic gates, an OR gate can be constructed from an AND gate and three inverters. Therefore, all logic circuits could be made up of AND gates and inverters. Similarly,
$$AB = \overline{\overline{AB}} = \overline{\overline{A} + \overline{B}}$$

Sec. B-1   Elementary Logic Gates

A	B	C	B+C	A(B+C)	AB	AC	AB+AC
0	0	0	0	0	0	0	0
0	0	1	1	0	0	0	0
0	1	0	1	0	0	0	0
0	1	1	1	0	0	0	0
1	0	0	0	0	0	0	0
1	0	1	1	1	0	1	1
1	1	0	1	1	1	0	1
1	1	1	1	1	1	1	1

—Same—

Figure B-5 Proof of the left distributive law.

and it is seen that any logic circuit could also be constructed from OR gates and inverters. The fact that all combinational logic circuits could be constructed from just two basic building blocks is an important fact to anyone who is developing a new technology, such as a computer that is based on light instead of voltages and currents.

Although any logic circuit could be built from the gates given in Fig. B-2, there are other very simple gates that are considered to be elementary. They are the not AND (NAND), not OR (NOR), exclusive OR (XOR), and exclusive not OR (XNOR) gates shown in Fig. B-6. A small circle at an input or output of a logic symbol indicates an inversion. Therefore, the NAND and NOR have outputs that are the complements of the outputs of the AND and OR gates. For a NAND gate, the output is 0 if and only if both inputs are 1; and, for a NOR gate, the output is 0 if and only if either input is 1. The Boolean expressions for the NAND and NOR gates are $\overline{AB}$ and $\overline{A + B}$, respectively.

An XOR gate differs from an OR gate in that its output is 1 if and only if exactly one input is 1, but *not both*. Technically, XOR is not a Boolean operation but, for convenience, the symbol $\oplus$ is used to algebraically indicate an XOR. An XOR can be expressed in terms of complementation, addition, and multiplication in the following two ways:

$$A \oplus B = A\overline{B} + \overline{A}B = \overline{AB}(A + B)$$

The XOR operation is commutative and associative (see Exercise 5).

The XNOR output is the complement of the XOR output and its Boolean expression is:

$$\overline{A \oplus B} = \overline{A\overline{B} + \overline{A}B} = \overline{A\overline{B}}\,\overline{\overline{A}B} = (\overline{A} + B)(A + \overline{B}) = AB + \overline{A}\,\overline{B}$$

The XNOR output is 1 if and only if the two inputs are identical and therefore, an XNOR gate is sometimes referred to as an **equivalence gate**.

The AND, OR, NAND, and NOR gates shown in Figs. B-2 and B-6 have only two inputs; however, they can easily be generalized to *n* inputs by the following rules:

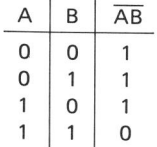
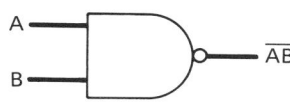

(a) NAND

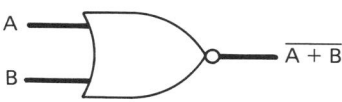

(b) NOR

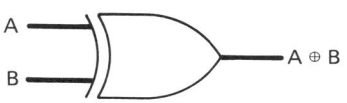

(c) XOR

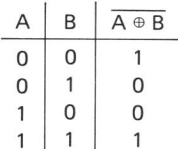
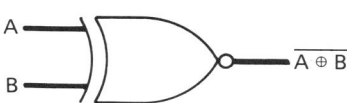

(d) XNOR or equivalence

Figure B-6 Other elementary gates.

AND—output is 1 if and only if all inputs are 1.
OR—output is 0 if and only if all inputs are 0.
NAND—output is 0 if and only if all inputs are 1.
NOR—output is 1 if and only if all inputs are 0.

Figure B-7 uses gates that have more than two inputs to implement the expression

$$A\overline{B}C + (A + \overline{B} + C)(\overline{A + B + C}) + \overline{AD}$$

Until now, all inputs and outputs have been taken to be 0s and 1s and we have not been concerned with the physical entities use to represent them. For the logic gates, these entities are almost always two voltage levels. If they are

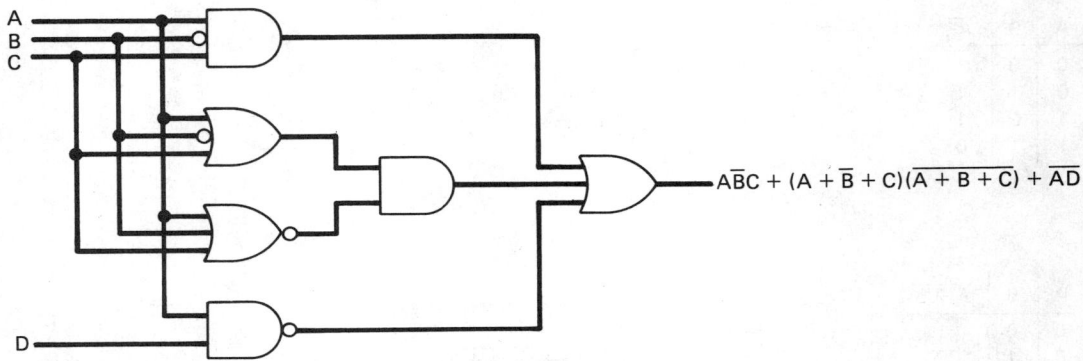

Figure B-7 Logic circuit that includes 3-input gates.

voltage levels and the higher voltage represents 1, the gate is then called a **positive logic gate**. If the lower voltage represents 1, it is a **negative logic gate**. Sometimes a computer will include both sections based on positive logic and sections based on negative logic. When both positive and negative logic are present, it may be better to use H for high and L for low instead of using 1 and 0. Most semiconductor manuals use Hs and Ls instead of 1s and 0s to define their logic gates. This designation gives the input/output relationships directly in terms of voltages and the designer can use gates either as positive or negative logic.

Negative logic gate symbols are different from their positive counterparts. Both sets of symbols are shown in Fig. B-8. The positive logic symbols are the same as those given in Figs. B-2 and B-6 and the negative logic symbols are the same as the corresponding positive logic symbols except that inversions are added to all inputs and outputs. Note that any positive logic circuit can be replaced by an equivalent negative logic circuit by simply replacing all positive gates with negative gates.

The truth table in Fig. B-9 shows that a negative AND and a positive OR are equivalent and can be implemented by the same electronic circuit. Similarly, the other gates that are directly across from each other in Fig. B-8 are equivalent. (The proof of this statement is requested in Exercise 7.)

Note that the gate symbols defined here and used in this book as a whole are the older, standard symbols. The IEEE, in conjunction with the International Electrotechnical Commission (IEC), has established a newer set of standard gate symbols. These newer symbols, which are specified in IEEE standard 91-1984, all have rectangular shapes and are differentiated by notations within the rectangles. The reason for using the older symbols in this book is that the distinctive shapes make it easier to recognize the various gates. The IEEE gate symbols are only part of an extensive set of symbology and, although we have chosen not to use them, they do provide a concise way of presenting logic circuitry and are particularly useful to those who must implement logic using electronics.

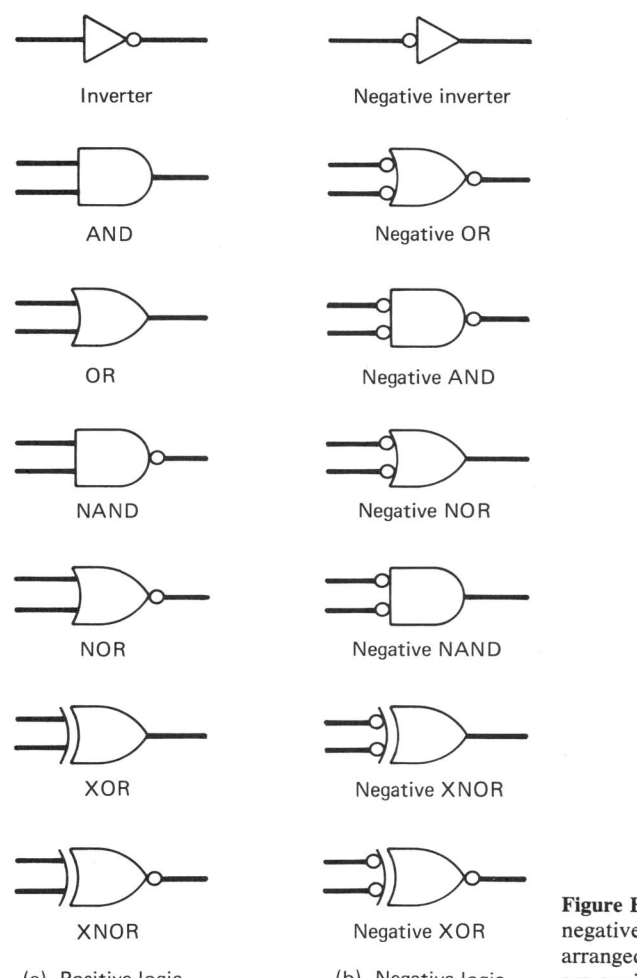

Figure B-8 Summary of positive and negative elementary logic gates arranged so that gates in the same row are equivalent.

(a) Positive logic (b) Negative logic

A	B	A+B	$\overline{A}$	$\overline{B}$	$\overline{A}\overline{B}$	$\overline{\overline{A}\overline{B}}$
L	L	L	H	H	H	L
L	H	H	H	L	L	H
H	L	H	L	H	L	H
H	H	H	L	L	L	H

← same →

Figure B-9 Proof of equivalence of a positive logic OR gate and a negative logic AND gate.

Sec. B-1 Elementary Logic Gates

B-2 COMBINATIONAL LOGIC DESIGN

In general, mathematical modeling is used to optimize a design, predict the results that will occur from various situations, or determine the important factors related to the feasibility or economics of the system being modeled. The modeling procedure

1. Finds the mathematical model for the given system.
2. Uses the model to make the necessary simplifications, predictions, and so on.
3. Determines the final design of the system from the final form of the model.

In the case at hand, modeling is used in the design of logic networks as follows:

1. Determines all the input/output relationships that must be true for the network being designed and puts them into a convenient tabular form.
2. Uses the table resulting from Step 1 to find a Boolean expression for each output that relates the inputs to that output.
3. Simplifies, or perhaps optimizes, the expressions resulting from Step 2.
4. Uses the expressions resulting from Step 3 to develop the desired logic diagrams.

If only a modification of an existing design is desired, Steps 1 and 2 could be replaced with:

Finds the Boolean expressions for the outputs of the given network.

In the preceding discussion, three design aids have been introduced: truth tables, Boolean expressions, and logic diagrams. Because truth tables are primarily used to originally define a logical network, Boolean expressions are needed for minimization, and logic diagrams are needed to actually put the network together, a designer must be able to convert from one form of a network's description to another. In particular, a designer must be able to perform the conversions shown in Fig. B-10.

As a tabular listing of the outputs for all possible inputs, a truth table serves as the definition of the network to be designed. It can normally be obtained from a precise statement of what the network is to do. For example, suppose that a three-input network is needed that will output a 1 if the majority of inputs is 1 and, otherwise, it is to output a 0. In other words, if X is the output and A, B, and C are the inputs, then

$X = 0$ if none or exactly one input is 1.

$X = 1$ if any two or all three inputs are 1.

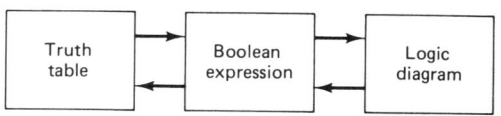

Figure B-10 Conversions needed during the design process.

This statement can be easily used to obtain the following truth table:

A	B	C	X
0	0	0	0
0	0	1	0
0	1	0	0
0	1	1	1
1	0	0	0
1	0	1	1
1	1	0	1
1	1	1	1

Once the truth table is established, a Boolean expression for each output is needed, i.e., a truth table to Boolean expression conversion must be made. There are two approaches to this problem. The first uses the facts that

1. A product is 1 if and only if all of its factors are 1.
2. A sum is 1 if and only if at least one of its terms is 1.

Therefore, a Boolean expression for an output can be derived from a truth table by forming a product for each row for which the output is 1 and then adding these products. Again, considering the voting example above, we will first examine the fourth row in the truth table and note that $X_3 = \overline{A}BC$ is 1 if and only if $A = 0$, $B = 1$, and $C = 1$. For the sixth, seventh, and eighth rows

$$X_5 = A\overline{B}C \text{ is 1 if and only if } A = 1, B = 0, \text{ and } C = 1$$

$$X_6 = AB\overline{C} \text{ is 1 if and only if } A = 1, B = 1, \text{ and } C = 0$$

$$X_7 = ABC \text{ is 1 if and only if } A = 1, B = 1, \text{ and } C = 1$$

Also

$$X = X_3 + X_5 + X_6 + X_7 = \overline{A}BC + A\overline{B}C + AB\overline{C} + ABC$$

is 1 if and only if at least one of the variables X_3, X_5, X_6, and X_7 is 1. Any combination of values for A, B, and C other than those given in the definitions of X_3, X_5, X_6, and X_7 will cause all of the terms in the output X to be 0 and thus will cause X to be 0. An expression such as the one given for X in this example is called a **sum of products**.

Alternatively, the output expression could have been based on

1. A sum is 0 if and only if all of its terms are 0.
2. A product is 0 if and only if at least one of its factors is 0.

In this case, a sum is formed for each row for which the output is 0 and then these sums are multiplied. For the voting example, note that

$$X_0 = A + B + C \text{ is 0 if and only if } A = 0, B = 0, \text{ and } C = 0$$
$$X_1 = A + B + \overline{C} \text{ is 0 if and only if } A = 0, B = 0, \text{ and } C = 1$$
$$X_2 = A + \overline{B} + C \text{ is 0 if and only if } A = 0, B = 1, \text{ and } C = 0$$
$$X_4 = \overline{A} + B + C \text{ is 0 if and only if } A = 1, B = 0, \text{ and } C = 0$$

Therefore

$$X = X_0 X_1 X_2 X_4 = (A + B + C)(A + B + \overline{C})(A + \overline{B} + C)(\overline{A} + B + C)$$

is 0 if and only if at least one of the variables X_0, X_1, X_2, and X_4 is 0. The **product of sums** solution is, of course, equivalent to the sum of products solution obtained above. (Note that either of the above procedures proves the earlier statement that all combinational logic circuits can be constructed from elementary gates.)

The reverse conversion for getting a truth table from a Boolean expression can be accomplished by finding the value of the output expression for each possible input and noting these values in the truth table. This could possibly be done more quickly by establishing columns in the table that contain values for intermediate subexpressions. Figure B-11 gives a truth table that defines

A	B	C	D	$\overline{AD}$	$\overline{CD}$	$X = \overline{AD} + B + \overline{CD}$	$\overline{A} + C$	$C + D$	$Y = (\overline{A} + C)(C + D)$
0	0	0	0	0	0	0	1	0	0
0	0	0	1	1	0	1	1	1	1
0	0	1	0	0	1	1	1	1	1
0	0	1	1	1	0	1	1	1	1
0	1	0	0	0	0	1	1	0	0
0	1	0	1	1	0	1	1	1	1
0	1	1	0	0	1	1	1	1	1
0	1	1	1	1	0	1	1	1	1
1	0	0	0	0	0	0	0	0	0
1	0	0	1	0	0	0	0	1	0
1	0	1	0	0	1	1	1	1	1
1	0	1	1	0	0	0	1	1	1
1	1	0	0	0	0	1	0	0	0
1	1	0	1	0	0	1	0	1	0
1	1	1	0	0	1	1	1	1	1
1	1	1	1	0	0	1	1	1	1

Figure B-11 Obtaining a truth table from Boolean expressions.

$$X = \overline{A}D + B + C\overline{D}$$

$$Y = (\overline{A} + C)(C + D)$$

After having found the desired output columns (the seventh and tenth columns), the designer could redraw the truth table without the intermediate columns (the fifth, sixth, eighth, and ninth columns).

Finding the logic diagram that corresponds to a given Boolean expression is the easiest of the conversions shown in Fig. B-10. It is simply a matter of drawing the gates that represent the operations in the expression and then connecting them together. For example, the diagram in Fig. B-12(a) can be obtained from

$$(A\overline{B} + D)\overline{C} + BD$$

by scanning the expression from left to right and drawing the gate symbols as the scanning takes place. Then, by noting the variables involved in the operations, the gate symbols can be connected.

For complex expressions, a more systematic approach may be easier. By using the distributive law to multiply out the expression to obtain a sum of products, one could then form a logic diagram by complementing all variables whose complements appear in the expression, draw a row of AND gates to get the products, and use an OR gate to get the sum. Using the same expression as in the above example, we get

$$(A\overline{B} + D)\overline{C} + BD = A\overline{B}\overline{C} + \overline{C}D + BD$$

which corresponds to the diagram in Fig. B-12(b).

A similar systematic approach consists of factoring an expression to get a product of sums. Once again, consider the expression

$$(A\overline{B} + D)\overline{C} + BD = (\overline{C} + D)(B + \overline{C})(A + D)(\overline{B} + D)$$

Fig. B-12(c) can be obtained by complementing the necessary variables, using OR gates to implement the sums, and then using an AND gate to produce the output.

The design of the voting network discussed at the beginning of this section could be completed by simplifying the output as follows:

$$\overline{A}BC + A\overline{B}C + AB\overline{C} + ABC = \overline{A}BC + ABC + A\overline{B}C + ABC + AB\overline{C} + ABC$$

$$= (\overline{A} + A)BC + (\overline{B} + B)AC + (\overline{C} + C)AB$$

$$= BC + AC + AB$$

$$= A(B + C) + BC$$

The first equality is justified because an existing term (in particular, ABC) can be repeated as many times as desired without changing the value of the expression. Two equivalent logic diagrams for implementing the voting network are shown in Fig. B-13.

The reverse conversion, that of obtaining an output Boolean expression from a logic diagram, is also very straightforward. It can be accomplished by tracing backward from the output to determine all gates that contribute to the output and

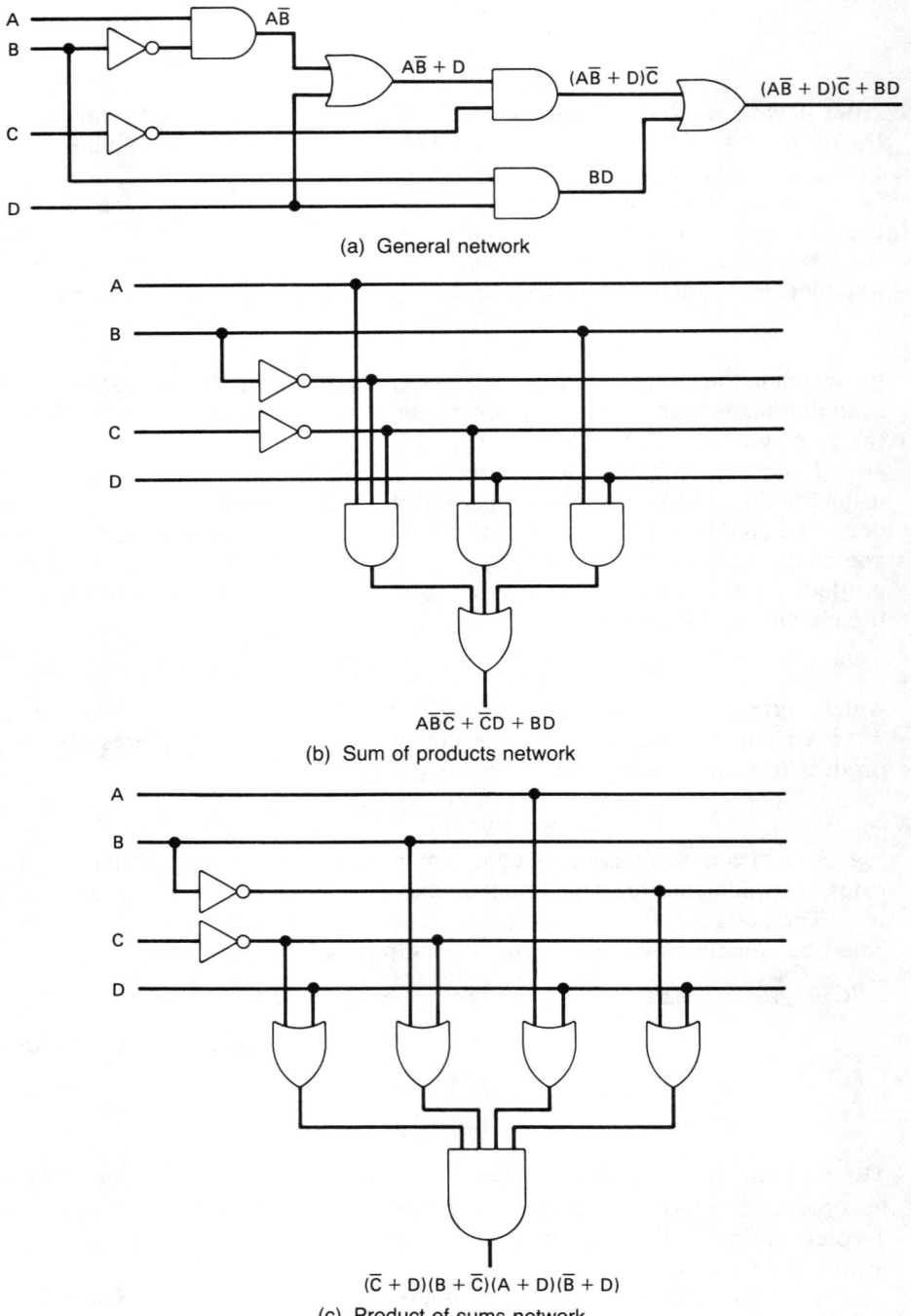

Figure B-12 Equivalent logic diagrams for a typical Boolean expression.

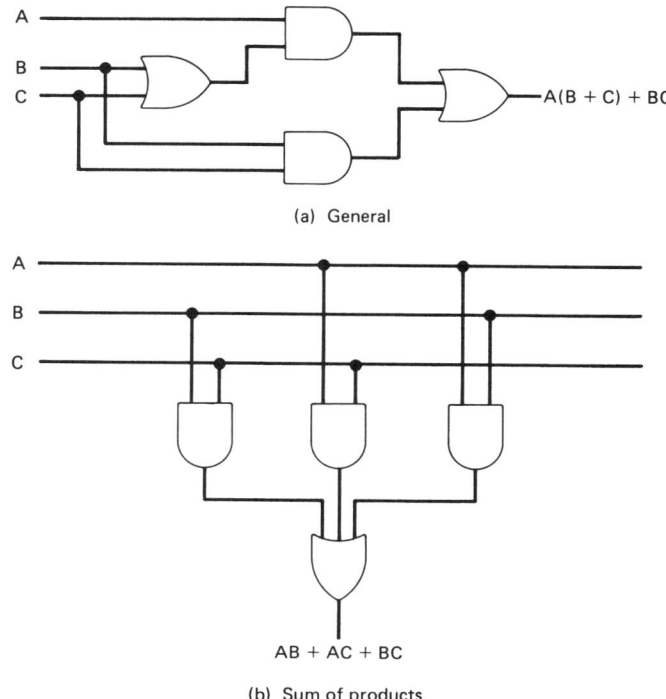

Figure B-13 Voting circuit designs.

then moving forward and finding the Boolean expressions for the outputs of these gates. This is demonstrated in Fig. B-14.

At this point it is clear that one of the principal problems confronting a digital designer is that of reducing a Boolean expression, thereby permitting it to be implemented using fewer gates. The purpose of the remainder of this section is to describe a design tool, called a **Karnaugh map**, that permits such reduction by visual inspection. Before we introduce Karnaugh maps however, a few preliminary definitions are needed. As we have seen, there are two standard Boolean expressions that can be obtained for an output in an arbitrary truth table: the sum of products expression and the product of sums expression. The occurrence of a variable or its complement in an expression is called a **literal**, and a term in a sum of products that includes a literal for every input is called a **minterm**. Similarly, a sum in a product of sums that includes a literal for every input is called a **maxterm**. For example, if A, B, and C are the inputs, then in

$$A\overline{B}C + \overline{A}BC + A\overline{C}$$

$A\overline{B}C$ and $\overline{A}BC$ are minterms and $A\overline{C}$ is not a minterm. For

$$(\overline{A} + B + \overline{C})(A + \overline{B} + \overline{C})(\overline{A} + C)$$

$\overline{A} + B + \overline{C}$ and $A + \overline{B} + \overline{C}$ are maxterms, but $\overline{A} + C$ is not.

Sec. B-2 Combinational Logic Design

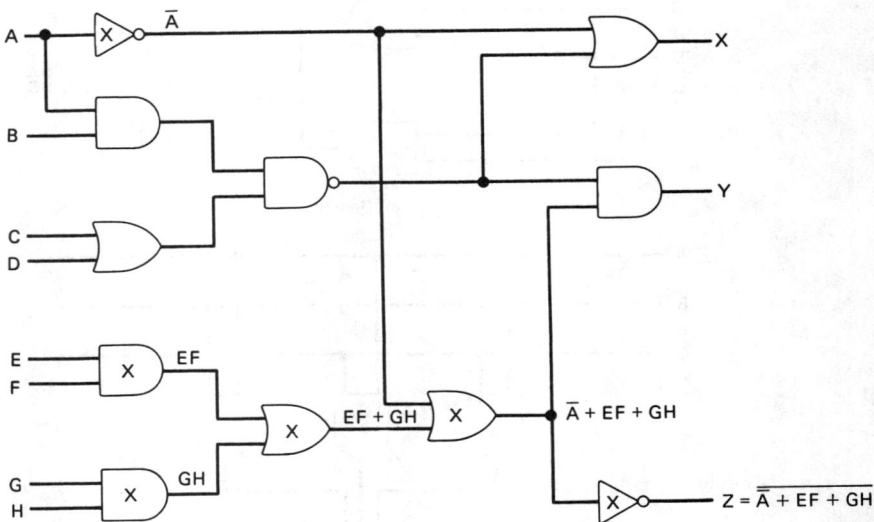

Figure B-14 Finding the Boolean expression for an output by tracing backward to find the contributing gates.

A Karnaugh map is nothing more than a truth table for a single output that is organized in a special way. It consists of an array of squares, such as those in Fig. B-15, where each square corresponds to a row in the truth table. The symbol(s) at the top indicates the variable(s) associated with the columns and the symbol(s) on the left indicates the variable(s) associated with the rows. The value of the output for each input is put in the corresponding square, as shown in Fig. B-16. Therefore, for each 1 in the Karnaugh map, there is a minterm in the output's sum of products expression, and for each 0 there is a maxterm in the product of sums expression. From either the truth table or the Karnaugh map, the following output expressions could be produced immediately:

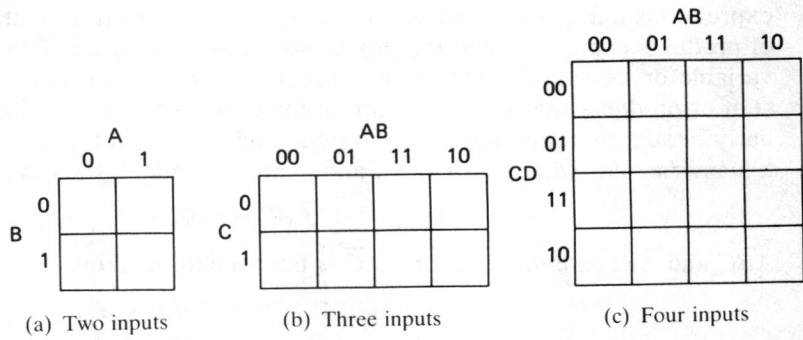

Figure B-15 Examples of Karnaugh map constructions.

514 Logic Level Design App. B

A	B	C	X
0	0	0	0
0	0	1	0
0	1	0	0
0	1	1	1
1	0	0	0
1	0	1	0
1	1	0	1
1	1	1	1

	AB			
	00	01	11	10
C 0	0	0	1	0
1	0	1	1	0

X = ABC + AB$\overline{C}$ + $\overline{A}$BC

Figure B-16 Truth table and its associated Karnaugh map.

$$X = ABC + AB\overline{C} + \overline{A}BC$$
$$= (A + B + C)(A + B + \overline{C})(A + \overline{B} + C)(\overline{A} + B + C)(\overline{A} + B + \overline{C})$$

Minimization of expressions using Karnaugh maps is based on the fact that if S is a sum of a subset of the minterms and

$$S = PQ$$

where Q consists of all possible combinations of a subset of the inputs, then

$$S = P$$

This is so because if Q consists of all possible combinations of a subset of the inputs, then $Q = 1$. The reason a Karnaugh map helps simplify an expression is that its rows and columns are arranged so that all possible combinations of the various subsets of inputs are adjacent, thus making it easy to spot such combinations.

In the example shown in Fig. B-16 the 1's appearing in the 11 column correspond to the minterms $AB\overline{C}$ and ABC. The sum of these terms can be factored as follows:

$$AB\overline{C} + ABC = AB(\overline{C} + C) = AB$$

The two 1's in the bottom row correspond to the minterms $\overline{A}BC$ and ABC, and

$$\overline{A}BC + ABC = (\overline{A} + A)BC = BC$$

These groupings are indicated in Fig. B-17(a) and result in

$$X = ABC + AB\overline{C} + \overline{A}BC$$
$$= ABC + AB\overline{C} + ABC + \overline{A}BC$$
$$= AB + BC$$

Note that because $P + P = P$, a minterm, i.e., a 1 in the map, may be used in as many groupings as desired.

Because a sum of all combinations of one variable consists of two terms, of

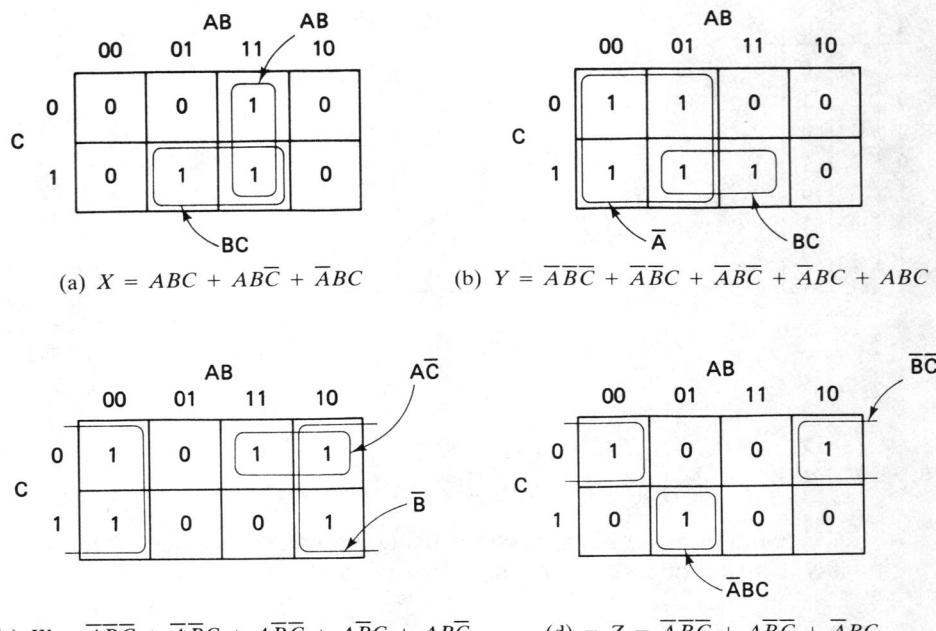

Figure B-17 Minimization of three-variable outputs.

two variables consists of four terms, of three variables consists of eight terms, etc., a designer must look for adjacent groups that include 2^n, $n = 1, 2, \ldots,$ ones. The larger the grouping, the greater the reduction in the number of literals and minterms. If the Karnaugh map of Y is as shown in Fig. B-17(b), then

$$Y = \overline{A}\,\overline{B}\,\overline{C} + \overline{A}\,\overline{B}C + \overline{A}B\overline{C} + \overline{A}BC + ABC$$
$$= \overline{A}(\overline{B}\,\overline{C} + \overline{B}C + B\overline{C} + BC) + BC(A + \overline{A})$$
$$= \overline{A} + BC$$

The products that correspond to maximum groupings are called **prime implicants**.

A three-variable Karnaugh map should be considered to be a cylinder with the left column being adjacent to the right column. Therefore, if the map for W is as shown in Fig. B-17(c), then the prime implicants are $\overline{B}$ and $A\overline{C}$, and

$$W = \overline{B} + A\overline{C}$$

A fourth example is given in Fig. B-17(d). In this example, the prime implicants are $\overline{B}\,\overline{C}$ and $\overline{A}BC$, and

$$Z = \overline{B}\,\overline{C} + \overline{A}BC$$

Note that in all of the above examples the variables that do not change in a grouping are the variables that appear in the corresponding prime implicant.

A Karnaugh map of a four-variable output is shown in Fig. B-18(a). The prime implicants are $A\overline{B}$, $A\overline{C}\overline{D}$, and $\overline{A}B\overline{C}$, and

$$X = A\overline{B} + A\overline{C}\overline{D} + \overline{A}B\overline{C}$$

The minterm $AB\overline{C}\overline{D}$ could also be covered by $B\overline{C}\overline{D}$; therefore, it is also true that

$$X = A\overline{B} + B\overline{C}\overline{D} + \overline{A}B\overline{C}$$

and it is seen that the prime implicants used in the final expression are not unique.

For purposes of adjacency, the four-variable Karnaugh map is to be considered as a doughnut-shaped surface that is formed by first attaching the top to the bottom to obtain a cylinder and then attaching the left and right ends to obtain a doughnut shape. When this is done, the top is adjacent to the bottom, the left side is adjacent to the right side, and the four corners are adjacent. To demonstrate these relationships consider the example shown in Fig. B-18(b). The output for this map is

$$Y = \overline{B}\overline{D} + \overline{B}C + \overline{A}B$$

In this example, note that the minterm $\overline{A}\overline{B}CD$ was not picked up by simply adding it to the others; it was covered by forming a grouping of four even though only one 1 was left to be included. Thus, only two literals were required in the third term instead of four. Once again, note that the larger the groupings the better.

Karnaugh maps can also be used for attacking problems involving five or six inputs. For these cases multiple four-input maps are used, as shown in Fig. B-19. So that adjacencies can be used to find prime implicants, the four-input maps should be viewed as if they are in a stack. For the six-variable case the $E = F = 0$ map should be on top followed by the $E = 0$, $F = 1$ map, the $E = F = 1$ map and the $E = 1$, $F = 0$ map, respectively. The top and bottom maps are considered to be adjacent. The output indicated by the five-variable map shown

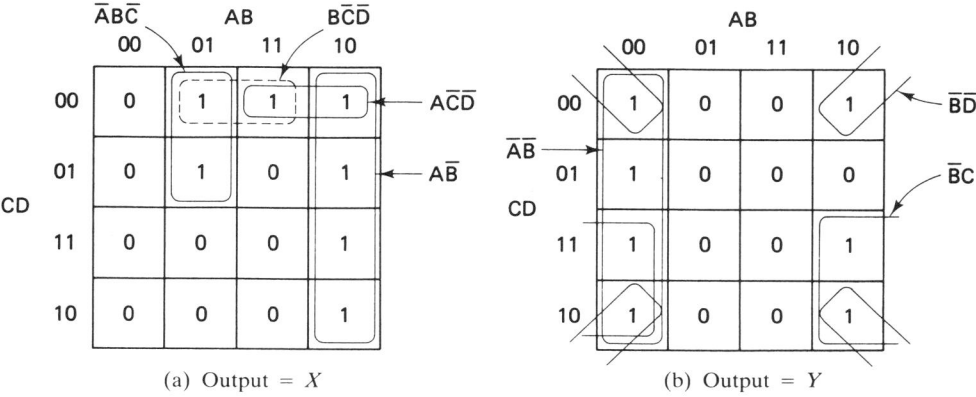

Figure B-18 Examples of four-variable outputs.

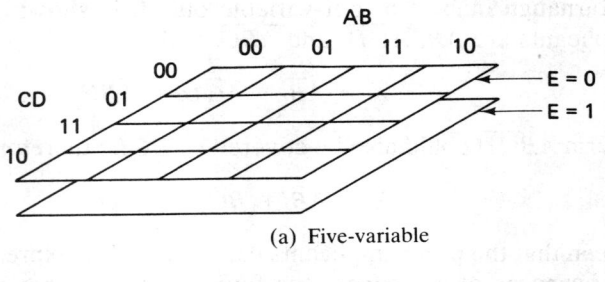

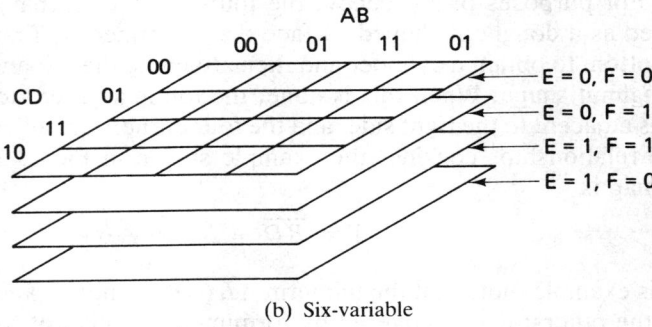

Figure B-19 Construction of five- and six-variable maps.

in Fig. B-20 is

$$X = \overline{AD}\overline{E} + ABD + ADE$$

As an example of a complete network design using a Karnaugh map, consider the problem of developing a network that compares the binary numbers $A = A_2A_1A_0$ and $B = B_2B_1B_0$ and output a 1 if $B > A$. The Karnaugh map describing the network is given in Fig. B-21(a). From this map we get

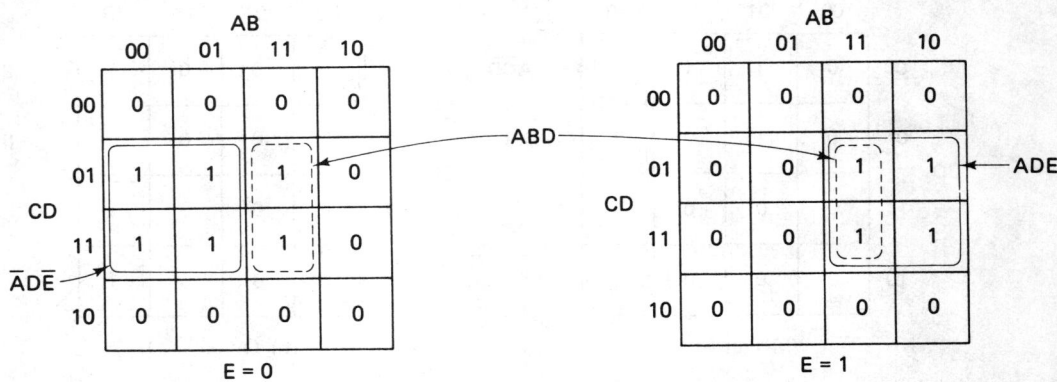

Figure B-20 Five-variable example.

$$X = \overline{A}_2 B_2 + \overline{A}_2 \overline{A}_1 B_1 + B_2 \overline{A}_1 B_1 + \overline{A}_2 \overline{A}_1 \overline{A}_0 B_0$$
$$+ B_2 \overline{A}_1 \overline{A}_0 B_0 + \overline{A}_2 \overline{A}_0 B_1 B_0 + B_2 \overline{A}_0 B_1 B_0$$

A network for implementing the comparator is shown in Fig. B-21(b).

Our ability to visualize only three dimensions and the fact that only two variables may be associated with each dimension limit the use of Karnaugh maps when working with more than six inputs. Although they can be used to help solve problems involving more than six variables, the use of adjacencies to spot prime implicants is limited to only six variables at a time.

The possible use of XOR and XNOR gates is indicated in a Karnaugh map with a diagonal pattern. This type of map is demonstrated in Fig. B-22. In Figs. B-22(a) and B-22(b) the outputs are

$$X = A\overline{B} + \overline{A}B = A \oplus B$$

and

$$Y = \overline{A}\,\overline{B} + AB = \overline{A \oplus B}$$

For the map in Fig. B-22(c)

$$W = \overline{A}(B \oplus C) + A(\overline{B \oplus C}) = A \oplus B \oplus C$$

and for the map in Fig. B-22(d)

$$Z = \overline{A}\,\overline{C}(B \oplus D) + A\overline{C}(B \oplus D) + CD$$
$$= \overline{C}(B \oplus D) + CD$$

Needless to say, it sometimes takes some ingenuity to make optimal use of XOR and XNOR gates. A more elegant way of designing a comparator using XNOR gates is given in Sec. 3-3-2.

To arrive at a product of sums, note that the Karnaugh map of $\overline{X}$ is obtained by interchanging the 1s and 0s in the Karnaugh map of X. Then the sum of products expressed for $\overline{X}$ is found and DeMorgan's laws are used to complement $\overline{X}$ to obtain X as a product of sums. For example, let the Karnaugh map for X be the one shown in Fig. B-23(a). By finding prime implicants using groups of zeros it is seen that

$$\overline{X} = A\overline{B} + AD$$

Therefore

$$X = \overline{\overline{X}} = \overline{A\overline{B} + AD} = \overline{(A\overline{B})}\,\overline{(AD)} = (\overline{A} + B)(\overline{A} + \overline{D})$$

By interchanging the 1s and 0s in the column and row labels as shown in Fig. B-23(b) and interchanging the use of the ANDs and ORs

$$X = (\overline{A} + B)(\overline{A} + \overline{D})$$

could have been obtained directly.

Finally, because for some designs some input combinations cannot occur, the outputs corresponding to these combinations are optional. These combinations

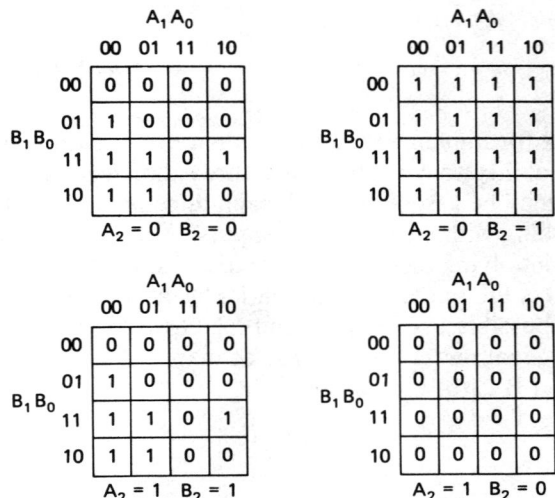

(a) Karnaugh map

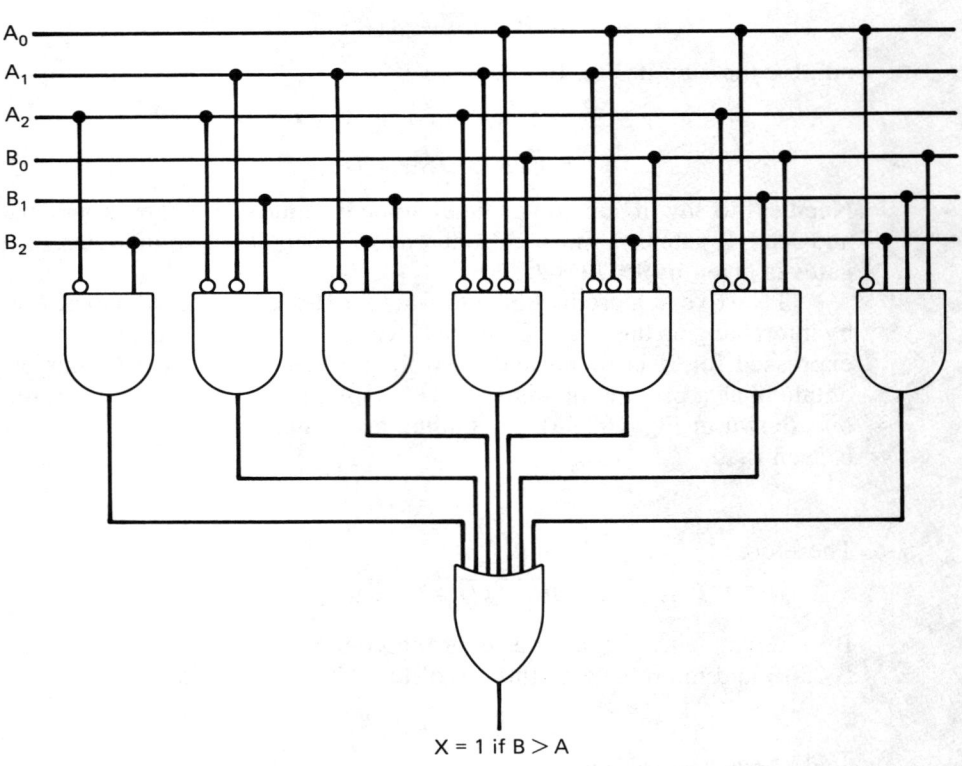

$X = 1$ if $B > A$

(b) Logic diagram

Figure B-21 Design of a 3-bit comparator.

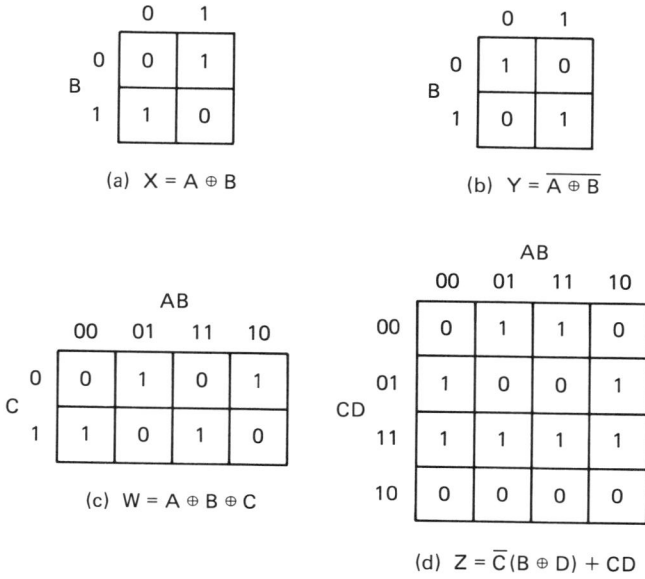

Figure B-22 Examples of maps that indicate the use of XOR and XNOR gates.

may be chosen to be either 1 or 0 as is convenient to the minimization process. They are represented by X's in the Karnaugh map and may or may not be included in the prime implicants. For the output whose map is shown in Fig. B-24, it is useful to include the minterm $A\bar{B}C\bar{D}$ in a prime implicant, but it is not useful to include the minterm $\bar{A}BC\bar{D}$ in a prime implicant. The minimized output function is

$$X = A\bar{B} + AC$$

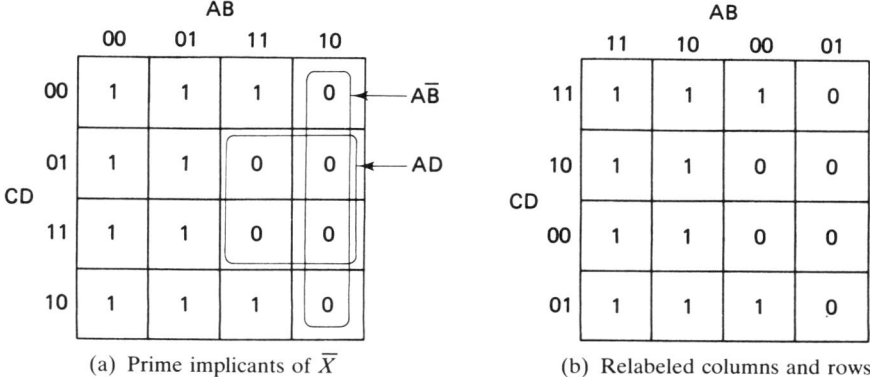

(a) Prime implicants of $\bar{X}$ (b) Relabeled columns and rows

Figure B-23 Example of finding a product of sums.

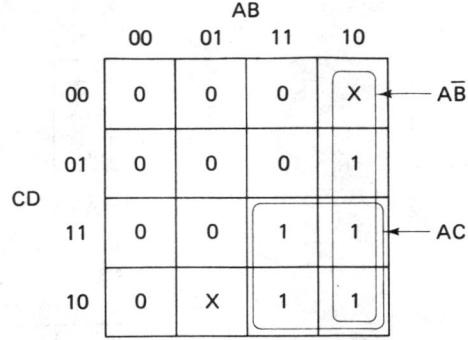

Figure B-24 Map with optional minterms.

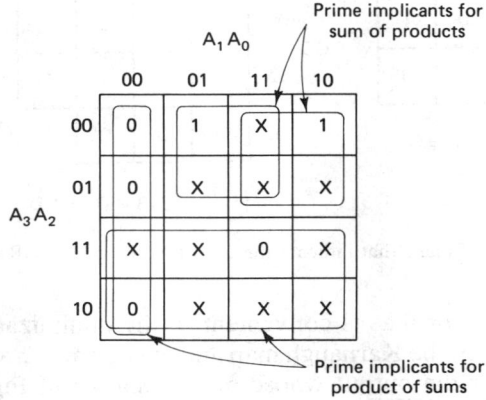

Figure B-25 Rotary switch example.

As a final example, suppose that a network is needed that will output a 1 at X if and only if the binary number $A_3A_2A_1A_0$ is greater than 0 and less than 3. Also, suppose that it is known that because the inputs are controlled by a rotary switch, at most one input can be 1 at any given time, except one switch position will allow all inputs to be 1. The needed Karnaugh map is in Fig. B-25. A sum of products solution is

$$X = \overline{A}_3 A_0 + \overline{A}_3 A_1 = \overline{A}_3(A_0 + A_1)$$

By grouping the 0s it is seen that the product of sums solution is the same, i.e.,

$$X = \overline{\overline{X}} = \overline{A_3 + \overline{A}_1\overline{A}_0} = \overline{A}_3(A_1 + A_0)$$

B-3 ELEMENTARY SEQUENTIAL CIRCUITS

Combinational circuits are characterized by the absence of memory (i.e., there is no means of retaining internal states and the outputs are strictly functions of the inputs) and feedback paths. In contrast, a sequential circuit must have both memory and feedback and the outputs depend on both current states and inputs.

Current states are considered to be the current memory contents and, at certain times, are fed back and combined with the inputs to determine new states and outputs.

In sequential networks, the variable time takes on a significant role, whereas combinational networks are considered to be time independent. It is usually necessary to define a sequential network according to its inputs and outputs over a period of time instead of simply noting the input/output relationships in a truth table that ignores time. The chief aid employed in examining the time-dependent aspects of a sequential network is called a **timing diagram**. A typical timing diagram is shown in Fig. B-26. In this figure A and B are assumed to be inputs and X and Y are assumed to be outputs.

Time is measured horizontally, but the actual time scale is normally not given because the time between events is usually not known or is not important; only the order in which events occur is relevant. If a time is important, it is specified as shown in the diagram for the Y output. The vertical scale consists of two values, with the higher value corresponding to state 1 and the lower value to state 0. In the figure, A begins in the 0 state and B and X begin in the 1 state. The transition of A to the 1 state does not change the X output, but the subsequent transition of B from 1 to 0 causes X to change to 0. The change of A from 1 to 0 does not affect X, but the following transition of A causes X to change to 1. The output Y is shown to change states 25 μS after a change in X.

Sometimes the current state of a variable is unimportant and the timing diagram is to indicate only a change of state. The S-shaped curves superimposed on the timing diagram for Y imply that the state of Y at a particular time is unknown, but regardless of the current state, a change will take place at the indicated point. If the current state is 0, the state will become 1, and vice versa.

Elementary sequential circuits fall into a general class of binary electronic circuits known as **multivibrators**, which may be astable, monostable, or bistable. An **astable multivibrator** cannot maintain a fixed state but must keep switching back and forth between its states. A **monostable multivibrator** can take on two

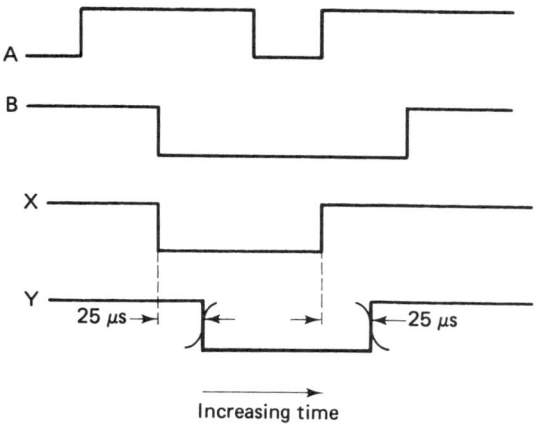

Figure B-26 Typical timing diagram.

states, but is stable in only one of them and can only temporarily stay in its unstable state. A **bistable multivibrator** is stable in either of its states and therefore can maintain either state indefinitely.

Most computer circuits are composed of groups of elementary circuits with each group operating in lockstep fashion. That is, each group maintains itself in a set of states until a certain event occurs (usually this event is a change in a voltage level or is a voltage pulse), at which time all elements in the group change their states simultaneously. The collection of groups may also have a central controlling mechanism. Any computer circuit or subcircuit that is controlled in this way is called a **synchronous circuit**. **Asynchronous circuits** operate independently from each other so that changes of states in one circuit are not necessarily time related to changes of states in other circuits.

B-3-1 Clocks

Synchronous circuits are normally regulated by trains of evenly spaced pulses generated by astable multivibrators called **clocks**. The constant length of time between pulses is called the **period**, the reciprocal of the period is the **frequency**, and the length of the pulse divided by the period (usually expressed as a percentage) is the **duty cycle**. The output of a clock whose duty cycle is 50% is given in Fig. B-27. Some electronic devices, known as **multiphase clocks**, output two or more identical pulse trains that are offset from each other in time. Multiphase clocks can be used to regulate activity in different sections of a computer circuit.

Three clock designs are shown in Fig. B-28. The first has a nonadjustable period that depends on the amount of time it takes for an inverter to change its output and the number of inverters used. The period of the second is primarily determined by the capacitance in the outer feedback loop and, because this capacitance can easily be set by a designer, is considered to be adjustable. Both of the first two designs have periods that may change with temperature or as the electronic components age; this is especially true of the second, which includes a capacitor. The third design avoids this problem by replacing the capacitor with a crystal oscillator. With a crystal oscillator controlling its period, this clock is highly stable and provides a constant frequency for a long time. More sophisticated clock circuits involving crystal oscillators can provide additional flexibility, such as adjustable duty cycles (see Fletcher [1]).

B-3-2 Monostable Multivibrators

When properly excited by an input, a monostable multivibrator temporarily goes to its unstable state and then returns to its stable state. This action normally results in a voltage pulse at the output whose width is the amount of time spent in the

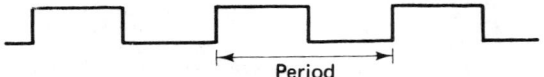

Figure B-27 Typical clock output.

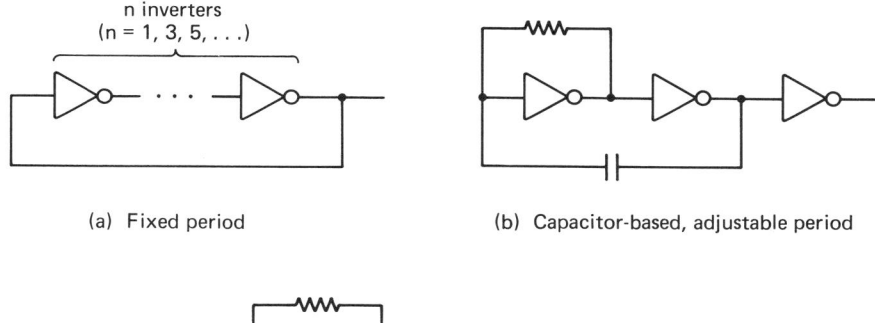

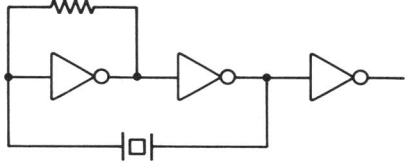

(c) Crystal oscillator controlled

Figure B-28 Clock designs.

unstable state. The symbol for a monostable multivibrator that is triggered by a 0 to 1 transition at its input and outputs a 1 pulse at its output is shown in Fig. B-29(a). If a small circle is placed at the input, then a 1 to 0 transition triggers the output. A small circle at the output indicates that the output is a 0 pulse (i.e., the pulse is inverted).

Figure B-29(b) shows a logic diagram for a simple monostable multivibrator that is triggered by a positive transition and outputs a positive pulse. When T goes to 1, the output of the left gate goes to 0. Because the voltage across the capacitor cannot change instantaneously, the input to the right inverter must also be 0, hence its output must go to 1. As the capacitor charges through resistor R, the input to the right inverter once again approaches 1. When this input reaches the voltage level that causes the inverter to switch, the output state will again go to 0. This change will cause the output of the left gate to return to 1 whenever the T input goes to 0, and will cause the capacitor to discharge. The width of the output pulse will be proportional to the product $(R + R_0)C$, where R_0 is the output resistance of the left gate.

The input pulse may return to 0 at any time after the output pulse is initiated; it does not need to wait until the output pulse is complete. However, the capacitor must have time to discharge completely before the next input pulse occurs, because a residual charge on the capacitor will shorten the output pulse. Generally, the capacitor is considered to be completely discharged after $4(R + R_0)C$ seconds.

Frequently, monostable multivibrator designs are more complicated than the one shown and provide more flexibility in adjusting the ratio of pulse width to time between pulses. Other common features include an inverted enable pin, which can be used to turn the multivibrator on or off, and a second input, which allows the output pulse to be triggered by either a positive transition or a negative

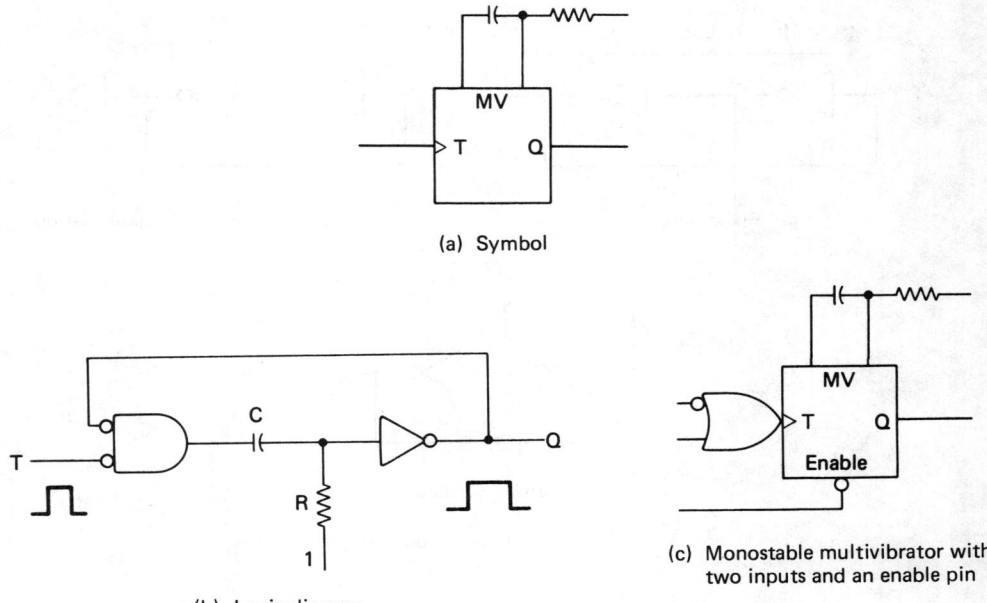

Figure B-29 Monostable multivibrators.

transition, according to which input is used. The symbol for indicating a monostable multivibrator with these features is shown in Fig. B-29(c). Some multivibrators also have outputs for providing both positive and negative pulses.

The uses of monostable multivibrators are varied. They could, for example, be used to send a pulse to one or more subcircuits in a computer to initiate actions in the subcircuits simultaneously. Also, a negative pulse could be used to hold off an action for a specified period of time (the width of the pulse).

B-3-3 Flip-flops

The bistable multivibrators of interest to us are those known as **flip-flops** that accept voltage levels at their inputs and output voltage levels. The use of flip-flops in designing computers is pervasive and is discussed at length in Chap. 3. The discussion here only introduces the different types of flip-flops and their associated terminology.

The simplest flip-flop is the set-reset (S-R) flip-flop shown in Fig. B-30. It has two inputs, S and R, and two outputs, Q and $\overline{Q}$, with $\overline{Q}$ being the complement of Q. When $S = R = 0$ and $Q = 1$, the output of the lower NAND gate is 0 and the feedback of this output into the upper NAND gate causes Q to be maintained at 1. If R is then raised to 1, the output of the lower NAND gate becomes 1 and the feedback forces the Q output to 0. This state remains 0 even after R is returned to 0 because of the feedback from Q. If, after R is lowered, S becomes 1, the Q

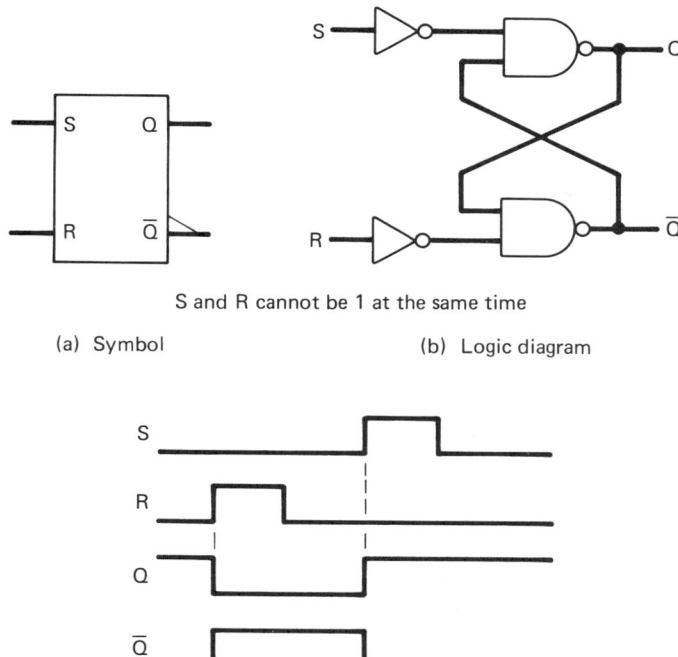

(a) Symbol (b) Logic diagram

S and R cannot be 1 at the same time

(c) Timing diagram of basic action

Figure B-30 S-R flip-flop.

output must once again become 1 and Q is forced back to 0. This activity is depicted in Fig. B-30(c). Basically, an S-R flip-flop is a 1-bit memory that can be cleared to 0 by applying a pulse to R, or set to 1 by applying a pulse to S, and whose contents can be monitored via Q or $\overline{Q}$. Note that S and R should never be 1 at the same time.

An important modification of the S-R flip-flop is to add a third input to control whether the S and R inputs are enabled or disabled. As shown in Fig. B-31, this input is most easily added by replacing the inverters with NAND gates and having the third input connected to both NAND gates. Frequently, flip-flops are synchronized by applying a common clock signal to their enable/disable inputs; therefore, these inputs are called **clock inputs** and are denoted by C. One should be cautioned, however, that quite often the clock input is not provided by a clock. Also shown in Fig. B-31 is a typical timing diagram of a clocked S-R flip-flop's activity. Note that, while the C input is 0, changes in the S and R inputs are ignored, but as soon as the C input goes to 1 the outputs are determined by the S and R inputs according to the definition of the S-R flip-flop given above.

A variation of the clocked S-R flip-flop is the data (D) flip-flop which is obtained by connecting the S input to the R input through an inverter as shown in Fig. B-32. While $C = 1$ the output of a D flip-flop is the same as its input, and while $C = 0$ this input is ignored.

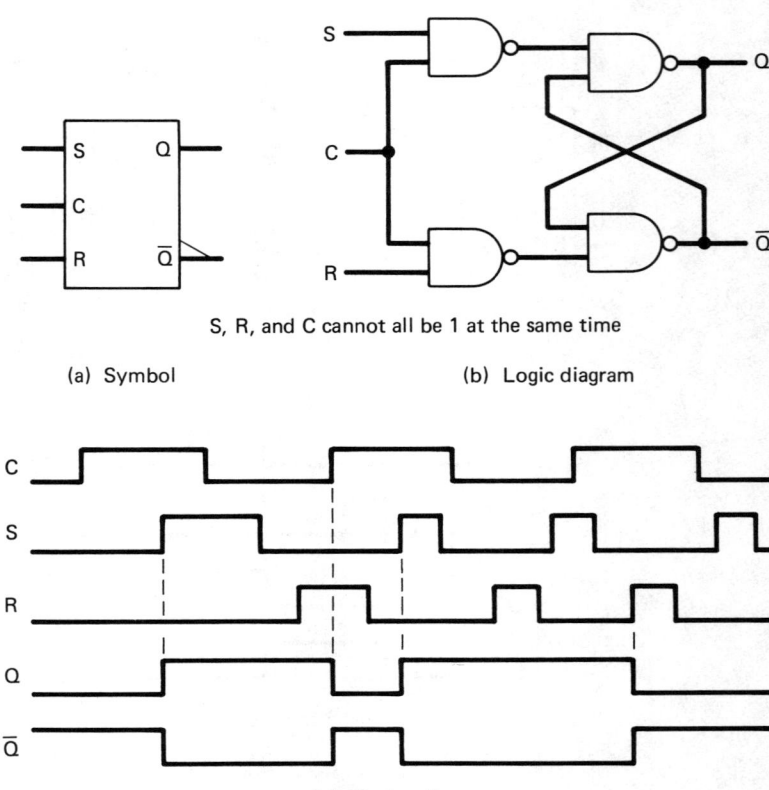

(a) Symbol (b) Logic diagram

(c) Timing diagram

Figure B-31 Clocked S-R flip-flop.

All clocked flip-flops that react to their inputs any time $C = 1$ are called **latches**. Alternatively, some clocked flip-flops are **edge-triggered** and can change states only when there is a 0 to 1 transition at C, **positive edge triggering**, or a 1 to 0 transition at C, **negative edge triggering**. Figure B-33 shows the symbols for positive and negative edge-triggered D flip-flops. The small angular shape at the C input is part of the IEEE standard. It means that action inside the sequential circuit can occur only at the time of a 0 to 1 transition at the marked input. If a

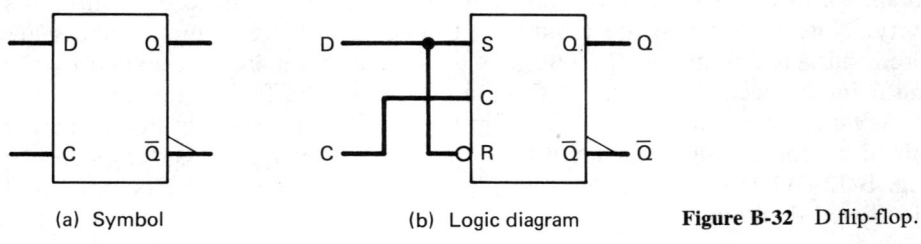

(a) Symbol (b) Logic diagram **Figure B-32** D flip-flop.

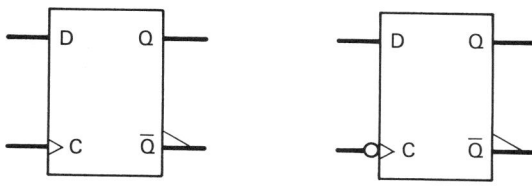

Figure B-33 Symbols for edge-triggered D flip-flops.

(a) Positive edge-triggered (b) Negative edge-triggered

small circle is also placed at the input, then the incoming signal is inverted and action is prompted by a 1 to 0 transition of the incoming signal.

Figure B-34 gives a set of timing diagrams that illustrate the differences between a D latch, a positive edge-triggered D flip-flop, and a negative edge-triggered D flip-flop. For the D latch, the output Q tracks the D input while $C = 1$, but while $C = 0$ the Q output does not change regardless of the activity at the D input. For positive edge-triggering, Q can change only when C changes from 0 to 1 and once Q has changed, it remains in its new state until the next 0 to 1 transition at C. In the example shown in Fig. B-34, at the time of the first 0 to 1 transition the D input is 0 and this causes Q to remain at 0; at the time of the second transition $D = 1$ and Q changes to 1; and at the time of the third transition, $D = 0$ and Q returns to 0. For the negative edge-triggered case, $D = 1$ when C first goes from 1 to 0 and therefore, Q goes to 1; during the next 1 to 0 transition, $D = 0$ and Q returns to 0; and, during the last 1 to 0 transition, $D = 0$ causing Q to remain at 0.

The remaining principal types of flip-flops are the J-K and toggle (T) flip-flops shown in Figs. B-35 and B-36. A J-K flip-flop is a clocked edge-triggered S-R flip-flop that has been modified by ANDing the outputs with the inputs. As does a 1 at the S input, a 1 at the J input when the triggering edge arrives causes Q to be set to 1; and, as with a 1 at the R input, a 1 at the K input when the edge arrives causes Q to be cleared to 0. However, unlike the S-R flip-flop for which $S = R = 1$ is not allowed, J and K may both equal 1 and, if they do, the J-K flip-flop outputs reverse their states (i.e., if $Q = 1$ it will become 0 and if $Q =$

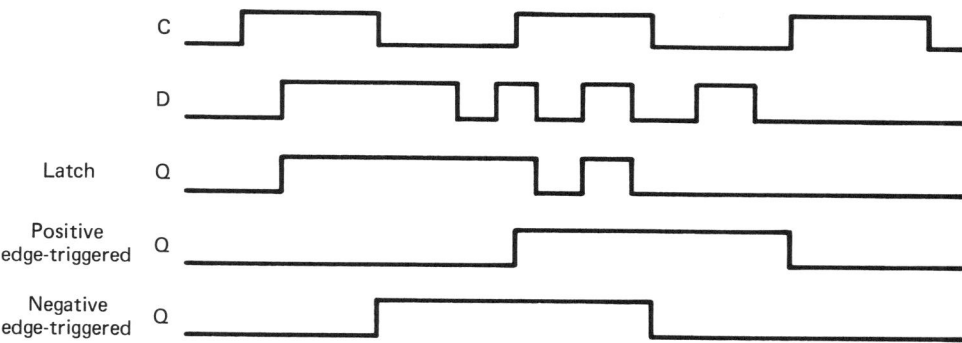

Figure B-34 Typical activity for the three types of D flip-flops.

Sec. B-3   Elementary Sequential Circuits

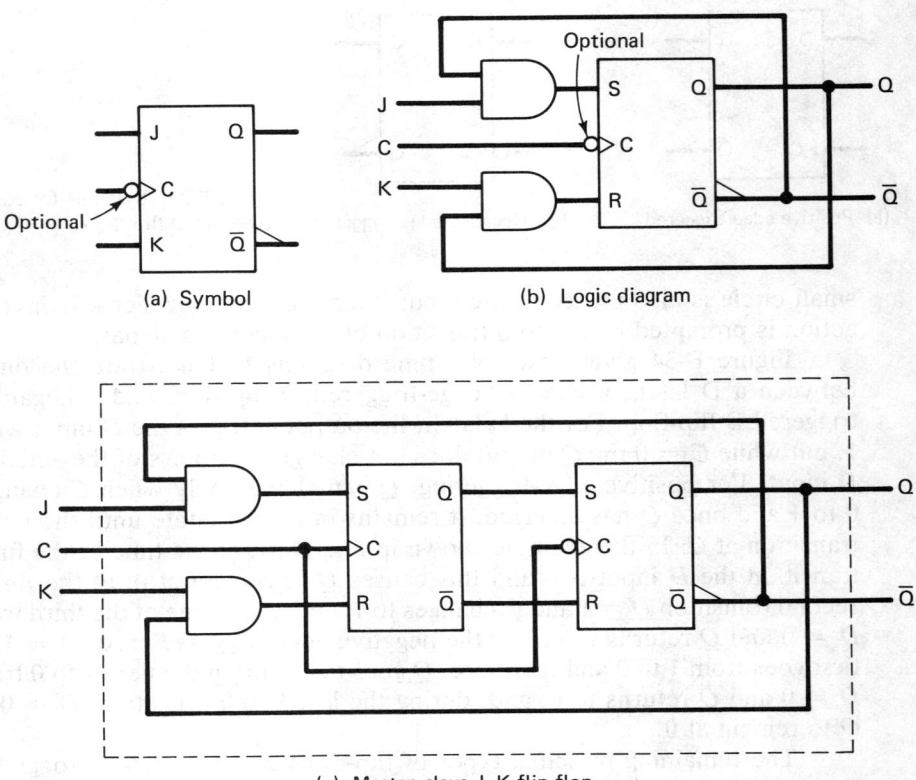

Figure B-35 J-K flip-flops.

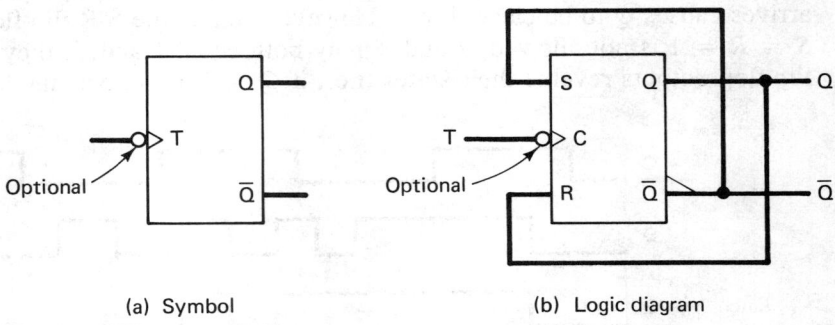

Figure B-36 T flip-flop.

0 it will become 1). A J-K flip-flop must be edge-triggered; otherwise, it would be unstable.

Shown in Fig. B-35(c) is an important variation of the J-K flip-flop that uses both edges of a C input pulse. The positive edge sets an internal state that is

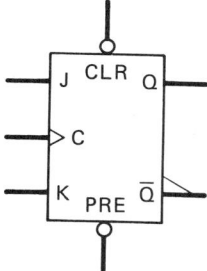

Figure B-37 Positive edge-triggered J-K flip-flop with clear and preset inputs.

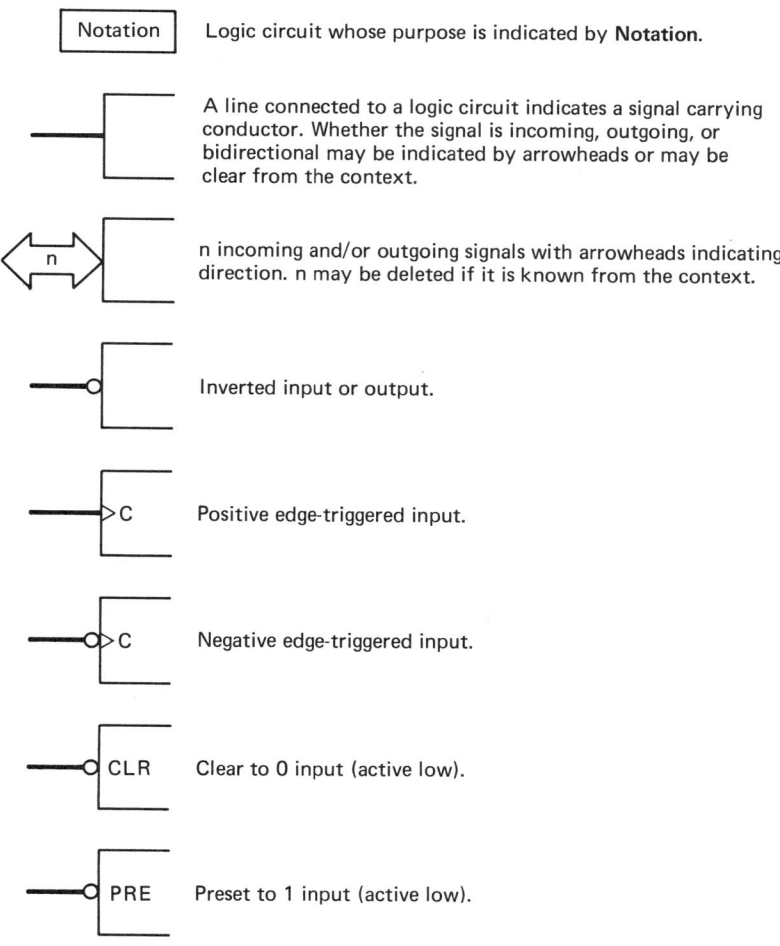

Figure B-38 Logic circuit symbols.

Sec. B-3 Elementary Sequential Circuits

passed to the output when the negative edge arrives. This variation is called a **master-slave J-K flip-flop** and its purpose is to isolate the output from the input.

The T flip-flop given in Fig. B-36 has only one input and is constructed from an S-R flip-flop by feeding Q and $\overline{Q}$ back into R and S, respectively. This feedback causes the outputs to reverse their states whenever the proper edge arrives. A T flip-flop must also be edge-triggered.

Common additions to a flip-flop are the clear and preset inputs shown on the J-K flip-flop in Fig. B-37. The clear (CLR) input provides a means of clearing Q to 0 at any time, regardless of the signal on input C. Similarly, the preset (PRE) input can set Q to 1. As indicated by the small circles, these inputs are inverted so that the clearing or setting is initiated by a 0 (negative going) pulse.

A summary of the symbols and notation used in this book is given in Fig. B-38.

REFERENCES

1. Fletcher, William I., *An Engineering Approach to Digital Design* (Englewood Cliffs, New Jersey: Prentice Hall, Inc., 1980).
2. Gibson, Glenn A., and Yu-cheng Liu, *Microcomputers for Engineers and Scientists* (Englewood Cliffs, New Jersey: Prentice Hall, Inc., 1987).
3. Barna, Arpad, and Dan I. Porat, *Integrated Circuits in Digital Electronics* (New York: John Wiley and Sons, 1973).
4. Hill, Frederick J., and Gerald R. Peterson, *Digital Systems: Hardware Organization and Design* (New York: John Wiley and Sons, 1973).

EXERCISES

1. Draw a logic diagram of a circuit whose output is
$$X = AB + \overline{A}(BC + \overline{B})$$
2. Determine the output X of the following logic circuit:

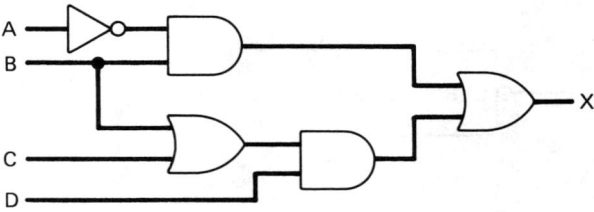

3. Prove the equivalences given in Fig. B-4.
4. Draw a logic diagram of a circuit whose outputs are:

$$X = \overline{B + D} + AB(C \oplus D)$$

$$Y = \overline{AD} + C \oplus D$$

5. Show that the XOR operation is commutative and associative.
6. Determine the outputs X and Y of

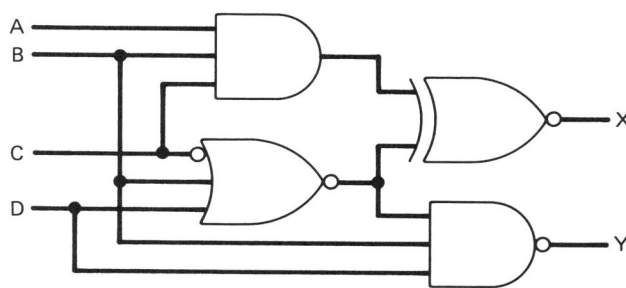

7. Prove that the gates that are directly across from each other in Fig. B-8 are equivalent.
8. Convert the positive logic circuit in Exercise 2 to a negative logic circuit and then reduce the number of inversions in the result by using the equivalences in Fig. B-8.
9. Prove the following equivalences:
   (a) $AB + A\overline{B}C = A(B + C)$
   (b) $(A + B)(A + \overline{B} + C) = (A + B)(A + C) = A + BC$
   (c) $AB + \overline{A}C + BC = AB + \overline{A}C$
   (d) $(X + Y)(\overline{X} + Z)(Y + Z) = (X + Y)(\overline{X} + Z)$
10. Given the following truth table, use both the sum of products method and the product of sums method to find Boolean expressions for each output:

A	B	C	X	Y	Z
0	0	0	1	0	0
0	0	1	0	1	1
0	1	0	0	1	1
0	1	1	0	0	1
1	0	0	1	0	1
1	0	1	0	0	1
1	1	0	0	0	1
1	1	1	0	0	0

Simplify each of the expressions obtained and draw a diagram of a logic network having the specified input/output relationships.

11. Given the network shown, find Boolean expressions for the outputs, simplify these expressions, and then draw an equivalent network using the simplified expressions.

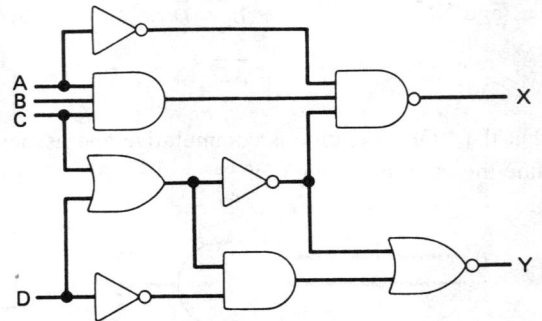

12. Design a four-input voting network that outputs a 0 if the vote is a tie or there are more 0 inputs than 1 inputs.
13. Find the Karnaugh maps for
    (a) $AB\bar{C} + \bar{A}BC + A\bar{B}C + \bar{A}B\bar{C}$
    (b) $\bar{A}BC\bar{D} + \bar{A}\bar{B}C\bar{D} + ABCD + \bar{A}BCD + \bar{A}\bar{B}C\bar{D} + \bar{A}\bar{B}\bar{C}\bar{D}$
    (c) $\bar{A}\bar{B}CD\bar{E} + \bar{A}\bar{B}CDE + \bar{A}BCDE + A\bar{B}CDE + \bar{A}B\bar{C}DE + \bar{A}BCDE$
14. Find the minimized sum of products for the following maps:

	AB			
	00	01	11	10
C 0	0	1	1	1
C 1	0	1	0	0

(a)

	AB			
	00	01	11	10
CD 00	1	0	0	0
CD 01	1	1	1	1
CD 11	1	0	0	1
CD 10	1	0	0	0

(b)

	AB			
	00	01	11	10
CD 00	0	0	1	1
CD 01	0	1	1	1
CD 11	0	1	1	1
CD 10	0	0	0	1

E = 0

	AB			
	00	01	11	10
CD 00	0	0	0	1
CD 01	1	0	1	1
CD 11	1	0	1	1
CD 10	0	0	0	1

E = 1

(c)

15. Use XOR and XNOR gates to simplify the output X defined by the following map:

	AB			
CD	00	01	11	10
00	1	0	1	0
01	0	1	0	1
11	0	1	0	1
10	1	0	1	0

X

16. Find the minimized product of sums for the maps given in Exercise 14.
17. Given the following truth table, use Karnaugh maps to find a simplified logic network that has A, B, and C as its inputs and X and Y as its outputs:

A	B	C	X	Y
0	0	0	0	0
0	0	1	0	0
0	1	0	1	0
0	1	1	0	1
1	0	0	0	0
1	0	1	0	0
1	1	0	1	1
1	1	1	1	1

(Note that a Karnaugh map of XY can be used to find the prime implicant that is common to both X and Y.)

18. Find a minimized sum of products expression for the output whose map is

	AB			
CD	00	01	11	10
00	1	0	0	X
01	0	0	0	0
11	X	1	1	X
10	1	1	1	1

19. Find a minimized product of sums expression for the map given in Exercise 18.

20. Because two Karnaugh maps are identical if and only if the mapped expressions are equal, maps can be used to show equality. Use a Karnaugh map to prove the following equality:

$$A\overline{C} + BC = A\overline{C} + AB + BC$$

21. If it takes 10 nS for a signal to pass through an inverter, what is the period of a clock constructed from nine cascaded inverters? What is its duty cycle?
22. Draw a symbol of a monostable multivibrator that is triggered by a 1 to 0 transition at its input, outputs a 1 (positive going) pulse, and has an inverted enable feature.
23. Draw a timing diagram that shows the S, C, and R inputs and Q and $\overline{Q}$ outputs of a clocked S-R latch, assuming that initially $S = C = R = Q = 0$ and the following sequence of events:

$$R = 1 \quad C = 1 \quad C = 0 \quad S = 1 \quad R = 0 \quad C = 1 \quad S = 0 \quad R = 1$$

$$C = 0 \quad S = 1 \quad S = 0 \quad C = 1$$

24. Rework Exercise 23 assuming that the S-R flip-flop is positive edge-triggered. Negative edge-triggered.
25. Complete the following timing diagram assuming a D latch. Positive edge-triggered D flip-flop. Negative edge-triggered D flip-flop.

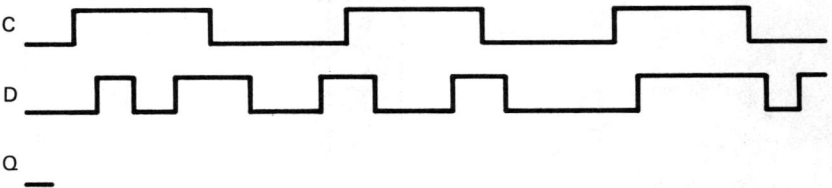

26. Complete the following timing diagram assuming a positive edge-triggered J-K flip-flop. Negative edge-triggered J-K flip-flop.

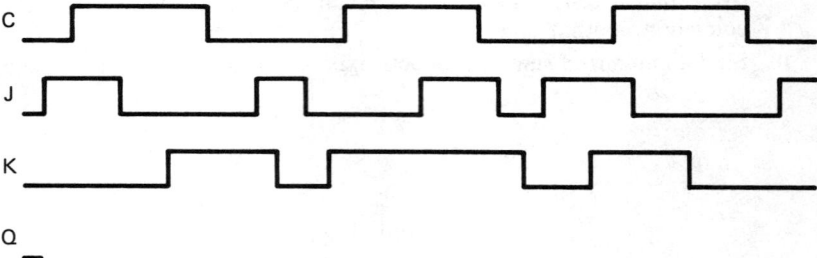

27. Use a timing diagram to show that if a clock signal is input to a T flip-flop, then the output of the T flip-flop is a clock signal whose frequency is half that of the input.

C

X16 Summary

This appendix summarizes the instruction set, assembler directives, and important properties of the hypothetical X16 computer. The X16's programming model is given in Fig. C-1 and the eight registers that are accessible to a programmer are given below along with their 3-bit addresses.

Register	R0	R1	R2	R3	R4	R5	SP	PC
Address	000	001	010	011	100	101	110	111

The addressing modes are designated by either three bits or six bits as follows:

Addressing Mode	Bit Designation
Immediate	010 or 111010
Register	000
Direct	011 or 111011 or 000011
Register indirect	001
Register indirect, autoincrement	101
Register indirect, autodecrement	111
Relative	110

For immediate and direct addressing, a mode is designated by only three bits if it is part of the first operand field of an instruction with a 7-bit opcode; otherwise, the mode is designated by six bits. For direct addressing, 111011 indicates the

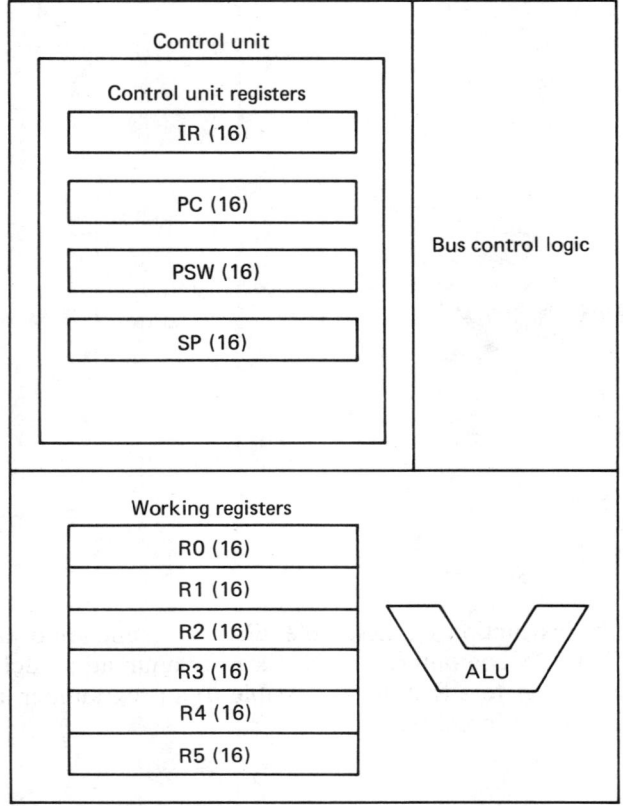

Figure C-1 X16 programming model.

address is of a memory location and 000011 indicates the address is of an I/O port.

The format of the PSW is:

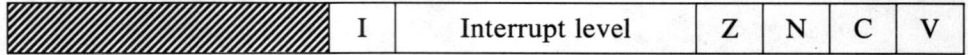

where the condition flags are the

Zero (Z) flag: Set to 1 if the result of an arithmetic/logic or shift/rotate operation is zero and cleared to 0 if the result is nonzero.

Negative (N) flag: Set to equal the high-order bit of the result of an arithmetic/logic or shift/rotate operation.

Carry (C) flag: For addition, it is set to 1 if there is a carry from the high-order bit position and for subtraction, it is set to 1 if a borrow is needed (i.e., the unsigned subtrahend is greater than the unsigned minuend). For shifts and rotates it is set by the bit shifted out of the operand.

Overflow (V) flag: Set to 1 if an addition or subtraction operation causes a signed overflow and cleared to 0 if it does not cause a signed overflow.

The *I* bit disables all interrupts when it is 0 and enables the interrupt system as a whole when it is 1, but even when the *I* bit is 1, only those interrupts with the same or a higher priority request level than is indicated by the 3-bit Interrupt Level field are recognized.

All instructions consist of a 4-bit, 7-bit, 10-bit, or 16-bit opcode followed by 0, 1, or 2 operand fields. They are 2, 4, or 6 bytes long, depending on the addressing modes used and the number of operand fields. The instructions are defined below using the abbreviations and symbols given in Fig. C-2. Except for the push and pop instructions, which are considered separately, the instruction definitions are divided into groups according to the number of bits in their opcodes. Each definition includes the instruction's assembler code format, abbreviated description, condition flag settings, and opcode in binary. For the condition flag settings

- u   means unchanged.
- s   means set according to the above rules.
- x   means left with an arbitrary value.
- 0   means cleared to 0.
- 1   means set to 1.

Each group of definitions is followed by the possible machine language formats for the instructions in the group. The halfwords drawn with dashed lines may not be present depending on the addressing modes being used.

Abbreviation	Meaning	Symbol	Meaning
OPR	Operand	→	Replaces
SRC	Source operand	(X)	The contents of X
DST	Destination operand	$\overline{X}$	Complement of X
NAME	Identifying name	∧	Logical AND
CONST	Constant expression	∨	Logical OR
LAB	Label	▽	Logical exclusive OR
R	Register	#	Immediate mode
M	Addressing mode	[R]	Register indirect mode
A	Memory address	[R]+	Register indirect autoincrement mode
D	Displacement		
I	Immediate operand	−[R]	Register indirect autodecrement mode
PORT	I/O port address		
OC	Opcode	LAB[R]	Relative mode
R0, R1, R2, R3, R4, R5	General purpose registers	—	Unspecified bit
IR	Instruction register		
PC	Program counter		
SP	Stack pointer		
PSW	Processor status word		
LC	Location counter		

Figure C-2 Glossary of symbols and abbreviations.

4-Bit Opcode Instructions

(Transfer, Compare, Addition, Subtraction, and I/O)

Assembler Code		Description	Flags	Opcode
MOVB	SRC, DST	(SRC) → (DST)	uuuu	1111
MOVH	SRC, DST			1110
CMPB	SRC, DST	(DST) − (SRC)	ssss	1101
CMPH	SRC, DST			1100
ADDB	SRC, DST	(DST) + (SRC) → (DST)	ssss	0101
ADDH	SRC, DST			0100
ADCB	SRC, DST	(DST) + (SRC) + (C) → (DST)	ssss	0111
ADCH	SRC, DST			0110
SUBB	SRC, DST	(DST) − (SRC) → (DST)	ssss	1001
SUBH	SRC, DST			1000
SBBB	SRC, DST	(DST) − (SRC) − (C) → (DST)	ssss	1011
SBBH	SRC, DST			1010
INPB	PORT, DST	(PORT) → (DST)	uuuu	1111*
INPH	PORT, DST			1110*
OUTB	SRC, PORT	(SRC) → (PORT)	uuuu	1111*
OUTH	SRC, PORT			1110*

* The in and out instructions differ from the move instructions in that, for an in instruction, the Source Register/Mode field must be 000011 and, for an out instruction, the Destination Register/Mode field must be 000011.

Addressing Modes: All are possible for SRC and DST except that DST cannot be immediate. PORT is an I/O port address specified by the Direct mode.

Machine Instruction Formats:

| OC(4) | M(6) | M(6) | I or A (16) | A (16) |

| OC(4) | R(3) | M(3) | M(6) | D (16) | A (16) |

| OC(4) | M(6) | R(3) | M(3) | I or A (16) | D (16) |

| OC(4) | R(3) | M(3) | R(3) | M(3) | D (16) | D (16) |

7-Bit Opcode Instructions

(Logical, Negate, Multiplication, and Division)

Assembler Code		Description	Flags ZNCV	Opcode
NOTB	SRC, DST	$(\overline{SRC}) \rightarrow (DST)$	ss00	0011100
NOTH	SRC, DST			0010100
ANDB	SRC, DST	$(DST) \wedge (SRC) \rightarrow (DST)$	ss00	0011000
ANDH	SRC, DST			0010000
IORB	SRC, DST	$(DST) \vee (SRC) \rightarrow (DST)$	ss00	0011001
IORH	SRC, DST			0010001
XORB	SRC, DST	$(DST) \triangledown (SRC) \rightarrow (DST)$	ss00	0011010
XORH	SRC, DST			0010010
TSTB	SRC, DST	$(DST) \wedge (SRC)$	ss00	0011011
TSTH	SRC, DST			0010011
NEGB	SRC, DST	$-(SRC) \rightarrow (DST)$	ssss	0011101
NEGH	SRC, DST			0010101
MULB	SRC, DST	$(DST)*(SRC) \rightarrow (DST+1):(DST)$	00xx	0011110
MULH	SRC, DST	$(DST)*(SRC) \rightarrow (DST+2):(DST)$		0010110
DIVB	SRC, DST	Quotient of $(DST+1:DST)/(SRC) \rightarrow (DST)$ Remainder of $(DST+1:DST)/(SRC) \rightarrow (DST+1)$	00xx	0011111
DIVH	SRC, DST	Quotient of $(DST+2:DST)/(SRC) \rightarrow (DST)$ Remainder of $(DST+2:DST)/(SRC) \rightarrow (DST+2)$		0010111

Addressing Modes: SRC may have any addressing mode, but if a register is used it must be R0. DST may have any addressing mode except immediate. For the multiply and divide instructions, DST must be a register with an even address.

Machine Instruction Formats:

| OC(7) | M(3) | M(6) | | I, D, or A (16) | | A (16) |

| OC(7) | M(3) | R(3) | M(3) | I, D, or A (16) | | D (16) |

App. C X16 Summary

10-Bit Opcode Instructions

(Branch, Shift, and Rotate)

Assembler Code		Condition	Flags ZNCV	Opcode
BREQ	OPR	$Z = 1$	uuuu	0000011100
BRNE	OPR	$Z = 0$	uuuu	0000010100
BUGT	OPR	$C \vee Z = 0$	uuuu	0000010101
BULE	OPR	$C \vee Z = 1$	uuuu	0000011101
BULT	OPR	$C = 1$	uuuu	0000011001
BUGE	OPR	$C = 0$	uuuu	0000010001
BSGT	OPR	$(N \triangledown V) \vee Z = 0$	uuuu	0000010110
BSLE	OPR	$(N \triangledown V) \vee Z = 1$	uuuu	0000011110
BSLT	OPR	$N \triangledown V = 1$	uuuu	0000011011
BSGE	OPR	$N \triangledown V = 0$	uuuu	0000010011
BRNG	OPR	$N = 1$	uuuu	0000011010
BRNN	OPR	$N = 0$	uuuu	0000010010
BROV	OPR	$V = 1$	uuuu	0000011000
BRNV	OPR	$V = 0$	uuuu	0000010000
BRUN	OPR	—	uuuu	0000011111

Addressing Modes: Only immediate, register indirect, and PC relative addressing are possible. The branch address is the operand and OPR indicates its location. The format of OPR is:

#LAB—immediate

[R]—register indirect

LAB—PC-relative (assembler determines the length of displacement).

Assembler Code		Description*	Flags ZNCV	Opcode
SLLB	OPR		sss0	0001110000
SLLH	OPR		sss0	0000110000
SALB	OPR	Same as shift	sss0	0001110010
SALH	OPR	logical left	sss0	0000110010
SLRB	OPR		sss0	0001110001
SLRH	OPR		sss0	0000110001
SARB	OPR		sss0	0001110011
SARH	OPR		sss0	0000110011
ROLB	OPR		sss0	0001111000
ROLH	OPR	LSB of result = C	sss0	0000111000
RORB	OPR		sss0	0001111001
RORH	OPR	MSB of result = C	sss0	0000111001
RCLB	OPR		sss0	0001111010
RCLH	OPR		sss0	0000111010
RCRB	OPR		sss0	0001111011
RCRH	OPR		sss0	0000111011

* All shifts and rotates are by one bit position.

Addressing Modes: May be any mode except immediate.
Machine Instruction Formats:

OC (10)	M(6)		A (16)

OC (10)	R(3)	M(3)	D (16)

App. C   X16 Summary

16-Bit Opcode Instructions

(No Operation, Halt, Set Carry, Clear Carry, Set Interrupt Field, Procedure Call, Procedure Return, Interrupt Return, Interrupt, and Test and Set)

Assembler Code		Description	Flags	Opcode
NOOP		No action	uuuu	0000000000000000
HALT		Halts all activity	uuuu	0000000000000001
SCRY		$1 \to (C)$	uu1u	0000000000110001
CCRY		$0 \to (C)$	uu0u	0000000000110000
INTF	CONST†	CONST $\to$ Interrupt field	uuuu	000000000001----
CALL	OPR	$(SP) - 2 \to (SP)$ $(PC) \to ((SP))$ $OPR \to (PC)$	uuuu	0000000000000010
RETN		$((SP)) \to (PC)$ $(SP) + 2 \to (SP)$	uuuu	0000000000000011
IRET		$((SP)) \to (PC)$ $(SP) + 2 \to (SP)$ $((SP)) \to (PSW)$ $(SP) + 2 \to (SP)$	*	0000000000000111
INTR	OPR	Interrupt sequence is executed. OPR indicates interrupt vector address.	**	0000000000000100
TESB	OPR	Set OPR and Z flag to 1 if OPR = 0; clear Z flag if OPR = 1.	uuuu	0000000000000101

† Low-order four bits are set according to CONST.
* Flags are filled from the stack.
** Flags are filled from Interrupt vector.

Addressing Modes: None are used; second halfword may contain OPR.
Machine Instruction Formats:

```
                              ┌── For CALL, INTR, and TESB
                              │   instructions only
                              ↓
┌──────────────┐         ┌──────────────┐
│    OC (16)   │         │    A (16)    │
└──────────────┘         └──────────────┘
```

Stack Instructions

Assembler Code		Equivalent Move Instruction or Description	Flags ZNCV	Opcode
PSHB	SRC	MOVB SRC, −[SP]	uuuu	1111
PSHH	SRC	MOVH SRC, −[SP]	uuuu	1110
POPB	DST	MOVB [SP]+, DST	uuuu	1111
POPH	DST	MOVH [SP]+, DST	uuuu	1110
PSHP		(SP) − 2 → (SP) (PSW) → ((SP))	uuuu	1110
POPP		((SP)) → (PSW) (SP) + 2 → (SP)	*	1110

* Flags are filled from the stack.

Addressing Modes: SRC may be any addressing mode and DST may be any mode except immediate. For PSHP the Source Operand field is a special case for which the bit combination 110010 is used to indicate the PSW. Similarly, for POPP the destination Operand field is 110010.

Machine Instruction Formats:

PSHB, PSHH, POPB, and POPH are move instructions.

PSHP

| 1110 | 110010 | 110 | 111 |

POPP

| 1110 | 110 | 101 | 110010 |

DIRECTIVES

Assembler Code		Description
DB	CONST	Reserves bytes
DB	CONST(CONST, . . . , CONST)	Reserves and preassigns bytes
DH	CONST	Reserves halfwords
DH	CONST(CONST, . . . , CONST)	Reserves and preassigns halfwords
DH	LAB	Reserves a halfword and preassigns the address of LAB to it
DW	CONST	Reserves words
DW	CONST(CONST, . . . , CONST)	Reserves and preassigns words
DD	CONST	Reserves doublewords
DD	CONST(CONST, . . . , CONST)	Reserves and preassigns doublewords

When space is only being reserved, CONST specifies the number of bytes, halfwords, words, or doublewords. For data preassignment, the constant outside the parentheses indicates the number of times the pattern of constants inside the parentheses is to be repeated. This constant is optional and if it is not present, it is 1. For preassignment of an address to a halfword, the address of LAB is put into the halfword.

Assembler Code			Description
NAME	EQU	CONST	CONST is associated with NAME so that whenever NAME appears in the assembler code the assembler replaces it with the value of CONST.
	ORG	CONST	Causes the value of CONST to be put into the LC.
	UNIT	NAME	Marks the beginning of a source unit and associates NAME with the unit. NAME is optional.
	END		Marks the end of a source unit.
	PROGRAM	NAME	Marks the beginning of a program and associates it with NAME.
	PROCEDURE	NAME	Marks the beginning of a procedure and associates it with NAME.
	ENDP		Marks the end of a program or procedure.
NAME	MACRO	DARG, ..., DARG	Marks the beginning of a macro and gives it a NAME. The DARGs are the *Dummy arguments* that appear in the template code.
	ENDM		Marks the end of a macro.
	EXTERNAL	LAB, ..., LAB	Indicates that the definitions of the labels are not in the current unit, but should be in units being linked to the current unit.
	PUBLIC	LAB, ..., LAB	Grants permission allowing the labels, which should be defined in the current unit, to be referenced by units that are linked to the current unit.

INTERRUPT FACILITY

The X16 facility for handling external interrupts receives its inputs from eight interrupt request lines numbered 0 through 7 with 7 having the highest priority and 0 having the lowest priority. It contains a priority encoder that outputs the number of the request with the highest priority. The request is recognized if the interrupt bit (bit 7) of the PSW is 1 and the output of the priority encoder is greater than or equal to the interrupt level (bits 6-4) of the PSW. If a request is recognized, an interrupt acknowledge is returned after the completion of the execution of the current instruction and the interrupt sequence is entered. The interrupt acknowledge causes the interrupt vector address, which is four times the number of the highest priority request (i.e., the output of the priority encoder), to be latched into the interrupt vector address register. The interrupt sequence pushes the PSW and PC onto the stack and then uses the interrupt vector address to input new values to the PSW and PC from the proper interrupt vector in memory.

Interrupts may also result from the execution of an INTR instruction. The interrupt sequence is the same as for external interrupts except that the interrupt vector address is obtained from the second word of the INTR instruction.

Index

A

Activation record, 155
Adder, 69–74
    full, 70
    half, 69–70
    look ahead, 71
    ripple, 70
    serial, 82–84
Address, 99, 108
    absolute, 192
    generator, 271
    relocatable, 192–94
Addressing, mode, 107–12, 408
    autodecrement, 134
    autoincrement, 134
    base, 110
    direct, 108–9
    immediate, 108
    memory indirect, 108–9
    PC relative, 110
    register, 108–9
    register indirect, 108–9
    relative, 108, 110
Alignment, 39–41
Analog signal, 323
Analog to digital (A/D), 201, 224, 234–35, 237
Arbitration logic, 370, 457–58
Architecture, 7
    internal, 243
    single bus, 8
    single processor, 8
Arithmetic/logic unit (ALU), 99–100
ASCII (American Standard Code for Information Innterchange), 18–19, 340
Assembler, 11, 119, 169–84
    constant, 120
        numeric, 120
        string, 120
    cross-, 171
    directive, 120, 196
    identifier, 120
        undefined, 184
    instruction, 119
    label, 120
        external, 195
        internal, 195
    language, 119–20
    mnemonic, 120
    self-, 171
Asynchronous transmission, 296, 326–27
Average access time, 340

B

Base, 494
Basic I/O system (BIOS), 427
Baud rate, 323
Best fit algorithm, 394
Bit, 18
Bit slice, 286–88
Block check character (BCC), 223, 331
Block transfer, 201, 221–23
Blocked state, 433
Boolean algebra, 502
Booth's algorithm, 29, 33
Bootstrap loader, 424
Branch instruction (*see* Instruction, branch)
Buffering, 431
    double, 224–25
    triple, 224
Bus, 7 (*see also* Link)
    access logic, 301–2, 309
    address, 296
    bandwidth, 460
    control, 296
    control logic (BCL), 9, 99–100, 243
    data, 296
    grant, 221
    internal, 249–58, 295
    local, 9
    request, 221
    system, 9, 295–300
    timing, 296–98, 458
Byte, 18

C

Cache memory, 371–80
    associative, 375–77
    direct mapped, 373–75
    fully associative, 377
    line, 372
    set, 372
    tag group, 372
Carrier, 323
Cathode ray tube (CRT), 228–31
    storage, 231
Character, 16
    string, 16
Checkerboarding (*see* Fragmentation, external)
Chopping, 35
Clock, 524–25

Cluster, 390–91
Code, 18
    alphanumeric, 18
Combinational logic, 508–22
Comite Consultif International Telephonique et Telegraphique (CCITT), 327
Command line interpreter (CLI), 10, 424
Compaction, 395
Comparator, 66–69, 518–19
Compiler, 11, 169, 184–91, 196–97
    optimizing, 190
Completion routine, 223
Complex instruction set computer (CISC), 284, 289
Computer, 2
    general purpose, 2–3
    special purpose, 2
    system, 4
Condition flag, 99, 117–19
Contention, 9
Context switch, 437
Continuum model, 462–64
Control:
    centralized, 456
    decentralized, 456
Control ROM, 271, 286
Control unit, 99–100
Counter, 77–79
    decade, 79
    synchronous, 79
Critical section, 444–47
Crystal oscillator, 524
Cycle stealing, 221
Cyclic redundancy check (CRC), 331

D

Daisy chain, 215, 309–10, 456–57
Data communications equipment, 320–22
Data flow computer, 466
Data selector (*see* Multiplexer)
Data type, 16–17
    abstract, 17
    atomic, 16
    basic, 16
    numeric, 16
        floating point, 20, 36–43
        integer, 20–36
    physical, 17
    text, 16, 18–20
    virtual, 17
Deadlock, 444–46

Decoder, 61–63
Demodulation, 323
DeMorgan's laws, 503, 159
Demultiplexer, 66
Digital signal, 323
Digital to analog (D/A), 201, 235
Direct access, 341
Direct memory access (DMA), 202, 220–27, 430, 443
  channel, 227
  controller, 221
  management, 224–27
Directory, 347
  root, 348
Dirty bit, 409
Disk/diskette:
  cylinder, 345
  formatting, 345
  hardsectored, 345
  sector, 345
  softsectored, 345
  track, 345
Display generator, 230
Division:
  nonrestoring, 30–31, 87, 140–41
  restoring, 30–31
Driver, 88, 302–4, 311, 314
  tristate, 88
Drum, 350–51
Duty cycle, 524

E

Electrical Industry Association (EIA), 327
  RS-232, 327–30
Emulation, floating point, 141
Encoder, 62–63
End around carry, 32
EPROM eraser, 362
Equivalence, logic circuit, 502

F

Fan-in, 57
Fan-out, 57
File, 340
  management system, 427
First fit algorithm, 394
Flip-flop, 526–32

  data (D), 527–28
  edge-triggered, 528
  J-K, 529–31
  master-slave J-K, 530, 532
  set-reset (S-R), 526–28
  toggle (T), 529–30, 532
Foreground/background system, 402–3
Format:
  binary, 21
  binary coded decimal (BCD), 21
    packed, 21–23
    unpacked, 21–23
  excess n, 39
  fixed point, 35–36
  floating point, 20, 36–43
    IBM, 42–43
    IEEE standard, 36–42
  1's complement, 24–25, 31–32
  sign-magnitude, 24
  10's complement, 32–33
  2's complement, 24–31
Fragmentation:
  external, 394, 403–5, 407, 415, 438–39
  internal, 389–91, 407, 415
Framing error, 326

G

Garbage collection (*see* Compaction)
Generating polynomial, 331
Granularity, 465
Guard bits, 42

H

Handshaking logic, 301–2, 311, 313
Hardware, 4–9
Hierarchical diagram, 145
Hit ratio, 371, 376–78, 381
Horner's rule, 495
Hypercube, 486–87

I

Incrementer, 96
Infix notation, 44
Inline code, 152
Input device, 5

Input/output (I/O):
  element, 7
  handler, 435, 442–43
  instruction, 201
  interrupt, 202, 207–20, 430–31, 443
  mapped memory, 238
  port, 200
  programmed, 202–7
  programming, 200, 430, 443
  queue, 441–43
  space, 200
Institute of Electrical and Electronics Engineers (IEEE), 327
Instruction, 10
  branch, 10, 99
    conditional, 99
    unconditional, 99
  compare/branch, 131–32
  cycle, 98, 100, 159
  execution, 10 (*see also* Macroinstruction, execution)
    time, 159–61
  fetch, 98
  format, 104–5
  LOCK, 467
  loop, 135
  machine language, 11
  memory transfer, 201
  repeat, 136
  test and set, 446
Integrated circuit (IC), 91
  technology, 92, 452
  yield, 92
Interface, 7, 294–95, 300–320
  link to link, 310–20
  selection logic, 311–13
Interleave, 368
International Standards Organization (ISO), 327
Interpreter, 11, 169–70
Interrupt, 207
  acknowledgment, 208
  external, 207
  facilities, 207
  internal, 207, 401–2, 429
  logic, 301–2
  management, 214–20
  maskable, 210–11
  nonmaskable, 210–11
  request, 207
  return, 209
  routine, 208
  sequence, 208
  software, 207, 402, 429
  vector, 209–10

K

Karnaugh map, 513–22
Keyboard, 227–29

L

Last-in, first-out (LIFO) stack (*see* Stack)
Latency time, 345–46
Link, 7, 294 (*see also* Bus)
  communications, 295, 322
  data, 295, 320–32
    standards, 327–30
  full duplex, 322, 461
  half duplex, 322, 461
  parallel, 294, 316–19
  serial, 294, 316, 319
  simplex, 322, 461
Linked list, 391–93, 398, 441
Linker, 169, 191–95
  map, 191
Literal, 513
Loader, 169, 195–96
Locality of reference, 368, 378, 411, 417
Location counter (LC), 178
Logic diagram, 502
Logic gate, 500
  elementary, 500–7
Logical unit number, 344, 348, 428

M

Macro, 157–59
  call, 157
  definition, 157
  expansion, 157
Macroinstruction, 246 (*see also* Instruction, execution)
  execution, 246–49
Magnetic bubble memory (MBM), 351–52
Magnetic tape, 340–45
Main memory (*see* Memory)
Manchester code, 323
Mask, 137
Masking operation, 137
Mass storage, 9, 339–52 (*see also* Disk/diskette; Magnetic tape)
  management, 389–98

Matrix operations, 486–87
Maxterm, 513
Memory, 6, 9, 99–100 (*see also* Cache memory)
   access, 7, 337
   access time, 363–67
   address, 99
   bandwidth, 337
   capacity, 337
   cell array, 353–55
   column select logic, 353–55
   dynamic RAM, 358–61
   element, 6–7
   fault, 406
   hierarchy, 7, 337–38, 380–83
   IC array, 353–54
   IC timing, 363–66
   location, 99
   logical structure, 339
   main, 352–69
   management, 399–405, 438–40
   mapped I/O ports, 238
   medium, 337
   module interfacing, 366–69
   multiple-port, 369–71
   nonvolatile, 337
   physical structure, 339
   protection (*see* Protection; Main memory)
   random access, 337, 353
   read only (ROM), 61–64, 356, 358, 361–63
      electrically alterable (EAROM), 363
      erasable PROM (EPROM), 362
      masked, 362
      programmable (PROM), 362
   read/write, 356
   referencing, 388–89
   refresh, 359–61
   removable, 337
   row select logic, 353–55
   static RAM, 358–59
   volatile, 337
   word, 353
Memory management unit (MMU), 405
Microcode, 12 (*see also* Microinstruction)
Microcontrol, 246, 265–83
   hardwired, 265–70
   microprogrammed, 265, 271–83
Microinstruction, 12, 246
   branch, 277–80
Microoperation, 246
Microprogram sequencer, 281, 286, 288

Miller code, 323
Minterm, 513
Miss ratio, 371
Mnemonic (*see* Assembler, mnemonic)
Modem, 323
Modulation, 323
   amplitude, 325–26
   frequency, 325
   phase, 325–26
Module, 145
   called, 146
   calling, 146
Monitor, 227–31
   graphics, 230
   raster scan, 229
Multiplexer, 64–66
Multiplier, 74–75
Multiprocessing, 9, 448–49, 452–69
Multiprogramming (*see* Operating system, multiprogramming)
Multivibrator, 523
   astable, 523
   bistable, 524, 526
   monostable, 523–26
Mutual exclusion, 444–46

N

Nanoinstruction, 282
Nanostore, 281–82
Node, 454
Nonreturn-to-zero level (NRZ-L), 323
Normalization, 39–41
Number systems, 494

O

Object file, 170
Opcode (operation code), 105–7
   field, 104
Open-collector gate (*see* Wire-ORed gate)
Operand, 104
   destination, 115
   field, 104
   immediate, 104 (*see also* Addressing, mode)
   implicit, 105
   source, 115

Operating system, 10, 422
   multiprogramming, 10, 403, 423, 431–43
   preemptive, 438, 442, 448
   single user, 10
   time shared, 438
   uniprogramming, 423–31
Output device, 5
Overflow, 25–28
   exponent, 38
Overhead, 434
Overrun error, 316

P

Packet, 330–32
Page, 407
   fault, 409–10, 440 (*see also* Memory, fault)
   frame, 407
Paging, 407–13, 416–17, 439–40
   demand, 409–10, 440
   table, 408
Parallel processing, 452
Parallel transmission, 81 (*see also* Link, parallel)
Parameter (*see* Procedure, parameter)
Parity, 75–77
   error, 316, 320
   even, 76
   odd, 76
Particle model, 462
Pipeline:
   collision, 476
   collision vector, 476
   delay stage, 479, 481
   efficiency, 472
   speedup, 472
   stage, 469
   throughput, 474
Pipelining, 453–54, 469–82
Pixel, 230
Plotter, 232
Polling, 206–7
Position, independent code, 194
Postfix notation, 44–45
Power consumption, 54–57, 356
Presence bit, 409
Prime implicant, 516
Printer, 231–32
Privileged instruction, 402
Procedure, 145–57, 208–9
   call, 146

   linkage, 151–52
   parameter, 149–52
      call-by-address, 149
      call-by-value, 149
      table, 149
   recursive, 155
   return, 146, 209
Process, 432
   loading, 438–40
   scheduling, 435–38
      priority based, 435
      round robin, 435
      synchronization, 447
   state vector, 435
Processing element, 6, 99–100
Processor status word (PSW), 99, 117–19
Product of sums, 57, 510, 514, 519, 521
Program, 4, 10
Program counter (PC), 99
Programmable logic array (PLA), 61–64
PROM programmer, 362
Propagation delay, 51, 53–54
Protection, 89
   file, 398
   key, 411
   paged memory, 411
   segmented memory, 413–15
Pull-up resistor, 89
Pure code, 448

R

Read only memory (ROM) (*see* Memory, read only)
Ready state, 432–33
Real-time clock, 234
Real-time executive, 448
Receiver, 88, 304–5, 311, 313
Record, 340
Reduced instruction set computer (RISC), 283–85, 289
Reduced state diagram, 478
Reentrant code, 447–48
Register, 80–82
   base, 404–5
   instruction (IR), 99
   limit, 401, 405
   set, 9
   shift, 80–81, 316, 319
   width, 80
   working, 99–100
Relocation factor, 192

Replacement policy, 375
  least recently used (LRU), 375, 409
Reservation table, 476–77
Reset, 264
  address, 265, 424
Resident monitor, 422
Resolution, 34
Resources, 9
  shared, 9, 443–47, 466–68
Return address, 146, 208
Reverse Polish notation (*see* Postfix notation)
Rounding, 35
  IEEE standard, 42
  Von Neumann, 42
Running state, 433

S

Scale factor, 34–35
Scoreboarding, 469
Seek time, 345
Segment, 405
Segment fault, 414–15
Segment limit fault, 413
Segment table, 413–15
Segmentation, 413–17, 439–40
Semaphore, 447, 464
Sequencing and control logic (SCL), 243
  horizontal design, 274
  vertical design, 274
Sequential access, 341
Sequential logic, 499, 522
  asynchronous, 524
  synchronous, 524
Serial transmission, 81, 326–27
Shared resources (*see* Resources, shared)
Side effect, 150
Signal path, 294
Skew, 54, 94
Software, 4, 10–12
Source file, 170
Stack, 45, 47, 142–46
  frame, 155
  pop, 45, 143
  push, 45, 142
  system, 425
  top of, 143
Stack pointer (SP), 99–100, 142
Start bit, 326–27
Starvation, 218, 307, 458
Stop bit, 326–27

Storage device, 5 (*see also* Memory; Mass storage)
String (*see* Character, string)
Subprogram (*see* Procedure)
Subtracter, 73–74
  half, 96
  full, 96
Sum of products, 57, 509, 514–15
Supercomputer, 489
Supervisor mode, 402
Swapping, 440
Swiss cheese effect (*see* Fragmentation, external)
Switching time, 51–53
Symbol table, 178–81
  external, 195
Synchronous transmission, 296, 326–27, 330
System call, 429
Systems programs, 423, 429–30
Systolic array, 74–75

T

Task synchronization, 464–66
Thrashing, 409–11, 417
Time constant, 52
Time slice, 438
Timer/event counter, 232–34
Timing diagram, 523
Topology, 454
  bus, 455–61
  complete interconnection, 455
  generalized bus, 455
  loop, 455, 461
  mesh, 455–56, 461
  star, 455–56, 461
Transceiver, 88
Transfer rate, 340
Translation lookaside buffer (TLB), 412
Translator, 169
Tristate gate (*see* Driver, tristate)
Truth table, 500

U

Underflow, exponent, 38
Unit, 170
User mode, 402

V

Valid bit, 378
Vector graphics, 231
Vector processing, 482–86
Virtual address, 406, 408

W

Wait state, 159, 300
Winchester disk, 349
Wire-ORed gate, 88–91
Working set, 411
Write back, 380
Write pulse, 364–65
Write through, 379

X

X16, 537–47
   addressing modes, 110–12, 537
   ALU, 257–59
   BCL, 301–9
   bus timing, 304–6
   condition flags, 118–19, 258–62, 538
   instructions, 340–45
      arithmetic, 124–29, 540–41
      branch, 129–32, 542
      call, 149, 544
      formats, 116
      I/O, 204, 540
      interrupt, 544
      interrupt return, 211, 544
      logical, 136–38, 541
      move, 122–24, 540
      PSW, 141, 544
      push/pop, 143, 545
      return, 149, 544
      shift/rotate, 138–41, 543
      test and set, 544
   interface, 313–15
   internal architecture, 252–65
   interrupt management, 215–18, 546–47
   interrupt sequence, 211, 546–47
   macroinstruction execution, 253–57
   microinstruction format, 279
   programming model, 110–11, 538
   PSW, 118–19, 258–62, 538
   opcodes, 105–7
   operand fields, 113